W9-BVX-681

The Global Issues of Information Technology Management

Shailendra Palvia
Babson College

Prashant Palvia
Memphis State University

Ronald Zigli
The Citadel

IDEA GROUP PUBLISHING

Senior Editor:	Mehdi Khosrowpour
Series Associate Editors:	Shailendra Palvia
	Prashant Palvia
	Ronald Zigli
Series Consulting Editor:	Maryam Alavi
Managing Editor:	Jan Travers
Copy Editor:	Karen Cullings
Printed at:	Jednota Press

Printed in the United States of America

Library of Congress Card Catalog No: 90-082964

ISBN: 1-878289-10-1

IDEA GROUP PUBLISHING

Global Information Technology Management Series

Senior Editor
Mehdi Khosrowpour, Pennsylvania State University

Series Associate Editors
Shailendra Palvia, Babson College
Prashant Palvia, Memphis State University
Ronald Zigli, The Citadel

Series Consulting Editor
Maryam Alavi, University of Maryland

First release of this series
The Global Issues of Information Technology Management
Edited by Shailendra Palvia, Prashant Palvia and Ronald Zigli

Upcoming in 1992
Global Information Technology Education:
Issues and Trends
Edited by Karen D. Loch and Mehdi Khosrowpour

For more information, or to submit a proposal for a book in this series, contact:

Mehdi Khosrowpour, Senior Editor
Idea Group Publishing
Olde Liberty Square
4811 Jonestown Road, Suite 230
Harrisburg, PA 17109
1-800-345-4332

Global Issues of Information Technology Management

TABLE OF CONTENTS

SECTION 3. GLOBAL INFORMATION SYSTEMS

SECTION 4. MULTINATIONAL ISSUES: TECHNOLOGY TRANSFER, ADOPTION, AND DIFFUSION

SECTION 5. NEW CHALLENGES FOR THE CIO

SECTION 6. ISSUES FOR THE MULTINATIONAL ORGANIZATION

SECTION 3. GLOBAL INFORMATION SYSTEMS

SECTION 4. MULTINATIONAL ISSUES: TECHNOLOGY TRANSFER, ADOPTION, AND DIFFUSION

SECTION 5.   NEW CHALLENGES FOR THE CIO

SECTION 6. ISSUES FOR THE MULTINATIONAL ORGANIZATION

DEDICATED TO:

Our parents: Chandmal and Lalita Palvia
                Anthony and Helen Zigli

Our wives: Rajkumari
                Madhu
                Kathie

Our children: Aseem, Anupam, Anjali
                Tanuj, Tanisha
                Ann, Andrea

ABOUT THE EDITORS OF THIS BOOK

Shailendra Palvia is An Assistant Professor of Information Systems at Babson College in Wellesley, MA. He received his Ph.D. from the University of Minnesota and has twelve years of industry experience. He has publishing widely in many journals and conference proceedings, and is a member of several professional organizations. He serves on the editorial review board of the *Journal of Microcomputer Systems Management.*

Prashant Palvia is an Associate Professor of Management Information Systems at Memphis State University. He received his Ph.D. from the University of Minnesota and has nine years of experience in industry. He has published extensively in journals and conference proceedings. he serves on several editorial review boards, and is the Associate Editor of *Information Resources Management Journal.*

Ronald M. Zigli holds a joint appointment as a Professor of Business Administration at The Citadel and Professor of Health Services Administration at The Medical University of South Carolina. He also serves as the Director of the MBA Program at The Citadel. He earned his BS degree in mathematics from the Ohio State University, and his MBA and Ph.D. degrees in management from Georgia State University.

PREFACE

Slowly and quietly, a revolution is under way. The predictions of futurists like Marshall McLuhan and Alvin Toffler are finally coming true, and the world is rapidly turning into a global village, where geographic distances, time zones and national borders are no longer barriers to business and trade. In today's shrinking world, in order to achieve and sustain competitive edge, a multinational corporation may have to buy raw materials from one country, use finances from another country, procure human resources from yet another country, manufacture finished products in a fourth country, and sell the finished products wherever possible. There is now truly a global dimension to all aspects and phases of business. Without a doubt, information technology (IT) has been a key factor in propelling and accelerating the globalization of businesses. In the past decade, IT has made almost revolutionary advances in hardware, software, telecommunications, and databases — all of which have brought us to the dawn of the complex yet exciting age of true globalization.

This book is a pioneering and comprehensive collection of chapters about the application and management of information technology at the global level. It is imperative that in order to effectively function in this new and complex environment, one must understand the myriad of issues, problems, and opportunities related to Global Information Technology Management. There are significant issues to be explored from several perspectives, e.g., the views of the practitioner, the educator, and the researcher. The editors have achieved this goal by including chapters written by well-known experts in the Information Systems field. Each chapter has been carefully chosen to provide the reader an insightful examination of important aspects of global information technology management.

The book contains twenty seven chapters, organized into six sections. Each section has a unique theme which is captured in the section introduction. The first section contains the introductory stage-setting chapter. It gives a broad overview of the global IT environment under which organizations have to operate, as well as it proposes an overall framework for the study of the subject. Section II, consisting of eight chapters, embarks on a detailed examination of the IT environment in different countries of the world — advanced as well as developing. Section III, containing six chapters, is about global information systems and includes frameworks and evaluations of such systems, and some applications. Section IV has four chapters concerning the adoption, diffusion, and transfer of technology within and between nations. Section V, in its two chapters, discusses the changing role and responsibilities of the Chief Information Officer operating in the global environment. Finally, the last section has six chapters that discuss various issues faced by the multi-national corporation in its pursuit of exploiting information technology to maximize its performance at the global level.

The book has significant educational value for both students in universities (and colleges) as well as managers in corporations. It would be ideal as a text for a graduate or a senior undergraduate course dealing with international aspects of business. It can also be used as a supplementary text for an Information Technology Management course or an advanced Information Systems course. The book has enormous practical value for managers, in general management, functional management and Information Systems management. It is applicable to all levels of management, especially to the senior and middle management levels.

All editors have contributed equally in the preparation of the book. Shailendra Palvia, the first editor, conceived the idea for the book project and provided the coordination in the initial phases. Prashant Palvia and Ronald Zigli shared the majority of the work in the final phases. The editors at this point would like to acknowledge their gratitude to several individuals. First of all, our deepest gratitude goes to the chapter authors who wrote the chapter manuscripts. They worked really hard in targeting the chapters to the needs of our readers as well as responding to extensive comments from the reviewers and the editors, all in a relatively short time frame. Authors, we truly appreciate your efforts! And, your efforts are reflected in the quality of the book. Our profuse thanks are also due to Idea Group Publishing, our publisher, and especially Mehdi Khosrowpour, whose initial encouragement and vision led us to embark on this ambitious project. Mehdi Khosrowpour and Jan Travers (also of Idea Group Publishing) provided constant support throughout the execution of the project. Our warm thanks also go to Donna Bailey who demonstrated the patience, and persistence to go through several handwritten and reworded drafts of letters, and put together the finished letters that were mailed to the authors and the publisher.

Finally, we solicit and welcome the comments of our readers so that future editions and works can benefit from their valuable feedback. We truly believe that we, along with our esteemed contributing authors, have laid the foundation for a new area in education and research, namely: "Global Information Technology Management". As a consequence, we hope to see and encourage more work in this important global arena.

Shailendra Chandmal Palvia, Boston
Prashant Chandmal Palvia, Memphis
Ronald Michael Zigli, Charleston

SECTION 1
GLOBAL ISSUES:
AN INTRODUCTION

This section sets the stage for the rest of the book. It describes information technology in the context of a global environment. As Marshall McLuhan pointed out long ago, we exist in a "Global Village." The traditional information systems department must undergo a metamorphosis, a transition to a Global Information System (GIS). This perspective was echoed by Michael Porter in his book , The Competitive Advantage of Nations, where he stated, "The availability and interpretation of information are central to the process of gaining competitive advantage..." (Porter, pp. 173,174). To understand this environment is an imperative. This chapter, written by Professors Prashant Palvia, Shailendra Palvia, and Ronald Zigli, begins that process by attempting to provide a listing and a discussion of key information technology and management information systems issues in different parts of the world. Specifically, the key issues germane to advanced countries, developing countries, and less developed countries are identified and assessed categorically. A comparative assessment of these issues is made and the stages of global information technology (IT) adoption are identified. This chapter ends with a suggested paradigm for future research and applications in global information technology.

1 Global Information Technology Environment: Key MIS Issues in Advanced and Less-Developed Nations

Prashant C. Palvia
Memphis State University

Ronald M. Zigli
The Citadel

Shailendra Palvia
Babson College

The key information technology (IT) and management information systems (MIS) issues in Europe, the United States and many other advanced countries in the world have been periodically identified and reported in the literature. In today's global society, however, the practice, application, and research of MIS must be extended to include the broadest range of nations, economies, and political systems. At this time, there is a paucity of MIS applications, research, reported in the literature for less developed or third world nations. In this chapter, we attempt to describe the global environment of information technology and information systems. It offers the readers a basic concept of the environment within which global information systems have to be developed and information technology has to be managed. Based on the existing literature and studies conducted by the authors, the important MIS issues in advanced, and less-developed nations are described.

In general, the important MIS issues in less-developed countries appear to be much more basic and operational in nature than those of advanced nations. Economic development "looms large" in the day to day and year to year decisions of MIS executives and computer vendors. Many developing nations are in the initial stages of MIS adoption and are plagued with operational and infrastructural problems related to software, hardware and data; limited education of managers and MIS personnel; limitations in the availability of trained personnel; and a plethora of other day-to-day problems. These "other" environments signify the need for the internationalization of MIS applications and research, and an active role by the advanced nations in providing technological assistance and facilitating technology transfer to these less-developed nations.

INTRODUCTION

In the past three decades, management information systems (MIS) and information technology (IT) have made major strides in advanced nations (e.g., in U.S.A., European countries, and Japan). In recent years, the rate of technology diffusion has accelerated exponentially; in fact the advancements in information technology during the last decade have been rapidly transforming industrialized societies from service economies to information economies. It is estimated that more than 50% of the GNP in the United States, Western Europe, and Japan is derived from information related technological activities. (Porat, 1977). Consequently, the MIS field remains very dynamic and ever-evolving. \ ?

While the advanced countries have enjoyed wide-spread use of information technology, IT has also started to make inroads into the lesser developed countries, due largely to declining costs of hardware and software, the advent of microcomputers, and advances in telecommunications. Furthermore, many multinational companies and government organizations are investing in global information systems and global information networks in the pursuit of international business and general societal welfare. Due to the application of information technology at a global level, the barriers due to national boundaries are beginning to disappear. In addition, many other countries (e.g., Korea, Singapore, India, China, the Soviet Union) are also making a determined effort to assimilate information technology as an important ingredient in their developmental infrastructure.

It is in this context of the global application of information technology that this chapter is written. Since many companies, government organizations, and MIS researchers have begun to have a global IT perspective, it is necessary to understand the global IT environment. We describe the global IT environment by identifying the key MIS issues in different countries. While addressing all key MIS issues worldwide is clearly infeasible, we describe these issues in selected countries at various stages of economic growth. The United Nations (Porat, 1977; Kalman, 1979) has classified countries according to their Computer Industry Development Potential (CIDP): Advanced (e.g., the United States, Canada, Japan, and Western European countries); Operational (e.g., Argentina, Brazil, Bulgaria, Greece, Hong Kong, Hungary, India, Mexico, Romania, U.S.S.R, and Venezuela); Basic (e.g., Albania, Chile, Cuba, Indonesia, Iran, Iraq, Jordan, Kenya, Libya, Malaysia, Nigeria, Pakistan, Panama and Thailand); and Initial (all others). Note that the terms: advanced, operational and basic countries roughly coincide with developed, developing and under-developed countries. (In this chapter, both developing and under-developed countries will be referred to as less-developed countries).

In recent years, many scholarly articles have appeared addressing evolving MIS issues in the United States (Ball & Harris, 1982; Brancheau & Wetherbe, 1987; Buday, 1988; Dickson et al., 1984; Hartog & Herbert, 1986; Martin, 1982; Moon, 1989; Rockart, 1979; and Wilder, 1989). Therefore, we have primarily used the key issues in the United States as representative issues for advanced nations. For an operational (developing) country, we have identified the key MIS issues in India; and for basic (under-developed) countries, we have identified the key MIS issues from Kenya and Zimbabwe. The rest of the chapter enumerates these country issues, describes them, and provides a comparative discussion. While the U.S. issues are derived from the reported findings from other authors (as referenced above), the India findings are based on the work of Palvia and Palvia (1990), and the Kenya/Zimbabwe findings are based on the work of Zigli (1990).

The benefits of identifying the global IT environment are manifold. Overall, the understanding of the environment helps accelerate the rate of absorption of information technology in less developed countries (LDCs). It helps advanced nations and multinational corporations to be sensitive to the needs of the LDCs, and it helps LDCs to learn from the experiences and conditions of the advanced nations. For example, in different countries, the differences in technology levels, national culture, economic stability, and social priorities all influence the assimilation of technology (McFarlan, 1986). According to Warren McFarlan (1986), differences in the application of technology exist for several reasons; primary among them being language, geographical distance, different organizational and institutional structures, culture, existing technology, labor cost tradeoffs, and the "not invented here" syndrome. Our "limited domain" approach to understanding global information technology environment issues should serve the cause of promoting international learning, technology transfer, and global cooperation.

KEY MIS ISSUES IN ADVANCED NATIONS

The United States is used as a primary example of the advanced nations given that there have been several studies conducted exploring the key MIS issues in USA (e.g., Ball & Harris, 1982; Brancheau & Wetherbe, 1987; Dickson et al., 1984; and Martin, 1983). Before reporting these issues, it would probably be helpful to review the U.S. economy and prevailing conditions.

The United States, like most Western European countries and Japan, has what is termed, a mixed economy. A mixed economy combines some of the basic features of capitalism and socialism (Schnitzer & Nordyke, 1983). In such countries, the economy relies on the market mechanism to allocate resources but government intervention is not uncommon and can influence the market significantly. In addition to the United States, Schnitzer and Nordyke cite France, Japan, the United Kingdom and West Germany (a term now obsolete) as prototypes of such economies. Although similar in some respects, there is considerable variation in these mixed economies.

The American economic system is dominated by business, government, and labor. In the business sector, industry is concentrated (in the hands of a few) in terms of employment and output. The government has always exerted some influence over the United States economy. In general, government intervention and participation has increased substantially over time. In the United States, the government not only regulates the manner of doing business in the private sector but, owns and operates certain types of business enterprises. It is a major provider of credit, collector of taxes, purchaser of goods and services, and the single largest employer in the United States economy. Government intervention through private agreements, quotas, tariffs, government loans, and subsidies softens the effects of free-market competition. Finally, labor, especially as manifested in labor unions, represents a third major force in the United States Economy. Although labor is still a significant force in the economy, labor union membership has been declining recently (Schnitzer & Nordyke, 1983).

The population of the United States was estimated to be approximately 247,498,000 in 1989. The total population is growing slowly and the age composition is maturing. The percentage of 16-24 year olds is expected to shrink until 1995. The Gross National Product hovers around $4.5 trillion and the per capita income falls somewhere between $16,000 and $17,000. The rate of inflation during the last three years ranged from four to six percent. Private capital stock, a determinant of productivity and the standard of living, fell in the 1980s relative to its level in the 1970s. Unemployment (seasonally adjusted) in 1982 was approximately 10.5% and in 1990 is estimated to be around 5.3%. Non-farm payroll and employment rose for seven consecutive years, but in 1989 had the smallest increase since 1986. This slowdown was most evident in manufacturing and service.

The major agricultural products in the United States include cattle, soybeans, dairy products and grain. In manufacturing, transportation equipment, food, machinery, and chemicals top the list. The major mineral products are petroleum, coal, and natural gas. Like most other developed nations, the United States is not self sufficient in terms of natural resources (e.g., oil). However, it does enjoy an abundance of many other resources.

It is within this context or one quite similar that the relevant or key

MIS issues for developed nations should be considered. Those issues are identified and discussed next.

Key Issue Ranks

The top ten MIS issues in the United States as ranked by U.S. information system executives and U.S. corporate general managers, in a study conducted by James Brancheau and James Wetherbe (1987), are shown in Table 1. A recent survey by the Index group (Buday, 1988) highlights the top ten MIS issues of 1989 for the USA and Europe (Table 2). The May, 1989 issue of CIO (Moon, 1989) documents the top ten issues based on a survey of one hundred and twenty information system executives representing a range of industries in Fortune 500 companies (Table 3). Most recently, a survey of the participants in a one day conference (organized by the Center for Information Management Studies at Babson College, Massachusetts on May 11, 1989) from England, France, Belgium, Luxembourg, Netherlands, India, and USA and as reported in Computerworld (Wilder, 1989) resulted in yet another list of key MIS issues (Table 4). While this list also shows non-U.S. issues, most non-

Item	IS rank	GM rank
1. Strategic Planning	1	1
2. Competitive Advantage	2	2
3. Organizational Learning and Use of IS	3	3
4. IS's Role and Contribution	4	5
5. Alignment in Organization	5	7
6. End User Computing	6	6
7. Data as a Corporate Resource	7	8
8. Information Architecture	8	9
9. Measuring IS Effectiveness and Productivity	9	4
10. Integrating Data Processing (DP), Office Automation (OA), Factory Automation (FA), and Telecommunications (TC)	10	10

KEY:
IS — Information Systems Executives
GM — General Manager (non-IS Executives)   (Source: *MIS Quarterly*, Vol. 11, No. 1)

Table 1: Top Ten IS Issues in the U.S.A.

```
┌─────────────────────────────────────────────────────────────┐
│                          INDEX                                │
│                                                               │
│  Top US Issues                  Top European Issues           │
│                                                               │
│  1. Using IS for Competitive    1. Using IS for Competitive   │
│     Advantage                      Advantage                  │
│                                                               │
│  2. Aligning IS and Corporate   2. IS Strategic Planning      │
│     goals                                                     │
│                                                               │
│  3. Educating Senior Management 3. Aligning IS and Corporate  │
│     on IS Potential and Role       Goals                      │
│                                                               │
│  4. IS Strategic Planning       4. Making IS Professionals more│
│                                    Business-oriented          │
│                                                               │
│  5. Developing an Information   5. Educating IS management on │
│     Architecture                   IS Potential and Role      │
│                                                               │
│  6. Data Utilization            5. Using IS to integrate across│
│                                    Business - tie             │
│                                                               │
│  7. Using IS to Integrate across 7. Data Utilization          │
│     business functions                                        │
│                                                               │
│  8. Making IS Professionals more 8. Developing an Information │
│     business-oriented              Architecture              │
│                                                               │
│  9. Measuring and Improving IS  9. Managing Organizational    │
│     Productivity                   Changes caused by IS       │
│                                                               │
│  10.Managing organizational     10. Measuring and Improving   │
│     changes caused by IS            Software Productivity      │
│                                                               │
│                                 10. Improving Software        │
│  (Source: Research Report on Critical Issues of  Development - tie │
│  IS Management for 1989 by Index Group Inc.                   │
│  conducted in October, 1988                                   │
└─────────────────────────────────────────────────────────────┘
```

Table 2: Top Ten U.S.A. and European IS Management Issues

U.S. countries included are advanced nations. These four listings are remarkably similar, and emphasize the strategic and organizational implications of technology. The issues reported by Brancheau and Wetherbe (1987) are reiterated below. The following review is heavily based on Brancheau and Wetherbe's article.

Rank 1: Strategic Planning: Strategic planning for information systems is a difficult and important issue for IS executives. It requires the ability to develop courses of action based on rapidly changing technology as

CIO
1.Communication with top management, functional managers, and end users (92%).
2.Improving productivity of application system development (76%).
3.Translating information technology into a competitive advantage (74%).
4.Developing the capability to handle sudden business changes and shorter system life cycles (73%).
5.Managing information resources, including data security and control and disaster recovery planning (69%).
6.Training and education of an organization's work force in the effective use of installed applications (66%).
7. Facilitating and managing end-user computing (57%).
8.Integrating office automation, data processing, communications, and manufacturing (53%).
9. Training and education of IS staff (52%).
10.Keeping current with changes in technology (50%).
(Source: *Trendlines, CIO,* Volume 2, Number 8, May 1989) conducted by Arthur Andersen and Company in August, 1988.

Table 3: Top Ten CIOs Concerns in U.S.A.

well as align them to the company's strategic business plan. Brancheau and Wetherbe also note that this issue has been perennially ranked first in similar U.S. studies.

Rank 2: Competitive Advantage: Much has been written in the past five years about the value of information systems as providing strategic advantage. Such systems, labeled as "strategic information systems for competitive advantage", have become essential weapons in the corporate arsenal for competitive advantage. Competitive advantage emerges from the creative application of technology directed at the value chain of the company (towards customers, suppliers, and competitors).

Rank 3: Organizational Learning: This issue refers to facilitating organizational learning and the use of information systems. Historically, information technology and information systems have stayed in the domain of IS managers. However, to obtain its full potential, this technology will have to pervade the whole organization. While some progress has been made in this regard, much more has to be done on a continuous basis. Education and development seem to be part of the solution to this need.

CIMS		
	U.S.	**Non-U.S.**
1. Rapport and credibility with Senior Management	1	2
2. Knowledge of the Business	2	3
3. Ability to recognize and exploit Strategic Business Opportunities	3	1
4. Long Range Vision and Plan	4	5
5. Skills Mix and Motivation of IS Personnel	5	4
6. More effective use of Telecommunications	6	9
7. The establishment of Overall Corporate IS Architecture	7	7
8. Employment of Effective Application Development Procedures	8	12
9. Improved Level of System Connectivity	9	8
10.Cost Control and Containment	10	14
11.Reporting Level of the IS Organization	11	10
12.Availability of a Tested Security/Back-up Plan	12	6

(Source: Conference on INFORMATION SYSTEMS IN TRANSITION) organized by the CENTER for INFORMATION MANAGEMENT STUDIES at BABSON COLLEGE, WELLESLEY, MA on May 11, 1989.

Table 4: Top Ten IS Executives' Issues Inside and Outside the U.S.A.

Rank 4: IS's Role and Contribution: While information systems have made dramatic advances in the past decade and have earned appreciation and respect from many managers, its full role and contribution are not fully understood. In some companies, IS is still regarded as an overhead or a service function. The concept of "information as a resource" is a new phenomenon which needs to be understood at all levels of management. In a sense, this issue may be contributing to some of the other issues cited earlier.

Rank 5: Alignment in Organization: The organizational location of the IS department has a direct bearing on its effectiveness and impact on the organization. Until a few years ago, the IS department, consistent with its service/overhead image, had been associated with a functional area, such as finance, accounting, and even personnel. With the new strategic importance of IT, the IS department is moving up in the organizational hierarchy. Titles, such as vice-president of information systems and CIO (Chief Information Officer), are not uncommon any more.

Rank 6: End User Computing: End-user computing has pervaded practically every organization in the USA, Western Europe, and other advanced nations. Thus, facilitating and managing end-user computing and its growth are vital concerns. While the productivity aspects of end-user computing are apparent, there still remain problems due to the lack of standardization, documentation, and quality control (Davis, 1982).

Rank 7: Data as a Corporate Resource: There is a growing realization in organizations that data and information need to be treated as a corporate resource, not bounded within the domain of a single person or single group, but for the good of the entire organization. The importance of information resource management, and mechanisms developed to enforce the concept speak to the importance given to this issue. Another trend in support of this issue is the establishment of large corporate databases, centralized or distributed, easily accessible by a large population of users.

Rank 8: Information Architecture: This issue has newly risen to the top ten category. Information architecture refers to a high-level map of the information requirements of an organization. It provides guidelines for the development of applications and it provides a link between the organizational goals, business processes, and the information requirements. By necessity, the task of developing information architecture requires expertise in both organizational as well as technical areas (something which is scarce).

Rank 9: Measuring Effectiveness: Measuring effectiveness and productivity in MIS has always been a murky problem. While the costs of developing information systems can be measured with a good deal of accuracy, the benefits remain largely intangible in today's systems and are hard to quantify. Further, no clear standards exist for measuring the productivity of key IS professionals (e.g., systems analysts, programmers, etc.). Given that a significant percentage of the annual budget goes to information systems, this concern is becoming increasingly important.

Rank 10: Integrating Information Technologies: One of the elements of obtaining the full value out of the information resource is the ability to integrate the different information technologies. Specifically, this USA study underscored the importance of integrating data processing, office automation, factory automation, and telecommunications. Both technical and organizational factors have to be addressed in order to successfully integrate these technologies.

Lower Ranked Issues: While the above were ranked as the top ten issues, telecommunications, human resources, and software development stood at the top of the lower ranked issues. Surprisingly, applications portfolio had dropped down to rank 16 in this study, compared to a rank of 10 in an earlier 1983 study. Also, while there seems to be a lot of interest in artificial intelligence, its ranking was relatively low (rank of 15) as was office automation.

KEY MIS ISSUES IN OPERATIONAL (DEVELOPING) NATIONS THE CASE OF INDIA

As stated earlier, we are reporting the key MIS issues in India, as an example of issues in an operational/developing country. These results are based on a study conducted by Palvia and Palvia (1990), and the discussion below heavily relies on their work. Before reporting the issues, we will once again set the stage by providing a brief description of the Indian environment and its economy.

India is the second most populous country in the world, behind China, with an estimated population around 850 million. India is unique in many respects. First, unlike many of its neighboring and other Asian countries, it has earned the distinction of being the largest democracy in the world by maintaining a democratic government ever since its independence from the British rule in 1947. Secondly, unlike United States, India is a very diverse nation of 26 states consisting of people who read, write, and speak diverse languages — thirteen regional official languages and hundreds of dialects; people who practice diverse religions — Hinduism, Jainism, Islam, Sikhism, Christianity, Buddhism, Judaism, Zoroastrianism; and people who live diverse cultures. The average literacy rate is about 40%. There exists a large number of highly educated and well trained people — especially in the medical, engineering, and computer science fields. While the relatively few urban centers are the hubs of economic activity, the masses (referred to by some as the teeming millions) live in small villages, constitute about 75% of the population, and are primarily involved in agriculture.

India has a mixed economy with very large public and private sectors. In many areas, the public sector fully controls or dominates industries (e.g., railways, airlines, banking). In general, businesses are heavily dependent on policies and regulations imposed by the government. The economy has sustained a 4% to 5% growth on an annual basis for many years till 1987. In fiscal 1988-89, it showed an impressive growth of 11% in real GNP (Dhir, 1991). Despite this growth, the existence of an affluent class, and a growing middle class, the country still has high levels of poverty. Since independence, the country has had seven five-year comprehensive plans for economic development; currently, it is in its eighth plan (1990-95). In the seventh plan (1985-90), the then Prime Minister Mr. Rajiv Gandhi placed heavy emphasis on computerization, telecommunications, and other hi-tech efforts (Menon, 1990). The current government of Mr. V. P. Singh has proposed a sharp shift in the pattern of investment from capital-intensive to labor-intensive areas, while maintaining the same level of investment and effort in the strategic and hi-tech industries. (At the last writing of this article, the government was undergoing another change of leadership).

The methodology used by Palvia and Palvia was based on data collected from top-level and middle-level managers who were knowledgeable and/or interested in computers and MIS. The issues were generated using the nominal grouping technique (Van de Ven, 1974) and brainstorming, and then were ranked by participants in two seminars in India. In addition, several managers were interviewed to obtain further insights into the key issues and to assess the general IT climate in the country. Before reporting the key issues identified in India, it is prudent to present a general discussion of the current state of IS and the emerging trends in computerization based on these personal interviews.

Computerization and MIS in India

The Shifting Emphasis of the Public Sector: As stated earlier, India has a mixed economy and the government exerts considerable influence on the economy, its industries, and business in general. The implication is that the government policies and laws determine the extent, type and pace of computerization that takes place. The former prime minister of India, Mr. Rajiv Gandhi, initiated the increasing use of information technology in diverse agricultural and industrial fields to accelerate economic growth. In addition, he took steps to promote the development of IS and computer technology within India, as well as import it from the technologically advanced countries. The government of Mr. V. P. Singh, although not so enthusiastic, sustained the previous initiatives. In summary, the climate and incentives from the government generally encourage businesses to acquire and use IS technology. Further, within the government itself, it seems that computerization is gradually alleviating the massive bureaucracy.

Increased Demand for Computer Science Programs: There is a high demand for computer science programs at the undergraduate level. The realization among high school graduates is that the discipline of computer science is going to be extremely rewarding for their careers throughout their entire working life. In fact, many consider computer science to be the number one career choice among all possible careers for high school graduates. Colleges, universities, and private schools are attempting to keep pace with this burgeoning demand. Still, there is fierce competition for the available slots, and only the "best" get into the superior programs. This trend among the youth has very positive implications for IS development especially in terms of the quality of information systems specialists in the labor pool. In the short-term, however, a scarcity of skilled human resources exists and limits the growth of information systems in business. Another side effect of this insatiable demand has been the mushrooming number of Computer Science programs. Unfortunately, many of these programs are hastily put together and are of poor quality.

Lack of Distinction Between Computer Science and MIS: Professionals and educators, in India, generally do not make a distinction between computer science and MIS (this is partly true in other countries also). We believe, along with many MIS professionals, that computer literacy is not the same as information literacy. While computer science emphasizes the hardware, systems software, and efficiency aspects of processing; MIS emphasizes the effectiveness, utility, and management aspects of information systems. In India, there seemed to be little recognition given to the importance of MIS in decision making and organizational effectiveness. This, we believe, is another negative element which will impede the level of IS adoption in organizations.

Assimilating Information Technology Through Microcomputers: Most businesses are buying microcomputers in lieu of larger mainframes in an effort to rapidly bring computers into the work place. This is not terribly surprising,since, for the most part, Indian businesses began using this technology in the eighties; just when microcomputers came into being. Perhaps it is universally true that it is easier for an organization to initiate computerization with microcomputers. In fact, the new model for technology adoption may be the micro-mini-mainframe sequence (Palvia, et al., 1987). The microcomputer movement has also brought a lot of people closer to technology much faster. The availability and user friendliness of microcomputer software, and increasing capability for rapid in-house software development are also positive factors in introducing and assimilating information technology.

The Bottleneck: Information Systems Implementation: Most executives believe that it is not difficult to develop quality information systems applications. The analysis phase may take a long time and may be difficult at times, but it can be done satisfactorily. Further, designing and programming applications is a relatively straight-forward process. Bu,t the real problem unfolds during implementation of the information system. Organizations face resistance from all constituencies, especially employee unions. Advanced nations have also encountered implementation problems in the past and still wrestle with such problems. However, this is one area where developing countries can learn from the failures and successes of the United States and other advanced countries. Successful implementation models which take behavioral and organizational factors into account (e.g., Schein, 1964) may be transferable with minor adjustments to less-developed nations. For example, user participation and top management commitment may alleviate some of the problems of implementation.

Mixed Vendor Shop is Commonplace: Developing countries, that are still in the initial stages of hardware and software production, are more likely to buy from other countries. Further, many of these countries are in the non-aligned block. This means that they are more likely to have trade relations with both the eastern and the western block of countries than the countries that are aligned to one of the blocks. Even within one block, there are many countries to choose from. The doors of opportunity open even wider with the political changes going on in Eastern Europe. A plethora of options in terms of hardware and software selection now exist. While this situation offers more flexibility, it also poses a major challenge in planning the information architecture and managing it.

Key Issue Ranks

The key issues in India are reported in rank order of importance in Table 5. The top eleven issues are discussed below (eleven, as there was a two-way tie for the tenth place). Lower-ranked issues are summarized at the end of this section.

Rank 1: Understanding and Awareness of MIS Contribution: There is a general lack of knowledge among managers as to what management information systems can do for a business. Thus the need for computer-based systems is not widely recognized. Unless the contribution of what MIS has to offer is clearly understood, advances in technological resources are not likely to be of much help. This lack of understanding is partly due to the availability of a large number of semi-skilled and skilled personnel capable of running manual systems.

Rank 2: Human Resources and Personnel for MIS: Given the relative newness of the field in developing countries and also other priorities in the national agenda, the importance attached to this issue is understandable. The scarcity of quality educational and training facilities in the areas of computer science and information systems for students as well as executives was overwhelmingly pointed out by the seminar participants. As a direct response, universities, colleges, and private training institutes are gearing up to the task of providing the much needed education and training. In addition, companies send employees to training seminars and special schools.

Rank 3: Quality of Input Data: This is an issue which came up as a surprise and refers to the age-old adage of GIGO (Garbage In Garbage Out). This issue has seldom surfaced in U.S. studies. It appears that, in developing countries, there is a lack of information literacy among workers as well as a less-than-adequate infrastructure for collecting data for computer processing. Some managers related experiences of excessive errors in data transcription as well as deliberate corruption of data. The underlying cause may be mistrust in or intimidation caused by computer processing resulting in carelessness, apathy and/or sabotage. In turn, these may be related to the lack of attention given to behavioral factors during the systems development and implementation.

Issue Name	Average Rank
1. Understanding/Awareness of MIS contribution	1.222
2. Human Resources/Personnel for MIS	1.519
3. Quality of Input Data	1.556
4. Educating Senior Managers about MIS	1.630
5. User Friendliness of Systems	1.769
6. Continuing Training & Education of MIS Staff	1.778
7. Maintenance of Software	1.808
7. Standards in Hardware and Software	1.808
9. Data Security	1.815
10. Packaged Applications Software Availability	1.889
10. Cultural and Style Barriers	1.889
12. Maintenance of Hardware	1.920
13. Aligning of MIS with Organization	1.923
14. Need for External/Environmental Data	1.926
14. MIS Productivity/Effectiveness	1.926
16. Applications Portfolio	2.038
17. Computer Hardware	2.053
18. MIS Strategic Planning	2.074
19. Effect of Country Political Climate	2.077
20. Telecommunications	2.111
21. Government Controls	2.259
22. Fear of Loss of Management Authority	2.538
23. Fear of Loss of Employment	2.667

Table 5: Key Management Information Systems Issues in India

Rank 4: Educating Senior Managers about MIS: This issue relates to the earlier top-ranked issue about understanding and awareness of the role of MIS, and suggests a partial solution to the problem. Once again, it appears that senior managers do not truly understand the full potential of information technology and need to be educated. One manager suggested that companies should send their senior managers to computer and information systems "appreciation" courses. The authors feel that education should go beyond computer and information literacy, into internalizing this knowledge by the use of business cases and practical hands-on training.

Rank 5: User Friendliness of Systems: The appearance of this issue among the top ten was also a surprise, as it is not mentioned at all in any of the recent U.S. studies. We feel that the importance of this issue in a developing nation may be attributed to several factors. First, users in a developing nation are generally novices and untrained in the use of information technology; thus they may not be at ease with the computer interfaces. Second, much of the software and systems are imported from western and/or advanced nations. This software is geared to the needs of people in the exporting nation and may not be user-friendly given the different needs and cultural backgrounds of users in the importing nation. One can make a hypothesis that the ergonomic characteristics of information systems are at least partially dependent on the cultural and educational background of the people using them.

Rank 6: Continuing Training and Education of the MIS Staff: The education issue comes up once again, since technology is rapidly advancing and MIS personnel need to keep pace with it. One of the problems reported was that many of the current training plans attempt to train a large number of people simultaneously at the expense of quality and in-depth coverage. Another training need expressed was to train MIS professionals relative to the business functions.

Rank 7 (tie): Maintenance of Software, and Standards in Hardware and Software: These two related issues were tied in rank. Maintenance of software can be a problem because of inadequate resources and competition for resources for new applications. Compared to developed nations, the developing countries may suffer from an inadequate supply of trained programmers. The problem may be compounded if the majority of the software is purchased as prepackaged software (rather than developed in-house). The maintenance effort is likely to be high if the quality/applicability of the purchased system is low. The quality of a system depends, in part, on the existence and enforcement of hardware and software standards, which brings us to the next issue.

The issue of standards in hardware and software becomes an important one in developing countries, since much of the software and hardware (especially hardware) is imported from several different countries. The problems of hardware/software standards in the United States alone are many; imagine the magnitude of these problems when one is dealing with hardware and software developed in several nations. While some international standards exist (e.g., in programming languages and telecommunications); the challenge is to develop an exhaustive set of standards, and then to enforce their implementation.

Rank 9: Data Security: In manual systems, the data does not have to be closely guarded since it is not highly vulnerable to breaches of security. As a result, many workers have developed the habit of using data casually and callously. With computerized systems, this attitude can cause data security and integrity problems. On the other hand, data security may not be a very big issue since the majority of systems in a developing country like India are still batch-oriented.

Rank 10 (tie): Packaged Applications Software Availability, and Cultural and Style Barriers: These two issues are tied in rank. An inadequate supply of MIS personnel (an issue discussed earlier) necessitates a reliance on packaged software. While some software may be available, more needs to be developed which specifically meets the business requirements.

It is the authors' perception that cultural and style barriers/differences always exist, although it is hard to quantify them. For example, in one government departmental office, secretaries and clerical people were mandated to use word-processing equipment. But as soon as the mandate was removed, they went back to typewriters and manual procedures. Apparently, they trusted their age-old equipment more, and also it gave them a greater sense of control. This example demonstrates the importance of the influence of prior conditioning and behavioral factors. As for a success story, the computerized reservation system for Indian Railways is an outstanding example. Indian Railways is the largest public employer in the nation with 8220 railway stations. The public was highly frustrated with the old manual and corrupt system, and were ready for any improvement. In behavioral parlance, they were "unfrozen" from the old system (Schein, 1964)). As a consequence, the on-line system has been a tremendous success.

Lower Ranked Issues: Maintenance of hardware was considered a problem. Many organizations were getting personal computers, and their maintenance had been a problem. Aligning of MIS with the organization has been one of the top ten issues in the United States; it was ranked thirteenth in the India study. According to an Indian manager, beyond alignment, the organizational culture and philosophy itself has to change to accept the role of MIS. The applications portfolio was not a major issue as most businesses were in the initial stages of information systems growth (Nolan, 1979) and are still computerizing the basic accounting applications. Also, for the same reasons, MIS strategic planning was not considered very important right now. Given the relatively recent entry into the MIS field, telecommunications is also considered a thing of the future.

Some new issues that emerged during brainstorming and personal interviews are: fear of loss of employment with computerization, fear of loss of control and authority by managers, effect of country political climate on the penetration of the technology, and government instituted controls. However, all of these issues were ranked at the bottom. We believe that some of these issues are important and are manifested or imbeded in some of the higher ranked issues.

KEY MIS ISSUES IN BASIC (UNDER-DEVELOPED) NATIONS: THE CASES OF TWO AFRICAN NATIONS

The two African countries of Zimbabwe and Kenya were used as examples of basic/under-developed countries (per United Nations literature). The key issues were identified in a study completed by Zigli (1990) and the following discussion is based primarily on his work. Before reporting the results, however, some general information about these two nations might be in order.

Zimbabwe (formerly Rhodesia), is a nation with a population in 1989 of approximately 9,987,000 and a land area of 150,803 square miles. There are two major cities, Harare and Bufawayo with populations of 730,000 and 415,000 respectively. Zimbabwe is divided into eight provinces and has a one-party Socialist form of government. Zimbabwe was a former British colony which achieved its independence (officially) on April 18, 1980. President Robert Mugabe was and still is the Head of State. The literacy rate is 50% for the general population. English is the official language but, Shona and Sindebele are also spoken. Religions are predominately those derived from the traditional tribal beliefs. Christians constitute a small minority group in this country. Zimbabwe has three major modes of transportation (air, rail and motor vehicles). In 1985 there were 253,000 passenger cars and 28,000 commercial vehicles in the country (The World Almanac, 1990).

Zimbabwe's economy could be characterized as diversified but largely agricultural and mining. Although a significant portion of Zimbabwe's gross domestic product (GDP) is derived from agriculture and mining, nearly 25 percent of GDP comes from manufacturing. Agriculture has been a fairly stable factor in the economy and recently showed a strong recovery in 1988 from the effects of a drought the previous year. Zimbabwe also exports a variety of products including ferrochrome, nickel, coffee, sugar, textiles, and clothing. In general, economic growth is expected to continue at 4 to 6 percent per year. The most serious problem in this country is unemployment with an unemployment rate averaging around 23 to 25 percent. Secondary school graduates have a very difficult time finding jobs. Another serious problem is the lack of investment, both foreign and domestic. Two areas of vulnerability for Zimbabwe's economy are its reliance upon South Africa for trade routes and its total dependency on imported petroleum (coal reserves, however, are immense). Inflation has been estimated at 8-15 percent. Zimbabwe does enjoy a favorable balance of payments position. In 1988, it had an estimated trade surplus of $450 million ("Foreign Economic Trends," 1989).

Kenya is a nation with a population in 1989 of approximately 23,727,000 and a land area of 224,960 square miles. There are two major cities, Nairobi and Mombasa with populations of 959,000 and 401,000 respectively. Kenya is divided into seven provinces and has a Republic form of government. Kenya too was a former British colony that achieved its independence on December 12, 1963. Jomo Kenyata was Prime Minister in 1963 and when Kenya declared its independence, he became its first president. In 1978, with the death of President Kenyata, the presidency passed to Daniel Moi who is still the Head of State. The literacy rate in Kenya is also 50% as it is for Zimbabwe. Swahili is the official language but, English is also spoken throughout the country. Approximately 38% of the people are Protestant, 28% are Catholic, 6% are Moslem and the rest are various other religions. Including the port city of Mombasa, Kenya has four major modes of transportation (air, motor vehicle, rail and ship) at its disposal. In 1985 there were 126.000 passenger cars and 103,000 commercial vehicles in the country (The World Almanac, 1990).

Kenya's economy could be described as predominately agricultural with fast growing service and manufacturing sectors. While non-subsistence agriculture accounts for approximately 30 percent of the monetary GDP, nearly 75 percent of the work force make their living on the land. Coffee, tea, and petroleum products are the major exports followed by other minerals and foodstuffs. Unemployment, like that of Zimbabwe is a major problem. The population growth far outstrips the growth in jobs and some analysts predict the unemployment rate in the year 2000 will be near 40 percent if nothing changes. Kenya's balance of payments has been typically weak ("Foreign Economic Trends," 1989).

The methodology used in the study of the two African nations was based upon the results of the India study. The same instrument (with minor modifications) was used to collect the data. Although a number of questionnaires were mailed and/or delivered to various information systems executives, too few were returned to provide enough information to draw any meaningful conclusions. Consequently, a number of in-depth personal interviews of senior information systems executives were conducted utilizing the same questionnaire as a basis for these discussions. Both sources of primary data were supplemented by information drawn from local trade publications and other secondary sources in the literature. These personal interviews were 'rich' in information going well beyond the issues cited in the questionnaire. Much broader concerns relative to the current environment of computerization and MIS in the African nations surfaced during these interviews. Some of these contextual factors are described below to give the readers a proper perspective.

Computerization and MIS in Kenya and Zimbabwe

Aging Hardware and Software: The computer industry in both countries appears to be competing in an environment that is strongly influenced by government and the lack of "hard foreign currency." This lack of foreign currency combined with a virtual absence of indigenous hardware and software production has resulted in an inventory of both which is quite old. Although this condition is changing, both countries are still far behind technologically. It is not uncommon, for example, to find first-generation and second generation hardware in many installations; a situation that clearly leads to a decided competitive disadvantage in the global marketplace.

Government Support and Policy: In both countries, the exigencies of their respective economies occupy most of the time and attention of government decision makers. The net effect appears to be that information systems, computers, and information technology in general take on much less importance and get less attention and support from government than is true for more advanced nations.

In Zimbabwe, President Mugabe has often expressed his intention to institute greater state control of the economy. At this point in time, however, Zimbabwe's diversified industrial sector remains privately owned. There is, however, a movement to gain greater equity control of foreign-owned firms in some industries. Additionally, imports are tightly controlled through import licensing which has the effect of moving prices up considerably affecting the information technology industries and others in the process.

In Kenya, President Moi has expressed increased support for education and the private sector and continues to encourage foreign investment. The espoused development policy of Kenya is designed to support the role of private enterprise in industry and commerce while limiting direct government participation in productive enterprises. Today, however, government support for information technology industries appears to be, at best, "lukewarm." Computers and information technology still seem to be perceived as "necessary evils".

Lack of Distinction Between Computer Science and MIS: In reviewing the curricula of the leading institutions of higher education in both countries, it seems clear that the distinction between computer science and information systems has not yet been clearly delineated. Although selected courses are interspersed in the business curricula (graduate and undergraduate), no obvious distinction seems to have been made between computer architecture and the management aspects of computer systems — giving the perception of treating hardware and software as an information system. In terms of personnel, the demand for talented information-literate people is apodictic, but no concerted effort to fill that need is apparent.

Mixed Vendor Shops are Common: In these two African nations, some existing hardware and software are archaic. The lack of "hard foreign currency" precludes the purchase of parts and thereby most repair work for computer hardware not to mention the replacement of existing mainframe computers. Consequently, when purchases of equipment are made, the equipment may come from many different countries and vendors. The result quite frequently, is a mixed vendor shop. The political changes in Eastern Europe further potentiate this problem. A plethora of options in terms of hardware and software selection now exist.Again, as in India, while this situation offers more flexibility, it also poses a major challenge in planning the information architecture and managing it.

Key Issue Ranks

The key MIS issues (based largely on personal interviews) for the two African countries are shown in Table 6. Given the nature of IT adoption in these countries, only seven issues emerged (two were tied) with any degree of consensus. These issues and other miscellaneous issues espoused by a few of the participants are discussed below.

Rank 1: (tie) Obsolescence of Computing Equipment: and Obsolescence of Operating and Applications Computer Programs: Of greatest concern was the state of obsolescence of computer equipment and software. The need for new computer equipment was viewed as urgent and" loomed large" in the minds of all information systems executives interviewed. The current inventory of computer equipment is aging fast and simply doesn't meet the needs of any organizations adequately. A major contributing factor is the balance of trade and more specifically, the shortage of "hard foreign currency" ("Boost for Banks," 1989; Moroney, 1989). Twenty years ago when these computers were installed they were considered to be state-of-the-art and efficient. Today, after 20 years, littleprogress has been made. These 20 year old computers have now gone through two or three iterations of emulations, and both efficiency and effectiveness have suffered. In Kenya, a burgeoning population and rapidly developing economy have exacerbated the problem. The short-fall of computer equipment in this nation is acute and impacts not only the private sector but the public sector as well (Mutambirwa, 1989).

Issue	Name	Rank
1.	Obsolescence of Computing Equipment (hardware)	1
2.	Obsolescence of Operating and Applications Computer Programs (software)	1
3.	Proliferation of Mixed Vendor Shops (hardware and software)	3
4.	Availability of Skilled MIS Personnel and Opportunities for Professional Development for MIS Managers and Non-Managers.	4
5.	Possible Government Intervention/Influence in Computer Market	5
6.	Establishment of Professional Standards	6
7.	Improvement of IS Productivity	7

Table 6: Key Management Information Systems Issues in Basic (Under-developed) Nations in Africa

Overall, both national infrastructures appear ill-prepared for advanced information technology at their present states of development ("How Does Kenya Fit?" 1989; Rushmere, 1989).

The inventory of software is also quite dated. Packages presently in use are largely emulators of word processors, and spreadsheets. Only recently have relational databases been introduced into both countries. The severe shortage of "hard foreign currency" precludes firms from purchasing software which leads to another interesting problem; an exceptionally high rate of software piracy (especially for microcomputers). Major systems development is a rare occurrence. According to one observer, there is simply no requirement for an integrated computerized manufacturing supply and distribution system given the fact that conglomerates are virtually non-existent. On the positive side, some contemporary software is being introduced. For example, the relational database package Oracle is now being distributed in both countries by local software firms. In Zimbabwe, this package has been installed at a major university.

Rank 3: Proliferation of Mixed Vendor Shops: Another issue is the mixed vendor shop. It appears that mixed vendor shops may have been the result of purchases of hardware and software made whenever the availability of foreign capital permitted using vendors most accessible at the time. It is seen as a major detriment to efficiency and productivity by a number of firms in the less developed nations surveyed (Rushmere, 1989).

Rank 4: Availability of Skilled MIS Personnel and Professional Development: Finding trained personnel and keeping existing information systems people current with the latest advances in IT are other vital concerns of information systems managers in these less developed nations. More specifically, many executives are of the opinion that people with computer skills and training nationwide are in short supply. They are being spread too thin and not enough new people are being trained (Hernandez-Lapuerta, 1989; Rushmere, 1989).

Rank 5: Possible Government Intervention in the Computer Industry: Concern remains high about government intervention in the computer industry thereby threatening to reduce competition and increase the probability of a monopoly. One government action that exemplifies such intervention in the industry is the issuance of import licenses to new, local businesses in an effort to encourage the growth of these small locally owned businesses. Unfortunately, a number of these new firms are selling their import licenses to existing, larger vendors. Both the sellers and the buyers realize substantial profits. One writer characterizes this practice as "profiteering." Another example of government action that influences the industry are the mandated markups for imported parts and equipment. As a result of these markups in these government controlled economies, virtual cartels have emerged, and the cost of computers, computer peripherals and computer software may be the highest in the world (Moroney, 1989).

Rank 6: Establishment of Professional Standards: The professional data processing societies in these two countries are very anxious to gain "official" approval authorizing them to establish or participate in the establishment of standards of behavior and expertise for data processing (MIS) professionals ("Computer Society Waits," 1989). It is hoped that the establishment of such standards will lead to better quality IS products and contribute to productivity.

Rank 7: Improvement of IS Productivity: Improving productivity is another issue of concern in these two nations. In general, this concern extends to all aspects and areas of information systems. There is usually considerable emphasis on productivity in the advanced nations, and serious efforts have been made to enhance productivity (e.g., use of fourth generation languages, and CASE tools). However, in the less-developed countries, while being recognized as a problem, productivity appears to take a back seat to other more pressing problems.

Lower Ranked Issues: The archaic hardware and software that exists in these two nations leads to an ever-widening technological gap and thereby a loss of competitiveness of the domestic businesses that depend upon such equipment. Information systems productivity and the erosion of the competitive position of firms were issues of some concern expressed by a few local executives. Additionally, it was the opinion of these executives that advances in hardware and software technology in the more developed nations continues to widen the competitive gap (Zigli, 1990).

Another issue cited by some executives is the question of the local manufacture of computer hardware. This strategy is seen by some as one way to increase the availability of computer hardware. This appears to be a polarizing issue with major computer vendors on one side and users (especially smaller firms) and the government on the other (Moroney, 1989). The major vendors (foreign based), as one would expect, oppose the local manufacturer of computer hardware while users and the government favor it. Perhaps, a short run solution to the computer hardware problem is the local manufacturer of microcomputers or the assembly of knock-down kits. The possibility of the establishment of local software houses is another equally controversial issue. Again, large vendors oppose local software houses and the government and users favor it. Many are convinced that the need for local software houses is desperate. It is clear that the computer industry is sadly lacking in terms of available software ("How Does Kenya Fit," 1989). Indeed, many view software as the prime determinant in the evolution of information technology for these economically less-developed nations (Rushmere, 1989). The solutions to the shortage of software vary from benign neglect, to in-house upgrading, to outright software piracy (Rushmere, 1989).

Still other information systems executives expressed concern about the future of local systems development. For example, one industry analyst ("How Does Kenya Fit," 1989) observes that no requirement for an integrated computerized manufacturing supply and distribution system is likely in the foreseeable future given the fact that conglomerates are virtually non-existent.

What was equally surprising in this study is what is not mentioned by the participants. For example, an understanding of MIS by senior executives does not emerge as an issue of significant concern. Using IS for competitive advantage is another issue that did not surface in the interview process. In general, the strategic dimensions of information technology do not seem to be as important as the operational issues. Indeed, it seems evident that most of the issues of greatest concern to executives and government officials closest to information technology are very fundamental and deal with very basic operational matters. Questions seem to revolve around the acquisition and upgrade of hardware and software. Finding supply sources and catching up with the technology are the main concerns of these executives. Central to most of the issues cited is the fundamental ability to do business — to purchase new equipment and/or computer software — all hinging upon the availability of "hard foreign currency". Obviously, the availability of currency is more of a problem for some less-developed nations than it is for others. The issues most germane to a nation are clearly influenced by the cultural, political, and economic climate indigenous to that nation. The resulting domestic IT infrastructure (or the lack of it) is a vital factor driving the absorption of information technology by businesses in less-developed nations.

A COMPARATIVE ASSESSMENT OF GLOBAL MIS ISSUES

Although, we had anticipated that there will be a core set of MIS issues common to all countries, such was not the case. However, there were some common issues between USA and India (advanced and operational countries), and then again there were some common issues between India and the African nations (operational and basic) countries. The situation appears to be as shown in figure 1. It seems that the issues of advanced countries are driven by strategic needs, the issues of developing/operational countries are driven by operational needs, and the issues of under-developed/basic countries are driven by IT infrastructural needs. As shown in Figure 1, there are some common issues at the borders of these three different types of needs.

Based on this categorization, we have formulated a hypothetical three-stage life-cycle model for IT and IS development in nations (Figure 2). In stage one, the infrastructure needs to be bolstered, which remains largely in the domain of governments and/or large powerful organizations. In stage two,

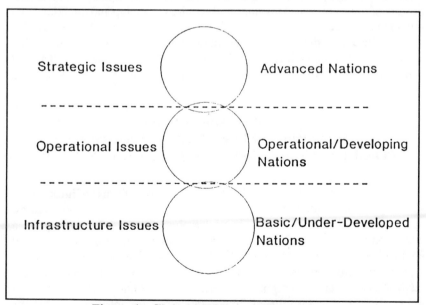

Figure 1: Global MIS Issues Comparison

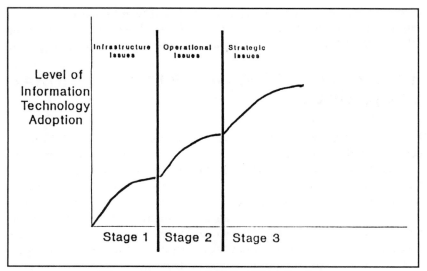

Figure 2: Stages of Global IT Adoption

the operational problems need to be addressed, which are in the realm of lower and middle management. Finally, when the organization matures in its use of the technology, then information systems and information technology can be utilized in a strategic manner to enhance the competitive and organizational posture of the company. This stage will require leadership and direction from top management.

Based on the above observations, we will discuss in the following sections the commonalities and differences between countries. Table 7 captures a comparative representation of issues in United States, India, and Africa.

A Comparison of Issues:
Advanced and Less-Developed Nations
(The United States, India and The African Nations)

The U.S. rankings reflect a level of maturity in the use of information systems. In the United States, and by extension in other advanced nations, operational and control issues are of less importance today having been addressed a long time ago. Now, the focus seems to be strategic value and applications. For example, the issues: strategic planning for information systems, gaining competitive advantage, IS's alignment in the organization, realization of data as a corporate resource, and to some extent the issue of information architecture are all important issues for information systems executives in advanced nations according to the studies cited here. Clearly, the

	USA				INDIA	AFRICA
	MISQ	INDEX	CIO	CIMS		
1. Strategic Planning	1	4	-	4	-	-
2. Competitive Advantage	2	1	3	3	-	-
3. Organizational Learning and Use of IS -Implementation	3	10	6	-	-	-
4. IS's Role and Contribution	4	3	-	-	1	-
5. Alignment in Organization	5	2	-	-	-	-
6. End User Computing	6	-	7	-	-	-
7. Data as a Corporate Resource	7	6	-	-	-	-
8. Information Architecture	8	5	-	7	-	-
9. Measuring IS Effectiveness and Productivity	9	9	-	-	-	-
10. Integrating DP, OA, FA, TC	10	7	8	6,9	-	-
11. Communication with top management, functional managers, and end-users	-	-	1	1	-	-
12. Knowledge of the business by IS professionals	-	8	-	2	-	-
13. Data Security, Back-up, and Disaster Recovery Planning	-	-	5	12	9	-
14. Improving IS Productivity	-	9	2	8	-	7
15. Skilled MIS Personnel, Continued Training for MIS Personnel, non-MIS Managers	-	-	9	5	2,4,6	4
16. Quality of Input Data	-	-	-	-	3	-
17. User-friendliness of Systems	-	-	-	-	5	-
18. Maintenance of Software and Software, Hardware Standards	-	-	-	-	7,8	1

(continued on next page)

Table 7: Top-Ranked MIS Issues in USA, India, and Africa

	————USA————					
	MISQ	INDEX	CIO	CIMS	INDIA	AFRICA
19. Availability of Packaged Software	-	-	-	-	10	1
20. Obsolescence of Computing Equipment (hardware)	-	-	-	-	-	1
21. Obsolescence of Operating and Applications Computer Programs (software)	-	-	-	-	-	1
22. Proliferation of Mixed Vendor Shops (hardware and software)	-	-	-	-	-	3
23. Possible Government Influence or Intervention in the Market	-	-	-	-	-	5
24. Establishment of Professional Standards	-	-	-	-	-	6

Table 7 (contd.): Top-Ranked MIS Issues in USA, India, and Africa

importance attached to these issues are evidence of the perception that MIS is a strategic weapon in the organization's arsenal (Wiseman, 1984). On the other hand, the less-developed nations are still struggling with the operational and infrastructural issues of information systems, and seem to attach little importance at this time to the strategic issues. This is not to imply that MIS development in developing countries has to necessarily parallel the "bottom-up" cycle experienced in the U.S. (i.e., in the sequence of EDP, MIS, DSS and SIS). It may be possible, with proper planning, especially for the operational/ developing nations, to work on operational issues and strategic issues at the same time. The viability of such an approach would depend on new initiatives, experimentation, and subsequent evaluation.

Another issue which is ranked high in the United States is end-user computing. This issue simply did not surface as important in the India or African studies cited here. An unanswered empirical question is "Do other less-developed nations share this perception?" In all probability, end-user computing may be a non-issue in developing nations because the critical mass of end-users in organizations has not yet been reached. Another important issue in the United States that seems relatively unimportant to IT executives in India and the two African nations is the integration of information technologies. Typically, U.S. executives are concerned with the integration of various technologies such as data processing, factory automation, office automation and telecommunications. The measurement of IS effectiveness and productivity is another issue considered to be of greater importance in the United States than in the developing countries in the studies presented here. In less-developed nations, unlike the United States, it would seem that the use of IS is not widespread enough to warrant the measurement of its effectiveness and productivity. It is clear that in the United States, there has been a strong interest in improving the productivity of IS developers and implementors and thereby its measurement. The proliferation of CASE tools, application generators, and fourth generation languages bear witness to the quest for productivity measurement and enhancement.

A Comparison of Issues: Advanced and Developing Nations (The United States and India)

Some IT issues are of importance to both India and the United States. One issue that is considered important to both nations is the understanding and awareness of MIS's role and contribution. It was ranked first for India. In two of the four surveys reported for the United States this issue was ranked third and fourth. Clearly, the message and the managerial perception is that in operational and advanced nations alike, information systems have a lot more to offer than most people realize. This, in a way, is encouraging and exciting for MIS professionals since the challenge for them is to continuously develop newer uses and applications based on the information resource.

Another issue of common importance is the need for the continuing education of MIS and non-MIS personnel about the role and contribution potential of MIS. Issues relating to this category ranked fifth and ninth in two of the four U.S. surveys and the importance given to related issues in the India survey were second, fourth, and sixth respectively. This outcome is very understandable, when one considers the rapid pace at which information technology has been changing and shaping the way in which business is conducted.

In two of the four U.S. surveys reported, data security, back-up and disaster recovery planning emerged as fifth and twelfth in importance, while for India the importance ranking was fifth. It seems that data security and the ability to recover from a disaster are basic business requirements for the long term survival of an organization, irrespective of its country affiliation.

A Comparison of Issues: Advanced and
Under-Developed Nations
(The United States and The African Nations)

As previously stated, there are few issues that are common to information systems executives in both the United States and the African nations. There are two issues, however, that are cited by both groups. These notable exceptions are "The Improvement of IS Productivity" and "The Availability of Skilled MIS Personnel". The first issue in the African study ranked 7th , 8th in the CIMS study (United States executives), 9th and 10th in the Index Group study (United States and European executives respectively) and 2nd in the CIO study. The second issue was ranked 4th by African executives, 5th by the CIMS respondents, and 9th by the subjects in the CIO study. These two issues, however, had no ranking in the MISQ study. It seems logical and comes as no surprise that these two issues are critical for less-developed nations, since development of the often desperately needed skilled personnel is a challenge to the less developed nation's institutions of higher education and the attraction of expatriates to fill these positions is unlikely. Of course, some institutions are better prepared than others to meet this educational need. It is not uncommon, however, for these institutions not to have adequate (let alone state-of-the-art) hardware or software to train these people.

A Comparison of Issues: Developing and
Under-Developed Nations
(India and The African Nations)

When comparing the results we find few areas where there is a commonality of issues between the operational/developing and basic/under-developed countries. The issue, "Availability of Skilled MIS Personnel" is one exception having been ranked 3rd by African executives and 2nd/4th/6th in the Indian study (results varied by subcategory). Also common to both groups are issues related to software. In India, the maintenance of software is a concern, while the obsolescence of software is a an issue in the African nations. In our opinion, both issues essentially highlight exhibit the same problem, since one issue leads to the other. Also, the mere existence and the ready availability of requisite software are issues of concern in both developing and under-developed nations.

CONCLUSIONS, IMPLICATIONS, AND FUTURE RESEARCH

While key MIS issues have been periodically identified in the United States, there is no assurance that these same issues are applicable to other countries or even other types of countries. It does seem clear, however, that the issues relevant to the United States may be more applicable to advanced nations, than they are to the less-developed nations. When examining the MIS issue of the advanced, operational/developing, and basic/under-developed countries it seems clear that each group has a number of unique sets of key MIS issues. In the advanced nations, the issues appear to be driven by strategic needs; in the operational countries, by operational needs; and in the basic countries, by IT infrastructural needs. There are precious few issues that seem to be common to all nations. A greater degree of commonality was observed between advanced and operational nations, and operational and basic nations. One could infer that as countries progress through stages of economic growth and IT adoption, the relevant issues change in a predictable fashion from the basic structural concerns to those that are strategic in nature. If true, then the less-developed countries could and should benefit from the experiences of the more economically advanced countries.

To the extent that future research supports these limited domain studies, more generalized conclusions may be reached relative to less-developed countries. It is to be hoped that future studies relative to key IT issues of other countries can be correlated in such a way as to establish the basic rudiments of a theory for global IT assimilation and strategy formulation. It is likely that such a theory will be quite complex and a function of not only economic development but the nation's political system, culture, educational opportunities, available natural resources, and other elements of the national infrastructure. A useful and convenient taxonomy might be to consider the components of such a theory as consisting of domestic elements, multinational elements, and global elements. Some factors are indigenous and unique to each nation (e.g., national infrastructure, educational institutions etc.), others are common to a subset of nations or a region (e.g., Europe 1992, and OPEC), and still other factors are truly global in nature (e.g., transborder data flows, overall global economic development, state of the art of technology, etc.). The dimensions of such a model are shown in figure 3, but such a model must be enriched and validated.

Much research needs to be done in the international MIS arena. The studies cited and conclusions drawn in this chapter are just a beginning. Since the dawning of the information age, we all are members of an information based global village (McLuhan, 1964). The stakes are high and the competitive

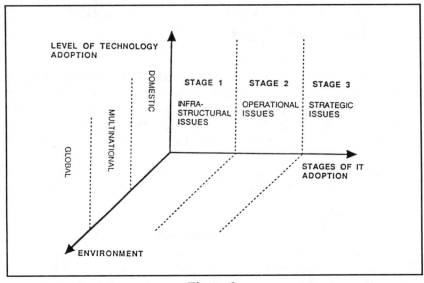

Figure 3

environment intense. The advanced nations can ill afford to permit the information gap between the less developed nations and advanced nations to become much greater. There is a need to understand the state of IT absorption in different countries. We need to know what the effects are, if any, of technology levels, social/cultural differences and national priorities on IT adoption and IS issues. Are there stages of IS growth and if so what are they in other countries? Nolan's stage model (Nolan, 1979) is widely quoted in the literature. Is the stage model relevant in understanding the development of IS in other nations, or are less-developed countries experiencing a different kind of growth? Further, given the IT environment in a specific country, how does that government and indigenous organizations exploit this knowledge to maximize the adoption of information technology at the local and global levels.

The important issues in a country dictate its educational and research agenda as well. What should be the goals of MIS education in different countries and how might they be achieved? What should the composition be of MIS majors in different countries and what should the blend of technical and managerial content be in the curriculum? Further, the differences between the advanced nations and the less-developed nations point to the need for technology transfer, mutual learning and international cooperation in certain areas. What are these areas, and how might they be exploited for mutual advantage? Physical boundaries between nations are steadily losing meaning due to the trend toward globalization spurred by this information technology. It is clear that we need to assimilate and take advantage of this growing knowledge base.

These are important but largely unanswered questions; it is imperative that we begin to address them now.

References

Ball, L., and Harris, R. (March, 1982). SMIS Member: A Membership Analysis. *MIS Quarterly, 6*(1), 19-38.

Boost for Banks. (August, 1989). Computer and Telecom News pg. 1.

Brancheau, J., and Wetherbe, J. (March, 1987). Key Issues in Information Systems Management. *MIS Quarterly, 11*(1), 23-45.

Buday R.S. (1988). Critical Issues of Information Systems Management. *Index Group Report.*

Davis, G.B. (1982). Caution: User-Developed Systems Can Be Hazardous to Your Organization. *Proceedings of the 17th Annual Hawaii Conference on System Sciences.*

Dickson, G.W., Leitheiser, R.L., Wetherbe, J.C., and Nechis, M. (September, 1984). Key Information System Issues for the 1980's. *MIS Quarterly, 8*(3) 135-159.

Dhir, K. (1991). The Challenge of Introducing Advanced Telecommunication Systems in India. *Global Information Technology Management*, Idea Group Publishing, Harrisburg, PA.

Foreign Economic Trends and Their Implications for the United States. (June, 1989). *Zimbabwe.* Prepared by the American Embassy in Hearare, U.S. Department of Commerce, Internal Trade Commission, Washington, D.C.

Hartog, C., and Herbert, M. (December, 1986). 1985 Opinion Survey of MIS Managers: Key Issues. *MIS Quarterly, 10*(4), 351-361.

Hernandez-Lapuerta, F. (1989, Zimbabwe Supplement). A Lack of Skills and Policy. *Computers In Africa, 3*(4), 43.

How Does Kenya fit into the Bigger Picture? (1989). *Computers In Africa, 3*(6), 25-31.

How Good is Zimbabwean Software? (1989, Zimbabwe Supplement). *Computers In Africa, 3*(4) 23-24.

Kalman, R.E. (1979). Effective Information Technology: Criteria for Selecting Appropriate Technologies under Different Cultural, Social, and Technical Conditions. *IFAC Symposium, Milan, Italy.*

Martin, E.W. (September, 1983). Information Needs of Top MIS Managers. *MIS Quarterly, 7*(3), 1-11.

Martin, E.W. (June, 1982). Critical Success Factors of Chief MIS/DP Executives. *MIS Quarterly, 6*(2), 1-19.

McFarlan, F.W. (December, 1986). Editor's Comments. *MIS Quarterly, 10*(4).

McLuhan, M. (1964). *Understanding Media: The Extensions of Man.* McGraw-Hill, New York.

Menon, M. (July 21, 1990). India and Computers: A Necessity for Modernization and Growth. *India Tribune.*

Moon D.V. (May, 1989). (Andersen Consulting - 312-507-2375). Trendlines: A Sweeping Generalization. *CIO - the Magazine for Information Executives, 2*(8).

Moroney, S. (1989, Zimbabwe Supplement). Africa's Potential IT Leader for the 1990s. *Computers In Africa, 3*(4), 17-19.

Moroney, S. (1989). Local Manufacture: A Hot Issue for the 1990s. *Computers In Africa, 3*(4), 25-26.

Mutambirwa, R. (August, 1989). Urgent Need for New Computers for PTC Billing. *Computer and Telecom News,* pg. 1.

Nolan, R.L. (March-April, 1979). Managing the Crisis in Data Processing. *Harvard Business Review,* pp. 115-126.

Palvia, S., Palvia, P., and Meile, L. (1987). Classification of Computers: From Many Classes to a Simple Dichotomy. *Proceedings of 1987 North American Conference of IBSCUG* (pp. 174-178).

Palvia, P., and Palvia, S. (1990). Key Management Information Systems Issues in a Global Society: A Comparison Between U.S. and India. Working Paper, Memphis State University.

Porat, M.U. (1977). *The Information Economy.* Washington, D.C.: U.S.Department of Commerce.

Rockart, J.F. (March-April, 1979). Chief Executives Define Their Own Data Needs. *Harvard Business Review, 57*(2), 81-93.

Rushmere, M. (1989, Zimbabwe Supplement). Education Scrambles to Catch Up. *Computers In Africa, 3*(4), 40-43.

Schein, E.H. (1964). The Mechanism of Change. In Benson, Schein, Steels, and Berlin (Eds.). *Interpersonal Dynamics.* (pp. 199-213). Homewood, Illinois: The Dorsey Press.

Software- The Computer Industry's Achilles Heel? (1989, Zimbabwe Supplement). *Computers In Africa, 3*(4), 21-22.

The Computer Society Waits for Recognition. (1989, Zimbabwe Supplement). *Computers In Africa, 3*(4), 36-37.

The World Almanac and Book of Facts (1990). New York: Scripps-Howard. pp. 725,726,772.

Van de Ven, A.H., and Delbecq, A.L. (December, 1974). The Effectiveness of Nominal, Delphi, and Interacting Group Decision-Making Processes. *Academy of Management Journal, 17*(4), 605-621.

Wilder Clinton (CW Staff). (May 22, 1989). Foreign and US executives see eye-to-eye on the top IS issues. *Computerworld, and Proceedings of the CIMS conference in Babson College,* Wellesley, MA.

Wiseman, C., and MacMillan, I.C. (Fall, 1984). Creating Competitive Weapons from Information Systems. *Journal of Business Strategy.*

Zigli, R.M. (1990). Rank Order of African MIS Issues Based on Personal Interviews with Selected Information Systems Executives. Working Paper, The Citadel, Charleston, SC.

SECTION 2
THE GLOBAL PERSPECTIVE:
SPECIFIC ISSUES IN ADVANCED AND DEVELOPING NATIONS

Section 1 described the global environment from a macro or overall perspective. The eight chapters in this section are more specific, focusing on issues, problems, and challenges related to information technology management in different parts of the world.

The first chapter was written by James A. Senn, who examines the impact the "New Europe" will have on information technology after 1992. He begins with a discussion of the political and economic changes anticipated during the unification of Western Europe and the potential impact that these changes may have.

The next two chapters, written by Anthony Verstraete and Ewan Sutherland respectively, move the focus to Eastern Europe. Interest by scientists and experts in information technology in this part of the world has been almost explosive following the significant economic and political changes.

The remaining chapters in this section center on issues indigenous to developing and less developed countries. Elia V. Chepaitis examines several broad questions about planning and control relative to the effective utilization of information technology in less developed countries (LDCs). Krishna Dhir describes the technological revolution taking place in India in telecommunications while Christine Specter and Sundeep Sahay describe an evolving crisis of major proportion in developing nations relative to the rapid and uncontrolled depletion of natural resources and general environmental decline. Finally, Tom Iverson presents two case studies of organizations located in the United States territory of Guam to illustrate the difficulties in designing an effective mix of information technologies in such an environment and Lech Janczewski introduces a number of very unusual environmental problems rarely considered by computer manufacturers in the design of their products.

2

Assessing the Impact of Western Europe Unification in 1992: Implications for Corporate IT Strategies

James A. Senn
Georgia State University

A new Europe, with the trade borders down, is under construction. As a result, corporate practices are changing, both to enjoy new opportunities and to safeguard existing successes. This paper examines the Europe 1992 program, focusing on the distinguishing factors behind the emerging European Community. Questions for evaluating the strategies of businesses wishing to compete in the new Europe are explored. Key information technology issues are examined with an eye toward the role computer and communications systems will play as firms examine their competitive alternatives.

INTRODUCTION

The playing field for business around the world continues to change at a rapid rate. Evolving political adjustments, economic changes, and the infusion of new technologies are among those elements contributing most to the evolution. The formation of huge trading regions will further shape the face of competition for years to come. Canada and the United States have taken the first step toward a North American trading block. Pacific Rim nations have for some time now been regarded as a trading region (Ohmae, 1985). But the most attention is being given to Europe as December 31, 1992 approaches and with it the next step in the evolution of the European common market.

This paper explores the characteristics of the European Community and the role information technology (IT) will play in changing corporate strategies for the new Europe. The first section describes the community's move toward 'Europe 1992,' including the political structures that have been put in place to manage the community. In the second section, progress in three key areas will be summarized. Part three examines the implications for international firms wishing to compete successfully in the New Europe and parts four and five focus on the heightened role information technology may play for all competitors in the European Community and six key IT issues players must address.

BACKGROUND: CHARACTERISTICS OF THE EUROPEAN COMMUNITY

Although the emergence of the European Community (EC) is captivating corporate practitioners and researchers alike, it is not a new development but one that began 30 years ago. At that time, the European countries of Belgium, Federal Republic of Germany, France, Italy, Luxembourg, and The Netherlands banded together for the purpose of improving the political and economic opportunity in and among their respective states.

The community has been transformed from a time of "Europessimism", in which the countries felt they could not compete successfully against Pacific Rim and North American firms, to a new optimism—a "europhoria"—which we have come to know as 'Europe 1992.'

Evolution of European Community

The European Community began to take shape in 1951 with the Treaty of Paris (Exhibit 1), which established the European Coal and Steel Community (European Unification; Working Together). Designed to encourage the pooling of coal and steel production and consumption, the treaty also brought France and the Federal Republic of Germany together. For the first time in history, national governments were asked to delegate a part of their sovereignty to another authority that independently could make decisions on behalf of member states. The six countries signing the treaty expected the group to become a unified European body, setting in motion a process they hoped would ultimately include a single European constitution.

The Treaty of Rome, signed in 1957, was the next major evolutionary step It established the European Economic Community (EEC), the Common Market and Euratom (for communication on nuclear energy). To non-Europeans, there was little visible change for a number of years after the Treaty of Rome. Although Common Market members continued to interact with one another, the Market was perceived as a European phenomenon that had little

Date	Event	Effect
April 1951	Treaty of Paris	Established European Coal and Steel Community (ECSC)
		Initial members: Belgium, Federal Republic of Germany, France, Italy, Luxembourg, and the Netherlands.
March 1957	Treaties of Rome	Establish European Economic Community (EEC), such as the Common Market and Euratom; consists of initial six member states
January 1973		Denmark, Ireland, and the United Kingdom join the European Economic Community
January 1981		Greece joins the European Economic Community
April 1985	Consolidation of European Institutions	Member countries sign a treaty merging ECSC, EEC, and Euratom
February 1986	Single European Act	Endorsed "white paper" outlining a strategy to create a true common market by 1992. (EEC henceforth referred to as the European Community (EC)).
January 1986		Spain and Portugal join the European Community bringing to 12 the current number of member nations
31 December 1992	Single European Community	Target date to remove trade restrictions outlined in the Single European Act.

Exhibit 1: Key Events on Path To Europe in 1992

affect on other countries, either politically or economically.

In 1985 the various European institutions were consolidated. Member countries signed a treaty merging the ECSC, EEC, and Euratom. A sense of rebirth was occurring and with it a feeling that European states could and should become more competitive economically. The rebirth became most evident when the European Commission (Exhibit 2), the Executive branch of government for member countries, published a white paper entitled "Completing the Internal Market" (Completing The Internal Market). The document proposed and discussed new objectives for member states and it identified measures to be taken and issues to be addressed in reaching a fundamental objective: establishing an internal market without the obstruction of national borders. It identified 300 actions (later reduced to 279) needed to bring about the single internal market and to diminish the effects of uneven economic development between the northern and southern states. It also provided for weighted voting on the issues to achieve a balance between the needs and wishes of large and small states.

The white paper was endorsed by the Council of Ministers, consisting of heads of government from each member state. A target of December 31, 1992 was chosen for completion of the internal market—a date coinciding with the expiration of the next commission's term of office.

The Single European Act was perhaps the most significant event in the development of the EC. It was perceived as a sign for other countries to note that Europe intended to reach the objectives of a single market and totally transform the global competition among different regions.

Legal Institution	Description
European Commission	The executive branch, responsible for proposing community legislation and monitoring conformance. Consists of 17 commissioners each serving four-year terms. (Referred to as The Commission).
European Council of Ministers	Responsible for final decision on ways to be applied throughout the EC. Consists of Foreign Ministers and heads of government from 12 member states. (Referred to as The Council).
European Parliament	518 members directly elected by states to five-year terms. Exercises democratic control over running of the EC and ensures laws are drawn up according to democratic process.
Court of Justice	The judicial branch. Thirteen judges appointed by agreement between governments. Passes judgment on disputes arising from the application and interpretation of Community law.

Exhibit 2: Decision Making Units of European Community

Overcoming Market Obstacles

The white paper identified three categories of obstacles to an integrated market:

  • *Physical barriers*
Controls related to the movement of goods and people between countries within the European Community that serve as barriers to trade

Examples: passport control for EC members; transport documents and regulations, such as drivers' licenses and truck and lorry sizes

  • *Technical barriers*
Conditions or standards for the procurement of goods and services, or structural obstacles to the application of the evolving European Community policy

Examples: Product content definitions, mutual recognition of services, regulations on movement of capital, and homogeneous policies on residence permits.

  • *Fiscal barriers*
Barriers in the areas of indirect, direct, and excise taxes

Examples: Variations in value added taxes (VAT) between countries within the EC, differences in income tax assessment, and duties imposed on goods and services.

Each barrier is firmly rooted in national concerns. As expected, attempts to remove them are prone to various forms of resistance from political and commercial sources.

SUMMARY OF PROGRESS

A great deal of activity has taken place since issuance of the white paper and passage of the Single European Act. This section reviews both progress and prognosis using the framework of physical, technical, and fiscal market barriers.

Removal of Physical Barriers

A great deal of effort has been devoted to the removal of physical barriers inhibiting the movement of goods and people. EC members see both opportunity and danger in removing the effect of borders between countries.

Creation of Single Administrative Document: The introduction of the single Administrative Document on January 1, 1988, was a major breakthrough. It was designed to ease the movement of goods across state borders. Truck and lorry drivers, for instance, find that this single document replaces as many as 100 individual forms (sometimes weighing more than 30 pounds) that have controlled import/export and transit.

A community tariff program was also prepared at the same time. As it is implemented, border procedures should be eased further. Border crossings, that used to take more than one hour between each country, are becoming fast and relatively "hassle-free." Hence, drivers' travel distance has expanded substantially.

While the Single Administrative Document does simplify procedures, it does not eliminate the need for paper forms and manual review. It appears that the EC will be obliged to consider implementation of electronic data interchange (EDI) as an additional means of simplifying border controls. Since firms are increasingly reliant on EDI, they may want to use it between governments as well as between firms, eliminating further the use of paper documents and manual procedures to manage inter-country commerce.

Movement of Plants and Animals: Approximately one-fourth of all measures identified in the white paper refer to the movement of plants and animals across borders—an indication of the magnitude of concern in this single area. Countries differ in sanitation standards and in their desire to protect against certain problems. For example, the disease rabies does not exist in Great Britain. Thus officials want to continue border checks that safeguard against its importation. In addition, technical, rather than political, issues often lie at the heart of many of the countries' regulations on the movement of plants and animals. Hence, the political agencies have much greater difficulty in passing new legislation.

It is unlikely that legislation will be in place and border controls eliminated in this area by 1992.

Movement of People: Implementation of a common EC passport eases the flow of travelers between countries for visits. However, movement of professionals is a much wider area of concern. The ability of individuals to move from state to state to practice their profession is of particular importance. In the past, there has been an unwillingness of one country to recognize the professional or educational qualifications from other areas. This reluctance was inhibiting the single-market objective in many ways.

All EC countries agreed in mid-1988 to recognize university degrees from all institutions as equivalent in meeting professional qualifications. The only area of exception is for legal professions (e.g., lawyers and certified public accountants) where individuals are required to pass a certification examination or complete a six-month course of study. Similar progress is occurring in the trade professions (e.g., plumber or electrician) with little difficulty expected.

Cultural and language differences will, however, be a moderating factor in the tendency of skilled professionals to move from the less developed regions of the EC to the more developed regions. Technology and business practices will move more readily than the people behind them.

Removal of Technical Barriers

Standards, procurement of goods and services, and local content in manufactured goods are the areas where technical barriers have been of greatest concern.

Establishment of EC Standards: National and product regulations and standards have traditionally been significant obstacles to inter-country trade. Development of uniform standards has been very slow. The white paper concluded that neither mutual recognition of another country's standards nor harmonizing the existing European standards would suffice.

Standardization is developing under a different approach. The two-fold strategy states that:

> • Selected standards related to essential requirements must be harmonized at the EC level. These standards are essential requirements of health and safety as well as consumer and environmental protection.

> • European standards (that is, Europe-wide rather than EC-wide) will be formulated by the relevant standards bodies, such as the European Standards Committee (CEN) and the European Electrotechnical Standards Committee (CENELEC).

In the interim, countries are free to develop their own standards as long as they conform to the essential requirements at the EC level.

The areas deemed most important for standardization by the commission include information technologies, telecommunications, construction and food products. Progress to date, however, is both inconsistent and slow.

Local Content and Rules of Origin: An emotional topic of legislation focuses on the local content in manufactured goods—the proportion of the value added work performed within the EC. Local content guidelines are aimed at eliminating competition from vendors who manufacture parts and products outside of the EC and do no more than assemble shipped parts within the community in an attempt to be considered a European manufacturer.

Local content requirements are defined in two ways. Products purchased by governments must contain at least 50 percent EC content. Local vendors can be given preference in the awarding of procurement contracts if their bids are no more than 3 percent higher than those submitted by non-EC firms.

The second case addresses the strong EC anti-dumping sentiment, that is, the government disapproval for non-EC companies that sell their foreign-made products at low cost in order to gain market share. The commission established guidelines foreign firms must follow in order to be considered an EC manufacturer and to avoid anti-dumping penalties. The so-called "screwdriver law" requires that products must contain at least 40 percent local content, that is components made within the EC. Most affected by the law are firms that assemble finished products within the EC using assemblies and parts imported from outside the EC (i.e., they only need to use limited effort—a screwdriver so to speak—to complete the manufacturing process). Although the law is directly aimed at foreign automobile manufacturers, the impact will be felt in other industries as well.

Removal of Fiscal Barriers

Taxation and movement of capital are, like transportation, formidable barriers to inter-country trading.

Taxation: The levying and collection of taxes is a particularly troublesome area for the commission. Commission members' concern with the harmonization of taxes triggered early efforts to make the necessary changes in national taxation.

Value added taxes (VAT) have traditionally varied significantly between countries. Since VAT is a factor in virtually every product and service, a disparity across countries affects the ability of a firm to market across state borders. Yet the commission also recognizes that it cannot unilaterally impose a standard tax rate without damaging the economies of the states who rely heavily on VAT for a large portion of their revenue. Consequently, the commission is moving initially toward establishment of an allowable range of variation. EC law will permit states to vary tax rates between the highest and lowest rates levied by the states. Up to five percentage points variance on items of necessity and six percent for others will be allowed.

Uniformity is, however, an objective for excise taxes. The commission has proposed, but not yet implemented, a uniform excise tax. Implementation is questionable in the near term because of extremely adverse reaction from EC member states.

Movement of Capital: Bonds and securities, long-term commercial transactions, short-term monetary instruments, personal bank accounts, and loans are all areas of concern. Such a broad range of issues means many individuals and businesses are affected by any changes here. Yet the commission has been able to move quickly. States have agreed to full liberalization of capital in every area. Changes are being implemented, with all states scheduled to be fully liberalized by 1992.

The creation of a uniform monetary system and a central bank are both a logical outgrowth of the move toward an internal market. Although there was initial resistance from Great Britain, the government's decision in October 1990 to join the European monetary system makes it clear that the direction is toward achieving both of these objectives.

ASSESSING BUSINESS STRATEGIES IN THE EUROPEAN COMMUNITY

Each new directive aimed at implementing features of the Single European Act as it related to commerce brings about change in the business communities throughout Europe. The playing field is changing rapidly as a result.

New firms are entering Europe. Other national firms are expanding to do business in new regions of the EC (Friberg, 1989; Goette, 1990; Jeelof, 1990; Magee, 1989). All firms are having to assess their status in at least four areas: their past and future competitiveness, basis for logistical support, management and reporting structures, and production capacity.

Assessing Competitiveness

Existing firms may find that their future is much different. Even a company currently competing successfully in the EC must examine its basic competitive strategies, determining the reason for current success. The following are representative of the questions corporations must answer:

• Do cost advantages accumulate from European-wide manufacturing programs?

• Have tax barriers served to keep competitors out of markets in which a particular firm competes, thus creating an artificial advantage?

• Have tax policies created artificial prices and thus margins and profits that will be dramatically altered in an open market?

• Have internal border controls protected national firms from international competition?

• Are differentiated products, developed to meet national market needs only, the basis of success? Are their features suitable for transEuropean competition?

Current cost advantages may disappear as tax structures are harmonized and border controls relaxed. Similarly, differentiation may not remain significant if competitors currently operating within national boundaries take on a European nature, in effect becoming new competitors in an expanded market.

It is clear that in the future products will have to compete on the basis of landed cost (e.g., all manufacturing costs, taxes, and shipping charges included in full). With internal barriers down, all competitors, whether based in Europe or elsewhere, will be on a more nearly equal basis within particular markets.

Assessing Logistics Support

The removal of cross-border obstacles to trade will mean faster and cheaper distribution of goods and services is essential. Logistics systems will take on added importance for manufacturing and distribution firms, meeting new requirements where the movement of materials and finished products is no longer constrained by border controls. The inability of a firm to reach a market, in effect a form of protective barrier for national businesses in the past, may vanish. All firms will be able to transport goods further and more quickly, and at a lower cost than ever before. Broader distribution networks will be a fundamental requirement for successful pan-European competition.

Assessing Management and Reporting Structures

The above changes suggest that *from the viewpoint of business processes,* the EC must be treated as a single region rather than a set of individual countries. Companies will be obliged to reexamine management strategies and reporting structures, emphasizing pan-European structures.

Similarly, marketing strategies may be shaped by demands for new forms of product pricing and delivery. Buyers are changing their manner of negotiating with suppliers, insisting on a single point of interface for contract and price negotiation. They are consolidating purchase orders to negotiate new quantity purchase levels. Single European contracts will often be negotiated in place of, say, a dozen national contracts for lower quantities and higher prices. (Yet the firm will be obliged to deliver and bill according to national norms.)

A large number of multinational firms have already made these adjustments. Many others have been treating Europe as a single region for many years. However, European firms themselves must adjust since they have traditionally focused on their native markets and perhaps those physically adjacent states.

Assessing Production and Distribution Capacity

Many corporations currently active in the EC operate multiple facilities developed to meet distinct national needs or to avoid transport hassle. Harmonization of laws and taxation policies may turn them into excess facilities, dispensable as their owners seek to shed excess capacity. Scale advantages may be possible where they were infeasible in the past.

On the other hand, firms wishing to establish a European presence may consider investing in manufacturing capacity within the EC. This is particularly true for those corporations accustomed to manufacturing products in their non-European locations and importing them into the EC. As legislation has made clear, true product manufacturing, not just assembly capability, will be an important criteria for the EC's local content decisions.

Strategic alliances (Lynch, 1990), mergers, and acquisitions are increasing in frequency (Exhibit 3). A growing number of European firms are using such strategies to establish a broader market presence, often acquiring facilities or arranging partners in other regions of the EC. Non-European firms are either purchasing European corporations or creating alliances (Exhibit 4). It is clear that the playing field will continue to change, and with it the rules of competition and criteria for success.

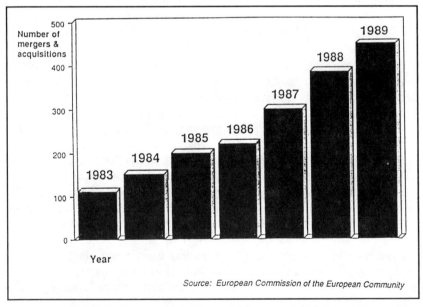

**Exhibit 3: Mergers and Acquisitions for 1000 Largest
European Companies**

Target nations	ECU million	Total Number of Deals
United Kingdom	20,831	237
Fed Rep of Germany	5,710	215
France	5,386	191
Italy	4,121	104
Spain	2,689	128
Netherlands	1,883	98
Belgium	1,285	61
Sweden	762	34
Denmark	543	34

Acquiring nations	ECU million	Total Number of Deals
United States	13,803	185
France	9,674	167
Fed Rep of Germany	6,647	128
United Kingdom	5,512	281
Italy	1,681	52
Japan	1,481	54
Sweden	1,381	120
Belgium	1,016	27
Switzerland	926	82

1 European currency unit (ECU) = approximately $1.10
Adapted from Translink's European Deal Review

Exhibit 4: Cross-Border Acquisitions Involving EC Firms During 1989

AREAS OF INFORMATION TECHNOLOGY IMPACT

The use of information technology to facilitate efficiency and individual support in the traditional lifestream applications is a fact of business life. All enterprises must make certain that such data processing systems are in place and working properly. But those systems alone are no guarantee of competitiveness in the EC or elsewhere.

Yet information technology is playing a central—indeed strategic—role in the competitive plans emerging from the meeting rooms of firms interested in the EC. While seemingly innovative strategies have been attributed to leading firms in the IT literature (Keen, 1988), the same strategies are actually essential ones for EC competitiveness. Corporate plans and information systems strategies are closely intertwined. Five strategies are most evident.

Strategy 1: Compress Business Response Time

Removing time from business processes (Stalk & Hout, 1990) is a necessity, not an option. From the development of new products to acceptance and fulfillment of orders, elapsed time is a barrier to business. Removing time from these processes creates advantage.

Logistics systems will change most dramatically in the Europe of 1992. It appears that firms will be obliged to provide delivery of products or materials to any point within the 12-member community within 24-hours. Removal of customs delays and harmonization of taxes associated with travel will promote quickly movement of freight. However, rapid delivery must be accompanied by an efficient order-to-ship cycle, and that is where information technology will be essential.

A large, multinational automobile manufacturer established its European parts center in Belgium. The center coordinates the distribution of all parts for the manufacturer and connects with dealers in Belgium, France, Germany, and the United Kingdom through videotext systems. Telephone links are used to interconnect with other countries. The center uses its information and communication systems to handle inquiries, accept orders, and fulfill requests quickly. Without the responsive logistics system, the firm would be unsuccessful in the unified market.

Strategy 2: Facilitate Mass Customization

There is a limit to the homogenization that can take place in the European Community. Twelve cultures simply will not become one; history, language, and social differences will prevent that. Hence, business will be obliged to accommodate local taste in the majority of the products and services it provides.

The customizing of products (Davis, 1987) to meet local taste will often depend on information technology-based flexible manufacturing systems that can be configured to manufacture a quantity of a product and then be adjusted quickly to produce a different product. Each time, manufacturing efficiency and quality levels are retained for both short and long runs.

In spite of the best intentions of the EC organizations, there will still not be one "Europe" but 12 separate countries. Firms will have to decide where Pan-European strategies can prevail and where local tastes must be accommodated.

A well-known foods European foods manufacturer is closing its regional factories located throughout Europe and consolidating production of individual brands into single factories. It is equipping the factories with flexible manufacturing systems that will drive costs down while enabling the firm to gain economies of scale in manufacturing.

Strategy 3: Enable Local Presence

As firms expand outside their national boundaries to establish a local presence in the EC, they will look to information technology as a way to maintain links to the home office. Transmission of customer order information in a timely fashion to meet the response-time targets discussed previously will certainly be one requirement. But local presence also means full service and support to buyers. Hence, there should be links to databases, engineers and technicians, and advisers, depending on the needs of a firm. The linkage will be electronic and transparent as time and distance barriers are erased. This strategy will be repeated many times.

Long-established firms will undoubtedly face new competition. For example, firms in the financial service industry will face new competitors, even if those competitors do not establish a specific facility in a state. The European Court of Appeals moved that a corporation legally established in one country can write insurance policies in another without having to establish a branch or subsidiary in that country.

A growing number of firms across diverse industries will carefully unfold a strategy of local presence. An umbilical cord in the form of digital communication networks and computer support systems will ensure that service and reporting meet the standards that have enabled the bank to gain its dominant position. Customers will be unaware whether information to respond to their queries originates in their local office or at corporate headquarters.

In businesses where strong local sales forces are needed to deal with customers, centralized sales systems will be difficult, even unworkable.

Local accommodation will not, however, be a panacea. Differing accounting procedures, tax laws, and other government policies will make it necessary for operation companies to exercise a considerable degree of autonomy.

A leading European bank has developed a multi-country presence that it supports through a comprehensive communications network and computer support system. The bank is now expanding to offer both banking and insurance activities throughout the EC. Local presence is an integral part of the strategy. The firm's communications system will ensure that service and reporting meet the standards of the bank and EC bodies. Customers will be unaware whether information to respond to their queries originate in the banking office where they are located or at the home office.

Strategy 4: Aid in Managing Europe as a Region

The focus on many firms will become Pan-European, rather than national. Hence, the Community will be recognized as a region for business.

Products, marketing, distribution, and packaging must remain responsive to local markets and to cultural issues. Yet the company must operate within a trans-European venue. "Business as usual" will mean balancing trans-European strategies with local tactics.

Marketing strategies are being shaped by the need to have new guidelines for the pricing and delivery of products. As mentioned earlier, buyers are already changing their manner of negotiating with suppliers, consolidating purchase orders and writing single European sales contracts, not individual national contracts. Conversion rates and pricing, perhaps in European currency units (ECUs—a form of currency used in commerce and made up of a combination of EC member money units) may further alter marketing strategies and policies.

Pricing, contracting, and sales management complexity may actually increase. Firms will find it impossible to keep pace unless they develop comparable marketing and sales support systems that provide information structured according to a regional view.

European contracting will increase. It will be virtually unmanageable if information technology is not integrated into the quotation, contracting, and delivery processes.

Companies in the computer and automobile industry typify the change going on across industries. In response to customer requests, the firms now quote prices for products based on Pan-European sales totals, even though the units are delivered through individual state marketing organizations. Local sales representatives are compensated based on units sold and delivered.

Strategy 5: Aid in Driving Down Cost of Operations

Cost management will grow in importance. EC leaders expect that prices will be average 5 to 6 percent less than those prevailing before passage of the Single European Act. Yet it is unlikely that the savings will result from personnel reductions (the social issues of unemployment and codetermination are topics of high-level importance).

Reduced inventory ratios should be achievable through central distribution centers. Such centers will be successful, however, only if rapid stock replenishments are possible. Changed transportation patterns may also reduce business costs. These are only examples, however. Heightened competition will increase the pressure on managers to reduce costs.

KEY INFORMATION TECHNOLOGY ISSUES

Good internal systems alone are not a basis for competitive success in the evolving European community, nor a firm information systems strategy. This section raises six questions IT executives must consider for EC competition (and for global business).

Abililty to Interconnect. To what extent can the firm interconnect with key suppliers and customers? What information can be exchanged? Many firms will learn that their systems are not currently designed for the type of interconnection that will be needed to meet the objectives of compressing business time and overcoming distance barriers. Cross-country and cross-application connectivity will both be fundamental.

IT managers and executives alike must recognize that the decision to share information, in order to obtain business advantages, will raise questions about other basic business systems. It is difficult to conceive of a situation where a decision to do business electronically will not touch all business systems—accounting, purchasing, inventory management, order processing, and even compensation systems.

Reach Across Markets. To what extent can a firm span consumer markets to acquire sales and demand information effectively? The ability of an organization to reach across markets is growing in importance. Since local accommodation is an essential characteristic of business, it is essential that both suppliers and customers be interconnected with decision making groups. Although the strategies vary, information technology is frequently the means to achieve the desired result.

Some manufacturers use sample stores to determine what is selling and therefore what items to manufacturer for a local market. Others rely on sharing of sales data, manufacturing schedules, and material requirements to ensure production needs are met, perhaps utilizing "just-in-time" methods. Often value-added networks and electronic data interchange are the means for accomplishing these business strategies.

Synchronization of Policy and Technology. To what extent are technology questions and policy questions jointly addressed and synchronized? Firms moving toward flexible manufacturing as a vehicle for meeting local taste or individual market needs have taken the easy step by making the decision to proceed. Among the many difficult choices that follow are such policy issues as whether to rely on single source suppliers, to pay higher parts and material costs on a per unit basis in order to achieve improved quality and long-term costs, and whether to share manufacturing and inventory capacities with partners who may be suppliers for one product line and competitors of another.

Likewise, a decision to share information does not mean the technology will facilitate the sharing. Firms may utilize different communication vendors, varying protocols and standards, or rely on proprietary systems while partners use open architectures. Information technology questions are at least as important as policy issues. Both IT managers and corporate officials must consider them together, meaning they must have an open line of communication between them.

Suitability of Technology Platform. Does a coherent information technology platform exist or is such a platform planned? Firms who are aggregating their capabilities at the EC level will often find that national operations were built from individual designs relying on local technology. This may be particularly troublesome if decisions were made years ago to use the technology of a major computer or communications vendor in the country of interest.

Many firms will find they do not have an information technology platform but rather a series of incompatible facilities, and worse yet, incompatible application systems. Selecting information technology options that will support a pressing application need, without regard for the larger platform, can only address a short-term IT need, often on a temporary basis.

Long-run advantages will accrue only to those firms who establish a platform which can be drawn on repeatedly as new applications, and new features for existing systems, are added. Criteria for selecting workstations, local area networks, value-added carriers, and database systems are the starting point for a foundation, not the end-point. The latter requires a full evaluation of information delivery requirements.

In selecting a platform, tough decisions about vendors will have to be made. Some vendors do not provide a coherent product line (on the hardware or the software side) that can serve as the basis for an information technology platform.

Application Location. To what extent should processing be distributed? The choice of a hardware and software platform on which to build EC-wide applications will raise many challenges, as it does in any large system. The need to meet local market requirements may result in a tendency toward distributed functionality and localized data. Price/performance trends in computing and data communication supports this tendency as will the continued evolution of high-power workstations, attractive mid-range systems, and effective networking techniques. On the other hand, the need to be responsive at corporate levels will in some instances suggest a centralized system and large processor platforms.

The Galileo system, Europe's first airline computerized reservation system, will give travel agents access on one screen to information about member airlines, including British Airways, Aer Lingus, Al Italia, KLM, TAP, and COVIA. The system is designed to provide response to travel agents in less than four seconds. Developers had the option of using a distributed architecture, taking advantage of powerful processing platforms linked by networking.

Developers ultimately decided to concentrate all computer applications in a single processing center rather than distributing the information across several sites. Distribution would have meant partitioning the database across various centers. That in turn would mean a devising a way for splitting the inventory of seats for flights across different computers which in turn means that the seat information for a specific flight would not be synchronized. Additional access time to locate and assemble all inventory information could mean the difference between a travel agent locating a seat in time or losing it to another agent.

Common Systems. Should information systems be common or tailor-made? The growing importance of accommodating local taste while achieving the levels of effectiveness firms need to be competitive multinationally also raises a question of uniformity across information systems. Should applications be tailor-made to fit local needs or common across markets, thus having a universal design?

Increasingly multinational firms are emphasizing common systems. They define data standards, processing characteristics, and application interfaces. Local development teams carry out the implementation, giving them ownership and involvement. At the same time, they pass back experience that may influence common system features as the applications evolve.

CONCLUSIONS

Key words for business in the changing Europe of 1992 will be time, distance, cost, flexibility, and customization. As EC directives alter the ground rules for competition, firms will have to scrutinize more carefully how and where they do business. The mix of competitors will continue to change, with European-based firms shifting their market focus and their territories of interest. Foreign competitors will continue to enter the market as well, often bringing with them new tactics and a Pan-European focus, unhindered by a tradition of nationalism.

Information technology will be increasingly viewed and utilized as an integral element for firms on the competitive playing field. Basic lifestream systems, aimed at productivity and efficiency must be in order. However, such systems will only enable a firm to step on to the field. More than ever before the ability to enter markets, serve customers, and respond to market changes will be influenced by the ability of a firm to interrelate corporate strategies and information technology capabilities, drawing on vision and infrastructure at the same time.

References

Davis, S.M. (1987). *Future Perfect,* Reading, MA: Addison-Wesley.

Completing the Internal Market, Office for Official Publications of the European Communities, Luxembourg.

European Unification: The Origins and Growth of the European Community, Office for Official Publications of the European Communities, Luxembourg.

Friberg, E.G. (May-June, 1989). 1992: Moves Europeans Are Making. *Harvard Business Review, 67*(3), 85-89.

Goette, E.E. (March/April, 1990). Europe 1992: Update for Business Planners. *Journal of Business Strategy, 11*(2), 10-13.

Jeelof, G. (April, 1990). Europe 1992: Fraternity of Fortress. *Communications of the ACM, 33*(4), 412-417.

Keen, Peter G.W., (1988). *Competing In Time,* (updated edition) Cambridge, MA: Ballinger.

Lynch, Robert Porter, (March/April, 1990). Building Alliances to Penetrate European Markets. *Journal of Business Strategy, 11*(2), 4-9.

Magee, J.F. (May/June, 1989). 1992: Moves Americans Must Make. *Harvard Business Review, 67*(3), 78-84.

Ohmae, K. (1985). *Triad Power,* New York: Free Press.

Stalk, G. Jr., & Hout, T.M. (1990). *Competing Against Time.* New York: Free press.

Working Together: The Institutions of European Community, Office for Official Publications of the European Communities, Luxembourg.

Illustrations and opinions in this report are based on information obtained from interviews with members of the European Community headquarters and executives in Europe and the U.S., from communiques from European Community directorates and from published sources.

3 Information Systems in the Soviet Union and Eastern Europe:
Opportunities Under Perestroika

Anthony Verstraete
Pennsylvania State University

The successful transfer of Information Technology to the former Soviet Bloc nations will be an important achievement in the conversion of Eastern European economies to a free and viable market economy. However, numerous issues must be resolved before such technology transfer can be successfully completed. Strongly centralized management structures, top heavy and conformist decision making apparatus and arcane labor practices must be faced. Legal and political hurdles involving restrictions on joint venture activities, difficulties in interpreting and enforcing agreements, and barriers to the free flow of data must all be surmounted. Problems concerning the availability and suitability of hardware, software, and communications technology must be overcome. This chapter identifies such salient issues and suggests strategies for dealing with them effectively.

INTRODUCTION

The recent events which have shaken the economic infrastructure of the Soviet Union and its satellite nations have been viewed by many observers in Western countries as an opening door to new opportunities for strengthening trade between the West and the nations belonging to the Soviet Council for Mutual Economic Assistance [COMECON]. With the specter of "Fortress Europe" suppressing trade with Western Europe and growing competition with other Pacific Rim nations, the prospect of new trading partners in Eastern Europe is quite welcome.

Of these new trading prospects, one sector of our economy which holds special interest is information technology and services. The United States and its western allies have seen a tremendous boom in the percentage of the GNP devoted to this sector. U.S. based multinationals belonging to this group including such giants as AT&T and IBM as well as hundreds of smaller firms are looking toward these opening markets for opportunities to sell information system products and services. They see peristroika's promise for business privatization resulting in thousands of new enterprises eager to obtain information technology from the west. Other western interests in the opening of Eastern Europe are focusing on the opportunities for joint ventures which could capitalize on the east's low labor costs and well educated work force. They hope to use computer based management systems to evaluate business potentials and for planning, organizing and controlling the joint venture.

Transferring information processing technology to Eastern Europe is not a simple matter of signing trade or joint venture agreements and locating marketing channels or relocating systems architectures currently in operation in the west. As with technology transfer anywhere, a complex set of interrelated factors will determine which information system products will find acceptance and how they should best be introduced. Issues involving economic, political, legal and other socio-cultural aspects of organization have often been identified in the success and failure of international technology transfer ventures elsewhere in the world. We have, from lack of opportunity, little direct experience with the Soviet Bloc counties in such endeavors.

In addressing the problems of transferring information technologies to Eastern Europe, we must be careful not to ignore the unique cultural identity of each nation. Recent political events have underscored this enduring cultural plurality. Maruyama (1990, p. 90) warns against simplistic approaches toward implementing management systems: "In East Europe, Romanians are highly individualistic and adversarial while the Poles are more mutualistic. Each country has its own cultural characteristics." A wealth of comparative management studies from Western Europe effectively demonstrates national and large regional differences in management attitudes and practices which could influence the design, implementation and use of information systems (Hofstede, 1981; Laurant, 1983). We unfortunately lack similar studies from Eastern Europe. However, overall similarities can be detected in certain socio-cultural attributes of the eastern slavs, and these tendencies have been reinforced over the years of domination and influence from Moscow. For example, a fundamental feature of eastern slavic society is a preference for strong, paternalistic centralized leadership. Deeply rooted in slavic family and village organization, this patriarchal relationship tends to extend to include all authorities within and beyond the village, a pronounced feature of the culture of the eastern slavs which has been sustained during centuries of centralized totalitarian rule. (Fitzsimmons, Malof, & Fiske, 1960).

This chapter will explore what is known concerning information systems within Eastern Europe at present, both from a technical stance and from an organizational perspective. It will serve as a survey comparing current knowledge concerning the diffusion of information technologies and the channels through which such diffusion occurs. Of special importance will be the differentiation of formal government agencies responsible for promulgating 'informatization' within the U.S.S.R. and its former satellites. Also, this chapter will examine informal infrastructures in Eastern European society which could either be obstacles to technology transfer or serve as vehicles for spreading these new technologies.

ISSUES IN INFORMATION TECHNOLOGY TRANSFER

This section reviews what is currently known from recently published and private sources concerning the diffusion of information technology in Eastern Europe, what changes to expect under perestroika and obstacles which may be encountered. Since reliable figures on the rate and extent of the adoption of information systems are unavailable, what little evidence as can be offered is more anecdotal than empirical. We will examine a wide range of evidence concerning economic, organizational, political, legal, and technological aspects of Eastern European society, and draw inferences concerning how the identified conditions might impact attempts to transfer information technologies under Gorbachev's policy of perestroika.

Economic Issues

How has perestroika been developing in the economy? I must say, frankly, that all our efforts toward changing the structure of the national economy, transferring it on to the track of intensive development, and accelerating scientific progress prompted even more urgently the need for a radical reform of the economic mechanism and for restructuring the entire system of economic management (Gorbachev, 1987, 83).

For the last seventy years, the Soviet Bloc system of "economic management" was characterized by the creation of gargantuan industrial complexes controlled from the top under the direction of ministries whose decisions were based upon social and political motivation rather than by profit making incentives. A key role in answering Gorbachev's call for a monumental "restructuring" is the development and implementation of information systems designed to aid rational management decision making and move its loci down toward the operational levels. It is the quest for informatization, a term used in Soviet Bloc government for the effort to introduce information technology. Among the issues which must first be considered is the economic scale of the organizations targeted for information system modernization (large industrial complexes to small incipient businesses) and the design of information systems to support the vastly different accounting and reporting objectives of managers in the Soviet Bloc economic system. This was not, and is not yet, a "free" economy as we know it in the west, and there is a corresponding lack of a free flow of information: "...information is only publicized if it will help shape the society or mold it. A common pool accessible to all does not exist in any serious form except where it is operationally unimportant. An information marketplace...does not exist" (Malik, 1984).

The economic incentives for domestic and foreign investment in information systems in Eastern Europe are obvious. The combined population of the Soviet Union and its former satellites is about 400 million individuals, which represents an enormous market potential as well as an educated and low cost labor pool for joint manufacturing ventures. From an international perspective, information systems can be viewed as a tool to capture these potential markets or facilitate venture management. From the domestic viewpoint, information systems represent a way of improving operations within the huge, inefficient eastern european industrial complexes. Almost all production is currently concentrated in large scale industries. Small scale industries are almost non-existent, nor are there many small independent business operations. But the long lead times and high costs of implementing modern information processing systems within large scale industries, coupled with the difficulties in recouping such investments over the short time frame preferred by most western investors, represent obstacles to technology transfer to this scale of enterprise.

Hope has been expressed for introducing information technologies within more modest start-up "cooperatives" , a term synonymous with small privately owned businesses in the Soviet Bloc. However, the American rags-to-riches tales of young entrepreneurs who start small companies that grow into multimillion dollar enterprises may never have many Soviet Bloc counterparts. Those in the west who anticipate a huge market for small business systems might temper their enthusiasm. The inflated estimates of the number of cooperatives recently formed is a misleading indicator of market size. The majority of those registered exist only on paper and are not, nor may never be, truly operational entities. Until now almost all of those cooperatives which do actually operate exist as an alternative market outlet to serve in obtaining and distributing goods, rather than for creating new products or services. In a recent interview Nikolai Petrakov, one of Gorbachev's top economic advisors, acknowledged "widespread hostility to the cooperative movement." (Berlin, 1990) In the eyes of many citizens, cooperatives are just another disagreeable manifestation of black marketeering. Dyson (1990) reports the comment of a computer programmer who preferred not to work for cooperatives because he considered it too dangerous to associate himself with such unpopular (and presumably temporary) enterprises. Nevertheless, the small cooperatives which do provide marketable products or services, rather than the behemoths of Soviet Bloc industry, may provide the most fertile ground for the introduction of innovative information technologies, and may be the best route to pioneering informatization. They possess the least structural resistance, and their size permits rapid implementation and pay backs.

Accounting Information Systems

The effects of long domination of Soviet Bloc accounting systems within the Eastern European economy will pose among the greatest challenges to the transfer of information systems technology. The difficulties of transferring accounting information systems or using existing outputs from Soviet Bloc accounting systems are overwhelming. In a recent report on Hungry, Fuhrman (1990) bemoans "There are no proper accounting systems, and accounting fraud is a way of life among bureaucrats whose jobs depend more upon meeting paper goals [rather] than on producing real products."

This situation is related to a strong, venerable underground economy which exists in parallel to the officially sanctioned economy, deeply entrenched in the peasant economies of the pre-soviet era. The "official" and "unofficial" economies are mutually interdependent, although the underground activities and cash flows are, by definition, undocumented. In fact, the term "cash flow" is misleading...much of the underground economy rests upon bartering goods and services where no rubles are exchanged. Ruble equivalents assigned by government agencies to these goods and services are often meaningless since such products are unobtainable at such official rates!

From the point of view of western business, such underground activity is often considered as bribery, fraud, and corruption. A Japanese management expert recently complained "In some East European countries...bribing became more rampant than in free market economies where one has to maintain some level of productivity and cannot live entirely on bribes. But in a nonfree market system, one can live on bribes" (Maruyama, 1990). However, labeling behaviors unacceptable in western culture with disapprobative terms can be counterproductive. Managerial differences in ethical values are often rooted in the host country's culture and will resist attempts at change (Davis, 1988). Accepting money or favors for services rendered, as well as manipulation of data to support beliefs and policies, is normally accepted behavior in many non-western business settings, not just Soviet Bloc nations, and continue to be a problem in business relationships with the United States even after years of bilateral business relations.

Accompanying the problem of undocumented payments for products or services rendered and falsified information, is the problem of interpreting the legitimate accounting data reported by information systems. Financial ratios generated from these systems are often misused when applied to foreign operations because of differences in accounting practices and misinterpreted because the U.S. investor does not understand the economic environment that influences all financial ratios in the Soviet Bloc economic environment. Choi (1983) warns that accounting information, which relies heavily on symbolic representation of enterprise activities, may undergo further misinterpretation because a given symbol may assume different meanings in different cultural contexts. In the economic systems of Eastern Europe, almost any financial ratio or other economic indicator will not be directly comparable with its western equivalent.

Manufacturing Information Systems

Many years ago Berlinger (1959), in his classic comparative studies of managerial decision making in the U.S. and the Soviet Union, found that production data could not be taken at face value in the Soviet Bloc system. On the sending end, managers would falsify reported production or underestimate real productive capacity. Fabrication or distortion of information would be expected, and compensatory adjustments would later be made by those receiving and interpreting such information provided they understood the cultural norms of expected distortion. According to Berlinger, much of this behavior stems from the system of bonuses; a system which has been a strongly entrenched aspect of management rewards dating from pre-soviet czarist days. Gorbachev (1987, 20) acknowledges this problem: "...bonuses began to be paid and all kinds of undeserved incentives introduced...that led, at a latter stage, to the practice of padding reports merely for gain."

Because such practice is long standing and socially institutionalized, any attempts to introduce accurate computer based reporting systems are certain to be greeted with hostility and resistance, and widespread tampering and sabotage may result. Even in the unlikely event that the production data available from Soviet Bloc manufacturing systems is accurate, its interpretation still remains a problem for western managers. For examples, we may look again to the problems involved in measuring production. Manufacturers in much of Eastern Europe count all of their productive output as earned revenues, even though the products may not be actually sold. Inventory and accounts receivable are equally uninterpretable. Therefore, the standard information models used to determine the performance of enterprises in the west are not easily transferable to Soviet Bloc nations. Paul Hoffman, an Arthur Anderson partner who was recently involved in a joint venture deal in the Soviet Union, frustratedly comments "Their model just doesn't capture such things as costs or profits" (Sternthal, 1990). It is doubtful if this situation will change in the near future, in spite of perestroika.

ORGANIZATIONAL MANAGEMENT ISSUES

We realize that the rates of economic restructuring are in no small degree held back by the bulky nature and inadequate efficiency of the managerial apparatus...Redistribution of rights between the central departments and the enterprises is not proceeding smoothly. The apparatus of the ministries and ministers themselves are unwilling to give up the habit of deciding minor matters themselves (Gorbachev, 1987, 91).

Organizational structure in Eastern European nations has long been characterized by its highly centralized and rigid nature. Observers have noted that such tendencies predate the Soviet era, and are deeply rooted in Slavic culture. (Berlinger, 1959; Fitzsimmons, Malof & Fiske, 1960). Gorbachev's own admission of frustration in the failed attempt to decentralize decision making authority and in reducing "bulky, unwieldy and bureaucratic structures" is telling.

Centralization of Management

In the West, recent advances in information system technology, and the management infrastructures which support it, have been characterized as a growing federation of decentralized systems. Such architectures may be inappropriate for Eastern European organizations. Transfer of IS technology to Eastern Europe requires that these technologies be adapted to fit the organizational structures they are intended to support. Accompanying these issues are a variety of salient topics concerning the nature of managerial attitudes toward information and its "legitimate" use in business and society.

Factories in Eastern Europe are characterized by strongly centralized, rigidly formalized structures. There is a corresponding tendency towards bureaucratic specialization which is deeply rooted in the organizational makeup of Eastern European enterprises. The combination of centrality of decision making and the fragmentation of decision authority among specialists results in a situation where management "...is unlikely to be able to alter the size of its own labour force or its supervisory echelon, to spend capital sums, to specify the exact equipment it prefers, to embark on a new product line, to spend capital sums, to vary prices, to change its sources of supply, to reorganize departments, to determine its selection and training methods." (Kuc, Hickson & McMillan, 1980, p. 266).

Management Decision Making Processes

To those attempting to achieve a computer integrated manufacturing environment, or to introduce rational management schemes based upon MIS reporting systems, such a finding severely impacts the assessment of organizational feasibility. It would appear that the tendency towards strong rigid centralized control is strongly reinforced by a cultural tendency to discount individual decision making responsibility which probably predates the Soviet era. It finds voice in the statement made to a westerner by a Russian businessman that "No decision is a safe decision in the Soviet Union. You commit yourself to any course of action, and you increase your chances of being wrong by 50 percent" (Barium, 1990).

Relaxing the stultifying effects of a rigidly centralized organizational structure was a key goal of Gorbachev, who complained that the old soviet management system was "severely centralized, every assignment regulated down to the last detail." Under these conditions, the introduction of new technologies such as information systems becomes extremely difficult. One of the Soviet Bloc's most severe practical problems is how to foster evolving technologies within particular and specific structures of ministerial responsibility. "The technology not only adds to ministerial power, it can also redistribute it; and thus, for some, diminish it. And the further up the ladder, the more difficult the technology becomes to introduce" (Malik, 1984, p 42).

A Soviet systems expert from the U.S.S.R. Academy of Sciences, in commenting upon recent attempts to loosen such centralized control in these government ministries themselves, observes that the management functions and tasks inherent in the middle level are instead performed at the headquarters and that the management bodies of divisions still remain in the headquarter units. Attempts to separate these bodies from the headquarters and turn them into profit centers have failed for varying reasons (Rapoport, 1989).

Among the difficulties encountered in decentralization efforts, concerns the retention of control of profits for such purposes as construction of new enterprises, social programs, and so forth. According to Rapoport's report, "...management decentralization, implemented nowadays in the course of radical reform, is based upon the first function -- control of everyday operations -- being completely delegated to enterprises, and the second -- management of centralized funds -- being retained by the state management bodies" (Rapoport, 1989, p. 444). This assures that the Soviet Bloc organization can still not, in this era of perestroika, be effectively governed by information systems modeled around western concepts of profitability as a basis for rational management decision making.

Labor Management

Among the significant problems in integrating information systems into the organizational structure of Eastern European countries lie in labor conditions in those countries. Observers have noted that labor in Eastern Europe is characterized by absenteeism, featherbedding, waste, pilferage, and a general lack of work ethic in comparison to industrialized market economies (Kennedy, 1990). Within such an organizational environment, hostility towards the intrusion of information technologies, which would be viewed as an onerous attempt at controlling labor inefficiencies would likely lead to attempts to subvert or sabotage such systems.

LEGAL AND POLITICAL ISSUES

Activity and initiative developing within the framework of law should be given every support and encouragement...Let's strictly observe the principle: everything which is not prohibited by law is allowed (Gorbachev, 1987, 108).

There is a joke in Moscow concerning the place "Principle"; in Principle, any legal activity is permitted; the only trouble is no one knows where to find principle! (Dyson, 1989). What is allowed, in reality, is often unclear and, even if allowed, may be ill advised. Transferring technology available from the western private sphere requires surmounting complex legal hurdles. Restrictions still exist in the west limiting the exportation of certain information technologies to the Soviet Bloc nations. In addition, negotiations and contracting for the sale of equipment and services in Eastern Europe is quite dissimilar from western practices, and extra-legal systems operate in parallel, and often in replacement of, formal law. Issues of legally sanctioned piracy of hardware and software add to the tangle of legal problems encountered in moving western information technology eastward.

Restrictions on Joint Ventures

The soviet fear of becoming exploited slaves toiling for the profit of foreign owned operatives has led to the creation of several legal restrictions on foreign ventures. Investment capital is scarce, yet until recently attempts to attract foreign investment have been stymied by insistence that western investors be barred from majority ownership. More recently, such restrictions on equity participation have been relaxed in view of the unrealistic nature of such demands. However, especially considering the xenophobic character of the Eastern Slavs, it is reasonable to predict that further attempts to place restrictions on western ownership and the expatriation of earnings will occur.

Interpreting and Enforcing Legal Agreements

Adding to the legal impediments to investment in high technology transfer are fears of defaults on payments, inability to expatriate funds in hard currency and nationalization of foreign investments. The Japanese Ministry of International Trade recently warned Japanese businesses it will not extend its customary trade insurance to Soviet Bloc trade ventures following a string of defaults on payments. Valery Kazikaev, president of the U.S.S.R. Union of Managers and active in the promotion of joint ventures, recently acknowledged this high risk is discouraging foreign investors, remarking that "Many companies are scared, but those who don't risk, don't win" (Sternthal, 1990).

To win requires careful study of the complex and often ambiguously worded legal documents and rulings. For example, recently issued guidelines by the U.S.S.R. concerning foreign investment contained this ominous clause: "All foreign currency expenditures of a joint venture, including transfer of profits and other sums due to foreign partners and specialists, shall be covered by proceeds from sales of the joint venture's products on foreign markets" (Bart, 1989). Practically, this would restrict investment in information technology in the development of industry for domestic markets, since such investment would currently require the use of hard currencies to purchase information technology unavailable within Eastern European nations. Other clauses from the same set of guidelines permit "liquidation" of joint ventures by unilateral decree of the U.S.S.R. Council of Ministers and require unanimity on "fundamental issues"; essentially giving them the legal right to unilaterally veto business decisions and terminate business relationships. The problems and legal restrictions on sending domestic earned profits abroad can lead to some creative finance. For example, Pepsico's highly profitable operation in the U.S.S.R. was repaid by resorting to the old pre-soviet barter system...they were compensated in vodka, which they then exported to sell abroad. The Soviet Bloc information industry, unlike its beverage, is not yet able to offer an equally saleable product.

The rapid change in political/legal decision authority further complicates the picture. A Western firm with established ties in the Soviet Union had received a commitment of support to proceed on a joint venture from a major industrial ministry, only to discover upon a subsequent visit that the minister had been replaced and that responsibility for the decision concerning the joint venture now lay with a different ministry (Laurita & McGloin, 1988). In another recently reported case (Kiam, 1990) Remington's attempts to embark on a joint enterprise were thwarted when the first agreement painstakingly arranged through the local Chamber of Commerce fell through, and subsequent dealings with the Soviet Minister of Industry failed because of unrealistic constraints concerning the acquisition of components. Large scale information systems typically require long lead times to implement in western nations. Delays in negotiation and bureaucratic changes in the loci of decision authority will certainly result in even greater delays in Eastern Europe.

If the legal barriers posed by central government structures such as the Council of Ministers provide little assurance, the decentralization of authority only exacerbates the problem. For example, John Minneman, Chase Manhattan's Moscow representative, has remarked that in the past foreigners could rely on contractual agreements, as they were all signed by the Ministry of Foreign Trade which was scrupulous in honoring such agreements. Now, thousands of state-owned enterprises can negotiate their own agreements, but there is little certainty that the agreements are enforceable (Smith, 1990). A new bilateral investment treaty is, as this is being written, under negotiation with the Soviet Union, and if signed may reduce contractual risks.

Data Flow Restrictions

Considering the sensitive nature of information systems in organizations, it is virtually certain that the legal right to collection and use of information will be among those fundamental issues. An especially sensitive area of prime interest to foreign participants in joint ventures with the Soviet Bloc nations concerns transborder data flows. Transmitting data across national borders involves a complex set of laws and overlapping jurisdictions which pose many problems even for flows among western allied nations (Chradran, Phatak & Sambharya, 1987).

TECHNICAL ISSUES

We have drawn lessons from the decisions taken by the United States and other Western countries to refuse to sell the Soviet Union advanced technology. That is perhaps why we are now experiencing a real boom in the fields of information science, computer technology, and other areas..." (Gorbachev, 1987, 94).

However, there appears to be little evidence to support Gorbachev's claim to such a boom in information technology. Most computers currently available in Eastern Europe are illegally obtained or poor, unreliable copies of western produced mainframes (mainly IBM 360/370 family), a hodge-podge of mid-range computers of various makes which complicate interconnectivity and data transfer problems, and around 200,000 micros, of which about half are IBM clones from Sweden or Asia. Parts and repair expertise are both in short supply, and it is difficult to say how many computer facilities are in working order. Interconnectivity problems are exacerbated by primitive telecommunications facilities.

Hardware

The attempt to introduce computers in Soviet Bloc management practice long predates the period of glastnost and perestroika. The attempt to establish within its industries what the Soviets called automatizirovannaya sistema upravleniya [ASU], which roughly translates as "Automated Management Systems," has been ongoing since the sixties. But the endeavor, like all officially sanctioned activities within the Soviet Bloc system, was relegated to the control of the centralized ministries. Objective reports of implementation success or failure are unavailable from the ministries themselves but the general consensus, both within and outside the Soviet Union is that most ASUs have failed to meet their expectations.

Technical initiatives to develop computer applications were fragmented between various ministries and their appendages. Analyzing the structure of the Soviet Bloc computer industry involves learning a Russian "alphabet soup" of state committees, ministries and special bureaus and institutes. Production of mainframe computers has been assigned to the Ministry of Radio Industry [MINRADIOPROM] whereas responsibility for application programming was delegated to the Ministry of Instrument Construction, Means of Automation and Control Systems [MINPRIBOR]. Responsibility for microcomputer production has been variously assigned to several agencies. The State Committee for Science and Technology [GKNT] used to be the primary body in charge of policy decisions relating to the production and use of information systems, but their duties have been partially reassigned to the newly formed State Committee for Computer Technology and Informatics [GKVTI]. The Bureau of Machine Building, a staff organization of the Council of Ministers, attempts to coordinate the diverse activities, but has failed to achieve success. In spite of numerous attempts at reorganization, the Soviet Bloc computer industry remains complex and decision making far removed from the user community (Hebditch, 1988).

By the end of the sixties, those in charge of computer systems development decided to emulate the IBM 360 systems design in lieu of pursuing their own architectures. These copies eventually were redesigned to duplicate the IBM 370s, but technical difficulties abounded: in migration from older machines, in the availability of critical peripheral units, in high failure rates due to faulty components, and so forth. (Davis & Goodman, 1978) The Soviet Union's five year plan for the last half of the eighties dictated that over a million PCs be produced -- only a few fault plagued models were ever delivered.

Software

According to McHenry & Goodman (1986), the low level of hardware has "...impeded the introduction of complicated tasks, reduced the confidence of management in its ability to rely on the computer for anything critical, and lengthened the time needed to design and implement systems." Software is equally poor in design and reliability. The Soviet ministry in charge of software development was mandated to develop a standard number of "tasks" for selected applications. However, those tasks chosen for implementation were done so on the basis of their ease of development rather than upon their impact on efficiency or effectiveness of the enterprise.

Eastern Europe boasts a number of "experienced" programmers, but such experience is in the production of code -- much of it assembly code. In terms of software engineering technique, project management, the design of modern user friendly interfaces, and so forth, the Eastern European programmers are quite unsophisticated. As with Soviet Bloc labor in general, few incentives exist to encourage software innovations by programmers. Alexei Pazhitnov, muscovite author of the popular computer game TETRIS, serves as an example. Although his game sold widely in the west, he did not profit directly. Instead, the rights are owned by the academy for which he works. He hopes to market future games through the JV Dialouge cooperative, a joint venture involving Microsoft (Dyson, 1989), but there are currently few joint ventures offering such an outlet for programming creativity. Moreover, it is likely that Pazhitnov is an exception whose talents are not shared among most Soviet Bloc production programmers.

Data Communications

In the United States and Western Europe, the early growth of computer communications was greatly facilitated by the existence of a well established telephone network. With lines in place, only a modem was required to transfer data. In Eastern Europe, telephones are relatively scarce, and access to lines are controlled by powerful Ministries of Postal, Telephone, and Telegraph Service [PTT]. The U.S.S.R. reports only 13 phones per 100 inhabitants, and the switching technology is primitive (Kudriavtzev & Varakin, 1990). Complaints are frequent concerning long waits for obtaining telephone lines for new enterprises, and problems in establishing connections to installed lines. Digital switching equipment is unavailable, making the implementation of integrated digital networks an impossibility now and for the foreseeable future. Knowing this, an American executive of a major telecommunications company was puzzled by the request of an official of the Soviet PTT for "digital" phones until he realized that the man was simply referring to touch-tone phones to replace the rotary dial phones (Barnum, 1990). The transmission lines are of such poor quality that either special lines must be installed or a search conducted through which only one in every 20 or 30 lines is found adequate (Grahan, 1986).

The primitive telephone network conditions, along with the unavailability of leased lines or alternative networking resources, assures that most information systems will be insular or restricted to LAN configurations which can be installed without resort to the government communication monopolies. A report from a recent meeting of Eastern European members of the International Telecommunications Society indicates that the government PTT Ministries are strongly entrenched and that little progress is being made toward deregulation (Steffens, 1990).

Transferring technology to the Soviet Bloc countries is in some ways aided and in other ways hindered by the existing technological environment in Eastern Europe. Insofar as the large mainframes copy the IBM 370 technology, it will be a relatively easy task to retrofit Soviet Bloc equipment found in Eastern Europe with imported equipment. However, because of the very high failure rates of the Soviet Bloc mainframe computers, it is questionable if such upgrades are cost effective. Failure rates for Soviet Bloc made microcomputers are also high, and due to the lack of replacement boards and trouble shooting expertise, repairs may take months. Managers, therefore, cannot rely on computers for routine operational support.

Because the approval and acquisition of computer equipment is still fragmented among ministries, and must conform to their standards and policies, efforts to "leap frog" Soviet Bloc information systems into the 21st century are likely to be thwarted. Even if technically modern and reliable hardware and software can be imported or produced locally, there still remains the challenge of interconnectivity posed by the primitive Soviet Bloc telecommunications industry. Finally, although not yet officially reported, it must be assumed that most technological systems implemented in Eastern Europe will be under higher risk of misuse and sabotage than similar systems in the west.

IMPLICATIONS FOR PRACTITIONERS OF INFORMATION TECHNOLOGY TRANSFER

The lack of practical experience in designing and implementing information systems in Eastern Europe means that, until a wide base of implementation experiences is available, we must govern our approach based upon the indirect evidence reviewed above. Several inferences can be drawn concerning the types of systems architectures most likely to meet the organizational environments of Eastern Europe, the techniques best used to transfer information technologies, and the management methods needed to assure smooth implementation and operation.

One overwhelmingly predominant feature of Eastern European organization universally mentioned is its extreme emphasis on centrality, with decision making emanating from the top and seldom allocated to lower echelons. Within such an environment, the personal computer will serve a far different role than it has in the west, where its introduction enhances individual autonomy. In the west, spreadsheets were quickly embraced because of the flexible modeling potential they offer. In Eastern Europe, individuals are less likely to be motivated to use the tools in this manner. If used at all, templates which provide standard solutions to guide routine operations would be a more likely way to utilize spreadsheets. Spreadsheet products would best be implemented as fully developed applications requiring no local modeling activity.

Conversely, expert systems on PC platforms, especially those designed to facilitate routine procedural or diagnostic operations, would fit well within the organizational and technological infrastructure of Eastern Europe. We are faced with an undertrained work force in an area which has tremendous labor and market potential. Given the abundance of low cost labor, and the high cost of automation such as industrial robots and lack of experts to train and supervise labor, the guidance offered by expert systems applications would seem highly feasible.

One of the most promising potential markets is for database applications. Since information (data) is often regarded as a means of legitimizing established authority and control, rather than as a means of obtaining control or gaining a competitive edge over others, accuracy of data may not be important. "Data does flow, lots of it. It is data aimed at the production of statistics...tables constantly pass before you, yet little data is available on what went wrong in a time scale for you to be able to affect it...[it] eschews comparisons across the board.." (Malik, 1984).

Database technology in the United States is sold with the promise of providing a greater diversity of views and creative access of the data resource, as well as enhancing accuracy by reducing informational inconsistencies inherent in data redundancy. These advantages may not, except in certain scientific applications, appeal to traditional Soviet Bloc management. A great potential for marketing database technology exists in the Soviet Union, but database products should currently be promoted on their ability to restrict user views to those deemed legitimate, to limit access, and to prohibit "unauthorized" data values. Reducing data redundancy and thereby eliminating inconsistencies may not be viewed as an advantage, as they are in the West.

Local Area Networks, insofar as they can be simply installed and be independent of the government PTT communications monopolies, have far reaching potential. Complaints concerning communication problems abound in Eastern Europe. The ability to interconnect offices in the same or closely adjacent buildings, especially if it can be achieved through installing low cost twisted pair lines, would allow great efficiency improvements. Here, however, the implementer must carefully tread through the maze of legal restrictions concerning the installation and use of private communication networks. It can be predicted that the PTTs will zealously guard their monopolies, and attempt to restrict LAN implementations, especially if they involve integrated voice/ data communications.

In conclusion it should be emphasized that the problems and obstacles noted in this chapter can be surmounted or avoided when the systems practitioner is made aware of such pitfalls and armed with a knowledge of feasible strategies. What is very clear is that success cannot be achieved on a short term basis. Success in transferring information technologies to Eastern Europe will come only after years of patient accumulation of experience and the careful nurturing of the nascent information systems. Introducing information systems will require patience and flexibility in redesigning information systems to respond to the economic and cultural demands of local managers. The period during which reforms of perestroika take place promise to be tumultuous, and the timid may wish to avoid the fray. But the enormous potential is there to be exploited by those with the courage, patience and foresight to do so.

References

Barnum, C.F. (1990). Americans as seen from behind the iron curtain. *International Executive, 31*(3), 47-48.

Berlin, R.K. (1990). Can the russians really reform? *Fortune. 121*(10), 117, 120-121.

Berlinger, J. (1959). Managerial incentives and decision-making: A comparison of the United States and the Soviet Union. *Comparisons of the United States and Soviet economies, Part 1.* Washington D.C.: Joint Economic Committee of the Congress of the United States. 349-376.

Burt, J.A. (1989). Considering a joint venture with the russians: What you can expect. *The International Executive, 31*(3), 8-13.

Chandran, R., Phatak, A., & Sambharya, R. (1987). Transborder data flows: Implications for multinational corporations. *Business Horizons, 30*(6), 74-82.

Choi, F.D.S. (Spring/Summer, 1983). Analyzing foreign financial statements: The use and misuse of international ratio analysis. *Journal of International Business Studies, 14*(1), 113-131.

Davis, H.J., & Rasool, S.A. (1988). Values research and managerial behavior: Implications for devising culturally consistent managerial styles. *Management International Review, 28*(3), 11-20.

Davis, N.C., & Goodman, S.E. (1978). The soviet bloc's unified system of computers. *ACM Computing Surveys, 10*(2), 93-122.

Desai, P. (1989). *Perestroika in perspective: The design and dilemmas of soviet reform.* Princeton: Princeton University Press.

Dyson, E. (1989). High risks, distant payoffs. *Forbes, 114*(13), 117-120.

Dyson, E. (1989). Three weeks that shook my world. *Forbes, 143*(12), 103-105.

Fitzsimmons, T., Malof, P., & Fiske, J.C. (1969). *U.S.S.R.: Its people, its society, its culture.* Human Area Relations File Survey of World Cultures. Mayflower Publishing Company, London.

Fuhrnam, T.P. (1990). Doing business in the dark. *Forbes, 115*(4), 50-51.

Gorbachev, M. (1987). *Perestroika: New thinking for our country and the world.* New York: Harper & Row.

Graham, L. (June, 1986). Russia's non-revolution. *Personal Computing,* 222.

Hofstede, G. (1981). Culture and organization. *International Studies of Management and Organization, 10*(4), 15-41.

Hebditch, D. (1988). The structure of the soviet IS industry. *Datamation, 34*(16), 24, 26.

Kennedy, P.J. (1990). Doing business in the new Eastern Europe: A risk profile. *International Executive, 31*(6), 7-13.

Kiam, V.K. (1990). Eastern Europe: The new entrepreneurial frontier. *International Executive, 31*(5), 9-13.

Kuc, B., Hickson, D.J., & McMillan, C. (1980). Centrally planned development: A comparison of Polish factories with equivalents in Britain, Japan, and Sweden. *Organizational Studies, 1*(3), 253-270.

Kudriavtzev, G.G., & Varakin, L.E. (1990). Economic aspects of telephone network development: The USSR plan. *Telecommunications Policy, 14*(1), 8-14.

Laurent, A. (1983). The cultural diversity of western conceptions of management. *International Studies of Management and Organization, 13*(1-2), 75-96.

Laurita, T., & McGloin, M. (1988). US-Soviet joint ventures: Current status and prospects. *Columbia Journal of World Business, 23*(2), 43-51.

Malik, R. (July 8, 1984). Communism vs. the computer: Can the USSR survive the information age? *Computerworld*, 35-48.

McHenry, W.K., & Goodman, S.E. (1986). MIS in soviet industrial enterprises: The limits of reform from above. *Communications of the ACM, 29,* 1034-1043.

Maruyama M. (1990). Some management considerations in the economic reorganization of Eastern Europe. *Academy of Management Executive, 4*(2), 90-91.

Rapoport, V. (1989). Consistency and change: Flexible organization structures. *Systems Practice,* 2(4).

Smith, L. (1990). Can you make any money in Moscow? *Fortune, 121*(1), 103-107.

Steffens, M.B. (1990). Reform in Eastern Europe. *Telecommunications Policy, 14*(1), 87-89.

Sternthal, S. (1990). Soviets aim for trade pact. *Insight, 6*(28), 40-41.

Telecommunications in Eastern Europe

4

Ewan Sutherland
University of Stirling

Following the political changes in Eastern Europe there is an opportunity for the countries to make good the gap in their telecommunications infrastructure and to develop for the first time value-added services. To achieve this requires a considerable liberalisation and enormous change in the regulatory regime. Telecommunications operators can usefully be separated from the traditional post and telephone authority and can then be privatised. Joint ventures are a very useful way forward in improving the manufacturing sector. Foreign firms, with expertise and capital can contribute enormously to these developments, always provided the circumstances are attractive.

INTRODUCTION

In parallel with the immense political changes in Eastern Europe there has been an unprecedented opening up of these economies. The 'dead hand' of state bureaucracy was withdrawn creating a political and economic uncertainty which has permitted the re-emergence of ideas thought to be long forgotten. Writing in 1990, one can see only the stirrings of change; for good or ill Eastern Europe will reverberate with change until well into the next century.

The apparent aim of the peoples of Eastern Europe is to achieve the same standard of living of Western Europe and to do so as quickly as possible. They are seeking membership in the European Community and are enthusiastic about meeting the political and economic conditions this would require; they have already jumped at democracy and seem willing to accept the free market with open arms. How long this will last is less certain. People will be confronted with inflation, unemployment and bankruptcies followed by the economic and political counter-measures which governments will be obliged to use. The transition will be painful for both individuals and society.

The 'liberation' of Eastern Europe by the Red Army at the end of World War II left the region under Communist domination. Countries were forced to undergo a perversion of economic development along Stalinist lines, leaving legacies of aging and inappropriate heavy industry which has distorted their economies and polluted the environment. While Western Europe has entered the information economy Eastern Europe retains high levels of employment in extractive and primary industries (See Figure 1).

Eastern Europeans accept that in almost all areas of technology they have fallen behind and they now want to acquire Western technology in order to catch up; telecommunications is no exception. The infrastructure of cables and exchanges is 20 to 25 years behind Western Europe, while telecommunications-based services are almost non-existent.

In this author's opinion, this backwardness has been caused mainly by misguided governmental policies, economic weakness and mismanagement which have resulted in prolonged under-investment in telecommunications. Reliance on the division of the manufacturing of telecommunications equipment among Eastern European countries made the position worse, through the

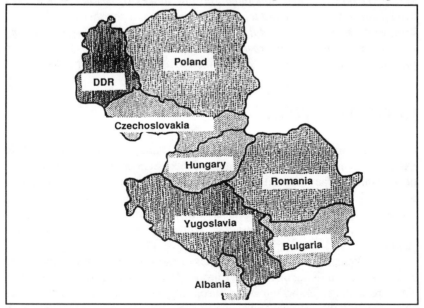

Figure 1 :   Map of Eastern Europe

failure of most countries to deliver to an acceptable quality. There was a total absence of consumer feedback, blocked by the rigid structure of ministries and monopoly telecommunications operators. Under-development also resulted from the trade restrictions imposed by the United States of America and its allies through COCOM (the Coordinating Committee on Multi-lateral Export Controls).

Decisions taken in Eastern Europe are unlikely to have any significant effect on the pace or direction of global technological change in telecommunications. Those changes are difficult for any country to control or influence including the United States of America and the European Community. Therefore, Eastern European countries must go along with technological changes and not try to go in other directions. Where they can control events is in the rate of assimilation of Western technology, now that trade restrictions have, in large measure, been lifted. Willingness to open markets and to create business opportunities in telecommunications are the key considerations, raising questions of regulation and the operation of market forces.

This chapter sets out to describe and analyse the state of telecommunications in Eastern Europe as they appear in 1990. The pace of development of both telecommunications and of political and economic events in Eastern Europe is such that the 'half-life' of the chapter is short. The interested reader may care to follow up developments in newspapers, weekly journals and specialist newsletters. The USSR has been excluded because it is significantly different from the rest of the Socialist Bloc countries, both in its existing infrastructure and the way in which it seems to be developing.

THE REGULATION OF TELECOMMUNICATIONS

Technological advances have radically altered telecommunications in the last forty years. Systems have become: smaller, faster, cheaper, more reliable and easier-to-use. The well known phenomenon of convergence of computers and communications has not only linked two separate technologies but forced together two very different areas of application and two previously distinct markets.

New services have been established using the new technologies. The boundaries between old services have been all but eliminated and it is difficult to see new barriers lasting any length of time. The established trading patterns and the economies of scale of the telecommunications industry have been overturned. Both business and domestic markets have been revolutionised.

The use of telecommunications has made services tradeable in ways that could not previously have been imagined. For example, Reuters has been transformed from a rather staid, if extremely respectable, provider of newspaper stories into a very dynamic provider of financial information and a rival to stock exchanges (DTI, 1990).

Telecommunications now underpins much of modern business. Sectors such as airlines rely on telecommunications day-to-day and minute-to-minute for their operations. Electronic data interchange has become an essential part of the basis on which manufacturing and distribution companies operate (Benjamin et al, 1990). Coordinating a business across organisational boundaries has become much easier with telecommunications. It is often as easy to conduct business between firms as within a firm. Similarly, the significance of national boundaries has been eroded.

General economic pressures have led to a re-examination of subsidies to, and cross-subsidies within, telecommunications authorities and monopolies. Political changes in Western Europe, Japan and the United States of America have helped drive this re-regulation. The 1980s were a time for free markets, though this may not be true of the 1990s. France Télécom, British Telecom and the Deutsche Bundespost have all undergone and continue to endure significant changes. The political ideas behind re-regulation are now being applied in Eastern Europe where there are no 'sacred cows' and change can be even more rapid. Poland and Hungary are already in the process of privatising their PTTs and of introducing competition.

Deregulation, in the strict sense of abolition of all controls, is impossible. Instead countries have been driven to some alternative form of regulation - re-regulating telecommunications. Indeed, one must express some concern that too much faith is being placed in the operation of the free market and that the role of state regulation and intervention is being overlooked. It may seem perverse to suggest sending in Western regulators to help, nonetheless they could provide vital assistance. One lesson which can be learned for the West, is to make the telecommunication operators pay for the regulators.

There have been massive structural changes in the telecommunications industry. The end of vertical integration of services and equipment has almost been reached; its last traces are dying out. Distribution of service has occurred through greater accessibility. Production of exchange equipment is controlled by a few global firms who can carry the massive research and development costs and have the sales volume to recover these costs. At the same time telephones have become a commodity market, though with their relatively low labour cost they remain open to European manufacturers, probably those making 'white' or 'brown' goods or possibly computers.

The recent regulatory changes made by the European Community will most probably spill over into Eastern Europe. The rapidly evolving single internal market in value-added services must be an important factor in developments in Eastern Europe. The development of the data services market is less clear, but will be subject to considerable change in the early 1990s.

No Longer a Natural Monopoly

The traditional view of telecommunications in Europe, East and West, was of a state monopoly with a number of industries providing the necessary telephones, exchanges, and other services. These became known as PTTs (post, telephone and telegraph authorities). State control or sponsorship was considerable and could, therefore, be seen as a form of vertical integration.

Telecommunications has, for all practical purposes, ceased to be a natural monopoly. It is no longer a single business providing black bakelite telephones to shops, offices and homes on a grudging basis. Telephone 'lines' (the media) can be traditional copper cables, microwaves, satellite transmissions, or optical fibre. The multiplicity of sources of access lines has ended the monopoly, since there can now be competition without wasteful duplication of infrastructural investment.

In the past, the economies of scale were of vital importance, they are less obvious with current technologies. For example, Mercury Communications Ltd. was able to build its figure-of-eight optical fibre backbone for England in a very short period of time and has since extended its network to reach much of the United Kingdom population. Telecommunications has ceased to be a labour intensive process characterised by gangs of unskilled and semi-skilled workers laying cables under streets or stringing wires between telegraph poles. Instead, the key to success lies in quality of service and innovation, (e.g., mobile telephony and value added networks).

Ownership of the Means of Production, Distribution & Exchange

The basis of communism lies in the state ownership of the means of production, distribution and exchange (Marx, 1848). It is all too evident that in Eastern Europe state ownership no longer matters.

Telecommunications industries and PTTs have been under total control. The traditional PTTs of the inter-war era were, in the late 1940s, consolidated into state controlled enterprises closely linked to their supply industries.

An important part of the problem of developing telecommunications lies in ending the state ownership of the PTTs. If everybody owns the PTT then, in effect, nobody owns it. If it is sold to the public then the sale is biased in favour of those with capital who would be able to buy shares; mainly people favoured by the old regimes. Managers cannot be allowed to achieve ownership through a management buy-out, that would simply consolidate those already in power and reflect nothing more than a change of employment. Given the highly inefficient nature of PTTs and the need for changes in organisational culture and technology it is absolutely essential to restructure organisations. Vesting control of these PTTs in the hands of existing management would be little short of foolhardy, since it would make these telecommunications changes almost impossible.

Sale of the PTT or a spun-off telecommunications operations to the workforce (a buy-out) as a whole is equally problematic. In Eastern Europe, it is necessary to differentiate between ownership by the workers and contracts of employment. Employees of the PTT have no especial right to own the firm. Indeed this could be a serious handicap given the overmanning in the PTTs and the necessary changes. This would require, however, employee share ownership programmes (ESOPs) which do play an important role in rewarding staff, especially senior staff.

One important responsibility of ownership is the ability to raise money (capital). Capital markets in Eastern Europe are almost non-existent and are unlikely to develop in the immediate future. Therefore firms must develop a form of ownership which allows them to take advantage of Western sources of finance, to participate in joint ventures and, eventually, to raise money from local markets.

Regulation of Competition

The view of the ancien régime favoured only a very modest growth. Today, the new objectives are to develop and to catch up; which imply a new regulatory regime. Cross-subsidisation between services is out of favour; it is seen as inefficient.

There seem to be five scenarios for regulation.

State monopoly: retaining total control by the state, providing services as and when government considers it appropriate.

Regulated private monopoly: licencing one or more providers of telecommunications on a non-competitive basis, but with government restrictions on activities and profitability.

Heavily regulated competition: more than one telecommunications operator, whose activities operate under the control of government but also driven by the profit motive.

Lightly regulated competition: more than one telecommunications operator

with each having considerable degrees of freedom for firms to compete in some or all sectors of the market if they so wish, subject to some constraints.
Unregulated competition: removal of all constraints on operations in telecommunications, allowing any company to offer any service.

The traditional trade-off is that an organisation is granted a monopoly in exchange for a guarantee of 'universal service' and acceptance of control over its prices and/or profits. In Eastern Europe this has not been the case, in the sense that monopolies failed to provide a universal service. The historical view of universal service was the guarantee to provide a telephone to any location, even the most isolated. In the 1990s, a basic telephone is of little value, when the advanced urban resident can expect two fully digital lines of 64K bits per second and businesses from 2M to 140M bits per second.

In this author's opinion, although attractive, a national optical fibre grid is to be avoided. As an investment in infrastructure it cannot have a high priority. Its attractions lie in allowing revenue to be made from transmitting television signals. However, mixing television and radio with telecommunications adds complexity and confusion to very different regulatory regimes. Whilst a fibre grid might result in valuable technological advances, it would be extremely expensive. Further, it is not at all clear that consumers would be willing to pay for this innovation. It could prove to be a very costly white elephant.

If competition were permitted, different network providers would be obliged to interconnect. Where interconnection occurs and the use of services from other suppliers is necessary then the sharing of revenues would probably have to be regulated. If the services were non-competitive, then there would have to be regular reviews of tariffs and quality of service.

If it were decided that there should be a monopoly service in addition to competitive services, then a boundary between the two would have to be fixed. A company providing both regulated and unregulated services is almost impossible to regulate since it involves untangling the allocation of various overheads, transfer pricing, and the like. Whatever else, if there is to be a boundary, it must be sustainable. In the United States of America, the Federal Communications Commission has had considerable difficulty with this problem; trying to keep up with its Computer I, II and III judgments.

There is one practice of Western Europe that Eastern Europe might usefully go along with and that is the adoption of standards which could be applied from the Atlantic to the Soviet border, if not all the way to the Ural Mountains. This would require the adoption of both Open Systems Interconnection (OSI) and Open Network Provision (ONP) conventions. It would also require the Eastern European countries to join the European Telecommunications Standards Institute (ETSI).

Instead of national certification of equipment, countries should recognise each countries' approval of equipment type which would simplify matters for larger users and suppliers. Some care would still be necessary since there might be problems with the connectivity of some modern equipment to the rather antiquated systems of Eastern Europe.

Potential New Entrants

It is difficult to judge how much interest there will be in the markets of Eastern Europe. Whilst the urban centres of Bucharesti, Budapest, Praha, Sofia, Warszawa and Dresden are attractive prospects, the problem is to find vendors who would be willing to provide telecommunication services to rural Transylvania, Macedonia or Galicia. Finding an appropriate balance between services in urban and rural areas may prove quite difficult.

There is a very strong trend towards globalisation in industry in general and in telecommunications in particular (Bartlett & Ghoshal, 1989). Eastern Europe is one geographic area with the potential for massive economic growth, probably the largest such area in the world. There remains, however, many problems to be solved. AT&T and the regional Bell operating companies (Bell South, Nynex, etc) are active in Western Europe and are assessing the opportunities in Eastern Europe.

Proximity to Western Europe means that reformed PTTs must be considered as possible actors in Eastern Europe. Of all these reformed PTTs, those in the United Kingdom are probably the fastest movers. For example, British Telecom acquired US-based Tymnet and Dialcom and Cable and Wireless plc, a long established international operator, is currently building its 'Global Digital Highway'. Although other large European PTTs like Deutsche Bundespost Telekom and France Telecom are slower, they should not be forgotten.

It would be difficult, if not impossible, for Eastern European PTTs to defend themselves against a Western onslaught. Western firms enjoy significant economies of scale, advanced technology, marketing skills, high levels of service and reserves of 'hard' currency. Indigenous East European firms in other sectors have neither the technology nor the money to competitively enter the telecommunications market.

Governmental Policies

Various governments and politicians often endeavour to pursue several policies at once, which tends to be confusing. This is true in both Eastern and Western Europe and the telecommunications industry is no exception. For example, telecommunications is used to boost applications of high-technology and, by location of manufacturing industry, to reduce unemployment in a particular city or region. Today, there is a considerable need to build up the telecommunications infrastructure in order to meet domestic demand, to support existing and, more importantly, new businesses and to attract inward investment.

The telecommunications industry has traditionally been the subject of governmental interest because of the long standing close relationship between various governments and the telecommunications industry. This is more pronounced in Eastern Europe than in Western Europe where the links are quite strong. For example, the United Kingdom's 'System X' telephone exchange programme involved close collaboration between British Telecom and its major suppliers: GEC, Plessey and STC.

Most PTTs are an important source of government income through taxation, appropriation of profits, or cross-subsidies. It is unlikely that Eastern Europe countries will be willing to give this up, at least in the short term. It is difficult to estimate the magnitude of these revenues since few statistics are available and those are of questionable reliability. For example, the Czechoslovakian and Polish PTTs showed earnings of 7,484M Crowns and 50,663M Zloty respectively in 1988 (UIT, 1990).

All Eastern European countries appear to be very enthusiastic about inward investment. It is likely that these countries would accept almost anything, especially if it had a technological component. However, they will soon discover that once the first wave of euphoria is over they are in a very competitive market. Eastern European countries will face competition from such organizations as the Irish Development Authority and the Scottish Development Agency which have considerable experience in attracting such investments. The Irish have recently been attracting 'back office' operations from the United States of America using very sophisticated telecommunications links (Doz, 1986).

Two potential bottlenecks in telecommunications growth are manpower problems (ranging from skilled labour to management) and in supplies, particularly as they relate to quality. These are issues that will have to be addressed by governments as soon as possible.

INFRASTRUCTURE FOR ECONOMIC DEVELOPMENT

The economic development of Eastern Europe is being constrained by many factors one of which is their poor telecommunications infrastructure. This is likely to remain the case for the medium term, given the limited funds for investment and the enormous numbers of conflicting national priorities and 'special cases'. Economists and politicians will have to address these and many other issues in the next few months and years.

Figure 2 shows the relationship between gross domestic product and the number of telephone lines in a country. The cause and effect relationship between the number of telephone lines and economic activity is uncertain. Whether the number of telephone lines enables economic activity or economic activity allows the purchase of telephones is unclear. What is clear, however, is the very strong correlation between these two variables. It is impossible to position Eastern European countries on the graph, since there are no reliable figures for their gross domestic products. However, it is anticipated that each country's GDP will be low, though not as low as the number of telephone lines might suggest (Kudriavtzen & Varakin, 1990).

The European Community is implementing its Special Telecommunications Action for Regional development (STAR) programme which is designed to develop the infrastructure for telecommunications of Ireland, Greece, Portugal and Spain. The objective is to bring the telecommunications provisions in these countries up to the standards of the other eight members of the European Community (Martin, 1990).

The IT sector of the economy outstrips conventional sectors in terms of value-added and jobs created. Telecommunications can be used to improve productivity, flexibility, and quality in other sectors and is important in terms

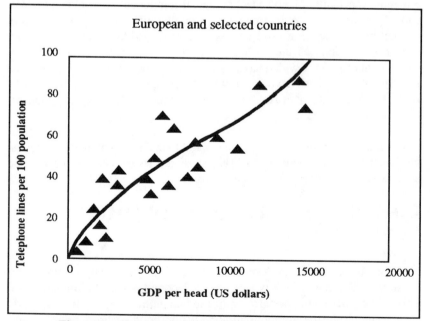

Figure 2: Telephone Lines Versus GDP per head
[Source: International Telecommunications Union]

of process innovation, (e.g., the development of multi-location research and development facilities in automobile companies). Whole new areas of economic activity are created, (e.g., value added services). It is also a way of linking the production and consumption processes, (e.g., customer reservation systems). The interconnection within and between firms leads to synergy in the creation of knowledge and 'know-how' which in turn encourage the spread of small innovations, an increasingly important factor for modern firms.

If firms from Western Europe, Japan and the United States of America are to be attracted to invest in Eastern Europe, then all these telecommunications infrastructures will have to be raised to world standards. Likewise, if Eastern European firms are to operate in western markets they will need to be able to adapt to modern telecommunications-based technologies and make the necessary changes to their organisational structures and processes. This will require money, in 'hard' currency, and a number of considerable organisational changes.

Financing Growth

Countries in Eastern Europe have for a long time had non-convertible currencies and this seems likely to continue; certainly in the short term. Control over the limited supplies of 'hard' currencies by Eastern European countries have been stringent and subject to very bureaucratic procedures. Such procedures were deemed necessary to ensure that use of 'hard' currencies met the priorities of central governments, the Communist Party and the Council for Mutual Economic Assistance (CMEA). In most cases, when policies for 'hard' currencies were developed, recognition was not given to the importance of telecommunications. Moreover, access to 'hard' currency was possible only after long delays and the judgments of many officials, involving the arbitrary and often 'corrupt' execution of power.

Today, the availability of 'hard' currency has scarcely improved and will only get better slowly. Governments may have changed, but full convertibility will have to wait for strengthening of their economies. In the interim, it is important for each country to ensure that some progress is made in the uses of 'hard' currency. It should be recalled that the United Kingdom went through considerable economic anguish trying to restore convertibility in the late 1940s. The former German Democratic Republic has been able to follow a very different route to strengthen its currency from the rest of Eastern Europe, namely, through re-unification though even that is proving to be a painful process.

Looking at telecom development in Western Europe, it is interesting to note that in the United Kingdom in the late 1970s and early 1980s a limit was placed on public sector borrowing. Since British Telecom was part of the state any borrowing was treated as government borrowing. As part of fiscal policy, state borrowing was minimised to control inflation. This experience may be of interest to Eastern Europe, given that state borrowing in Eastern Europe is likely to be restricted for the foreseeable future which implies that telecommunications development will be held back, so long as telecommunications remains in the public sector. Revenue from customers is very difficult to predict, therefore, one cannot be sure to what extent telecommunications can be made self-financing. It is difficult to know how much people and firms will actually spend on telecommunications services.

One other obvious source of 'hard' currency lies in increased tourism. Eastern Europe is already undergoing such a boom. Special facilities could be given in the sure and certain reward of 'hard' currency which could be channelled into infrastructure.

The World Bank (IBRD) is already active in supporting telecommunications projects. It has recently been joined by the European Bank for Reconstruction and Development (EBRD).

PRIVATISATION

The British Government would very much like to export its policy of privatisation to Eastern Europe and is supported in this by the United States of America. It has been obliged to understate the value of firms in order to sell them successfully. It is nearly impossible to arrive at a statement of the real value of the PTTs in Eastern Europe. Existing assets are a poor guide and, in any case, are of little utility in valuing such firms. A discounted cashflow might be a better guide, if it were not so difficult, if not impossible, to calculate. To arrive at a discounted cashflow, it would be necessary to know the revenues from telecommunications operations, which is problematic and then it would be necessary to take into account inflation and exchange rates, two more monumental problem areas.

What attracts investors from Eastern and Western Europe alike is the potential for development. Desirable as the current political changes in Eastern Europe are, the political instability they bring makes investment still very risky. Whilst a relapse into Communism is unlikely, a switch to the extreme right is not impossible. Telecommunications companies rely on a stable, regulatory regime, so that many stages short of nationalisation could destroy confidence, (e.g., the ability to repatriate profits).

Reforming the PTTs

Of all firms, the telecommunication companies have endured the greatest organisational changes. It is no surprise that Kanter (1984) chose to look at organisational change at Meridian Telephone. Following privatisation, British Telecom has undergone massive changes in organisational culture (Brunnen, 1989).

Privatised telecommunications operators have to exchange a close and often comfortable relationship with government for one of greater risk, namely, an 'arm's length' relationship. The bureaucratic culture must give way to one which is commercial. This is likely to be a major problem in Eastern Europe where the only real alternative to the 'dead hand' of party bureaucracy is a narrow minded technocracy. A technological solution is not what is needed; rather it is vital to look after the customers, for the first time in decades.

Attitudes must change from facility expansion or production to a market orientation. Integrated Services Digital Network (ISDN) is probably the last major technological development which the Western PTTs will be able to impose through the brute force of monopoly and oligopoly. The balance of power has changed, with control slipping away from the PTTs. The computer manufacturers and, increasingly, the users themselves now expect to have a say in telecommunications developments.

In Eastern Europe the scale of the problem of catching up is of such a magnitude as to require a degree of central direction. However, this must be focused on the clear needs of business users. Beyond an initial period where central direction can be justified, it will be necessary to develop marketing skills.

PTTs can no longer be seen as a sink for unemployment: Czechoslovakia 25,000, Hungary 73,000 and Poland 64,400 (UIT, 1990). They must become 'lean and hungry' if they are to compete and survive. Freedom from government control will allow firms to pay full market salaries. This may prove important at a time when governments will be using pay restraints as an economic lever to control inflation.

The effects of digitalisation of the network alters the skills balance in PTTs, it requires massive retraining of staff in technical skills. It also changes many job definitions, causing people to be re-assigned. Individual jobs cease to be narrowly defined and become broadly based. With the development of new skills, jobs expand. As part of slimming down the organisation, individuals acquire more responsibility, which is an unprecedented phenomenon in Eastern Europe.

The retraining and development of the workforce coincides with a severe manpower shortage. Although the potential rate of growth of the telecommunications market is high, the lack of a suitably trained staff will limit the ability of firms to respond to demand. A sophisticated telecommunications firm requires a broad range of technical, managerial and marketing skills. One cannot allow able people to opt out, it is necessary to retrain and motivate employees, though there are advantages to all parties if some staff leave to create their own telecommunications-based businesses.

National economies of scale have long since been achieved. Today, the processes at work are the gaining of global economies of scale and scope. These processes have to be managed carefully, a joint venture presents interesting challenges for the organisational cultures and processes of both sides.

There is a need to keep internal records of telephone ownership and maintenance in a commercial way, that is, related to profit centres. There is a considerable need to develop management and financial accounting procedures in order that the firms become auditable. Commercial accounting practices, rather than mere book-keeping, are necessary if a proper return on investment is to be calculated for investors.

Using sophisticated computer systems, the information from transaction processing can be distilled to provide a potentially valuable data base which can be exploited to determine how to meet customers' needs. Initially this will be limited in value, but would grow rapidly to supplement market research.

Market Research

In the conventional sense, market research is almost impossible in Eastern Europe. Eastern Europe lacks simply the necessary staff trained to carry out the studies and to analyse the findings.

The public themselves have no understanding of how to answer the researcher's questions; they have never had to do so in the past. Telecommunications is not an easy subject on which to conduct research, especially with the general public. The key objective of market research is to determine their willingness to pay for telecommunications services. It would be all too easy to get undifferentiated but positive responses.

Even if people were able to answer these questions the extent to which their personal position and the nature of their employment will alter is immense, consequently changing their responses. State-run industries are being sold off or bought out, start-ups and spin-offs will be legion. Today, individuals have little idea of what is to come.

BEYOND THE PLAIN OLD TELEPHONE SERVICE

The existing telephone service in Eastern Europe is, being kind, poor. The availability of telephone lines is limited; new towns and housing estates may wait for years to get a telephone exchange. Dialling a number usually takes

	Population	Lines /100	Deficit	Missing Lines	Cost US$M
Bulgaria	8,959,000	28	22	1,970,980	4,927
Czechoslovakia	15,534,000	25	25	3,883,500	9,709
East Germany	16,624,000	23	27	4,488,480	11,221
Hungary	10,627,000	16	34	3,613,180	9,033
Poland	37,456,000	13	37	13,858,720	34,647
Romania	23,897,000	8	42	10,036,740	25,092
Yugoslavia	23,641,000	14	36	8,553,314	21,383
TOTAL	136,738,000			71,782,000	116,012

Note: No statistics are available for Albania.

[Source: UIT, 1990 and author's estimates]

Table 1: The Missing Lines

several attempts, and all too often, one still gets a wrong number and/or a crossed line. The switching equipment is analogue or quasi-digital with poor levels of reliability. There are very few international lines; and international direct dialling is quite limited. The service is difficult and irritating to use.

Even where growth has occurred, its often not what it appears to be. For example, although there has been a considerable growth in the number of lines in Bulgaria this is due to the production of a telephone exchange based on a sixty year old design. These are cheap to produce, but of mediocre quality.

The cost of bringing the service up to Western European standards (50 lines per 100 population) is high, indeed, almost prohibitive. This is made worse by the virtual necessity of using 'hard' currency to pay for these systems, or for large parts of the system. Table 1 shows the scale of the problem of lines needed to reach the standard of Western Europe. The costs are expressed in US dollars.

The cost of a telephone line is approximately, US $2,500, comprised of: construction and operations $700, switching systems $400, local network transmission $500 and other equipment $900.

The production of fully digital exchanges in Eastern Europe was, until very recently, extremely limited. Poland manufactured a very few digital exchanges, while others produced quasi-digital exchanges. Joint ventures have been established or are being developed in Czechoslovakia, Hungary, Poland and Yugoslavia involving divisions of Alcatel, Northern Telecom and Siemens.

Digital Services

The conventional packet switched services (X.25) that make up the public switched digital networks (PSDN) of Western Europe are almost non-existent in Eastern Europe. Yet these are essential for computer-computer communications for on-line transaction processing (OLTP) and value added services. Bulgaria has recently launched its 'Bulpac' X.25 service on a modest scale, linked to DATEX-P in Germany to provide access to international traffic.

In contrast to the West, Eastern Europe has almost no academic networks. In the past, the European Academic and Research Network (EARN) declined to accept members from CMEA countries, because of COCOM regulations. Recently, Hungary, Czechoslovakia and Bulgaria have all been offered membership. Also, universities have been experimenting with wide area networks (Huzar and Kalis, 1988).

Digitalisation for data services is not a very attractive path, since access to any data network by telephone dial-up is almost impossible, given the poor quality of many of the public telephone networks. High quality access is only possible using direct connections and leased lines, which are expensive and difficult to provide. The engineering effort necessary to provide and maintain these lines is considerable. Existing public exchanges simply cannot handle data traffic.

To develop a mass market for digital services in Eastern Europe will require a significant improvement in the public telephone network. However, it will be relatively straightforward to provide limited services in city centres to meet the demands of business, especially overseas firms.

The future of packet switching is closely tied to the success of Integrated Services Digital Network (ISDN). If ISDN succeeds, then most traffic will transfer to channel switching. For the present, ISDN must remain a medium-term goal in Eastern Europe. This allows Eastern Europe to wait for the results of the experiments in France, Germany and other Western European countries which will provide both technical information, and more importantly, application services.

In the Highlands and Islands of Scotland there is an initiative to accelerate the introduction of ISDN. The intention of making available high quality telecommunications services in this isolated geographical region is to attract inward investment and to encourage local business in the use of information technology. The initiative is adding to an already substantially large digital network, consequently the incremental cost is low. Therefore, although the idea might seem applicable conceptually to Eastern Europe, it is less clear how one would implement it.

The longer term goal of Integrated Broadband Communication (IBC) is so far off as to be largely irrelevant. Even in Western Europe the applications of IBC are not easy to anticipate.

Mobile Communications

Given that no Eastern European country has an established mobile telephone network, the problem is to see how such networks can be developed and how they can be linked to the existing infrastructure. There now exists an agreed standard for mobile communications in Western Europe and this should be extended eastward.

It is unlikely that any Eastern European country would build its own mobile telecommunications network. Cellular systems are too sophisticated, too expensive, have too low a priority and would take too long to develop. Instead they are entering joint ventures or licensing the technology from the West.

The former German Democratic Republic was connected in early 1990 to the West German cellular network (C-Netz) for a trade fair at Dresden. Interestingly, the link had to be made by satellite in the absence of suitable microwave or optical fibre lines. The Deutsche Bundespost has provided mobile telephony along the autobahn between Berlin and West Germany and is now expanding that service to cover the major cities of what was East Germany. Developments in the rest of Eastern Europe will be slower. The World Bank has provided $5 US million for a cellular telephone service in Budapest to be operated by Magyar Posta (the Hungarian Post Office) and US West (FT East European Markets, 6 October 1989).

The success of mobile telecommunications depends, in part, on access to the conventional national and international telephone networks. Given the low penetration rates in these countries and problems with obtaining connections, mobile telephony is less attractive than in Western Europe. A further problem is that one cannot use the existing network of inter-exchange links and exchanges, therefore, it is necessary to build a dedicated network which adds to the cost.

In Western Europe there is a strong correlation between high levels of penetration of mobile telephony and liberality of the licensing regime. Approximately 3 or 4 mobile 'lines' per 100 population is found in the more liberal countries, mainly Scandinavia. Whereas, only one tenth or one hundredth of that level is found in more conservative countries. If mobile telephony is to succeed it is essential that the regulatory regime be liberal. Although the potential of the market in Eastern Europe is considerable, its value compares unfavourably with those of West Germany, France, Spain, Switzerland and Italy. The potential for expansion of mobile services in Western Europe is still very great, though constrained by inertia of the various PTTs and governments. Importantly, customers have the money to pay for such systems and, if allowed, the inclination.

Hugo Dixon argued in the Financial Times that Eastern European countries should go directly to mobile telephony which could reach a large business group relatively quickly (Financial Times 5.ii.90) Whilst this might meet part of their requirements, there is a counter argument for going to optical fibre for the higher bandwidth and greater flexibility. Fibre provides the opportunity for other chargeable services, notably television; which is, at best, poorly provided in Eastern Europe.

There is also an opportunity to develop radio-paging. However, this will be closely tied to the development of a telephone network, since use assumes ready access to telephones. The alternative form of mobile communications, personal communication networks (PCNs), will also have an important role to play once the technology is fully developed and unit costs have fallen. All of these developments are likely to be pan-European.

Value Added Networks

At present, value added services are almost non-existent in Eastern Europe. However, there are a small number of users accessing data bases in the West for important governmental and commercial purposes.

A popular videotext service such as the French Minitel would currently be very difficult to provide, though not impossible. The local call to the exchange followed by a data call to a service provider is not feasible. The French system relies on digital services which do not exist, are too limited in coverage or could not cope with the load a successful Minitel-type service would generate. Moreover, the public telephone network could not provide the quality of connection necessary. However, it might be possible to use the much less successful British approach with a local rate call to a local computer running the necessary software and a copy of a down-loaded data base (Sutherland, 1990).

Electronic mail services are being considered by several Eastern European countries. However, opportunities for such a service are limited by poor infrastructures. The use of electronic mail to access telex could be a key consideration since penetration levels for telex are very low. Both British Telecom and Mercury Communications Ltd used this route to attract customers to their electronic mail services. It is also possible to bundle together an attractive range of services with access to other value-added services, (e.g., on-line data bases).

Voicemail is growing with remarkable rapidity in Western Europe and North America ranging from 20% to 40% per annum. Like facsimile systems, its attraction is that anybody can use it, no matter how much they dislike computers. If necessary, text messages can be synthesised into voice output. Voicemail has the major advantage of working on even noisy telephone lines, provided the necessary connections can be made.

Voicemail is extremely attractive for Eastern Europe. It avoids any problems with the cyrillic character sets of Bulgaria, Romania and the USSR. There is a need to replace existing PABXs with modern versions which often contain voicemail facilities. The most obvious constraint is the low density of telephones. It may be necessary to await the adoption of telephone answering machines, though that stage may be bypassed.

The poor analogue infrastructure makes access to data bases difficult but not impossible, discouraging the large scale use of remote services. There are relatively expensive international tariffs for telephone calls. In larger institutions there must be considerable competition from data bases on CD-ROMs which provide up-to-date information and at no cost for additional access.

The most likely way in which host services will develop is through the opening of gateways on data networks. Services could then be built up to a mix of domestic services and access to foreign services which should be attractive to customers. This approach is being used in the Scottish Highlands and Islands to establish the Network Services Agency in order to:

1) overcome the reluctance of VANs suppliers to market to such a low density market.
2) meet the unique requirements of local economies.
3) coordinate disparate initiatives by government and information providers.
4) stimulate the production of services and to gain experience.

The services being provided are intended to allow local users to access remote databases, together with some transactional services, (e.g., tele-shopping & home-banking).

There is an opportunity to stimulate the provision of reliable information about Eastern Europe to other parts of the world as people and firms fall over themselves to invest and to do business there. Equally, Eastern European firms will increasingly want access to the information and data bases of Western Europe, Japan and the United States of America. It would be possible, for example, to encourage new newspapers to go to 'high-tech' printing in order that their text be available in on-line databases.

THE TELECOMMUNICATIONS SUPPLY INDUSTRY

Conventionally, the various telecommunications sectors (customer premises equipment, private branch exchanges, public exchanges, transmission equipment, basic services and enhanced services) have been vertically integrated. This is true also in Eastern Europe, though the mechanism is one of state direction or 'tutelage' rather than that of a commercial monopoly or oligopoly. The industry is further complicated by the allocation of tasks and industrial sectors between CMEA member countries which creates a very artificial division of activities. Many manufacturing operations were established to meet the needs of a domestic market and to supply excess production to the USSR and/or other CMEA countries. However, changes in the USSR have brought Eastern European firms into direct competition with Japanese, North American and West European firms. The effective loss of the USSR as a market has been a major blow to the telecommunication industries of Eastern Europe.

Much of the IT industry in Eastern Europe has been specially created in order to imitate the technology of the West, or has degenerated to a point where it can do little else. Telecommunications is no exception, therefore, it must restructure or collapse.

Unfortunately, the appropriate management skills are almost non-existent. However, there is a great willingness either to learn the skills or to make way for people younger and less 'tainted' by the old political systems. In particular, recent Western trends in quality management have passed Eastern Europe by. Quality is a particularly serious problem in Eastern Europe. Generally, quality is very poor.

Joint Ventures

The telecommunications industry has been altered enormously in recent years by the forces of globalisation. What were once cosy national industries have chosen, or more often been obliged to meet, foreign competition. Consequently, old protected and fragmented national markets are quickly disappearing.

The multi-national corporations interested in investing in Eastern Europe are fully integrated, serving a world market. Their technology is far too valuable to sell and there is no incentive for them to do so. For example, it costs more than US$ 1 billion to develop a new telephone exchange system. A licence for telecommunications services seems to offer the best option, with the government taking a fee for allowing the transnational company to make its profit.

New and more liberal legal frameworks for joint ventures are generally in place in Eastern Europe. However, they are untested and will certainly change. Some prize industries have already been captured. For example, General Electric has bought the Hungarian light bulb manufacturer, Tungsram, and there are already many suitors for Skoda, the Czech car manufacturer.

However, there are few, if any, obvious candidates in telecommunications.

Hungaria Telecom is currently being separated from Magyar Posta and privatised. Fully 50% of the shares are likely to be disposed of, 20% within Hungary to private investors and 30% to a foreign telecommunications operator. This pattern is likely bring the best of both worlds, domestic ownership with foreign capital and international expertise.

An assessment of the capacity of Eastern European countries in research and development is fraught with difficulties. Published research indicates that there are strengths in theoretical and mathematical areas (Boyanov & Angelinov, 1989). Research seems good given the resources that are available, which is not much. Such research, however, has been weakened by being government driven; often by the personal whims of ministers and bureaucrats. In many cases, research and development is not 'developing' but copying. Like manufacturing, research was broadly shared with other CMEA countries.

Research is very much stronger than development. This is mainly because there is little, if any, understanding of the market.

Secrecy and Security

Secrecy has been an important consideration in telecommunications. For example, in the USSR, private ownership of facsimile machines was unknown until very recently. The U.S.S.R. even used and still uses non-standard protocols in its telephone network to ensure total state control of traffic. However, Eastern Europe has been less extreme in this than the USSR Nonetheless, telephone networks in many factories are not connected to public telephone networks.

The Coordinating Committee on Multi-lateral Export Controls (COCOM) banned the export of a variety of equipment, including telephone exchanges, multiplexors and telecommunications software for computers. These rules are now being relaxed considerably, though the Trans-Siberian fibre optic cable was vetoed, because of the advanced technology required.

CONCLUSION

One of the critical factors for the success of any contemporary business is its ability to interconnect both within and between firms; to such an extent that the significance of company boundaries is being severely eroded. Consequently, business processes and networks are being redesigned. Such connectivity relies on the use of telecommunications in many forms. Few of the developments in Western Europe and North America are, as yet, known in

Eastern Europe.

The demand for improved telecommunications in Eastern Europe is great and the supply and service industries for telecommunications must and will grow. The necessity of telecommunications for business operations ensures that this growth will occur. The question is how fast will this growth be and what direction will it take. The factors to watch are the strength of demand and the willingness to pay. The known constraints are poor management, inattention to customer service and old technologies.

The Appendix sets out in some detail a suggested 'national agenda' which could be applied to the countries of Eastern Europe, though it could be used with some modification in some less favoured regions of Western Europe. It is not intended to be prescriptive but to indicate the areas where attention should be focused.

Regulation is much more important than privatisation in order to balance conflicting objectives. Put simply, there is not much to privatise and a lot to invite in. To succeed in developing the use of telecommunications services, partnerships and collaboration are essential anywhere in the world. In Eastern Europe the scale of this problem is so great and the available effort so limited that collaboration will be an absolute necessity for success. Joint ventures represent one very attractive way forward, provided they can be made to work for all parties involved.

Much of what is readily available is really assembly work which has little future and is subject to fierce competition from other countries. Governments must try to get the best available deals and be ready to build up the appropriate industries. To be competitive, the future Eastern European countries need to be able to participate in the information economy.

In the short term, developments will be externally driven by offers of joint ventures and funding from the World Bank and EBRD. At the same time, they will be constrained by COCOM and by the inclination and ability (or lack thereof) to respond to Western offers.

It is necessary to avoid dogma of any sort and instead to be pragmatic. This will require Eastern European governments to learn how to regulate, when to intervene and when to keep out of the various telecommunications industries.

References

Bartlett, C., and Ghoshal, S. (1989). *Managing across borders*, Hutchinson, London.

Boyanov, K., and Angelinov, R. (1989). *Network Information Processing Systems*. North-Holland, Amsterdam.

Benjamin, R., de Long, D., and Scott Morton, M. (1990). Electronic Data Interchange: How much competitive advantage? *Long Range Planning, 23*(1), 29-40.

Bruce, R., Cunard, J., and Director, M. (1986). *From Telecommunications to Electronic Services.* Butterworths, London.

Brunnen, D. (1989). Developing an Enterprise Culture at British Telecom. *Long Range Planning,* 22(2), 27-36.

Commission of the European Communities. (1987). Green Paper. Brussels, COM (87) 290 Final.

Department of Trade and Industry. (1988). *Evolution of the United Kingdom Communications Infrastructure.* HMSO, London.

Department of Trade and Industry. (1990). *Electronic Trading Cases.* HMSO, London.

Dixon, H. (February 5, 1990). How the East can Jump Ahead. *Financial Times,* 15.

Dizard, W., and Swensrun, B. (1987). *Gorbachev's Information Revolution - controlling Glasnost in an electronic era.* Centre for Strategic and International Studies, Washington, DC.

Doz, Y. (1986). Government Policies and Global Industries. pp 225-266. In *Competition in Global Industries,* Porter, M. (ed.)., New York: Free Press.

Financial Times. (1990). *East European Markets.* London.

Financial Times. (1990). *Fintech 1 - Telecommunications Markets.* London.

Huzar, Z., and Kalis, A. (1988). Some Projects of Wide Area Networks in Poland, pp 465-474. In *Governmental and Municipal Information Systems* edited by Peter Kovacs and Elek Straub, North-Holland, Amsterdam.

Kanter, R. (1984). *The Change Masters.* Allen and Unwin, London.

Kudriavtzen, G.G., and Varakin, L.E. (1990). Economic Aspects of Telephone Network Development. *Telecommunications Policy, 14*(1), 7-14.

Martin, W.J. (1990). The European Communities' STAR Programme and demand for advanced telecommunications services. *International Journal of Information Resource Management, 1*(4), forthcoming.

Marx, K. (1848). *The Communist Manifesto.*

Sutherland, E. (1990). Minitel - the resistible rise of French Videotext. *International Journal of Information Resource Management, 1*(4), forthcoming.

Union Internationale des Telecommunications. (1990). Annuaire statistique des telecommunications du secteur publique - 17 edition. Geneve.

Appendix A
A NATIONAL AGENDA FOR TELECOMMUNICATIONS

Aim: To be an active participant in the global information economy by the year 2000.

Infrastructure
1.To establish more and better international telephone links (new exchanges and lines).
2. To convert the core national network to fibre optic cables with fully digital switches.
3 .To bring the penetration level of telephone lines up to the level of leading Western European countries.
4 .To ensure provision of a full range of mobile services (paging, cellular and personal communication) fully integrated into Western Europe.
5 .To establish digital exchanges to serve central business districts of cities and large towns, industrial complexes and science parks.

Services
1 .To establish one or more digital services (X.25) accessible to the majority of businesses, with full international links.
2. To encourage the formation of companies to provide value-added services.
3. To encourage service firms to locate in the country.
4. To make governmental information available for trade by value-added service providers (e.g. census data).

Manufacturing
1. To establish one or more joint ventures with Western firms to build digital telephone exchanges.
2. To develop the existing manufacturing base in customer premises equipment, where necessary through joint ventures with western firms.

Regulation
1. Separate telecommunications from the postal services.
2. Study re-regulation processes worldwide.
3. Create a free market in customer premises equipment.
4. Licence providers of cellular and personal communication networks. The licenses should be subject to a requirement for joint ventures with local firms to manufacture equipment. They would also require licenses to undertake to migrate to a fully digital service and to guarantee to provide a stated minimum coverage of the population within three years.
5. Licence providers of value added networks subject to use of Open System Interconnection and Open Network Provision.
6. Authorise resale of excess capacity on both national and international leased lines.
7. Authorise type approval of equipment on the most liberal basis possible, recognising type approval from other countries.

8. Freely licence earth stations for satellites.

9. Join the European Telecommunications Standards Institute.

10. Encourage the creation of a telecommunication user group.

Stimulation

1. Creation of at least one designated 'teleport'.

2. Subsidise the development of an infrastructure for less developed regions.

3. Identify and promote examples of the best practice in the use of telecommunications.

Education & Training

1. Introduce the teaching of management in courses for telecommunications engineers.

2. Introduce the teaching of telecommunications in courses for managers.

3. Ensure the provision of post-experience courses on telecommunications management.

Fiscal

1.Raise capital by selling the telecommunications operator within three years.

2.Tax the telecommunications operators and new licensees as ordinary firms.

Notes

1.The *Financial Times* on a daily basis gives good coverage, supported by specialist newsletters on Eastern Europe and Telecommunications. The *Economist* is also quite good as are the specialist EIU reports. Predicasts publish an *East European Alert*.

2.Alcatel NV was created by the merger of the telecommunications interest of ITT and Compagnie Generale d'Electricite. Philips merged its telephone exchange interests with AT&T in a joint venture called APT. Siemens and the UK-based General Electric Company (GED) jointly acquired Plessey in 1990.

3.Until recently, all Eastern European countries operated currencies which could not be freely converted. These are termed 'soft', (e.g., the Bulgarian Lev) as distinct from 'hard' currencies which can be freely converted, (eg., Deutsche Mark).

4.There is no sensible conversion rate for currencies, making their value difficult to calculate in Deutsche marks or Pounds Sterling.

Acknowledgements: Prof John Beaumont (University of Bath), Dr Gabor Gulacsi (Budapest), George McKendrick (International Telecommunications User Group), Gillian Marcelle (British Telecom), Svetoslav Tintchev (Sofia) and to the British Council for funding for a trip to Sofia.

Information Systems in Lesser Developed Countries:
Seminal Questions in Planning and Control

5

Elia V. Chepaitis
Fairfield University

The strategic importance of information technology (IT) has increased for both developed and underdeveloped nations because of changing patterns of economic development and because of global resource movements and dependencies. Lesser Developed Countries (LDCs) must adopt information technology for developmental needs and to remain competitive in a global economy.

Yet the challenge of effective planning and control has increased, complicated by the constancy of technological, business, and socio-economic changes. In addition, the needs of most LDCs in the 1990s are enormous and resources are limited. Judicious systems design is paramount in the identification of goals and the selection of appropriate technologies.

The problems of planning and control in LDCs have been studied primarily outside of computer information systems: in economics, anthropology, sociology, and political science. The failure in those disciplines to differentiate the unique characteristics and potential of information technology from other technologies has produced egregious divergence between theory and practice, and few constructive lessons for underdeveloped economies.

Research into information systems success in newly industrialized countries such as South Korea identifies not only technical and non-technical benefits for developing areas but also germane issues in systems design and implementation. Input from information systems professionals is vital to optimize the opportunities which LDCs face in IT transfers.

INTRODUCTION: THE STRATEGIC VALUE OF IT FOR LDCs

Financial and economic indicators—indebtedness, inflation, GDP/capita, the balance of trade, savings and investment data, literacy rates, public health statistics—denote the precipitous decline of developing nations as a group in the 1980s. Thirlwall (1989) sees parallels with the Great Depression of the 1930s in collapsing commodity prices and in the deterioration in excess of 10% in the terms of trade for LDCs. In fact, continuous debt rescheduling and the threat of defaults have been necessary to avoid severe economic disruption, especially in non-oil LDCs. In addition, the diversion of both foreign aid and investment capital to emergent Eastern Europe and to established markets threatens sources of external aid in the 1990s. Finally, the growing exigencies created by the oil crisis and the refocusing of attention on the Middle East threatens to further dilute Western aid to lesser developed countries.

THE EMERGENCE OF THE GLOBAL MARKET

The emergence of the global market accelerated the decline of most LDCs, and increased dependence on the global capitalist system. Lesser developed nations have found that they cannot develop markets in isolation, and that pricing is impacted by global investment and resource movements beyond their control or anticipation. Proposals for poor nations in the southern hemisphere to delink from northern trade and seek autarchic solutions are therefore not feasible.

Clearly, alternate economic restructuring is in order. The example of prosperous newly industrialized countries (NICs), such as India and the Pacific Rim nations, is instructive. Some, such as Taiwan and South Korea, founded world-class knowledge industries and leapt to advanced nation status, albeit unevenly. Their experience shows that investment in information systems can serve as a catalyst for economic reform and repositioning.

Computer technologies, global markets, and transnational information systems have enormous potential to trigger growth mechanisms for nations at every level of development(Information Computer Communications Policy [ICCP] 1989). In fact, computerization is becoming more congruent with LDC resource endowments and cultures because of five technological trends: miniaturization, customized applications, ease of use and development, decreasing costs, and the addition of intelligence to goods services, and processes.

Well-designed information technology (IT) conveys significant competitive advantages to small producers and can conserve scarce resources such as capital, labor, know-how, and materials. The lowering of IT's cost/performance ratio, together with enhanced systems flexibility, holds significant promise for cash-poor developing nations.

In fact, it is increasingly evident that unless LDCs computerize and provide connectivity, their political and economic decline relative to developed nations will probably accelerate. Gricar and McCubbry (1989) emphasize the pivotal importance of Electronic Data Interchange (EDI) to preserve market and developmental opportunities, and deplore past failures to invest adequately in technologies such as telephone systems. Hills (1990) cites difficulties which LDCs face in planning and controlling improvements in the telecommunications infrastructure needed for EDI:

1. pressures from foreign business users,
2. changes in international communications, mitigated by the intercession of the International Telecommunications Union,
3. foreign currency shortages,
4. shortages of trained personnel, and
5. the late start in perceiving the strategic value of telecommunications.

Hills also cites financial constraints which inhibit appropriate systems selection and lead to long-term maintenance and training problems. The World Bank, lender of last resort, is curtailing telecommunications project funding. Both bilateral and commercial loans, on the other hand, often do not permit recipient LDCs to choose technology.

Nonetheless, poor nations must pay the technological ante, build connective communications and improve infrastructures in areas such as education. Reliable information systems are vital to develop surplus economies and to maintain viability in the global marketplace, particularly given changing patterns of economic development.

INFORMATION TECHNOLOGY AND PATTERNS OF ECONOMIC DEVELOPMENT

Two models are useful to depict changing patterns of economic development and to illustrate the seminal role of information systems in the economies of lesser developed countries. These countries typically possess subsistence or below subsistence economies. An overdependence on agrarian and foraging activity, as well as factors such as a high birth rate and poor resource endowments, inhibits the creation of surpluses and broader economic activity.

The traditional pyramid of economic development (Figure 1) is being turned on its ear, supplanted by a two-stage model characterized by a narrow channel from a subsistence to a surplus economy which is dependent upon IT-capability (Figure 2).

To borrow an adjective from Soshana Zuboff (1988), nations, like work groups, will be divided into informated "haves" and non-informated "have-nots". LDC connectivity with suppliers, distributors, customers, and sponsors is vital to maintain a toe-hold in the world market. Marginal economies also require appropriate computer information systems for optimal resource management, flexible and self-supporting administrative and production systems, and reliable information retrieval.

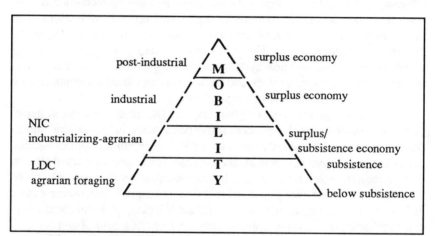

Figure 1: Traditional Pattern of Economic Development

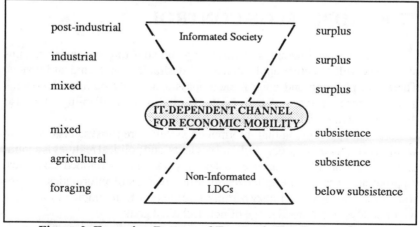

Figure 2. Emerging Pattern of Economic Development

THE PROBLEM OF PLANNING

Ayres (1990) identifies the convergence of telecommunications and computers as the fifth major technological transformation since 1770. The first long wave of technical and economic change represented the shift from charcoal to coal; the second, the application of steam to textiles and transportation; the third derived from steel production, mechanization, electrification, and telephones; and the fourth featured synthetic materials and electronics.

Each long wave accelerated economic growth and produced spurts of associated technological innovation and convergence. Within the fifth wave, information technology features revolutionary and capital technologies, generic tools which generate new technologies and novel combinations. The information revolution is a revolution, not an evolution, characterized by major discontinuities, unprecedented innovations and juxtapositions, at accelerating speed. Although information systems can offer predictable short-term improvements in products, services, and resource management, the depth and the tempo of change mitigate against rigid planning.

The margin for error is slight in fragile LDC socio-economic systems. In general, endemic problems—debt and dependencies, infrastructural underdevelopment, fragile cultures, and swings in leadership and policy—make underdeveloped areas less than ideal candidates for IT and long wave effects. Therefore, although vital strategically, computerization is undeniably problematic for cash-poor over-populated areas wary of capital-intensive processes and labor-saving equipment, especially for areas lacking well-educated workers. Significant obstacles to optimal long-term systems control and for economic development must be taken into consideration in planning.

THE PROBLEM OF CONTROL

LDCs need secure, self-sustaining and adjusting systems at reasonable costs with effective applications and desirable non-technical impacts. Therefore, planning and control encompasses not only traditional systems goals—security, privacy, data integrity, flexibility, and reliability—but also developmental, social, and political change.

An appreciation that information systems are subsystems operating within local economies, socio-cultural contexts, and political realities is central to the selection of appropriate technology in underdeveloped countries. Appropriate design both optimizes the effectiveness of informatics and resource management, and also permits information technologies to act as a major catalyst for a broad range of non-technical goals.

Unless the multiple impacts of information technologies are appreci-

Figure 3. Confluent and Overlapping Change Areas

ated and controlled, however, inappropriate and uncontrolled technologies can wreak egregious economic, social, and political havoc in underdeveloped countries. Business and systems professionals are challenged to secure systems which cannot only create wealth, but also serve as conduits for developmental improvements which can be more significant than the introduction of computer and communication technologies itself.

Formidable challenges confront policy makers, entrepreneurs and systems professionals in the introduction of appropriate information technology and management to underdeveloped countries. Systems designers must consider opportunity costs, affordability, and cultural compatibility.

Is controlled LDC information management possible? Four sets of overlapping dynamics complicate the problem of control: the dynamics of changing technologies, of changing global business practices, of developmental needs, and of available resources such as finance, leadership, know-how, and human capital (Figure 3).

METHODOLOGIES

Programs for both technical and organizational goals demand long-term planning and flexibility, including a willingness to restructure organizations and work cultures. Inter-enterprise partnerships, novel resource management and substitution, and assistance from nongovernmental organizations can assist impoverished governments to pursue strategic priorities. In addition, the foundation of competitive information industries and profit centers should not be ruled out. In the long term, LDCs need not only linkage to the global market and more efficient internal management, but also platforms for new enterprises. As systems in developing areas become refined, the outflow of saleable expertise, invention, and services should follow.

LITERATURE: THE DOMINANCE OF THE APPROPRIATE TECHNOLOGY SCHOOL

Problems of planning and control have been examined primarily in developmental theory and in disciplines other than computer systems. Computer technology transfer issues have remained not only unresolved but also poorly formulated. Since the literature has been dominated by sociology, political science, and economics rather than information systems, research parameters and themes reflect research interests which evolved from historical events, such as decolonization, rather than from experience in systems development.

Since the late 1960's, beginning with the economist E.F. Schumacher, the appropriate technology (AT) movement addressed problems caused by inappropriate technological transfers to lesser developed countries (1973). From Jacques Ellul (1964) to Arnold Pacey (1984), AT scholars concentrated on the displacement of traditional norms by technocratic values. References to computer applications focused on costly, undebugged, unsuitable, socially-disruptive technologies shipped without customization to the Third World. It was seldom noted that these costly, undebugged, disruptive technologies plagued developed nations also, and were symptomatic of immature technology rather than neo-colonial exploitation.

The AT school established a powerful thirty-year tradition of prejudice against high-tech solutions and innovative systems for developing areas. However, 1990s state-of-the-art tools often are optimal, cost-effective, friendly, tested and assonant technologies for underdeveloped economies. Although the appropriate technology group impacted academic disciplines and foreign aid, Eckaus (1987) states that AT failed, employing dubious criteria, insufficient data, and ill-defined parameters.

Divisions within the school, as well as a bifurcation of theory and practice, diluted its efficacy. Durbin (1989) notes that two branches were often in conflict: Science, Technology, and Society (STS) which was anti-technology and anti-establishment, and Science, Technology, and Public Policy (STPP) which was pro-technology but antispecialist and multi-disciplinary. As a consequence, an appropriate information technology school has yet to be established and grounded by the referent disciplines or by systems professionals.

Although the AT groups failed to provide comprehensive and timely answers to LDC dilemmas, it did identify some important issues in the cultural impact of technological innovation. The groups, however, failed to deal with the problem of plural cultures and technological transfers, a problem inherent to a global economy and to computer systems. Not only the culture of host LDCs, but also other cultures often must be considered: the receiving enterprise, the vendor, the nation of the technology's origin, sponsors, LDC subgroups such as third-nation managerial classes, and minority workers must be considered (Chepaitis, 1990).

For example, preferences for bilingual or multilingual software, multilateral needs for standard menus and commands, vendor maintenance practices, licensing options, and legal constraints on transborder information flows represent significant tactical choices in systems development. In addition, developing nations themselves, because of other priorities, particularly in centrally-planned economies, may see cultural compatibility as a minor consideration in technology transfers. For example, the Peoples Republic of China has purchased turnkey systems with English language software to accelerate application development.

EXPERIMENTS IN TECHNO-NATIONALISM

Reich's article (1987) in the *Atlantic* on techno-nationalism, the effort to nationalize and restrict access to IT know-how, examined the paradox of resistance to techno-globalism. Techno-nationalism, the movement to develop and nationalize discrete information industries, affected Brazil (Adler, 1986; Botelho, 1987), India (Grieco, 1982), and South Africa (Alant, 1988). These countries established varying degrees of technological autarky to escape external dependencies. They also invested in controlled research and development to improve upon existing systems.

Remembering the opportunity costs of funding a national computer industry, the case of Brazil is instructive. In 1990, Brazil is $115 billion in debt. Yet, according to Boritz, Brazil failed to develop adequate human resources and training capacity. Furthermore, Brazil cannot support vital transfers such as auditing systems. Although Brazil invested heavily in the production of Apple clones, the investment was probably misdirected. Resources could have been applied instead to constructing global linkages and to developing human capital, to optimize existent information systems (Fleury, 1988).

Techno-nationalism offered a compelling if misguided solution to the twin problems of dependency and inappropriate technology. The campaign to control information systems through nationalized computer industries elevated IT research to a national priority, but produced significant anomalies and uneven development, particularly in the case of Brazil, which in 1990 experienced a $118 billion deficit and continues to import foreign applications

(Boritz, 1989).

Techno-nationalism has declined as an economic ideal, and less attention is directed toward the politicization of control. Third World countries do fear any technological dependence which would enhance the West's "triangle of domination" (Prebisch, 1964): the control of finance, know-how, and management. This triad of Western control emerged with the spread of multinational enterprises after the Second World War. However, nationalization is of limited value for developing nations in the 1990s. Global enterprises with minimal national ties are supplanting Western-based MNEs and global connectivity is a necessity.

Most literature on cultural congruence and on national control is not only dated, but also of slim value for policy and programs in which sweeping social or economic change is desired. This is particularly true when technology transfer is designed to serve as a catalyst for both technical and non-technical changes.

THE BIFURCATION OF THEORY AND PRACTICE

Case studies of technology transfers lack direct applicability, but do illustrate strategic techniques to optimize IT. It is seldom possible for an LDC to replicate the adult literacy, munificence, or entrepreneurial advantages of technological leaders and early followers, nor is it desirable to adopt aging technologies. Unfortunately, the worsening debt/equity ratio for LDCs and rampant globalization in the 1990s also constrain planners in technology selection.

Third World countries must compromise, to create pockets of literacy, investment, and solvent industries. The resultant benefits are uneven, and undesirable side effects often represent the result of market trends or policy decisions rather than inherent technology-related liabilities. For example, in concentrated service and product industries located in Mexico's maquiladoras, laborers work for 55 cents an hour, burn out quickly, and move on to less stressful but less remunerative occupations. Mexico's data entry and industrial sweat shops are globally competitive because of low wage rates, but the identical technology is not exploitative in other economies.

China's central planners imported billions of dollars worth of computer equipment without the electricity, phone system, training, or managerial expertise to support the technology (Maier, 1986). Yet what seems wasteful to the West is often tolerable and typical of crash programs within centrally planned economies. Here, the political decision to leapfrog technologically subsumes other systems considerations.

In Third World nations, the success of IT is decidedly uneven, but instructive. Many publicized successful computer applications have been in public administration or services: utilities (Andima & Orungu-Olende, 1987), transport (van Oudheusden, Khan and Mohammed, 1987), customs and taxation (Corfmat,1985), housing (Struyk, 1987), health, or agricultural planning (Babington, 1987), rather than in the private sector. It may be that researchers lack access, motivation or funding to investigate the private sector. On the other hand, government and relief agencies may possess superior resources for the acquisition and control of successful IT, or may be better positioned to build on existing bureaucracies and to attract well-educated labor.

Case studies, ranging from the Persian Gulf (Buckley, 1987) to Southeast Asia (Yoshida, 1988) to Latin America (Alvarez, Smiley, & Rohrmann, 1985) consistently support Maier's findings, that a major cause of substandard IT performance in LDCs such as the Peoples Republic of China is entrenched managerial resistance and bureaucratic prerogatives and practices which have endured a millenium. Frequently, the conversion of the managerial class, top-down commitment, and effective software and operations training emerge as pillars of successful CIS implementations.

NON-TECHNICAL BENEFITS

Not only are information systems vital for entry into the global market, but they can produce economic, socio-cultural, and political benefits in underdeveloped countries. Among the economic goals which can be facilitated are: enhanced munificence, debt reduction, better infrastructures (Figure 4), long-term job creation, resource substitution, and the foundation of new industries and services. For example, the conversion of financial and information divisions into profit centers provides such benefits. Furthermore, provisions for appropriate expert systems and ongoing employee training compensate for local educational deficiencies. Well-negotiated, long-term agreements with global allies can include assistance in systems maintenance, and vendors, suppliers, distributors, and EDI (Electronic Data Interchange) associates can reduce uncertainties by pooling expertise, information, and opportunities with partners, clients, and policy makers in underdeveloped countries.

For many cash-poor LDCs in search of exportable goods, information-intensive processes can expand the traditional range of marketable products, creating "economies of scope" within traditional manufacturing, agriculture, and extractive industries and preserving the viability of small-scale and highly diversified enterprises.

The social benefits of judicious technological selection include channeling benefits of improved resource management, employment and educa-

---

Appropriate IT Transfer: Economic and Infrastructural Improvements

---

1. computer-aided services:
    medical diagnosis
    rural resource management: decision-support
    CAI in formal education
    adult instruction and training
    coordinated distribution of services through information
      sharing

2. satellite/telecommunications applications:
    thematic mapping: holistic planning and development geology
    shipping and offshore facilities
    coastal and littoral development
    land use
    weather

3. support for strategic projects:
    computer-assisted development of natural products
    controlled development of natural resources
    reduced dependence on imported or costly
      chemically-processed and synthetic products

4. economic benefits:
    development of human resources and mobility
    low energy consumption
    generation of consumer electronics
    variegated labor-intensive, capital-intensive, and
      knowledge-intensive options available
    enhanced resource management and substitution
    development of highly diversified and localized applications
      complements and seldom displaces other economic activities
    develops export-oriented, often capital, industries
    generates additional enterprises: economies of scale and
      of scope created
    job creation in spin-off industries and infrastructural
      projects
                                        Source: Chepaitis (1989).

Figure 4. Infrastructural and Developmental Improvements

tion, and superior products and services to disadvantaged groups such as women and workers displaced from failing native industries. Conversely, inappropriate and uncontrolled IT may lead to electronic data entry sweat-shops, deskilling, wage differentials, and structural unemployment. Computerization can inform not only through connectivity but also through improved formal education, informal education, educative participation in global citizenship, and empowerment through information access, handling, and sharing. In addition, expert and reference systems supplement skills and expertise in management, trades and professions.

For example, earthquake disaster programs developed for construction along the San Andreas fault in California greatly reduced mortality and damage, in marked contrast to the devastation in Armenia in 1989. Cornell and Berkeley have studied the behavior of buildings and soils, earthquake energies, and optimal design for structural analysis and earthquake-resistant designs which would not be possible using non-electronic technologies. Disease, drought, crop infestation, floods, landslides, typhoons and other natural disasters recur in many LDCs, often contributing to poor economic and social development. Computer-assisted forecasting, preparation, prevention, and recovery can vastly extend available expertise and resource management.

Other products designed for field work and remote applications in the West are ideal for extending scarce expertise in the Third World by enabling remote experts to gather and interpret medical, market, environmental data. Hand-held computers, mobile tracking systems, voice and image scanners multiply the channels through which information can be gathered, handled with a minimum of training, and utilized.

Shortages of valuable human resources are relieved by decreasing the demand for highly-skilled production workers or additional managers for extensive reporting or project management. In health care, diagnostics, monitoring, emergency care, and recordkeeping can both extend the effectiveness of existing health workers, and accelerate the utilization of medical technology.

It is true that computerization subverts traditional societies. Computerized work, atomic workstations, self-pacing, literacy, and transferable skills—all encourage development of individual identities apart from group roles. New technologies and job opportunities accelerate the decline of long-standing social values and collectivist ideals which emphasized the security and survival of the group rather than individual well-being. The reluctance to eradicate tribal, colonial, rural, or religious tradition and rankings may not be universal. Historically, elites have been less kind and less efficient than markets in apportioning class, security and choice for individuals. Changes in the labor market reduce overpopulation, maternal and infant mortality, and the incidence of poverty. According to the Population Crisis Committee, birth rates fall dramatically when women have opportunities for wage-earning employment, especially in the Third World.

Externally and internally computer technologies alter the distribution of power. A major consideration in systems selection is whether information systems tighten or loosen foreign control and non-nationals' privileges. Internally, guarantees of security and privacy are costly, but must be pursued before implementation. On the other hand, public access to communications and to news of global events in 1989-1990 illustrated global information's constructive and democraticizing effects in evolving political systems.

The potential for political abuses is significant. The emergence of global technology coincides with declining autonomy for impoverished nations. In fact, the instability caused by financial and economic malaise increased the potential for foreign and internal interventionism, facilitated by information gathering and surveillance. Foreign parties utilize information technology at present to monitor austerity programs, military strength and environmental problems.

Computer programs already assess anti-government sentiment in the Third World for U.S. policy (Richardson, 1987), and the capacity for domestic LDC surveillance and internal repression is nascent. Just as, unexpectedly, Soviet communism took root in a pre-industrial, pre-democratic country in 1917, defying Marx's predictions, so Big Brotherism may appear in the weak socio-economic systems of underdeveloped areas.

Politically, information resources tend to be democratizing and educative, but guarantees of security and privacy must be incorporated into system design. The technical feasibility for Big Brotherism, combined with local histories of periodic instability and dictatorship, increase the possibility of unprecedented information control and behaviour monitoring through information systems. Also, foreign control of information systems and transmissions could result in a new technological imperialism. External monitoring of cocaine production and trade, as well as environmental devastation, while perhaps pursuing worthwhile goals, may set dangerous precedents for external data gathering and ownership.

If 24-hour global news services such as CNN and widespread information access were curtailed, IT has the singular potential to concentrate the distribution and exercise of power, mass communications, privacy, and behavior control. However, IT at present is less feared as an internal dictatorial tool than as a pernicious incursion into traditional societies, Westernizing and homogenizing cultures at breakneck speed.

OPTIONS AND SOLUTIONS

A broad spectrum of cultures and economics development typifies emergent nations. Across that spectrum, computer technology will intensify rather than relieve stress on traditional values, processes, and social structures as LDCs adopt competitive solutions.

The most strategic investment for LDCs in the 1990's is in the infrastructure needed for communications and education. Communications capabilities and skilled labor are vital for electronic data transfer and expert resource management, for nations to remain viable in the global marketplace, as major actors, or even as suppliers and distributors. Infrastructural improvements are needed for top-down and bottom-up education.

In a free flow of information, holistic views of markets, resources, and constraints increase the commonality of purpose and mass education regarding mobility, competition, consumer expectations, and political goals. Communications and information technologies are symbiotic, transmitting together instantaneous and unedited image, voice, and data at declining costs and increasing integrity, timeliness, and quantities.

Computerization promotes dual economies, within LDCs as a whole and within specific industries (Wirth, 1987). Socio- technological dualism and pluralism are included in the costs of LDC self-determination in the next century.

Comparative advantage increasingly accrues to the producer of processed materials, finished products, skilled labor, substitutable and mobile factors of production, and fluid resource management. Information technology is a common link between all these factors, and vital to the survival of underdeveloped countries.

Studies of the role of microelectronics and computerization in newly industrialized countries can identify options for computer-aided development. In South Korea, micro-electronics and textile industries spearheaded a dramatic break from poverty to munificence (Woronoff, 1983). Korea plunged into informatics, an area which promoted progressive resource management. Information technology was suitable also because of the lack of dependence upon costly imported raw materials; furthermore, IT required little energy consumption.

The Korean experience is germane for LDC development. Except for a few large producers such as Gold Star and Daewoo, informatics is characterized by intensive, small operations and even putting-out systems. Microelectronics complemented Korea's natural endowments and created as two by-products a well-trained labor force, a major long-term asset, and an improved living standard. Microelectronics is non-polluting, provides relatively good profit margins, and is export-oriented.

Although work in informatics, especially data entry, is scandalously arduous, it often represents an improvement for the predominantly female labor force in contrast to their former occupations. Through information handling, adult literacy spreads through informal education, through non-governmental enterprises, and workers acquire transferable skills.

A variety of economies are suitable for the highly variegated electronics and information industries. In Korea, resource endowments needed for different industry sectors range from labor-intensive (components), to capital-intensive (consumer products), to knowledge intensive (industrial equipment, data processing).

The expansion of computer industries was encouraged by direct and indirect government incentives in financing, taxation and administrative control, and marked by the development of a variety of organizational structures: foreign-owned, joint ventures and local companies. Informatics flourished amidst relative and absolute declines in other sectors, did not exacerbate the failure of older industries, and opened significant new avenues for economic development, worker mobility, and trade surpluses.

The impact of computers in the Third World is tied to developmental issues. Ill-chosen technologies may augment unemployment, devalue skills, dehumanize and bankrupt socio-economic systems. However, technology transfer techniques are improving. More acumen is available to introduce technology by stages, preferably through prototypes with a high likelihood of success, targeted at well-prepared user-groups and lucrative applications.

Burgeoning service industries in insurance, hotel and airline reservations, accounting, shipping, and information retrieval encourage educational investments in human capital by domestic and foreign employers, as well as governments and other agents. From production to data collection, education is the one prerequisite always needed to extract value from the best technologies. From the workshop to the global network, public and corporate policy is required to control systems selection to optimize human development as well as economic growth, and to channel benefits to those groups in most need.

CONCLUSION

Information technology transfers represent both a threat and an opportunity to populations in developing areas. Market forces accelerate the dispersion of valuable technologies, but intelligence and control is vital to capture and distribute CIS's benefits.

In the 1990s IT management and control will continue to be affected by many factors external to LDCs: the continued globalization of multinational enterprises, increased competition, a shifting focus of trade and investment toward Europe, the relative economic decline of the U.S., and innovative business behaviour by the Pacific Rim nations. The progressive decline of the planned economies and superpower demilitarization may redirect foreign aid and investment.

Political and business leaders frequently lack the will and the expertise for vision and control. Yet, without rigorous systems analysis together with social and economic planning and control, market-driven IT selection may exacerbate financial distress, social divisions, and economic immobility. Nonetheless, LDCs must adopt competitive technologies, and controlled computerization holds vast promise.

Computer professionals have little policy-making or economic development experience, training, *pro bono* tradition, or organization to assist them in optimizing the transfer of changing IT technologies to LDCs. However, no group is better equipped to share responsibility, accountability, and leadership in CIS planning and control.

References

Adler, E. (1986). Ideological 'guerrillas' and the quest for technological autonomy: Brazil's domestic computer industry. *International Organization, 40*(3), 673-705.

Alvarez, J., Smiley, S.M. & Rohrman, F. (1985). Informatics and Small Computers in Latin America, *Journal of the ASIS 36*(4), 259-267.

Andima, Haron S. and Arungu-Olende, Shem. (1987). The use of microcomputers for financial modeling of a public utility system in a developing country. *Microprocessing and Microprogramming, 19*(2), 110-118.

Ayres, Robert (1990). Technological transformations and long waves: Part I. *Technological Forecasting and Social Change. 37*, 1-37.

Babington, E.A. (1987). Installing a computerized planning system in Ghana. *Long Range Planning, 20*(4), 110-117.

Boritz, J. Efrim. (1989). Bye, bye Brazil. *CA Magazine, 122*(11), 36-43.

Botelho, A.J. (1987). Computers: A third world country builds its own. *Technology Review, 90*(4), 36-45.

Buckley, Pamela (1987). This is no way to automate. *Management World, 16*(6), 24, 26.

Chepaitis, Elia V. (1990). Cultural constraints in the transfer of computer technologies to Third World countries." In *Technology for International Development*, Mtewa, Mekki, ed. New York: St. Martins Press, 1990.

Chepaitis, Elia (1989). Information technology and infrastructural improvements in developing countries. *Conference on Organizations and Information Systems: Proceedings.* University of Maribor. Bled, Yugoslavia, I, 249-256.

Corfmat, Francois. (1985). Computerizing revenue administration in LDCs. *Finance and Development, 22*(3), 45-47.

Durbin, Paul T. (1989). Technology studies against the background of professionalization in American higher education. *Technology in Society, 11*, 439-445.

Eckaus. R.S. (1987, Winter). Appropriate technology: The movement has only a few clothes on. *Issues in Science and Technology*, 62-70.

Fleury, Paulo Fernando. (1988). The implementation of the Brazilian computer industry: Its complexity and potential impacts. *Technology in society, 10*(10), 29-43.

Garson, Barbara. (1988). *The Electronic Sweatshop: How Computers are Transforming the Office of the Future into the Factory of the Past.* New York: Simon and Schuster.

Glenn, Jerome C. (1985). Helping countries help themselves. *Futurist, 19*(6), 33-35.

Gricar, Joze and McCubbrey, Donald. (September 13-15, 1989). Electronic Data Inter-change as a means of stimulating international trade. *Proceedings of the International Conference on Organization and Information Systems,* Bled, Yugoslavia. 36-37.

Grieco, J.M. (1982). Between Dependency and Autonomy: India's Experience with the International Computer Industry. *International Organization 36*(3), 609-632.

Hartmann Heidi, ed. (1986). *Computer Chips and Paper Clips: Technology and Women's Employment.* The National Research Council. The National Academy Press.

Hills, Jill. (1990). The telecommunications rich and poor. *Third World Quarterly, 12*(2), 71-90.

ICCP [Information Computer Communications Policy], (1989). *Information Technology and New Growth Opportunities.* OECD. Paris.

Maier, John. (1986). When the sun goes down, so do China's computers. *Computerworld, 20*(14), pp. 57-66.

Noble, David E. (1986). *Forces of production: A social history of industrial automation.* New York: Oxford University Press.

Pacey, Arnold. (1984). *The Culture of Technology.* Cambridge: MIT Press.

Population Crisis Committee. (1988). Country rankings of the status of women: Poor, powerless, and pregnant. *Population Briefing Paper,* Washington.

Prebisch, Raoul. (1964). Toward a new trade policy for Development. *Proceedings of the United Nations Conference on Trade and Development,* New York: United Nations.

Reich, Robert B. (1987). The rise of techno-nationalism. *Computers in Society.* Guilford, CT: Dushkin Publishing, 54-60.

Richardson, John M., Jr. (1987). Violence and repression: Neglected factors in development planning. *Futures, 19*(6), pp. 651-668.

Rybcyzynski, Witold. (1985). *Taming the tiger: The struggle to control technology.* New York: Penguin Books.

Schumacher, E.F. (1973). *Small is beautiful: Economics as if people mattered.* New York: Harper and Row.

Struyk, Raymond J. (1987). The housing needs assessment model. *Journal of the American Planning Association, 53*(2), 227-234.

Thirlwall, A.P. (1989). *Growth and development,* 4th ed. London: Macmillan Education.

van Oudheusden, Dirk L. and Khan, Mohammed L.R. (1987). Planning and development of rural road networks in developing countries. *European Journal of Operational Research, 32*(3), 353-362.

Yoshida, Tsuji (1988). Japan helps to promote computerization in developing countries. *Business Japan, 33*(7), 61-62.

Wall Street Journal. (November 14, 1988). The case for low tech. *The Wall Street Journal Reports: Technology.*

Wirth, Arthur G. (1987). Contemporary work and the quality of life. In *Society as Educator in an Age of Transition,* ed. Kenneth D. Benne and Steven Tozer. Chicago: University of Chicago, 54-87.

Woronoff, Jon (1983). *Korea's economy: Man-made miracle.* Seoul: Si-sa-yong-o-sa Publishers.

Zuboff, Shoshana (1988). *In the age of the smart machine: The future of work and power.* New York: Basic Books, Inc.

The Challenge of Introducing Advanced Telecommunication Systems in India

6

Krishna S. Dhir
The Citadel and The Medical University of South Carolina

There is a technological revolution taking place in India. India has undertaken a major program to improve its telecommunications and supporting systems. The focus is not limited to the urban centers. Villages, and remote areas, throughout India are being exposed to satellite based telecommunications. Telecommunications is deemed as critical to India's efforts to improve the lot of its people as health, food, environment and education. This chapter presents an overview of the change taking place in India through the introduction of advanced technologies in telecommunications.

INTRODUCTION

Global telephone networks cover only about 800 million people out of a world population of about 4.5 billion. About 75 percent of this coverage is concentrated in 9 countries. Three quarters of the world's population live in countries with 10 telephones or less for every 100 persons. Over half live in countries with less than one telephone for every 100 persons. Nevertheless, the International Telecommunication Union (ITU)'s Independent Commission for World-wide Telecommunications Development, chaired by Sir Donald Maitland, recommended in December 1984, that,

> ... by the early part of the next century virtually the whole of mankind should be brought within easy reach of a telephone and, in due course,

the other services telecommunications can provide. That should be the overriding objective ... (Maitland et al, 1984).

The next century will be upon us in less than a decade. And yet, the Maitland Commission was quite aware that,

> Achieving this will require a range of actions by industrialized and developing countries alike ... While telecommunication is taken for granted as a key factor in economic, commercial, social and cultural activity in industrialized countries and as an engine of growth, in most developing countries the telecommunications system is not adequate even to sustain essential services. In many areas there is no system at all (Maitland et al, 1984).

Developed countries no longer think in terms of separate networks for voice, telex, data, etc. Through the Integrated Services Digital Network (ISDN) concept, the consumers in these countries can access a variety of services, including voice communication, data transmission and video services, through a single connection. Access to telephones in the less developed countries, however, is far less than in Europe, Japan or North America (see Table 1). The disparity in network capabilities among them is even greater.

The less developed countries of the world, over a relatively short period of time, have arrived at the telecommunication technology crossroads.

Country	Main lines per 1000 population
Sweden	615
U.S.A.	409
W. Germany	403
Japan	367
Hong Kong	304
Singapore	292
Bahrain	161
Republic of Korea	141
Brazil	50
Mexico	47
China	5
India	4
Indonesia	3
Tanzania	2
Zaire	0.7

Source: ITU; Telematics India, March 1988, 39.

Table 1: Telephone Densities in Selected Countries

In the past many of these countries, including India, opted for technologies in an unplanned, piece-meal manner. Today they find it necessary to carefully study their needs and constraints and to diligently plan their future. They have to take into account their commitment to national development, advanced and rapidly developing technologies available in the developed nations, constraints of a host of demands on their limited resources, and often overwhelming basic needs of their people.

India, as one of the relatively more developed of the less developed countries, has elected to opt for some of the most advanced telecommunication technologies. There is a technological revolution taking place in India. While it struggles to feed, clothe and shelter its poor, India is also active in space. Its efforts to improve its telecommunications systems are not limited to the urban centers. Villages all over India are being exposed to satellite-based systems. But for a poor country like India, introducing advanced telecommunication systems is a monumental task. This chapter describes how the introduction of such advanced technologies is changing India.

THE SCALE OF INDIA'S TELECOMMUNICATIONS PROBLEM

It is estimated that the population of India is between 800 and 850 million. This accounts for about one sixth of the world population! India is a nation consisting of many different cultures, whose people speak many languages. Average literacy is around 40 percent. While nearly 350 million Indians live in the Gangetic plains, the rest of the population is dispersed throughout India's 3.3 million square kilometers area. In India, there are 3,126 towns with an urban population of about 23 percent of the total. This population has access to only about 45,000 payphones. The ratio is 1 payphone for 3,600 people. In rural India, the picture is quite different. Seventy seven percent of India's population, living in 575,936 villages, have access to a mere 33,000 long distance telephones. While the average population per village is 1,190, 92.7 percent of the villages have a population of less than 2,000 (Murthy, 1987, 9).

INDIA'S ASPIRATIONS

In 1987, the economy of India was growing at 4 to 5 percent annually, and industrial output at 6 to 7 percent annually. In the fiscal year 1988-89, India showed an impressive growth of 11 percent in its real gross domestic product (GDP). Despite this performance, India's economy faces a number of serious problems, such as persistent power shortages, a large and growing number of financially insolvent industrial units, and a large central budget deficit (Anonymous, 1987; 1989b). Indian planners are concerned that after four decades of planning, the objective of ensuring employment and a moderate standard of living for India's poor remains unfulfilled. To address these concerns, the Government of India, in its Eighth Five Year Plan, has announced a major revision in its priorities. The Government proposes to reduce its expenditures, during the 1990-95 period, in the capital-intensive areas of the economy and increase it in the labor-intensive areas, except in strategic and high technology industries. The development of energy and infrastructural facilities including telecommunications and transportation are to be emphasized along with the production of intermediate and capital goods. The Government's industrial policy strives for international competitiveness in selected areas such as steel, electronics and machine building (Anonymous, 1990b, 3).

THE SEVEN TECHNOLOGY MISSIONS

India has committed itself to seven ambitious multi-billion dollar technology missions during its Seventh Five Year Plan (1985-90), aimed at generally improving standards of living in India, with emphasis on rural India. These missions, with a total budget of about US$ 2.8 billion (INRs. 50 billion, at US$ 1.00 equal to INRs. 18.00), pertain to:

(i) rural drinking water,
(ii) immunization,
(iii) oilseeds,
(iv) literacy,
(v) revitalizing wastelands,
(vi) infant mortality, and
(vii) telecommunications.

Clearly, India regards telecommunications to be as critical to its efforts to improve the lot of its people as health, food, environment and education. This philosophy is not an easy one for India to adopt. The challenges it faces in health, food, environment and education areas are enormous.

India looks to technology to address its challenges. The Technology Mission on rural drinking water, for instance, hopes to provide potable drinking water to 100,000 villages within two years, deploying modern technologies to increase the drilling success rates and water purification. For maximum impact, the focus is on villages where people have to walk at least 1.6 kilometers to fetch water. Similarly, the Immunization Mission's objective is to protect 20 million children and 25 million pregnant women against illness and death attributable to six major vaccine preventable diseases. Under the Literacy Mission, the goal is to increase the number of people who are functionally literate by 10 million people per year in the age group 15-35. The number of illiterates in this age group is about 116 million. The Oilseeds Mission is geared to reduce the imports of edible oil from the US$ 555 million (INRs. 10 billion) a year to a fifth of that figure by increasing the domestic production of oilseeds.

The Telecommunications Mission, generally known as the Mission Better Telecommunication, has set out to modernize India's telecommunications systems and to correct the communications imbalance between rural and urban India. Over 85 percent of the total 4.3 million telephones lines in India are concentrated in urban centers. About 60 percent of the total number of lines are located in 25 cities. There are about 13 thousand telephone exchanges in India, with about 28 percent of these in urban centers and the remaining 72 percent in rural areas (Raghavan, 1990). For the urban areas, the aim is to provide telephone connections on demand, and both voice and non-voice communication facilities. In rural areas, the aim is to bring a public telephone to every village. Presently, India has over 133,000 speech circuits, 35,000 telegraph circuits, 22,000 route kilometers of coaxial/symmetrical cables, 26,000 route kilometers of microwave radio systems, and a few hundred kilometers of optical fiber. At the beginning of 1986, there were 32 (29 fixed and 3 transportable) satellite earth stations (Murthy, 1987, 9). By 1995, there will be 88 satellite earth stations in India.

Telecommunications is Given High Priority

The first 35 years of independence saw very little development in telecommunication. The development achieved was more for necessity, and was at best slow and at worst nonexistent. This record has extracted a heavy price. For instance, in 1987, 5,000 people perished in the town of Morvi, in Gujarat, when the Machu Dam gave way. A substantial loss of human life could have been averted if only the telephone at the dam site had been functioning properly. Desperate attempts by local staff to inform authorities of the impending collapse could not succeed due to the defective on-site telephone (Anonymous, 1988a, 38). As a result of such tragedies, the old notion that the telephone is an item of luxury has finally been given up. Ambitious plans have been formulated and are being implemented to prepare India for the 21st century.

In order to promote rapid development in all aspects of telecommunications, including technology, production and services, the Government of India has consolidated all telecommunication and electronics programs under a new Telecommunication Commission. This Commission has a wide range of authority. It is responsible for formulating the policies of the Government; for preparing the budget for each financial year; and for implementing the Government's policies concerning telecommunications. The Commission, within the limits of the budget approved by the Parliament, has the power of the Central Government in both administrative and financial matters. The Commission also has the power to frame its own rules and procedures. It is not clear whether the Commission is accountable to the Government or the Parliament, and if it is, to what extent. This ambiguity does create problems from time to time, such as the instance of conflicts between the Commission's Chairman, Mr. Satyen 'Sam' Pitroda, and the Union Minister of Communications, Mr. K.P. Unnikrishnan. These conflicts resulted in Mr. Pitroda's role as the Chairman of the Telecommunications Commission being reaffirmed, though his role as Special Advisor to the Government of India on Technology was eliminated. There is little doubt of the great emphasis being put on the telecommunications systems development by the Government of India. This was a high priority area in Prime Minister Rajiv Gandhi's administration, and remained no less important an area in Prime Minister V.P. Singh's administration.

India feels that it is poor partly because it missed the industrial revolution. The years of colonization did not help its cause of development. Indians are now fearful of missing the information revolution. They see that the technologically more advanced options are, in many instances, more economical. This perspective has led to the provision of the Indian National Satellite (INSAT) series. INSAT 1B cost India millions of dollars. However, a lower technology ground based system would have cost trillions. Similarly, India's Eighth Five Year Plan seeks to deploy the latest technology in fiber optics in and between major centers, such as New Delhi, Calcutta, Bombay and Madras (Williamson, 1990). The infusion of new technologies along with the antiquated systems already in place, has created a hodgepodge of technology in the country. In the large cities, modern digital switching systems exist in parallel with the older step-by-step systems. Only a short distance away from the major cities one can find 1920 style manual telephone exchanges. Thirty percent of Indian telegraph offices still use the Morse Code.

INDIA's SELF-RELIANCE STRATEGY

For less developed countries, the problem of choosing a telecommunications technology is confounded by the ever changing and ever increasing sophistication of new and emerging technologies in industrialized nations. Planners are continually faced with the obsolescence of technologies that form the basis of their plans. The alternatives available to the less developed countries are examined below.

Alternative Strategies

Strategies for telecommunications development vary widely depending on the degree to which they rely on foreign technology and investment. They range from the direct purchase of telecommunications products through international bidding, to efforts to develop an indigenous technology capability with minimum foreign participation. The technology acquisition strategies adopted by less developed countries are often a combination of the following three categories:

    (i) The direct transfer of technology, which may involve an outright purchase of the technology;

    (ii) The absorption of technology, which involves initial participation of a foreign partner, either through joint ventures or direct investment, with the degree of foreign investment phased out over time; and,

    (iii) The self-reliance strategy, involves the development of indigenous technologies.

Hong Kong, Malaysia, Singapore, Thailand, and the OPEC countries, have purchased foreign technologies directly. For less developed countries, direct purchase of technology is often an expensive proposition. They use this strategy in combination with the other strategies. Brazil and Korea have experimented with the absorptive strategy, and so have Algeria, Argentina, Indonesia, and Turkey. India has decided to develop indigenous capabilities in telecommunications. Algeria, Brazil, China, Iran, Korea, Kenya, Portugal, and Zimbabwe are doing the same (Ambrose, 1988).

The Dilemma of Technology Acquisition

For a less developed country, both the direct purchase of technology and the absorptive strategy are not easy alternatives to follow. The environment in most of these countries is primarily rural, steeped in an agriculture-based culture which has evolved over thousands of years. The transfer of the technologies from developed countries to less developed countries is not a simple matter. Even those technologies which have been developed within the agricultural framework of the developed countries are often difficult to transfer. For instance, the farm culture in many developed countries is that of a large scale industry. It is constituted of big businesses, and it utilizes expensive farm machineries too large for the small scale, primarily family oriented operations one finds on small parcels of land in less developed countries. In the absence of massive land areas needed to operate heavy equipment, the highly capital intensive systems of the developed countries often fail to replicate comparable economies of scale in less developed countries. As a result, the differences in structure and scales of economy, and in culture, can compound the problems of transfer of higher level technologies, such as those of telecommunications, manyfold.

The strategy of self-reliance, too, is not easy to follow. Keeping abreast of rapid advancements in digital, optical and software technologies is difficult even for the largest global suppliers. Mergers and joint ventures are common (e.g., AT&T and Philips, Siemens and GTE, ITT and Alcatel, Italtel and Telettra). If these multi-billion dollar multi-nationals have difficulty supporting the levels of research and development spending required to keep up with these technologies, how can the financially-strapped less developed countries hope to keep up, much less catch up?

Developing Indigenous Technology

India has chosen to seek self-reliance with limited foreign technology inputs. To some extent, China is doing the same. India's strategy combines protectionist trade policies with efforts to develop indigenous technology. Direct foreign investment is avoided. In selecting a technology, consideration is given to several factors such as universality of application, flexibility, high capacity, cost, ease of maintenance, and indigenous production. Where necessary, foreign assistance may be sought to build plants, and to license technology. Both India and China have had to purchase a substantial share of their telecommunications needs from outside as they wait for their indigenous technology efforts to bear fruit.

Developing an indigenous capability in telecommunications requires the following prerequisite elements (Ambrose, 1988):

(i) basic science and technology capability;
(ii) engineering expertise in the areas of materials, micro-circuitry, power, etc.;
(iii) advanced software engineering expertise;
(iv) skilled labor;
(v) network planning expertise;
(vi) management expertise, particularly in the area of logistics and production; and,
(vii) capital.

Developing countries typically have few of these resources. Yet some of the less developed countries have shown encouraging and impressive progress. Korea has designed the TDX-1 digital local exchange and the KD-4 digital channel bank. Brazil's Telebras has designed its Tropico digital concentrator and switching family (Ambrose, 1988). China is developing an indigenous fiber optics industry (Williamson, 1990), and India has developed an indigenous digital exchange. India has been self-sufficient in switching and microwave transmission production for decades. It is fortunate to have a large technical manpower base, government support, and experience in the development of analog electronic technology.

The Slow Road to Development

Despite the benefits that come with an indigenous technology capability in telecommunications, a self-reliance strategy, whether absorptive like Korea's or protective like India's, results in considerable lags in technology implementation. Self-reliance efforts slow the introduction of new technology to the telecommunications network. Those countries that purchase telecommunications equipment with high levels of indigenous content typically are at the bottom of the scale in terms of main line density of connections (Ambrose, 1988).

In India, as in Brazil, much of the equipment going into the telecommunications networks is manufactured indigenously. At the same time, both have established indigenous research and development efforts that have made important progress in the areas of digital switching, optical transmission and software development. Nevertheless, their networks are over 90 percent electromechanical. By contrast, those countries that are purchasing foreign technology directly are rapidly developing digital networks. Even Korea lags in implementing digital technology. Having decided upon analog electronic designs in the early 1980s digital plans have been slow to develop as Korea waits for its suppliers to earn an adequate return. Only about 10 percent of Korea's network is now digital (Ambrose, 1988, 41).

Indian planners are not impressed by these observations. In their factories they plan to produce the Strowger exchanges of yesteryear (the first ever automatic exchange, invented by A.B. Strowger in 1889) well into the next decade. Some electromechanical manufacturing facilities are only five years old; production is projected through the mid-1990s to achieve payback. Indian planners feel that the price they pay in slow development is justified. The Maitland Commission's report, *The Missing Link*, points out that the less developed countries incur heavy costs in pursuing the absorptive strategy because spare parts supply contracts associated with purchases of foreign technology are very rarely respected (Maitland et al, 1984). Consequently, brand-new equipment becomes virtually obsolete several years before the end of its nominal life. These concerns are compounded by the rise in merger activity and a continuing shakeout in the industry.

Indian planners stress that by buying foreign technology directly they would forego the benefits of indigenous electronic research and development to other sectors of the economy, such as transportation, energy and health. Direct acquisition of foreign technology would also deprive the domestic economy in other ways. For instance, it would inhibit indigenous development of technology and its associated benefits, such as the creation of a local, value-added contribution to the GDP, creation of jobs, reduction of foreign exchange requirements, and the development of technologies more appropriate for the local needs. India's indigenously developed rural automatic exchange, for instance, features a high throughput for application in high-density populations in remote areas. It consumes less power, and it does not require air condition-ing. In a country where the balance of payments is so critical that only six to eight weeks of foreign exchange is available for imports, the planners feel compelled not to import products that would primarily serve 'elitist consump-tion' (Anonymous, 1990a, 5). They favor technologies which generate employment, use indigenous natural resources, and promise progress towards improving the lot of the poor.

MISSION BETTER COMMUNICATIONS

Mission Better Telecommunications was launched in February 1987. It is aimed at correcting the deficiencies in the country's networks and modernizing them to a limited extent to the satisfaction of subscribers. The mission covers planning, operation, training and research activities.

The Objectives

The objectives of Mission Better Telecommunications include the following, among others:

(i) Improvement of telecommunication availability, accessibility, reliability and services of the present network using existing re-sources, with marginal investment, through improved productivity and customer interface.

(ii) Provision of basic satisfactory voice and non-voice telecommuni-cation services nationwide to the client constituencies of government, business, institutions, urban areas, suburban areas and rural areas.

(iii) By the year 2000, achieve targets of 20 million telephone lines, more than 2 million public phones, and growth in rural telecommuni-cation.

(iv) Integration of the overall telecommunication development with other national modernization programs on education, water, energy, health, transportation, housing, etc.

(v) Development of a work ethic and a culture within the administrative organization and the bureaucratic infrastructure which are conducive to the efficient achievement of the mission's objectives.

Action Plans

Action plans have been drawn up for each of the objectives which are called "mini-missions." The resulting improvements in various parameters are continually monitored at all levels. For instance, the action plans for improvement in quality of telephone service consists of the following activities (Hiregange, 1988):

(i)   Induction of electronic exchanges;
(ii) Replacement of unserviceable electromechanical systems;
(iii) Replacement of overhead lines in subscriber loops with drop wires;
(iv) Replacement of old underground cables which are fault prone;
(v)   Replacement of heavy overhead alignments of bare wires by underground cables;
(vi) Replacement of heavy overhead trunk alignments of bare conductors by insulated wires until rural communication link is replaced by radio links and fiber-optical systems;
(vii) Pressurization of all junction cables and primary cables;
(viii) Laying new primary and junction cables in ducts;
(ix) Increasing the availability or reliability of junction circuits by inducting pulse code modulations systems in existing cables; and,
(x)   Providing reliable power supply systems.

Emphasis is being placed on value analysis and value engineering. For instance, Indian planners would like to minimize the use of voice communications in large business organizations and in Government departments, such as the Railways, so that a given amount of investment can transmit more information. Non-voice transmission can cost as little as 1 percent of that of voice communication!

The Challenges

The major challenges identified by the planners are the following:

(i) The technological challenge is that of indigenous product development;

(ii) The productivity challenge is that of the quantum leap required in product availability and surplus;

(iii) In the area of service, the major challenge is that of achieving customer satisfaction;

(iv) The decentralization required in the bureaucratic decision making process with financial authority, autonomy and flexibility offers a major financial challenge; and

(v) Creation of a new work culture and a new work environment offers an administrative challenge.

The Eighth Five Year Plan calls for the doubling of the entire telecommunication network. It's objective is to increase the total number of subscriber lines to 9.5 million by 1995. This growth is to be achieved without growth in size of the administrative organization. The primary constraint pertains to materials. For instance, Indian Telephone Industries Limited is required to produce 500,000 lines per year. Only half of this will come from digital switching technology. The rest must come from other technologies for which Indian Telephone Industries Limited is not geared at the present time. It is not clear where this production will come from. It is conceivable that India might add 1 million lines to the current capacity by the third year of the Eighth Five Year Plan, resulting in a shortfall of 250,000 lines. Out of the 4.8 additional million lines desired by 1995, India might manage to realize 4 million lines. The funds for this growth are to be derived from revenues, surplus and depreciation. This funding source will account for about 80 percent of the total spending. In effect, the growth will be subsidized by the urban telecommunications systems users. Consequently, the central government has allocated rather limited budget for the program, and is primarily limited to the foreign exchange required.

INCOME AND EXPENSES

In the mid-80s, the combined yearly revenues of the telecommunications industry world-wide were estimated around US$ 250 billion. Since then, according to the World Bank, the less developed countries have become poorer and the developed countries richer. A study by the ITU estimates that for the development of telecommunications, the less developed countries collectively require a total investment of about US$ 12 billion. Unfortunately, about 60 percent of this investment has to be made in foreign currencies, causing serious hardship for the less developed countries (Bhattacharjee, Singh & Colhando, 1989, 57).

Expenditure Schedule

India's plans call for the addition of about 20 million telephone connections and 2 million public telephones over the 12 year period from 1988 to 2000. Indian planners expect to spend around US$ 37 billion and add about 15.1 million connections and 1.1 million public payphones, and to build up an adequate infrastructure for a reliable service as well as to provide the essential telecommunications services for business, industry and administration (Raynor, 1989; Sangal, 1989, 32). Of this, US$ 3 billion was earmarked for fiscal 1989. Roughly US$ 10 billion is to be distributed from 1990 to 1995, and the remainder between 1996 and 2000. Of the total investment the Government of India will contribute only about half. The rest will come from private investors, both domestic and foreign (Raynor, 1989). While one telephone line costs around US$ 1,555 (INRs. 28,000) in Indian urban areas, a village telephone costs from US$ 5,555 (INRs. 100,000) to US$ 8,333 (INRs. 150,000). This suggests a requirement of billions of rupees to be generated by the urban sector which is already paying and supporting the entire Indian telecommunications services. Through satellite, radio and other technologies, India's Telecommunications Research Center is attempting to reduce the cost of a village telephone to US$ 745 (INRs. 13,400), which is even less than the average cost of providing a telephone in urban areas. If this low cost materializes, the total investment in rural communications would be US$ 467 million (INRs. 8.4 billion) against US$ 3.33 billion (INRs. 60 billion) estimated to install a phone in every village.

Successful implementation of the plan will require a considerable infrastructure and advance preparation for connections to be provided in subsequent years. To improve reliability and service, obsolete and worn out equipment will also require replacement and rehabilitation. The investment costs per connection provided will, therefore, rise significantly in the initial years of the plan. The figure will, however, come down in later years as the number of connections added each year starts rising sufficiently. According to Sangal (1989), the yearly investment as a share of the GDP, at current prices, may peak at 0.64 percent compared to the current figure of less than 0.4 percent.

Adequate Surplus

Telecommunication services have, over the years, generated adequate income and surplus. The bills for services have generally been rendered and collected in a businesslike manner and surpluses reinvested on a continuous basis. The income as a share of the GDP at current prices has risen from 0.54% to 0.61% even though tariff increases have not kept pace with wholesale and consumer price indices. During 1978-88 period, telecommunication

Year	Income	Operating Expenses		Capital Related Expenses		Surplus
		Staff	Others	Deprecia-tion	Interest & Dividends	
1978-79	308.6	111.1	29.4	30.0	15.0	122.8
1979-80	341.7	126.7	33.3	33.9	15.6	132.2
1980-81	380.0	151.7	40.0	38.3	17.8	132.8
1981-82	446.1	180.6	44.4	42.2	24.4	155.0
1982-83	545.0	223.9	60.6	50.0	35.6	176.1
1983-84	633.9	256.7	63.9	61.1	48.9	203.3
1984-85	729.4	303.9	76.1	74.4	68.3	206.7
1985-86	774.4	349.4	87.2	89.4	94.4	111.7
1986-87	928.9	431.7	123.9	143.3	118.3	335.0
1987-88	1277.2	483.3	175.6	136.7	146.7	
1978-88	6365.3	2618.9	734.4	699.4	585.0	1575.6

Adapted from: Telematics India, February 1989, 32.

Table 2: Income, Expense and Surplus from Telecommunication Services (1978-1988) in US$ Millions (US$ 1.00 equals INRs 18.00)

Year	Investment made	Internal Resources				Borrowing
		Surplus	Depreciation	Others	Total	
1978-79	145.0	122.8	30.0	1.1	153.9	(8.9)
1979-80	154.4	132.2	33.9	1.1	167.2	(12.8)
1980-81	176.7	132.8	38.3	1.1	172.2	4.4
1981-82	273.9	155.0	42.2	2.8	200.6	73.3
1982-83	311.7	176.1	50.0	1.7	227.8	83.9
1983-84	387.2	203.3	61.1	2.2	211.1	176.1
1984-85	469.4	206.7	74.4	7.8	288.9	180.6
1985-86	509.4	153.9	89.4	1.1	244.4	265.0
1986-87	571.1	111.7	143.3	25.6	280.6	290.6
1987-88	777.8	335.0	136.7	0.6	477.8	300.0
Cumulative Total	3776.7	1729.4	699.4	45.0	2424.4	1352.2

Adapted from: Telematics India, February 1989, p.32.

Table 3: Investment in Telecommunications & Sources of Funds (1978-1988) in US$ millions (US$ 1.00 equals INRs 18.00)

services generated an income of US$ 6.4 billion (INRs. 114.6 billion) and, after meeting fully the operating expenses and depreciation, and paying over US$ 585 million (INRs. 10.5 billion) to the general revenues as dividend and interest charges, were left with a net surplus of over US$ 1.67 billion (INRs. 31.1 billion) which was reinvested as retained earnings (Sangal, 1989; also see Table 2).

Taking the 10-year period again, an investment of US$ 3.78 billion (INRs. 67.98 billion) was made, financed to the extent of 64 percent from internal resources, US$ 1.73 billion (INRs. 31.13 billion) by way of retained earnings and US$ 700 million (INRs. 12.59 billion) by way of accretions to the depreciation fund. Only US$ 1.35 billion (INRs. 24.3 billion) has been financed by way of borrowing (see Table 3).

Income Projections

In projecting income, it has been assumed that there will be no substantial increase in tariffs. In arriving at operating expenses, it has been assumed that:

(i)the inflation rate will not exceed 7 percent per year on average,
(ii) the staff costs per employee will rise exponentially at the rate at 10 percent per year on average,
(iii) other operating costs (covering consumables, power, transportation) per telephone connection will rise at an exponential rate of 7 percent per year (in line with the general rate of inflation),
(iv) there will be a continuous improvement in productivity as measured by number of telephone connections per employee,
(v)the low dividend bearing capital borrowing will not be available from the general revenues, and
(vi) the cost of borrowing will be about 12 percent per year through a suitable mix of 13 percent and 9 percent interest bearing public bonds.

Taking the 12-year period, it will be possible to finance the plan entirely from internally generated resources. It will, however, be necessary to borrow some funds during the initial build-up period. The total borrowing will work out to about US$ 3.33 billion (INRs. 60 billion) during the initial eight-year period. Thus in terms of a direct tangible contribution, adequate telecommunication development holds the potential of generating better than 1 percent of the GDP as income and almost 40 percent of that income in the form of savings that can be invested.

Contribution to the Economy

The contribution of any sector to the economy needs to be considered from a number of different perspectives. In the case of telecommunications, these include:

(i) direct tangible contribution through income generated,
(ii) indirect tangible contribution through savings to users,
(iii) intangible benefits to the economy through effective and instantaneous communication made possible,
(iv) contribution through growth and services upstream, contribution to international trade generally and in telecommunication products especially, and
(v) contribution through substantial growth of employment, direct and indirect.

By one estimate, if India could meet all demands for telecommunications services by the year 2000, it would generate over US$ 1.11 billion (INRs. 20 billion) a year in funds that could be used for other nation-building activities (Anonymous, 1990a, 9).

RECENT ACHIEVEMENTS

The Government of India's Department of Telecommunications has performed impressively in recent years (see Table 4 for recent trends). It exceeded the targets of the Seventh Five Year Plan with a year to spare. It exceeded its plan of adding 1.33 million lines of net switching and 1.1 million telephone connections before the end of the Seventh Five Year Plan by actually adding 1.5 million lines and 1.3 million connections, respectively. During 1988-89 alone, the Department of telecommunications added a record 477,000 lines of net switching capacity against the previous year's 340,000. Also, 367,000 new phone connections were installed during the same year against the previous year's 313,000. Subscriber Trunk Dialing (STD) facility expanded remarkably during the year, with 213 stations offering the facility (nationally and globally) against only 93 the year before. Today 710 stations have STD facilities with access to 177 countries. In the same year, 77 rural automatic exchanges, designed and developed on the indigenous technology of India's Center for Development of Telematics' (CDoT) and manufactured by the Indian Telephone Industries Limited, were commissioned. And to improve STD services, 19 digital trunk automatic exchanges with a capacity of 34,500 lines were also commissioned (Anonymous, 1989a).

	1977	1987
Telephones:		
No. of telephones	1.6 mil.	4.3 mil.
No. of villages with long distance public telephones	6787	24959
Percentage of strowger exchanges	67	50
Percentage of crossbar exchanges	16.5	29
Percentage of manual exchanges	16.5	10
Percentage of electronic exchanges	0	11
No. of trunk automatic exchanges (TAX)	13	35
No. of digital TAX	0	7
No. of metered call units per digital exchange lines per day	7.82	12.9
No. of effective trunk calls	123 mil.	215 mil.
No. of stations on national subscriber dialing	55	403
No. of point-to-point Subscriber trunk dialing	102	123
No. of countries available for international subscriber dialing (ISD)	1	164
No. of towns where ISD is available	2	444
No. of persons on waiting list	183000	1125000
Percentage demand (working lines and waiting list) satisfied	87	76
Average time on waiting list	3 years	4.5 years
Telex:		
No. of telex exchanges	82	220
Percentage of strowger exchanges	100	30
Percentage of electronic exchanges	0	70
No. of subscribers	18050	34109
Telegraph:		
No. of offices	23760	36235

Source: Anonymous. Telecom watershed decade. Telematics India, April 1988, 34.

Table 4: Indian Telecommunications through 1977-1987

During the first four years of the Seventh Five Year Plan, 377,000 lines of old switching equipment were replaced by electronic switching equipment; during 1988-89 alone about 123,000 lines of old or worn out equipment were replaced. The Department of Telecommunications has also claimed success under Mission Better Communication as follows (Anonymous, 1989a):

> (i)the local call success rate improved 97.4 percent;
> (ii)the STD call success rate improved 78.3 percent;
> (iii)the telephone fault rate came down from 35 to 17.5 per

100 stations per month; and

(iv) the telex fault rate came down from 62 to 25.5 per 100 stations per month (all improvements being recorded since April 1, 1986).

Meanwhile, investments of US$ 25 million (INRs. 450 million) during 1989-90 and US$ 222 million (INRs. 4 billion) during the Eighth Five Year Plan are planned to upgrade the quality of telecommunication services to the international level. The upgrading of services is expected to be completed by 1995, subject to availability of finance and material. Some measures already taken include the following:

(i) installation of digital electronic exchanges, introduction of push-button telephone instruments,

(ii) replacement of old and worn out exchanges by digital ones,

(iii) use of jelly-filled cables and cable ducts,

(iv) use of a high grade medium, like optical fiber system, for junctions; and

(v) large scale use of computer aids for fault detection and repair and for cable and subscriber records.

DEMAND

Until recently, the telecommunication services demanded were basically the public telegraph service and the public telephone network. The telex was introduced in India only in 1963-64. With the sophistication of the economy, demands have arisen for new services such as data transmissions and facsimile. The rural demand for telephone connections and extending the network to rural areas continues to be most pressing challenge.

Urban Demand

The urban demand for telephone service can be considered in two parts:

(i)the demand for private telephone connections for the exclusive use of a subscriber; and

(ii)the demand for public payphones for common use by many people, particularly those who are unable to lease a private connection for their exclusive use.

There are 10 million Indians in the upper middle class. This population has been investing in consumer goods on a great scale (see Table 5). A color

Quantity	Item	Amount
		(US$ billion)
		(US$ 1.00 equals INRs. 18.00)
-	Equity shares of companies	2.22
3 million	Black & white or color television sets	0.62
0.6 million	Refrigerators	0.28
0.1 million	Passenger cars	0.56
0.60 million	Motorcycles & scooters	0.40
-	Telephones	0.67

Adapted from: Telematics India, March 1988, 25.

Table 5: Indians' Private Investments, 1986-87

television set costs about US$ 800 to US$ 1100. The millions waiting for telephone service would invest from US$ 1000 to US$ 2000 towards equity shares of a telephone company if they were guaranteed, beside their share-holding, a telephone within two or three years. Table 5 shows that telephones claim greater share of private investments than transportation items like passenger cars, or motorcycles and scooters, and entertainment items like television sets (Chowdary, 1988).

The registered demand for telephones grew at an exponential rate of about 10.3 percent per year during 1978-88. The actual rate of growth of demand is believed to be double this rate. During the same period, supply grew at an exponential rate of about 8.2 percent per year. Consequently, the waiting list, representing the demand-supply gap, has risen from about 119,000 to over 1.31 million in 10 years. The gap has grown at an average exponential rate of 21 percent per year (Sangal, 1989; also see Table 6).

Rural Demand

In India's rural areas, where the bulk of the country lives, meeting the demand for private telephones is out of the question. India cannot afford it. Therefore, the focus is on public payphones for common use by many. A study in rural regions of the state of Andhra Pradesh found that when a community telephone was available in a farming village, even the poorest people were willing to pay a hefty share of their month's income to use it. Had there been no telephone for urgent calls, they would have carried the message in person, or by bus, even at the loss of several days' wages. The villagers' biggest complaint about their telephones was the unreliability of the service, not the expense (Pai, 1988, 39).

As on April 1	Registered Demand (millions)	Working Connections (millions)	Waiting List (millions)	Average Waiting Time (mos)
1978	1.92	1.73	0.19	-
1979	2.11	1.87	0.24	-
1980	2.35	2.02	0.34	18
1981	2.60	2.15	0.45	22
1982	2.89	2.30	0.59	27
1983	3.12	2.47	0.66	30
1984	3.41	2.67	0.74	33
1985	3.74	2.90	0.84	32
1986	4.20	3.17	1.03	33
1987	4.61	3.49	1.13	33
1988	5.11	3.80	1.31	34

Average annual exponential rate of growth:
    10.3%   8.2%   21.3%

Source: Telematics India, February 1989. 32.

Table 6: Growth of Telephone Demand, Working Connections and Waiting Time During 1978-1988

Considerable travel is necessitated due to inadequate telecommunications facilities. To communicate, telephone, if available, is cheaper than personal travel, even by the cheapest means of transportation, by a factor of 7 to 12. For shorter distances, the telephone is cheaper than mail. The telephone provides an effective, cheaper alternative for face-to-face communication.

A study in 52 countries found that a one percent rise in the number of telephones per 100 population between 1950 and 1955 contributed to a rise in per capita income between 1955 and 1962 of about three percent. It also found that the poorer the country the greater the benefit. Interestingly, the home telephone was a greater economic boon than the telephone in the place of business (Pai, 1988, 39). This may well have to do the accessibility of the home telephone. There are social benefits, too. In rural areas, the telephone is used far more for emergencies than it is in the cities.

India's record on providing public telephones, both in rural as well as urban areas, has been dismal. In rural areas, out of 575,936 villages only about 33,000 had public payphones in March 1988. In urban areas, too, for a population of about 160 million there were only 45,000 payphones or only one payphone per 3,600 people. It is proposed to provide at least one public telephone in every small village and at the rate of one for a population of 500 in larger villages, towns and cities. This will require 600,000 public payphones in rural areas and another 600,000 in urban areas. It is further proposed that a substantial number of these payphones be assigned individuals to provide answering services. Such an arrangement would create jobs.

RURAL COMMUNICATIONS

The planned efforts to provide rural telephone services in India had a modest beginning almost 25 years ago when small automatic exchanges and public telephones were installed. Later, in the seventies, a policy was framed to provide fully subsidized telephones without the hope of even minimal revenue. Still later, further changes were made in the policy and plans. In spite of these attentions, and possibly due to these frequent changes in policies, rural areas were generally neglected (Bhattacharjee, Singh & Colhando, 1989).

Recommendations of the Sarin Committee

On March 31, 1987, there were 24,961 out of the 575,936 villages connected by telephone. In the late 70's and early 80's, the Indian government commissioned several studies on telecommunication needs in rural areas (for example, see Murthy, 1987, 159-162). These were considered by the Sarin Committee on Telecommunications in 1981-82, which in its seventh report concluded that "... despite the poor financial returns, there are strong reasons for extending telephones to all areas of the country and all sectors of the population" (Anonymous, 1988b). Sarin's Committee noted that telecommunications is essential not only as a social service, but as an economic and public health resource. Telecommunication services are necessary for coordinating the distribution of water and power for agriculture, for early warning of severe weather, locusts and epidemics, for rendering assistance for accidents, fires and crime, and so on. A minimum provision of telecommunications is essential for promoting social change and rural economies. The Sarin Committee recommended that the Government provide a long-distance public telephone located within 5 kilometers of every village by 1990. The ITU conference on Asia and the Pacific also recommended this (Anonymous, 1988b).

To implement this recommendation, Indian planners divided the entire country into clusters of villages forming hexagonal cells symmetrical in shape and 5 kilometers in size, excluding uninhabited regions, such as deserts and mountains. The task of identifying the central villages in each hexagon was entrusted to the National Council for Applied Economic Research. Under the new plan adopted in 1984, there are 46,858 hexagonal cells. This count makes allowances for forests, mountains, deserts and other uninhabited areas. Of these, by late November 1987, only 35,000 cells had been provided either with telephone exchanges or long distance public telephones. At a rate of 1,200 cells per year, the target may be reached in 1997. Of the 575,936 villages, 529,078 remained to be provided with one telephone each. Assuming that only local transmission lines (using open-wire) are to be provided in these villages, the task is almost impossible to complete. The material required will be too extensive, and he time frame will be too long. As for costs, the average budgeted cost for a village telephone at present is US$ 5,555 (INRs. 100,000) for a Public Telephone open-wire line, and US$ 8,333 (INRs. 150,000) using the Multi-Access Rural Radio (MARR) system. At this rate, the total cost of providing telephone service in every village in India will run into an astronomical figure of more than US$ 33.33 billion (INRs. 600 billion) (Murthy, 1987, 15-16).

ALTERNATIVE TECHNOLOGIES

A large number of villages in India are in remote regions. They have remained socially and economically underdeveloped. The absence of telecommunication facilities has contributed to their backwardness. In the past, costs, the lack of an adequate infrastructure, and difficulties in staffing, compelled the use of open wire based communication facilities. Today, a number of alternatives are being considered by Indian telecommunications planners. These are discussed in the next five sections:

UHF Systems

Telecommunications officials have proposed a 30 to 120 channel digital UHF system as one of the more practical solutions for rural communications. A large number of UHF systems are planned for rural and remote communications incorporating integrated switches/rural automatic exchanges which serve both the local network and the long distance networks. On the face of it, this approach may not appear entirely satisfactory as the demand may be much less than what is anticipated. It is expected, however, that the demand would increase when the benefits of telecommunications become apparent to the users. In addition, this approach has an inherent growth potential and is futuristic since it can easily be switched over to integrated digital network.

VHF Systems

Single channel or small VHF systems with 4 to 6 channels may be appropriate for areas having limited traffic, where cost is an important consideration.

Multi-Access Rural Radio

The MARR is another suitable technology. This is being developed indigenously through technology transfer. The Long Distance Public Telephone (LDPT) can be installed as a terminal in the MARR rural radio circuits, allowing more than one user to benefit from it.

Satellite Systems

Satellite communication is most effective in providing communications to remote areas like the mountain and island territories. Small earth stations can either independently provide essential communications or supplement other terrestrial media to link remote and inaccessible areas. An extensive use of low cost earth stations using INSAT Series has been envisaged. As many as 500 earth stations of different sizes are expected to be commissioned during the Eighth Five Year Plan.

The space technology developed by the Indian Space Research Organization is already providing various services to rural areas, such as meteorological observations for precise adverse weather forecasts, remote-sensing multi-spectral environment and agricultural data, national communications, and radio and television broadcasts. India began satellite communications over 10 years ago. Its most spectacular achievement in remote sensing was the launching of the small Rohini satellite in 1983. Eventually India hopes to become autonomous in space activities. It seeks to use a space based remote sensing system for a survey of natural resources and for domestic management of agriculture, forestry, geology and hydrology.

Open Wire

Despite some major disadvantages of open wire systems, in a large number of situations open wire alignments will continue to be the most cost-effective and feasible solution for the immediate future.

Although remote and inaccessible areas are best served by satellite earth stations, cost considerations and technical constraints suggest that an approach of using a balanced mix of open wire, radio system and satellite communication is more judicious.

SATELLITE COMMUNICATIONS

Arthur C. Clarke put forth the concept of a communication satellite in 1945. As he points out, the electronic digital technology offers

... forms of communication that are cheap and ideally suited for people who cannot read. It gives the Third World a chance to leapfrog into the space age, without investing in the expensive copper-wire networks that slow down the industrialized world's telecommunications advance (Pai, 1988).

It has always been evident to the Indian planners that the rural and remote regions would benefit greatly from a satellite based telecommunications systems. Though India is not as vast as Canada or Australia, the Indian planners have shown a keen interest in the experiences of these two countries. Canada's 25 million people live in few large cities and a number of settlements scattered throughout its the 30 million square kilometers. Today Canada has 160,000 route kilometers of microwave and over 100 earth stations connecting some 20 million telephones. Similarly, Telecom Australia once faced serious communications problems between cities and rural settlements. Like Canada, Australia was forced to evolve a system that could network a vast region.

Prior to 1983, television reached just 28 percent of the Indian population. It was served primarily through transmissions from four major metropolitan cities, namely, Bombay, Calcutta, Madras, and New Delhi, linked by microwave towers. In 1988 there were about 250 transmitter relayed programs from the Government owned and operated Doordarshan's television studios in New Delhi, bounced off a powerful S-band transponder on INSAT-1B. By 1990, about 423 transmitters will do this job. Over 70 percent of the population can now tune in to Doordarshan's programs, a rate of expansion that would hardly have been possible through terrestrial links. The satellite is most efficient when a common program is beamed to the entire nation. However, with preference being expressed vociferously for programs in regional languages, more and more such programs are being produced. Commercials designed for the urban populations are being viewed by rural communities, giving rise to increased consumerism in villages. The markets for detergents, soap and toothpaste are increasing at a rate as high as 25 to 30 percent in some rural regions.

A major proportion of satellite capacity has been assigned to telecommunication (mainly telephone) services. The satellite two-way voice circuits and the digital trunk automatic exchanges in major towns with the satellite circuits extended to them has widened the reach and quality of subscriber trunk dialing service. Similarly, National Informatics Center's NICNET is a nationwide satellite-based two way data communication network that links the various central and state government offices across the country. This facilitates communications across all levels, from district governmental headquarters, to State capitals and to the departments of the central government. The network system uses micro earth stations equipped with 1.8 meter diameter parabolic antennas. In remote northeastern regions, small aperture terminals provide access to the satellite for rural telegraphy networks. Through timely satellite based meteorological forecasts, numerous lives have already been saved from the devastation of cyclones.

CREATION OF JOBS

In implementing its telecommunications plans over the next decade, the Government of India will spend about US$ 25 billion (INRs. 450 billion) to purchase capital goods and US$ 8,333 million (INRs. 150 billion) to purchase services required to operate and maintain the telecommunication systems. This expenditure will be considerably greater than the expenditure over the previous 10 years and will naturally provide an impetus to industries and services upstream. A large number of highly sophisticated and not-so-sophisticated equipment and products will be needed.

The development of telecommunications services will result in a substantial increase in highly skilled jobs in the construction, operation, maintenance, and research and development service industries, and other industries upstream. The substantial earnings of people employed directly in the telecommunication sector will generate many additional jobs ensuing from the need for goods and services by these employees and their families. Most jobs, however, will be generated by the construction, operation and maintenance of the telecommunication services. Even with substantial productivity gains, 1978-88 saw an increase of about 95,000 full-time jobs, the gross standing at 251,000 in April 1988. During the 12 year period 1988-2000, another 175,000 full-time jobs could be created, even while continuing gains in productivity are realized (Sangal, 1989).

Apart from direct full-time jobs, telecommunication operations in rural areas will provide about one million supplementary jobs for the rural under-employed, and about one million jobs through public payphones. For instance, each public payphone in every one of the 575,936 villages may be manned by an individual responsible for its operation and maintenance.

The earnings of employees engaged directly in telecommunications will give rise to substantial increase in demand for products and services, housing, food, clothing, education, health, transport, entertainment, etc. These demands effect economic sectors that are highly employment-intensive (see Table 7).

Activity	1987-88	2000

1. Full-time regular
  a) Directly in construction, operation
    and maintenance & allied activities
	350,000	528,000

b) In specialized telecommunication manufacturing industries	35,000	38,000
c) In allied other industries	10,000	12,000
d) Building construction	3,000	4,000
Total	398,000	582,000
2. Total full-time regular employment		

Casual, supplementary employment in
  construction and in looking after
  payphone of attended type
	150,000	1,000,000

3. Indirect to provide goods and services to directly employed full-time	300,000	500,000

Source: Telematics India, February 1989, 32.

Table 7: Gross Estimate of Employment in Telecommunication Sector in The Economy in 1987-1988 and in 2000

GOVERNMENT MONOPOLY IN TELECOMMUNICATIONS

Telecommunications services have generally been owned and controlled by various governments as an extension of the postal system. The underlying principle of this natural monopoly is that the economies of scale are realized only if the service is provided without competition (Chowdary, 1988). Until the 1950s, when the transistor was invented, the pace of development of telecommunication, and particularly telephone technology, was slow. For instance, in the United States, it took several years to install the first million telephones, but in the 1960s, 5 to 10 million telephones were added annually. In the early decades, the United States experimented with a competitive market. Users had to subscribe to several companies to reach different individuals by phone. The chaotic conditions forced the United States government to intervene and threaten nationalization. The industry proposed the alternative of territorial monopolies. This proposal favoring regulated monopolies over "wasteful" competition was adopted. Historically, in Europe and in European colonies elsewhere, telegraph, and later telephone, telex and other telecommunications services were owned and controlled by Government which already owned and operated the postal service.

With the advent of new technologies of the transistor, large and very large scale integrated low-cost circuits, memory chips and micro-processors, telecommunications became increasingly computer oriented. The boundary between pure telecommunications and computers started to diminish. Subsequent growth of telecommunications was influenced by various factors, including:

(i)a spectacular decrease in the cost of computer memory,

(ii) reduced competition,

(iii)the widespread availability and use of cheap micro-processors,

(iv) extension of telecommunication services to the transmission of information as indistinguishable from information processing, and

(v) reduced prices through mass production leading to universal affordability.

Consequently, the argument of the need for economies of scale as a rationale for a government monopoly is weakened (Chowdary, 1988).

The Government of India's Department of Telecommunication is generally faced with the challenge of providing services in a market which is growing even faster than anyone imagined. The per capita telephone revenue in India is about US$ 222 (INRs. 4,000) per year. This is about 1.6 times the per capita national income in India, as compared to about 0.05 times the per capita national income in industrialized nations (Chowdary, 1988). The Government's plans to finance nationwide telecommunications expansion from surpluses of the current revenues amounts to an indirect taxation of the current subscribers whose demands are not being fully met. These subscribers have not always received a fair treatment from the government-owned monopoly and have often suffered severe hardships. Until recently, for instance, the payment of bills was a problem for subscribers in Bombay. Bills would come in late through the post, payment counters were few in number, and consequently queues were long. Fear of disconnection forced people to wait in long lines in the rain or hot sun, for hours at a time. Telecommunications authorities have only recently accepted the suggestions of allowing payment of bills in nationalized banks. With that, a major irritant has now been removed (Anonymous, 1988a). In India, there are very few telephone subscribers' associations. However, there are increasing calls for privatization of the telecommunications services in India. It is argued that with technology undermining natural monopoly, prices of electronics driven telecommunications are falling, and the possibility of unrestricted entry and investment in the market, the volume of business in a free market system could be very high.

CONCLUSION

India was one of the first countries to introduce telephones shortly after its invention. The Department has had a tradition of service for 105 years! As in other sectors of the economy, there is a crucial need to convert the present class economy into a mass economy. Fortunately, modern technology is available to effect such a change. The country should seek to obtain the most modern technology available. In this regard, the example of France is relevant. Only 15 years ago, the French system was considered to be one of the worst in Europe. But a determined effort by the French Government turned this around and made it one of the best in Europe today.

Lack of Bold Decisions

Quite often the Indian Government's efforts are frustrated because of lack of determination on the part of its planners and their inability to make bold decisions. Thus high frequency radio, which has given Australia the best communication in rural areas, could not be deployed in India in spite of the fact that the technology was readily available. Government control of telecommunications has prevented development in these areas. The Government has not allowed the industry to deploy mobile radio which is less cost-intensive.

Changing Techologies

Today, telecommunication technology becomes obsolete every two to five years. For planners in less developed countries this short technology cycle is problematic. They are continually tempted to revise their developmental plans to take advantage of new, superior, more exotic technologies. Pressures on them can be enormous. An Indian executive states,

> ... We have been making a lot of plans but suddenly one finds that some foreign country has developed certain special types of equipment and we immediately change our plans. Here, we must make the final plan ... taking into account the equipment which is available today and freeze the design. It may not be the very best for implementation ... but it should be accepted. (Anonymous, 1990a, 7).

While India has already committed itself to a digital technology in the urban areas, it has not yet frozen the rural technology. India should freeze its plans, and the specifications for rural technology, for a certain period of time, say from three to five years. It should concentrate on the implementation of existing plans.

Local Planning

The United Nations General Secretary U. Thant once stated:

> ... In human affairs, we have reached a point where it is no longer the possession of resources that is going to matter - of far greater importance is the kind of decision that we make on the use of the resources that are available to us (Anonymous, 1990a, 17).

India needs to bring the benefits of its planning to the lowest possible level. India needs to encourage planning at the local or community level. Information collected in Delhi must percolate to the 575,936 villages. Modern technological tools, such as satellites and computers, must be designed to provide data and information to village-level planners to assist them in a plethora of decisions such as where tube-wells should be drilled, where trees are to be planted, what is the optimum composition and amount of fertilizer to be used, and so on. Dr. Vikram Sarabhai's advice to India still holds:

> ... Our initial backwardness, our late arrival on the scene and the meagre investments that we have made in the past for these activities should no longer be allowed to be our major handicaps ... This we can do if we visualize and develop the right kind of policies, if we make right kind of investment and above all if we decide to move forward with confidence in our ability to reach the goals (Anonymous, 1990a).

References
Anonymous. (March 2, 1987). Business Outlook Abroad: India. *Business America, 10*(5), 22-23.

Anonymous. (January, 1988a). Subscriber Woes. *Telematics India,* 38-40.

Anonymous. (May, 1988b). Dialing into Rural Telecom. *Telematics India,* 4.

Anonymous. (June, 1989a). Give the Devil his dues. *Telematics India,* 23.

Anonymous. (October 9, 1989b). Business Outlook Abroad: India. *Business America, 11*(20), 19-20.

Anonymous. (February 2-4, 1990a). *Information Technology Trends* (Special Supplement on

Seminar and Exhibition). New Delhi: Telematics India.

Anonymous. (Monday, May 28, 1990b). Indian cabinet gives approval to 5-year plan. *The Asian Wall Street Journal*, 3.

Ambrose, W.M. (March, 1988). Goal: Self-Reliance. *Telematics India*, 38-42.

Bhattacharjee, A., Singh R., and Colhando, K. (May, 1989). The missing link. *Telematics India*, 56-57, 60.

Chowdary, T.H. (March, 1988). Is monopoly the answer. *Telematics India*, 24-25,27,29.

Hiregange, N.R. (November, 1988). Better Telecom: Mission a success. *Telematics India*, 34-35.

Maitland, D. and associates. (1984). *The Missing Link*, Report of the Independent Commission for World-wide Telecommunications Development. Geneva, Switzerland: International Telecommunication Union.

Murthy, B.S. (November, 1987). *A Phone in Every Village*. New Delhi, India: Telecommunications Research Center, Department of Telecommunications, Government of India.

Pai, M.R. (January, 1988). Subscriber woes. *Telematics India*, 38-40.

Raghavan, T.C. (May 30, 1990). Deputy Director of General Planning, Telecommunications Commission of India, Personal communication.

Raynor, B.C.P. (January 23, 1989). Crackle, crackle ... It's India on the line. *Electronic Business*, *15*(2), 72,74.

Sangal, D.K. (February, 1989). Assured Telecom: Brighter Economy. *Telematics India*, 29,32,35.

Williamson, J. (March 26, 1990). Asia's high-fiber diet. *Telephony*, *218*(13), 40-47.

Information Technology for Natural Resource Inventory and Monitoring in Developing Countries

7

Christine N. Specter and Sundeep Sahay
Florida International University

There is growing international awareness of the environmental crisis confronting our planet. Approximately ten billion hectares of environmental regimes are threatened, including tropical and boreal forests, polar and glacial ice margins, rangelands, and coastal zones. The majority of these critical areas are in developing countries. Most developing countries are suffering major losses of their natural resource bases as they pursue economic development in the face of large and growing populations. While such problems are of direct and immediate concern to the developing world, the degradation and depletion of environmental resources has a substantial impact on all nations. Given the size and complexity of the environmental crisis, international collaboration is required if the challenge is to be met. An essential requirement for effective response is the gathering of reliable, cost-efficient information over large geographic areas on a repetitive basis to monitor environmental changes. Remote sensing technology provides the required mechanism for this purpose. It is information technology which integrates data gathering capabilities of computers for the storage, manipulation and access of data and the telecommuting powers of satellites for transmission of data to ground receiving stations for further diffusion to the end users. This chapter identifies the technology transfer process as the major issue related to the successful application of remote sensing and proposes an information systems model for the remote sensing technology transfer process, an understanding of which is a necessary first step in solving the problem of natural resource inventory and monitoring for developing countries.

REMOTE SENSING AS INFORMATION TECHNOLOGY

Information technology broadly involves hardware and software which facilitate codification, processing and diffusion of information by integrating computer power with telecommunications capabilities. Remotely sensed data, collected by sensors on aircraft and satellites is coded into digital formats using onboard computers and transmitted to ground receiving stations. Digital information is stored on computer useable media, called computer-compatible tapes, and is diffused through networks of companies and agencies in the private and public sectors. The data can be processed, analyzed, and interpreted to provide valuable information concerning the status of the biosphere, land and water resources, and cultural features, e.g. cities, archaeological sites, roads, and canals. (See Appendix A for a technical definition of remote sensing.)

Through the provision of this information, remote sensing technology can assist those responsible for making decisions related to land use planning; agricultural production; exploration, development, and conservation of natural resources. In many cases this method of data collection is most economical; remotely sensed data is less expensive per unit of information collected than through more traditional means, e.g., sending survey teams into the field. Also, large amounts of data can be collected rapidly in situations where time is of the essence in decision making. The repeat coverage offered by the satellites means that temporal comparisons can be made which are critical in detecting changes in natural resource conditions.

REMOTE SENSING AND TELECOMMUNICATIONS

Public technology is a term used to categorize large scale, capital intensive technologies which form a subgroup of high technologies (Jequeir, 1976). Remote sensing and telecommunications are information technologies covered under the public technology domain. They share similarities both in the technical and policy aspects related to their application.

Technical factors

Both remote sensing and telecommunications technologies are used for capturing and transmitting basic information. In the case of remote sensing the data relates to basic environmental factors like land cover, vegetation and forest area. This data has utility for multiple earth resources applications such as agriculture, land use, water resources, and forestry. Telecommunications provide dynamic communication links over which a variety of voice, video and data messages are transmitted.

Both remote sensing and telecommunications involve the use of satellite technology, but the types of satellites used are different. Telecommunications uses satellites in geosynchronous orbit (maintaining a position over a single location along the equator) at altitudes of about 33,000 km for data transmission. On the other hand, remote sensing uses polar orbiting satellites (travelling in longitudinal orbits from the North to the South pole) for data collection. Landsat, for example, circles the globe at 920 km height above sea level, fourteen times per day, collecting data in 185 km swaths (strips of land which are imaged as the satellite passes over). Data is downlinked through a tracking and data relay satellite system or directly to ground receiving stations.

Policy Factors

Decisions to invest in telecommunications and remote sensing systems are made by national governments with central planning and centralized decision making characterizing the implementation process. This is especially true in the context of developing countries, where there is relatively less privatization of these industries as compared to developed countries. The technology once transferred is owned and operated by national governments for the purpose of producing outputs in line with public welfare. These factors result in inherent similarities in the policy aspects relating to the technology's transfer and utilization.

The major obstacles encountered in the transfer of telecommunications and remote sensing are also perceived to be similar. The major obstacles in the transfer of remote sensing technology were found to be related to economics, equipment, political and organizational factors (Specter, 1988). A thematic analysis of literature relating to transfer of telecommunications technology suggested similarities in the obstacles encountered (Zamora, 1989). The authors are currently conducting research to validate these findings.

COMMERCIAL ASPECTS OF REMOTE SENSING

In 1988 the remote sensing industry achieved sales in excess of $500 million, including sales related to both satellite and aircraft data collection. Approximately $250 million was comprised of sales of remote sensing data, image procesisng, and other value-added products and services and an additional $250 million for purchases of necessary hardware and software for analysis and interpretation processes (Anonymous, 1988a). The market is expected to grow. Expert forecasts of the rate of growth vary widely, with estimates for 1997 annual sales ranging from one billion dollars (Department of Commerce, 1988) to six billion dollars as reported in *Aviation Week and Space Technology* (Anonymous, 1988b). Differences in estimates reflect differences in opinion regarding the rate of technological breakthroughs, degrees of success in educating potential users about the value of remote sensing data, as well as the ability of providers to offer specific information that is directly responsive to the needs of the various market segments.

Information Providers

There are over 165 U.S. companies active in the production, processing, and interpretation of remotely-sensed data (Morain & Thome, 1990). Approximately half of these focus their activities on satellite data, the other half on aerial photography. For more than a decade, the United States held the lead in satellite remote sensing, as evidenced by the launch of five Earth resource satellites, beginning in 1972 with the launch of Landsat-1. However, the French launched SPOT-1 in 1986, and these two systems are now engaged in a battle for market share. Foreign competition is intensifying from both governments and companies in Europe, Japan, the U.S.S.R., Canada, India, and Brazil.

In general, companies engage in two types of activities: 1) activities related to the "space segment", (i.e., designing, launching, maintaining remote sensors and satellites); collecting data and transferring that data back to Earth; and 2) the "ground segment," (i.e., processing and integrating data with geographic, physical, demographic, and economic data) in order to provide the types of information required by users. According to *Aviation Week and Space Technology*, the latter set of activities, referred to as the value-added business, is ten times larger than that of the space segment, as defined by annual revenues (Anonymous, 1988a). Geographic Information Systems (GIS) technology which merges spectral (remotely-sensed) and spatial data has gained substantial recognition over the past decade because this combination of data provides the specific types of information required by end users who must address resource management issues. There are five products and service categories (Morain and Thome, 1990). Each of these five categories is described briefly below.

1) **Data Products** include processed satellite data in the forms of photographic images or digital computer tapes.

2) **Ground Data Acquisition and Processing Systems** refers to ground receiving stations, and hardware and software required to make necessary data corrections to account for sensor and space-craft induced errors and to prepare data for interpretation.

3) **Satellite Image Processing and Interpretation Services** are provided by consulting firms that provide customized processing and interpretation of remotely-sensed data for clients that do not have internal capabilities or who need assistance in carrying out these activities.

4) **Information Products and Services** go beyond data processing to deliver information based on remotely-sensed data that is tailored to the unique needs of each customer. Information can be provided in terms of reports, tables, and images.

5) **Research Services, Applications Development, and Market Research** are used to develop and test customized techniques for processing, analyzing, and interpreting remotely sensed data. This category also includes research activities concerning the remote sensing market.

The Global Marketplace

The U.S. government accounts for 56 percent of current purchases; this figure is expected to decrease to 40 percent by the year 2000 (Department of Commerce, 1988). U.S. commerical users comprise 22% of the worldwide market for remotely-sensed data products and services; non-U.S. users comprise the remaining 22%. Each of these latter two markets is expected to grow to 30 percent over this decade. However, these figures do not reflect the relative needs that these user groups have for the data, but instead reflect their relative purchasing power. The largest need, internationally, lies with non-U.S. governments, most especially those in the developing world (Morain & Thome, 1990).

APPLICATIONS OF REMOTE SENSING IN DEVELOPING COUNTRIES

Initial Successes

In one declaration of achievement regarding remote sensing technology transfer efforts, the Landsat program was called "one of the most successful technological programs in the history of the U.S...a major part of this success linked to the transfer of this technology to the Third World" (Thibault, 1985). Since the early 1970s, there has been as increasing interest in these applications, particularly ways in which the data can be used by developing countries in the process of natural resources monitoring and development.

The Agency for International Development (AID) has played a lead role in funding and transferring this technology to the Third World. AID funding of remote sensing technology transfer (RSTT) rose from approximately seven million dollars in 1978 to close to twelve million dollars in 1979. That year marked the peak in RSTT assistance. While expenditures have fallen since the late 70s, funding of RSTT projects averaged over six million dollars per year during the period 1981-1985 (AID, 1985). Table 1 indicates the categories of development projects that benefited from the application of remote sensing technology. Projects took place in over 50 developing countries during this period. Regional projects and regional remote sensing centers extended these benefits to an even broader group of developing countries. Examples of the types of activities are provided in Table 2. These are divided among applications grants and projects, the establishment and support of regional and national remote sensing centers, and education/training opportunities in the U.S. and abroad.

General Land Remote Sensing	$9,516,450*
Agriculture/Forestry	6,340,090
Hydrology	4,104,400
Geology/Geography	1,050,000
Regional Remote Sensing Centers	6,772,000
Atmospheric Remote Sensing	5,140,173
Onchocerciasis Control	400,000
Total Remote Sensing Activities	$33,323,113

Source: AID Bureau of Science and Technology. "Civil Land Processes Research from Space". Unpublished report to the Land Processes Subcommittee, Committee on Space-Based Earth Science Research, for the White House Office of Science and Technology Policy, 1985.

*Projects listed in this category deal with all three land remote sensing categories, i.e., agriculture/forestry, hydrology, and geology/geography.

Table 1: AID Foreign Assistance for Remote Sensing Technology Transfer 1981-1985

Grants
Bangladesh: map of haor areas for third rice crop
Bolivia: explore iron formations
Cameroon: develop resource management techniques
Chile: inventory resources
Haiti: measure sugar cane
Lesotho: investigate snowfall and drainage patterns
Pakistan: map river sediment loads for new port location
Peru: identify and map aguaje palm
Philippines: assist development of Mindoro Island
Sri Lanka: measure rice crop
Swaziland: locate ground water
Thailand: survey agriculture
Zaire: provide map base

Projects
Costa Rica: forest survey
Bolivia: population census
Senegal: resource inventory
Upper Volta, Togo, Benin: Onchocerciasis (river blindness)-free area survey
Morocco: geological mapping
Mali: range management
Kenya: population census
Bangladesh: weather satellite station
Dominican Republic, Jamaica, Costa Rica, Ecuador, Bolivia, Morocco, Thailand, Philippines, and Indonesia: agricultural crop estimates

Centers
Regional: Nairobi,Kenya; Ouagadougou, Upper Volta; Bangkok, Thailand; 2 planned for Latin America

National: Cairo, Egypt; Tunis, Tunisia; Kinshasa, Zaire; others planned for Younde, Cameroon; Damascus, Syria; and Katmandu, Nepal

Training
EROS Data Center
South Dakota State University
University of New Mexico
Overseas in Argentina, Peru, Botswana, Senegal, Sudan, and Nepal

Source: Technology Application Center. Remote Sensing: A Technology for Economic Development. New Mexico: University of New Mexico, n.d.

**Table 2: Examples of Remote Sensing Technology Activities
Funded by the U.S. Agency for International Development
1970s-1980s**

THE UNFULFILLED PROMISE

While it is true that many development projects have benefitted from the application of remote sensing technology, the brief review of the major market segments provided below indicates that the potential value of remote sensing information to the developing world has not been fulfilled. The three major segments are mapping and surveying (30% of the market), vegetation monitoring and management for agriculture and forestry (20%), and geological studies for energy and minerals exploration (18%) (Brachet, 1990). If one considers that agriculture, forestry, energy production, and mining generate at least half the gross national product of many developing countries and account for even larger portions of livelihoods and employment (World Commission on Environment and Development, 1987), and that mapping provides an underlying foundation upon which to build a natural resource information base, it would seem reasonable that a significant portion of the available data would be purchased by developing country governments. However, this is not the case as illustrated by the examples given below.

Mapping

The largest group of users of remote sensing data are involved in mapping activities. Outside the U.S., only 20% of the world has been adequately mapped (Metrics, Inc., 1981). This percentage is even lower among developing countries. Turning to Africa as an example, only seven countries on the continent have been mapped at a resolution in the range of 1-40,000. (Six of these countries are among Africa's smallest, the exception being South Africa (Laing, 1989).

Vegetation

Remote sensing information for agriculture can provide input for decisions related to planting, irrigation, crop health and yield, pest management, and pricing. Major companies within the forestry industry rely on remote sensing data for forestry inventory, soil moisture, burning plans, yield forecasts, and pest management. However, developing country governments have lagged behind other users in applying the technology in these critical areas (United Nations Committee on the Peaceful Uses of Outer Space, 1990). For example, the Tropical Forestry Action Plan (TFAP) with its secretariat at the Food and Agriculture Organization (FAO), endorsed by over 60 tropical countries, places an emphasis on policies and practices leading to sustainable use (FAO, 1988). However, there is growing concern among participants that there is no plan to monitor the impact of the TFAP, and therefore its level of success can not be evaluated.

Geology

Remote sensing technology can provide information for better decisions related to minerals and energy exploration, including the mapping of fault lines that suggest the existence of oil and gas reserves, and vegetation anomalies that suggest the presence of certain minerals. However, 90 percent of all data used by the geology community is purchased by the 50 largest companies in the world engaged in exploration (General Dynamics Space Systems Division, 1987). This inequality in the distribution of information suggests that developing countries' governments are not as well informed as exploration companies about the value or extent of the resources they hold. This can be a serious disadvantage at the time of negotiation of leases and/or sales of these resources to the exploration companies.

THE ROLE OF ENVIRONMENTAL MONITORING IN DEVELOPING COUNTRIES

Countries Face Environmental Bankruptcy

For most developing countries the process of economic development has involved massive losses of their major source of economic capital: natural resources (MacNeil, 1989). Nonrenewable resources (e.g., oil) are disappearing and renewable resources (e.g., tropical forests) are being depleted at rates that defy regeneration. Each year six million hectares of productive dryland turn into worthless desert and over eleven million hectares of tropical forest are destroyed.

During the 1980s the international development community has come to realize that sustainable economic development will not be possible unless current environmental degradation processes are reversed and effective environmental management will require the widespread adoption of environmental monitoring using satellites (WCED, 1987). Given the fact that there are approximately 10 billion hectares of critical environmental regimes, including portions of tropical and boreal forests undergoing change, polar and glacial ice margins, desert boundaries and coastal zones (most of these in developing countries), remote sensing technology must be employed as a means of collecting the enormous volume of data required to detect change in these crucial areas (Specter & Raney, 1990).

Issues of Global Concern

The environmental crisis is a global concern. Global warming and ozone depletion are tied to environmental degradation in both developed and developing countries. Widespread desertification and deforestation threaten global ecosystems fundamental to life as we know it.

The fact that the 1989 Summit of the Group of Seven (Canada, France, Germany, Italy, Japan, United Kingdom, and the United States) has been called the "Green Summit" suggests that international commitment to environmental action is growing. A proliferation of institutional responses has been observed at international, national and local levels. Some initiatives focus on the need for policy reform, giving consideration to economic, political, and institutional factors in decision making processes. A major example is the TFAP (Hazlewood, 1989).

Other initiatives focus on the need to provide environmental data through satellite monitoring. One of the leading programs is the Earth Observing System (EOS) of NASA (NASA, 1984), an estimated $30 billion undertaking (David, 1990) that will collect data through a variety of satellite remote sensors after a 1997 launch date. The purposes of EOS are to observe, catalogue, analyze, and understand the Earth's systems for "global change" research.

Space observations will be carried out through remote sensors carried on a series of polar-orbiting platforms launched over the next two decades. It is expected that this will be an international endeavor, with complements being furnished by other countries, (e.g., members of the European Space Agency, Japan, and Canada). This program is expected to generate a flood of data equal to the information content of the U.S. Library of Congress per week. Current plans are to make this data available to the global change research community. EOS is not geared to provide policy-related information that would be useful to national decision-makers who must respond to environmental degradation (Cremins & Katula, 1990).

EOS data will be distributed partially through commercial market mechanisms, and partially through government subsidies. Purchases by EOS investigators will be funded through NASA; other U.S. researchers and those affiliated with EOS participating countries will have access to EOS data at the incremental costs of reproduction and delivery. Other users (those from non-participating countries, including many developing countries) will have access to EOS data only on a commercial basis consistent with Landsat distribution processes. Specifics of these arrangements are yet to be determined (NASA, 1990).

In general, there have been few attempts to incorporate remotely sensed data into global natural resource inventory and monitoring activities, nor to tie remotely sensed data to environmental action plans in developing countries.[1] One might conclude that this failure is due to technical problems in applying the technology, but this is not the case. Interpretation techniques and those required to handle large volumes of data required for global monitoring have developed substantially during the past decade and do not present barriers to the technology's application (Specter & Raney, 1990).

Given increased recognition among members of the international community concerning natural resources depletion and environmental degradation, particularly in the developing world, why is it that the developing countries comprise such a small percentage of the users of remote sensing information? The current technology transfer process must be understood in order to answer this question. There are two significant components to this process which deserve attention: 1) the international technology transfer process; and 2) domestic technology transfer process within the context of developing countries.

A SYSTEMS PERSPECTIVE ON THE PROBLEM

Rationale

A systems approach provides a useful perspective on the technology transfer and utilization process. It provides a broader perspective which can lead to an understanding of current processes and necessary initiatives that must be undertaken if remote sensing is to be applied in support of environmental management.

Taking a systems approach to the technology transfer process, our attention is focused on the relevant institutions and the technology transfer network that connects them. The term "transfer network" refers to the lines of communication and diffusion corresponding to the paths that the technology (data, equipment, training etc.) takes as it is disseminated. The technology transfer process is comprised of system inputs, the transformation process, and outputs. These three items together represent the simplest systems model (Luthan, 1976). "Inputs" represent those elements that are fed into the technology transfer system, such as data, equipment, and human resources. The transformation process indicates the changes which the inputs undergo as they pass through the system. Transforming organizations are those responsible for turning the "raw material", technology, into information that can be applied to environmental monitoring and management. "Outputs" indicate the results of the process, i.e., environmental outcomes that would have not occurred without the application of the technology. The systems model would not be complete without including "Contextual Factors". Macroeconomic, political, and social factors in the developing country will have a significant impact on the ability of the transfer network to function. Managers of the technology transfer system may be able to influence these conditions, but they are beyond the manager's direct control.

Numerous authors have taken a systems perspective in analyzing technology transfer and diffusion processes (Frame, 1983; Rogers, 1983; Robinson, 1989; and Roman, 1980). Likewise, a number of professionals in the field of remote sensing have urged that knowledge gained from remote sensing technology transfer (RSTT) be used to build a conceptual model of the transfer system (Hankins, 1977; Levin, 1978; Pala, 1980; and Voute, 1982). In the field of information systems, McFarlan and McKenny (1982) have looked at technology diffusion at an organization level, dividing the process into stages of technology identification and investment, experimentation, learning and adaptation, rationalization and management control and widespread technology transfer. In light of these earlier studies, a study of RSTT to developing countries was undertaken recently, based on the systems perspective.

The study began with comparative case studies of the transfer and utilization processes in Thailand and Zaire. Thailand was chosen for three reasons: 1) it is recognized as one of the most successful developing countries in absorbing remote sensing technology; 2) the technology transfer system to and through Thailand is relatively well-developed; and 3) there is considerable information available about the system in Thailand. Zaire was chosen for the comparative case analysis because remote sensing technology transfer to Zaire has been recognized as unsuccessful. The opportunity to compare such differenct outcomes offered the potential of providing insights regarding critical factors in the technology transfer process.

As the available material was analyzed, it became apparent that the process could be described from a systems perspective. The transfer network in Thailand was effective. Inputs (e.g., funding, training and data products) flowed through the system, allowing the technology to bear fruit. Provider organizations in the United States were well connected to the National Research Council (NRC) in Thailand. This technology source point cooperated with those in-country organizations which transformed this information technology into outputs. Success could be measured in terms of the number of completed development projects that relied, at least in part, on the application of remote sensing technology to reach completion (Specter, 1989).

The process in Thailand could be compared with that in Zaire. As of 1980, few development projects had made use of remote sensing technology (Stancioff, 1981). The transfer network was not well developed. Government agencies that might have benefited from access to the technology were not connected to the country's recipient organization. It was apparent that obstacles existed which blocked the flow of technology through the transfer pipeline. From these case studies it is apparent that the RSTT process could be modeled as a system. The resulting model could provide valuable information to managers of the transfer process by identifying the system's critical elements and demonstrating the interrelations of its organizational actors.

OBSTACLES TO TECHNOLOGY TRANSFER AND UTILIZATION

A review of the literature on remote sensing technology transfer clearly indicates the existence of obstacles that impede the flow of the technology to developing countries. In keeping with the systems perspective, these are presented below as obstacles related to system inputs, the transformation process, system outputs, and contextual factors.

System Inputs

Data Costs and Accessibility . Numerous sources have identified the cost of data as a significant barrier in the transfer process (Elkington & Shopley, 1988; Morain & Thome, 1989; Specter & Raney, 1990). The costs of both hard copies of imagery and computer compatible tapes were mentioned (Odenyo, 1984; Araya, 1982). A number of experts believe that the lengthy procedures and lead times required to obtain necessary data created serious obstacles to utilization (Nanayakkara, 1978; Malingreau, 1984; Araya, 1982).

Equipment Costs and Procurement Procedures. While authors have identified the costs associated with the purchase of data processing equipment as a major barrier to the technology transfer process (Paul & Wigton, 1984; Abiodun, 1977; Staples, 1980), these costs are falling dramatically each year (Elkington & Shopley, 1988). Some sources mentioned difficulties associated with the process of importing necessary equipment (Perez, 1972; United Nations, 1982).

Lack of Human Resources. Lack of experienced personnel was mentioned by a number of sources (Honey et al., 1984; Bartolucci et al., 1980; Shelton & Estes, 1979; Hossain, 1978; Voute, 1982). One source went so far as to say that certain developing countries in Latin America could not use available computer compatible tapes due to the lack of trained personnel (Staples, 1980).

Transforming Processes

Organizational Variables/Parameters. The size, structural complexity, and traditions of organizations in developing countries were viewed as factors which could affect the outcome of RSTT projects significantly, both the rate of acceptance, and the rate of diffusion (DuBois & Bruce, 1978). The institutional environment must be examined closely. Roles and responsibilities of these institutions must be established and agreed upon. Sufficiently strong and frequent communication paths must be set up among cooperating institutions (Sharp, 1979).

System Outputs

Remote Sensing and Unacceptable Solutions. In certain situations the information made available through remote sensing could suggest solutions that could undermine the current power structure, or undermine individuals who are making decisions regarding natural resources for their own self gain. In these cases, it is the potential outputs of the technology transfer system that would halt the flow of technology. For example, in 1977 the U.S. Agency for International Development helped the Costa Rican government devised a national forest survey using Landsat data. The survey showed that the existing levels of deforestation were unsustainable. The Costa Rican government responded by moving its remote sensing specialists to other positions (Elkington & Shopley, 1988).

Contextual Factors

Economic Constraints. Macroeconomic factors were perceived as representing a major obstacle to the technology transfer process (Paul & Wigton, 1984; Levin, 1978; Abiodun, 1977; Greenblat et al., 1974). Many developing nations lack sufficient foreign exchange to pay for the importation of necessary data, equipment, and technical assistance (Odenyo, 1984; Schweitzer, 1971).

Political Constraints. "Frequently the most important influences upon regional development are social and political in origin, since they may determine whether innovation and change are to be sought or powerfully resisted" (Youssef et al., 1980, p. 97). Government officials in developing countries must be involved in all stages of the RSTT process (Shaffer, 1980; Levin, 1978).

Social Constraints. Numerous authors believe that the social environment of the country represents a critical RSTT factor (Levin, 1978; Hossain, 1978; Greenblat et al., 1974). Some of the necessary characteristics for a successful RSTT program include social stability, an orientation toward the future, a professional labor force, and intellectual adaptability (Youssef et al., 1980). The issue of labor displacement must be considered. Many sources indicate that the "high-tech" nature of RSTT exacerbates problems in the transfer process (Sovain et al., 1980; Dubois & Bruce, 1978; Hossain, 1978). The historical setting may be extremely important to the transfer process. It requires "wide experience with conventional remote sensors" (Araya, 1982, p. 26).

Based on this literature review, factors that hinder or halt the flow of technology from providers to end users have been identified. There is substantial overlap among the critical elements identified by various authors. The systems perspective provides a useful framework for examining these factors.

Further research, based on the comparative case analyses and the literature review, led to a global survey of over 650 experts from 66 countries (Specter, 1988). Results of the survey revealed factors crucial to technology transfer success. These were related to system inputs (appropriate computer equipment, adequate data distribution patterns and reasonable costs, and the experienced personnel); the transformation process (cooperation and coordination among relevant organizations in developing countries); and contextual considerations (economic and political factors, and confidence in the future of Earth observing satellite systems). Later studies have supported the systems perspective as a tool for better understanding of the technology transfer process (Gayle and Specter, 1990; Specter, 1990).

THE INFORMATION SYSTEMS MODEL FOR REMOTE SENSING

The proposed information systems model for remote sensing describes the various factors involved in the application of remote sensing to resource inventory and monitoring in developing countries. The proposed model is a first step towards formulating a stage model for remote sensing technology transfer in response to resource inventory and monitoring demands. Both the international transfer of technology and the domestic transfer of technology within the recipient country are included in the model and the various policies which affect the process are identified.

The organizations included in the model are the international organizations, the public and private sectors in the provider nations, and the governments and transforming organizations in developing countries who utilize remote sensing technology for resource inventory and monitoring applications. Most of these organizations are government agencies; the number of remote sensing businesses in the private sector in developing countries is minimal.

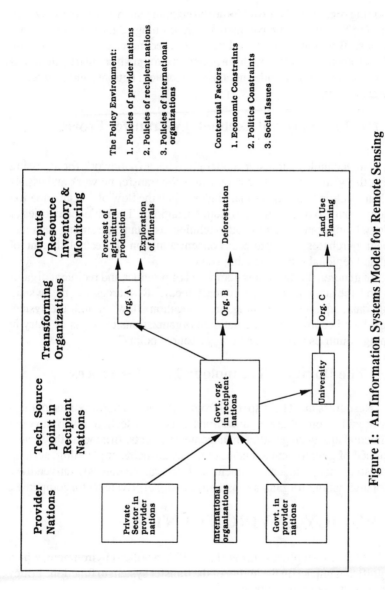

Figure 1: An Information Systems Model for Remote Sensing

Transforming organizations provide the throughput which converts the system elements (equipment, technical manpower, training, data and funds) into applications. Both the international transfer of technology and the domestic technology transfer take place within a policy environment created by three sets of policies, those of: 1) provider nations; 2) recipient nations; and 3) international organizations.

The International Technology Transfer Process

The technology transfer model provides a framework for assessing the interactivity and interrelationships within the transfer network and assists in the identification of obstacles that hinder or halt the flow of this information technology from provider nations to recipient nations. The major categories of technology being transferred include technical assistance, training, data and equipment purchases, and projects concentrating on the establishment of national and regional remote sensing centers.

In general, the system is composed of provider and recipient organizations and the networks which connect them. Resources for the system (funding, data, equipment, training, and education) flow through the system from developed country and international organizations to points of entry in developing countries termed "technology source points".

The Domestic Technology Transfer Process

Resources must be dispersed from technology source points to transforming organizations, those organizations that use the technology to carry out environmental monitoring and/or management projects. In general, the system is comprised of government agencies (e.g., departments of planning, agriculture, forestry, mapping, environment and natural resources), universities, offices of international organizations, and occasional private sector companies.

THE POLICY ENVIRONMENT

The transfer process takes place within a policy environment, which has a significant impact on the ability of the transfer system to function. Policy concerns result from three sources:

1. Policies of technology providing nations
2. Policies of technology receiving nations
3. Policies of international organizations

Examples of some of the policies that have major impacts on the transfer and utilization of remote sensing technology for natural resource monitoring and management are discussed below.

Policies of Provider Nations

There is growing concern in Congress that commercial pricing of remotely-sensed data from Landsat has a negative impact on our efforts to monitor and manage environmental change (Lawler, 1990). The current U.S. pricing policy which is based on the Remote Sensing Act of Congress of 1984, has a marketplace philosophy. Other countries have followed suit, including France and Canada. The appropriateness of this philosophy has to be examined against the fact that developing countries would find the data too expensive at even one tenth of the cost (Morain & Thome, 1990).

The contradiction regarding the pricing of remotely-sensed data products arises from its treatment as a product being sold through the market mechanism rather than as a public good. One of man's loftiest goals, preservation of the environment, will likely require a new perspective on the pricing of environmental data, not just in the United States, but also among other satellite-launching nations. The October 1990 Earth Observations and Global Change Decision Making Conference marked the first time that leading spokesmen for the national space agencies of Europe and Japan went on record stating that the urgency of global environmental change research has begun to soften their countries' plans to sell satellite data at expensive commerical rates (Isbell, 1990). Canada's top space executive, Larkin Kerwin, said that while data from their upcoming Radarsat will be sold at commercial rates, low-cost arrangements with Third World countries that cannot afford the data might be possible.

Another policy being hotly debated within the U.S. government deals with the decision to invest $30 billion in EOS. Fred Wood, project director of the Office of Technology Assessment study, "Helping America Compete- The Role of Federal Scientific and Technical Information," comments that "the longer-term programs [EOS] are fine, but they won't help the policy makers as soon as we need...For a few tens of millions of dollars you can get a better understanding of global change within a year or two [using remotely-sensed data currently available]" (David, 1990, p. 9).

In addition to the policy concerning the level of investment in EOS, there is a policy question regarding current distribution plans for EOS data. Current data distribution mechanisms will allow scientists to access the data, but they are not geared to providing policy-related information to decision-makers. If EOS data is to reach these users, the EOS data policy must be reviewed and expanded. Data management and distribution in the service of sustainable development in the Third World would require a substantial further investment in resources to analyze and interpret EOS data for the benefit of non-scientific communities (Wagner & Duchin, 1990).

Policies of Recipient Nations

At a national level, it is often found that available remotely sensed data is not utilized for sustainable use of natural resources. This is understandable if we recognize the perspective of "users", those individuals who are in the position of deciding if, and how, remote sensing will be used within the developing country context. The term "user" in the remote sensing literature relates to individuals and organizations with diverse needs for remote sensing information. The primary assumption made is that the users are apolitical and their primary interest is the efficient allocation of natural resources (Aronoff, 1986). This does not hold true in most developing countries where decisions regarding use of remotely sensed data is taken by politicians.

National policies of sustainable development are extremely difficult to realize given the severe economic problems faced by many developing countries. Efforts to reduce high levels of international debt may encourage national decision-makers to export unsustainable levels of natural resource exports. In the interest of maintaining the existing power structure, politicians may make decisions that reflect short-term goals rather the long-term good of the society. In the face of these constraints, it is encouraging to see newly industrializing and developing countries that are moving toward the use of remote sensing in sustainable development policies. Brazil is a case in point. Through the early 1980s deforestation was a planned policy in Brazil. Landsat data was used for more efficient stripping of the Amazon forest (Elkington & Shopley, 1988). However, in recent years Brazil has taken a leadership role in activities aimed at a better understanding of deforestation processes through improved satellite monitoring. In 1988 the Brazilian government initiated a program called "Our Nature" to establish conservation policies for the country's natural resources (INPE, 1990). As part of this program the Instituto de Pesquisas Espaciais (INPE) conducted a survey of the extent of deforestation in the Brazilian Legal Amazon in 1989.

Another example of a developing country that is moving toward the use of remote sensing for sustainable development is Costa Rica. The Institute of Agrarian Development (IDA), which controls a substantial portion of all land in that country, has established a Scientific Advisory Commission. One of the members of the Commission was brought in expressly to advise IDA regarding sustainable development projects in rural areas, particularly those using remote sensing technology for monitoring and management.[2]

Educational policies in developing countries have a significant impact on their ability to absorb remote sensing technology from the space-launching nations. Studies have shown that one of the major obstacles to the transfer process is the lack of educated and trained human resources (Specter 1988; Gayle & Specter 1990). Systematic education in the newer and important areas frequently is not provided in developing countries, particularly in space science. Therefore, national government support, both short-term training and longer-term, four-year degree programs in relevant fields is crucial. A lack of appropriate policies is sometimes attributed to overlapping responsibilities for space programs among various departments and agencies (Singh, 1990). Given the economic constraints facing developing countries, certain analysts are suggesting a broad-based space education initiative with support provided through developed countries or international organizations (United Nations Committee on the Peaceful Uses of Outer Space, 1989; Singh, 1990).

Policies of International Organizations

A major problem of utilization arises from inconsistencies in international policies regarding data availability to developing countries. After many years of discussion and debate, the 1986 Principles Relating to Remote Sensing were adopted by the United Nations General Assembly. The Principles enabled and authorized states, nongovernmental entities, and international intergovernmental organizations whose membership is composed of states that are parties to the 1967 Treaty on Principles Governing the Activities of States in the Exploration and Use of Outer Space, including the Moon and Other Celestial Bodies to engage in remote sensing activites. The Principles documented the acceptance of the "Open Skies" policy, meaning that there are no limitations on the fundamental right of sovereign nations to acquire data from space. The policy of "Open Access" to remotely-sensed data is seen as providing a balance to this lack of national privacy (Christol, 1990). The special needs of developing countries were formally recognized, particularly their rights of access to data and information about their territories (Christol, 1988). Principle XII declared that sensed states should have access to data on a nondiscriminatory basis and at reasonable costs. Access through the marketplace philosophy, however, does not imply compatibility with this principle, due to the wide differences in purchasing power of nations. Using gross national product per capita as a measure of the economic wealth, there is a least a one hundredfold difference between the purchasing power of the poorest developing countries and that of the wealthiest countries.

Utilization is also affected by the absence of effective mechanisms to subsidize the cost of remotely sensed data required for environmental action programs. Recent policy statements of international organizations reflect a growing interest in the environmental aspects of development; however, these policies are yet to be realized. Since the vast majority of funds to support remote sensing activities in developing countries come from international organizations (Morain & Thome, 1990), it is important that these organizations give consideration to backing their policies with increased funding for remote sensing activities aimed at improved environmental monitoring.

CONCLUSION

Remote sensing technology transfer to developing countries has been analyzed, using an information systems framework. A common goal, environmental preservation, underlies the need for integrating data collection on environmental parameters with utilization by decision makers responsible for environmental monitoring and management. The systems perspective suggests the need to focus on more application-oriented research leading to closer and more effective linkages between remote sensing technology providers and institutions interested in applying the technology to environmental conservation and development. Also, further research is needed to study the impacts of the policies of developed countries, developing countries, and international organizations on the technology transfer process. The authors hope that the proposed information systems model sheds light on these critical areas and provides directions for future initiatives.

References

Abiodun, A. The transfer of remote sensing technology in the developing Nations: An Observation. *Proceedings of the Eleventh International Symposium on Remote Sensing of Environment*, Environmental Research Institute of Michigan, 1977, pp. 339-351.

Agency for International Development, Bureau of Science and Technology. Civil land processes research from space. Unpublished report to the Land Processes Subcommittee, Committee on Space-Based Earth Science Research, for the White House Office of Science and Technology Policy, 1985.

Anonymous a. Growth, stability predicted for commercial space ventures. *Aviation Week and Space Technology*, March 14, 1988, pp. 108-110.

Anonymous b. Remote sensing: New applications gain acceptance. *Aviation Week and Space Technology*, February 15, 1988, pp. 63-64.

Araya, M. Main advances and needs in Chilean remote sensing programs. *Proceedings of the Sixteenth International Symposium on Remote Sensing of Environment*, Environmental Research Institute of Michigan, 1982, pp. 25-42.

Aronoff, S. Political implications of full cost recovery for land remote sensing systems. *Photogrammetric Engineering and Remote Sensing*, 1986, *51* (1), 41-45.

Bartolucci, L. Phillips, T. & Davis, S. Building locally adapted remote sensing programs in developing nations. *Proceedings of the Fourteenth International Symposium on Remote Sensing of Environment*, Environmental Research Institute of Michigan, 1980, pp. 179-186.

Brachet, G. The market for SPOT data after four years of operation. *Proceedings of the Twenty Third International Symposium on Remote Sensing of Environment*, Environmental Research Institute of Michigan, 1990.

Christol, C.Q. International law and remote sensing. *Space commercialization: Launch vehicles and programs*, 1990, (126), pp. 140-158.

Christol, C.Q. Remote sensing and international space law. *Journal of Space Law*, 1988, *16*, (1), 25, 37-38.

Cremins, T. and Katula, B. Making sense of remote sensing. *Space News*, June 18-24, 1990, pp. 15-16.

David, L. Report: Exploit existing data before taking EOS plunge. *Space News*, August 13-19, 1990, p. 9.

Department of Commerce. *Space commerce: An industry assessment*, Washington, D.C., 1988.

DuBois, F. & Bruce, B. Remote sensing technology transfer: The Canadian-Peruvian approach. *Proceedings of the Twelfth International Symposium on Remote Sensing of Environment*, Environmental Research Institute of Michigan, 1977, pp. 203-211.

Elkington, J. and Shopley, J. *The shrinking planet: U.S. information technology and sustainable development*, Washington, D.C.: World Resources Institute, 1988.

Frame, J. *International business and global technology*. Lexington Mass.: Lexington Books, 1983.

Food and Agriculture Organization, in cooperation with the World Resources Institute, The World Bank, & the United Nations Programme. *The tropical forestry action plan*. Rome: FAO, 1988.

Gayle, D. and Specter, C. Managing the transfer of technology for development: Remote sensing applications for the Caribbean Basin. *International Journal of High Technology Management Research*, 1990 (forthcoming).

General Dynamics Space Systems Division, *Atlas G/Centaur mission planner's guide*. April 1983, complete revision April 1987.

Greenblat, E., Lowe, D. & Summers, R. Evaluation of ERTS data utilization in developing countries. *Proceedings of the Ninth International Symposium on Remote Sensing of Environment*, Environmental Research Institute of Michigan, 1974, pp. 1509-1515.

Hankins, D.B. *Building a model for a remote sensing technology transfer program in northern California*, NASA-sponsored final report, Arcate, California, 1977.

Hazlewood, P. Interview in Washington, D.C., August 8, 1989.

Honey, F., Lyons, K. & Wright, G. Development of digital image processing in a developing country: A case study from Papua New Guinea. *Proceedings of the Eighteenth International Symposium on Remote Sensing of Environment*, Environmental Research Institute of Michigan, 1984, pp. 511-520.

Hossain, A. Transfer of remote sensing technology to benefit of developing countries. *Proceedings of the Twelfth International Symposium on Remote Sensing of Environment,* Environmental Research Institute of Michigan, 1978, pp. 213-216.

Isbel, D. European, Japanese officials endorse low-cost scientific use of EOS data. *Space News,* October 29-November 4, 1990, pp. 3, 20.

INPE. *INPE Space News,* 1990, *1,* (1), 3-5.

Jequier, N. ed. *Appropriate technology: Problems and promises.* Paris: Organization for Economic Co-operation and Development, 1976.

Laing, W. Recent experience in defining remote sensing needs and effective implementation plans for Africa. Presentation to the United Nations international meeting of experts on the development of remote sensing skills and knowledge, University of Dundee, Dundee, United Kingdom, June 28, 1989.

Lawler, A. Landsat policy disavowed. *Space News,* June 18-24, 1990, pp. 1, 20.

Levin, S. The role of science and technology in development. *Proceedings of the Twelfth International Symposium on Remote Sensing of Environment,* Environmental Research Institute of Michigan, 1978, pp. 11-15.

Luthan, F. *Introduction to management: A contingency approach.* New York: MacGraw-Hill Book Co., 1976.

MacNeill, J. Strategies for sustainable development. *Scientific American,* 1989, *261* (3), 155-165.

Malingreau, J.P. Remote sensing and disaster monitoring: A review of applications in Indonesia. *Proceedings of the International Symposium on Remote Sensing of Environment,* Environmental Research Institute of Michigan, 1984, pp. 283-293.

McFarlan, F.W. & McKenney, J.L. "The Information Archipelago - Gaps and Bridges, *Harvard Business Review,* 1982, *60* (5), 109-119.

METRICS, Inc. *Satellite remote sensing market forecast: 1980-1990.* 1981.

Morain, S.A. and Thome, P.G. *America's earth observing industry: Perspectives on commerical remote sensing.* Hong Kong: Geocarto International Centre, 1990.

Nanayakkara, C. Problems associated with organizing remote sensing applications in a developing country. *Proceedings of the Twelfth International Symposium on Remote Sensing of Environment,* Environmental Research Institute of Michigan, 1978, pp. 1665-1670.

NASA. Earth observing system, working group report, 1, NASA/Goddard Space Flight Center, Report No. NASA TM-86129, August 1984.

Odenyo, V. The regional sensing facility for eastern and southern Africa. *Proceedings of the Eighteenth International Symposium on Remote Sensing of Environment,* Environmental Research Institute of Michigan, 1984, pp. 207-213.

Pala, S. A working concept of remote sensing technology transfer: *Proceedings of the Fourteenth International Symposium on Remote Sensing of Environment,* Environmental Research Institute of Michigan, 1980, pp. 1653-1660.

Paul, C. & Wigton, W. Remote sensing and the development process. *Proceedings of the Eighteenth International Symposium on Remote Sensing of Environment*, Environmental Research Institute of Michigan, 1984, pp. 201-205.

Perez, J. Remote sensing in Mexico. *Proceedings of the Sixteenth International Symposium on Remote Sensing of Environment*, Environmental Research Institute of Michigan, 1972, pp. 1-13.

Robinson, R. Toward creating an international technology transfer paradigm. *The International Trade Journal*, 1989, *4* (1), 1-19.

Rogers, E. *Diffusions of innovations* (3rd ed.). New York: Free Press, 1983.

Roman, D. *Science, technology, and innovation: A systems approach.* Columbus: Grid Publishing, Inc., 1980.

Schweitzer, G. Remote sensing and international development. *Proceedings of the Seventh International Symposium on Remote Sensing of Environment*, Environmental Research Institute of Michigan, 1971, pp. 161-164.

Shaffer, L. Remote sensing technology transfer: The politics of international cooperation. *Proceedings of the Fourteenth International Symposium on Remote Sensing of Environment*, Environmental Research Institute of Michigan, 1980, pp. 199-205.

Sharp, J. Guidelines for evaluating remote sensing demonstration projects. *Proceedings of the Thirteenth International Symposium on Remote Sensing of Environment*, Environmental Research Institute of Michigan, 1979, pp. 1167-1176.

Shelton, R. & Estes, J. Integration of remote sensing and geographic information systems. *Proceedings of the Thirteenth International Symposium of Environment*, Environmental Research Institute of Michigan, 1979, pp. 463-483.

Singh, R.N. Broad-based space education: Prerequisites for space commercialization. *Space Commercialization: Launch vehicles and programs*, 1990, *126*, pp. 217-225.

Sovain, P., Davis, S. & Adrien, P. Remote sensing decoded: Meeting the challenges of multidisciplinary and international technology transfer. *Proceedings of the Fourteenth International Symposium on Remote Sensing of Environment*, Environmental Research Institute of Michigan, 1980, pp. 205-218.

Specter, C. An International Space Year Policy for developing and newly industrialized countries. *Space Policy*, 1990, *6*, (2), 117-130.

Specter, C. Obstacles to remote sensing commercialization in the developing world. *International Journal of Remote Sensing*, 1989, *10* (2), 359-372.

Specter, C. & Raney, R. Observation of Tropical Forests by C band radars: Proposed ten year project. *Proceedings of the 1989 ASPRS/ACSM Fall Convention*, Cleveland, Ohio, September 17-20, 1989, pp. 133-143.

Specter, C. Managing remote sensing technology transfer to developing countries: A survey of experts in the field. *Photogrammetria,* 1988, *43* (1), 25-36.

Specter, C., & Raney, R. Constructive trends in data policy in support of global and environmental monitoring. *Global and Environmental Monitoring Techniques and Impacts,* Victoria, Canada, September 17-21, 1990 (forthcoming).

Stancioff, A. Annual report for the year 1980, ERTS-Zaire, final report. Contract No. AID/afr-c-1483. Spectral Data Corporation, New York, 1981.

Staples, J., "The remote sensing barrier: How to penetrate it. *Proceedings of the Fourteenth International Symposium on Remote Sensing of Environment,* Environmental Research Institute of Michigan, 1980, pp. 613-621.

Thibault, D. Vice President of International Marketing, EOSAT. Speech at the joint government affairs program of the American Congress on Surveying and Mapping and the American Society for Photogrammetry and Remote Sensing, Rosslyn, Virginia, October 17, 1985.

United Nations. *Report of the United Nations Conference on the Exploration and Peaceful Uses of Outer Space.* Vienna, Austria, 9-12 August 1982.

United Nations Committee on the Peaceful Uses of Outer Space. Report on the United Nations international meeting of experts on the development of remote sensing skills and knowledge, organized in cooperation with the government of the United Kingdom of Great Britain and Northern Ireland and hosted by the University of Dundee, Dundee, United Kingdom, June 26-30, 1989. UN doc. no. A/AC.105/438, January 3, 1990.

United Nations, United Nations general assembly resolution # 41/65 December 1984.

Voute, C., "Satellite remote sensing for developing countries: Prospects and constraints. *Proceedings of an EARSel-ESA Symposium,* ESAP - 175, 1982, pp. 196-197.

Wagner, T.W. and Duchin, F. CIESIN Interdisciplinary Task Force on Land Surface Changes, Environmental Research Institute of Michigan draft report, October 1990.

World Commission on Environment and Development. *Our common future.* Oxford: Oxford University Press, 1987.

Youssef, A., Kabakibo, A. & Shahrokhi, F. The Syrian Arab Republic remote sensing center to meet national and regional needs. *Proceedings of the Fourteenth International Symposium on Remote Sensing of Environment,* Environmental Research Institute of Michigan, 1980, pp. 97-101.

Zamora, J., Obstacles to the Transfer of Telecommunications Technology, an unpublished report, 1989.

End Notes

1. This was the conclusion of many participants at the international conference, Global Natural Resource Monitoring and Assessments: Preparing for the 21st Century, Venice, Italy, 24-30 September 1989.

2. In July 1990 Dr. Christine Specter was appointed to serve a four-year term on the Scientific Advisory Commission of the Costa Rican Institute of Agrarian Development (IDA).

3. For a more complete discussion of remote sensing technology, refer to Szekielda, K.H.,ed. *Satellite Remote Sensing for Resources Development.* United Kingdom: Graham and Trotman, Ltd., 1986.

APPENDIX
Remote Sensing Defined[3]

Remote sensing is the detection, recording, and analysis of electromagnetic radiation. Various types of sensors are used to measure this radiation along the spectrum from extremely short, high frequency wavelengths; through the range of frequencies associated with visible light; to long, low frequency wavelengths. Since all elements of the Earth's surface have distinctive electromagnetic signatures, the detection of these radiation values allows us to analyze the global environment. The most commonly used remote sensing system is that of aerial photography. Special films and cameras allow one to extend information obtained through the visible range of the electromagnetic spectrum into the range of ultraviolet and infrared radiation. The Multi-Spectral Scanner (MSS), the major data source on Landsat 1-3, provided electromagnetic radiation information in four bands in the visible light to near-infrared range.

Landsat 4 and 5 each carry a Thematic Mapper (TM) which differs from the MSS in that it has seven bands instead of four at higher levels of resolution. Information collected through the MSS and TM is transmitted in digital format directly to ground receiving stations, or indirectly through the Tracking and Data Relay Satellite System (TDRSS). This digital information is stored on computer compatible tapes. Data received in the U.S. is archived at the U.S EROS Data Center in South Dakota. This data can be purchased by both U.S. and foreign nationals.

The data may be analyzed in two forms. First, images can be interpreted visually. Black/white/gray images of one of the electromagnetic bands allows the expert to focus on particular environmental features. For example, bands 4 and 5 are best for detecting cultural features such as urban areas and roads; band 6 and 7 are best for detecting bodies of water. False color or color-infrared composite images can be constructed by combining band information. This process generates images similar to color photography. However, the colors do not have the same meaning as those viewed with the naked eye. For example, vegetation ranges from pink to dark red; bodies of water appear blue (shallow or with sedimentation) to black (clear and deep). Second, the data may be digitally analyzed through a computer-assisted spectral pattern recognition system. This sophisticated method is particularly useful to large areas analysis.

All the products of remote sensing mentioned above share a number of characteristics that make them invaluable in the exploration and analysis of the Earth's surface. These characteristics include:

1. Improved spatial context- The ability to analyze a large area of land in a single image. Each image data set covers an area of 185x185 km.

2. Improved temporal context- Since each Landsat satellite circles the same portion of the Earth every 18 days, changes in the Earth's surface can alert researchers to oncoming problems.

3. Degree of resolution; Each unit of observation (pixel) covers an area 79x79 meters. Each MSS image data set contains over 30 million observations.

It is important to note that the best use of remote sensing from space incorporates aerial photography and field site analysis in order to clarify and check ground classification determined through space technology.

8 Information Technology Issues on Guam

Thomas Iverson
University of Guam Station

Managers must continuously assess the current state of technology to adequately plan improvements to their information systems. Part of this assessment is to weigh the advantages of new technology relative to the costs. In this chapter, two unrelated projects are used as case studies to illustrate the difficulties of determining the appropriate technological mix in an insular and developing economy. The projects demonstrate the need to adjust decision criteria to reflect the typical shortage of skilled labor and the high transportation costs which are common in insular economies. An emphasis on reliability and standards contributes to improved choices in systems design.

Four trends in information technology are chosen as likely candidates for adoption in new designs in insular areas. These are: graphical user interfaces, fourth generation languages, local area networks, and presentation graphics.

INTRODUCTION

Living on Guam provides experiences that enhance one's sensitivity to the problems of developing countries. An island economy, moreover, exhibits an economic isolation which creates additional problems. Stable power supplies, real-time communications, and skilled human resources are luxuries that most researchers in the U.S. take for granted. Two years of teaching and consulting in Micronesia have provided an interesting series of anecdotes regarding the implementation of information systems.

Story telling, however, may not be the best way to add to our stock of knowledge. A general theory of insular economies could be very useful to practitioners in such locations. One step in that direction is to discuss the characteristics that most markedly alter the design and implementation of insular information systems and the choice of technological mix. While this chapter only deals with the setting on Guam, projects are underway which may lead to a more general theory by providing evidence from surrounding islands.

The traditional economic development framework (Nafziger, 1990; Hagen, 1980) emphasizes the relationship between choice of technological mix and input costs. Consideration of input costs leads one to the "appropriate technology." The choice of appropriate information technology depends on an accurate assessment of input costs. Two projects on Guam, supervised by the author, are used to illustrate the peculiarities of information technology (IT) choice and management in a developing, insular economy.

The two projects are discussed in a somewhat disjointed manner, perhaps testing the patience of the reader. The intent is to illustrate both macroeconomic and microeconomic applications of the main arguments. The first section of this chapter provides background information regarding Guam and the two projects. The second section describes methodologies of the projects. The third section provides general observations regarding insular economies and information systems costs. The fourth section discusses specific relevant trends in modern technology. In the fifth section, the projects are used as case studies to illustrate the general principles. A final section provides a summary and caveats.

BACKGROUND

A Developing, Insular Economy

Guam is a territory of the United States, with a political status similar to the Virgin Islands and Puerto Rico. It is surrounded by the archipelagos of the new Micronesian nation- states. With a sea area greater than the land area of the United States, Micronesia consists of: the Commonwealth of the Northern Marianas Islands, the Federated States of Micronesia, the Republic of Palau, and the Republic of the Marshall Islands. Each of these new nations consists of many small islands, often separated by hundreds of miles of ocean.

Touted as the "Hub of the Pacific Rim," Guam's location and climate have dictated its economic role. A significant American military force has been present since the end of World War II. Strategically, Guam and neighboring islands play an important role in American military foreign policy. Guam's near proximity to Japan (less than four hours by commercial aircraft) has fostered its new role as a major vacation destination for Japanese tourists.

Guam has many of the characteristics of newly independent former colonies. After World War II a dependency relationship weakened the local entrepreneurial base and resulted in drastic declines in locally managed businesses. Expatriates, or what Nafziger (1990, p. 292) terms "marginal individuals" are prevalent in all levels of business management.

Guam's civilian population is about one hundred and thirty thousand. While an accredited, land grant university of more than two thousand students exists, programs of study are limited in technological and information areas. No degree programs are offered in Computer Science, Engineering, or Management/Computer Information Systems.

Information systems are unsophisticated as a rule, but there is a large enough installed base for a small IBM service outlet, one major chain (ComputerLand), and several full service computer stores. RCA, an MCI company, provides telecommunication services through TYMNET, including MCI Mail, CompuServe, Dow Jones, Westlaw, and others.

Viewed under the framework of development economics, Guam is a moderately well-off developing country. Long life expectancy, low infant mortality rates, and moderately high incomes provide the picture of an economy well beyond the provision of basic needs. Recent statistics would reveal a current state of dramatic economic growth and prosperity with coincidental measures of crime and environmental degradation.

The economic growth is almost entirely due to the rapidly expanding tourism sector. The mixed blessing of rapid growth due to tourism investment has caused new concerns about the ability of the island to absorb the consequent physical and social changes.

In 1984 the public and private sectors were about equal, an indication of the heavy dependency on the U.S. that has existed since the end of World War II. By 1990, the private sector was twice as large as the public sector (the latter remaining constant through the period). This explosive growth in the private economy has outpaced the ability of the local government to monitor and control.

This environment, then, is somewhat unique. A politically stable, full employment economy with moderate inflation seems like a politician's dream. However, concerns have surfaced about the involvement of local people in the development prosperity. One government agency in particular had the foresight to see the need for a study to determine the effects of rapid growth on the economy of Guam.

The GEDA Project

Guam is governed by an executive branch (Governor, Lieutenant Governor) and a unicameral legislature. Major players in the executive branch include: the Bureau of Planning, the Department of Land Management (and the associated Territorial Land Use Commission), the Departments of Commerce and Labor, the Guam Environmental Protection Agency, and the Guam Economic Development Authority (GEDA).

GEDA is charged with the responsibility of providing incentives to foster and direct economic development. GEDA's statutory authority enables a wide variety of tools to accomplish this task. The GEDA board of directors sought a re-examination of their policy focus. A small group of researchers from the University of Guam, led by the author, designed a two-phase study to 1) determine the aggregated impact of proposed new development projects, and 2) design strategies for the agency to direct and channel economic growth in a positive manner.

The LAN Project

In 1989, the College of Business and Public Administration of the University of Guam received a special legislative appropriation to design and install an instructional Local Area Network (LAN). The author chaired a faculty procurement committee and also served as the College's Academic Computer Coordinator throughout the design stage.

The existing lab was typical of a "first generation" computer lab. Built with donated hardware and software, and augmented through small grants, the lab was an administrative nightmare. A collection of Apple IIs with a variety of disk drives and monitors were in place. A MacIntosh network represented the most sophisticated hardware platform. A mixed collection of IBM PCs, some with monochrome, some with CGA color monitors, and all with worn disk drives completed the picture.

Six different dot matrix printers were in use, three different models just to support the IBMs. Five different word processors were made available. Software was "checked out" on an honor basis. Lab assistants (part-time student workers) were hard pressed to provide support. Most of the microcomputers were in use without surge protection and a large portion of the College's support budget was allocated to maintenance contracts.

The activities that provided the experience for this chapter were carried out through the period roughly corresponding to the '89-'90 school year (for Northern Hemisphere institutions).

METHODOLOGY

Research in emerging technologies or in unique settings often precludes the use of sophisticated methodologies. Frequently there is no track record of empirical work to use as a guide. The lack of good data is a nagging problem. Theories may be difficult to model, or may not be well formed. Opinions do form, however, as seemingly independent observations begin to cluster into cause and effect relationships.

As Weill and Olson (1989) note, in an article of considerable comfort to those who find themselves caught in this stage: ". ..the field is still emerging from the contingency theory stage and many researchers are uncomfortable with the lack of a central MIS paradigm" (p. 77). We are in the throes of change due to the Information Revolution, entering a period of interdisciplinary research and the re-examination of central paradigms in the social science disciplines. In their study of (mainstream) published material, Weill and Olson (1989) lament the lack of variety in MIS research and argue that "A generally more subjectivist, less functional, and less deterministic approach is needed" (p. 79).

The examples cited in this chapter are not presented as evidence of empirical research. Instead, they are anecdotes which serve to buttress observations regarding IS implementations in insular and developing nations. Still, the methodologies, albeit somewhat eclectic, are worth discussing. Two very different approaches were taken to the two projects.

The GEDA Project Methodology

The approach to the planning problem posed by GEDA was twofold. We wanted to avoid becoming "island-bound" in our perspective and we needed to collect base data from the relevant government agencies.

Researchers conducted a series of site visits in relevant areas. These included: the Virgin Islands, Hawaii, Georgetown (KY), Great Britain, and Portland (OR). Selection criteria for these sites included: 1) insular nature of the economy, 2) massive Japanese investment, and 3) well-articulated government policies.

Concurrently, a mailout of requests for master planning documents achieved an approximate 50% response rate (about thirty planning documents). These plans were content-analyzed for the presence of 1) accountability (assignment of responsibility and quantifiable objectives) and 2) readability (formatting, use of graphics, length).

A simple data base was built to track the development projects. This facilitated analyses based on size, location, rooms, workers, etc. Considerable "legwork" was necessary to collect information from the relevant government agencies. Observations from this inductive stage of the project contributed to a broader understanding of IT management issues on the island.

The work was reviewed periodically by a task force, representing the agencies that would be involved in implementing new strategies. Mindful of Churchman's dictum (1968, p. 75) "the system is always embedded in a larger system," the objective was to ameliorate concerns that one agency was studying (and therefore, "criticizing") the planning efforts of other agencies.

The preliminary findings of the study project were presented in a public forum (Iverson & Blanchard, 1989). Subsequent feedback and follow up work developed a greater understanding of the public sector information systems on Guam.

The LAN Project

A small steering committee was established to design and procure the instructional LAN. The author, who was also serving as the Academic Computing Coordinator for the College, chaired this committee. Surveys, memos, and individual consultations were used to involve faculty. Software demonstrations and educational efforts ameliorated conflict.

A broad range of materials were consulted for tips and implementation guidelines. Local vendors were invited to submit pre-proposals and to provide input into the development of the Request for Proposal (RFP). Off-island vendors were also contacted for preliminary pricing information.

TECHNOLOGICAL MIX AND THE INSULAR ECONOMY

Introduction

Insular economies differ in many ways. These include: the sociopolitical system, language, culture, currency, autonomy, and infrastructure. Aspects held in common are: the susceptibility to economic shocks, reliance on imports, lack of balance in composition of the economy, relatively high transportation costs as a portion of total product cost, and the absence of borders. A general model would incorporate all of these factors. Building on the common features, but allowing for the unique aspects of each island, perhaps a model could generate an insular "filter" to provide an efficient implementation framework.

Guam is a U.S. Territory. Most information technology comes from the U.S. mainland. Thus, the projects discussed in this chapter do not shed light on problems relating to differences in sociopolitical system, currency, language, or autonomy. The intent of the discussion, instead, is to demonstrate how the isolation due to the insular nature of Guam's economy leads to a different design than for a comparable (mainland U.S.) locale.

The phrase "technological mix" is used here to represent a particular combination of available techniques. Economists distinguish between "techniques in use" and "technology." Mansfield (1988), defines the latter as ". ..society's pool of knowledge regarding the industrial and agricultural arts" (p. 8). Information technology may be employed in a wide range of combinations, or mixtures. Input costs influence this choice. Hardware, software, support, and labor costs must be examined.

Input Costs

There is no doubt that computing hardware has fallen in price, both in nominal and real (inflation-adjusted) terms (Cash & McLeod, 1985). Powerful micros now have the capabilities of minicomputers. Perhaps more important in an environment subject to frequent power outages and high humidity is the greater environmental tolerance of PCs versus minicomputers.

In an insular economy, the shipping cost of components is disproportionately high. Reliability saves money, as the cost (measured in both time and money) of shipping products back for repairs or replacement is relatively high. Insular economies do not have a support grid to ensure a steady source of electricity, resulting in frequent power outages. An uninterruptible power supply becomes a necessity for most systems.

Software prices have risen, but not dramatically, when one considers additional features and the option to purchase network licenses. Observation indicates that software may be used longer (revised less often) in the insular economy. Viewed as a long term investment, the premium prices required for some of the better software packages are not considered prohibitive.

Support costs may be viewed in several ways. Telephone support from a software vendor may be a moot point for those who are working in an insular economy (Guam, for example, does not have access to free "800" numbers). Internal support (developing software) is very expensive where programming expertise is scarce and costly. Small insular economies tend to become captive to an individual programmer or vendor, leading to high maintenance costs.

Projecting Information Systems (IS) labor costs is difficult in the changing scenarios typical of insular economies. A key aspect is the presence of an institution of higher education, specifically one that has a Computer

Science (CS) or Management Information Systems (MIS) program. Size of domestic markets becomes an issue again, as many islands do not have the installed base necessary to make training and support cost-effective for a wide range of software. Sending personnel off-island or bringing support people from off-island location may be cost prohibitive.

The traditional economic development framework focuses on the capital/labor ratio and the prices of these two inputs. Less developed countries generally employ more unskilled labor within their "appropriate technology" than do developed countries (Nafziger, 1990). Local educational institutions play a major role in determining IS labor costs. Small insular economies generally fit the pattern of the less developed country, with scarce skilled labor and surplus unskilled labor. Guam is an exception in the latter respect. The economy has grown so fast that unskilled labor is imported.

Wages have improved in most of the Pacific Rim countries, and Guam is no exception. Both employment and wage growth have been particularly strong in the past few years. The wage growth, however, is primarily in skilled jobs, as migration of unskilled labor is relatively unchecked. The high demand for skilled labor has not generated a corresponding move to develop domestic programs to supply more skilled labor.

The explanation for such labor paradoxes may lie in the degree of human capital formation. Studies which measure the pecuniary returns to continued doses of education find diminishing returns to this public investment. Nafziger (1990) cites studies conducted through the period 1957-1978 and reports that "returns to primary education were 24 percent per year, secondary education 15 percent, and higher education 12 percent" (p. 239). Whether viewed in this perspective or simply as a luxury, new programs in computer science and information systems are apparently seen as prohibitively expensive.

The University of Guam, for example, has over two thousand students but is not able to offer degree programs in computer science, engineering, or information systems. The dearth of technical knowledge in the domestic labor force becomes a limiting factor in the design and implementation of systems. As a territory of the United States, there are no labor restrictions between Guam and mainland USA. Japan, in contrast, places severe restrictions on outside workers. With no domestic supply source, then, each IS professional must be recruited and often subsidized to relocate on Guam. One can generalize, therefore, and argue that the high cost of skilled IS professionals relative to semi-skilled operatives will lead to designs that require less skilled input and maintenance.

How do these relative price differences affect the choice of technological mix? A decision matrix will give extra weight to techniques which require little support and are reliable. Hardware and software prices are relevant but less important factors.

Alternative technological mixtures are measured through this resulting cost matrix. To illustrate, four recent IT trends are discussed in relation to the peculiarities of the insular economy. The trends are: Graphical User Interfaces (GUIs), Fourth Generation Languages (4GLs), Local Area Networks (LANs), and Presentation Graphics. Conjecture regarding the four trends in an insular economy will be followed by their application to the two applied projects.

FOUR TRENDS IN INFORMATION TECHNOLOGY

Graphical User Interfaces

The GUI of the MacIntosh and the PC-based Windows is particularly appealing to the novice (and those who are not accomplished typists). Intuitively, the mouse input and use of icons may be desirable in multilingual and multicultural environments. On Guam, English is a second language for a sizeable minority of the residents. The tighter control placed on applications by working through the graphical interface may lead to fewer user errors. There seems to be much promise for enhanced productivity through the GUI.

However, GUIs for the (dominant) IBM-and-compatible market have been relatively expensive, with few options among the available software applications. It is too costly to experiment with new software releases in an environment of very limited support availability. A "wait and see" attitude is likely to prevail until the new applications are debugged.

Fourth Generation Languages

The dearth of programming expertise on Guam makes 4GLs seem particularly attractive. The high cost of training makes it very difficult to build and maintain systems using third generation languages. A review of the government financial information systems in Micronesia in 1985 applauded the widespread adoption of a standard (turnkey) accounting package. The consultants recommended placing more resources into training, documentation, and security rather than into the areas of programming (Grosh & Blandford, 1985).

The ease of use of 4GLs, however, is not without a price. They generally require a more sophisticated, thus more expensive, hardware platform. As with all software innovations, initial results are somewhat exaggerated and experience lowers one's expectations. The early, glowing reports of the benefits of 4GLs (Davies and Hale, 1986; Green, 1985) were followed by more sober analyses of the operating inefficiencies of the 4GLs (e.g., Bordoli & Jenkins, 1990).

The happy marriage of powerful, inexpensive processors and relatively mature 4GLs is likely to cause a shift in technologies in some of the more remote, insular economies. The efficiency advantage of procedural languages over 4GLs (e.g., COBOL over FOCUS in the Bordoli & Jenkins study) can be eliminated by swapping out a processor. To clarify, the slower FOCUS language running on a 486 PC (or a 33 megahertz 386 PC) will easily outperform COBOL on an IBM AT.

LANs

LANs provide lower unit costs through the sharing of peripherals and the licensing of network software. This immediate pecuniary impact is often decisive in the purchasing decision. The impact on work group productivity through email or group decision support software may also influence the decision. Modifications to supported software are simplified in network designs, since one only changes the programs on the file server. Designs in which the workstations have disk drives offer another advantage. The clean separation of programs (maintained by the network supervisor) from data (the responsibility of the user) is easily implemented.

Several factors, though, cause for caution in implementing LANs. By nature, most local area networks are installed in a multi-vendor environment. The burden this places on servicing and troubleshooting the LAN is a significant cost factor. The skill of managing a network must be developed and maintained. There is a definite change in perspective necessary in moving from "personal computing" to "network computing."

Presentation Graphics

The dedicated graphics packages are entering their second generation. No longer difficult to use, these packages are now more visually appealing with the higher resolutions found in both monitors and printers. Display devices for overhead projectors have also advanced considerably in quality, offering another output medium.

A reasonable hypothesis is the positive relationship between the use of graphics and acceptance by clients in a multilingual society. This should also be true where general education levels are relatively low, and where jargon may obfuscate meaning. Of course, it is generally accepted that visual information enhances understanding in practically all settings.

CASE STUDY RESULTS

The GEDA Project Results

In discussing "national" IT environments, Cash, McFarlan and McKenney (1988) list nine issues which affect the coordination and transfer of technology. Three of these are particularly germane to Guam: 1) the availability of IT professional staff, 2) general level of IT sophistication, and 3) technological awareness. As discussed earlier, Guam would score low in each category, due to the lack of professional degree programs in these areas and the expense to recruit and retain skilled professionals.

Guam's economy prior to the tourism boom and subsequent to World War II was endemic at best, at worst it was a modern welfare state. There was little need for sophistication within public sector agencies. During the recent expansion due to tourism, the public sector on Guam has not added resources to deal with the dramatic surge in the private sector. A sophisticated information system was not expected, then, as research commenced. What was surprising was the disparity that existed among the different departments. All land records were maintained in manual form, with poor organization and controls. Agencies with statistical responsibilities (Commerce, Labor) generally had more sophisticated users, generally using contemporary mainstream software and hardware. The Bureau of Planning was conducting a pilot project with a relatively sophisticated Geographical Information System (GIS) software. This was a relevant issue, as growth planning requires careful coordination across agencies, and the relevant agencies had markedly different capabilities to deliver information.

It is not clear if this differential allocation of resources with the government of Guam was haphazard or planned. Viewing local government as a firm, one could argue that Guam is experiencing the not-uncommon development of multiple technology assimilation patterns (McFarlan & McKenney, 1982). The experience with the Geographical Information System, though, was illustrative.

There seemed to be general agreement that a GIS (utilized by all government agencies) was a desired goal. The development of a usable model, however, was viewed as expensive and time consuming. As noted by Shangraw (1986), in his study of public sector managers, the level of computer expertise may influence systems design. Lack of trust in the GIS concept may have influenced the reluctance to develop a full-blown GIS for the island. No champion appeared within the public sector to educate the decision makers and build support for this solution to the planning dilemma.

While experimenting with new software and display devices, a significant finding of our study group was that verbal arguments that did not sink in were immediately grasped when accompanied by a graphic presentation.The project was redirected to reduce the emphasis on the written report and focus on a series of "slideshows," which illustrated the results using three dimensional graphics.

Preliminary results were presented in two public forums, a university conference and a session with the GEDA Board of Directors. The visual impact of these presentations facilitated the direct conveyance of a range of complicated issues and data in a rather short period of time.

Within two months of the presentations, the study appeared on the front page of the local newspaper, in the "Letters to the Editor," the editorial section of the paper, and in the Guam Business News. Independent efforts of other groups to raise growth issues and concerns have contributed to a new public awareness. Most recently, an effective ban on further development incentives has been imposed by Executive Order of the Governor.

The macroeconomic problem demonstrated by this case is the need for self-realization within the decision structure of the public sector in insular economies. Specific resources must be devoted to overcoming the lack of knowledge and sophistication regarding new technologies. This is particularly advisable in a rapid growth scenario such as the boom on Guam. Possible solutions might be drawn from analogy between these agencies under pressure and strategically dependent firms. Cash and McLeod (1985) identify the requisite processes as "technology forecasting, tracking, research and development, introduction and management of new technology" and recommend two approaches:
". ..(1) establish an organizational unit with specific responsibility for these processes, and (2) use a contingency framework for the design of ongoing administrative infrastructure to effectively manage new technology" (p. 5). There seems to be no natural catalyst for this effort. A macroeconomic approach to this problem calls for specific policy legislation.

The LAN Project Results

As an example of a microeconomic application, the appropriate technology for a local area network is determined by examining relevant input prices and developing a decision matrix. The desire to provide a futuristic learning atmosphere or to utilize the leading edge of technology must be tempered by the risk and costs associated with this technology.

The College of Business and Public Administration (CBPA) of the University of Guam serves about eight hundred students. An early decision to serve the instructional needs of the College with a LAN was made for two main reasons: 1) the sharing of peripherals (a large hard disk, laser printer, and scanner), and 2) lower software costs. Contributing factors were the future use of groupware and email among faculty and the immediate separation of software and data (thus students were responsible for their data and the College was responsible for network software).

Experienced faculty were quick to advise not to "go state-of-the-art" with the new configuration. Their experience reflected the difficulty of getting support for untried systems and the likelihood of system failure under our poor (physical) environmental conditions.

The planning cycle for hardware was assumed to be five years. A distributed system based on PC technology was selected as most practical for a business-based curriculum. Software standards were chosen from the mainstream (Lotus, WordPerfect, and dBase). Standards lead to improved training and support capabilities, and continuity (particularly in education, where texts and support materials are geared to specific software packages).

The network topology, hardware, and software were selected with reliability and low maintenance as major criteria - again from the mainstream. An ARCNET LAN with IBM PS/2 Model 30/286 workstations provided the core of the lab. The older 8088/86 machines were avoided due to the fear of obsolescence. Two IBM PS/2s with 80386 processors (Models 70 and 80) were bridged as file servers. Networking capabilities were provided by Novell software. A major determinant in this configuration was the existence of several similar configuration on-island. Some of the analysis and design activities followed prescribed procedures unique to network designs (Kibirige, 1989). Consideration was given to adequate message transfer rate of the network topology and attention was devoted to products with high mean time between failure statistics (adjusted for the number of nodes).

To provide support for this new design, the Lab Supervisor was sent off-island for training. This was an expensive mistake, as the person was later reassigned and the training was not successful. The true cost of this mistake was quite high, including the travel and workshop costs ($4,000 U.S.) and the cost to contract with a local vendor to provide the installation and to train a new network manager ($7,000 U.S.). There is a need for more studies of turnover in the insular economy to determine when it is wise to train and develop internal resources. This often desirable objective may be cost-prohibitive in many cases.

Particularly humorous (in retrospect) was the relationship with vendors. An attempt was made to purchase items on island where the price differential was not exorbitant. Local vendors were given a ten percent preference but, beyond that, good public relations were desirable as were timely support and maintenance.

When items were purchased off-island, invariably problems arose with communication, delays in shipping, and returned merchandise. One of the vendors went bankrupt, another would selectively go incommunicado when unable to deliver supplies. Fax, telephone, and shipping costs were considerably higher than projected.

SUMMARY

It is dangerous to generalize from isolated examples. These anecdotes do not form any sort of general theory of insular economies. It remains a somewhat aloof objective. Yet, it is hoped that policy makers, consultants, and program officers will recognize that insular economies have certain systemic features that require additional care in information technology transfer.

From a macroeconomic perspective, policies that encourage the "appropriate technology" should be carefully articulated. Incentives for local manufacture could be appropriate; local government might designate a fostering and controlling agency to manage the assimilation of new technology; price preference for local vendors might be advisable, recognizing the social value of the development of on-island support.

It does seem clear that several trends are combining to cause a shift in technological choice in this area:

1) Graphical User Interfaces are strong candidates for success in insular and developing countries. Reluctance to try new ideas and products, however, will most likely delay widespread use until the second generation of GUI software is available. The rapid development of the PC-based Windows and OS/2 indicate that this second generation may materialize very soon.

2) The hardware costs relative to support and programming costs have fallen radically. Now 4GLs are fast enough to implement on 386 and 486 micros. Awareness of this new technology may be a barrier, but the possibility of abandoning the environmentally sensitive minicomputer configurations for the PC platform may be a strong incentive.

3) Networks are no longer leading edge technology and are thus attractive in areas of limited support. Mainstream network operating systems are well designed and relatively error-free. A solid experience base in standard technologies has lead to a wide range of training materials and support channels.

4) Presentation graphics proves to be a powerful means of presenting information. Written and verbal communication should be supplemented wherever possible with concise and simple graphics.

Each of these trends shows some promise for the insular economy. It is hoped that research will continue to identify characteristics both of the developing nations and those with problems unique to their insular status.

For those who are familiar with the "So What?" arguments in refutation of Bertalanffy's General System Theory I would argue that yes, it is important to be able to generalize about such things. We are seeking underlying structures and processes that may be of little immediate benefit but may contribute in a broader sense when viewed in an appropriate context.

References

Bordoloi, B., & Jenkins, A.M. (1990). An Experimental Investigation of Comparative Operating Efficiency of a 4GL (FOCUS) and COBOL in a Workstation Environment. *Journal of Microcomputer Systems Management, 2*(1), 26-37.

Cash, J.I., & McLeod, P. L. "Managing the Introduction of Information Systems Technology in Strategically Dependent Companies." *Journal of Management Information Systems, 1*(4), 5-23.

Cash, J.I., McFarlan, F.W., & McKenney, J.L. (1988). *Corporate Information Systems Management.* Homewood, IL: Irwin.

Churchman, C.W. (1968). *The Systems Approach.* New York, Dell.

Davies, T.R., & Hale, W.M. (1986). Implementing a Policy and Planning Process for Managing State Use of Information Technology Resources. *Public Administration Review, 46*(Special Issue), 516-518.

Green, J. (1985). Productivity in the Fourth Generation: Six Case Studies. *Journal of Management Information Systems, 1*(3), 49-63.

Grosh, G. & Blandford, D. (1985). *Trust Territory of the Micronesia: Computer System Review.* Austin, TX: Tools & Techniques.

Hagen, E.E. (1980). *The Economics of Development.* Homewood, IL: Irwin.

Iverson, T., & Blanchard, J. (November 16, 1989). An Overview of Development Trends on Guam: The UOG-GEDA Study Project (paper presented to *The 10th Island Conference of Public Administration.*

Kibirige, H.M. (1989). *Local Area Networks in Information Management.* New York: Greenwood Press.

McFarlan, F.W., & McKenney, J.L. (May-June, 1982). The Information Archipelago—Maps and Bridges. *Harvard Business Review.*

Nafziger, E.W. (1990). *The Economics of Developing Countries.* Englewood Cliffs, NJ: Prentice Hall.

Shangraw, R.F. (1986). How Public Managers Use Information: An Experiment Examining Choices of Computer and Printed Information. *Public Administration Review, 46*(Special Issue), 506-515.

Watson, H.J., Carroll, A.B., & Mann, R.I. (1987). *Information Systems for Management: A Book of Readings.* Plano, TX: Business Publications, Inc.

Weill, P., & Olson, M.H. (1989). An Assessment of the Contingency Theory of Management Information Systems. *Journal of Management Information Systems, 6*(1), 77-79.

Factors of Information Technology Implementation in Under-Developed Countries:

9

Example of the West African Nations

Lech J. Janczewski
University of Auckland

The issue of a wider introduction of Information Technology (IT) to the West African countries should be analyzed by considering three separate groups of problems: technical, economical and cultural. For the successful implementation of IT, all three must be tackled.

Technical problems. Computer equipment manufactured in West Europe and North America can be implemented in West Africa but unfortunately does not appear to be well suited for the special climatic and other conditions characteristic of West Africa, such as high humidity, high temperatures, dust and fluctuations in the power supply. Also, telecommunications systems of the proper quality are virtually non-existent.

Economical problems. Total fund requirements for the average IT investment are quite substantial in comparison with the cost of labor. This may encourage companies to promote a manual operation rather than invest in computers.

Cultural problems. Computers, the products of western civilization, are adjusted to the culture of their developers. African cultures are quite different and as a result, their implementation there may lead to psychological stress. Developers of information technology should be aware of this fact and adjust their systems accordingly.

INTRODUCTION

Q: What is a difference between a line printer and a dot printer?
A: In output the functions of the line printer will come out in written form.
But in a dot printer, it will be in an oral form.

Authentic answer from "General Evaluation Test" for data process-
ing personnel, Government of Niger State of Nigeria.

The above illustrates the type of problem that may be faced by data processing managers working in under-developed countries. Such countries are caught in an almost "no-win" situation. On the one hand, the introduction of Information Technology (IT) on a wider scale is a must if these societies want to maintain contacts (industrial cooperation, trade, etc.) with advanced nations. On the other hand, the direct introduction of IT may lead to significant losses for the users. The various governments of West African countries seem to understand these problems and significant numbers of students are sent every year to Western World tertiary educational organizations to study Computer Science and Information Systems. Also, many specialists from these countries are hired by West African governments and private organizations to help these countries design and run their own information systems. The problem is, however, that both groups of specialists receive basic training in data processing problems as they are perceived by contemporary societies in The United States of America and countries in Western Europe. This knowledge directly implemented in other environments may, in fact, work against the desired goals.

The following chapter is based upon the author's three year work on a computer project in West Africa, and studies of the countries of the region. The chapter examines two closely associated issues:

1. The potential technical, economical and cultural problems in mplementation of Information Technology in the ries of the region.

2. Possible methods of solving these problems, which may allow foreign and local investors to achieve a higher level of effectiveness and efficiency from their computer installation.

THE REGION

West Africa (Figure 1) is a vast stretch of land located on the northern side of the Gulf of Guinea, from Senegal on the West, to Cameroon on the East. It encompasses the most populous (over 106 million people) country of Africa - Nigeria; one of the richest countries (GNP per capita: US $960) - Cameroon; one of the poorest countries (GNP per capita: US $ 200) - Burkina Faso; and the smallest country - Gambia (territory of only 10,240 sq km). Climate varies from a rain forest on the south along the Gulf of Guinea, to semidesert in the interior (around 1000 km north off the coast). (World Bank, 1988 and Macdonald's Encyclopedia, 1976).

Most of the countries of the region gained their independence from England or France around 1960. Hence, depending on the country, either French or English is the official language of that West African country. These languages are a binding factor, given the astounding number and variety of local languages and dialects.

Most of the countries of the region started as western-style democracies. Some exhibit the clear influence of the political systems of Eastern Europe. Later, in the majority of the countries, military forces or local "strongmen" took over. Thehistory of the region is an almost never ending string of coups and counter-coups, sometimes separated by short periods of democratic rule.

Because of the climate, and despite very primitive agricultural systems, countries of the region produce enough food to feed the rapidly growing population. Also, agricultural products are in many cases the only commodities exported and the only source of 'hard' currency.

Exportation of oil, after its discovery in the 1960s, became a very important source of income for some of the countries of the region, especially for Nigeria. This country is at present one of the world's 15 biggest producers of crude oil (United Nations, 1986). The oil boom at the beginning of the 1970s had a dramatic impact on the economy of that country. Easy money encouraged unrealistic spending. Many ambitious projects started, but the lack of rational planning and qualified cadres plus the drop in oil prices on the international market at the end of 1970s forced investors to slow down, even to completely stop their projects. The countryside and cities are dotted with such abandoned projects. September 1990 hikes in the price of crude oil (Iraq - Kuwait conflict) on the world market may reactivate some of these projects but in view of the country's debt, in the range of US $20 billion, may have a rather limited effect.

In the meantime, cities started expanding rapidly, like Lagos, one of the biggest African cities, with an estimated population of around 2.8 million in 1983 (The New Encyclopaedia Britannica, 1986). Urban growth far exceeded and still exceeds the ability of these West African governments to create jobs and provide even basic services for city inhabitants. Power failures or switch-offs and water supply stoppages are frequent, telephone networks are working only in theory, and the crime rate and corruption exceeds anything

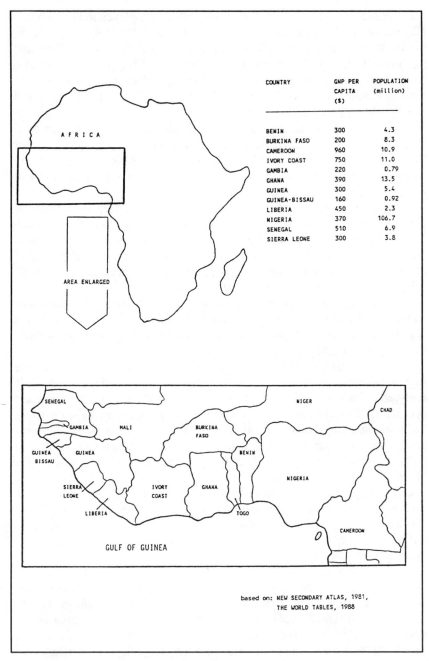

COUNTRY	GNP PER CAPITA ($)	POPULATION (million)
BENIN	300	4.3
BURKINA FASO	200	8.3
CAMEROON	960	10.9
IVORY COAST	750	11.0
GAMBIA	220	0.79
GHANA	390	13.5
GUINEA	300	5.4
GUINEA-BISSAU	160	0.92
LIBERIA	450	2.3
NIGERIA	370	106.7
SENEGAL	510	6.9
SIERRA LEONE	300	3.8

based on: NEW SECONDARY ATLAS, 1981,
THE WORLD TABLES, 1988

Figure 1: West Africa

known in North America. Many local governments now are not facing the problem of how to manage development, but rather how to survive (in both an economic and political sense).

The lack of political and economical stability in these countries make any investment in information technology very difficult. Solutions for these problems are not easy and/or quick. But even if we assume that stability could be achieved in the near future, there are other factors, equally important for successful implementation of information systems. These factors are discussed next.

WEST AFRICAN CLIMATE

Most data processing equipment imported to this region is not fully prepared to withstand local conditions. At best, the equipment is manufactured according to "tropical" conditions, which generally refers to high temperatures and humidities. This is not enough. For electronic equipment to work properly in this part of the world, the following factors must be considered.

Temperatures

Along the coast the temperature fluctuates between 20 and 30 degrees Celsius (Figure 2). Further north, in the proximity of the Sahara Desert, the temperature may easily rise above 40oC during a day and fall to 17 degrees at night. The most popular roofing material in Africa is corrugated iron, which is an excellent heat conductor. Sun heats the flat roof quickly and the heat penetrates through it and the ceiling into the rooms below, resulting in temperatures inside well above 40 degrees Celsius. Air conditioners solve this problem, but due to frequent power failures this solution is not completely reliable. Hence, computer equipment should be designed to withstand temperatures up to 50 degrees Celsius at least.

Humidity

In the interior, rainfall is scarce, but along the coast may reach over 400 cm per year. It is mostly in the form of storms, during the rainy season, with heavy atmospheric discharges and strong winds. In a matter of one hour, 20 cm of rain may fall. As a result, in Conakry, Guinea, the monthly rainfall in May exceeds 125 cm and the mean annual rainfall is over 500 cm, while in the north rainfall is less than 5 cm with practically no rain from December to February (New Secondary Atlas, 1981).

Humidity of the air during the rainy season, therefore, is extremely

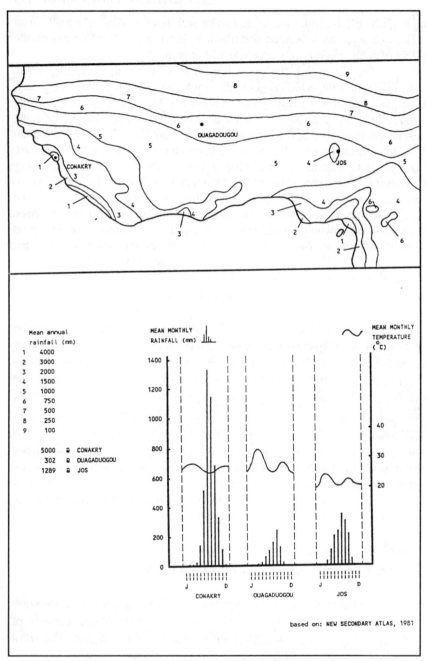

Figure 2: Climate in West Africa

high. Quite often condensed water can be seen pouring down the walls in an office or home - an indication that humidity has reached 100 %. Imagine the effect of such condensation on electronic apparatus!

The air during the rainy season is very clean, except for some industrial pollution, which is generally not heavy. However, there are other, more serious problems. During the "heat time" (December to March) a strong wind called Harmattan blows from the direction of the Sahara Desert, bringing vast amounts of sand in the form of very fine dust. The effects of Harmattan wind may be observed as far away as a hundred kilometers north of the coast. To an observer, this dust looks like fog, sometimes thin but sometimes so heavy that automobile drivers are forced to switch on their headlights. The dust is so fine that it penetrates everywhere. The damaging effects of dust to electronic equipment, especially to external memories and electro - mechanical switches, are common knowledge. Data processing equipment imported to this region must be well protected against dust if it is expected to be used for several years.

Sterility

Organic contamination is often overlooked but is a logical extension of the problem of equipment working in environments with high temperatures, humidity, and a lot of dust. This dust, which may penetrate computer equipment, carries bacteria and other microorganisms. High temperatures and humidities inside electronic apparatus set up very favorable conditions for their intensive growth, especially if the equipment is not used continuously. The internal parts of computers including wires and circuits boards start to coat with a layer of microorganisms, which often chemically react with the substratum to the point of destroying it completely. Among data processing communities, many stories have been circulated about mice causing the disruption of computer installations, but in Africa the real danger comes from these micro-organisms.

IT TECHNICAL ENVIRONMENT

However well-protected against the hostile environment, computer equipment may still not be used successfully in West Africa, because of problems relative to the technical infrastructure of the region. The most significant components of that infrastructure are discussed below.

Power Supply

The quality of the power supply in most West African nations is poor because of the overloading and low quality of the power grid. This alone may interrupt the work of data processing equipment, but much more dangerous are the frequent storms with extremely powerful electrical discharges. Often power lines are built very close together, even to the point that the conductors touch each other. Consequently, Quite powerful power spikes may be inducted from a line hit directly by lightning to other nearby lines. Travelling in a heavy storm with powerful winds and electromagnetic discharges along two such power lines is an unforgettable experience!

Low quality electrical power supply may be the result of not only climatic or economic conditions existing in these countries, but also to the legislation protecting power authorities. In each of these countries, power authorities are run as state-owned enterprises (such as the Nigerian Electrical Power Authority) and legislation protects them very effectively so that the quality of their performance may not be challenged (Federal Government of Nigeria, 1975).

This low reliability of the power supply forces most homeowners and businesses to install their own power generators on their premises. Usually, after a heavy rain and the resulting power cuts, West African cities are filled with noise and covered with smoke emanating from all these miniature power plants.

Telecommunication

Modern societies can not exist without the development of telecommunication networks, and West African governments seem to understand this. A number of formidable problems still exist, however:

1. Investments in telecommunication are expensive and together with low GNPs such investments are more difficult.

2. Intercity links must be based on microwave or satellite connections not only because of the climatic conditions oned earlier, but also because of the simple fact that cables are a very sought after material and may literally be stripped from the poles by local people.

3. Investors apparently are interested in developing systems which will survive only the warranty period and do not care about the needed years of reliable service to follow. The author had a chance to observe work of a team laying intercom systems in the building where he worked. They were laying cables

violating the most fundamental principles of the job - like forcing cables through narrow, sharp-edged openings. The author's intervention to the manager was met with comments of: "Mind your own business, besides, the network will work." It was predicted that problems would occur within a month after commissioning the network and unfortunately, that is exactly what happened.

In conclusion, the telecommunication system in these countries may be characterized by the following factors:

First, the telecommunication networks are not extensive. For example, the telephone book (including yellow pages) of Nigeria, with a population exceeding 100 million people, is the size of one volume of the New York telephone directory. In a city of around 100,000 people you may expect to have around 1000 telephones. In West Africa, generally, there has not been sufficient investment in this technology.

Second, the telecommunication networks rarely function properly, especially after storms. Connections, including international links, may be disrupted for several days. Quite recently, this author could not connect to a telex number in Nigeria for a week. The quality of a telephone connection will generally depend on the proximity of a satellite or microwave station, since major cities are connected via radio links rather than through wires.

Third, although most of a network may be automated, the number of channels available is often not adequate. The common practice is to use operators' services instead of direct dialing. If you are on good terms with the local operator, your waiting time will be insignificant, but if you criticize their services, you are doomed!

Fourth, many organizations aware of the state of the government telecommunication network, build their own radio link systems, based on short wave or microwave transmissions. Quite often these systems are more reliable. An example is Kramer - Italo's network in Nigeria.

Maintenance and Servicing

A very important part of any successful IT implementation is the maintenance and servicing of the equipment. An information technology manager running a Data Processing shop in West Africa is facing a set of problems not known to his/her equivalent in the United States of America.

First of all, the n Time Between Fault and Attempt to Repair measured in days rather than in hours. If a service center is located in the same city then service may not be a problem but if the site is remote from that service center, then repairs may take some time to complete. Poor telecommunication networks make contact with such a service center quite difficult and then the question of transport arises. Even with the best effort and good will of all parties concerned, it may be impossible for the repairperson to reach the destination within a day or two.

Second, there is a question of the ability of the serviceperson (his/her knowledge). This kind of job requires an extremely good understanding of the equipment in question. Such a person is rarely willing to travel around the African countryside, since much better-paying jobs may be found in developed countries.

Third, local maintenance is usually rudimentary at best because the number of qualified people who understand how a computer works, and could perform reliable maintenance, is very small. In general, knowledge of technical matters is fairly limited. For example, during the recruitment of staff for the computer center, this author was approached by one man who explained that he was interested in taking the job of maintenance engineer. He was then presented with a fuse box with its cover removed and live wires hanging outside (as left after repair by a local electrician). He was asked if he thought everything was in order. The man examined the wires carefully and said, that in his opinion, everything seemed to be OK. This lack of understanding of the need for maintenance will be addressed later in the text.

The fourth problem associated with maintenance and servicing is availability of spare parts. Predictably, the cost of parts is very high, partly because of transport expenses from the country of origin. Additionally, countries of Western Africa are facing serious financial constraints. Direct imports from Europe, Japan or United States usually take some time, owing to the fact that most business organizations need to file applications for securing 'hard' currency for purchase of spare parts. Processing of such applications may take a long time, even months. Some materials are, of course, manufactured locally (e.g. print-out paper), but quite often they are of inferior quality.

INFORMATION TECHNOLOGY ECONOMIC ENVIRONMENT

In the text so far, technical and technically related factors influencing successful implementation of Information Technology in West Africa have been presented. The economic environment in which IT is supposed to work is equally important and is presented below.

Recently TIME magazine (Beyer, 1990) wrote: "Throughout the 1980s, [African] political leaders told their constituents that times would be

lean for a few years under the belt - tightening polices and would then turn rosy. But their deadlines are long
past, and their promises are unfulfilled. According to a World Bank report last year, the gap in per capita income between sub - Saharan Africa [West Africa is a significant part of this group] and the rest of the Third World keeps widening. In 1988 the contrast was U.S. $330 versus an average U.S. $750 for all developing countries. The nations of black Africa, home to 470 million people, together have the purchasing power of Belgium, a country of only 10 million. ... A wave of strikes and protests prompted by economic grievances has turned political. At the same time, the IMF and the World Bank have begun to press African regimes to liberalize their politics as well as their economies. ... With its current debt of $135 billion roughly equivalent to its gross national product and its debt - service obligations equal to half its export earnings, sub - Saharan Africa faces an intolerable situation that has produced instability and promises to breed more."

The above is perhaps one of the best current descriptions of the state of the economy in countries of the region. Very low GNP per capita places heavy burdens on every aspect of life in these countries. Discussion of aspects important to the IS investment follows.

Methods of Investment

Procedures for implementation of Information Technology in developed countries such as in Europe or North America are well researched and follow the typical patterns of a project life cycle, whether "prototype" or "classical" (Capron, 1986). At the beginning of the whole process of investment a feasibility study is performed. Results of this study indicate whether the investment is sensible, preferred lists of types (if not exact models) of equipment and software are compiled, and a more detailed study follows resulting in the formulation of a Request for Proposal (RFP), which is sent to various vendors - or design and programming work begins.

Investment in IT in under-developed countries seems to follow this pattern. Upon close inspection, however, the differences between the theoretical model and reality are much greater than it appears. Some typical patterns of investment in IT in these countries are:

Turn-key project. These are the most common instances of installation of larger mainframes, more complicated networks and computer-supported manufacturing systems. Information technology turn-key projects are usually parts of larger projects. A good example of such investment is the ICL system supporting an oil refinery in Kaduna, Nigeria, which was ordered together with the plant. Sometimes, the construction of a computer center and the installation of computer(s) becomes a turn-key project itself, as in the case of the installation at the Nigerian Ports Authority in Lagos. In these cases a detailed configuration is determined by specialists closely associated with the vendor organization, directed mainly by their general knowledge of the type of plant, factory, business organization or government agency the installation should support. In many cases the vendor organization is located abroad and IT specialists have only a rudimentary knowledge of local conditions. On the other hand, locals quite often do not show a good grasp of information technology. As a consequence, it is likely that the resulting configuration will be ill-matched to the real requirements. Further, the assumption that every party involved in these investments is genuinely interested in building an effective and efficient installation is questionable.

Locally controlled IT projects. The turn-key projects described earlier have a common characteristic: the role of local government (or rather investors) is essentially limited to providing general guidance to projects and securing funds. In locally controlled projects, the investor is also responsible for the direct control of the IT investment - usually provided through hiring the services of an IT consultant or consulting firm. Often the quality of these consultants is not verified and results can be disastrous. Two such examples may be quoted. The computer center at the University of Ilorin (Kwara State of Nigeria), had air conditioning provided by a set of window-type air conditioners loosely mounted in wall openings, which were bigger than the units themselves. Many more mistakes had been made (fortunately rectified later) in the case of a computer center at the Ministry of Finance and Economic Planning, Minna (Niger State of Nigeria), where designers located an auxiliary power source (diesel/generator unit) in the middle of the building and planned to install louver-type windows in the computer room. Apart from the qualifications of the consultants, inferior quality of locally-controlled IT projects is affected by the following:

- Financing of projects is less secure. The lack of funds may slow work down to a virtual halt for many years (e.g. the case of the Ministry of Finance and Economic Planning, Minna, Nigeria).

- The same lack of funds prevents smooth planning of particular investment phases. Erection of walls is so important (and costly) that nobody wants to talk about ordering a raised floor or suspended ceiling.

- Locally-controlled IT projects may become the easy target of power game, which may influence the quality of work.

Small projects. The methods of investment described so far deal exclusively with large (expensive) projects with a price tag in the range of a hundred thousand dollars. These projects are important, as they are considered milestones of IT development in a country, but equally important is a range of small systems, mainly desktop types, installed nation-wide. These systems are strongly 'application package' oriented. This means that they were installed with one task in mind, like running accounting operations, payroll, general ledger, etc. These installations rarely use in-house or tailor-made packages; they are based on the off-the-shelf products and usage is mostly limited to the basic functions. The decision to invest in a particular hardware and software package is mainly done on an ad hoc basis: the owner of the company brings a system back from an overseas trip, the director of the company has a meeting with an energetic salesman, and the like. Such purchases imply that the feasibility phase of investment in such cases is practically non-existent. Also, very rarely is any further development of that software performed, like debugging or upgrading to a newer software version.

Gifts. A number of IT systems are brought to under-developed countries in the form of gifts donated by international organizations, companies or individuals. In such cases, it is less meaningful to talk about even the most rudimentary feasibility studies since the usual procedure is to get the equipment first, find a recipient later and then suggest a possible implementation approach.

It would seem that these are the most popular methods of investing in IT in under-developed countries. As a matter of fact, most investments in other fields are arranged along similar lines. All of these methods may by characterized by the following features:

1. Very rarely is any investment in IT based on a solid analysis of facts aimed at finding real requirements for Business Information Systems, verification of data flows, optimization of configuration, software, etc.

2. In a considerable number of cases, the consultants called in t have proper experience of designing and running IT systems in the given environment (climate or business).

3. Unfortunately in the case of many under-developed countries and West African countries in particular, corruption appears to be a fact of life. Neglecting its existence would be very dangerous. The governments of West African countries do try hard to limit this custom as much as possible, introducing specific legislation, and imposing strict penalties, but with little effect. Dash ("gift" in Hausa language) is a way fe. Such a social attitude does

not support objective planning.

Data Processing Equipment Prices

Table 1 clearly illustrates one of the biggest problems of computerization in under-developed countries and West African countries in particular:

• Prices of similar types of equipment are generally higher in West Africa than they are in industrialized countries and with the growing complexity of the equipment this price gap is increasing.

• Much lower GNP per capita makes IT equipment even more inaccessible including even the most simple pocket calculator. In 1986, the average person in the United States could buy 1748 of these devices (for the equivalent of GNP apita), while the average person in Nigeria could ase only 32. For more powerful equipment the rence is even more substantial.

These differences in prices indicate that many applications feasible in the United States or Western Europe cannot be justified from an economic point of view in Africa. It may be cheaper in many cases to hire a team to do the job manualy than to install a computer.

Country	United States of America	New Zealand	Nigeria
GNP per capita (GNP/P) $USD	17,480	7,460	640
Price of mid-range systems (P1) $USD	75,000	85,000	280,000
Price of simplest calculator (P2) $USD	10	15	20
P1/(GNP/P)	4.2	11.3	437
P2/(GNP/P)	0.00057	0.0002	0.03

Table 1: Relations Between Various Data Processing Equipment and GNP

Why are prices of IT equipment higher in these countries than in the United States or Western Europe? Many factors are involved. For example:

- The equipment must be fully imported with shipments usually transported by air.

- High local taxes.

- Maintenance and servicing of the equipment is much more costly than in developed countries.

CULTURAL PROBLEMS OF COMPUTERIZATION

The importance of the climate and economic environment for IT implementation is well known. However, equally important is the general educational level of a society and its culture. Of course, in any society one may create "oases" of different customs, cultures, and technology. Such oases may function well but, by definition, their influence on the whole society would be fairly limited. Computers are a product of western civilization. Anybody trying to implement them on a wider scale elsewhere must be aware of the potential problems arising from these cultural differences. The most important are outlined below.

General Education

Basically, countries of this region offer free primary education to all children. However, due to limited teaching cadres and financial constraints, the level of education is generally very low (and not accessible to all). On the surface, the school programs look impressive: very often prepared with the help of Western World scholars, and covering most of the subjects taught in the developed world. Some educational institutions in larger cities look exactly like world class junior or senior schools or universities. This picture rapidly changes with increasing distance from main population centers. Tastefully decorated, air-conditioned lecture theatres become mud huts with thatched roofs, no windows or doors, no tables, chairs or school benches. Handbooks are subsidized but their cost is still above the financial limits of poor families and very often these handbooks are not even offered in adequate quantities. Some books are sold only to specific groups of people - for example, handbooks for a particular subject may be sold in a university store only to students enrolled in that subject.

Another problem in education is the shortage of "qualified" teachers. Teachers' colleges are perhaps the most popular type of school in this region of the world but the number of teachers educated there is not enough, without regard to the very basic of education at those colleges. West African governments understand these problems and try to help by offering teaching positions to expatriates. The problem is, however, that these offers are not attractive to the majority of candidates. There is not a different scale of salaries for locals and foreigners. Expatriates receive some additional benefits (like free travel to their countries of origin, etc) but still their salaries are much lower than their equivalent in the United States or Western Europe. For example, a high school teacher in Nigeria (Niger State Government, 1984) may earn the equivalent of US $8,000 per annum. Of course such a salary is sufficient to support a teacher's family locally, but would not allow for any savings. Frequent discussions with these teachers allowed this author to make another observation: apart from some distinctive groups of people devoted to helping African nations at some cost to themselves (like a group of volunteer teachers from Canada), many who came to Africa to teach wanted to escape from their own surroundings, or from their social or family problems. All these factors indicate that the quality of services offered by some of these teachers coming from developed countries may not be of the highest standard.

It is worth noting that these working conditions seem to be attractive to only one group: university teachers from Eastern Europe. Owing to the exorbitant exchange rate of dollars on the black market in communist countries, even savings of one hundred dollars would be worth a lot there. In the late 1970s and in early 1980 many universities of the region were dominated by highly qualified teachers from such countries as Hungary, Poland or Yugoslavia (e.g. The University in Accra, Ghana, The University in Zaria, Nigeria). With changing economic and political situations in Eastern Europe these numbers started declining rapidly.

Even the best-educated and motivated expatriate teachers may not be very effective. Often they lack knowledge of local customs and due to their temporary status do not tend to integrate with the local community. African culture is tied to family and/or group activities. The fact of being an outsider with a different background may severely limit the reception or acceptance of a particular teacher.

All these factors contribute to the fact that on average, the academic level of most graduates is appears to be very low. The quotation which started this chapter is one example of this. The person who gave this answer claimed to be a graduate from a local high school who had attended a "computer training course".

As a result, local software products may not be of the highest technical standard, and may have a lot of software "bugs" in them. For example, during work on a payroll system for a Nigerian State Ministry, this author discovered that the taxation algorithm did not correspond to the taxation table. Nigeria uses a progressive taxation model and with few exceptions, taxes are calculated using the taxation tables printed by the Government Printing Office. These taxation tables come in two volumes of A3 size (297 x 420 mm) and cover calculated taxes for incomes up to the equivalent of around US $40,000 per annum with an entry for each last dollar and for every month. A detailed analysis showed that in almost every month for a specific range of incomes (around the introduction of the next progression), taxes were calculated incorrectly and many entries were missing entirely. The interesting point was that the mistakes evidently resulted from a wrongly-designed algorithm, rather than somebody's deliberate action. A suggestion to inform the Federal Ministry of Finance was turned down, as the verification of all taxation tables in the country would be too costly.

Further Examples of Cultural Differences

Some other observations made by the author also suggest that educational and cultural factors may hinder the implementation of computers in West Africa and possibly other under-developed countries.

For example, teaching COBOL to a group of about 20 adults was extremely difficult. The students had no problem memorizing simple instructions, programs or the COBOL structure. The real problem appeared to be understanding how loops operated and especially how the verification of condition for staying in the loop worked. It seemed clear that the students were having serious problems understanding the meaning of a formula or algorithm. Most of them were good at arithmetic and the utilization of pocket calculators but had considerable difficulty with the meaning of even simple formulas like $(a + b) / c$.

The second example illustrates a problem relative to planning. In the city where the author used to live, the water supply was provided by sets of electro-mechanical water pumps. Of course, standby units were built and when one main unit was damaged, these standby units restored the water supply to the town. However, no effective action was taken to repair the main unit and when the standby unit was also damaged (much later), parts of the city were deprived of water for two weeks. Spare parts were airlifted from Europe and this operation cost a fortune. A regular order for parts placed on time and repair of the main unit just after it broke down would have cost considerably less (not to mention that the population was forced to arrange a water supply for themselves).

The above concludes the presentation of the most important factors

Group of Problems	Comments
1. Climate	
Temperature	May exceed 50oC
Dust	Very heavy during December-February
Humidity	Up to 100% during rain season and along the coast
Sterlility	Accumulated dust and humidity creates favorable conditions for microorganism growth
Atmospheric discharges	Very heavy during storms
2. Technical and Economic Environment	
Power supply	Frequent power cuts, voltage out of range
Telecommunication	Very sparse, not reliable especially during rain season and outside major cities
Service	Very expensive and very long response time
Maintenance	Practically non-existent
Methods of investment	Lack of proper feasibility studies
Cost of IT components	Relatively 10 to 100 times more expensive than in developed countries
3. Cultural	
General education level	Very low, on average 26%-45% first level school enrollment
Planning	Problems with planning of more complicated procedures

Table 2: Summary of IT Implementation Problems in West Africa

to be considered by anybody planning to install computer systems successfully in West Africa. A summary of the problems is outlined in Table 2.

SUGGESTED CHANGES TO IT EQUIPMENT AND PROCEDURES

The identification of factors influencing the effective and efficient implementation of Information Technology in West Africa must be followed by suggestions for dealing with the outlined problems.These suggestions are presented.

Changes in Design of Hardware

Computers and associated electronic equipment working in the West Africa region must be well protected against high humidity, high temperature, dust and microorganisms. Currently equipment imported to this zone does not meet these requirements. For instance, examine the layout of components in a typical

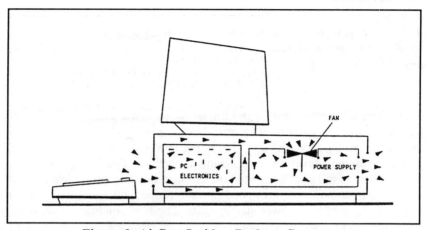

Figure 3: Airflow Inside a Desktop Computer

desktop computer. This is quite a popular arrangement.

It is obvious that the major source of heat in the unit is the power supply unit. With the built-in fan for cooling, air is forced to enter the unit ventilating other components (PC electronics) as well - which also means that a lot of moisture or dust may penetrate the machine. This creates very favorable conditions for (accelerates) corrosion and other processes, such as the growth of microorganisms, which may quickly lead to a malfunction. Information technology equipment intended to work in these countries should have some built-in protection against such processes.

The first step towards achieving this seems to be simple in concept but difficult and costly in realization: a total seal of the machine's electronics. All power components should be mounted near or on the inside of the cover with radiators (and fans, if required) outside. Sealed type keyboards should be used for the same reasons. This solution is widely used in military applications.

The unanswered question is how to deal with floppy disks, both 5.25" and 3.5" sizes. Diskettes are formidable collectors of dirt (especially the 5.25" type), despite protective covers. Protection with the usual sleeve envelopes is not sufficient. The use of sealed boxes during transport and storage is highly recommended. The author recalls that after travelling 700 km over African roads during Harmattan season, dust clearly penetrated inside a 5.25" disk's envelope placed in an attache case.

The other problem is that dust and humidity may gradually penetrate the computer interior via the slot used for loading floppy disks. A good preventive technique would be the implementation of a disk lock mechanism, used in the very early stages of floppy disk technology. In those devices a flap was mounted over the slot, open only during loading or removing of the diskette.

To preventthe development of microorganisms, a good method would be to coat the interior of machines with a layer of sterilizing, anti-mold or similar compound.

Power Supply

An unreliable power supply has forced the mass implementation of local back-up power generators, with attached diesel engines. The quality of these units is generally good and data processing equipment could be connected directly to these units in cases of interrupted power supplies (Datapro Reports, 1989). There is still a problem with a variation in the main power level due to changes in load and atmospheric conditions. It is not enough to implement fuses and built-in stabilized power supply units. The best solution seems to be powering the IT equipment through a stabilizer/separator in the form of an electric motor-flywheel-power generator. Such a solution is costly but highly effective. Such a system is installed in many larger computer installations such as in the ICL House in Lagos, a city with a very low quality of public power supply. The staff there did not register any malfunctions, which may be traced to the quality of the power supply.

Feasibility Studies

The analysis of methods of investment in West African countries concluded that a significant number of IT investments were and are still carried out without proper feasibility studies based on a sound knowledge of the local conditions.

To perform such tasks successfully, the teams responsible should:

• have a thorough knowledge of the subject (i.e. Information Technology),

• have a good understanding of the local conditions, both in terms of climate as economy,

• have high moral standards.

The first two conditions are obvious, In this section we will concentrate on the latter. The problem is that due to the political, economic and cultural history of this part of the world, corruption seems to be a way of life. The economy is powered (or rather, slowed down) by bribes. It is customary to include in the price of a contract (especially signed by a government agency) a sum of 10 to 30% which is used for "convincing" managers to sign a contract or their advisers to recommend signing of it. It is therefore always a risk, that a particular consultant will not be objective in his/ her recommendations.

The only sensible way to overcome this would seem to be to establish an agency, operating under the supervision of an independent sponsor which would specialize in performing or verifying the validity of feasibility studies. This agency should employ both types of experts: in Information Systems - for expertise relative to the technical problems - and others, with good understanding of the local economy, customs, etc. Financing of this agency could be split between local (or federal) governments and international agencies like United Nations Educational, Scientific and Cultural Organization (UNESCO). The agency could charge some token fee for their consultative work. Arrangements should also be made to eliminate the possibility of bribing the experts. There are many ways to achieve this, for example: short contracts with high salaries for experts with stipulated anonymity of a decision. Each IT investor could be made aware of the existence of the agency, but of course not forced to use its services. Depending on the availability of human resources, the agency could be staffed both with African and Western World experts. Due to the pressure which might be brought to bear on local experts, some rotation would be necessary: for instance, an expert should not evaluate projects from the city of his/her origin, etc.

Creation of the suggested agency would not have an immediate impact on computers and related equipment already installed in the region but may have a sustained effect on the effectiveness of future IT systems.

A good umbrella for such an agency could be the Intergovernmental Informatics Program (IIP) established by the General Conference of UNESCO at its twenty-third session in 1985, with the aim of solving some of the problems of disparity in the development of Informatics around the world, (UNESCO, 1985). The purpose of the IIP is to promote informatics as a factor in national development, particularly in the poorest countries through:

• training in informatics at all levels, particularly for specialists and trainers;

• development of an informatics infrastructure such as networks and their associated services;

• software development through software engineering and tools,

• development of national policies directed towards the integration of informatics in development plans;

• basic and applied research on software and hardware such as the development of expert systems or the use of microprocessors (Tanahashi, 1985).

This agency is not the final solution to the problem. It is rather a temporary measure. In the opinion of the author, the universities of the region should play a key role in the adaptation of IT to local needs. The developed world may be the source of technical expertise, but tailoring technology must be done locally.

The first important task for the tertiary education organizations in the countries of this region should be the preparation of guidelines for designers of software (including documentation) and for needed curriculum adjustments to address the local level of education.

HANDLING THE PROBLEM OF CULTURAL DIFFERENCES

The generally low educational level of many West African societies and the potential problems that may result from cultural diferences between that group of nations and the advanced countries require some changes to existing Information Systems and those being developed. The first priority seems to be the modification of documentation for popular software packages.

An approach that might be useful is exemplified by the documentation for the dBASE IV package, distributed by Ashton-Tate. One of the more important aspects of this documentation is the description of Application Generator (AG) facilities. The AG allows a user not familiar with the dBASE language to assemble fairly large applications by using menu-driven functions (Ashton-Tate, 1988). The problem is that a number of functions incorporated in the AG make it difficult to understand for someone without considerable exposure to IT. Presumably, it would be better to design a fairly large database management system and to show how to dleete those parts not required for particular applications (or how to modify it).

In addition, the development of a manual, for any procedural language would be extremely helpful. Of course, grammar and vocabulary must be discussed, but a number of typical applications should also be provided with discussion on how to tailor the language to specific requirements.

These suggested changes may or may not lead to optimal applications, but at a minimum should provide error-free solutions.

GNP VERSUS INFORMATION TECHNOLOGY INVESTMENTS

All the changes to hardware, software and procedures suggested in the previous sections of this chapter lead to one conclusion: a higher cost for IT investments in West African countries. This, combined with the fact that present prices are already higher than in most developed countries (taking official exchange rates into consideration) and that many West African countries have a very low income per capita, all make IT equipment there even more inaccessible. Does this mean that it is not worth performing a cost/benefit analysis, since it would probably give negative results at the end, or that generally, IT implementation is not feasible? No!

Obviously, a cost/benefit analysis should always be performed. The question is, however, which factors are important enough to be included in such an analysis. The following points seem to be worthy of consideration.

1.The first question an African IT potential investor should ask himself or herself is whether the possible implementation really requires the use of a computer. Unfortunately, in many cases the standard line of thoughtseems to be "I have a problem with calculation of..., what about buying computer?" A West African government agency known to the author had a four year delay in the preparation of its annual financial report. It is doubtful whether the installation of even the most modern equipment would speed up the processing of that report. A better organization of the work should presumably have been implemented beforehand. In the organization cited, the archive had a room filled knee-deep with papers so that a search for a particular document literally meant digging through papers for a couple of days resulting in an even bigger mess, since nobody bothers to put documents back in any order.

2.A number of applications must be supported by computers due to the international connections of some organizations. The question then becomes, "What type of equipment should be installed to realize these communications," rather than "Is the computer a feasible option?" Many of banks in the region use ancient "open record computers" (calculators with printing facilities) and cashing a cheque at the branch office which holds the account takes between an hour and a whole day, while cashing a cheque from another city may take two weeks or more!. These kinds of delays can not be tolerated in international business.

3.There are also applications that require computer support despite the fact that it would be cheaper (theoretically) to employ humans. These applications include cases when human replacement would be too difficult to manage and control especially with respect to possible errors. We also have to realize that working conditions (temperatures, humidity, dust) are difficult even for locals. The efficiency of work after lunch is clearly lower than it is before. Another important fact of life is that, apart from the coastal zone of West Africa, the majority of the population in this region are followers of Islam. According to

Islam, during Ramadan Feast, which lasts over a month, eating or drinking from sunrise to sunset is strictly forbidden. This has a visible effect on the performance of many individuals. Hence such tasks as preparation of production plans, ships' manifests etc., must be supported by computers.

4. Should any investor, after consideration of all the factors mentioned, decide to engage in IT, he/she must be certain that the equipment will last for many years, much longer than in developed countries. The suggested changes in hardware designs are aimed directly towards reaching this goal. Unfortunately, this also means that the investor should take into consideration developments which may take place many years from now.

Only after taking the above factors into consideration should any investor engage seriously in an IT project. The rest of a feasibility study should concentrate on finding a simple and reliable solution to IT development, taking into consideration the climate, technical, infrastructure and social conditions mentioned above.

CONCLUSIONS

In the late 1960s and the beginning of the 1970s, depreciation of computers to 10% of their initial values was estimated to take about 12 years. In 1978 this period was shortened to seven years (Cortada, 1980). Today, the common practice is to write-off equipment after three or a maximum of four years. In the case of software, these periods are much longer and some specialized applications may even last twenty years. Recently, one of the biggest data processing organizations in New Zealand, DATABANK, announced a major modification of one of its banking systems which was originally written in IBM System /370 Assembler Language. The rapid shortening of the life span of computer hardware is related to progress in electronics and 'tough' business conditions which exist in developed countries. More and more sophisticated applications are used by business organizations and as a result computers must grow in both speed and processing power.

This phenomenon is well-known to business managers and Information Systems specialists in developed countries. As mentioned previously in this chapter, the same does not hold true in the under-developed world and West African countries in particular. There, a different logic should be implemented, specifically:

1. Many African business problems should be solved first before embarking on even the most rudimentary computerization program. As mentioned above, it is pointless to install a computer if there are no desks in an office and documents

are not kept in any particular order. Unfortunately, many organizations are launching computerization projects without bothering to improve their organizational and procedural structures (especially in the case of government organizations).

2. The next step after streamlining organizational and procedural structures should be to determine whether or not computer power is necessary to communicate with the outside world (within the country and overseas). A typical example would be the branch office of an international bank. If the answer is YES, then a feasibility study should be initiated and concentrate on the question of how to provide this link in the most reliable but simplest way. Reliable telecommunication is essential!

3. Computerization for internal needs should be introduced only if it is proven that the given operation cannot be performed manually. Economic factors should focus on examining the cost of IT investment versus the cost of hiring and supervising additional staff, taking into consideration the speed of generating results. This point is presumably the most significant difference in the method of investing in IT in developed countries and African countries.

4.All investors in IT in West Africa should build their systems to last for many years. This means that they should demand from IT manufacturers protective measures against the local climate, as described earlier in the text. Also, they should protect their premises against humidity, dust and an unreliable power supply.

5. Software development should be limited to an absolute minimum. Instead, tailoring, detailed testing and careful documentation of packages should be undertaken before using such a package.

References

Ashton-Tate Corporation. (1988). *Using the dBase IV Application Generator*. Torrance, CA: Ashton-Tate Corporation.

Beyer, L. (1990). Continental Shift. *TIME. 21*. pp 14-15.

Capron, H.L. (1986). *Systems Analysis and Design*. Menlo Park, CA: The Benjamin/Cummings Publishing Company.

Cortada, J. *EDP Costs and Charges* (1980). Englewood Cliffs, NJ: Prentice Hall Series in Data Processing Management.

Datapro Reports on Information Security. (1989). All About Power Continuation Products (Report No IS 44 -001). Delran, NJ: McGraw-Hill.

Federal Government of Nigeria. (1975). Nigerian Electrical Power Authority Act. Lagos, Nigeria: Federal Government Printer.

New Secondary Atlas. (1981). London: Collins-Longman.

Niger State Government. (1984). Contract Agreement for Overseas Officers. (Form No GEN.69E). Minna, Nigeria: Niger State Government Printer.

The New Encyclopedia Britannica. (1986). Chicago: Encyclopedia Britannica.

Macdonald's Encyclopedia of Africa. (1976). London: Macdonald Educational.

Tanahashi, T.K. (1985). *Informatics and Third World Development: Perspective and Prospect for an Intergovernmental Programme.* (Publication No 63925). Paris: UNESCO.

United Nations. (1988). *Statistical Yearbook 1988.* New York: United Nations.

UNESCO. (1985). *Report No 6, General Conference 23rd Session, Sofia.* (Publication No 67836). Paris: UNESCO.

World Bank. (1989). *From the Data Files of the World Bank, Edition 1988-89.* Baltimore: The John Hopkins University Press.

SECTION 3
GLOBAL INFORMATION SYSTEMS

The number of multinational firms has grown almost exponentially. As a result, the role, responsibilities and perspective of the Chief Information Officer (CIO) have changed dramatically. Firms operating in a global environment must have global information. Building such a GIS is made easier if one has a framework for its design and that is the subject of the first chapter in this section by William R. King and Vikram Sethi. The authors propose a definition for Transnational Systems (TNS) and a specified domain and environment of these systems. This chapter is followed by one written by Chetan S. Sankar and P.K. Prabhakar which identifies and examines in greater detail the issues and components of a GIS.

The impact of EDI is examined by Roger Clarke, Persio DeLuca, Jose Gricar, Takeshi Imai, Don McCubbrey, and Paula Swatman. They note that since the 1960s, Electronic Data Interchange has been the subject of concern to many information systems executives.

The fourth chapter, by Kranti Toraskar offers a comprehensive, multidimensional framework for a global information system predicated upon the attributes of a GIS.

The focus changes to decision support systems and the role they play in global information systems in the next chapter by Vicki L. Sauter. She discusses, at length, issues that designers may encounter relative to the acceptance, use, and success of a DSS in different national cultures. The last chapter in this section written by George Ballester and Edmund Marcarelli addresses many of the problems indigenous to a GIS within a specific industry. In this case, that industry is international investment.

10

A Framework for
Transnational Systems

William R. King and Vikram Sethi
University of Pittsburgh

This chapter develops a framework for understanding the role and character of Information Systems (IS) and Information Technology (IT) in a transnational environment. Several recent studies have pointed to the need for the active management of transnational IT. These studies have adopted a rather narrow perspective of transnational systems and have discussed issues in areas such as international standards and telecommunications services. Few studies have attempted to present a comprehensive framework in order to offer an integrated agenda for research and discussion. This chapter will address this gap in IS research by explicating the dimensions of transnational systems and the environment in which these are instituted. Four categories of transnational interactions, of interest to the IS function, are differentiated: Intracorporate Transactions; Transactions with an Intergovernmental/Transnational body; Host Government Transactions; and Reactive Transnational Interactions. Different interactions such as bilateral/multilateral agreements are identified as the environment of transnational systems. Several different kinds of studies which can be developed from this framework are identified. In addition, several research hypotheses are developed to guide future research.

A recent management study noted the trends toward continued globalization and the increasing competitiveness of markets (Arthur Young, 1989). The study also noted that the fiercely competitive global marketplace of the 1990s can be attacked through well-managed Information Technology (IT).

The phenomenon of globalization is neither new nor unexpected. International interdependence was a dominant theme in Secretary George Marshall's speech at Harvard in 1947 that led to the establishment of the Organization for European Economic Cooperation (OEEC), the predecessor of the Organization for Economic Cooperation and Development (OECD). However, the character of interdependence is inherently and markedly different today. Increases in global trade have been followed closely by a rapid growth in services transactions and paralleled by international monetary transactions and foreign direct investment. In this environment of interdependence, the enhanced role of Information Systems (IS) and Information Technology will be a major issue that business executives will face in the future. This is underscored by Highbarger (1988), who notes that most organizations are discovering that IS support and the use of IT are their best sources of competitive advantage (CA) in the international marketplace.

The global organization has extensive needs for information. Dyment (1987) expresses this imperative in the context of an integrated control system and notes:

> The global corporation may have a product that was designed in a European country, with components manufactured in Taiwan and Korea. It may be assembled in Canada and sold as a standard model in Brazil, and as a model fully loaded with options, in the United States. Transfer pricing of the components and assembled product may be determined with an eye to minimizing tax legality. Freight and insurance may be contracted for relet through a Swiss subsidiary, which earns a profit subject only to cantonal taxes. The principal financing may be provided from the Eurodollar market based in London. Add the complexities of having the transactions in different countries, with foreign exchange hedges contract gains and losses that sometimes offset trading losses or gains, and one has a marvelously complex management control problem (p. 20).

Despite the above need, many companies lack an understanding of the nature of IS and IT that is required to manage in a global environment. Along with a lack of corporate understanding is a lack of research in the area. Ives & Jarvenpaa (1990) note that little has been written about global IT strategy or global IT activities. According to Cash et al. (1988), research is inadequate because it involves the difficult task of integrating concepts from the quite different disciplines of IS and International Business.

This chapter develops a framework for understanding the role and character of IS and IT in a transnational environment. Specifically, this chapter undertakes the following tasks:

1. Define the concept of Transnational Systems (TNS);

2. Specify the domain of TNS;
3. Specify the environment in which TNS are instituted; and
4. Evaluate the utility of the proposed framework regarding its descriptive and normative capabilities.

We first summarize past research that has focused on managing IS in a multinational corporation. We then describe a model of transnational interactions and note different kinds of interactions pertinent to IS. These interactions are then developed to explain TNS. Implications of the model are derived. The chapter concludes with a discussion of how the framework is useful to researchers.

A REVIEW OF IS IN MULTINATIONALS

IS literature related to multinationals can be categorized into five areas: general issues, planning, decision support, transborder data flows, and contingency approach. The following highlights the main themes and studies in each area.

General Issues

The main focus of some studies has been on IS issues faced by multinational corporations and, to some extent, on how they may be addressed.

According to Kelley (1980), when firms install IS overseas, they encounter problems such as lack of appropriately qualified systems and support engineers, difficulty in obtaining emergency service, poor quality communications equipment, and government bureaucracy. He thus recommends that IS should choose hardware vendors who can provide service and support internationally, employ equipment that is easy to use, be prepared to spend more time in IS installation and operation, and interact with foreign governments through a native.

Carlyle (1988) emphasized the problem of data management and noted that the emergence of global markets has multiplied the problems of getting the right data in the right amount to the right place at the right time. His study revealed that IS executives of some large multinationals were addressing the data problem by using electronic data interchange (EDI) and structured query language.

An overall framework for categorizing transnational IS issues was developed by Mandell and Grub (1979). They suggested that linkages between the parent and subsidiaries could be divided into four types: organizational, data, technology, and communications. Each linkage presents a unique set of issues and problems.

Planning

Several studies have discussed IS planning in multinational corporations. Buss (1982) underscored the need for IS planning and noted the lack of any planning frameworks. He observed that multinationals differ greatly in the arrangement of hardware and software and on the role of corporate IS. Further, he argued that "this diversity of approaches is confusing and there are few models to follow." He recommended that multinationals should plan their IS by creating the right organizational framework and by defining the roles of key players.

A more comprehensive planning framework was developed by Selig (1982), who suggested that multinational IS planning should be comprised of six phases: environmental analysis, examination of issues and opportunities, strategic analysis of alternatives, strategic objective setting and commitment, systems development methodology, and follow-up and measurement. His comparison of this normative planning process with the actual planning practices of 25 U.S. multinationals revealed that while the broad steps were similar, there were differences in structure and detail. Selig concluded that the differences were attributable to contingency factors such as product and industry diversity and corporate roles.

Decision Support

Another set of studies describes the characteristics of specific types of IS that may provide decision support in multinationals. Based upon an assessment of decisions that are made in an international environment, Iyer and Schkadi (1987) broadly outlined the nature of effective data support systems, decision support systems, and executive support systems. The issues involved in building decision support systems and their use for multinationals were further described by Iyer (1988) in a case study. He detailed how an organization developed, implemented, and utilized a decision support system for evaluating alternatives for foreign investments in manufacturing facilities.

Adopting a more normative approach, Eom et al. (1987-88) developed a decision support system to help financial managers choose a global financing strategy. The system uses a goal programming model for multiple criteria decision making and enables managers to consider multiple, conflicting objectives such as costs, foreign exchange risks, political risks, and managerial motivation goals.

Transborder Data Flows

Issues related to transborder data flows and their effects on multinational organizations comprise another area of study. Transborder data flows are movements of machine readable data across national boundaries (Sauvant, 1986). This area is of increasing concern because regulation of transborder data flows and international communication "may make or break companies doing business multinationally during the next decade" (Moore, 1984, p. 30). Previous literature has studied the nature of transborder data flows in the context of trade in services (Sauvant, 1986); third world needs (Shields & Servaes, 1989); sovereignty effects (Branscomb, 1986); and privacy mandates (Maisonrouge, 1981).

Contingency Approach

Finally, a few studies have attempted to establish the contingencies under which various IS recommendations should be followed. In one such study, Thompson et al. (1989) suggested that two factors - degree of market integration and degree of home country rule - be used to categorize firms into one of four globalization stages: domestic, empire, UN, and war games. They then outlined the salient IS management concerns for each stage.

In a similar analysis, Reck (1989) matched three fundamental multinational operating strategies for corporations with IS management concerns. The types of strategies studied are - imperialistic, multidomestic, and global - and these strategies define IS issues such as technology architecture, data architecture, and communication architecture.

THE TRANSNATIONAL CONCEPT AND TRANSNATIONAL SYSTEMS

In order to develop an organizational framework, we seek points of reference from a model of transnational interaction and, based on this framework, use the term "transnational" to describe IS and IT operating across state boundaries.

As discussed, the IS literature related to multinationals is not extensive. However, these existing studies have delineated IS issues facing multinationals and have also suggested some recommendations for IS management. The usefulness of these studies, nevertheless, is significantly undermined by the fact that little is known regarding the conditions under which some IS issues may be more important or some IS management recommendations, more appropriate.

In order to present a formal framework, we seek points of reference from a model of transnational interactions. The term "transnational" was first presented formally by Keohane & Nye (1972) in their seminal work, Transnational Relations and World Politics. They defined transnational interactions as "the movement of tangible or intangible items across state boundaries when at least one actor is not an agent of a government or an international organization." The entities involved in transnational interactions are called "transnational actors". Correspondingly, "transnational organizations" can be defined as transnational interactions institutionalized (Skjelsbaek, 1972).

The Nye-Keohane model sets forth the following:

- Transnational interactions involve actors across state boundaries.
- Interactions between transnational actors involve a systematic transfer of tangibles or intangibles.
- The formulation of transnational interactions is independent of the extent and scope of their interaction, and the concept therefore is broad and general.

Although the transnational model presents an alternative perspective of international relations, it has been extremely influential in focusing attention on private transnational actors (private organizations such as MNC's, interest groups, churches, and foundations). This theory is, however, general and basic to understanding how any transnational interaction takes place. Since information technology is one very important mechanism that facilitates, sustains, and promotes transnational interactions, the model proposed by Keohane & Nye is a useful starting point for developing a theoretical background for discussing the role of transnational IS and IT.

Based on the above, we refer to information systems and technology in use by transnational actors in the support of transnational interactions as Transnational Systems (TNS). At a general level, this definition is broad enough to include:

a. Systems such as global financial systems that interconnect all subsidiaries;
b. The management issues involved in setting up such systems;
c. The process involved in assisting and developing subsidiary IS operations; and
d. Subsidiary IS operations within a global framework.

The spectrum of activities thus included under TNS are: establishing IS at subsidiaries; involvement of subsidiary IS in the functioning of the global organization; policy making and strategy formulation for the subsidiary IS; and

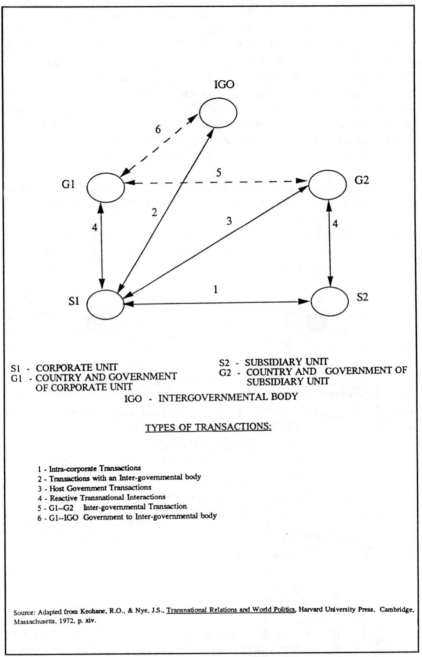

IGO

6

G1

5

G2

2

4

3

4

1

S1

S2

S1 - CORPORATE UNIT
G1 - COUNTRY AND GOVERNMENT
OF CORPORATE UNIT

S2 - SUBSIDIARY UNIT
G2 - COUNTRY AND GOVERNMENT OF
SUBSIDIARY UNIT

IGO - INTERGOVERNMENTAL BODY

TYPES OF TRANSACTIONS:

1 - Intra-corporate Transactions
2 - Transactions with an Inter-governmental body
3 - Host Government Transactions
4 - Reactive Transnational Interactions
5 - G1--G2   Inter-governmental Transaction
6 - G1--IGO Government to Inter-governmental body

Source: Adapted from Keohane, R.O., & Nye, J.S., Transnational Relations and World Politics, Harvard University Press, Cambridge, Massachusetts, 1972, p. xiv.

Figure 1: A Model for Transnational Interactions

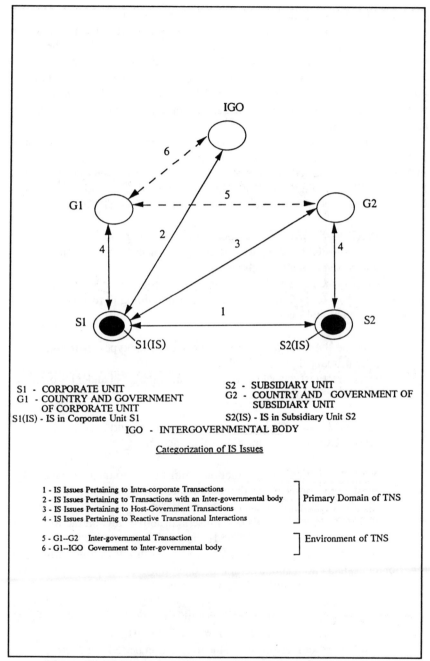

Figure 2: IS Issues Pertinent to Transnational Interactions

IS architectures linking the subsidiary to the corporation.

In order to develop the above general issues, we present below the Nye-Keohane model of transnational interactions. This model is shown in Figure 1. In the Nye-Keohane model, G1 and G2 refer to governments, S1 and S2 to societal units, and IGO's are inter-governmental organizations. For the purposes of this chapter, however, S1 is a corporate unit in the home country with G1 as its government. S2 is a subsidiary unit in the host country with G2 as its government.

The model can be used to describe the different categories of transnational activities. Since S1 and S2 are parent and subsidiary organizations, IS functions which occur within these organizations are shown as darkened circles S1(IS) and S2(IS) in Figure 2. Within each category of transnational activity, we can therefore identify different issues pertinent to IS. These are:

•S1(IS)—S2(IS): IS issues pertaining to intra-corporate transactions;
•S1(IS)—IGO: IS issues pertaining to transactions with an
inter-governmental body;
•S1(IS)—G2: IS issues pertaining to host-government transactions;
•S1(IS)—G1; S2(IS)—G2: IS issues pertaining to reactive
transnational interactions.

It is the thesis of this chapter that these four types of transactions constitute the primary domain of TNS.

The other two types of interactions in the figure, not under the premise of transnational interactions, are:

•G1—G2: Inter-Governmental Transactions; and
•G1—IGO: Government-IGO Transactions.

These two varieties of interactions form the environment of TNS. The domain and the environment are shown in matrix form in Figure 3.

The first row and column of the matrix in Figure 3 are the primary domain of TNS. In the framework presented above, all interactions that emanate from or end at a firm are defined to be within the domain of TNS. Also, since governments and IGO's are identified as both exogenous influences (environment) and endogenous actors (for example, S1(IS)—G1), the framework is more dynamic, multileveled and influenced by multisectoral assumptions. This according to Toyne (1989) is useful in including the modifying effects of factors such as the interaction of national markets, national industrial policies, international agreements, and international institutions.

Table 1 presents an outline of the transnational model and its constituent components. Different transactions are summarized, and this scheme is

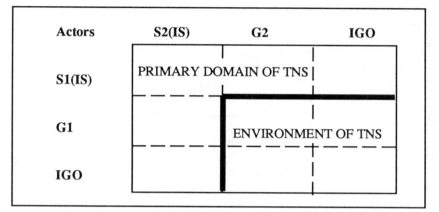

Figure 3: The Domain and Environment of TNS

followed in this chapter.

IS issues important to intra-corporate transactions relate to the design of parent-subsidiary IS interface. Some representative questions are: Given the organizational structure and strategy of the corporation, what is the role of subsidiary IS? What is the IS architecture most suited for the global corporation and the subsidiary?

IS functions pertaining to transactions with an inter-governmental body deal with questions of international standardization and regulation, for example, in the area of telecommunications. The user community's input into such areas is necessary to avoid restrictive national business practices; for example, those resulting from incompatible standards.

Some countries, especially developing countries, are wary of information technologies and restrict their use by MNCs within their boundaries. This skepticism arises from three sets of issues shown in Table 1—political, economic, technological, and socio-cultural issues. For example, e-mail is a primary tool for global firms; however, it is not available in most developing countries. Matters relating to the choice of technology and systems under these conditions are included in IS issues pertaining to host-governmental transactions. Reactive transnational interactions relate to matters of regulatory oversight and public policy in response to transnational activities. One example of IS issues under this category is the review of proposed European Community (EC) IT and telecommunications standards by the U.S. user community and the actions of the United States Trade Representative thereof. Other examples relate to input into the General Agreements on Tariffs and Trade (GATT) negotiation process and the International Telecommunication Union (ITU) regulations through national governments.

Several studies can be identified within each of the above categories. These are shown in Figure 4.

1. **Intra-Corporate Transactions**
   a. Pertaining to the IS function only
      i. Organizational Linkage
      ii. Architectural Linkage
         1. Data subarchitecture
         2. Applications subarchitecture
         3. Communications subarchitecture
         4. Technology subarchitecture
      iii. Personnel Linkage
   b. Pertaining to the support function of IS

2. **Transactions with an inter-government body**
   a. Technical Issues
   b. Regulatory Issues

3. **Host Government Transactions**
   a. Political Issues
   National security, access to information resources, free access to information, trans-border data flows.
   b. Economic Issues
   Protection of intellectual property rights, ownership of information, value of information, taxation of information.
   c. Technological Issues
   Governing the use of communication facilities, technology transfers.
   d. Socio-Cultural Issues
   Protection of the needs of the individual versus the needs of the society, NWICO.

4. **Reactive Transnational Interactions**
   Formulation of national information policy especially in response to differences in policies in other countries and their impact on the transnational interaction of the firm.

5. **Environment of TNS**
   a. Bilateral Agreements
      i. Canada-U.S. Free Trade Agreement
      ii. U.S.-Israel Agreement
   b. Regional Agreements
      i. OECD Guidelines for Data Protection
   c. Multilateral Agreements
      i. Services in the GATT Framework

Table 1: Components of the Domain and Environment of TNS

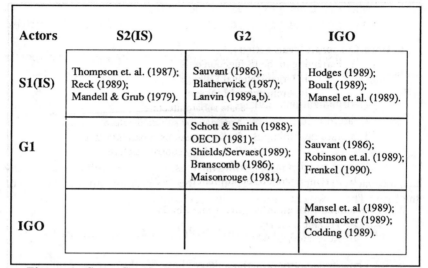

Actors	S2(IS)	G2	IGO
S1(IS)	Thompson et. al. (1987); Reck (1989); Mandell & Grub (1979).	Sauvant (1986); Blatherwick (1987); Lanvin (1989a,b).	Hodges (1989); Boult (1989); Mansel et. al. (1989).
G1		Schott & Smith (1988); OECD (1981); Shields/Servaes(1989); Branscomb (1986); Maisonrouge (1981).	Sauvant (1986); Robinson et.al. (1989); Frenkel (1990).
IGO			Mansel et. al (1989); Mestmacker (1989); Codding (1989).

Figure 4: Some Studies in the Domain and Environment of TNS

THE COMPONENTS OF TRANSNATIONAL SYSTEMS

This section develops each of the transactions mentioned above in detail and the IS issues related to each transaction. There is a greater degree of emphasis on intra-corporate transactions, primarily because of its importance.

Intra-Corporate Transactions

Intra-corporate transactions provide the interface between the corporate unit and its overseas subsidiaries. The primary function of this interface is to:

1. organize subsidiary operations such that they are in congruence with the operations of the parent;

2. render more effective corporate planning and the deployment of IS and personnel, while maintaining sensitivity to local characteristics of the subsidiaries; and

3. integrate subsidiary operations into corporate "architectures" to attain efficiencies.

IS issues related to intra-corporate transactions follow from the above and, as can be seen from Table 1, may be dichotomized into:

•those pertaining to the IS function only; and
•those pertaining to the role of IS in supporting business objectives.

The first type (IS only) refers to the means with which the corporate IS unit links with the subsidiary IS unit. These can be separated into:

1. organizational linkages;
2. architectural linkages; and
3. personnel linkages.

The second type (supporting business objectives) refers to the means and the extent to which TNS contribute to the global competitive advantage of the firm. These two categories are considered next.

Transactions Pertaining Solely to the IS function

These transactions are the linkages between the corporate unit and the subsidiary IS unit. By linkages we imply relationships within separate areas which are open to the specification of scope and strength of the relationship. For example, one component of organizational linkage is subsidiary participation in the corporate strategic planning process; "participation scope" refers to areas in which the subsidiary participates while "participation strength" refers to the subsidiary's degree of involvement. As shown in Table 1, linkages may be categorized into three types - Organizational, Architectural, and Personnel - and are explained below.

Organizational Linkages. Organizational linkages refer to the design of subsidiary IS organizational structure, control systems and reporting procedures as well as the subsidiary's participation in the functions of the corporation as a whole.

Several variables must be taken into account when organizing subsidiary IS functions. Based on study by Egelhoff (1989), these may be divided into company-specific or subsidiary-specific variables. Company-level variables include organizational structure and organizational strategy (Weill & Olson, 1989). Some subsidiary-specific variables are the information dependency of the subsidiary, the importance of the subsidiary, and the ownership of the subsidiary.

Several past studies have concluded there is no standard organizational structure for multinational operations and that organizational structure varies with business conditions. For example, Franko (1974) notes that organizational changes in European companies have typically occurred as a result of specific changes in the competitive environment. Davis (1976) traces the general patterns of organizations as a stage model starting with an export division, graduating to an international division, and then to a global product structure. Similar studies by Keegan (1974), and Stopford & Wells (1972) have shown a wide variation in organizational structures. Egelhoff (1989) summarizes the various types of organizational structures as functional divisions, international divisions, geographical regions, and product divisions.

There have also been different conceptualizations of global strategy. Porter (1986) categorizes international strategies on the basis of two factors: (1) the configuration of activities; and (2) their coordination. Configuration refers to the location in the world where each activity in the value chain is performed. Coordination refers to how these activities in different countries are coordinated. Based on these two factors, four dimensions of strategy are identified. These are: (1) an export-based strategy; (2) a country-centered strategy; (3) a simple global strategy; and (4) a complex global strategy. Other taxonomies of global strategies include Fayerweather's (1980) four strategy patterns (the dynamic high-tech model, the low-or-stable technology model, the advanced management skill model, and the unified logistic labor-transmission model) and Herbert's (1984) four general strategies (volume expansion, resource acquisition, reciprocity, and integrated operations).

Egelhoff (1989) notes that information dependency of the subsidiary may have a significant effect on the design of the parent-subsidiary interface. Information dependency refers to the dependence of the subsidiary on the parent for information regarding functions such as marketing, manufacturing, product design, and technology.

The importance of the subsidiary refers to the knowledge contribution of the subsidiary to the corporation, also called intra-corporate knowledge flows (Gupta & Govindrajan, 1989). Knowledge contribution is through a flow of skills, capabilities, and strategic value across the parent-subsidiary interface. Subsidiaries may thus be divided into the following categories based on knowledge flows: global innovator, where the subsidiary is an important source of knowledge to other units; integrated player, where the subsidiary has a high level of knowledge about input as well as output; implementer, where the subsidiary depends on the parent for knowledge; and local innovator, where the subsidiary develops its own knowledge for use in its local environment.

The last factor of importance is that of subsidiary ownership. Ownership can range from 100%-owned by the parent to joint ventures with a foreign firm. Several ownership formats exist, with each differing by the extent to which the parent has control over the subsidiary.

Having identified the above variables, we next discuss their impact on the organization of IS functions. Given the nature of organizational linkages, what can we infer regarding IS? A primary inference is that a variety of variables (organizational structure, strategy, product diversity, and the subsidiary's information dependency, importance, and ownership) may affect

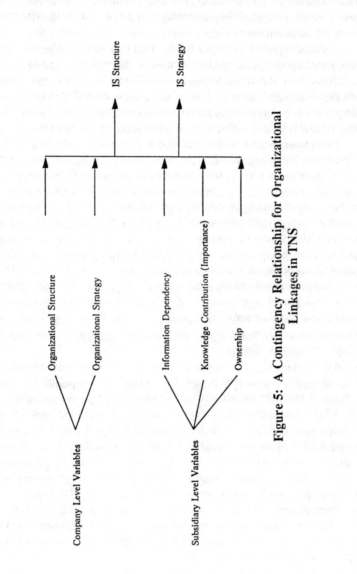

Figure 5: A Contingency Relationship for Organizational Linkages in TNS

the parent-subsidiary IS relationship. The major result of the above discussion on organizational linkage is the formulation of a classical MIS contingency relation of the form shown in Figure 5.

Although the relationship in the figure is driven by two sets of variables, those variables cannot be taken to be independent. For example, a greater information dependency of the subsidiary would perhaps dictate a different organizational strategy than if the information dependency of the subsidiary were low. Further, the figure shows only those variables of interest to organizational linkages and is later expanded to include other transactions.

Three studies can be noted that have followed a contingency approach as in Figure 5, while using different dimensions of strategy and structure.

In, perhaps, the first study to relate IS design variables to multinational strategy, Thompson et al. (1989) describe the changes in IS focus and policies based on the business strategy planned and followed by international corporations. They propose three models as international business strategies: empire - in which foreign subsidiaries operate as branch offices with their activities dictated by corporate headquarters; United Nations - in which a multinational corporation manages its activities like a portfolio and the corporate headquarters facilitates business strategy but lacks the power to enforce it; and global war games - in which international operations are integrated and a firm's competitive position in one country is significantly influenced by its position in other countries. The above strategies dictate IS management concerns. Thus, IS organizational structure in an Empire must be hierarchical; decentralized in United Nations; and matrix in Global War Games. Similarly IS planning is centralized in an Empire, decentralized in United Nations, and dispersed in Global War Games. In a very similar analysis, Reck (1989) proposes three multinational strategies: imperialistic, multidomestic, and global. IS, then, must be organized differently for each strategy. For example, IS organizational structure must be hierarchical for an imperialistic firm, decentralized for a multidomestic firm, and matrix for a global firm. Similarly, IS planning must be centralized for an imperialistic firm, decentralized for a multidomestic firm, and dispersed for a global firm.

Panepinto (1990) reviews a research study to note that firms may choose one of four major architectural alternatives depending on their preferred style of management. Thus a company that prefers a centralized management structure should design a global information system that maintains most functions at a central site, while a company that prefers a more loose management matrix should push data processing and network management out to different regional units.

While the above studies have been important steps towards understanding TNS, it must be noted that just as the empirical testing of the existence of these stages is lacking, so is their influence on IS variables. For example, there has been considerable focus on the centralize-decentralize design dimension. Pantages (1989) notes that centralization is the norm in the highly successful Texas Instruments worldwide system. Similar characteristics are noted by Mees (1981), and more cautiously by Kerr (1989), who points out that "Where the power lies within a corporation is an important factor in the globalization process." On the other hand, Main (1989) uses the term "glocalize" to discuss the need for local responsiveness and decentralized decision making. The extent to which the corporate office controls the strategies and operations of its overseas subsidiaries and the appropriate mechanism to achieve headquarters control have also been discussed by other studies, such as those by Doz & Prahalad (1981) and Dyment (1987). They note that the complexity of environment demands greater control whereas pressures to be responsive to local environment demand decentralization.

The implications are not restricted to the corporate office. Kerr (1989) describes the change in IS personnel relationships as they grow closer to the end-users in independent business units (IBU's) at the cost of corporate IS strategies. An extension of this argument to the area of TNS, where subsidiary units are in a different environment, may lead corporate IS to reformulate their corporate strategies. From a theoretical perspective, the concept of multiple loyalties in an international organization was first reported by Guetzkow (1955). Loyalties to the home unit versus loyalties to the international organization was the primary thesis of his report which discussed how the functioning of an international unit can be strengthened by moving away from national loyalties. By an adaptation of this theory, we can speculate that adherence to subsidiary norms may hinder the progress of central IS strategies.

ii. Architectural Linkages. Under architectural linkage we consider four IS subarchitectures: Data, Application, Communication, and Technology (Wardle, 1984). Data subarchitecture refers to the classification and organization of data resources; application subarchitecture addresses the current and future applications in the company; communications subarchitecture deals with the flow of data within the organization and with the outside world; technology subarchitecture addresses the relationship of hardware devices and systems software forming the technological infrastructure.

The content of the subsidiary's database is a vital input to the corporation. Data subarchitecture deals with the format of the database content maintained by the subsidiary. Mandell & Grub (1979) classify the subsidiary database into standardized, quasi-standardized, and free form depending upon whether there is complete corporate specification of information, standardization in certain functional areas, or total database dependency. The standardization of codes is another area of concern, and it may also fall anywhere in the standardized-nonstandardized continuum. The need to coordinate data structures and the management of databases in a universal fashion across various functions and subsidiary units is stipulated as the primary function of data subarchitectures.

Under application subarchitecture we note that the application software for overseas locations is often slow and poorly supported (Datamation, April 1, 1988). One option noted by Cash et al. (1988) is the use of applications developed at the corporate headquarters with modifications for location-specific hardware and processing requirements. Standardization of applications has also been observed for organizations such as Federal Express (Runyan, 1989; Pantages, 1989). However, organizations such as Rhone-Paulene grant considerable freedom to subsidiaries to develop their own applications. The achievement of an integrated computing environment in a multinational corporation is then the focus of the application subarchitecture. It depends upon such factors as the in-house development and support of applications versus subscription to external vendors.

Communications subarchitecture relates to the theme of integrating communications facilities and the emphasis on connectivity which are perhaps nowhere so evident as in a transnational corporation. The integration of voice and data technologies is a business imperative in the international environment, yet organizational and technical obstacles may persist (Datamation, April 1, 1988). Some of these are the integration of the telecommunications group with the IS group by resolving personality problems between the two groups, and the choice of leased versus public switched networks.

Studies such as that by King & Premkumar (1989) have outlined factors pertinent to telecommunications planning. These are: business factors, technology factors, organizational factors, and environmental factors. In addition to these, several areas of concern when developing an international communications strategy can be subsumed under country specific factors. Some of these are: (1) compatibility of equipment; (2) differences in operating standards; (3) communications infrastructure of the country (voice vs. data lines; leased lines); (4) the telecommunications regulatory regime (private vs. PTT); and (5) services offered by local telecommunications companies.

Several authors have also noted the use and benefits of the use of electronic data interchange (EDI) and the probable advantages from integrated services digital network (ISDN) (Szewczak & Snodgrass, 1989). Others have noted practical problems with the use of EDI. Purton (1989a) mentions, in particular, the problems of standardization, security and illegal access to networks. Etheridge (1988) notes the costs involved in up-front development and installation as well as those of network operation. Other authors have mentioned the lack of standards across countries for EDI. For example, the West German Teletex administered by the Deutsche Bundespost, the GTDI (Guidelines for Trade Data Interchange), and the EDIFACT (Electronic Data Interchange for Administration, Commerce, and Transport) used in the rest of

Europe show significant differences. Similar problems exist with the ISDN, which differs in such areas as in signaling protocols (Purton, 1989b).

The choice of hardware and the need for standardization across units are the most noted issues in the technical subarchitecture. Incompatibility of equipment, for example, was noted as a main concern by the Telecommunications Roundtable (Datamation, 1988). Runyan (1989) notes the examples of companies such as Federal Express which use the IBM AS/400 as a current computer of choice across subsidiary units. In opposition to the need for standardized hardware is the need for local support. For example, Marriott Corporation opted for NCR point-of-sale systems in Poland since IBM could not be supported locally (Runyan, 1989). This lack of integration techniques and products is preventing many organizations around the world from progressing with the implementation of new technologies and the use of IS in end-user environments.

With the wide variations in systems availability across units, subscription to common standards such as Open Systems Interconnections has been accelerated by registration with the International Standards Organization. The concept of open systems promises the advantages of flexibility and cooperative processing between dissimilar systems and is a major source of competitive advantage. The European Commission, for example, created in 1981 an Open Systems Interconnections-based open systems platform for the European community. Similar steps are under way with the Software Industrial Generalization and Maintenance Aids project, launched by Japan's Ministry of International Trade and Industry.

iii. Personnel Linkages. This area refers to the functions of planning and staffing, appraisal and compensation, selection and socialization of IS personnel in subsidiaries. Three major issues have been noted by Schneider (1988) in human resource management for multinationals: differentiation versus integration; autonomy versus control; and national versus corporate boundaries. Each of these issues is equally important to the personnel function in IS.

Regarding the first issue, Kobrin (1988) notes that, all things equal, a local national who speaks the language, understands the culture and the political system, and is a member of the local elite is more effective than an expatriate employee. On the other hand, the demands for integration require that employees identify with firm-wide rather than with local objectives. The second issue is that of autonomy versus control. There is a certain need for a subsidiary to be autonomous, and excessive control may cause severe morale problems and resistance. However, a multinational requires up-to-date information on a large number of local environments and an understanding of how local conditions affect the worldwide system. This presupposes a greater degree of corporate control over subsidiaries. Thirdly, in order to develop a strong corporate loyalty, multinationals often resort to frequent and multiple transfers. However, this often results in the erosion of national identity in favor of corporate identity (Schneider, 1988). Authors such as Sweet (1990) have firmly advocated the hiring of local personnel when installing or operating international networks. He notes, "One way to help ensure the success of an international project is to involve local people. They know the language, the culture and are more easily accepted than staff from the U.S." (p. 29).

Transactions Pertaining to the Role of IS in Supporting Corporate Objectives

Managing IT for competitive advantage has been the thrust of several studies in the IS area, and several frameworks deal with the means by which IT may be used to achieve sustainable advantage. Most of these frameworks have adapted the Porter models of competitive forces (1980) and value chain (1985) in order to show the impact of IT on the five competitive forces (customers, suppliers, competitors, substitutes, and barriers to entry), three strategies (cost leadership, product differential, and focus), and the value-added chain. Other approaches have used different frameworks. These include a focus on information resource assessment (King, 1984) and the customer resource lifecycle (Ives & Learmonth, 1986).

Few authors have, however, explored the link between IT and global competitive advantage. Grant (1989) notes the extent to which IT has allowed firms to provide services internationally and observes that "Information technologies have nullified the imperative of a physical presence and, in doing so, have opened up vast possibilities" (p. 103). IT has made feasible the provision of transnational services in sectors such as agriculture, education, health, transportation and financial services. Firms that can exploit such opportunities can develop considerable competitive advantage. Dyment (1987) contends that time (doing things faster) is one source of strategic advantage. As noted by Merrills (1989), this strategy is used by firms such as Northern Telecom. Within multinationals, the use of technologies such as electronic funds transfers and electronic data integration (Tate, 1989) are based on the same principle. As noted by Mees (1981), an automated system not only speeds up the flow of money but provides the information necessary to control the cash and preserve it for the company as long as possible. For example, the basis of Reuters' strategy is the breadth of its databases, its constantly developing communication network and the provision of real time news and data.

While most of the above studies have reported examples of transactions, there is a lack of a theoretical framework to understand the role of TNS in global competitive advantage. Perhaps one reason for the lack of studies is that the concept of global competitive advantage is itself not well developed. Some representative studies and their implications for IT are reviewed here.

Global competitive advantage can be segregated into location-specific comparative advantage and firm-specific competitive advantage (Kogut, 1985). The first is based on the fact that different factor costs exist across countries and lower costs of a factor in one country relative to another favor the industries that use this factor intensively. Firm-specific competitive advantage is obtained through some proprietary characteristic of the firm. In a similar analysis, Shanks (1982) notes that global competition is an interaction of two sets of factors: economic advantages and strategic strengths (company-controlled factors).

The bifurcation of global competitive advantage into competitive and comparative advantages presents several possibilities. Firms that operate in same/similar countries cannot exploit comparative advantage sources. In such cases IT must focus on maintaining firm-specific competitive advantage. The transfer of systems that have been used at the home of the parent can be one option, although this presupposes a lack of barriers (regulation, technology, market structure). On the other hand, similar firms that operate in different countries cannot exploit competitive advantage. However, since they operate in different environments, IT must focus on sources of comparative advantage. Patterns of sourcing and a focus on logistics are examples of targets for exploiting comparative advantage. Finally, a model where firms operate in an environment with both comparative and competitive advantages generates a complex pattern of activities. As noted by Kogut (1985), sources of global comparative advantage are the relative superiority of configurations of locations, comparative advantages and product/market decisions. This interplay of factors must be the focus of IT.

In keeping with the above discussion, Figure 5 is expanded to include IS architecture and the management of IS personnel for the global organization. Two additional independent variables are included in the figure: industry-specific variables which determine sources of competitive advantage and country-specific variables which provide comparative advantage for global operations. The expanded framework is shown in Figure 6.

Transactions with an Inter-Governmental Body

Transactions between a corporate unit and an inter-governmental unit can take place in several areas and can be categorized as technical or regulatory. Technical interactions refer to matters such as standards while regulatory interactions refer to transactions with organizations such as the International Telecommunications Union (ITU) and matters pertaining to the General Agreement on Tariffs and Trade (GATT).

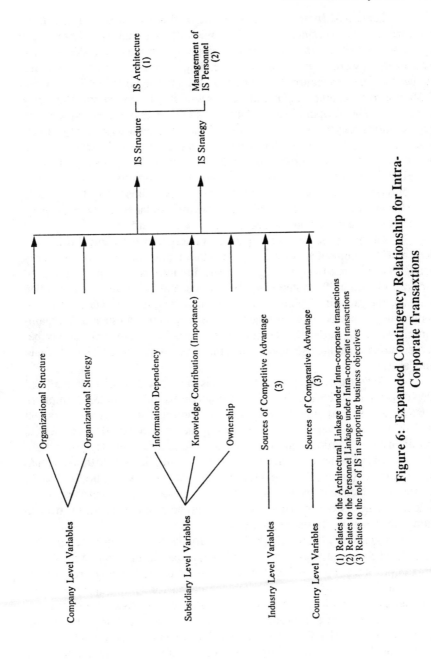

Figure 6: Expanded Contingency Relationship for Intra-Corporate Transaxtions

Technical Interactions. The role of the user in standards-setting organizations is increasing. This has been noted at a national level, for example by Hodges (1989). The trend toward open systems and the demand for interoperability are the two main forces leading to the rise of user groups such as the 486 Standardization Committee and the Open Software Foundation. Both groups are examples of organizations working toward common industry standards. The Corporation for Open Systems is another example of an organization bringing together vendors and users to establish products compatible with the Open Systems Interconnections standards. Similar examples can be seen in Europe. Boult (1989) reports the formation of a pan-European group called Istel'92 formed by the IS managers of 20 network operators in Europe. The purpose of Istel includes cross-border leased lines, Electronic Data Interchange and File Transfer and Management standards, network security, and UNIX standards as promulgated by X/Open Co. Ltd.

The need for user participation in international technical organizations and international standards implementation organizations is particularly strong, as evidenced by the high demand for international network-based services, electronic data interchange, distributed databases, the boost for open systems, the growth of global networks, data centers and data havens. A congruence of perspectives between the users, vendors and standards organizations will help in developing coherent international standards simply because consensus at the user level deters the development of different de facto standards.

ISDN has for long been forecast as the foundation of a standardized global communication system. However, incompatibilities in ISDN implementation across countries may render this promise ineffective. Crockett (1990b) reviews several of the incompatibilities which would force users to install different terminal equipment in various countries and may prevent use of advanced ISDN-based applications. What this implies for the transnational firm implementing ISDN in several countries is that it would not be able to standardize on a single vendor's terminal equipment. This would result in a lack of volume discounts on international equipment purchases and the need to train employees on multiple systems.

Regulatory Interactions. Various regulatory systems are also in existence. The international telecommunications regime anchored in the ITU is an example of the coordination of telecommunication activities and regulation. The 13th ITU plenipotentiary conference called for setting up appropriate national and international mechanisms to formulate and review telecommunications policies. The same report also noted that delegates from 30 countries appeared to accept that ITU should be involved in policy issues at national and international levels. This is largely because compatibility requirements for networks and services rests on, at least, de facto standards and minimally consistent patterns of behavior, which are notably different among geographical and national territories.

While members of the ITU recognized telecommunications as a strategic asset, telecommunications and IT issues have also been prominent at the negotiations of the GATT—the international trade regime. The telecommunications annex, currently under review under GATT, is designed to establish the first set of network regulations requiring carriers to adopt reforms beneficial to users.

A consistent pattern of international technical and regulatory practices is a prerequisite to information services and information transfers required by a global firm. A major advantage to transnational firms from this provision would be a greater choice of private-line services, reduced prices, greater choice of equipment vendors, ability to resell network services and build shared networks, and the use of proprietary private network standards. A second benefit is noted by Crockett (1990a), who quotes Edward Regan, vice president of strategic network planning for Manufacturers Hanover Trust Company: "Anything we do to cut the cost of international telecommunications and make it easier to build international networks would flow directly to our company's bottom line... This treaty [GATT telecommunications annex] could give the U.S. a competitive advantage. It would make it easier to deploy international network services, which is something U.S. companies excel at" (p. 45).

Another benefit of global telecommunications liberalization to transnational users is that of using their home market experience to their advantage in foreign markets. For example, as a Network World (1990) editorial notes, U.S. firms have grown accustomed to using private networks and IT to support their business strategy. This, however, is impossible to do in a country which does not permit private networks or makes such usage extremely costly. Network-based inter-organizational systems which have been a major source of competitive advantage in the U.S. may well be technically infeasible in countries with monopoly telecommunications regimes. Therefore reforms as postulated by ITU and GATT can prove to be of significant advantage to U.S. users.

Finally, we need to note that the manner in which interactions such as those above can be facilitated is unclear. User interest groups for IT and their role in formulation and agenda setting are areas not discussed in past research but are certainly important for further study.

Host-Government Transactions

The essence of host-government transactions is the effect of information technology on the state and the corresponding reactions of states to the introduction, use and development of information technology. Both the effect of IT and the reactive stance adopted by states are dependent on factors such as national industrial development, national IT sector development, and the capabilities of regulatory organizations.

We categorize issues pertinent to this section into four broad issue areas: political, economic, technological, and socio-cultural.

National sovereignty is perhaps at the core of political issues concerning IT. Sovereignty implies the right of a nation over its resources and over matters of ownership, distribution, and use of these resources. Insofar as information is a national resource, IT (such as remote sensing by satellite, direct broadcast by satellite, and TNS) renders the national control of information ineffective. The second political concern is that of intrafirm transborder data flows. Multinational firms, mostly headquartered in developed countries, are thought to have the ability to control global operations including those in less developed areas through the use of IT. This is construed to mean that there is no transfer of management expertise or IT-generated benefits to the less-developed nations. This further implies that developing countries become more dependent upon nations with greater IT development and consequently less sovereign.

Economic issues relate to the development of indigenous IT industries, productivity and employment, and trade issues. Many nations have adopted restrictive policies against MNCs in order to encourage the development of indigenous industry. This is especially true of the IT sector. In addition, the emphasis in developing countries has been on the acquisition of technology to support developmental strategies. While it is recognized that IT improves productivity in all economic sectors, concerns for immediate technological unemployment and displacement have often hindered the adoption of IT by developing nations. Another reason for a slower adoption process is the restriction these countries apply to foreign direct investment (FDI). The nature of information products and services (for example, their intangibility) makes some degree of FDI essential. For example, computer software can be traded; however, in order to support it, the supplying company would need some kind of presence in the importing country. With the increase of IT services and their trade, the requirements for FDI have become even greater. As Leeson (1984) points out, "IT may shift the structure of international commercial relations away from traditional export and import patterns and towards the establishment of foreign subsidiaries through foreign direct investment" (p. 109). However, as noted earlier, FDI policies in developing countries often prove to be at odds with IT trade requirements.

Technological issues relate to the differential development of IT resources among countries and its impact upon the industrial competitiveness of a country. Within developing countries, technological concerns emanate from fears that they may become dumping grounds for obsolete technologies and be denied access to international markets and networks. The lack of a communication infrastructure in these countries connotes their dependence on MNCs and world markets for appropriate technology. This often results in concerns that IT is increasing the tendency for worldwide centralization or concentration of information and technology in a few countries. Moreover, as service sector activities become more global, access to international networks becomes imperative and this need further exacerbates the differences among countries. For example, Riddle (1988) notes that the SWIFT network has few links in developing areas. Similar is the case of major worldwide news agency networks. Even though developing countries have demanded and obtained reduced rate access to international networks, the tendency among these countries has been towards restrictive IT related policies and protectionism.

As an example of socio-cultural issues, a study by Parthasarathi (1988) describes some issues in the use of IT in India. Using an example from the banking industry in India, he writes:

> The most decisive factor in computerization in banks [in India] has been the willingness of the various employee[s] unions. At present, unions have agreed to install a maximum of 3,500 computers by September, 1987, for front-line operations in branches handling 1,000 vouchers or more per day. This will cover about 1,200 branches. The unions have also agreed to allow the use of machines of memory capacity up to 256 KB for banking operations in the branches. In return, the IBA [Indian Banks Association] has offered Rs. 350 per month as a special allowance to employees handling such machines. The bank management are keen to install 2,500 additional machines before September, 1988, and another 2,500 before September, 1989, covering about 4,800 bank branches in three states. (p. 55)

Perhaps this is an extreme example of restrictive IT practices, but it does point out that transnational firms need to coordinate business practices with host government policies and social group interests.

Reactive Transnational Interactions

Reactive transnational interactions include the formulation of national information policy especially as applied to changes required by policy actions in other countries and their impact on domestic firms.

For example, the National Telecommunications and Information Administration (NTIA), in formulating an outline for U.S. policy (NTIA, 1983), called for an extensive role of the private sector in policy development and noted that "as direct beneficiaries or victims of many policy decisions, private firms have a critical stake in the nature and effectiveness of governmental decision making." (1983, p. 25). Several goals were noted by the report.

These include the free flow of information worldwide; a free and competitive marketplace for telecommunications and information services, equipment, and facilities; and non-political international organizations. Many of these proposals were included in the Telecommunications Trade Act of 1988 (U.S. Congress, 1988), which called for ensuring the international right of attachment, right to market, right of access, transparency, and non-discrimination in the international provision of services.

Similar actions can also be seen in various technical areas. One example is the work of the United States Council for International Business. The Council represents American business interests in the major inter-governmental institutions and to the Executive and Legislative branches of the U.S. government. The Council, for example, extensively reviewed the European Commission's Green Paper on the Development of the Common Market for Telecommunications Services and Equipment (United States Council of International Business, 1988) and suggested a review of a number of revisions in the Open Network Provision (ONP) proposed by the European Commission.

THE ENVIRONMENT OF TRANSNATIONAL SYSTEMS

In this section we will examine the two transactions: inter-governmental (G1—G2), and government-IGO (G1—IGO) that make up the TNS environment (as shown in Figure 2). These transactions primarily translate into bilateral, regional, and multilateral negotiations regarding issues which deal directly or indirectly with IT.

Before summarizing trade negotiations, we need to discuss how IT relates to governmental agreements.

The fundamental use of IT is in the provision of services. This use can be thought of in terms of: (1) the provision of specialized information, i.e. applications; and (2) the telecommunications infrastructure which transports this specialized information to the user. When these services cross national boundaries, we speak of trade in services. Services trade and the role of IT in this trade has been increasing over the past few years. However, while international (bilateral, regional, and multilateral) agreements exist for regulating the trade-in-goods, none or few exist for services. Hence, the emphasis since 1980 has been on developing a framework to regulate their trade. IT as a provider of services, constitutes a core issue area in all services agreements. For example, the telecommunications annex currently under review by GATT negotiations requires regulators to permit the unrestricted movement, storage, and processing of information across national borders. Similar requirements can be seen in other international agreements and some of these are summarized below.

The bilateral negotiations between Canada and the U.S. resulted in the signing of the Free Trade Agreement (FTA) in 1988. The FTA incorporates provisions that cover transactions in services. The computer and telecommunications services agreement is the most extensive of the sectoral pacts. This will provide non-discriminatory access by add-on users to the basic systems; maintain existing rights of access; and limit anti-competitive practices. The agreement also contains provisions with regard to transborder data flows and access to databanks (Schott & Smith, 1988). Transborder data flows have been an issue in bilateral relations. For example, in a statement before the Subcommittee on Telecommunication, Consumer Protection, and Finance (U.S. Congress, 1981), Oswald Ganley noted that of special concern to the American business community is Paragraph 157(4) of the Canadian Banks and Banking Law Revision Act, 1980, which requires data processing of all primary records in Canada.

Another example of bilateral agreement on services is the agreement between the U.S. and Israel concluded in 1985. The agreement deals with goods and a separate article relates to services in general.

At a regional level, the Organization for Economic Cooperation and Development (OECD) has taken several steps to build an understanding of services. Several sectoral studies have been instituted to identify barriers to trade in services and transborder flow of data. For example, in 1981 the OECD Member Countries developed guidelines to harmonize national privacy legislation and ensure international flow of data. In addition, the U.S. proposed a draft text of a TDF Declaration in January, 1982. In 1985, a revised version of this text of The Declaration on Transborder Data Flows was adopted by the OECD Council of Ministers. The Declaration calls for promoting access to data, seeking transparency in policies relating to services, and developing common approaches when dealing with issues related to TDF.

At the multilateral level, the emphasis has been on the inclusion of services in the GATT. GATT has traditionally dealt with trade in goods. The idea of services was first raised by the United States in the Trade Act of 1974 which included services in the concept of international trade. The U.S. campaign in 1982 for the inclusion of services was strongly opposed by the developing countries. The opposition arose from two concerns: the legal incompetence of the GATT in services; and the inapplicability of the rules of the GATT to services. Finally, the Ministerial Meeting in Punta del Este, Uruguay, in September, 1986, agreed to establish a 'parallel-track' negotiation on trade-in-services.

The primary objective of international trade negotiations is to provide firms with a fair and free environment to carry out commercial transactions. Within this perspective telecommunications, data, and information services constitute a primary service sector since they govern the infrastructure within which many other services are traded.

IMPLICATIONS FOR FUTURE RESEARCH

Several types of both descriptive and normative studies can be conducted for each constituent transaction category in the framework of Figure 2. These studies can be confined to a single dimension or discuss multiple dimensions. For example, studies within intra-corporate transactions can focus on the identification and verification of variables that affect the parent-subsidiary interface. Similarly, studies pertaining to host-government transactions can focus on strategies for dealing with host governments with respect to the introduction of IT and how this choice reinforces or opposes national IT policies. What conflicts are faced by transnational firms and how are these resolved? — are some representative questions.

Research can also address interaction among dimensions. For example, some representative areas are the impact of host-government policies in designing IS interfaces between the parent and the subsidiary. How does the IT policy in a country force a firm to alter the way in which it does business? Does this lead to a loss of competitive advantage for the firm?

Another classification scheme for research studies can be developed based on categories developed by Toyne (1989). Based on his work, three types of studies can be proposed: (a) Work Coordination Studies; (b) Domain Consensus Studies and (c) Ideological Consensus Studies. Although a more abstract distinction, this categorization provides a rigorous discussion of the ideas presented earlier. These categories are discussed below. In addition, several past studies which can be thought of as representative in each category are noted as examples in order to clarify each type of study.

Work coordination refers to the patterns of exchanges, cooperation, and coordination agreed to by international exchange actors (Toyne, 1989). This includes, for example, studies dealing with the nature of subsidiary involvement, which systems operate at the local level and which at the global level; and what vendors are used where. For example, Carlyle (1988) described the use of EDI and SQL in a large multinational; while Kelley (1980) recommended that IS should choose hardware vendors who can provide services and support globally. At the national level, work coordination studies deal with issues such as local content regulations. For example, Sauvant (1986) describes the nature of the informatics policy of Brazil and its effect on transborder data flows. Lanvin (1989a, b) considered several factors that need to be considered in order to allow for a productive integration of developing countries in the network economy.

Toyne (1989) defines domain consensus as the result of the interaction of economic, social, and political considerations and the exercise of influence by one or more actors. Thus, domain consensus refers to such things as the level and intensity of competition for the exchange. For example, Buss (1982) notes that IS management in international information processing can range from "not involved" to "totally responsible", with all shades in between. Selig (1982) developed a six-phase process for multinational IS planning. At a national level, interactions with inter-governmental organizations are some examples of domain consensus studies. The study by Mansell et al. (1989) notes the extent to which patterns of behavior among countries must change in order to take advantage of telecommunications in developing strategic advantage for users.

Ideological consensus refers to the agreement among exchange participants concerning the nature of an exchange (Toyne, 1989). Some examples are the degree of agreement concerning the stability, fairness and predictability of relationships, and the effectiveness and efficiency of interorganizational relationships. Schneider (1988) describes how MNC's often resort to frequent transfers of personnel in order to develop strong corporate loyalty. Kobrin (1988), however, shows that this leads to a lack of understanding of local conditions. At a national level, the MacBride Report (UNESCO, 1980) describes the disparate views among developing and developed countries regarding the concentration of news media and information technology. Lanvin (1989a, b), in a similar context, describes the change that must occur in order for the developing countries to overcome their fear of network monopolization.

The above three categories are some examples of the type of studies that can occur in each transaction type of the framework.

CONCLUSION

Naisbitt and Aburdene write in Megatrends 2000 (1990):

The movement to global free trade is being driven by an alliance between telecommunications and economics that permits you to deal with a business associate in a Tokyo office from a mountain perch in Colorado as if you were across a table - sharing conversation and documents... We are laying the foundation for an international information highway system. In telecommunications we are moving to a single worldwide information network, just as economically we are becoming one global marketplace. We are moving toward the capability to communicate anything to anyone, anywhere, by any form - voice, data, text, or image - at the speed of light (p. 23).

At the center of the global economy is the transnational firm which is and will continue to be the focal point for the convergence of transnational theory, political-economic propositions, and international business guidelines. Information and communications systems are a core technology for the transnational enterprise and as such demand a more integrated and rigorous analysis than that undertaken in the past.

This chapter is one step towards this goal. Based on a general framework of international relations, we have proposed a definition for TNS and specified the domain and environment of these systems. By identifying a significant number of variables, the chapter presents a broad perspective of the many relationships that exist in the global environment and impact IS. What is needed next is some ordering of these variables and an analysis of their interdependence. The several classifications of future research areas developed in this chapter can be particularly useful in doing so. Not only do we propose descriptive, normative studies but also suggest a more rigorous analysis in work coordination, domain consensus and ideological consensus studies.

Finally, the research framework presented here can be used directly or adapted for several empirical studies, and it is hoped that further research in each of the areas identified in this chapter can serve to develop an integrated theory of the transnational systems and technology.

References

Arthur Young. (1989). *The landmark MIT study: management in the 1990s.*

Blatherwick, D.E.S. (1987). *The international politics of telecommunications.* Berkeley: University of California.

Boult, R. (1989, September 1). Europe's one-stop telecommunications market. *Datamation, 64-*17.

Branscomb, A.W. (1986). Global governance of global networks. In Branscomb, A.W. (Ed.), *Towards a law of global communications networks.* New York: Longman.

Buss, M.J. (1982). Managing international information systems. *Harvard Business Review,* 153-162.

Carlyle, R.E. (1988, March 1). Managing IS at multinationals. *Datamation,* 1-4.

Cash, J.I., Jr., McFarlan, F.W., & McKenney, J.L. (1988). *Corporate information systems management: the issues facing senior executives.* Irwin.

Codding, G.A. (1989). Financing development assistance in the ITU. *Telecommunications Policy,* 13-24.

Crockett, B. (1990a, May 21). Treaty could reform international network rules. *Network World*, 43, 44.

Crockett, B. (1990b, March 26). Different flavors of ISDN hamper global net users. *Network World*, 1, 45.

Davis, S.M. (1976). Trends in the organization of multinational corporations. *Columbia Journal of World Business*, 59-71.

Doz, Y.L., & Prahalad, C.K. (1981). Headquarters influence and strategic control in MNC's. *Sloan Management Review*, 15-29.

Dyment, J.J. (1987). Strategies of management controls for global corporations. *The Journal of Business Strategy*, 7(4), 20-26.

Egelhoff, W.G. (1989). *Organizing the multinational enterprise.* Ballinger Publishing Co.

Eom, H.B., Lee, S.M., Snyder, C.A., & Ford, F.N. (1987-88). A multiple criteria decision support system for global financial planning. *Journal of Management Information Systems*, 94-113.

Etheridge, J. (1988, October 1). EDI In Europe. *Datamation*, 14-15.

European regulatory reform stands to benefit U.S. users. (1990, March 26). *Network World*, 22.

Fayerweather, J. (1980). *Management of international operations.* New York: McGraw-Hill.

Franko, L. (1974). The move toward a multidivisional structure in European organization. *Administrative Science Quarterly, 19*(4), 493-506.

Frenkel, K.A. (1990). The politics of standards and the EC. *Communications of the ACM, 33*(7), 40-51.

GATT. (1987). Ministerial declaration of the Uruguay round, part II: negotiations on trade in services. *Basic Instruments and Selected Documents*, 33rd Supplement, 19ff.

Grant, J.C. (1989). Global trade in services: a corporate perspective on telecommunications and data services. In Robinson, P., Sauvant, K.P., & Govitrikar, V.P. (Eds.), *Electronic highways for world trade: issues in telecommunications and data services* (pp. 701-720). Westview Press, Inc.

Guetzkow, H.S. (1955). *Multiple loyalties.* Princeton, New Jersey: Center for Research on World Politics, Princeton University.

Gupta, A.K., & Govindrajan, V. (1989). *Knowledge flows and the structure of control within multinational corporations.* Working Paper.

Herbert, T.T. (1984). Strategy of multinational organizational structure: an interorganizational relationship perspective. *Academy of Management Review, 9*(2), 259-271.

Highbarger, J. (1988, May 4). Diplomatic ties: managing a global network. *Computerworld*, 44-47.

Hodges, P. (1989, September 1). User power grows. *Datamation*, 61-64.

Ives, B., & Jarvenpaa, S.L. (1990). Global information technology: some conjectures for future research. *Proceedings of the Twenty-Third Annual Hawaii International Conference on Systems Sciences* , 127-137.

Ives, B., & Learmonth, G.P. (1986). The information system as a competitive weapon. *Communications of the ACM, 27*(12), 1193-1201.

Iyer, R.K. (1988). Information and modeling resources for decision support in global environments. *Information & Management, 14,* 67-73.

Iyer, R.K., & Schkadi, L.L. (1987). Management support systems for multinational business. *Information and Management, 12,* 59-64.

Keegan, W.J. (1974). Multinational scanning: a study of the information sources utilized by headquarters executives in multinational companies. *Administrative Science Quarterly,* 411-421.

Kelley, N. (1980). Checkpoints for international data systems. *Infosystems, 8,* 44-48.

Keohane, R.O., & Nye, J.S., Jr. (1972). *Transnational relations and world politics.* Massachusetts: Harvard Business School Press.

Kerr, S. (1989, October 15). Cutting through network control. *Datamation,* 30-34.

King, W.R. (1984). Exploiting information as a strategic business resource. *Policy and Information, 8*(1), 1-8.

King, W.R., & Premkumar, G. (1989). Key issues in telecommunications planning. *Information and Management, 17,* 255-260.

Kobrin, S.J. (1988). Expatriate reduction and strategies control in American multinational corporations. *Human Resource Management, 27*(2), 63-75.

Kogut, B. (1985). Designing global strategies: comparative and competitive value-added chains. *Sloan Management Review,* 15-28.

Lanvin B. (1989a). Economic development in global networks. *Fourth Meeting of the ThinkNet Commission,* Atlanta.

Lanvin, B. (1989b). Ethics and technology. *Workshop #4.* University of Guelph.

Leeson, K. (1984). *International communication.* The Netherlands: Elsevier Science Publishers B.V.

Main, J. (1989, August 28). How to go global - and why. *Fortune,* 70-76.

Maisonrouge, J.G. (1981). Regulation of international information flows. *The Information Society, 1*(1), 17-30.

Mandell, S.L., & Grub, P.D. (1979). Survey of multinational corporate computer-based information systems. *European Journal of Operational Research, 5,* 359-367.

Mansell, R., Morgan, K., & Holmes, P. (1989). European integration and telecommunications:

restructuring markets and institutions. Paper Presented for the European Association for Evolutionary Political Economy Conference.

Mees, P. 1981, May). How the computer helps handle the cash. *Euromoney*, 143-145.

Merrills, R. (1989). How Northern Telecom competes on time. *Harvard Business Review*, 108-114.

Mestmacker, F.J. (1989). Towards a new international telecommunications regime. *Transborder Data & Communications Reports*, 222-235.

Moore, S. (1984). Information managers must face the international communication web. *Data Management*, 30-32.

Naisbitt, J., & Aburdene, P. (1990). *Megatrends 2000. Ten new directions for the 1990s.* New York: William Morrow and Company, Inc.

NTIA. (1983). *Long range goals in international telecommunications & information: an outline for U.S. policy*, Committee Print, S.Prt. 98-22.

OECD. (1981). *Guidelines on the protection of privacy and transborder flows of personal data.*

Panepinto, J. (1990, May 29). Management style dictates form of global networks. *Network World, 7*(22), pp. 29-31.

Pantages, A. (1989, September 1). TI's global window. *Datamation*, 49-52.

Parthasarathi, A. (1988). Informatics for development: the Indian experience. In Haq, K. (Ed.), *Informatics for development. the new challenge.* , 41-83. North South Roundtable.

Porter, M.E. (1986). Competition in global industries: a conceptual framework. In Porter, M.E. (Ed.), *Competition in global industries.* Boston, Massachusetts: Harvard Business School Press.

Porter, M.E. (1980). *Competitive strategy.* New York: Free Press.

Purton, P. (1989a, August 1). Grappling with global digital networks. *Datamation*, 72-81.

Purton, P. (1989b, March 1). Europe's electronic trading bloc. *Datamation*, 13-14.

Reck, R.M. (1989, August 1). The shock of going global. *Datamation*, 67-69.

Riddle, D.I. (1988). International cooperation in informatic services. In Haq, K. (Ed.),*Informatics for development. the new challenge.*,185-207. Islamabad, Pakistan: North South Roundtable.

Robinson, P., Sauvant, K.P., & Govitrikar, V.P. (Eds.). (1989). *Electronic highways for world trade: issues in telecommunications and data services.* Westview Press, Inc.

Runyan, L. (1989, December 1). Global IS strategies. *Datamation*, 71-78.

Sauvant, K.P. (1986). *International transactions in services: the politics of transborder data flows.* Westview Press.

Schneider, S.C. (1988). National versus corporate culture: implications for human resource management. *Human Resource Management, 27*(2), 231-246.

Schott, J.J., & Smith, M.G. (1988). Services and investment. In Schott, J.J., & Smith, M.G. (Eds.), *Canada-United States free trade agreement. the global impact*, 137-150. Washington, D.C.: Institute for International Economics.

Selig, G.J. (1982). *Strategic planning for information resource management: a multinational perspective.* UMI Press.

Shanks, D.C. (1982). Strategic planning for global competition. *The Journal of Business Strategy*, 80-89.

Shields, P., & Servaes, J. (1989). The impact of the transfer of information technology on development. *The Information Society, 6*, 47-57.

Skjelsbaek, K. (1972). The growth of international non-governmental organizations in the twentieth century. In Keohane, R. & Nye, J.S. (Eds.), *Transnational interactions and world politics* , 70-95. Harvard Business School Press.

Stopford, J., & Wells, L.T. (1972). Managing the multinational enterprise. New York: Basic Books.

Sweet, W. (1990, June 4). Knowing local customs Is critical for global projects. *Network World*, 29, 32.

Szewczak, F.J., & Snodgrass, C.R. (1989). ISDN as an information resource for strategic management of multinational firms. *Information Resource Management Journal*, 15-25.

Tate, P. (1989, July 1). The battle for Europe. *Datamation*, (83)3-6.

Telecommunications realities: a users roundtable. (1988, April 1). *Datamation*.

Thompson, J.M., Faigle, T.W., & Short, J.E. (1989). We are the world. *Information Strategy: The Executives Journal*, 43-44.

Toyne, B. (1989). International exchange: a foundation for theory building in international business. *Journal of International Business Studies, XX*(1), 1-18.

UNESCO. (1980). *Many voices, one world.* Anchor Press.

U.S. Congress. (1988). *Omnibus trade and competitiveness act of 1988, public law 100-418, 100th congress.* H.R. 4848, 19USC 2901.

U.S. Congress, House, Committee on Energy and Commerce. (1981). *Telecommunications and information products and services in international trade. Hearings before the subcommittee on telecommunications, consumer protection, and finance, 97th congress, 1st session, 1981.* S.No. 97-59.

Ungerer, H. (1988). *Telecommunications in Europe.* Office for Official Publications of the European Communities.

United States Council of International Business. (1988). *Statement on the report by the analysis and forecasting group (GAP) on open network provision (ONP).*

Wardle, C. (1984). The evolution of information system architectures. *Proceedings of the ICIS*, 205-217.

Weill, P., & Olson, M.M. (1989). An assessment of the contingency theory of management information systems. *Journal of Management Information Systems, 6*(1), 59-85.

11

Key Technological Components and Issues of Global Information Systems

Chetan S. Sankar
Auburn University

P. K. Prabhakar
AT&T Bell Laboratories

Global information systems are developed using software application packages that communicate via world-wide backbone telecommunications networks. These networks are complex and are composed of a variety of components. Among the components are host computers, telecommunications equipment, networks, protocols and network management systems. Skilled technologists and managers integrate these equipment and networks to create global telecommunications networks. These networks are used by end-users and MIS staff to build and maintain the global information systems. Understanding the technical issues in building, installing, and maintaining these global networks is a prerequisite for development of global information systems.

INTRODUCTION

This chapter highlights the issues in designing, installing, and maintaining global telecommunications networks from a technical point of view. In order for a reader to understand the discussion on the issues, we provide an overview of all the technical components necessary to make this chapter self-sufficient. The functions of these components are made clear by showing how they fit together to produce global networks which in turn support global information systems. A reader who is already familiar with the details of the technological components can go directly to the section on "Issues in Designing and Implementing Global Networks."

A manager of a company charged with designing and implementing a global information system has to be aware of the difficulties and complexities in creating global networks. The material in this chapter would provide this awareness to the managers in a top down fashion using three sections.

The first section of this chapter describes the applications that could be performed using global telecommunications networks. The major applications discussed are the transmission of voice, data, text, and video information to users located at different places in the world.

The second section of this chapter identifies the key technological components of these global telecommunications networks. The key components identified are: equipment (computers, terminals, PBXs, FAXs, multiplexers, and others), transmission networks (analog, digital; public, private; switched, packet), protocols (OSI and SNA standards), and network management systems. Since the number of products in each component category is large, we do not provide a detailed discussion of the components. For more detailed information about the components, the readers can refer to the text books by Stalling (1990) and Elbert (1989). After a brief discussion of these components, the benefits of building global networks using these components are listed. The material in this section becomes the basis for understanding the next section on global issues.

The third section of this chapter highlights the issues associated in designing, installing, and maintaining global telecommunications networks. Examples are provided to illustrate the importance of understanding the global issues. Companies are beginning to integrate their voice, data, text, and video networks and manage them using sophisticated network management systems. For these companies, the need to resolve these issues is critical.

In summary, a current or future telecommunications or information systems manager will become aware of the complexity of technical issues involved in setting up a global telecommunications network by reading this chapter.

APPLICATIONS OF GLOBAL TELECOMMUNICATIONS NETWORKS

The primary functions of global telecommunications networks are to transmit and receive voice, data, text, and video information among the divisions and customers of governments and multi-national corporations. Instantaneous transmission of messages with little delay is becoming critical to many of these corporations. These functions provide the basis for building sophisticated global information systems.

Many companies have separate global voice, data, text, and video networks to fulfill applications needs of different divisions. As an example, a division of a multi-national company may provide information systems based on up-to-date stock market information of individual companies in many countries. This division could incorporate the current stock market information in decision support systems, expert systems, or data processing systems thereby helping improve the decision making ability of their customers. Obtaining current stock market information on-line using global data networks is critical for this division. Similarly, another division of the company could use the international 800 services to obtain orders for buying and selling stocks. High reliability and availability of the global voice networks is critical for this application to be successful.

Companies have developed separate global voice and data networks to take care of such applications (Figures 1 and 2). Figure 1 shows an example of global data transfer among countries. In this example, a stock broker in New York shares information with stock brokers in Rome and Frankfurt. The stock broker in New York may initiate a stock transaction in stock of an Italian company for a customer. This transaction is sent to a front end processor (FEP) in New York, which then transmits it to Rome using a private line. This private line may have been leased from a regional Bell Operating Company, AT&T or MCI or Sprint, and several foreign PT&Ts (Posts, Telephone and Telegraphs). The data is sent to the mainframe at Rome within a few minutes and the transaction is completed. The Rome office sends a confirmation message to New York and sends a duplicate copy of the transaction to the head office at Frankfurt. Thus, a data network is made up of terminals at customer sites that send and/or receive data from central data bases and mainframe computers (central processing units) at remote locations. Multiplexers are used at the customer premise to combine many different data calls to a high bandwidth facility. This can save substantial costs in long distance transmission across countries. Telephone carriers such as AT&T and MCI provide private line services which are dedicated lines. These dedicated lines or 'pipes' carry large amounts of data traffic between customer locations. The 'pipes' may be across satellite facilities such as AT&T's Skynet Service or through undersea cable such as AT&T's International ACCULINK Digital Services.

The stock broker can conduct a video teleconference with the broker at Rome. Once the call is set up, both the brokers can see each other on a TV screen and talk together. A camera takes the picture of the speaker and sends it to a coder-decoder (codec). The codec converts the picture to digital signals and sends it to a multiplexer. The multiplexer then combines these signals with other data and voice calls and transmits it to Frankfurt. The multiplexer at

Frankfurt delivers the appropriate signals to a codec, which converts the signals to show the picture and receive the voice of the sender. Major carriers offer special services whereby international video conferencing can take place. Companies can subscribe to this service from the carriers.

Figure 2 shows an example of global voice communication among countries. In this example, stock brokers at New York talk to the stock brokers at Rome and Frankfurt using regular international long distance lines. The equipment and network used to send this voice information can be totally different from the data network. The phone of the stock broker at New York is routed through a Private Branch Exchange (PBX) at the local company building. The basic features of a PBX provide for central answering mechanism, ability of calling within the company, and can provide special call features. The PBX at New York is connected to large switches of the Bell Operating System and then to the long distance company. They in turn are connected to the telecommunications carriers (PT&Ts) of Italy and Germany and from there to the company's PBX in Rome and Frankfurt. The calls go through the public network that is shared with all other customers. When the stock broker at New York rings the broker at Frankfurt, a physical connection is established between the two using the facilities of all the carriers. This line is used to transmit the voice call and is disconnected when either broker hangs up the phone.

The stock brokers can transmit documents globally using fax machines. The fax machine converts the characters in the paper to digital signals that are then converted to analog signals using a built-in or external modem. These analog signals can be transmitted using the voice network and the fax machine on the other side can interpret and print the pages.

These global networks need to be managed and controlled by network management systems so as to assure reliability and availability of the network. The network management systems are used to monitor each equipment and facility in the network and report the health of the network. Network management systems are complex software systems that receive and analyze messages from the equipment and facilities in the network. These systems detect service degradations on the network early and lead to maintenance actions thereby reducing service disruptions. A maintenance action could be to decide new routes in case of failures of existing routes and to implement new routes. When a facility fails, higher priority traffic could be routed onto other facilities, thereby minimizing disruption in service. These actions lead to overall improvement in quality of transmission.

Failure to understand differences among these components globally could lead to incompatibilities and problems in using the global networks effectively. The next section of this chapter explains the technical information about the major components used in creating global telecommunications

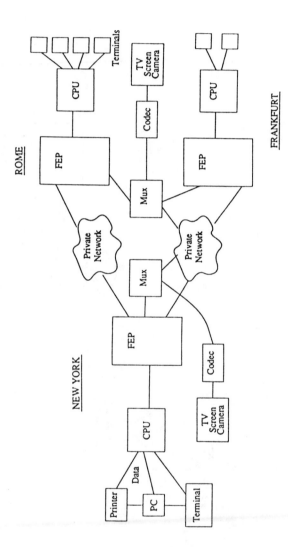

CPU - Central Processing Unit
FEP - Front End Processor

Figure 1: Data Network

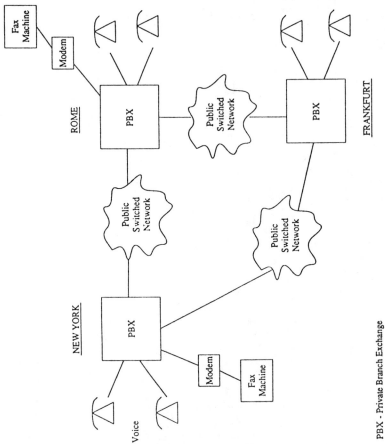

Figure 2: Voice Network

PBX - Private Branch Exchange

networks. A reader familiar with the technical information on the components can skip this section and go to the section on "Issues in Designing and Implementing Global Networks."

TECHNICAL INFORMATION ON COMPONENTS USED IN GLOBAL NETWORKS

Global telecommuications networks use several components such as equipment, networks, standards, protocols, and network management systems in transmitting voice, data, text, and video information across countries. This section describes each of these major components.

Many varieties of equipment are used in supporting applications of the global network, as shown below.

Application	Major equipment
Data	Terminals, data sets, computers, front end processors, multiplexers, controllers
Voice	Phones, switches, PBX
Text	Fax machines
Video	Codecs, video cameras and display systems

These equipment are used to produce a large amount of messages that need to be transmitted across the world. Both private and public networks are used to transmit this information. These networks are made up of multiplexers, digital access cross-connect systems, terrestrial cables, satellites, and radio systems. The data traffic is frequently transmitted using packet networks, whereas voice is is usually not transmitted via packet networks.

Standards and protocols are essential so that an equipment manufacturer can produce equipment that can interface with other vendors' equipment. Similarly, the networks have to work according to standard protocols so that the transmission medium of different countries can be connected together.

A new but important aspect of global information systems is the network management system that functions as the brain of the network. Real-time fault and performance information from the equipment and network can be collected and analyzed to provide centralized control of the network. We briefly discuss each of these components.

Equipment

A data network is made up by connecting the terminals or personal computers at an end-user's desk to other end-users using powerful computers, front end processors, and multiplexers. Computers can be divided into four major categories: super-computers, mainframe computers, minicomputers, and microcomputers. Computer terminals are available in many different varieties. Many of them are general purpose, although some of them are special purpose (such as the Automated Teller Machines keyboard). Multiplexers combine voice, data, and video traffic from several points to a single stream for transmission on high capacity digital facilities and vice versa. By combining traffic, a company can lease a high capacity facility from a PT&T, thereby generating significant savings. Multiplexers are available to multiplex and demultiplex traffic up to 56 Kb/s, 1.544 Mb/s, 2.048 Mb/s, 45 Mb/s, and 275 Mb/s.

A voice network is made by connecting the telephones at a customer's desk to a local PBX and then connecting them to a private or public network. The common carriers, such as AT&T and MCI, use expensive and powerful switching equipment to connect the voice network. The switching equipment is an essential component of global networks. They also vary in capacity and can be classified as: super large switches, large switches, mini- and micro-switches. Super large switches (such as 4ESS) are used by PT&Ts and telephone companies to route traffic. These switches can handle up to 670,000 calls. Large switches such as AT&T's 5ESS are used at the local offices and are designed for modular growth. They can handle up to 300,000 calls. Mini- and micro-switches are used at customer premise and can handle both voice and data traffic. They can be Key systems, Private Branch Exchanges (such as AT&T's Definity product lines) and CENTREX services. CENTREX service is usually provided by the local Bell Operating Company.

Facsimile (FAX) equipment is used for transmission of text material across the network. These machines have become cheaper and there are many vendors to choose from. A critical decision is to identify the protocols that are supported by a FAX machine and assure that the FAX machines at the other end can use those protocols. FAX boards can also be installed in personal computers so that files can be directly stored by a computer and there is no need for paper input/output. FAX machines are being widely used and have taken away volume from the overnight mail companies.

Transmission Networks

Transmission networks take traffic from one point and deliver it to another point. These networks can be broadly classified as: analog, digital; private, public; switched, packet. Common carriers have built international services using these networks to fulfill specific customer needs, such as International 800 services, International Satellite Services etc.

A network connecting different end points has to be designated analog or digital and then it can only function in that mode. It will be capital intensive to change analog to a digital network or vice versa since connecting equipment and repeaters have to be changed. An analog network operates on the principle that traffic is sent as continuous electrical signals. A digital network sends only 0s and 1s through the network using electrical signals. Any signal degrades after a certain amount of distance. Repeaters are used to regenerate the signals. In an analog network, repeaters may introduce distortions since the wave form can change. In a digital network, a 0 is represented by a particular frequency and 1 by another frequency; the transmit and receive 0s and 1s are identified by being given different frequency ranges. Thereby, digital signals could be transmitted and received using just four frequency values. This makes it easy to identify the digit in a repeater and to regenerate an exact signal. Thus digital networks provide more reliable transmission and most new networks are built to provide digital transmission of data.

A public network is shared by many users and the user is assured of services but has no idea how the traffic is routed. The traffic at a common carrier's office is routed using either public or private networks. A public network can accommodate differing bandwidth facilities (from 2.4 kb/s to 295 Mb/s). This network is used by many companies and the general public. The traffic of a customer may be routed on different facilities each day. Hence, some customers lease a private line network from the common carriers. These private networks contain facilities that are reserved for the use of specific customers. A private network guarantees the routing of traffic for a customer and also enhances privacy and security of the traffic. Companies received a major incentive to build their own global private networks with the installation of TAT-8 during 1988. TAT-8, a trans-Atlantic fiber optic cable (Foley, June 1989), is capable of carrying 40,000 voice calls simultaneously and went into commercial service during December 1988 (Taff, 1989). The technology lets TAT-8 providers offer fully digital transmission circuits with almost instantaneous response time.

Most networks use a circuit-switched or a packet-switched mode to communicate across the globe. In a circuit-switched mode, for each call, a direct connection is established between the caller and receiver for the duration of the call. Even if the caller and receiver do not transmit any messages, the connection is on. For example, when you dial into a network such as Compuserve from your home personal computer, you have a direct connection to the local computer and the line is dedicated for your use. In contrast, a packet network can let multiple customers use the same facility more efficiently. An example is of dropping a letter at a mail box. It reaches the receiver, but the customer does not have a direct connection to the receiver. Similarly, in a packet network, the message of the sender is divided into many different packets and mailed to the receiver. The equipment at the receiving side puts these packets together and makes a complete package. Packet networks have similar inefficiencies as a postal system; the sender has no guarantee of delivery, only partial messages may reach the receiver, etc. A successful use of packet network is the Bitnet or Arpanet used by faculty members at Universities and research institutions to communicate with each other.

Protocols

In order for information to be exchanged between one entity (any equipment or network) and another, they have to "speak the same language." The rules by which these entities exchange data and commands are referred to as protocols. The contents, messages, and timing of communications should conform to mutually accepted conventions. These conventions are referred to as protocols that may be defined as a set of rules governing the exchange of data between two entities. The key elements of a protocol are:

• Syntax: Includes such things as data format and signaling levels.
• Semantics: Includes control information for coordination and error handling.
• Timing: Includes synchronizing the clocks used by the different pieces of equipment.

Figure 3 shows the various protocols used between entities in a file transfer application.

There are a wide variety of ways in which these protocols may be implemented. In order that there may be some order in the way the protocols are developed, there have been attempts to standardize protocols. Many standard making bodies are in existence. Some of the more important ones of relevance to global information systems are:

• International Organization for Standardization (ISO): This is a voluntary, nontreaty organization whose members are designated standards bodies of participating nations, and nonvoting observer organizations. One of ISO's technical committees (TC97) is concerned with information systems. This committee developed the OSI model and is developing protocol standards at various levels of the model.

• International Telegraph and Telephone Consultative Committee (CCITT): This is an U. N. treaty organization made up of primarily the Postal, Telegraph, and Telephone (PT&T) authorities of the member countries. The U. S. representative is the Department of State. As its name implies, CCITT is involved in a broad range of communication areas. The organization works closely with ISO on communication protocol standards.

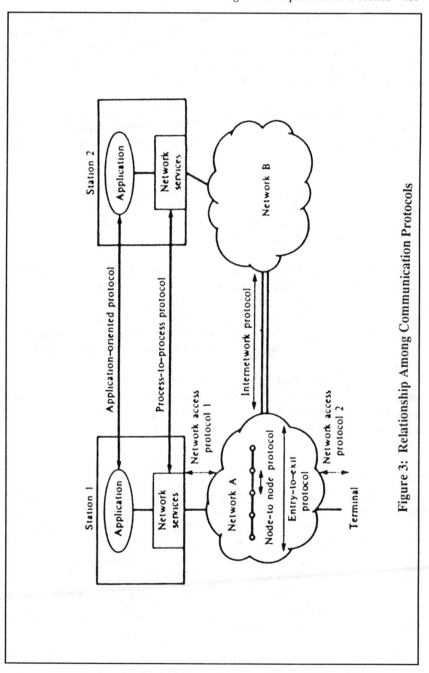

Figure 3: Relationship Among Communication Protocols

• American National Standards Institute (ANSI): This is a non-profit, non-governmental organization composed of manufacturers, users, communications carriers, and other interested organizations. It is the national clearing house for voluntary standards in the U.S. It is also the designated voting member of ISO for the U.S. ANSI's interests roughly parallel those of ISO.

• Electronics Industries Association (EIA): This is a trade association of electronics firms and a member of ANSI. It is concerned with primarily the standards that affect layer 1 of the OSI model (the physical layer, more on that later).

• Institute of Electrical and Electronics Engineers (IEEE): This is a professional society that is also a member of ANSI. Their concerns have been primarily with the lowest two layers of the OSI reference model (the physical and the data link layers, more on that later).

• European Computer Manufacturers Association (ECMA): This is composed of computer suppliers selling in Europe, including the European divisions of some American companies. It is devoted exclusively to cooperative development of standards applicable to computer technology. ECMA serves as a nonvoting member of CCITT and ISO and also issues its own standards. Because of the rapidity of their efforts they have considerable influence on OSI work.

The International Standards Organization (ISO) has created a reference model for Open Systems Interconnection (OSI). In addition, IBM has been using its SNA architecture to provide data communications for its customers. We will discuss both these architectures.

OSI Reference Model

OSI model (Figure 4) defines the functionality that must be provided by the networks. The rationale behind the creation of the OSI model was to create a standard and to eliminate the proliferation of vendor specific networks.

The model describes the communication between an end-user's terminal of one host computer, intermediate nodes and other end-user's terminals using seven layers. Since the functions of each layer are well defined, standards can be developed independently and simultaneously for each layer. Changes in standards in one layer need not affect already existing software in another layer, since the boundaries between the layers are well defined.

A message from the sending host may pass through many different nodes before reaching the destination host. The layers 4 through 7 are called end-to-end layers since they are invoked only by the two end systems that are

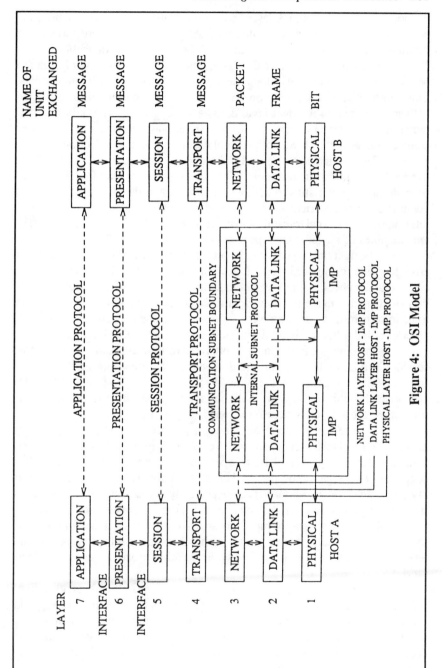

Figure 4: OSI Model

the hosts. Layers 1, 2 and 3 describe the communication between a host and node, or between nodes at all intermediate points. These are termed the "chained layers" because they are invoked throughout the connection.

The horizontal lines in the figure represent the passing of information between "peer" layers; that is, layers at the same level in two different systems. This communication defines a protocol. The vertical passing of information between a level and the next level defines the interface. The only physical movement of information is at the interfaces and over the physical layer connection. All other layers of protocol define "virtual" connections.

The physical layer (layer 1) is responsible for the transmission of bits over a communication channel. This layer provides the functional and procedural characteristics to activate, maintain, and deactivate the physical connection. The electrical and mechanical characteristics provide the physical interface to the external transmission media. RS-232C, RS-449, X.21 and V.35 are examples of physical layer protocols.

The data link layer (layer 2) protocol is responsible for providing an error-free line for higher layers. It accomplishes this task by providing error and sequence checking and by implementing a system of time-outs and ac-knowledgements that enables a transmitter to determine the frames that need to be re-transmitted due to an error. The unit of transmission at the data link layer is called a frame. In addition, flow control is provided at this layer.

The network layer (layer 3) provides routing and congestion control services to higher layers. In addition, network accounting and statistical functions are contained in the network layer. These bottom three layers comprise the chained layers. All hosts and nodes have to contain and implement these layers whenever a communication takes place.

The four layers above the chained layers are the end-to-end layers that are implemented in the sender and receiver hosts. Layer 4 is the transport layer. This layer accepts messages from layers above it, breaks them into smaller segments if necessary, and passes them to the network layer. The transport layer also ensures that all pieces arrive correctly at the destination host. This layer multiplexes several sessions over a single network connection or, conversely, it uses several connections to provide a high data rate for a session that requires it. Finally the transport layer has the responsibility to establish and terminate the connection between two application processes across the net-work.

The session layer (layer 5) is responsible for establishing and manag-ing the connection between two applications running on the sending and receiving hosts. Session establishment typically requires agreement on a set of parameters that will be in effect for the session. This layer is also responsible for recovery from a transport failure. The session layer provides the commu-nication controls between the users.

The presentation layer (layer 6) provides user services. This enhances communications by providing text compression, file format conversion and encryption services.

The application layer (layer 7) is the user interface to the network. It provides commonly required services such as the File Transfer Access and Management (FTAM) protocol, Electronic mail (i, e., Message Handling System), and the Virtual Terminal Protocol. The application layer may provide protocols that are specific to a particular application, such as an interbank transfer protocol, an airline reservation protocol etc.

Efforts are being made by vendors of global information systems to subscribe to the standards of the OSI model. Adherence to this model and related standards will make it easy to interconnect the equipment and networks of different vendors in the future.

Systems Network Architecture

Systems Network Architecture (SNA) is a hierarchical architecture introduced by IBM in 1974. This is the most widely used architecture for data transmission in the world (60%) and specifies how IBM's products connect and communicate with one another. It is a closed system architecture and does not confirm to the OSI model. All machines in an application path must use IBM's SNA in order to communicate and understand each other.

SNA is a hierarchical network in which a host machine controls one or more communication controllers. Each communication controller communicates with remote cluster controllers, and each cluster controller may in turn control several devices. Figure 5 illustrates a typical SNA based network.

The Host Processor controls all parts of the network. It provides capabilities such as computation, program execution, access to data bases, directory services, and network management. The telecommunications related access method resides in the host. It logically controls the flow of data through a network, provides an interface between application related subsystems and the network, and protects application subsystems from unauthorized access. VTAM (Virtual Telecommunications Access Method) is an example of this.

Application subsystems also reside in the host and are responsible for such functions as retrieving and updating information, processing jobs remotely, and presenting graphics information on displays and printers.

The communication controller manages the physical network, controls the communication link, and routes the data through the network. The Network Control Program resides in the communication controller. It routes data and controls its flow between the front end processor and other network resources. The cluster controller controls the workstation input/output operations and the devices connected to them. Workstation are the input/output

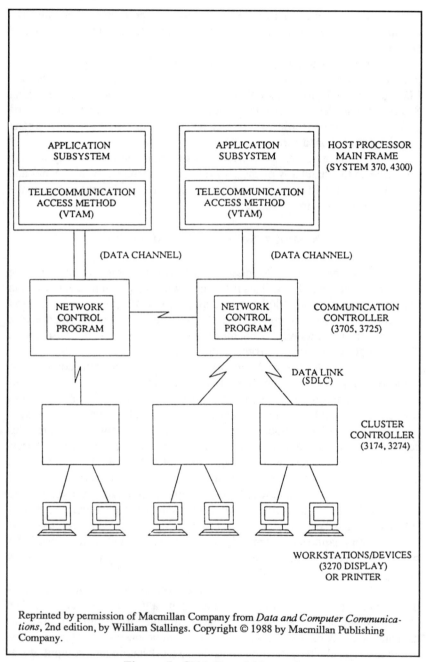

Figure 5: SNA-Based Network

devices enabling network users to access the network and send and receive information.

The communication controller and the cluster controller may be geographically far from one another and use transmission media such as telephone lines, microwaves, optical fibers, and coaxial cables. SDLC (Synchronous Data Link Control) provides a reliable data link over the transmission media.

Network Management Systems

In a limited sense, network management refers to the control of specific pieces of equipment that are remote from the controlling organization. However, in its broader sense network management is the total control, allocation, maintenance and management of the network and equipment from a business perspective. In order for this to occur, a company requires skilled personnel and sophisticated network management systems. A network management system provides many different features and we describe the features of AT&T's Unified Network Management Architecture (UNMA) here.

This architecture is intended to provide a unified view to a customer of many different network management systems that control equipment and networks at customer premises, local exchange carriers, and AT&T services. AT&T's UNMA classifies the functions included in any network management into the following categories:

• Configuration/Name Management- This provides the ability to name and configure the equipment used in the network. This includes inventory management, configuration management, directory management, change management and provisioning.

• Fault Management- This provides the ability to deal with network problems as they occur. It includes diagnosis, repair, testing, status supervision, and network backup/reconfiguration.

• Performance Management - This provides the ability to monitor the network so that problems can be forecasted and actions taken before disaster strikes. It includes monitoring the performance of the network based on user-defined acceptability parameters, performing trending and analysis, and generating exception reports based on user-designated thresholds.

• Accounting Management - This provides the ability to bill end-users for the use of the global information systems. It can help in developing budgets by maintaining information on network component pricing and network user

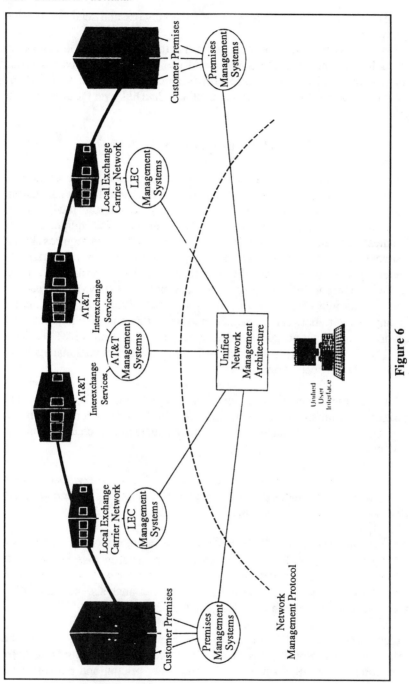

Figure 6

statistics.

• Security Management - This provides the ability to secure the network from unauthorized users. It establishes and maintains the network access and permission levels for end users as well as network managers.

• Network Planning - This provides an ability to plan and design networks for the future. It combines information on usage trends, network growth, performance, and external information for network design and for forecasting network needs.

• Operations Management - This ensures that the network is performing at its peak performance. It does this by incorporating the proper resource mix of people, support systems, procedures, training and information into a model network operations control center.

• Programmability - This permits users to tailor network management functions to their specific needs by customizing generic network management systems from vendors.

• Integrated Systems Control- This provides a facility for network managers to perform end-to-end management across all equipment and networks by allowing all resources to be tied together into a single, easy to use interface.

This section has briefly described the technical functions of the major components used in global networks. The reader can obtain more detailed information by reading the books by Stallings (1990) and Elbert (1989). These components are integrated to form global networks. These global networks form the basis for designing and implementing global information systems.

Benefits of Global Information Systems

A global information system for a corporation is designed, built, and maintained by its telecommunications staff using the components described above. The major benefits of building such an information system are:

1. Employees and customers in different countries can quickly and efficiently make voice calls, move data, send facsimiles, and confer using video teleconferencing systems.

2. Employees may need to use only seven digits to dial worldwide. This function eliminates the need for employees to use the public international

telephone network, thereby reducing expensive bills. At the same time, employees find it easier to dial another country using just seven digits rather than dialing 15 to 20 digits using the typical international telephone network. Seven digit dialing has been made possible by changing the software of the digital switches.

The corporation can also encourage employees to use international phone links to enhance business since the cost is already underwritten by the global network. Thus, each division could afford to call overseas often, and, at the same time, pay less than what they had been paying in the past.
3.Employees and customers are able to exchange data and files in real time without regard to geographical and political boundaries. The network provides an ability to use Electronic Data Interchange (EDI) in all the countries where the global network is supported. Even if a location in a country does not have a direct connection to the global network, employees can access this network by dialing the local country's node and transmitting information through that node. They thereby can replace expensive international telephone calls with cheaper domestic phone calls.

4. Employees and customers feel that the network is transparent. The network management center becomes the sole agency where the employees and customers report problems in the network. The network management center identifies the location of the fault, contacts the appropriate agency, and resolves the problem. Thereby, the complexity of the network operations is transparent to the employees and customers of the global network.

5. The network can be operated with minimal disruption of service, increased reliability, and a high percentage of availability.

Line managers in multi-national corporations are beginning to understand that they can obtain these benefits by implementing global networks. Hence, the MIS and telecommunications managers are increasingly required to design and implement such global networks. Some of them do not realize the issues and technical difficulties in designing such networks. The next section lists some of the problems and issues associated in globalizing the telecommunications networks.

ISSUES IN DESIGNING AND IMPLEMENTING GLOBAL NETWORKS

Designing and implementing global networks by appropriately combining equipment, networks, protocols, and network management systems in different countries is a complex task. A knowledge of the issues involved in deploying these components world-wide is important to telecommunications and MIS managers involved in setting up global information systems for their companies (Ergas and Okayama, 1984; Harper, 1989). Some of the major globalization issues are discussed below.

Equipment

Major issues in equipment are type approval, power requirements, and practices of the common carrier in a particular country.

Many countries require equipment of foreign vendors to be "type approved," that is, approved by the local telecommunications carriers as safe to be connected to the network. This process can take from a few months to many years. Any modification to the equipment may have to be type approved again before being used. For example, a multi-national corporation had implemented a domestic network using a particular brand of T1 multiplexers. These multiplexers were supported by an excellent network management system that provided back-up and rerouting capabilities in case of failure of any link. The top management at the multi- national corporation decided to expand this network management system globally. But, technically it was not possible since that brand of T1 multiplexer was not type approved in the foreign country. It took more than a year of negotiation and technical work before that T1 multiplexer was allowed to be used in the foreign customer premise of the multi-national corporation. The management has no option but to wait out this delay.

Another issue is that basic power standards differ across countries. The power specifications in the U.S.A. is 110/120 Volts, whereas it is 220/240 Volts in Europe. In addition, an equipment vendor has to adhere to any other technical standards each common carrier may impose before the equipment can be connected to the network. For example, the T1 multiplexer worked at 110/120 Volts and had to be modified to work with 220/240 Volts so that type approval could be obtained.

Frequently, the local telecommunications carrier may also insist on using equipment from preferred vendors only, thereby restricting a company's choice of equipment. In many countries, the common carrier is a Government monopoly and permits only the installation of locally produced equipment in the customer premise. For example, though type-approval was obtained for the T1 multiplexer in one European country, it could not be automatically deployed in other countries in Europe. Hence, many vendors do not have sufficient financial incentive to get their equipment type approved in different countries. This seriously limits the number of countries where a multi-national company can deploy its equipment to provide excellent services to their internal customers.

Multiplex Level	North America (Mb/s)	Japan (Mb/s)	Europe (Mb/s)
1	1.544	1.544	2.048
2	6.312	6.312	8.448
3	44.736	32.064	34.368
4	274.176	97.728	139.264
5		397.200	

Figure 7: Transmission Rates for Digital Hierarchy of North America, Japan, and Europe

Transmission Networks

Major issues in networks are differences in bandwidth of facilities, analog to digital encoding, quality of facilities, signaling, echo cancellation, compression techniques, and services.

The standards for bandwidth differ across countries. Figure 7 shows the differences in the bandwidth among Europe, Japan, and North America.

In Europe, the Conference of European Telegraphs (CEPT) standard hierarchy is used. In North America, it is the American standard. CEPT uses 30 channels in a 2.048 Mbps facility, whereas the North American standard uses 24 channels and 1.544 Mbps facilities. This immediately raises the issue of how to transport 24 channels or 1.544 Mbps over a 2.048 Mbps bearer and vice versa. This problem arose in the earlier cited example of the T1 multiplexer being modified to suit European conditions. In this case, an additional piece of equipment called a remultiplexer was used to convert the U.S. 1.544 Mb/s traffic to European 2.048 Mb/s facilities and vice versa. Installation of this extra equipment made it more expensive for the customer to obtain the same services globally than on a domestic network. Recently, a few of the telecommunications vendors of developed countries are working together so that these differences in the network are transparent to a customer.

The vendors in the U.S.A. use a method of converting analog voice to a digital signal called the 'mu law'. In Europe another method called the 'A law' is used. These encoding schemes make a big difference in the provisioning of PBXs in the global voice network. Telecommunications staff have to make the appropriate modifications to the PBXs connected in this network so that the voice calls are completed without any problems.

The telecommunications quality of the network in each participating country depends on the level of technology used in each network. The level of technology varies widely around the world. For example, the U.S.A. network is being rapidly digitized with a corresponding improvement in quality. On the other hand, in several European and other countries, large portions of the network are still analog. When a circuit traverses both an analog and a digital network, the quality is worse than if the circuit were entirely digital. Similarly, some countries may use fiber technology, whereas others may be just using 4-wire twisted pair for transmission of information. The quality and performance characteristics of these facilities differ. Some PT&Ts do not provide any guarantee on the performance level of their facilities. Hence a customer's end-to-end data or voice performance may be affected more by the low-grade facilities that traverse only a few miles long in a country. Thus, the quality offered to customers is necessarily a compromise worked out between the PT&Ts. The quality of the global network for a customer might drop dramatically if the facilities go through countries that do not provide good quality facilities.

Incompatibilities in signaling systems among countries introduce the need for additional pieces of equipment to bridge the differences. For example, a bit value of "1" in one country signals that the line is busy and the caller gets a busy signal. In another country, the same value of "1" signals that the line is available and the caller hears the phone ring. Even within adjacent countries such anomalies may exist. An example of such a situation is between the U.K. and France and between the U.S and Mexico. Additional pieces of hardware and /or software have to be introduced to "invert" the bits and rectify the anomaly.

To reduce echo in voice networks, echo suppressors/cancelers are deployed throughout the network. This deployment is based on facility lengths. Usually deployment of these echo suppressors is based on the individual vendor's quality and reliability objectives. In a global network, echo cancellation equipment is deployed by many different common carriers. A customer may have to persuade some of these PT&Ts to improve the deploy-ment of echo cancelers/suppressors in their networks to provide better quality to the global network.

Often, for reasons of economy, data compression technique are used for packing more information within the same bandwidth. This technique affects the quality of transmission of text using fax machines, since they are usually sent over voice lines. When an end-to-end circuit connecting the sender and receiver goes across several of these compression equipment deployed in separate national networks, the overall quality of the transmitted text degrades significantly.

The transmission networks are used by common carriers to market specialized services such as 800 services. Each common carrier makes up their own list of such services and frequently they are not compatible with one another. Hence, a customer used to a particular service in a country may not be able to expand that service to another country quickly. The features of the services offered by other common carriers differ widely and it may take years to expand the services to other countries. Recently, common carriers of some countries have collaborated with each other and are marketing a set of common services to multi-national customers.

Standards/Protocols

Major issues in protocols are diverse standards and differences in implementation. One troublesome issue is the existence of several standards for the same equipment or network. With so many standards-making bodies, there is a good possibility of the standards being different even though they may be addressing the same layer protocols. In addition, many vendors do not follow the standards and set up their own standards. For example, the T1 multiplexers marketed by Timeplex, Infotron, NET, and AT&T use their own proprietary schemes to transmit the network management information among the multiplexers. Such proprietary standards compel a customer to deploy the multiplexers from the same vendor all around the country and the world. Frequently, it is not possible to mix and match these multiplexers in the global network.

Another issue is the variety of implementations that is possible even within the same standard. Two countries may implement the same standard differently. A standard may allow certain bits to be used at the discretion of the national carrier for its own purpose. This may be used by two countries in a way that can produce incompatibilities. This means that one may have to carefully examine the implementation of standards in different countries. Widespread use of the OSI and other standards by common carriers and equipment vendors could reduce these incompatibilities in the future.

Network Management Systems

Major issues in network management systems are configuration and name management, responsibility for managing the network, differences among vendors, coordination among carriers, automation of operations, and definition of technical terms across countries.

It is difficult to keep track of the equipment and networks used within a country; this issue becomes enormous when a company wants its NMS to capture the information about the global network using data bases. Frequently, equipment gets moved around or the network is changed in a foreign country without updating the data base. The multi- national company has to set up procedures and implement them so that the inventory information is up-to-date.

Who manages and controls the global network is also an important issue. The customer portion of the network is managed by the customer in different countries. The common carrier portion of the network is managed by each individual common carrier. When a problem is reported in the network, the customers at different locations and the common carriers have to coordinate among themselves to resolve problems. The longer they take to resolve problems, the longer an end-user is kept waiting for services. For global networks, a wait of one to two days to fix troubles in an end- to-end connection is common. Recently, this wait has been reduced with the implementation of sophisticated network management systems. When a customer's network spans several countries and, consequently, the network of several carriers, the question of control becomes important. Specific procedures have to be agreed to by the carriers and the customer on the extent of control. For example, the customer may be able to view the network and see where the problems are and what they are. The customer may also be able to send test signals and monitor the health of the network. However, the carriers may retain the right to change the configuration of the equipment that forms a part of the network. The carriers, in turn, have to agree amongst themselves on the procedures through which these reconfigurations can occur.

Vendors of different equipment and networks market specific network management systems to manage that equipment or portion of the network. These network management systems differ in their representation of the same objects. A network maintenance person has to learn these different network management systems in order to manage and control the global network. Vendors and standards-making bodies have been working to resolve this problem by providing unified user interfaces. IBM has released a product called Netview that provides an integrated view of the customer's network management systems. It also has facility for other vendors to send network management information to Netview. AT&T has proposed Unified Network Management as another approach in integrating network management systems and has released products under this approach. Implementation of AT&T's UNMA is based on standard interfaces to integrate the network management systems of several vendors and common carriers (Figure 6) into a more cohesive network management system. AT&T is currently working with other vendors, common carriers, and international standards groups to ensure that UNMA is compatible with OSI architecture.

Coordination among carriers is another major issue. The major difference in a global network from a purely domestic network is the involvement of many telecommunication carriers in each country. For example, when communicating between locations in the United Kingdom and the U.S., British telecommunications providers such as Mercury Communications or British Telecom are involved in setting up the communication facilities along with a carrier in the United States, such as AT&T or MCI. Setting up the circuit is a cooperative effort between the British carrier and the U.S. carrier. The two carriers have to come to an agreement on several technical issues, such as the compatibility of the equipment used, how the facility is to be tested and maintained, and the type of testing that should be done to ensure the reliability of the facility. When a company leases a private line from the carriers, they may have to go to both carriers and order the communication facilities separately. The company has to separately negotiate with the carriers from the two countries. Efforts are being made by carriers to provide a one stop shopping service, thereby eliminating the need for businesses to go to several PT&Ts to order their service.

The degree of automation among telecommunications carriers differs, making network management a difficult task globally. In the U.S.A., many maintenance and operations activities have been automated. Using specially developed systems, a technician in a work center can rapidly sectionalize and isolate the cause of the problem. In Europe, as well as in Asia and South America, the level of automation is not as high as in the U.S.A. The effect of this is that it may take longer for problems to be isolated. A customer in the U.S.A. who is accustomed to having his problems fixed quickly is often surprised at the time it takes to fix problems on the international circuit. In general, it is fair to say that international circuit problems take longer to fix.

Another issue in network management is what a technical term means to the customer and to the different common carriers who have to resolve a problem in the network. For example, the carriers and the customers have to agree among themselves about what constitutes a fault or a trouble and on the criteria for degradation. The definition of what is a trouble and when a trouble report will be accepted varies among countries and an agreement has to be reached beforehand about what constitutes a trouble to ensure a smooth functioning network.

Companies are beginning to integrate their voice, data, fax, and video networks to resolve some of these issues. Using an integrated network, companies can monitor the network all the way to their customer premises in other countries. This can fulfill an important requirement of top management to have a central view of the network and thus obtain instant information about the health of the network. The company's central NMS can have information on how the network is performing, major outages, what efforts are being undertaken to fix them, and degradation of performance on some facilities. They can use this information to reroute traffic or to adopt other strategies so that the global business runs without interruption. Hence, integrated global information systems and effective network management systems to manage them are becoming a priority of MIS and telecommunications managers.

SUMMARY

The benefits of implementing global networks are just starting to be realized; many new information systems can be designed and implemented using such networks. Governments and large companies will be able to monitor and control their information technology resources in different parts of the globe instantaneously. Developing such networks also exposes the technical issues and problems in connecting the equipment and networks of different vendors. Standardization of the major components of the network would hasten the development of such networks. Integrated network management systems are beginning to provide the confidence to telecommunications managers that maintenance of such global networks is a feasible task. An understanding of the technical issues in designing global networks is a prerequisite in utilizing these networks to form innovative and new global information systems. A new cadre of systems engineers is beginning to master these issues in leading telecommunications companies.

References

Elbert, B.R. (1989). *Private Telecommunication Networks*, Artech House, Norwood, MA.

Ergas, H., and Okayama, J. (1984). *Changing Market Structures in Telecommunications*. North-Holland, Amsterdam.

Foley, J. (June 5, 1989). GE Blazes Global Path" *Communications Week, 251,* p. 1, 49.

Harper, J.M. (1989). *Telecommunications Policy and Management*. Pinter Publishers, London.

Smith, D.R. (1985). *Digital Transmission Systems*. Van Nostrand Reinhold Company, New York, p. 10.

Stallings, W. (1990). *Business Data Communications*. Macmillan Publishing Company, New York, NY.

Taff, A. (December 26, 1988/January 2, 1989). Undersea cable may herald lower prices. *Network World,5*:(52), p. 11-12.

12

The International Significance of Electronic Data Interchange

Roger Clarke—Australian National University
Persio DeLuca—Arthur Andersen, Sao Paulo, Brazil
Joze Gricar—University of Maribor, Yugoslavia
Takeshi Imai —Intelligence Engineering Association, Tokyo
Don McCubbrey —University of Denver
Paula Swatman—Murdoch University, Perth, W.Australia

Most discussions of Electronic Data Interchange have been from the viewpoint of a single organisation, although in some cases the perspective of an industry sector has been adopted. This chapter considers the international aspects of EDI.

An introduction is provided to EDI generally, and to the various classes of EDI services, especially Trade EDI systems. Determinants of the diffusion process are then discussed. The role of EDI in international trade is considered, and both positive and negative aspects identified. The transborder nature of many industry sectors is noted. Consideration is given to the ways in which governments are likely to be involved in using EDI, in stimulating it, in regulating it and in both unintentionally and intentionally retarding it. Policy issues for transnational corporations are discussed, and a research agenda is proposed.

INTRODUCTION

Electronic Data Interchange (EDI) is a term referring to a class of inter-organisational applications of information technology. Although the history of EDI is readily traceable to at least the 1960s, it is only in the 1990s that its potential is being realized.

The impact and implications of EDI for individual organisations are coming to be understood. More slowly, the meaning of EDI for industry sectors and for individual countries is also being appreciated. To date, however, relatively little attention has been given to EDI's international significance. This chapter addresses that issue.

The chapter commences by providing a definition of EDI, identifying its benefits and examining the various kinds of EDI applications. The factors are then discussed which are important in understanding the diffusion process whereby EDI comes to be applied. EDI's international impacts and contributions to global value chains are identified. Broader implications for the international order are identified, and policy issues for governments and transnational corporations discussed. Finally, a research agenda is proposed.

BACKGROUND TO EDI

A popular definition of EDI is "the standards-based computer-to-computer exchange of inter-company business documents and information" (Coathup, 1988). Application of EDI beyond its original area of product ordering and delivery systems has resulted in a fuller definition being needed. In this chapter, following the structure of Brawn (1989), the essential elements of EDI are defined to be:

> • direct communication between applications (not merely between computers);
> • the use of an electronic transmission medium (normally a value-added network) rather than the despatch of storage media such as magnetic tapes and disks;
> • the use of one of: electronic mail boxes for 'store and collect' transmission and delivery of documents; forwarding and delivery of urgent documents ('store and forward'); or real-time document exchange; and
> • the use of structured, formatted messages based upon internationally agreed standards (enabling messages to be translated, interpreted and checked for compliance to a set of standard rules).

EDI systems represent a class of organisational application of data communications. They are more specifically targeted than generalised services such as electronic mail, file transfer and remote data entry, and generally build on such products. On the other hand, they are less precisely targeted at business needs than products such as Just-in-Time inventory management systems and Quick-Response retail systems.

Although the early applications of what became known as EDI were undertaken in the United States, the idea's origins have an international flavour, since they are traceable back to the 1948 Berlin Airlift, where the task of co-ordinating airfreighted consignments of food and consumables (which arrived with differing manifests, languages and numbers of copies) was addressed by devising a standard manifest to be filled in by aircraft before unloading (Brawn, 1989).

The replacement of physical transport of paper and magnetic media by electronic transmission commenced during the 1960s, initially in the rail and road transport industries. The standardisation of documents was a necessary concomitant to that change. In 1968 the United States Transportation Data Coordinating Committee (TDCC) was formed, to coordinate the development of translation rules among four existing sets of industry-specific standards (McNurlin, 1987). A more significant move towards standardisation came with the X12 standards of the American National Standards Institute (ANSI), which gradually extended and replaced those created by the TDCC.

At about the same time, the U.K. Department of Customs and Excise, with the assistance of SITPRO (the British Simplification of Trade Procedures Board), was developing its own standards for documents used in international trade, called Tradacoms. These were later extended by the United Nations Economic Commission for Europe (UNECE) into what became known as the GTDI (General-purpose Trade Data Interchange standards), and were gradually accepted by some 2,000 British exporting organisations (Schatz, 1988).

Problems created by the trans-Atlantic use of two different (and largely incompatible) sets of standardised documents have been addressed by the formation of a United Nations Joint European and North American working party (UN-JEDI), which began the development of the EDIFACT (Electronic Data Interchange for Administration, Commerce and Transport) document translation standards. By the end of the 1980s, only two EDIFACT documents had been completed (a purchase order and an invoice), but a full range of business documents was in the process of being developed and approved (e.g. Carter, 1989).

EDI's direct impacts include labour-savings in the areas of data transcription, controls, and error investigation and correction; and fewer delays in data-handling. The resultant benefits are (e.g. Hill, 1989):

- improved inventory management;
- better control of transport and distribution;
- reduced administration costs;
- the possibility of more flexible buying strategies;
- better cash management; and
- improved trading partner relationships.

The indirect benefits may prove to be even more significant, but can only be obtained from closer integration among related functions within different organisations: it is not the replacement of paper by electronic messaging which provides EDI's strategic capabilities, but the associated changes in operation and function within and between organisations which EDI links make possible. For example, Rochester (1989) cites the case of Levi Strauss which, through its Quick Response system LeviLink, has achieved a complete vertical integration of the company's entire apparel manufacturing and marketing cycle (including the replenishment of inventory, the management and reconciliation of purchase orders, the receipt of goods, the processing and payment of invoices, the capture of point-of-sale information and the analysis of market trends). This focus on achieving integration across organisational functions and between organisations is what distinguishes EDI from other forms of electronic transaction, and makes EDI a strategic application of IT.

EDI's implications have been closely examined by many authors, but generally from the perspective of an individual organisation, or in some cases an industry sector or a particular country. Much less attention has been paid to the international significance of EDI, and the purpose of this chapter is to consider that question, by drawing on the experiences of specialists from a variety of countries.

This chapter first discusses a number of important factors relating to the technology of EDI, and the process by which the technology is coming to be applied in many different contexts, and for many different purposes. Some particular international impacts are then discussed, and it is proposed that the focus of future attention must be EDI's application throughout the value chains of each international industry sector.

A TAXONOMY OF EDI SYSTEMS

EDI Systems may be differentiated on the basis of a variety of different factors. This section identifies and briefly discusses five factors. The first is the mode of communication by which documents are transmitted.

The most basic mode of communication is direct transfer from the originator to the recipient. However, where the intended recipient is not currently able or willing to accept delivery (e.g. due to malfunction or unavailability of the equipment or the transmission medium), the transmission must be deferred and re-tried until it succeeds. A development on such simple 'point-to-point' systems is the 'store-and-forward' mode, in which an intermediary stores the document, and takes over the responsibility for achieving delivery, thereby freeing the originator to continue with other tasks.

A further development is 'store-and-collect', using an electronic mailbox. Under these arrangements, an enterprise can transmit a document and have it stored by an intermediary (typically a third-party EDI services supplier) until the addressee calls for the contents of his mailbox. For such arrangements to be effective, there generally needs to be an expectation of frequent clearances of mailboxes by all participants, e.g. at least daily and in many industries considerably more frequently.

Finally, some systems depend on 'on-line' communications, whereby the parties to the transaction are directly connected in an on-line session. Arrangements involving on-line sessions among participants have generally been referred to using terms such as 'electronic trading' and 'electronic markets'. The term 'EDI' has been conventionally used only for systems utilising off-line modes of communication. The distinction is arbitrary, and will shortly become a hindrance. Hence, in this chapter, the terms 'EDI' and 'electronic trading' are both used generally, irrespective of the mode of communication.

Another distinction which can be usefully drawn is between alternative patterns of organisational participation in EDI. Some systems have a star topology, with a single organisation having independent links with many others. This is typical of a system sponsored by a single organisation dominant in its industry or region, particularly where the sponsoring organisation seeks competitive advantage from those links.

An alternative to such a 'one-to-many' system is a 'many-to-many' system, in which each participant uses the system to communicate with a number of other participants. This is typical of a collaborative system sponsored by an industry association. The technical difficulties are significantly greater, and in such systems it has generally been found convenient to use an intermediary, which acts as a clearing house or communications hub, and is operated by one key player, a cooperative, or a specialist third party.

A further form of EDI system is the 'incremental paper trail' (Swatman & Swatman, 1989a), in which a document is initiated by one party, and progressively added to by a succession of other organisations, culminating in a completed document against which action can be taken. This is the form of Trade EDI systems, discussed in the following section of this chapter.

A related factor is the degree of 'openness' of the system. At one extreme participants may form a 'closed user group' permitting access only to member organisations (as is the case with the bank-operated Society for Worldwide Interbank Financial Telecommunications – SWIFT). At the other extreme, any organisation may connect to the system and send documents to and/or receive documents from any other participant.

A third classification basis is the source of the standards upon which EDI systems are built. Some protocols are proprietary, i.e. owned by a particular company. Others are used within a particular industry sector within a particular country (e.g. the national banking systems in many countries). Still others are standard within a particular industry but across national borders (e.g. in aviation). Some standards apply to all industry sectors, but only within one country (e.g. the United States' ANSI X12 and IEEE standards). Some standards are established by international organisations (in particular ISO and CCITT). Some standards, particularly those promulgated by ANSI, have become well-established outside the geographical area for which they were originally designed.

A further way in which EDI systems can be categorised is according to the environment in which they are applied. One such class, Trade EDI systems, is of such importance that it is dealt with in its own section, below. Another special class is the variety of systems serving the travel and tourism industry. Airline reservation systems pre-date EDI's development (e.g. Copeland & McKenney, 1988), and such systems are therefore commonly considered as EDI-like rather than as EDI systems. These applications are becoming increasingly standardised, with the active involvement of the worldwide industry body, the International Air Travel Association (IATA).

There are many other areas to which EDI principles and EDI software packages are applicable. Libraries have significant volumes of flows among themselves, e.g. for inter-library loan requests. Government agencies are increasingly accepting documents via electronic lodgement, particularly in taxation, the regulation of corporations, and land information. National statistical authorities and commercial market research enterprises are increasingly seeking to collect statistical information as a by-product of companies' transaction processing, using EDI.

An additional way in which EDI systems may be classified is according to their geographical or jurisdictional extent. Many such applications are local to a country, or even to a jurisdiction (e.g. a State, Province, Land, département or canton) within a country. Others are inherently international, including travel and tourism, and industries based on natural resources originating in the agricultural, pastoral and mining industries. Some EDI applications administered by agencies of national governments are explicitly concerned with international matters, including visa and migration application processing, and consular and trade-related enquiries. There are also areas, such as communications between the surveillance and investigative agencies of different countries, where routine international transaction flows may benefit from EDI.

TRADE EDI SYSTEMS

The origins of EDI are to be found in the trade and transportation of goods, and this continues to be a major area of application. There is an increasing trend toward conceiving of schemes which facilitate trade across a wide segment of an economy, rather than just corporation-based schemes or even schemes serving specific industry-sectors. This ensures that all transportation modes (rail, road, sea and air) are able to be more conveniently integrated into the system, and that related services such as finance and insurance can also be involved (e.g. Emmelhainz, 1988).

Trade EDI begins with the creation of a contract. However, the manner in which purchases and sales of goods and services are effected varies considerably. Conventionally, the three stages in the development of a contract are:

- the transmission by one party to one or more other parties of an 'invitation to treat', by which is meant any communication (documentary or otherwise) which indicates that the first party is interested in purchasing or selling an identified class of goods or services. Invitations to treat include advertisements, sales catalogues and invitations to tender. The recipient parties may or may not have been identified by the initiating party; for example the invitation may have been explicitly addressed to known parties (e.g. to a set of pre-qualified tenderers), or may have been broadcast or placed in a publicly accessible location (e.g. 'yellow pages' directories of suppliers of particular classes of goods and services, which are maintained by some other organisation);

- the transmission by one party to another specific party of an 'offer', by which is meant any communication (whether documentary or not) proposing the purchase or sale of specified goods or services, and containing explicit terms and conditions, and/or explicit or implicit reference to additional terms and conditions conventionally used in the particular context in which the contract is struck (e.g. the specific norms of the industry sector or jurisdiction); and

- the transmission by the offeree to the offeror of an 'acceptance' of a specific offer, by which is meant any communication (whether documentary or not) accepting an offer previously made concerning the purchase or sale of specified goods or services. Where a communication contains alternative or additional terms and conditions, it is generally a revised offer rather than an acceptance.

Beyond the point at which a contract comes into existence, a great many activities occur and many different documents are created, such as delivery date enquiries, delivery schedules, notices of despatch, notices of receipt and non-receipt, and invoices. There may also be additional documents involving third parties, such as notices to responsible authorities where the cargo is hazardous or oversize. These documents tend to vary in name and form between industries. All such documents could in principle be transmitted as structured electronic documents, using any of the modes identified in the previous section. The term 'Trade EDI systems' embraces electronic transmission of both the contract-related and the logistics-related documents.

Many types of business are essentially localised, because they deal in perishable goods (e.g. soft fruits) or heavy low-value materials (e.g. sand-

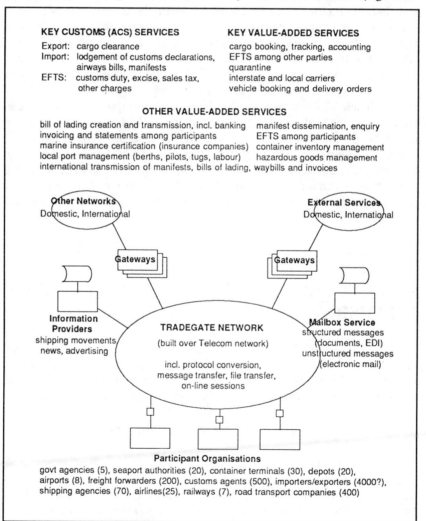

KEY CUSTOMS (ACS) SERVICES

Export: cargo clearance
Import: lodgement of customs declarations, airways bills, manifests
EFTS: customs duty, excise, sales tax, other charges

KEY VALUE-ADDED SERVICES

cargo booking, tracking, accounting
EFTS among other parties
quarantine
interstate and local carriers
vehicle booking and delivery orders

OTHER VALUE-ADDED SERVICES

bill of lading creation and transmission, incl. banking
invoicing and statements among participants
marine insurance certification (insurance companies)
local port management (berths, pilots, tugs, labour)
international transmission of manifests, bills of lading,

manifest dissemination, enquiry
EFTS among participants
container inventory management
hazardous goods management
waybills and invoices

Other Networks
Domestic, International

External Services
Domestic, International

Gateways

Gateways

Information Providers
shipping movements
news, advertising

TRADEGATE NETWORK
(built over Telecom network)

incl. protocol conversion,
message transfer, file transfer,
on-line sessions

Mailbox Service
structured messages
(documents, EDI)
unstructured messages
(electronic mail)

Participant Organisations
govt agencies (5), seaport authorities (20), container terminals (30), depots (20),
airports (8), freight forwarders (200), customs agents (500), importers/exporters (4000?),
shipping agencies (70), airlines(25), railways (7), road transport companies (400)

Exhibit 1: International Trade EDI – Australia's Tradegate

quarrying), involve personal services (e.g. customised computer systems), or are created and nurtured by local laws (e.g. accounting and tax advice publications). The majority of the early Trade EDI systems were designed and implemented within national boundaries, partly because of the large volumes of such within-country commercial activity, and partly due to the significantly greater complexity of international trade.

To large corporations, however, national borders are historical relics which create unnatural barriers to business. It is more natural to think of world-wide industry sectors for aluminium and wool than to think of a large number of national aluminium and wool sectors linked via international trade. Even in regions such as Western Europe, whose nations have significant cultural and historical differences, and in which warfare raged less than 50 years ago, economic considerations are leading to rationalisation of trade arrangements.

To support trade in large multi-nation regions, and worldwide, International Trade EDI systems are emerging. These presuppose the existence in member-nations of domestic networks which enable the efficient capture of relevant export-related data in electronic form, the transmission of data to the importing country, and the receipt and handling of that data in that country. Exhibit 1 provides a schematic representation of the Australian trade-related EDI system which is being developed around the Australian Customs Service (ACS). Tradegate's early phases are in operation and subsequent phases are under construction.

KEY CONSIDERATIONS IN EDI TECHNOLOGY DIFFUSION

The general theory of technology diffusion is fairly well understood (e.g. Rogers, 1983). This section identifies and discusses key factors which determine the rate at which EDI is adopted, and the extent to which it is able to contribute to the operations of corporations and government agencies.

Infrastructure Requirements

For EDI to be tenable, a number of pre-conditions must be satisfied. One requirement is for a sufficiently sophisticated and reliable data communications network to be available, extending at least to the major industrial and commercial centres. This is the case in all industrialised countries, and the pre-condition is increasingly satisfied by newly industrialised economies (NIEs). It is not so readily satisfied by less developed countries (LDCs), such as the countries of Africa and Oceania. Since some of these countries are important sources of raw materials for the industrialised world and the NIEs, this may be a problem as much for the advanced countries as for the LDCs. Furthermore, although satellite communications are technically feasible, they remain expensive and not wholly reliable.

A second infrastructural requirement is that clerical staff must have basic skills in the use of computers, and of computer-based systems. Since so-called 'personal computers' popularised and democratised computing, 'computer literacy' is in many cases becoming adequate, even in less technologically advanced countries. The emergence of 'information literacy' is slower,however.

In addition, corporations must have technical experience and capabilities in relation to computing and telecommunications, and the capital to invest in further specialised requirements. With the increasing availability from third parties of EDI interfacing packages and even of complete turnkey systems, this particular barrier is becoming less significant, at least in the richer countries.

Early Competitive Orientation

The first few EDI applications, in the U.S. transportation industry, were developed by a particular industry sector to facilitate the movement of goods. During the 1980s, however, the emphasis shifted to closed networks connecting a single corporation with its suppliers and/or customers, and usually using proprietary protocols. A considerable amount was written and said during this period about EDI as a competitive application of IT (e.g. Benjamin et al, 1988).

It seems likely that in a few circumstances, EDI may indeed be a valuable weapon whereby sustainable competitive advantage may be able to be achieved. Certainly the recent experiences of Japan, a relative latecomer to EDI, suggest that some corporations believe so, with corporation-based systems in the automobile, food, steel, textile, marine transportation and electronic equipment industries. In several sectors in the United States and in Japan, a single large company has implemented an EDI system, and required its suppliers to interface with it. In Australia, there is one instance of a 'dominant-corporation' EDI scheme, and three other company-based schemes in which one corporation (the iron and steel giant BHP and two aluminium smelters) dominate the industry and commerce of a geographical region.

Subsequent Collaborative Orientation

In the majority of industry sectors, however, at least after the early flush of excitement is over, it appears that a sector-based scheme is more likely to dominate. This is partly because competitors tend to move to neutralise a single corporation's advantage, and partly because industry and regulatory bodies tend to perceive a successful scheme to be anti-competitive.

Although sector-based collaboration might seem to reduce the competitiveness of the industry concerned, EDI tends to open up new possibilities for competition among participants. Corporations benefit from EDI only if they organise themselves to do so, by investing in technical capability and know-how, and adapting their internal procedures and structures to the new environment. Dynamic companies not only reduce costs, but also increase the service level they offer their clients, and discover new ways of leveraging on their existing comparative advantages. Inflexible companies, on the other hand, lose market share and either adapt or withdraw from the sector. Cooperative, sector-based schemes therefore benefit the sector's clients, and hence the economy and society as a whole.

Two effects which have been remarked upon in the United States are 'de-sourcing' and 'partnering'. De-sourcing refers to organisations decreasing the number of alternative suppliers from whom they source any particular raw material or component. They are able to do this because of the improved reliability of their suppliers resulting from improved intra- and inter-corporate information flows. The natural extension of this is partnering, which is a form of tighter, EDI-induced vertical integration or alliance between corporations.

Naturally counter-instances can be found. Although few EDI failures have been documented to date, an instance has been reported in the Australian business press of a duopolistic sector (book-distribution) in which each of the two companies began to develop their own system for installation in bookshops and libraries throughout the country, but both then, in a classic stand-off, cancelled their developments. Several years later, there is still no sign of a collaborative venture to replace the withdrawn competitive ones.

The Distribution of EDI's Benefits

It is unlikely that all organisations would be equally well placed to reap the benefits of EDI. In many circumstances, economies of scale enable large companies to benefit more than smaller ones, but at least as regards the IT components this does not appear to be the case with EDI. Smaller companies, whose needs can be satisfied by 'off-the-shelf' PC-based packages, and whose operations are more flexible, tend to be able to implement EDI very quickly. Large corporations, on the other hand, must make significant modifications to long-standing internal applications running in mainframe/ 'dumb' terminal environments rather than on networked PCs or on server/ intelligent workstation configurations.

There is some evidence, however, that the overall business benefits which EDI offers advantage larger corporations at the cost of smaller ones. In the United States, for example, the development of partnering is generally expected to favour larger suppliers. Another factor noted in Japan has been that closer coupling of supply chains into Just In Time (JIT) streams is having the effect of transferring the costs of investment in buffer stocks from the (generally large) downstream manufacturers to the (generally smaller) low-level components suppliers.

A further aspect is that many corporations which are not large enough to dominate their business partners are only slowly realising the anticipated benefits of their investment in EDI because their partners are not adopting it, or adapting to it, sufficiently quickly.

Third-Party Network Services

For several reasons, there is an increasing tendency for even the largest organisations to contract with third parties for the supply of networking services, rather than perform the function themselves. One reason is that, in sector-based schemes, each company prefers to concentrate its energies on its own 'competitive advantage' or 'distinctive differences', rather than on services such as EDI which underlie those differences. Another is that the network services must assure participants of the confidentiality and integrity of their documents, and trust is easier to invest in a third party than in a competitor. A further advantage of third-party networks is that the infrastructure costs can be shared across a variety of different EDI networks, rather than all being absorbed by one. The nature of services provided by third-party network vendors is shown in Exhibit 2.

A further advantage of having the network run by a third party is that inter-networking is facilitated. Many companies which sell components or supplies to multiple industries face the spectre of needing multiple pieces of computing equipment and network connections, or at least multiple software packages, in order to interface with multiple sector-based EDI systems. A third-party network supplier is in a position to offer such companies a service whereby they will accept transactions in a format compatible with one standard, and deliver in a format compatible with another. The cross-linkage of various EDI services is thereby facilitated.

In some countries, such as Australia, there has been a proliferation of organisations endeavouring to sell network services, and a shake-out is expected in due course, as it becomes apparent what business volumes the contenders have been able to attract (Takac & Swatman, 1989). Although many would regard this as a sign of a healthy market-place, an industry sector may be disrupted by the withdrawal or failure of the network supplier with whom its members had contracted.

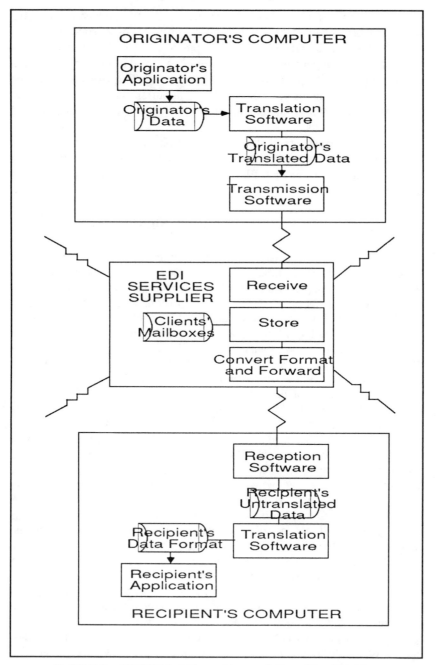

Exhibit 2:   EDI Third-Party Network Provider Services

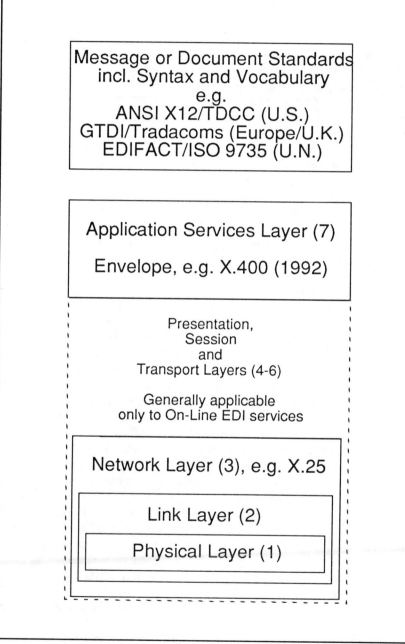

Exhibit 3: Standards Underlying EDI

The Standardization Issue

Standards are making a vital contribution to the infrastructure of EDI (e.g. Dawkins 1988, Scott 1988, Carter 1989 and Hollands 1989). The areas in which standards are needed range from underlying data communications protocols to applications software interfaces. Exhibit 3 depicts the International Standards Organisation's Open Systems Interconnection (ISO OSI) reference model, which has been particularly important to the current proliferation of EDI systems.

ISO's lower three Layers (1-3) of data communication standards provide a reliable message transmission medium, upon which inter-organisational business solutions can depend. The intermediate three Layers (4-6) provide on-line sessions between end-points, and are therefore less relevant to the current mainstream of EDI which uses 'store-and-collect' or 'store-and-forward' rather than direct on-line communications between business partners. The uppermost Layer (7), however, provides a number of services to applications, such as file transfer and electronic directories, and most critically for EDI's purposes, electronic message management or 'e-mail' services.

Although the X.400 standard appears likely to become the dominant electronic messaging standard, several different Layer 7 'message envelope' protocols will co-exist for some time, with third-party network suppliers providing protocol conversion between X.400 and earlier standards. Within the 'electronic envelope' which standards like X.400 provide, a further level of standards is needed, to specify precisely how the message itself is to be interpreted. Several such electronic document standards have been established to facilitate EDI. Of particular importance are TDCC and its successor ANSI X12 in the United States, Tradacoms and its successor GTDI in the United Kingdom and elsewhere in Europe, and EDIFACT which is a more recent international movement to produce worldwide standards.

A further group of standards appears likely to develop as EDI extends throughout the commercial world. This would specify the interfaces between EDI systems and the humans within user organisations. As more organisations take advantage of EDI, greater system inter-connection will be required. It is a hindrance for users of multiple EDI systems to have to become familiar with the separate front ends written by system providers. A single EDI front-end (particularly for the PC-based EDI systems generally used in small organisations) would simplify connection and make the concept of multiple connectivity less daunting.

It should not be assumed, however, that the use of standards guarantees success in EDI. In any given aspect of EDI there is unlikely to be a single standard, nor is it even necessarily true that any one standard will tend to dominate, and hence become the reference point. The need for protocol conversion, probably as a network service, is not a mere interim measure, but is likely to be a long term feature of EDI systems. In addition, standards, of necessity, tend to ossify existing technical solutions and industry practices, and therefore represent a barrier to future change.

A further aspect of standards is the length of time and the amount of negotiation which is required from the time a standard is mooted until it is actually approved. A period of some years may elapse before clearly written explanations are available. Major players in the market invest a great deal sending staff-members to participate in standards-setting processes, in order to ensure that they can design and construct products which comply with forthcoming standards (Berg & Schumny, 1990).

Motivations, and the Source of Payback

Some EDI schemes have been embarked upon because they provide the opportunity to lower the labour costs of data transmission. This arises from the rationalisation of purchasing activities, reduction in the volume of paper-handling, and a decrease in the incidence of transcription errors. Particularly in countries with high inflation and interest rates, there has been a desire to implement EDI in order to decrease the lags in the order-placement process, and so keep buffer stocks low; and to increase the control over cash flows.

Beyond these essentially defensive purposes, much more positive motivations have also been evident. In Trade EDI Systems, for example, both the companies concerned and the exporting country stand to gain from quicker handling of cargo. EDI has been seen in some countries as a means of improving the efficiency of waterfront industries, by speedier, less redundant and less error-prone data flows, and by using the opportunity to undertake significant change in operational practices. Meanwhile in Japan, an important stimulus has been the trend towards more frequent orders for smaller quantities, which in turn arises from increased product diversity and emphasis on Just In Time (JIT) manufacturing inventory systems.

Cultural Factors

A number of other considerations can be lumped together under the term 'culture'. Of especial importance is the openness of borders, variously to trade, investment, business and tourist travel, and industrial and commercial innovations. There are also questions of the cultural and lingual compatibility of a country with its potential partners, and particularly the proportion of the country's working population which has mastered the *lingua franca* of contemporary international trade, English.

A further matter of considerable consequence is the strategy, policies, actions and consistency of the national government. In some countries, such as Australia, the Government has designed an export-oriented strategy and carried that strategy through into action, such that the Australian Customs Service has been one of the key players in the development of Trade EDI. In others, such as Brazil, foreign exchange controls, and very slow appreciation of and adoption of EDI by government agencies actively retards developments.

INTERNATIONAL IMPACTS OF EDI

This section investigates a number of aspects of EDI which are of especial significance at an international level. It commences with a discussion of EDI's role in international trade, followed by consideration of trade blocs and impediments to trade. The role of standards is then re-assessed.

EDI's Role in International Trade

Efficient communications are an important factor in international trade, not so much because of their direct costs, but because poor quality or slow communications can give rise to considerable indirect costs, delays in the delivery of goods, increased investment in buffer stocks, and disruptions in manufacturing processes.

EDI services are critical in both the large central ports, and in remote locations. In both the exporting and the importing zone, containers are handled several times in quick succession, for example at the original point of loading, in a dockside park, onto a small vessel in a feeder port, and off the small vessel and onto a large ship in a major port. Electronic documentation preparation and transmission, and service availability at all handling points, is vital to the efficiency of these activities.

Materials such as coal, iron ore, bauxite, oil and wheat are not containerised, but instead transported by special-purpose bulk carriers, in many cases of enormous capacity. Because there are relatively very few transactions involved and the transit time of the loads is appreciable, it would be reasonable to expect that conventional communications by paper and telex or fax would continue to be satisfactory until such time as electronic communication becomes the norm. It is apparent, however, that the large resources companies are already sophisticated users of computing and telecommunications for a variety of other purposes, and are tending to be early adopters of EDI.

Economic and Trading Blocs

EDI appears to be becoming a factor in the maintenance of existing groups of nations with close economic ties, and in the emergence of new blocs. The European Community's EC '92 programme of 285 reforms will "effectively make a single trading market of 12 disparate nations ... The need for standardised inter- organisational links which EC'92 requires will mean a rapid proliferation of electronic networks, TBISs [Telecommunications-Based Information Systems] and the expertise to manage both ... The best-known and most important example of the co-operative systems group is Electronic Data Interchange" (Swatman and Swatman, 1989b).

The prospect of Fortress Europe, no matter how hotly denied by Europeans themselves, seriously concerns their other trading partners: "The energy and reality of substantial change are irrefutable: European business and political leaders are forcing the pace. If the outcome is anywhere near as radical as some Europeans hope, the American eagle and the so-called Asian dragons are about to meet a kind of European wolf pack" (Magee, 1989).

Whether or not the EC '92 programme results in a fortress built against outsiders, or a purely internal improvement in European trade efficiency, the electronic links provided by EDI will be a major factor in its success: "the single European market is all about the 12 member states working as one. Every procedure which improves business communications helps us to attain the single European market. EDI will accelerate our attainment of the single European market" (Purton, 1989). It is not yet clear whether other trading blocs are perceiving EDI to be a key factor in their future operation.

Economic and Trading Blockages

Research into the role of EDI within the European Community needs to be complemented by projects to assess the impacts elsewhere. There are as many Western European nations outside the EC as there are members, and these include some (such as Switzerland) which have very high volumes of trade with EC members. In addition, the enormous changes in Eastern Europe during late 1989 raise questions about the inter-linkage of trade, and of trade EDI systems, across what was until so very recently the Iron Curtain. Some Western European nations, both in the West (e.g. Switzerland and Austria) and the East (particularly Yugoslavia and Hungary), have recognised the contribution that EDI services may make to the retention and further development of their trading relationships with the European Community (McCubbrey & Kunin, 1989).

Elsewhere, Americans are very concerned about their access to

European markets (e.g. Magee, 1989). More distant countries, such as nations in Africa, South America, and the South Pacific which export food and minerals which European countries cannot produce, fear the bargaining power of a united Europe. There would appear to be scope for nation-groupings based not on physical proximity but on economic complementarity, such as 'tundra and tropics' and 'industrial and bread-basket' cooperations. Effective communications via EDI would play a key facilitative role should such international economic alliances develop.

Different countries, however, have differing abilities to participate in EDI schemes. It seems likely that, all other things being more or less equal, the trading companies of the major economic players will prefer to deal with countries with whom quality communications links exist. This would tend to work against the less developed countries, most of whom lack the capital to finance telecommunications infrastructure, and the workforce skills to fulfil the major countries' expectations.

EDI and Standardization

EDI has added pressure to the widespread demand for commonality of the underlying data communications services. International harmonisation is being greatly facilitated by the adoption by many national standards bodies of standards promulgated by international bodies, particularly ISO, whose Open Systems Interconnection (OSI) reference model has provided the general framework, the Consultative Committee on International Telegraphics and Telecommunications (CCITT) and UN-JEDI.

This movement is being accelerated by the EC'92 programme: "the greater standardisation of systems - both those from suppliers and those being used within user organisations - is likely to be one of the most significant consequences of the single market" (Tate, 1989); and "several Commission programmes focus on the improvement of the European Data Communications networks and already much work has been done in the area of standards and development to provide a common IT infrastructure" (Hardy, 1988). One of the most significant elements involved in the large-scale rationalisation of Europe's inter-organisational systems is the creation of a single Trading Document to replace the 35 separate documents previously required for trade within Europe.

In the United States, it is perceived that international EDI has been held back by differences between standards. The long-standing document standards, particularly X12, need to be mapped onto newer standards, particularly EDIFACT. For the most part this should not prove to be an enormous barrier, although it will take time before the EDIFACT family of standards is completed, and further time before reliable protocol conversion software is readily available. Some mis-mappings between the different families of standards is inevitable, and some rationalisation may have to be undertaken. For example, the United States' X12 standards' 2-character State-code is a little inconvenient for such countries as Australia (which uses a 3-character code), and its 5-digit Zip-field is rather more inconvenient for such countries as the United Kingdom and Canada (which use 6-character Postcode strings including both alphabetic and numeric characters).

The early industry-sector systems were closed networks using industry-specific protocols. As the quality of third-party services has improved, and with developments in standards, there has been an increasing tendency for networks to be open, to be operated by specialist suppliers, and to use national and international standards. This has been fairly apparent in the United States, and very clear in such countries as Australia, Brazil and Yugoslavia, which have come into EDI late, but have adopted them quickly.

It is less apparent in some other countries, particularly Japan, where the strength of the large companies is considerable, and the cultural leanings towards independence and even insularity are strong. It appears that proprietary and industry-sector standards may remain dominant for some time in Japan, and that third-party networks may not make a significant impact until they are able to offer conversion among industry and national protocols, and gateways out to international EDI networks. On the other hand, Japan is highly internationally oriented, through its trading houses, its enormously successful manufacturing industries, and more recently its overseas investments and the tendency of some of its corporations towards internationalisation. The need to adopt international standards when dealing internationally may bring about more rapid change in Japan's domestic systems than is currently foreseeable.

EDI IN CORPORATE AND GLOBAL VALUE CHAINS

The notion of the 'value chain' (e.g. Flaatten et al, 1989), reproduced in Exhibit 4, identifies the succession of activities by which a corporation adds value to its raw materials, and delivers its product to its customers.

Extension of the value chain notion to the level of the industry sector provides a basis for evaluating EDI's potential contributions. Exhibit 5 provides an example of the form which a model specific to any particular industry might take. The succession of organisations involved is identified, together with key supporting organisations. At successive points along the

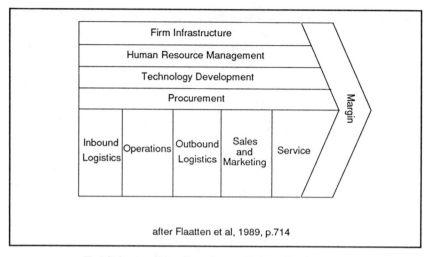

after Flaatten et al, 1989, p.714

Exhibit 4:   The Corporate Value Chain

chain, the flow of materials between the participants is enabled through electronic trading and electronic support for logistics.

This model does not purport to be generally applicable, because EDI is a broad class of service, and must be specialised in order to provide direct benefits to particular enterprises. For example, SWIFT in the international banking sector, Just In Time systems in manufacturing and some service sectors, and Quick Response systems in the retail sector, can be regarded as implementations of EDI principles in particular contexts. The example in Exhibit 5 is oriented toward goods-related industries, and a quite differently structured model is necessary for services-related EDI in such areas as banking, insurance, stock exchange trading and settlement, travel and tourism, libraries, taxation returns, and statistical collection and market research.

The enterprises in an industry value chain are most easily conceived as separate companies, with EDI as a means of providing value to organisations in the chain (e.g. wheat-grower, miller, bread manufacturer and foodstuffs retailer). However the enterprises may be separate profit-centres within the same conglomerate, or cost-centres within the same division of a single conglomerate. Hence, as EDI services mature, they may also have much to offer vertically integrated corporations in efficiently linking their own point-of-sale operations with inventory, purchasing, materials-handling, manufacturing and accounting systems.

There are many industries in which at least some of the steps in the value chain involve the flow of goods across national borders, and hence customs, quarantine, banking, insurance and other barriers must be negotiated. The model in Exhibit 5 incorporates some of those elements. The lessons being learned in Europe may prove highly valuable to all industry sectors and to countries throughout the world.

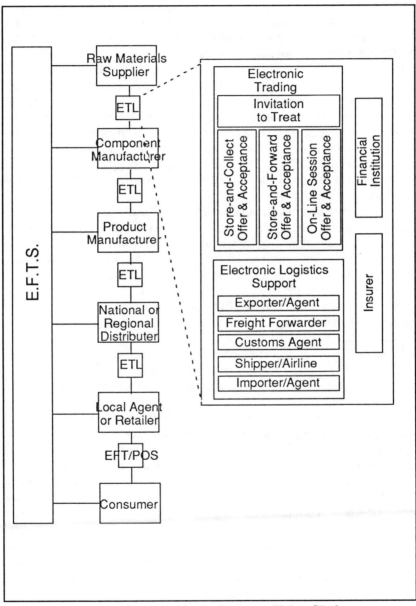

Exhibit 5: EDI in the Industry Value Chain

BROADER IMPLICATIONS FOR THE INTERNATIONAL ORDER

It seems likely that EDI systems will be imposed by large companies, mainly from advanced western nations, on the generally smaller companies in Newly Industrialized Economies (NIEs) and Less Developed Countries (LDCs). It is likely that these companies will be forced to have connections with a multiplicity of international EDI services running a variety of standards. There will be serious difficulties and long delays in upgrading the lesser-developed countries' infrastructures and human skills to the level necessary to take part in EDI. Hence it can be anticipated that many countries will encounter difficulties in taking part in the emerging new mechanisms of international trade. Because companies within LDCs will have difficulty participating in EDI, the influence of foreign and trans-national import-export houses within LDCs may well increase.

Many countries stimulate domestic economic development by biassing their purchasing toward local products. To the extent that EDI contributes toward more reliable, quicker and therefore cheaper international trade, local purchasing preferences will incur larger cost-disadvantages than before. If so, NIEs and LDCs may reduce the degree of local bias in their purchasing rules. Coupled with the moves to lower non-tariff trade barriers, EDI could therefore contribute to many less industrialised countries experiencing rapid structural change, perhaps amounting to de-industrialisation. The resulting replacement of domestic production by imports may place many LDCs in great economic difficulties. It is admittedly a long chain of cause-and-effect, but the disillusionment of many countries with the world order might be heightened, and there could be subsequent rounds of increased tariff and non-tariff protectionism.

A further potential effect of EDI is the facilitation of the monitoring of international trade, and the automation of customs duty collection. This may result in financial benefits for governments, but once again the rich nations are those most likely to be able to take advantage of the opportunity.

There are other potential impacts of EDI. For example, in common with other IT applications such as automated trading in stocks and shares, commodities and currencies, EDI might contribute to the more rapid transmission of economic shocks around the world, and hence increase economic instability. It is also possible that additional opportunities for cartels may emerge, based on regional groupings (e.g. the European Community) and/or factor-of-production groupings (e.g. the Organisation of Petroleum Exporting Countries – OPEC).

To the extent that EDI intensifies international interdependencies through trade, the sovereignty of nation-states will be diminished, and with it the likelihood of major (military) warfare between nation-states. However, to the extent that individual countries perceive (or pretend to perceive) internal economic malaise to result from outside interference, international tensions will be increased. The incidence of economically (as distinct from racially and politically) motivated terrorism and 'maverick-nation' behaviour may therefore tend to increase.

If, however, the nation-state divisions became less important, and the world were to divide into a smaller number of larger trading blocs, EDI might not help decrease the likelihood of inter-bloc warfare.

GOVERNMENT POLICY ISSUES

At an international level, the United Nations is involved in the development of regulations and standards for many aspects of EDI, from EDIFACT documents to the UNCID rules on legal aspects. Multi-national regional groupings, such as Europe's Single Unified Market, are involved in EDI schemes to create common trading documents and improve the flow of goods within the bloc. This section considers the ways in which the governments of nation-states and divisions within nation-states are likely to be involved in using EDI, in stimulating it, in regulating it, and in unintentionally and intentionally retarding it.

Governmental Use of EDI

The operations of many government agencies are capable of improvement through EDI systems. Potential applications include tendering for and purchase of goods and services, taxation return submission, submissions for benefits and subsidies (such as Medicare, pharmaceutical benefits and food stamps), land information systems, corporation registration systems, and the timelier and more accurate collection of statistics. Some government agencies have a direct interest in monitoring business transactions or volumes, e.g. those responsible for collecting customs and excise duties and sales tax, and law enforcement agencies which undertake transaction surveillance. It is therefore no surprise that some government agencies are active participants in EDI initiatives.

On the other hand, government agencies in most countries generally respond more slowly and ponderously to technological change than do private sector organisations. Such agencies may therefore experience considerable difficulties in rationalising their operations to achieve integration with EDI.

Governmental Stimulation of EDI

By acting as early adopters, governments can provide a stimulus for the development of the infrastructure and culture necessary for widespread use of EDI. An Australian survey undertaken in 1988 (Zinn and Takac, 1988) found that respondents expected government agencies (particularly those responsible for customs and taxation administration) would be the first to adopt EDI, probably within 2-5 years. Two further surveys found that there was considerable interest in and preparation for EDI among Australian government agencies (Swatman and Everett, 1990; Clarke et al, 1990).

Many national and regional governments have been involved in the emergence of EDI schemes, particularly for government purchasing and port management. International Trade EDI schemes have generally enjoyed significant involvement by interested government agencies (McCubbrey, 1990). For example, the U.K. GTDI document translation standards were largely traceable to the influence of Her Majesty's Customs, and the Australian Customs Service has been the prime mover behind the Australian Tradegate scheme (see Exhibit 1).

The majority of industrial collaboration, product development and even standardisation activity has been undertaken by corporations, industry associations and national standards associations, with limited involvement by their governments. Unnecessary intervention by governments in the development of EDI would be more likely to hinder rather than to assist in realising EDI's potential benefits. However, there are some areas in which government action may be beneficial, and even essential. At the very least, modifications are very likely to be required to various laws and court rules, particularly in the areas of evidence and contract, in order to facilitate EDI-based trade.

Governmental Regulation of EDI

The responsibility of national governments to regulate domestic activities may impose constraints on the development of EDI, in some cases through changes to the law. Depending on the nature of the domestic economy, some Governments may judge it necessary to encourage, for example, the emergence of third party networks, or their rationalisation. In Australia, the Government has clearly communicated its expectation that inter-connection among third-party network suppliers is to be achieved in the near future.

Beyond such exercises in persuasion, direct regulatory action may also be taken. In some industry sectors, an unacceptable degree of concentration may arise or market power may be abused, at least partly because of EDI, in which case trade practices, monopolies or anti-trust measures may be needed to ensure the survival of competition in the sector.

Governmental Inhibition of EDI

The governments of some countries may unintentionally retard the development of EDI, for example due to sheer bureaucratic sluggishness and unimaginativeness, or because investment in telecommunications infrastructure is perceived to be a relatively low priority for the country's limited capital resources. For example, both of these factors are operational in Brazil.

In some cases, EDI may be intentionally retarded for ideological, religious, strategic or political reasons, because the government seeks to maintain distance from the rest of the world. Although rapid change in Eastern Europe and the U.S.S.R. has seen many previously closed countries open their borders, a few substantially closed countries remain (including China, Iran, Albania and Myanmah – formerly Burma).

EDI might also be seen as contributing to greater cultural dominance by the economically and technically advanced countries, and hence a flattening out of cultures. Another potential threat to national sovereignty is that EDI may assist trans-national corporations (including not only manufacturing, transportation, finance and services companies, but also the major trading houses) to increase their influence over domestic economies. If it were perceived in this way, nationalist sentiments could result in some countries opposing EDI as an instrument of foreign domination.

There may also be circumstances in which a government would retard EDI for economic reasons. At present, the difficulty, cost and delays involved in international trade documentation represent a barrier to trade, and are hence a form of non-tariff protection of local industries. EDI has the effect of lowering that barrier, and hence exposing local industries to increased competition from industrialised countries. EDI might therefore work to the disadvantage of some countries, perhaps to the extent of contributing to de-industrialisation. If NEIs and LDCs detect serious threats to industries they perceive as being strategically important, they could reasonably be expected to defend those industries by placing barriers in the way of (generally overseas-sponsored) EDI developments.

TRANSNATIONAL CORPORATION POLICY ISSUES

EDI is a form of information technology with significant potential to change business practices. Unless senior management in large corporations appreciate this, and commit to EDI as a strategic measure, they may find themselves implementing 'perpetual pilot' schemes, which perform adequately within the confines of a particular application, but fail to deliver the economies possible from a top-down implementation.

Areas which have been suggested as demanding attention include interfaces between the corporation and its customers and suppliers, both within the country of manufacture and internationally; freight-forwarding, port systems, and document exchange with banks and international carriers; and the ability to automatically select the appropriate transmission medium depending on partner capabilities (Ulrich, 1990).

It is highly likely that, in utilising their freedom of self-determination, nation-states will impose differently conceived and inconsistent requirements on international enterprises. Corporations and industry associations need to monitor such developments, and actively lobby national governments and international agencies such as the General Agreement on Tariffs and Trade (GATT) to prevent such inconveniences from arising. In order to protect their interests against intentional restraints, corporations need to establish and maintain liaison with governments. They can thereby be positioned to take advantage of opportunities for creative 'win-win' strategies, and to avoid the unnecessary exercise of power over national governments and economies.

North American, European and Japanese corporations rely on many LDCs for resources which they cannot acquire from within their own geographical areas. There is hence a risk that these companies may impose (possibly ill-fitting) technology on LDCs rather than reduce trade with them. It is in the interests of multi-nationals and the richer countries to provide advice to LDCs regarding the development of their IT infrastructure and contribute to the associated education and training (McCubbrey & Griçar, 1989). It may be argued that transnational corporations should go further, and provide direct financial and technical assistance to countries in which they operate, to support the establishment of the necessary infrastructure, and perhaps also to ameliorate any adverse economic impacts.

RESEARCH OPPORTUNITIES

To date, only limited research has been undertaken on the impact of EDI applications on individual corporations, industry sectors, workforces and national economies. If, as seems to be the case, this application of information technology is a very significant strategic measure, then much more research needs to be undertaken. Exhibit 6 identifies areas in which research is necessary. Some of the most urgent include study of the actual benefits and costs of EDI in particular companies; the nature and extent of the impact on employees, and on organisational structures and processes; and industry-

- **Case studies of industry sectors which are adopting within-country EDI:**
  - origins, stimulus and politics of the adoption process (competitive cf. collaborative use of IT)
  - impact on logistics (incl. delivery lags, buffer stocks)
  - economic costs and benefits, particularly in relation to staff productivity
  - organisational impact, incl. structures and processes
  - staff impact, incl. task re-definition, re-skilling, job displacement
  - organisational and systems adaptation to achieve competitive advantage
  - application of EDI to internal data processing
  - industry-sector impacts, incl. organisational boundaries
  - impact on the bases of competition

- **Barriers**
  - legal constraints, both within individual countries and internationally
  - training requirements of company management and staff
  - costs arising from connection to multiple EDI systems
  - proprietary and industry cf. international standards

- **Case studies of corporations which are early-adopters of international EDI**
  - as above, and
  - resulting market-place advantages
  - the extent to which 'de-sourcing' and 'partnering' is occurring

- **Case studies of the integration of EDI within and with:**
  - Electronic Funds Transfer Systems (EFTS)
  - Just In Time (JIT) manufacturing and service systems
  - EFT/POS and Quick Response systems in the retail sector

- **Case studies of the approaches taken by governments in different countries, in particular:**
  - EDI applications in government agencies
  - bureaucratic constraints
  - parliamentary action on legal aspects
  - governmental stimulation and support
  - governmental regulation
  - potential benefits to government

- **Study of the technical and economic aspects of international EDI, including:**
  - single-company systems implemented in multiple countries;
  - VANs extending their services to multiple countries;
  - inter-operation of services in multiple countries
  - technical requirements of trading partners in Europe and North America

Exhibit 6: Research Agenda

- **Prototype development**
- common user-EDI interface
- protocol conversion software
- gateways to multiple overseas EDI systems
- EDI applications within corporations

- **Regional IT Infrastructure, in particular:**
- telecommunications channels and computer installations
- organisation of the commercial community
- computing skills-base and 'information literacy'

- **'telecommunications diplomacy'**

- **Case studies of early adopters of EDI within developing countries (LDCs)**

Exhibit 6: Research Agenda (contd.)

sector matters including the benefits and costs, reorganisation and re-definition, and the extent to which the competitive balance is changed.

Some of the difficulties which must be confronted are the need for suitable measures of costs and benefits, the subjectivity of many of the important variables (such as organisational change, the role of EDI in re-negotiating organisational relationships, and its impact on LDCs), the need for longitudinal studies to assess the technology adoption process, and the question of comparability of studies undertaken in different countries.

CONCLUSIONS

There are significant differences in the way in which EDI is perceived in different countries, and there are different histories and different future directions. In particular, different countries have different communications infrastructures, and appear to place different weight on the various objectives of installing EDI. However there are influences which are likely to bring about convergence during the coming decade, including the importance of international trade, and the economies available from applying international standards.

EDI's real international significance can only be appreciated if both international and industry sectoral factors are considered together. From the viewpoint of corporations, national borders are an artificial constraint, and it is in their interests to have these constraints removed. With the recent strong orientation of many national governments toward economic rationalism, many countries have perceived their own interests to also be served by the lowering of barriers, particularly non-tariff barriers.

Trade-related rules and documentation are non-tariff trade barriers, and many countries are acting to reduce the extent to which they stultify trade. EDI is an important element of the movement to remove barriers to international trade, and the implementation of International Trade EDI might be a potent force for further rounds of liberalisation of trade policies. There are, however, many difficulties in the development of these services, and globally operating and governments and trans-national corporations must carefully assess their policies in relation to these issues.

References

Baker M. (1989), 'Analysing the Costs of EDI' Proc. Conf. - EDI'89, IIR, Melbourne, May

Beer B. (1984). 'Legal Aspects of Automatic Trade Data Interchange', *Transnational Data Reporter* Vol 7, No 1, Jan-Feb, 52-57

Benjamin R.I., De Long D.W. and Scott Morton M.S. (1988). *The Realities of Electronic Data Interchange: How Much Competitive Advantage?*, Centre for Information Systems Research, Working Paper No. 166, MIT, Cambridge, January

Berg J. & Schumny B. (Eds.) (1990). *The International Standardisation Process* North-Holland, 1990

Blacker K. (1989). *The Use of EDI Across Industry Sectors* Proc. Conf. EDI - Benefits and Opportunities, IPS, London

Boucher C.M. (1989). *The EDI Dilemma*, Systems 3X & AS World, Vol 17, No 2, February

Brown R. (1989). 'EDI and Proving Your Transaction', *Proc. Conf. SOST'89*, Terrigal, NSW, Austral. Comp. Soc., Terrigal, May, pp.7-16

Brawn D. (1989). 'EDI Developments Abroad and How they Impact on Australia', *Proc. Conf. EDI - The Key to Profitability in the 1990's'*, Sydney, December

Carter S. (1989). 'Standards for EDI and Communications', *Proc. Conf. Gain the Competitive Edge with EDI*, IIR Pty Ltd, Melbourne, Australia, May

Clarke R.A., Pedler M., Swatman P.M.C. & Campbell P. (1990). *'Australian Federal Government Practices and Intentions Relating to EFTS, EFT/POS and EDI: A Survey Report'* Dept. of Commerce, Australian National University

Coathup P. (1988). 'Electronic Data Interchange' *Computer Bulletin*, June, 15-17

Copeland D.G. & McKenney J.L. (1988). 'Airline Reservations Systems: Lessons From History'. *MIS Qtly 12*,3 (September) 353-370

Dawkins P. (1988). *'Open Communications Standards: Their Role in EDI'* in Gifkins & Hitchcock (1988)

Emmelhainz M.A. (1988). 'Electronic Data Interchange: Does It Change the Purchasing Process?'

J. of Purchasing & Materials Mgt, Winter.

Flaatten P., McCubbrey D.J., O'Riordan D. & Burgess K. *'Foundations of Business Systems'* Dryden Press, 1989

Gifkins M. & Hitchcock D. (Eds.) (1988). *'The EDI Handbook'* Blenheim Online Publications, London

Hansen J.V. & Hill N.C. (1989). 'Control and Audit of Electronic Data Interchange' *MIS Qtly, 13,*4 (December) 403-412.

Hardy M. (1988). 'Opening up European Telecommunications - the Commission Perspective', *Proc. Conf. EDI* , London, November

Hill C.M. (1988). 'EDI - The Way Ahead', *Proc. Conf. EDI - The Competitive Edge,* I.I.R. Pty Ltd, Sydney, October

_____ (1989). 'EDI - The Competitive Edge', *Proc. Conf. SOST'89,* Terrigal, NSW, Austral. Comp. Soc., Terrigal, May, pp.193-208

Hollands D. (1989). 'Electronic Data Interchange (EDI) in the Australian Automotive Industry', *Proc. Conf. SOST'89,* Terrigal, NSW, Austral. Comp. Soc., Terrigal, May, pp.209-224

Hudson P. (1989)   'EDI The Emerging Technology for Document Productivity', *Proc. Conf. GTE '89,* Canberra, March

Langton Limited (1988). 'EDI for Competitive Advantage', Special Paper - *Proc. Conf. EDI* , London, November

Lyttle R.M. (1988). 'Will You be Proactive or Reactive on EDI?', *Systems 3X World, 16,* 11, November

Magee J.F. (1989). '1992: Moves Americans Must Make', *Harv. Bus. Rev.* May-June, 78-84.

McCubbrey D.J. & Griçar J. (1989). 'Electronic Data Interchange as a Means of Stimulating International Trade' *Proc. Int'l Conf. on Org. & Info. Sys.,* Bled, Yugoslavia, September 13-15

McCubbrey D.J. & Kunin J. (1989). 'A Universal Campus Identification/Transmission System Using Optical Memory Card Technology' *Proc. Int'l Conf. on Org. & Info. Sys.,* Bled, Yugoslavia, September 13-15

McCubbrey D.J. (1990). 'The State of EDI in the United States – 1990' *Proc. Int'l Conf. on Org. & Info. Sys.,* Bled, Yugoslavia, June 4-5

McNurlin B.C. (1987). 'The Rise of Co-operative Systems', *EDP Analyzer, 25,* 6, June

Patrick G. (1988). 'The Challenges of EDI Decision Making', in Gifkins M. and Hitchcock D. (eds) *'The EDI Handbook: Trading in the 1990's',* Blenheim Online Publications, London

Perry, N. (1989). 'Change Management in the EDI Environment', *Proc. Conf. EDI - The Key to Profitability in the 1990's,* Sydney, December

Purton P. (1989). 'Europe's Electronic Trading Bloc', *Datamation,* March 1, 76.13-76.14

Robinson D.G. and Stanton S.A. (1987). 'Competing Through Information Technology: Exploit EDI Before EDI Exploits You', *Information Strategy: The Executive's J.*, Spring, 32-35

Rochester J.D. (1989). 'The Strategic Value of EDI', *I/S Analyzer, 27*, 8, August

Rogers E.M. (1983). *'Diffusion of Innovations'* The Free Press, 3rd Ed., 1983

Schatz W. (1988). 'EDI: Putting the Muscle in Commerce and Industry'. *Datamation 34*, 6 56-64

Scott P. (1988). 'Trends in Communications', *Proc. Conf. EDI'88*, London, November

Sharpe D. (1989). 'EDI - The Legal Issues', *Proc. Conf. EDI - The Key to Profitability in the 1990's*, IIR Pty Ltd, Sydney, May

Skagen A.E. (1989). 'Nurturing Relationships, Enhancing Quality with Electronic Data Interchange', *Management Review*, February, 28-32

Spriggs S. (1989). 'EDI - There's a Whole Lot of Hustling Going On', *Hub*, Nov, 27-30

Swatman P.M.C. and Clarke R.A. (1990). 'Organisational, Sectoral and International Implications of Electronic Data Interchange' *Proc. Conf. Human Choice & Computers*, Dublin, July 1990, Int'l Fed. of Info. Proc., Geneva

Swatman P.M.C. and Everett J.E. (1990). 'Australian Involvement in Electronic Data Interchange - 1989', *Austral. Comp. J. 22*,3 (August)

Swatman P.M.C. and Swatman P.A. (1989a). 'EDI and Its Implications for Industry', *Proc. Conf. SOST'89, Terrigal, NSW*, Austral. Comp. Soc., May, pp.407-418

Swatman P.M.C. and Swatman P.A. (1989b). 'Europe's Single Unified Market - 1992 - A Spur to the Development of EDI?' *Proc Conf ACC '89*, Austral. Comp. Soc., Perth, W.A. September

Takac P. and Swatman P.M.C. (1989). 'A Discussion of Third Party Networks', *Proc. Conf. EDI - The Key to Profitability in the 1990's*, Sydney, NSW, December

Tate P. (1989). 'Europe's IS Execs Predict the Future', *Datamation*, March 1, 76:1-76:2

Ulrich H. (1990). 'The Effects of EDI on International Business Practices'. *Proc. 2nd Int'l Conf. of EDI Users*, San Francisco, July

Walsh D. (1989). 'Spreading the Word Internally - How to Gain Staff Commitment', *Proc. Conf. EDI - The Key to Profitability in the 1990's*, IIR Pty Ltd, Sydney, NSW, December

Weber R. (1989). 'Controls in Electronic Funds Transfer Systems: A Survey and Synthesis' *Comp. & Security 8*,2 123-127

Wilmot R. (1988). 'International Trends and Developments in EDI', *Proc. Conf. EDI '88*, London, November

Zinn D.K. and Takac P.F. (1988). *'Electronic Data Interchange (EDI) in Australia: Markets, Opportunities and Developments'*, Melbourne: Royal Melbourne Institute of Technology Press

Cost-Benefit Evaluation for Global Information Systems (GIS): Critical Issues and a Proposed Framework

Kranti Toraskar
Drexel University

The emerging phenomenon of Global Information systems (GIS) is examined from the standpoint of cost-benefit evaluation. The need for systematic research in this area is demonstrated through a multidimensional structure of the complexities of GIS. It is argued that the enormity of these complexities must not overshadow the socio-economic imperatives that need to be addressed through rational decision-making. Accordingly, a conceptual framework for research on cost-benefit evaluation of GIS is proposed, delineating its approach and method. The approach is characterized by a simultaneously Proactive, Comprehensive, and Multidimensional stance of the framework. The methodological implications of the approach are articulated in terms of specific research avenues which focus on (1) the operational as well as strategic character of GIS, (2) the similarities/differences of GIS with other types of information systems (IS), and (3) re-examining the very foundations of cost-benefit analysis (CBA) with regard to its application to GIS. The resulting recommendations are stratified along the levels of organizational hierarchy.

INTRODUCTION

As the multinational corporations face the challenges created by "internationalization of markets and competition" (Wind & Douglas, 1987), Global Information Systems (GIS) are emerging as a powerful trend in the business world today. The growing need for a global view of management, and thereby the need for GIS, is evident in the context of the strategic management of multinational corporations (Ohmae, 1989) (Reck, 1989). Additionally, the tremendous advances in the computer and communication technologies have provided the ultimate impetus for the growth of GIS.

Owing to the nature of their products, corporations in certain industries, such as electronics (Romei, 1989) and the financial industry (Schindler, 1987; Guptill, 1988), have been globalizing their information systems (IS) for nearly two decades. Today, corporations in other industries (e.g., semifinished goods, consumer electronics, and primary metals and chemicals) are also globalizing their operations and their IS, in response to a variety of international economic and political developments (Reck, 1989). These developments include the European Common Market, the changing political climate of Eastern Europe weakening the international trade-barriers, and the emergence of new industrial nations, such as Japan and Korea.

However, the phenomenon of GIS is still in such an embryonic stage, and the underlying causal factors so complex, that the major issues related to GIS can hardly be regarded as clearly understood at this time. On the one hand, the wide ranging panorama of such issues includes highly technical concerns, such as the need for international standards in communications technology. On the other hand, the political/economic concerns of various nations involved, and the socio-cultural complexities of managing multinational business operations are also important. At this embryonic stage of such a complex phenomenon as GIS, it is more important to first identify and formulate the major "problem areas" of related research, rather than to embrace specific solutions to problems that are not yet properly formulated. From the standpoint of systems planning and development, this chapter deals with one of the most important of such problem areas, namely, the cost-benefit evaluation of a proposed GIS. As the GIS phenomenon is still evolving, most of the current attention is focused on the dramatic developments of GIS in the field. Nevertheless, when the dust settles the cost-benefit issues and related difficulties are bound to become crucial for further developments in GIS. As demonstrated in this paper, the complexities of GIS suggest that the IS researchers ought to direct their attention to the costs and benefits of GIS right from the beginning of the GIS revolution.

The organization of the chapter is as follows. In the next section, we set the stage by reviewing prominent examples of GIS, and by delineating the major sources of complexities of GIS. Then, we review the literature on information systems (IS) evaluation in general, focusing on the foundations and the problems of their cost-benefit analysis (CBA). In the last section, the understanding and the insights obtained through this analysis are synthesized into a high-level conceptual framework for systematic research on cost-benefit evaluation of GIS. It is argued that the formidable challenge of applying cost-benefit methodology to this new genre of IS calls for a simultaneously Proactive, Comprehensive, and Multidimensional approach. The approach is elaborated through specific avenues for further research focusing on the methodological aspects of CBA, and on the comparison of GIS with existing types of IS. The resulting recommendations are found to be stratified along the levels of management and the organizational hierarchy.

GLOBAL INFORMATION SYSTEMS: A MULTIDIMENSIONAL COMPLEXITY

Although the term global information systems, or GIS, is not presently common in the IS literature, a variety of observations from the standpoint of information technology (IT) clearly reveal a rapidly growing number of corporate information systems that are global in scope, and are aimed at global connectivity (Craven, 1988). Companies as different as General Electric (GE), Caterpillar Inc., Coca-Cola company, Kraft Inc., and Scott Paper are adopting the global perspective for managing their business. A detailed account of the airlines reservation systems (Copeland and McKenney, 1988) suggests that the timing and emergence of GIS in a particular industry is a function of (1) the availability of the necessary communications technology, and (2) the globalization of markets which forces major corporations in that industry to adopt a global view of their business.

From the standpoint of the availability of necessary technology, corporations in the electronic and computer industry have a distinct advantage. For them, developing a GIS simply amounts to using their own product. Therefore, it is not surprising that many corporations in the electronic industry claim to have, or are developing, one of the largest computer communication networks. Such examples of GIS include: (1) Westinghouse Information Network (WIN) (Ruffin, 1990), (2) DEC's global applications in Computer-Aided Design (Romei, 1989), (3) Hewlett-Packard's worldwide data communications network (Van Rensselaer, 1985), (4) Honeywell's global distribution system (TDC3000) (Hurd, 1988), and (5) Texas Instrument's "single-image network" (Pantages, 1989-b) connecting its worldwide operations, customers, and suppliers.

As for responding to the globalization of markets and competition, the financial and insurance corporations may be the first to globalize their organizational information systems. The intangible, information-based character of their products and services may be a facilitating factor in this context. Major financial corporations like American Express (Guptill, 1988) and Bank America (Schindler, 1987) have been setting the GIS trend in terms of establishing global data networks, or GDNs, since the early 1980s. The Chase Manhattan

Bank (Dooley, 1990) and Citicorp (Heywood, 1989) seem to be following suit. The critical importance of the GIS capability for banking industry in general is noted by Burger (1990). In the insurance industry, Best's industry-wide aeon information service (Bestlink) appears to be approaching a global scope (Ojala, 1990).

In general, today, the trend towards GIS is apparent wherever businesses need to run worldwide operations, for example, the chemical industry. Dow Chemicals has been involved in implementing a 5-year strategy to link its customers worldwide (Brandel, 1989). Imperial Chemical Industries (ICI), another international giant of the chemical industry, has developed a worldwide document transfer network to support enterprise-wide planning and management (Pantages, 1989-a). Rohm and Haas Company is using the GIS approach to electronic mail, as well as to facilitate global business initiatives (Ostroff, 1990). Similarly, the Texaco Corporation now has a global data network linking its New York and London data centers for improved operational efficiency (Crockett, 1989).

The automobile industry appears to be poised for one of the world's largest private telecommunications networks (EDSNET) developed for the GM Corporation (Livingston, 1990). Major firms in the package freight industry, such as, UPS (Maglitta, 1990) and DHL (Savage, 1989), are also adopting different degrees of globalization for their information systems to gain a competitive advantage (Hastings, 1989). In sum, corporations as different as the Eastman Kodak (Ludlum, 1989), Woolworth Co. (Eckerson, 1988-b), and Chiquita Brands, Inc. (Brown, 1990) are moving toward using a GIS as an essential component of their business strategy.

The Multidimensionalities Involved in GIS

The wide-ranging panorama of the above examples of global information systems suggests that the phenomenon of GIS may be too complex to be understood simply as another category of information systems (IS). This suggestion becomes particularly convincing as one even attempts to recognize the different, and relatively independent, dimensions of the complexity of GIS. Below, we outline three such important dimensions through which one can begin to structure, and thereby understand, the complexities of GIS.

The Multinational Dimension: Although it is obvious that a global information system typically extends over several different nations, the scope of the complexities associated with this multinational dimension is not so obvious. Minimally, these complexities extend across three major realms, namely, the corporate, governmental, and the socio-cultural realms. In the broadest socio-cultural realm, the difficulties of developing and using a GIS amidst the ambiance of many different languages, management-styles, and cultural value-systems in general, have been reported in the literature (Burnson, 1989) (Bouldin, 1989) (Raptis, 1986). Motivated by their own national economics, nations tend to adopt trade policies and regulations that are generally unfavorable to foreign multinational corporations. Moreover, governments are also likely to change these policies and regulations in a rather unpredictable manner leading to additional business risk (Means, 1988). Even within a given multinational corporation, business-units located in different countries are likely to associate different degrees of gains/losses with the parent company's global strategies. The resulting inter-unit conflicts and competition can only compound the already noted complexities.

The Technological Dimension: Interestingly, the tremendous technological advances which made GIS feasible in the first place are also a source of added complexity for effective development and use of a global information system. GIS incorporate many diverse and competing technologies of electronic computers and communication. In addition, the rapidly changing nature of these technologies has important economic implications for GIS. Eckerson (1988-a) reports on the case of the GEONET system, (Manufacturers Hanover, Inc.) which had to be downsized due to the unanticipated advances in telecommunications technology. Even for a given technology, the designers of a GIS must be concerned with the compatibility of communication standards used in different parts of the world (for example, network protocols, character codes, and signal formats).

The Managerial Dimension: By the phrase "managerial dimension," here we refer to those sources of GIS-related complexities which are intrinsic either to the top management of the corporation, or to the structure of the GIS itself as it supports the various levels of management (Anthony, 1965). It is important to note here that, while the technological and multinational dimensions of GIS complexity are empirically obvious, the managerial or organizational sources of complexities are much more subtle.

Due to the high level of investments involved in a GIS, the top management of any multinational exerts a major influence on the development, and use, of GIS. Both the organizational structure and the management style of the corporation can seriously affect GIS development. Raptis (1986) specifically refers to GIS-related problems arising out of the differences between a multinational parent company and its foreign subsidiaries in terms of their marketing strategies and management styles.

The time-horizons required for development of GIS are fairly long, in the range of ten years or more. For example, several corporations such as Texas Instrument (Pantages, 1989-b), Hewlett-Packard (Van Rensselaer, 1985), and DEC Corporation (Romei, 1989) seem to have been developing their GIS for nearly two decades. Even with the shortening of these development periods due to industry learning, GIS projects are likely to require relatively longer time as compared to the traditional MIS applications. This long-range character of GIS is significant in the managerial dimension of GIS complexities, because the longer time-horizon calls for some prerequisite characteristics in the management organization, for example: (1) stable organizational structure, (2) long term commitment, (3) a requisite level of sustained participation, and (4) an entrepreneurial willingness to take the financial risk involved.

GIS: The IS Resource for All Levels of Management

Thus far, we have considered the influences of top management on GIS. However, a framework for cost-benefit evaluation of GIS will be incomplete without consideration of the *nature* and the *extent*, of the reciprocal impact of GIS on the managerial organization. Here, we must presume that the nature of this impact of GIS on management is beneficial, since all information systems (IS) are at least intended, and possibly expected, to improve managerial decision-making and the organizational performance. Strictly speaking, this normative assumption itself needs to be empirically tested in the context of cost-benefit evaluation. In contrast, a detailed examination of the GIS literature reveals that our intuitive notions concerning the *extent* of the influence of GIS on management may require significant modifications. As shown below, these modifications can be best understood in conjunction with Anthony's levels of management (Anthony, 1965).

Anthony's hierarchy of management levels is one of the most powerful integrating constructs used by management and IS researchers to describe the changing character of managerial activity across the organizational hierarchy. The three levels of management, or organizational decision-making, are designated as: (1) Strategic Planning (SP), (2) Tactical Planning and Control (TP & C), and (3) Operational Control (OC). Anthony's framework clearly differentiates these levels of management in terms of (1) the types of decisions which each level usually makes, (2) the typical time-horizons involved, and (3) the organizational scope and impact of these decisions.

Thus, the highest, or (SP), level of management typically deals with the long-range and organization-wide decisions with the greatest financial implications, for example, selecting the overall business direction and market strategy. In contrast, the tactical level (TP & C) is aimed at an effective execution of selected strategies. Here, the tactical issues of acquiring, organizing, and overseeing the proper use of resources become paramount. Finally, the operational control (OC) level of management is most intimately concerned with the day-to-day, short-term, decisions directly involved in running the operations.

Anthony's framework seems ideal for understanding the possible effects of GIS on management, for the following reasons. First, the MIS literature draws major distinctions with regard to the information requirements (such as, the source of information, its time-horizon, and the level of detail) of different management levels (Davis & Olson, 1985). Second, different management levels are commonly correlated with the different types of organizational information systems, such as, transaction processing systems (TPS), structured decision system (SDS), and decision support system (DSS). Against this background, below we interpret various field reports about GIS to develop a more objective understanding of the kind of support which a global information system can provide.

An Operational as well as Strategic IS: Everyone recognizes the fact that a global information system imparts a new world-wide connectivity to the day-to-day operational levels of a multi-national corporation. Depending on the need in a particular industry, this new genre of IS is capable of providing an hour-by-hour or even minute-by-minute computer report about simultaneous activities occurring in different parts of the world (Dalton, 1988). This operational level global aspect of the GIS support is rather self-evident in the field. In contrast, the strategic aspects of GIS, are not so easy to recognize. However, simply because "global" coordination of the operational levels cannot be realized without a GIS, it does not follow that GIS are useful for globalizing "only" the operational level activities. Below, we identify a wide variety of observations which reveal the strategic character of GIS.

Barkan (1989) defines strategic systems with the following key attributes: (1) They enhance customer relations, (2) They are traditionally viewed as being too complex and costly, (3) There is a high degree of business risk involved, and (4) They create new opportunities, rather than merely exploiting the existing ones. It is easy to see that these attributes of strategic systems, in general, apply rather perfectly to GIS also. It is not surprising, therefore, that many authors who formally discuss strategic information systems (SIS) (Kemerer and Sosa, 1988) (Vitale, 1986) actually refer to the same examples as the ones commonly cited in the GIS literature (e.g., American Airlines, American Hospital Supply Corp., Bank America, Citicorp).

The GIS literature itself provides some indications of the strategic importance of having such worldwide information systems in a multinational corporation. Even from a strictly technological perspective, Kennedy (1989) describes corporate communications networks as a "strategic asset" in that it is vitally needed for supporting long-range financial and organizational strategies. In the context of the airlines industry, Dalton (1988) emphasizes that a system which provides "minute-by-minute computer support" gives " an organization a strategic [as well as] operational advantage over its competitors." Dalton refers to such systems as the "strategic operations-support systems." Dorros (1990) also specifically recognizes the strategic underpinnings of geographically dispersed information networks in the airline industry.

The multi-level character of the linkage between a corporate organization and its global information system also appears inevitable from a more conceptual standpoint, since the transaction processing systems (TPS) provide "the base for all other internal information systems." (Davis & Olson, 1985, p.47) Similarly, in the context of strategic information systems planning (SISP), Moskowitz's (1986) emphasis on developing an organization-wide data-architecture essentially recognizes this multi-level character of GIS.

THE PARADIGMS AND PROBLEMS OF IS EVALUATION: A SYNOPSIS

In view of the multidimensional complexities discussed above, the challenge of cost-benefit evaluation of GIS already appears to be a difficult one. This challenge is compounded further by the methodological problems of evaluation of information systems (IS) in general. A high-level synopsis of the major paradigms and problems of IS evaluation is provided here for the necessary background and perspective.

The Variety of IS Evaluation Approaches

IS evaluation has long been recognized as an important aspect of MIS theory and practice (Nolan & Seward, 1974). And yet, the present state of the research literature in this area consists of little more than a set of divergent perspectives on the matter. Such perspectives include "information economics" (Parker, 1987), the "utility value" approach (Swanson, 1974), and the "economic value" approach (Senn, 1974). Nolan and Seward (1974) contrast the conventional "decision analysis" approach with the "user satisfaction" approach which seems to be attracting considerable research interest at the present time (Miller & Doyle, 1987) (Baroudi & Orlikowski, 1988). However, the development of specific methods and techniques of IS evaluation has thus far evolved mainly from the "implementation perspective" rather than the "information perspective" (Swanson, 1982), and is primarily aimed at the economic costs and benefits of proposed systems (Kleijnen, 1980).

For our purposes, the various approaches can be better understood as belonging to one of three major evaluation paradigms: (1) The Economic Paradigm, exemplified by cost-benefit analysis (CBA), (2) The Decision-making Paradigm, characterized by the decision analysis approach to IS evaluation, and (3) The Subjective Paradigm, represented by the user satisfaction approach. Among these, the most developed approach, with the longest track record, is the CBA or cost-benefit approach of the economic paradigm.

As observed by Horton (1985, p.12) "coming up with [new] approaches [to IS evaluation] is difficult." In contrast, considerable research commentary and feedback is available regarding the CBA methodology and its practice. Moreover, as compared to other evaluation methodologies, the linkages between IS evaluation and the broader contexts of systems approach and rational decision-making (Ackoff, 1962) appear to be relatively clearer in the case of the CBA methodology. Therefore, for the remainder of this chapter, we focus on the CBA methodology with regard to its application to GIS.

Rational Decision-making: The Foundation of CBA

The CBA methodology represents a formalized application of the rational approach, or "scientific method" (Ackoff, 1962), of decision-making to the decision-problem of systems planning and development. Thus, the methods and techniques of CBA, and the very notion of any kind of cost-benefit evaluation to assist a decision-maker, are ultimately rooted in the concepts of rational decision-making and the underlying systems approach. Therefore, an accurate understanding of these concepts is essential for: (1) correctly interpreting the methods of CBA, and (2) diagnosing the problems associated with the practice of CBA in the field of information systems.

Herbert Simon (1977), described the three principal phases of decision-making, namely: Intelligence, Design, and Choice. In this I-D-C model, the Intelligence phase involves "attention-directing" activities which "determine where... and what problems need attention... particularly problems originating from changes in the external environment." (Simon, 1977, p.128.) Effective intelligence activity actually uncovers dormant problems or decision-situations that are likely to become serious in the future. In contrast, the Design phase involves identification of the various courses of action for an already recognized problem, and the specification of methods and techniques for evaluating them. Finally, the Choice phase represents the final selection of a particular course of action by the human decision-maker(s) for actual implementation. The crucial importance of this phase, for practice, is underscored by several factors, such as environmental uncertainties and conflicting objectives.

The I-D-C model of decision-making is, of course, conceptually very valuable. However, the intimate connections between decision-making and the CBA methodology can be better appreciated through the detailed steps of rational decision-making process, summarized below:

(1) *Problem Recognition:* This step detects the very "presence" of a decision-problem, and identifies the corresponding decision-maker with certain "objectives". It closely corresponds with the intelligence phase of decision-making.

(2) *Problem Formulation:* This involves identifying "all" feasible alternative courses of action, existing as well as innovatively created. In addition, formulating a problem involves making explicit and comprehensive statements regarding the decision-maker's objectives, assumptions, as well as the decision-criterion.

(3) *Analysis and Evaluation:* This step refers to the use of appropriate analytical methods and techniques for evaluating the performance of each feasible course of action considered. The selection of specific performance variable(s), and their operational "measures," also becomes important at this stage.

(4) *Choice:* This stage integrates results of the preceding analysis and evaluation towards selecting the "best" course of action. In practice, this apparently simple step is complicated by the multiplicity of competing/ conflicting objectives and the trade-offs among them, as well as by various sources of uncertainty. Most of all, ultimately, the human imperatives and the prerogatives of decision-makers (charged with their responsibilities) make this the most challenging step from the standpoint of the practice of CBA.

(5) *Implementation and Control:* Beyond executing the selected course of action, this step focuses on "control," which involves an ongoing performance-monitoring, and taking necessary corrective actions. Due to this association with the lower levels of management (Anthony, 1965), this step of decision-making is delegated downward, and often neglected in practice. However, we must recognize that the control activities (namely, performance monitoring, diagnosis of deviations, and taking the corrective actions) themselves form a full-fledged decision-making process (Simon, 1977, p.43). Therefore, we regard this last step of decision-making to be just as important as any other step.

Planning and development of information systems is a special case of problem-solving, or decision-making, in general. As noted by Kroenke (1989, p. 134), the traditional sequence of systems development activities (namely, preliminary investigation, systems analysis, design, implementation, etc.) bears a remarkable resemblance with the decision-making steps. This correspondence between IS development and decision-making has major implications for the use of cost-benefit evaluations in practice. Specifically, although the economic evaluation of alternative IS designs points mainly to Step 3 of decision-making, the continuity of the various steps implies that the CBA activity must also ensure the logical validity and consistency among all five steps of decision-making.

The Problems of Cost-Benefit Evaluation of IS

The crucial connections between CBA and rational decision-making suggest that any practice of CBA which compromises or violates the principles of rational decision-making is likely to fall short of its goal, namely, assisting the decision-maker. What's important, such violations can potentially occur at many points in decision-making, for example, incorrect performance measure, neglecting some important course(s) of action, and so on. Therefore, we must examine whether the current practice of CBA in the field of information systems suffers from any significant departures from rational decision-making and scientific method. An examination of the relevant literature reveals three broad categories of problems which are described below.

The Problems of Perspective: Many observers in the field are questioning the applicability of CBA to information systems (IS) in general, and for certain types of IS applications in particular (Lay, 1985) (Inmon, 1987) (Rockhold, 1982) (Strassmann, 1988). The nature of related questions seems to be rooted in the fundamental differences in the overall evaluative perspectives of the major constituencies within an organization.

In this context, a major dichotomy appears between a *Business perspective and a Technology perspective* vis-a-vis the CBA process and the use of its results. In practice, those in charge of CBA activity are often biased with the information technology (IT) perspective. In contrast, the high level business managers have a broader business perspective, concerned with the organizational, and financial objectives. Doukas (1987) specifically points out these differences, and argues for a more organizational or business perspective in the practice of CBA. Another major dichotomy exists in terms of the *Efficiency versus the Effectiveness perspectives.* CBA efforts driven by the efficiency perspective are typically focused on the transaction processing or the operational level systems, and particularly on the cost of such systems. In contrast, the effectiveness perspective calls for evaluation of the planning and developmental aspects of IS, with the managerial and business-level objectives in mind.

The key to proper application of CBA methodology to information systems may be in recognizing the influence of such divergent perspectives on the very character, and conduct, of CBA. In particular, researchers must recognize the resulting differences in terms of the decision-maker's objectives, the feasible set of alternatives, and the decision-criteria which drive the CBA activity. Similarly, adoption of a particular perspective will favor specific CBA methods, and their associated tools and techniques. For example, a CBA effort driven by the efficiency perspective, will favor using the accounting tools and techniques of, such as, NPV or IRR.

The Problems of Methodology: The use of CBA in MIS also suffers from certain intrinsic problems which arise out of certain methodological difficulties. Two main areas of such difficulties are discussed below.

The Intangibility of Costs and Benefits: An overwhelming majority of problems involved in applying CBA to information systems point toward the intangibility associated with information systems (Smith, 1983), (Orli & Tom, 1987) (Rockhold, 1982). In this respect, the existing literature seems to view the intangibility problems primarily in terms of the adequacy of the existing techniques. However, beyond recognizing the inadequacy of certain techniques the present strategy has little to offer by way of solutions. Therefore, a fundamentally different approach may be needed to deal with the intangibility aspects of IS. Such an approach calls for serious research into the very meaning and use of fundamental concepts such as, data versus information, and decision versus action.

The Problems of Risk and Uncertainty: In practice, the issues of business risk and uncertainty are lumped together with the problems of intangibility. Strictly speaking, the problems of risk and uncertainty represent a special subset of the sources of intangibility. In the context of the Choice phase of decision-making (Simon, 1977), this particular subset plays a rather crucial role in the presentation and interpretation of CBA results, and the resulting decisions. Therefore, researchers need to specifically focus on the treatment of risk and uncertainty from the standpoint of CBA methodology as applied to information systems. Tate (1988) identifies business risk as the "third factor" which complicates IS-related decision-making, and therefore, the use of CBA in IS projects.

The Problems of Implementation: The realm of "implementation" has always been accompanied by its own brand of unique problems. As discussed earlier, the success of scientific method depends crucially on proper implementation and control of the chosen course of action. Thus, some of the problems associated with CBA implementations in practice may well be primarily due to the lack of adherence to the fundamental principles of CBA, either intentionally or inadvertently. King and Schrems (1978) point out the possible role of "advocacy" in the use of CBA in MIS. Clearly, an increased education of top managers, and IS staff, regarding the fundamental principles of CBA and their proper implementation can only help in this respect.

A FRAMEWORK FOR COST-BENEFIT EVALUATION OF GIS

In this section, we integrate our major insights into a broad-based framework for further work in the area of cost-benefit evaluation of GIS. This framework is derived by explicating a high-level "rationale" based on the foundations of scientific method, and by applying the same foundation principles to the problems of using CBA methodology. The three major planks of the framework resulting from this process are elaborated below. In view of the limitations of space, it should be recognized that the rationale, which is the generating force of the framework, is just as valuable for further research as the specific planks presented here.

The Rationale for the Proposed Framework

In arriving at the broad rationale for the framework, we apply the principles of rational decision-making and systems to the meta-level problem of applying the methodology of cost-benefit evaluation to GIS. As elaborated earlier, this meta-problem is characterized by (1) The complexities of GIS, and (2) The difficulties of applying CBA to information systems (IS) in general. The basic stance of our framework is based on this meta-level analysis, and can be described as being simultaneously Proactive, Comprehensive, and Multidimensional.

The Proactive Stance: The proactive stance of this framework simply suggests that the IS researchers should (1) aggressively anticipate and analyze possible problems involved in applying cost-benefit evaluation to GIS, and (2) develop the necessary research strategies and methodologies to deal with these problems. The default alternative to this stance is to take a purely "reactive" posture, and respond to the challenges of cost-benefit evaluation of GIS only as, and when, pressured to do so. As discussed below, there are simply too many indications against such a reactive stance in this matter.

First, the eventual need for an attention to cost-benefit evaluation of GIS is evident from the very nature of GIS. By their nature, GIS require enormous amounts of resources. Therefore, as the initial excitement wears off, and as the investors and top-management anticipate their payoffs from GIS, the pressures for some form of economic evaluation of GIS are bound to build in the future.

The only major argument against the proactive stance would be to point to (1) the multidimensional complexities of GIS, and (2) the difficulties of cost-benefit evaluation of IS in general. However, to be consistent with the principles of rational approach, our stance should be based on the need and potential value of cost-benefit evaluation of GIS, and not on the degree of difficulties involved. For one thing, whereas the potential value involved is relatively clear from the literature, the true measure of the anticipated difficulties cannot be obtained unless and until the research community goes ahead and makes some initial efforts in this area!

The Comprehensive Stance: By the comprehensive stance, we suggest that the GIS research agenda must not take a "limited" view of the challenges involved in cost-benefit evaluation of GIS. According to rational decision-making, a piecemeal approach is not desirable, especially during the initial "intelligence" and "formulation" activities of problem-solving. From the systems standpoint, Ashby's Law of Requisite Variety (1956, Chap. 7) would imply that, to deal with the complexities of GIS and their cost-benefit evaluation, we must use a correspondingly comprehensive and sophisticated solution strategy. A comprehensive stance for our framework suggests several implications for its operationalization in terms of an appropriate research strategy: (1) Focus on a re-examination of the CBA methodology as a whole, rather than on specific techniques, (2) Capitalize on experiences of CBA in other areas of information systems, specifically, MIS, DSS and the strategic IS (SIS), (3) Recognize the possible organizational "process-value" of engaging in the very process of cost-benefit evaluation.

The Multidimensional Stance: The multidimensional stance emphasizes the need to adapt and apply the fundamental methodology specifically to each of the three dimensions of the GIS complexity articulated earlier. We must interpret the fundamental concepts of CBA to address the specific issues which arise out of the multi-national, the technological, as well as the managerial complexities of global information systems. Clearly, the multidimensional stance is consistent with the comprehensive stance. However, this characteristic of our framework is so important that, it is best treated as a distinct element here. In the following sub-sections, we elaborate on some major implications of the above rationale in terms of the research agenda and methodologies that might be helpful for further work on cost-benefit evaluation of GIS.

Plank A: The Focus on Methodology

This plank arises out of the recognition that our interest in CBA here is primarily as a means toward an end, namely, the task of "IS evaluation" within the broader context of global information systems development. Given the tremendous difficulties of applying CBA to IS in general, perhaps we need to step back and first concentrate on the more fundamental concepts and on the methodological realms involved in cost-benefit evaluation of GIS. Following are the examples of such areas of investigation.

Re-examine the Fundamentals of CBA: First, we must re-examine the fundamental concepts, assumptions, and methods of CBA with reference to (1) its origins in rational decision-making and the scientific method, and (2) our intended application area, namely, GIS. Thus, fundamental notions such as costs, benefits, and objectives, need to be carefully scrutinized for their meaning in light of IS-related concepts of data, information, decision-making, operational value versus strategic value, and so on. Efforts of this nature are likely to result in a better understanding of the applicability of various CBA methods and techniques to GIS. Without such understanding, mechanistic application of the techniques, in itself, will not have a significant influence on the GIS developments in practice.

Integrate CBA with Planning and Design: Second, in the context of the comprehensive stance of this framework the methodological focus also means that we should look at *all* the phases of decision-making related to GIS development, rather than only the economic measurement of its cost-benefits. Specifically, we should expand the scope of the CBA activity backwards to the preliminary investigations involving the very identification of management's goals and objectives, and identification of *all* feasible courses of action. Thus, to be truly helpful towards the decisions related to GIS, the CBA projects need to be approached and conducted in a much more integrated fashion with the entire development cycle of GIS.

Identify the Generic Cost-Benefits of GIS: Another avenue for operating above the level of specific techniques is to identify the generic "categories" of costs and benefits of GIS, as a particular class of IS. As shown here, the literature on GIS enables us to make some progress in this direction. Sokol et al. (1989) emphasize the need for evaluating the specific types of risks (as well as opportunities) that may be unique to the internationalization of markets. Such risks represent a category of costs relevant in GIS development. From a technological standpoint of networking and data communications, Maire (1989) and Held (1988) discuss some important hidden costs (e.g., different cost-volume relationships in different parts of the world), as well as benefits (e.g., the greater relative payback) of the global networks. The downsizing of Manufacturers Hanover's GEONET system due to (1) the lower-than-projected volume of use, and (2) the new and better data services (Eckerson, 1988-a) clearly highlights the need for a better understanding of such generic costs and benefits of GIS.

Plank B: Learning from Other Areas of IS

Another major premise of this framework is that, although the CBA literature directly related to GIS is lacking at present, there is a significant amount of CBA literature in other, more established, domains of information systems (IS). GIS researchers must actively bring such relevant literature to bear upon the cost-benefit evaluation of GIS to provide a head-start for CBA research in this area.

In this respect, we see at least three major areas of IS literature of interest: (1) The evaluative literature on MIS in general, (2) The literature aimed at evaluation of decision support systems (DSS), and finally, (3) The more recent developments in the area of strategic information systems (SIS). Of these three areas, the fundamental relevance of the general evaluative literature on MIS, has been illustrated throughout this paper. Therefore, below we concentrate primarily on showing how the literature on DSS and SIS could provide valuable insights for work on the cost-benefit of GIS.

Learning from the DSS Experience: Due to the fundamental contrasts between a decision support system (DSS) and the traditional MIS, evaluation of a DSS involves characteristically different, and more difficult, challenges as compared to that of a traditional MIS application. The DSS literature reveals significant efforts to adapt the concepts of traditional IS development cycle, and CBA methods, to DSS. Such efforts include Keen's (1981) value analysis, and Keen and Gambino's (1982) concept of Adaptive Design of DSS. The literature also contains significant developments related to the methodological aspects of cost-benefit evaluation of a DSS. Although no consensus exists, the literature reveals the arguments in favor of applying the traditional CBA methodology to DSS (Thierauf, 1982), as well as the arguments identifying serious methodological and conceptual problems involved in doing so (McLean & Riesing, 1977) (Toraskar & Joglekar, 1990).

In order to see the relevance of such DSS literature for GIS evaluation, we must recognize certain parallels between the concepts of DSS and GIS. The most important such parallel is in terms of the increased complexities of both these new types of IS as compared to the traditional MIS. Thus, our technological and managerial dimensions of GIS complexities apply to DSS as well, albeit to a smaller degree. Similarly, just as we find GIS to be the all encompassing IS resource for all three levels of management, Schultheis and Sumner (1989) contend that the DSS concept supports all three phases of decision-making in Simon's I-D-C model. Since the three phases (namely, intelligence, design and choice) are themselves somewhat correlated with the different levels of management (namely, strategic, tactical and operational), we expect that the evaluative and CBA-related literature on DSS should provide important directions for GIS evaluation.

Finally, we note that the importance of applying any kind of evaluation methodology to DSS was not generally recognized in the early DSS literature. However, as the practice of DSS matured, the need for DSS evaluation (Keen, 1981) is now well recognized in the literature. Based on this experience with DSS, the researchers and practitioners of GIS can infer the potential need and importance of applying CBA to GIS.

Learning from the SIS Literature: Even though the literature on strategic information systems (SIS) is very recent, and still evolving, such literature should be regarded as being most relevant for the domain of GIS. The fundamental justification for this position is that there clearly are significant strategic aspects involved in the kind of support which GIS provides to the corporation. Thus, the concept of GIS overlaps with that of a strategic information system (SIS). This correlation between GIS and SIS is most evident from the role of information as a "strategic weapon" in today's competitive business environment in general, whether global or domestic (Webber, 1988) (Keen, 1988).

A lot can be gained from the SIS literature. First of all, this literature indicates the high degree of conceptual difficulties involved in evaluating these types of information systems (Kanter, 1987)(Marchand & Horton, 1986). Similarly, despite the initial excitement over SIS, the top management's resistance to these new and expensive types of IS is now acknowledged in the literature (Stretch, 1988) (Lederer & Mendelow, 1988) (Kemerer & Sosa, 1988).

The relevance of SIS literature for the evaluative research on GIS can also be seen from some specific suggestions found in the SIS literature. For example, when dealing with the decision-problems of planning and developing SIS, the concept of Strategic Information Systems Planning (SISP) (Lederer & Sethi, 1988) essentially calls for enlarging the scope of required analysis from the level of CBA to the wider realms of IS planning methodologies. This is quite consistent with our recommendations in Plank A, which calls for expanding the scope of CBA to integrate it with planning and design of GIS. Similarly, the high risk involved appears to be another common characteristic for both SIS and GIS, including the ironic risks associated with even the technical success of such systems. Vitale (1986) discusses a variety of risks of this type (for example, the legal costs of antitrust litigations), and emphasizes the need for incorporating such non-technical and long-term aspects in the cost-benefit evaluation of such systems. It is easy to see that these remarks are equally applicable to GIS as well.

Plank C: Addressing the Multidimensionality of GIS

The basic premise of this plank is that the cost-benefit evaluation of GIS will need to simultaneously deal with the major CBA-related issues along all three dimensions of the GIS complexity. Earlier, we elaborated the GIS complexity through its multinational, technological, and the managerial (or organizational) dimensions. Here, we outline some of the salient ways in which researchers could deal with the challenges created by this multidimensional complexity vis-a-vis application of CBA.

We consider this plank to be a rather crucial one, because, in a very real sense this is the "operational" plank which must deliver the thrust of this framework. The previous two planks were concerned with setting the general tone and the direction of this framework. In contrast, the following discussion focuses on the GIS complexity in the context of CBA, and has direct implications for possible research avenues in cost-benefit evaluation of GIS, as well as for a particular CBA project involving a specific global information system.

Independence of the Major Dimensions: In terms of specific guidelines toward concrete directions for research, it is suggested here that the complexities of cost-benefit analysis of GIS derive, in a large measure, from the multinational, technological, and managerial dimensions of the GIS complexity discussed earlier. Fortunately, as we noted there, these dimensions could be dealt with somewhat independently of each other. This decomposition approach should prove helpful at least during the initial phases of cost-benefit research on GIS. The approach seems especially applicable to the technological dimension, since typically the technological developments and their assessment precede in time, as compared to the developments in the other dimensions. Thus, if a particular technology is not available to the organization then the corresponding complexities of the cost-benefit analysis need not be investigated in any great detail. When the technology becomes available, the CBA-related consideration of the technology (for example, the risk of its becoming obsolete) could be carried out relatively independent of the multinational and the managerial dimensions.

In order to effectively deal with the complexities of the multinational character of GIS, we will need to access referent disciplines (such as, international law and politics) which we are not equipped with here. However, we are equipped to deal with the complexities of applying CBA methodology to GIS along the managerial or organizational dimension. Based on the insights gathered so far in this paper, below we propose a hierarchic view of our key recommendations related to cost-benefit evaluation of GIS.

Recommendations Along the Managerial Dimension: Our conception of the key recommendations is depicted in Figure 1. The figure emphasizes that the degree of applicability of many of our recommendations seems to vary along the three levels of GIS support for the management. The various aspects of GIS to be evaluated are conceptually separated in Figure 1 depending on the management level (Anthony, 1965) which they support. For example, a globally accessible database on international trade regulations may be viewed as an example of strategic aspects of GIS, whereas similar database on airline schedules would be an operational aspect of the GIS.

The recommendations which appear in Figure 1 arise out of the following major considerations related to our analysis. First, the GIS actually serves as an IS resource for all three levels of management. Second, the level of intangibility of the benefits (Toraskar & Joglekar, 1990) of information systems, as well as the overall difficulties of CBA, seem to increase monotonically as we move higher up in terms of Anthony's levels of management. Therefore, as indicated in Figure 1, the traditional methods and approaches to CBA may be useful mainly for the operational level aspects of GIS. In contrast, cost-benefit evaluation of the higher-level aspects of GIS may require fundamentally different and innovative approaches. Moreover, the continuum of the three levels implies that the application of CBA to the middle tactical level (TC) will require a blend of such competing methodological considerations.

In general, the recommendations appearing at the lower levels of

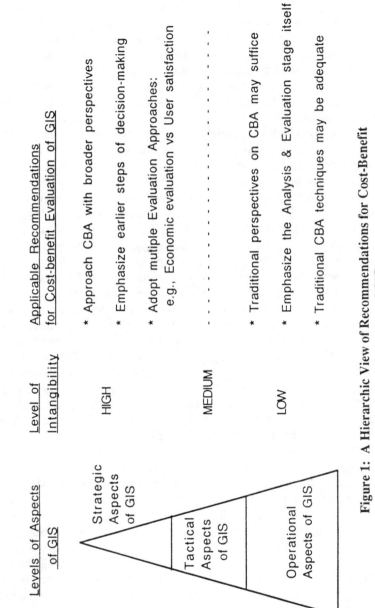

Figure 1: A Hierarchic View of Recommendations for Cost-Benefit Evaluation of GIS

Figure 1 follow the traditional view of CBA, and are self-explanatory. In contrast, the recommendations appearing across the strategic aspects of GIS need to be interpreted further. For example, the broader perspectives recommended for the CBA activity (both in research and in practice) imply that, when evaluating the strategic aspects of GIS we should be explicitly aware of the variety of perspectives (described earlier). Similarly, our recommendation for an emphasis on the earlier phases of the IS development translates into paying particular attention to the following issues: (1) A reliable explication of the firm's goals, (2) intelligence level activities pertaining to the larger economic and social environments, and (3) conducting the CBA activity in a more integrated fashion with the broader IS planning methodologies used by the organization (e.g., IBM's BSP methodology, or the SISP methodology). Finally, for cost-benefit evaluation of the strategic aspects of GIS it may be necessary to investigate the entire spectrum of the IS evaluation paradigms and approaches identified earlier.

CONCLUSION

If the principles of rational decision-making are valid for systems planning and management in general, then they must also be helpful for planning and development of related research activity itself. Accordingly, we have attempted to apply some of the basic principles of scientific method and rational decision-making to the research problem of cost-benefit evaluation of Global Information Systems or GIS. At present, systematic research efforts on cost-benefit evaluation of GIS have not been formulated and initiated. To make some progress in this direction, we have undertaken a special, meta-level, analysis aimed at assessing the need, or "demand" for, and the feasibility of a comprehensive research agenda for this new area of IS. Our analysis involved (1) a systematic account of the multidimensional complexities of GIS, and (2) bringing the existing literature on IS evaluation to bear upon the problem of cost-benefit evaluation of GIS. This analysis revealed a broad structure of the difficult issues involved in applying the concepts of CBA to global information systems.

The major findings of our analysis are logically integrated into a broad-based framework for continued systematic research on cost-benefit evaluation of GIS. A simultaneously Proactive, Comprehensive, and Multidimensional stance is adopted for the proposed framework for the purpose of developing concrete research directions and research goals. Guided by this stance, we have elaborated on three major planks of the framework, namely: (A) The focus on methodology rather than on techniques, (B) learning from other IS areas of CBA application, and (C) addressing the multidimensionality of GIS. The major recommendations arising out of these planks were outlined, and stratified along the three levels of management.

References

Ackoff, R. L.(1962) *Scientific Method: optimizing applied research decisions.* New York, NY: Wiley.

Anthony, R. N. (1965). *Planning and control systems: A framework for analysis,* Cambridge: MA, Harvard University Press, 1965.

Ashby, R. (1956). *An introduction to cybernetics,* London, England: Chapman and Hall.

Barkan, B. (1989). Strategic systems? Sez who? *CIO, 2*(6), March 1989, 11-14.

Baroudi, J. J., & Orlikowski, W. J. (1981). A short-form measure of user information satisfaction: A psychometric evaluation and notes on use, *Journal of Management Information Systems, 4*(4), Spring 1988, 44-59.

Bouldin, B. (1989). Culture has impact on data processing, *Software Magazine, 9*(8), June 1989, 73-77.

Brandel, W. (1989) Worldly leadership at Dow Chemicals, *Computerworld,* March 13, 1989, *23*(11), 63, 74.

Brown, J. (1990). Chiquita power-line net monitors bananas, *Network World, 7*(10), March 5, 1990, 13-14.

Burger, K. (1990). Banking goes global, *Bank Systems & Technology, 27*(2), February 1990, 34-37.

Burnson, P. (1989). The perils of going global, *Infoworld, 11*(33), August 14, 1989, 39-40.

Copeland, D. G. & McKenney, J. L. (1988). Airline reservation systems: Lessons from history, *MIS Quarterly, 12*(3), 353-370.

Craven, R. (1988). The challenge of enterprise-wide internetworking, *Telecommunications, 22*(10), October 1988, 31-37.

Crockett, B. (1989). Texaco looks to net technology for edge, *Network World, 6*(13), April 3, 1989, 19, 22.

Dalton, R. (1988). Strategies from the airlines, *Personal Computing,* March 1988, 83-84.

Davis, G. & Olson, M. (1985) *Management Information Systems,* McGraw-Hill.

Dooley, A. (1990). When a bank is more than a bank, *Computerworld, 23*(15), April 10, 1989, 30.

Dorros, I. (1990). Anyone, anytime, anyplace, *Telephone Engineer & Management* (supplement), 28-30.

Doukas, M. E. (1987). A perspective for IRM-related cost-benefit studies, *Records Management Quarterly,* July 1987, 15-17.

Eckerson, W. (1988-a). International bank reins in its worldwide network, *Network World, 5*(5), December 12, 1988, 1, 6.

Eckerson, W. (1988-b). Woolworth opts for EDI to keep pace in retail field, *Network World, 5*(51),

December 19 1988, 21, 24.

Guptill, B. (1988). American Express net puts users on top of the world, *Network World, 5*(36), September 5, 1988, 1, 37.

Hastings. P. (1989). Express services: A struggle for world domination, *Asian Business,* (Hong Kong), *25*(5), May 1989, 66-71.

Held, J. (1988). A manager's perspective on international communications: No more ugly Americans, *Network world, 5*(30), September 19, 1988, 33-38.

Heywood, P. (1989). Citicorp's scheme to shoehorn data into TV transmissions, *Data Communications, 18*(3), March 1989, 62-69.

Horton, F. (1985). *Information resources management,* Prentice-Hall, 1985.

Hurd, E. (1988). With a worldwide eye for profits, watch automation, *Transportation and Distribution, 29*(10), Sept 1988, 62-66.

Inmon, W. H. (1982). The hardware/personnel cost relationship: Separating fact from fancy. *Journal of Information Systems Management, 4*(2), Spring 1982, 48-53.

Kanter, J. (1987). Progress in tracking elusive ROI of new systems,*Directors & Boards, 11*(4), Summer 1987, 38-40.

Keen, P. G. W. (1981). Value Analysis: Justifying decision support systems, *MIS Quarterly, 5*(1), 1-14.

Keen, P. G. W. (1988). *Competing in time: Using telecommunications for competitive advantage.* Ballinger Press, 1988.

Keen, P. G. W. , & Gambino, T. J. (1982). Building a decision support system: The mythical man-month revisited, In Sprague, R., & Carlson, E. (Eds.), (1982), *Building effective decision support systems,* Englewood Cliffs, NJ: Prentice-Hall.

Kemerer, F. & Sosa, G. (1988). Barriers to successful strategic information systems, *Planning Review, 16*(5), Sept/Oct 1988, 20-23, 46.

Kennedy, M. (1989). Strategic responsibilities of corporate telecommunications managers, *Telecommunications, 23*(11), Nov 1989, 63-65.

King, J. L. & Schrems, E. L. (1978). Cost benefit analysis in information systems development and operation. *Computing Surveys, 10*(1), 1978, 19-34.

Kleijnen, J. P. C. (1980). *Computers and profits: Quantifying financial benefits of information.* Reading, MA: Addison-Wesley.

Kroenke, D. (1989). *Management Information Systems,* Santa Cruz, CA: Mitchell Publishing.

Lay, P. (1985). Beware of cost/benefit model for IS project evaluation, *Journal of Systems Management,* June 1985, 30-35.

Lederer, A. & Mendelow, A. (1988). Convincing top management of the strategic potential of information systems, *MIS Quarterly, 12*(4), December 1988, 525-534.

Lederer, A. & Sethi, V. (1988). The implementation of strategic information systems planning methodologies. *MIS Quarterly, 12*(3), September 1988, 445-463.

Lederer, A. & Sethi, V. (1989). Pitfalls in planning. *Datamation.* June 1, 1989, 59-60, 62.

Livingston, D. (1990). How EDS will build the worlds biggest private network, *Systems Integration, 23*(2), February 1990, 34-39.

Ludlum, D. (1989). Managing global networks, *Computer world, 23*(40), October 2, 1989, 86.

Maglitta, J. (1990). Eastern Europe move expands UPS horizons, *Computer World*, February 19, 1990, 79.

Maire, R. (1989). New ideas needed for global networking, *Data Communications, 18*(16), December 1989, 15-16.

Marchand, D. & Horton, F. (1986). *Infotrends: Profiting from your information resources.* New York, NY: Wiley.

McLean, E., & Riesing, G. (1977). The MAPP system: A decision support system for financial planning and budgeting, *Data Base, 8*(3), Winter 1977, 9-14.

Meador, C., & Keen, P. G. W. (1984). Setting priorities for DSS development, *MIS Quarterly, 8*(2), 117-129.

Means, G. E., & Bugos, B. (1988). Global views: The road to Rio, *CIO, 1*(7), June 1988, 16-19.

Miller, J., & Doyle, B. A. (1987). Measuring the effectiveness of computer-based information systems in the financial services sector, *MIS Quarterly*, March 1987, 107-117.

Moskowitz, R. (1986). Strategic systems planning shifts to data-oriented approach, *Computer World*, May 12, 1986, 109-119.

Nolan, R. L., & Seward, H. H. (1974). Measuring user satisfaction to evaluate information systems, In Nolan, R. L. (Ed) (1974), Managing the data resource function, 253-275, St Paul, MN: West Publishing.

Ohmae, K. (1989). Managing in a borderless world, *Harvard Business Review, 67*(3), 152-161.

Ojala, M. (1990). Insurance industry information online, *Online, 14*(1), January 1990, 71-74.

Orli, R. J. & Tom, J. C. (1987). If it's worth more than it costs, buy it!, *Journal of Information Systems Management, 4*(3), Summer 1987, 85-89.

Ostroff, L. (1990). Spinning systems in the Pacific, *Datamation, 36*(4), February 15, 1990, 129-131.

Pantages, A. (1989-a). The right is chemistry, *Datamation, 35*(16), August 15, 1989, 61-62.

Pantages, A. (1989-b). TI's global window, *Datamation, 35*(15), September 1, 1989, 49, 52.

Parker, M. M. Information economics: An introduction, *Datamation, 33*(23), December 1, 1987, 86-96.

Raptis, G. (1986). Managing multinational information systems, *Management Accounting, 67*(7), January 1986, 14, 29, 81.

Reck, R. H. (1989). The shock of going global, *Datamation*, (35), August 1, 1989, 67-70.

Rockhold, A. G. MIS feels pressure of ROI, cost/benefit analysis, *Infosystems*, July 1982, 90-92.

Romei, L. (1989). Distributing information on a global scale, *Modern Office Technology*, (34), May 1989, 100-102.

Ruffin, W. R. (1990). Wired for speed, *Business Month, 135*(1), January 1990, 56-58.

Savage, J. (1989). DHL sold on cosmopolitan UNIX, *Computer World, 23*(15), April 10, 1989, 30.

Schindler, Paul, Jr. At BankAmerica, GDN spells the difference. *Information Week,* October 12, 1987, 40-41.

Schultheis, R., & Sumner, M. (1989). *Management information systems: The manager's view,* Homewood, IL: Irwin.

Senn, J. (1974). Economic evaluation of management information systems,(MIDS), *Proceedings, National Meeting of the American Institute of Decision Sciences,* Atlanta, GA, 1974, 79.

Simon, H. (1977). *The new science of management decision,* Revised Edition, Englewood Cliffs, NJ: Prentice-Hall.

Smith, R. (1983). Measuring the intangible benefits of computer-based information systems, *Journal of Systems Management,* September 1983, 22-27.

Sokol, R., & Lipson, W. (1989). To spend or not to spend - Improving the evaluation of capital expenditures, *Industrial Management and Data Systems,* (7), 9-14.

Strassmann, P. (1988). Productivity, *Computerworld Extra* (supplement), June 20, 1988, 11-13.

Stretch, T. (1988). Overcoming resistance to strategic and executive IS planning and implementation, *Journal of Information Systems Management, 5*(1), Winter 1988, 63-65.

Swanson, E. B. (1974). Management information systems: Appreciation and involvement, *Management Science, 21*(2),178-188, 1974.

Swanson, E. B. (1982). Measuring user attitudes in MIS research: A review, *Omega, 10*(2), 1982, 157-165.

Tate, P. (1988). Risk! The third factor, *Datamation,* April 15, 1988, 58-64.

Thierauf, R. J. (1982). *Decision support systems for effective planning and control,* Englewood Cliffs, NJ: Prentice-Hall.

Toraskar, K. & Joglekar, P. (1990). Comments on price and value of decision support systems. *MIS Quarterly, 14*(1), March 1990, -12.

Van Rensselaer, C. (1985). Global, shared, local, *Datamation,* (31), March 15, 1985, 105-114.

Vitale, M. R. (1986). The growing risk of information systems success. *MIS Quarterly, 10*(4), December 1986, 327-334.

Webber, C. C. (1988). Information as a strategic weapon, *Best's Review,* December 1988, 101-103.

Wind, Y. & Douglas, S. (1987). The myth of globalization. *Columbia Journal of World Business, 22*(4), Winter 1987.

14 Cross-Cultural Aspects of Model Management Needs in a Transnational Decision Support System

Vicki L. Sauter
University of Missouri - St. Louis

The purpose of this chapter is to consider some problems associated with cross-cultural use of a decision support system. In particular, it illustrates the differences in modeling and model management issues that are likely to affect the acceptance, use and success of a system in use in multiple national cultures. Further, this chapter will provide guidelines regarding the parameters for design of the model management component of DSS.

Decision support systems (DSS) have been implemented widely to increase the use of dependable information and appropriate models. The goal of these systems is to aid decision makers by helping them obtain the information they need to understand problems, opportunities,and potential solutions (Alter, 1980; Sprague and Carlson, 1982). Since decision support systems are flexible (Hall, 1986), decision makers can adapt both the analysis itself and the reporting of results to be consistent with their own decision styles and information needs.

Decision support systems have proven their potential in supporting the task of managing domestic decision making (see, for example, Cooper et al., 1975; Henderson and Schilling, 1985; Keen, 1981; Walker et al., 1985; Wallace and Balogh, 1985; Zmud, 1983). There is substantial evidence to suggest they help decision makers to consider information more effectively and hence to make more informed choices (Bennett, 1983; Sprague and Carlson, 1982; Sprague and Watson, 1986). Furthermore, there is evidence that enhancing such decision support systems with increasing levels of "intelligence" can help even novice users to standardize the process of decision making and to improve the quality of its outcome (Harmon, Maus and Morrissey, 1988).

Decision support systems have the potential for even greater impact in assisting multinational decision making because the data needs are greater and the problems are more poorly defined. However, if not implemented properly, decision support systems have the potential for adding to the problems of transnational decision making. In order to exploit the benefits of decision support systems to improve multinational decision making, we need to be sensitive to a wider variety of issues and problems in their design than those generally considered in the design of domestic systems. The purpose of this chapter is to highlight those issues and problems.

For example, many transnational decisions address production options. These decisions may involve plants in multiple countries which produce the same (or similar) products, or they may imply having different components produced in multiple countries and assembled in one central location. Alternatively, the production process may have several stages of assembly, each in a different location.

Multi-plant and/or multi-staged production processes require significant coordination and communication to insure implementation of optimal strategies. However, the unique regulations and/or conventions associated with the other countries increases the complexity in planning; and this requires explicit consideration of all constraints associated with doing business in additional countries.

Such problems are often worse if the domestic plant is considerably larger and more important than the other plants. In such circumstances, planning tends to be one-sided: from the domestic plant to the foreign plants. The negative implications of such one-sided planning for transnational production processes have been well known for some time. For example, Skinner (1968) suggested that foreign plants have inadequate staffing at the middle to upper management levels. This causes inadequate emphasis on, and attention to, key control operations within the plant, such as quality control operations. Furthermore, because the appropriate levels of personnel either are not at the foreign plant or are assumed not to be at the plant, policy decisions generally disregard input from plant management. As such, there is no one in the planning process to share unique concerns and issues during planning. Finally, for a variety of reasons, the corporate headquarters does not stress communication between itself and its overseas plants. The people making the decisions have, at best, incomplete information about the plant, and the managers in the plant often have no information about upcoming plans. Although the situation has improved in the last twenty years, recent research identifies similar issues still affect the management of overseas operations (Carlyle, 1988; LaPalombara and Blank, 1987; Robey, 1987).

Decision support systems can help to make more relevant information available in a more usable form than could otherwise be accessible. They can also improve communication between the corporate office and the foreign operations by providing an effective vehicle for data and information transfer. Furthermore, decision support systems could simplify management of over-seas operations by providing help for administrators who may not have proper training, who lack sufficient experience or who are not familiar with corporate goals, procedures or policies.

Decision support systems can only help, however, if designed with a sensitivity to the needs of all users and an awareness of the problems of multi-cultural differences in needs. This chapter will highlight those issues with an emphasis on their impact upon the model management component of decision support systems. First, the chapter will summarize the international decision making literature. This will be followed by a brief discussion of how culture can affect decision making. The next section, will outline how one can operationalize the concept of "culture" so that its effect upon decision making can be studied. Finally, in the final section, the implications for the design of the modeling component of decision support systems will be drawn.

OVERVIEW OF DSS

A decision support system has three components: the dialog (or user-interface) component, the database component and the model management component. Each of these components has the potential for both realizing and inhibiting the promised benefits for improving transnational decision making and communication.

The Dialog Component

The dialog component provides the interface between the user and the DSS. With a well-designed dialog management component, the decision maker is no longer tied to the presentation modes chosen by someone else. With these systems, decision makers are in control of the information provided and the order of that presentation. They can query the system until they feel comfortable with their understanding of specific phenomena.

There is good reason to believe that there would be differences in preferences for user interface options for transnational systems. Researchers in the area of communication have long known that different cultures commu-nicate distinctively. Berger (1984; p. 43) notes that "even when they speak the same language, there are problems as a result of differences in education, class, level and cultural backgrounds." Once one begins to worry about transnational communication, one adds a new dimension to the problem.

Unfortunately, the user interface is the only way one can interact with the computer and may be the basis for interaction with other managers in a decision support system. One becomes totally dependent upon this interface for prompts that would otherwise come from "nonverbal cues" and other such tempering cues. Hence, different colors, size of representation (and relative size of representation), spatiality and contrast provide the "nonverbal cues" for the user interface. Words lose their intonation and the user becomes totally dependent upon their written context. Furthermore, the user begins to depend upon symbols and icons to convey more information. Even the way in which one moves from screen to screen or accesses information in a decision support system carries some significance.

This change in communication pattern is fine as long as everyone agrees to the meaning of the various cues. Problems occur, however, if there is a difference between the "codes" meant by the creators of the cues and the "codes" used by the consumers of the cues. Even the implications of a word can have very different meanings between cultures. For example, the Japanese interpret the word "pragmatic" to mean "tool user". There is every reason to believe that other less obvious problems of user interface would be different among cultures as well. Thus, if the dialog component is unacceptable to users, they will not use the DSS, and management cannot realize any potential that the rest of the DSS has for simplifying their tasks. Hence, the dialog component has an important direct influence on the ability of the user to realize the full potential of the system (Bostrom and Heinen, 1977; Zmud, 1979).

The Database Component

The second component of the decision support system, the database component, provides the ability to meld information from multiple databases, (e.g., plants or offices) for a specific analysis. Easy access to one or more databases and to a database management system can help managers view issues better.

One of the major difficulties in transnational management is insuring that everyone has necessary information at the appropriate time. Often the information is not available to suitable decision makers in a usable form or in a timely fashion. Consistent formats are often not used. Furthermore, problems of long delays in receiving the information especially from overseas plants is common. Even under comparatively good conditions, the corporate office has the information, but management in satellite plants, especially overseas plants, do not have all the information needed to plan future operations.

The advantage of a database in a decision support system is to eliminate the problems of data availability and consistency associated with traditional file processing systems with stand-alone data files. In particular, suitable management of the database component could give more access to information that would help not only in the actual planning, but in the communication about planning as well. First, since all relevant information can be retrieved from the same location and accessible in a similar format, the use of database technology greatly reduces the cost and effort needed to merge information from multiple sources. This is particularly true when the structures of these individual data files might not otherwise be uniform, as one might expect in different countries where standards might be different. Database organization also enables the users to obtain analyses at the appropriate level of aggregation easily. As a result, users can view the "big picture" of productivity and productivity by month or plant to help identify problems or opportunities. This facilitates the development of a wider variety of analyses, such as interplant comparisons, than would otherwise be possible. Further, it allows users to evaluate the issues from the perspectives of other decision makers. More important, though, is that the range of decision makers beyond the corporate office who could access and use appropriate information could be expanded. In this way, managers of an overseas plant could consider not only their production problems and opportunities, but also those of the company as a whole. They could therefore make more informed choices and be in a better position to understand decisions of the corporate office.

Second, because continuous collection and maintenance of data is encouraged in a database management system, careful management of the database component can increase the amount of information available to decision makers. Furthermore, since it minimizes the cost and effort needed to update data, the database component reduces problems associated with using data which are out-of-date or of questionable reliability. This allows the decision maker to examine phenomena over a longer period of time. For example, this might allow corporate decision makers to compare startup problems of overseas plants with those of domestic plants to determine political influences on operations. It could also allow comparisons of the plants at various stages to evaluate plant policies.

The Model Management Component

The model management component of a DSS, could also affect the ability of the DSS to meet the needs of transnational decision making. This component consists of a library of analytical tools and the means for managing those tools. It includes some pre-packaged analyses, the means for users to build their own analyses and the capability of integrating any of the analyses. The value of this component results from providing easier access to a wide variety of tools, some of which might be more sophisticated than those decision makers would otherwise employ.

The goal of the model management function is to enable users to select the appropriate models (from their points of view) to assist with a particular decision. That is, these functions ensure that analyses are consistent with users' decision styles and information needs. Important model management functions include: (a) showing the user what analytical procedures are available; (b) enabling the user to select the appropriate procedure and control certain aspects of its operation; and (c) documenting the critical assumptions and limitations of the basic procedures and the various user-controlled options associated with each analytical procedure (Sauter & Mandell, 1990).

Underlying the promises associated with improved productivity is an assumption that the decision support system will be designed with a particular user or type of user in mind. That is, the design of the models (and management of those models) must be attuned to reflect the people who will be using the system and the ways in which they will be making decisions (Sauter, 1985; Sauter, 1988). There is some controversy about what this means in the current context. After all, there are those who believe that there is one "correct" model to use for any decision and hence attention to transnational issues is irrelevant. However, each plant and division will have a different perspective and the different plants and divisions will be at a different stage of the decision making process. This results in their need to address different questions and hence need different models. Furthermore, management style is, at least partially, a function of the state of development and technology in a particular country or region (Evans et al, 1989). In light of the heterogeneity of the information needs and decision styles of decision makers (Sauter, 1984), it is unlikely, even without the cultural differences, that one could develop successful systems unless they included a wide variety of modeling capabilities.

There is evidence that the cultural differences exacerbate the problem. For example, some researchers have found that the use of models is influenced by the culture (and its norms) of the individual making the decision. (Evans et al, 1989; Hofstede, 1980) Different traditions and different values cause variations in the need to optimize, the variables to consider, and the methods by which to evaluate alternatives. The parameters of the problem to consider, in turn, will influence the choice of relevant models.

Of these three DSS components, the one that has received the least attention in the literature concerning cross-cultural issues is the model management component. Hence, it will be the focus of this chapter. Specifically, the chapter will provide guidance on what factors of culture need to be considered, and how they need to be considered in order to design model management systems for multinational corporations.

IS THERE A PROBLEM IN NEED
OF SOLUTION?

The central argument of this chapter is that designers of decision support systems should be sensitive to the differences among cultures when designing the model management component. The primary premises underlying this argument are that there exist differences in how people make decisions that can be attributed to cultural differences, and that it is important to represent these differences in the design of the modeling component of a DSS. Clearly, these premises need some justification. Unfortunately, an empirical literature addressing these premises does not exist. There is, however, a literature available regarding international management that addresses "management practices" and cross-cultural differences. In this context, management practices include the use of analytical tools, the use of measurements for control, planning, and communication (Drucker, 1974; Kobayashi, 1982) since these tasks are the ones for which a decision support system might be used.

Evans et al (1989) suggest that there are two theories regarding the impact of culture on management practices. One group of researchers has found that the general state of development of a country affects the management style. These researchers believe societal development implies a move of society as a whole and its values to Western values. This, in turn, causes management style to move toward a more Western style. The other hypothesis is that a particular culture is a dominant factor in managerial style and that unique cultural identity will be maintained even as society develops.

If the first group of researchers is correct, then it is less important to differentiate the modeling needs of cultures because they will all ultimately merge. That is, people in "developed" countries make decisions in some specified fashion and as other countries develop, they will adopt this process. Some studies support this perspective. For example, Al-Jafaray and Hollingsworth (1983) found no significant differences in the decision making practices in the United States and that in the Arabian Gulf region. This result is surprising considering that most other management practices did differ in these two regions.

Negandhi (1979) found that subsidiaries of American companies located in other countries adopted the formal decision making process of the parent corporation. His results held even for subsidiaries located in culturally different or economically different societies. This may, however, be attributable to the absence of decision making authority afforded to these subsidiaries. In another survey, Van Den Bulcke (1984) found that in American-based, transnational enterprises, decision making was severely restricted in about half of the organizations. This was true even if the host country was a "developed nation" with similar economic capabilities.

These results should be discounted significantly for the purposes of considering the implications for decision support system design. First, these researchers emphasized the formal aspects of the decision making perspective. That is, their studies highlighted issues such as the reports filed, the forms completed, the formal transmission of information and other issues associated with the official decision making protocol. While such studies are important, they are not relevant here. Decision support systems do not necessarily facilitate the formal aspects of the decision making protocol. Rather, decision support systems support informal decision making processes. These studies do not provide insights into the similarities or differences of the informal decision making procedures.

Adler (1983) found that the major impact of culture is on the ways in which individuals and groups work within systems. Ackermann (1981) further states that culture affects the ways of evaluating alternatives and experiences. In fact, he contends that values manifest themselves in all choices. Ankomah (1985) further notes that sensitivity to cultural differences and norms is necessary for a complete understanding of both how people evaluate goals and the kinds of information that might persuade decision makers. Hence, it would not be surprising if transcultural organizational structures did not differ substantially, even if their informal decision making needs might differ. This, in turn, suggests a need for special attention to modeling needs in multicultural organizations.

Second, as England and Harpoz (1983) suggest, it is only important to acknowledge differences when they are large both in an absolute and relative sense. These studies did not address decisions supported by decision support systems. It is possible that without decision support systems, there is not enough time or freedom to consider the variety of analyses one might want. Hence, it is not possible to capture the differences in needs in any meaningful fashion. However, such differences should be larger with the availability of decision support systems.

A substantial amount of research in international management, such as the study by Kelley, Whatley and Worthley (1987), support the alternative view that there are significant influences of culture affecting decision making styles associated with the societal culture in which the person works. The critical question is, of course, the degree of the effects and the aspects of decision making affected. A review of the literature suggests some interesting differences.

One difference in the decision making tendencies associated with different cultures involves the criteria considered in a decision making context. For example, in a comparison of managers in the United States and in Japan, Beatty, McCune and Beatty (1988) found there were significant differences in the compensation decision making.   Although managers in the two groups granted the similar average pay raises, there were substantial differences in the variances in those pay raises: Japanese managers awarded pay raises with very little variance, whereas managers in the United States granted raises with large variances.   The primary factor explaining those differences was the criterion emphasized in the decision making process. In the United States, managers emphasized job performance of the workers.   That is, workers received raises on the basis of how well they completed the tasks assigned to them. In Japan, managers emphasized the job worth.   These decision makers tended to put relatively little weight on how well people completed tasks assigned to them, but instead put significant weight on how important a job was to the good of the company or to the good of society.

Another study by Kanungo and Wright (1988) showed differences in the measures used in appraisal of potential employment. These researchers compared British and French managers and found that British mangers place more importance on individual achievement and autonomy than do the French. The French managers, in contrast, were more likely to emphasize security and comfortable working conditions.

Similarly, a study completed by England (1975) compared managers in the United States with those in Australia. In general he found that managers in the United States put a high value on profit maximization and growth in the consideration of new initiatives. Australians, on the other hand, placed a low value on those criteria. Instead they placed a relatively high value on employee welfare and egalitarianism in the consideration of such new initiatives.

Obviously these studies suggest that people of different cultures may choose to collect different information in support of similar decisions. Hence, if a decision support system is intended to support decisions in many cultures (as might be the case for a multinational corporation), one needs to be sensitive to those differences.   For example, if the systems are intended to measure productivity for a Japanese-American company, it might be necessary to include both the capability to track individual performance and the relative worth of a particular job.

In addition, these examples have implications for the modeling needs. Not only are these decision makers considering different criteria, they are considering criteria in different ways. For example, if the decision style is satisficing, a decision support system needs to have a strong statistical/ simulation component by which decision makers can gauge how well an action is meeting some goal. If decision makers who prefer to optimize some criterion will also be using the decision support system, it needs to incorporate optimization techniques as well.

Furthermore, the stages considered in making a decision differ among cultures. For example, Doktor, Kawase and Haig (1986) analyzed differences in the way managers in the United States and those in Japan conceptualized the productivity of a plant. They suggest that in the United States, the concept of productivity is from a management science perspective that emphasizes a strong planning component. As such, insuring productivity takes a "Think, Think, Do, Think" perspective. That is, managers in the United States follow a pattern of strategic planning, operational planning, production, and the quality control/feedback. Productivity from a Japanese perspective, on the other hand, comes from the skilled labor perspective that emphasizes activity. The Japanese managers, then, follow a "Do, Think, Do, Do" perspective to insuring productivity. That is, these managers follow a process of production, consideration of quality control issues, and more production. There is comparatively less time spent in the planning function. Clearly, managers in the United States require different information to utilize their approach. In addition, systems supporting the Japanese perspective on planning for improvements in productivity would not need the support for strategic planning and operational planning necessary for systems supporting managers in the United States. Managers in Japan, however, would require more statistical comparisons of historical trends.

Similarly, a study completed by Mallory et al (1983) of British and American subsidiaries located in Britain found differences in how decisions were approached. When considering major initiatives or cutbacks, British owned subsidiaries follow formal procedures of consideration within standing committees. They standardized both the criteria used in evaluation and the processes for evaluation of the criteria. In American owned subsidiaries, on the other hand, managers tend to rely upon informally assembled groups to consider such decisions. As such, there is a wider variation in the types of criteria and associated analytical procedures.

These differences in the number and form of the stages used to make a decision affect the kinds of information needed, the regularity of its use and maintenance, and the needs for models with which to analyze the data.

Finally, decision makers in different cultures are trained differently to make choices. Decision makers in the United States tend to come "up the ranks" in one department or area. Hence, they are accustomed to making decisions from a marketing perspective or a financial perspective or a production perspective. This tends to limit the kinds of analysis, or at least the emphasis of the analysis required by the decision maker. Japanese executives, on the other hand, are rotated among many departments to gain a wide range of experiences. Due to this policy, they are more likely to consider a wider range of issues in decision making than would their American counterparts. Hence, it would be more difficult to predict the models and model management capabilities of these decision makers.

These are some patterns in the international management literature that suggest that people make decisions differently across cultures. There are not obvious patterns, however, that can be adopted easily to design decision support system better. Such patterns can be derived only from further discussion of cultures and the dimensions of their definition. To facilitate that discussion, the next section will provide an operationalization of the concept of "culture" that can be used to illustrate the potential impact on decision support systems.

AN OPERATIONALIZATION OF THE TERM "CULTURE"

Cultural anthropologists have a variety of measures for defining and evaluating a culture. A culture cannot, as one might naively expect, be defined simply in terms of the nation in which it exists. Examination of only cross-national differences misses a wide range of characteristics that distinguish people and therefore might be useful for predicting their modeling needs (Ankomah, 1985; Negandhi, 1983). Consequently, for the purposes of this discussion, the focus includes dimensions of cultural differences, not generalizations about specific countries.

Kluckhohn and Strodtbeck (1961) identify five dimensions of cultural differences: (a) time orientation; (b) person-nature orientation; (c) activity orientation; (d) human nature perception; and (e) relational orientation. These are described below.

Time Orientation

The first of these dimensions, time orientation, describes the cultural interpretation and emphasis upon the temporal focus of life (Kluckhohn and Strodtbeck, 1961). This spectrum includes primary concern for past events, primary concern for future events, and primary concern for current events. Hofstede (1980) proposed a related concept of the relative linearity of time. His claim is that some cultures view time as linear, thereby having a beginning and an end. Other cultures view time as circular, without having obvious beginnings and ends.

Those with a strong emphasis on the past, value tradition and the continuation of that tradition. Their decision making emphasis is on the maintenance of the status quo simply because it exists. Those with an emphasis on the future, on the other hand, tend to be more interested in change, provided that change does not threaten the rest of their world.

This temporal orientation is likely to have an impact upon both the evaluation of alternatives and the informational needs of the decision makers as well. Decision makers with a strong "past" orientation will highlight historical data and the relationship of proposed practices to current practices when evaluating alternatives. Decision makers with a strong "present" orientation will want substantial monitoring capabilities in their decision support systems so they can maintain currency regarding current practices. Finally decision makers with a strong "future" orientation will emphasize alternative generation and simulation of future events in the decision support systems. That is, these decision makers would be concerned with how to change from the status quo to improve operations.

Hofstede (1983) linked attitudes toward time to the relative tendency toward uncertainty avoidance associated with different cultures. In particular, he claimed that people in different cultures had distinct patterns for addressing the ambiguity and uncertainty of the future. Cultures that accept the uncertainty will take risks easily. These individuals will be tolerant of opinions different from their own because they do not feel threatened by them. Cultures in which uncertainty is less well accepted attempt to create laws and facilities to shield their people from the unknown.

He found that the uncertainty avoidance level was, in turn, associated with two additional concepts, aggressiveness and a need for absolute truth. Those individuals with high uncertainty avoidance create security through aggressive intolerance for deviant behaviors and opinions and for any action and/or people who threaten their view of the world. In addition, these people seek absolute truth, usually in the form of a religion, as a way of explaining events and hence predicting the future. Cultures with low uncertainty avoidance, on the other hand, display tolerance and do not seek "absolute truths" because they accept each new change on its own merits.

The relative level of uncertainty avoidance of the culture will affect their decision making needs. For example, individuals in cultures with high uncertainty avoidance will want to have as great an understanding as possible about contingencies. To achieve that level of understanding, they will be more likely to want a greater number of alternatives to evaluate, and more information with which to evaluate the alternatives. In addition, when these individuals are faced with optimization results, they will seek more postoptimality analyses for evaluation. Finally, the high uncertainty avoidance culture is likely to be associated with more structured analysis and less ad hoc analysis.

Person-Nature Orientation

The person-nature orientation addresses the question of how a person views his/her relative dominance over fate. There are three ranges of interest for this dimension: subjugation-to-nature, harmony-with-nature and mastery-over-nature. People functioning in the first case believe there is nothing they can do to affect the future. These people do not believe in planning for future contingencies. Rather one simply accepts the inevitable. In the second case, people believe there is a one-ness between humans and nature and that it is important to maintain an appropriate balance between the two. Finally, people who believe in the mastery-over-nature emphasize their ability to overcome obstacles.

One of the implications of differences on this dimension is how one is likely to view the importance of planning. People in cultures that do not accept one's ability to influence the future do not participate in long range planning activities. In fact, decision makers in such cultures are more likely to emphasize reactive decision making. Since, in their view, it is difficult to influence things that will happen anyway, it is best to see what will happen and respond in the best fashion one can. Decision makers who adopt the mastery-over-nature orientation, on the other hand, are more likely to be interested in strategic and contingency planning. These people will be interested in improving the relative position of the organization in its environment and/or changing their own position in the organization.

Another feature that is likely to affect the use of decision support systems is the relative acceptance of technology among these groups. Those individuals who adopt the mastery-over-nature orientation encourage the use of technology as a way of meeting their goals. Individuals who adopt the subjugation-to-nature orientation are less likely to adopt technology easily. Hence, there may be significant differences among these groups in the likelihood of even using the decision support system, independent of its capabilities.

Evan (1975) associates the concept of "luck" with either the subjugation-to-nature orientation or, to a lesser extent, the harmony-with-nature orientation. Cultures adopting the subjugation-to-nature orientation believe that good things happen because of random luck. Hence, individuals in these cultures do not practice significant long-range planning or contingency planning because such activities are not relevant.

Harmony-with-nature oriented cultures believe that the more harmonious of a social structure and/or organizational structure one can create, the more "luck" one can attract for the organization. In these cultures, the top executives are likely to attempt to create harmony through meetings, gatherings, etc. This implies, in turn, that more of their responsibilities are delegated to lower levels in the organization. Hence, broader informational needs and greater authority are likely to be of less importance to such organizations.

Evan (1975) and Negandhi (1983) hypothesize that the person-nature orientation affects the formality of the socialization in the organization, the directions of communication and the output of the organization. In particular, they suggest that societies with a stronger mastery-over-nature orientation would have formal methods of socialization, multi-directional communication and high levels of output. Societies with a stronger subjugation to nature would be more likely to have informal methods of socialization, uni-directional communication and low levels of output. Hofstede (1983) verified the hypothesis regarding the levels of output.

Cultures which adopt the mastery-over-nature orientation require decision making analyses and review of analyses at various levels in the organization. Cultures adopting the subjugation-to-nature orientation, on the other hand, would need to have systems with strong controls over the types of information available at each level and the kinds of analyses that might be constructed.

Another implication is that conventions for decision making procedures, criteria, and models would be well established and structured in cultures with a stronger mastery-over-nature orientation. Cultures with a subjugation-to-nature orientation, on the other hand, would be more likely to adopt ad hoc analyses.

Activity Orientation

The manner in which people evaluate activity and accomplishments is the third dimension to consider when judging a culture. Note, this is not the active-passive dichotomy of which one normally thinks when considering activity. Rather, it is a description of the mode of expression and hence the mechanism by which activity should be evaluated.

Kluckhohn and Strodtbeck (1961) identify three major categories, the Being, the Being-in-Becoming, and the Doing orientations. Those adopting the "Being" orientation prefer spontaneous activity and spontaneous expression of attitudes. That is, people in this category do not accept planning or development of activities, and hence it is inappropriate to evaluate their activities against some planned agenda. Instead, people adopting this orientation believe that the worth of an alternative should be judged by what it "is", not what it can do. People who adopt the "Doing" orientation prefer activities with measurable outcomes that can be judged against objective standards. Those adopting this orientation attempt to plan their activities so as to meet some criterion of "getting the job done" as viewed by society as a whole. As one might expect, the cultures adopting the Being-in-Becoming orientation adopt a position somewhere between these two. These people focus on measurement of worth as a function of what an alternative "is" as do those from the Being orientation. However, they also believe that what "is" can develop into something better. Hence, their evaluations can include the ability of the alternative to improve itself or the organization over time.

In terms of decision making, this orientation will most significantly affect one's goal orientation and one's willingness to adopt standards. Clearly, those cultures which emphasize the "Doing" orientation are more likely to adopt more standards for evaluation and therefore more standardized evaluations of alternatives. Associated with this is a stronger tendency to depend upon optimization techniques of analysis. Cultures which emphasize the other two orientations are more likely to rely upon more descriptive measures of analysis to provide evidence of the relative worth of the alternative. Those in cultures emphasizing the "Being" orientation are more likely to be interested in current, static measures of worth, while decision makers in cultures emphasizing the "Being-in-Becoming" orientation are more likely to be concerned with historical data rating the development of the alternative.

Evans, Hau and Sculli (1989) believe this orientation is associated with a culture's relative levels of aggressiveness in management and decision making. Those cultures adopting the "Doing" orientation are seen as more aggressive and those cultures adopting the "Being" orientation are seen as more passive and defensive. More aggressive cultures are more likely to adopt efficiency as an important criterion for decision making, while more passive cultures are more likely to adopt social harmony as an important criterion for decision making. In addition, cultures that are more aggressive are more accepting of public disagreement, and therefore would be more likely to allow greater flexibility in the alternative generation and evaluation during decision making.

Human Nature Orientation

The fourth dimension identified by Kluckhohn and Strodtbeck (1961) is the view that a culture takes of the likelihood in finding innate "goodness" of human nature. They identify four categories of orientation of this dimension: neutral, evil, evil-good mixture and good. Underlying this dimension is the question of what motivates people in their actions. If one adopted the "evil" orientation, one would adopt an attitude that people are intrinsically bad. The result would be the need to adopt planning and management mechanisms that constantly control and discipline in order to obtain good results from the organization. If, on the other hand, one adopts the evil-good mixture orientation, one would claim a need for control mechanisms, but that lapses in performance should not be condemned.

In addition, they suggest that a subprinciple of mutability and immutability should be evaluated. That is, one should consider not only whether a culture views people as basically good, but whether they are unalterably good or whether that good is corruptible. Similarly, one should not only determine if people are basically evil, but also as to whether that can be changed. This also varies among cultures and affects whether managers believe in the ability to change basic viewpoints.

An obvious outgrowth of this dimension is the role of monitoring systems. In cultures in which the view is that people are basically evil, decision makers have a much greater need to observe people and/or projects quite carefully. The goal of such monitoring would be to detect problems as soon as possible. The more strongly one adopted the philosophy, the tighter such monitoring would be. If, on the other hand, one adopted the view that people are basically good, one reduces a need for monitoring. The goal in such cultures is not to detect problems, but rather to detect opportunities for development, growth and/or strategic advantage.

Evans, Hau and Sculli (1989) claim that the human-nature orientation also influences the flexibility exhibited toward managerial communication. The more a culture adopts an "evil" view of society, the less likely that superiors would want alternative opinions, especially from subordinates. Cultures that adopt a "good" view of society are more likely to tolerate conflict situations associated with debates of the relative merits of alternatives and methods for evaluating alternatives. In this latter case, decision makers through more levels of the organization need support from greater use of analytical tools, more alternative generation capabilities and greater information retrieval.

Relational Orientation

The final dimension identified by Kluckhohn and Strodtbeck (1961) is the relational orientation. Again the authors identify three basic categories by which cultures can be evaluated: lineal, collateral and individualistic. Lineal cultures emphasize the continuity of the group and hence the group goals have primacy in their decision making efforts. These groups are generally homogeneous in some fashion and want to stay that way. Individualistic groups, by contrast, value the autonomy of the members of the group. Collateral cultures represent a midpoint between the two extremes.

Cultures that emphasize the individualistic view emphasize achieving the goals of the individual above all others. These people may accept and pursue group goals, but only if they do not conflict with their own. Collateral societies, on the other hand, emphasize the goals and welfare of the extended group, such as the organization. Lineal cultures also emphasize the goals and welfare of the extended group. However, they also stress the importance of continuity of the group through time and ordered progression of individuals within the group.

The relational orientation, then, will affect what goals will be adopted and pursued in decision making. In addition, this orientation will also affect compliance with authority in considering alternatives and/or complying with contracts. Evan (1975) and Negandhi (1983) postulate that this orientation will affect the formalization of the socialization function and the direction of communication within an organization. They suggest that cultures that emphasize the individualistic component will have formal means of socialization within the organization and strong multidirectional communication among decision makers. Cultures that emphasize the lineal component, on the other hand, will have informal means of socialization within the organization and unidirectional communication. As stated previously, this will, in turn, affect the types of analyses and standards of alternatives considered, the need for controls on information within the organization and need for sharing of analyses among levels within the organization.

EFFECTS UPON A DECISION SUPPORT SYSTEM

There are few studies which have taken the additional step of applying these concepts about culture to the use of decision support systems; even fewer actually involve the use of empirical data in testing of hypotheses. However, there is some preliminary work being done. For example, Farn and Sun (1989) suggest that sensitivity analyses (within the model management function) for a group decision support system functioning in China would be useless because of the process of joint decision making. They contend that the cultural tendency among Chinese is to avoid conflict. Hence, it is not considered appropriate to pose "what-if" analyses in a group setting. On the other hand, in Japan, decision makers like to come to consensus in a group to avoid individual accountability. Such "what-if" analyses are likely to be well received in that setting.

Other researchers even believe that the preferences for specific analyses differ among various cultures. For example, Moore and his colleagues have found decision makers rely upon quite different models in developed countries than do their Third World counterparts (Moore and Bart, 1984). Similarly, there are researchers who contend (although they offer no proof) that Europeans and Japanese prefer more analytically driven solutions while Americans prefer heuristics or algorithms. They also contend that Europeans prefer normative models in their decision support systems while Americans prefer the ability to provide more descriptive models. Clearly, if there is a difference in preference for models among different cultures, their use and/or their support, this should affect the design of the decision support system for transnational organizations.

Based on the literature described in the previous section, one would expect observable differences in the preferences for design of decision support systems across cultures. There are five general aspects of the system on which one would expect differences. They are as follows.

1. The kinds of models used, including:
    - the choice of descriptive vs. optimization models;
    - the need for strategic planning and/or contingency models;
    - the use of standards in modeling;
    - the variables that will be used; and
    - the need for variety in the models available in the system.

2. The pre-modeling needs of a DSS, including the desirability of alternative generation capabilities.

3. The post-modeling needs of a DSS, including the desirability of "what if" capabilities.

4. Temporal aspects of the model, such as:
    - the temporal orientation of data to be used in the model; and
    - the choice between static and dynamic measures in the model

5. Desired access to the model, including:
    - the scope of the access to information, models or results; and
    - the choice between individual and joint use of the system.

The cultural dimension and its effect on each of these needs for a model management system were discussed in the previous section. A summary of the important relationships, however, are recapitulated below.

The literature suggests there might be differences in preferences for descriptive models vs. optimization models associated with the activity orientation of the culture and the uncertainty avoidance tendencies of the culture. Related to this is the hypothesis that there are different needs for contingency and planning models depending upon the person-nature orientation, the uncertainty avoidance and activity orientation. For example, cultures with mastery-over-nature orientation are more likely to emphasize strategic and contingency planning whereas cultures with subjugation-to-nature orientations are unlikely to practice strategic and contingency planning. Furthermore, one needs to differentiate when standards are adopted. The adoption of standards is associated with the activity orientation of the culture. In particular, "doing" cultures tend to encourage the use of standards for evaluation while "being" cultures do not adopt them. Of course, differences in the models that one expects to use will affect the variables and supporting data that should be maintained in the system. Finally, one needs to address the flexibility of the decision makers to select from a menu of appropriate analyses to support their choice process. The need for flexibility is associated with the a low uncertainty avoidance tendency, a high mastery-over-nature, a positive human-nature orientation and a highly individualistic orientation of the culture.

The literature also suggests that there would be differences between the needs for pre-model functions and post-model functions in the model management system. Alternative generation is the primary pre-model concern. The time orientation of the culture, uncertainty avoidance tendency and human-nature orientation affect the desirability of methods for generating alternatives to known problems or conditions. Those cultures that are future-oriented, have high uncertainty avoidance and/or have a "good" human-nature orientation are likely to want systems that facilitate alternative generation.

On the post-model side, is the desirability of building in informal, "what if" or post-optimality analyses. The uncertainty avoidance tendencies and the person-nature orientation of the culture are expected to affect the worth of these capabilities. In particular, high uncertainty avoidance tendencies and mastery-over-nature oriented cultures will value such ad hoc queries to determine the sensitivity of their solutions to potential changes in their environments.

Cultural norms will also affect the temporal orientation of the data that decision makers will expect in a decision support system. The time orientation of the culture and activity orientation affects the preference for current or historical data in an analysis. Cultures that emphasize the past and/or "being" or "being-in-becoming" societies will emphasize historical data availability in their systems. In addition, the human-nature orientation, the activity orientation and time orientation affect the desirability of monitoring systems as part of a decision support system and the kinds of information that should be maintained in such monitoring systems. Furthermore, the activity orientation and the time orientation affect the preference for static measures of merit of an alternative over dynamic measures of historical change. For example, societies that emphasize the value of individuals and their development (being-in-becoming) will require monitoring systems that trace growth of people, projects or organizations over time to support their decision making. This is in contrast to societies that emphasize simply the individual which would only need information about current performance, or societies that emphasize the achievements of individuals which would need comparisons to standards.

Another area in the design of decision support systems affected by the culture is the scope of the DSS to which members of the organization have access. In some cases, access to either information, models or results is expanded (limited) because of the need for more (less) people involved in the decision making process. For example, in cultures that emphasize the har-mony-with-nature orientation, lower levels of management need more infor-mation than in other societies, because upper management attempts "harmonizing" activities. Similarly, in cultures that believe that human-nature is basically good, information is available to greater numbers of people so as to generate more innovative solutions to problems. At other times, this access changes to limit the generation of alternatives, the questioning of assumptions or the direction of communication. The scope of the system seems to be affected by the person-nature orientation, the relational orientation of the culture, and the human-nature orientation of the culture.

The verification of these hypotheses requires the analysis and evaluation of users of decision support systems across cultures. Such analyses are being completed in the area of interculture management as described in an earlier section. As with management studies, they need to consider and operationalize the culture orientations described in the last section and the orientations directed by the organization and the environment in which it operates. However, in the short run, even sensitivity to these issues will improve our design of decision support systems.

References

Ackermann, W. (1981). Cultural values and social choice of technology. *International Soc. Sci. Journal, 33*, 447-465.

Adler, N.J. (1983). Cross-cultural management research: The ostrich and the trend. *Acad. Mgmt Rev, 8*, 226-232.

Al-Jafaray, A., & Hollingsworth, A.T. (1983). An exploratory study of managerial practices in the Arabian Gulf region. *J. Int. Bus. Stud., 14*, 143-152.

Alter, S.A. (1980). *Decision support systems: Current practice and continuing challenges.* Reading, MA: Addison-Wesley.

Ankomah, K. (1985). African culture and social structures and development of effective public administration and management systems. *Indian J. of Pub. Admin., 31*, 394-413.

Beatty, J.R., McCune, J.T., & Beatty, R.W. (1988). A policy-capturing approach to the study of United States and Japanese managers' compensation decisions. *Journal of Mgmt, 14*, 465-474.

Bennett, J.L. (1983). *Building decision support systems.* Reading, MA: Addison-Wesley.

Berger, A.A. (1984). *Signs in contemporary culture.* New York: Longman.

Bostrom, R.P., & Heinen, J.S. (1977). MIS problems and failures: A socio-technical perspective: Part I: The causes. *MIS Quart., 1*, 17-32.

Business International and Centre d'Etudes Industrielles (1972). *Managing the multinational: Preparing for tomorrow.* London: George Allen Unwin.

Carlyle, R.E. (1988). Managing IS at multinationals. *Datamation*, 54-66.

Collier, H. (1988). *Information flow across frontiers: The question of transborder data*. London: Infonortics, Ltd.

Cooper, D.O., Davidson, L.B. & Denison, W.K. (1975). A tool for more effective financial analysis. *Interfaces, 5*, 91-103.

Dickson, G.W., Desanctis, G. & McBride, D.J. (1986). Understanding the effectiveness of computer graphics for decision support: A cumulative experimental approach. *Comm. ACM, 29*, 40-47.

Doktor, R., Kawase, T., & Haig, J.H. (1986). Culture as a constraint on productivity. *Intl. Stud. of Man. and Org., 15*, 8-16.

Drucker, P. (1974). *Management: Tasks, responsibilities, practices*. New York: Harper and Row.

Emdad, A. (1990). Complexities in the transfer of information technology. *IBSCUG Quart., 2*, 4.

England, J.W. (1975). *The manager and his values*. Cambridge, MA: Ballinger.

England, G.W., & Harpaz, I. (1983). Some methodological and analytic considerations in cross-national comparative research. *J. Int. Bus. Stud., 14*, 49-73.

Evans, W.A., Hau, K.C. & Sculli, D. (1989). A cross cultural comparison of managerial styles. *J Mgmt Dev, 8*, 5-13.

Ghabu, A.J. & S. Al-Sakran (1988). The changing data processing environment in Saudia Arabia. *Information and Management,* 14, 61-66.

Ghertman, M. (1978). Strategic decision-making process: Practice or management? In M. Ghertman and J. Leontiades (eds.) *European Research in International Business*, Amsterdam: North-Holland Publishing Company, 49-67.

Gingras, L. (1988). The behavioral context of information systems in China: Chinese designer's models. Joint National Meeting of The Institute of Management Sciences and the Operations Research Society of America, Washington, D.C.

Hall, J.R. (1986). Communication to the membership of The Institute of Management Sciences.

Henderson, J.C., & Schilling, D.A. (1985). Design and implementation of decision support systems in the public sector. *MIS Quart., 9*, 157-161.

Hofstede, G. (1980). *Cultural consequences: International differences in work related values*. Beverly Hills: Sage.

Hofstede, G. (Summer, 1980). Motivation, leadership and organization: Do American theories apply abroad? *Org. Dynamics*.

Hofstede, G. (1983). The cultural relativity of organizational practices and theories. *J of Int. Bus Stud., 14*, 75-89.

Harmon, P., Maus, R. & Morrissey, W. (1988). *Expert systems*. New York: John Wiley and Sons.

Horn, B.R., & Ellis, D. (1988). Development information needs and uses in the Pacific Hemisphere community. In D.J. Wedemeyer and M.R. Ogden (eds.) *Telecommunications and Pacific Development: Alternatives for the Next Decade,* Amsterdam: North Holland.

Ibrahim, R.L.R. (1985). Computer usage in developing countries: A case study in Kuwait. *Information and Management, 8,* 103-112.

Jenner, S.R. (1982). Analyzing cultural stereotypes in multinational business: United States and Australia. *J. of Man. Stud, 19,* 307-325.

Kanungo, R.N., & Wright, R.W. (1988). A cross-cultural comparative study of managerial job attitudes. *J. Int. Bus. Stud, 14,* 115-129.

Katzan, H.S., Jr. (1980). *Multinational computer systems.* New York: Van Nostrand Reinhold Co., 63-82.

Keen, P.G. (1981). Decision support systems: Translating analytic techniques to useful tools. *Sloan Management Review, 22.*

Keen, P.G. (1979). Adaptive design for decision support systems. *Database, 12,* 15-25.

Keen, P.G. (1981). Value analysis: Justifying decision support systems. *MIS Quart., 5,* 1-16.

Kelley, L., Whatley, A., & Worthley, R. (1987). Assessing the effects of culture on managerial attitudes: A three-culture test. *J of Int Bus Stu, 19,* 17-32.

Keys, J.B., & Miller, T.R. (1984). The Japanese management theory jungle. *Acad. of Mgmt. Rev., 9,* 342-353.

Kluckhohn, F.R., & Strodtbeck, F.L. (1961). *Variations in value orientations.* Evanston: Row Patterson and Co.

Kobayashi, N. (1982). The present and future of Japanese multinational enterprises. *Int. Stud. of Man. and Org., 12,* 38-58.

Kwong, H.C. (1986). The practice of operations research in Malaysia and Singapore. *Omega: Int. J. of Oprl. Res., 14,* 333-344.

LaPalombara, J., & Blank, S. (1987). *Multinational corporations in comparative perspective.* New York: The Conference Board.

Licker, P.S. (1983). The Japanese approach: A better way to manage programmers? *Comm of the ACM, 26,* 631-636.

Lockett, A.G., Ahmad, R., & Turner, C. (1988). Managing system change requests in the development of a large and complex DSS. *DSS-88 Transactions,* Boston, MA, 177-189.

Lucas, H.C. (1981). An experimental investigation of the use of computer-based graphics in decision making. *Mgmt. Sci., 27,* 757-768.

Mallory, G.R., Butler, R.J., Cray, D., Hickson, D.J., & Wilson, D.C. (1983). Implanted decision-making: American owned firms in Britain. *J. of Man. Stud., 20,* 191-211.

Moore, J.H., & Narter, B. (1988). Senior executive computer use in the Americas: A study of U.S.A., Mexico and Brazil. Working Paper, Graduate School of Business.

Murray, T.J., & Tanniru, M.R. (1987). Selecting between knowledge-based and traditional systems design. *Journal of Management Information Systems, 4*, 42-58.

Negandhi, A.R. (1979). Convergence in organizational practices: An empirical study of industrial enterprises in developing countries. In Lammers, C.J. and Hickson, D.J. (Eds.) *Organizations Alike and Unlike*. London: Routledge and Kegan Paul.

Negandhi, A.R. (1983). Cross-cultural management research: Trend and future directions. *J Int. Bus. Stud., 14*, 17-28.

Peterson, R.B., & Shimada, J.Y. (1978). Sources of management problems in Japanese-American joint ventures. *Acad. of Mgmt Rev., 10*, 796-804.

Redding, G.S., & Casey, T.W. (1976). Managerial beliefs among Asian managers. In R.L. Taylor (ed.) *Proceedings of the Academy of Management 36th Annual Meeting*, 351-355.

Robey, D. (1987). Implementation and the organizational impacts of information systems. *Interfaces, 17*, 72-84.

Sauter, V.L. (1984). Some insights into the requirements for information systems of public sector decision-makers. *Policy and Information, 8*, 9-23.

Sauter, V.L. (1985). The effect of 'experience' upon information preferences. *Omega, 13*, 277-284.

Sauter, V.L. (1988). Evolutionary development of decision support systems: What issues are really important for early phases of design. *J of M I S, 4*, 77-92.

Sauter, V.L., & Mandell, M.B. (1990). Transferring decision support concepts to evaluation. *Evaluation and Program Planning, 13*, 349-358.

Sauter, V.L., & Joshi, K. (1990). Proposals for computer policies for developing nations. To appear in *Information and Management*.

Skinner, C.W. (1968). Management of international production. In R.N. Farmer (ed.) *International Management*, Belmont, CA: Dickenson Publishing.

Skinner, C.W. (1968). *American industry in developing economies*. New York: John Wiley and Sons.

Sprague, R.H., & Carlson, E.D. (1982). *Building effective decision support systems*. Englewood Cliffs: Prentice-Hall.

Sprague, R.H., & Watson, H.J. (1986). *Decision support systems*. Englewood Cliffs: Prentice-Hall.

Stabell, C.B. (1988). Towards a theory of decision support. *DSS-88 Transactions,* Boston, MA, 160-170.

Stabell, C., & Hennestad, B.W. (1987). The executive's operational code: Decision style or decision culture? Norwegian School of Management Working Paper 1987/5, Bekkestua, Norway.

Tobias, A.J. (1988). Today's executives in a state of readiness. *Software Magazine, 8*, a7-66.

Tricker, R.I. (1988). Information resource management: A cross-cultural perspective. *Inf. and Mgmt, 15*, 37-46.

Van Den Bulcke, D. (1984). Decision making in multinational enterprises and the information consultation of employees: The proposed Vredeling directive of the EC Commission. *Intl Stud of Man. and Org., 14*, 36-60.

Vinogradov, V.V. et al (1981). Towards an international information system. *Int. Soc. Sci. J., 33*, 10-49.

Walker, R.G., Barnhardt, R.S., & Walker, W.E. (1985). *Selecting a Decision Support System Generator for the Air Force's Enlisted Force Management System*. Rand Paper P-7149. Santa Monica, CA: The Rand Corporation.

Wallace, W.A., & Balogh, F.D. (1985). Decision support systems for disaster management. *Public Administration Rev., 45*, 134-146.

Wellman, D.A. (1989). *A Chip in the Curtain*. Washington, D.C.: National Defense University Press.

Witte, E. (1972). Field research on complex decision making processes: The phase theorem. *Int. J. of Mgmt and Org, 51*, 156-182.

Wolman, R. (1988). Taking software development back to Ireland. *InfoCenter, 4*(11), 42.

Zmud, R.W. (1979). Individual differences and MIS success: A review of the empirical literature. *Mgmt. Sci., 25*, 966-979.

Zmud, R.W. (1983). *Information Systems in Organizations*. Glenview, IL: Scott Foresman and Co.

15

The Impact of Global Information Technology on International Investment Managers and Custodians

George B. Ballester and Edmund A. Marcarelli
The Boston Company

Given the multiplicity of time-zones, national calendars, languages, laws and currencies, routing economic information around the world is no easy task for international investment managers and custodians. Navigating through different electrical, telephone, computer and satellite systems presents a worthy technical challenge to the developers of global information technology. The passage of the ERISA act and the growth of mutual funds have greatly increased the demands on such information technology. Dramatic changes in computer technology, both hardware and software, pose six questions for international investment firms:

1. What type of computer platform is the right one for each business function?

2. What is the most universal, reliable, cost-effective method for communicating trades to others?

3. How can the batch cycle be reduced, or even eliminated, to accomodate around-the- clock trading?

4. How can custody management data be organized more effectively in databases?

5. How can expert systems assist investment managers?

6. To keep pace with rapidly changing market conditions, how should software development teams be organized?

This chapter discusses the six questions and illustrates how the effective use of information technology aids an international investment firm by comparing operations at an investment firm that under-utilizes information technology with another investment firm which makes full use of information technology.

INTRODUCTION

As recent Group-of-Seven summits, European Economic Community meetings and American-Japanese trade negotiations evidence, the leaders of the major free-market countries have come to appreciate how interdependent their national economies have become and how important a measure of cooperation is for the prosperity of all. Such cooperation depends upon the pooling of trade and investment information. Given the multiplicity of time-zones, national calendars, languages, laws and currencies, routing economic information around the world is no easy task. Navigating through different electrical, telephone, computer and satellite systems presents a worthy technical challenge to the developers of global information technology.

International investment managers, and the institutions which provide custody services for the assets that they manage, play an important role in this process. As major users of global information technology, they constitute a significant force affecting the direction in which the technology grows.

To compete effectively, the international investment manager must master the twin technologies of information assimilation and distribution. International investment managers, whose clients include mutual funds, pension funds and endowments, look for the best investments in an intensely competitive environment where there are almost no international investment industry standards. In this arena, the international investment manager uses global information technology as a gladiator once used his shield and sword. To compete successfully, the investment manager must have timely, accurate, and complete information about the markets in which he is investing and about the banks and other financial institutions with whom he is dealing. The investment manager's worth will be measured by his ability to achieve the rate of return on the investments that the client expects. Data gathered from diverse sources such as market conditions or government fiscal and monetary policy changes must be assimilated by the investment manager, enabling him to make the decisions which represent his added value to the firm.

Distributing international investment information is a considerable challenge given the constantly changing business environment, rapid innovation in the technical environment, the diversity of software and hardware in use around the world, and the complexity of the networks needed to span continents and oceans. For example, one investment services product involves software written in two languages (German and English), using several computer languages, computer hardware from two major manufacturers, a telecommunications network which consists of leased lines and satellite links between no less than four data center locations, business operations staff in three countries, and clients worldwide. To the extent that a financial firm profits from the sale of global investment services, it profits from the global information technology which enables the service to exist.

There can be little doubt that information technology is the critical strategic tool for international investment management. Given the intense competitiveness of the field, changing economic conditions in the United States, Japan, and Europe, and rapid technological developments, the international investment managers and custodians who survive and prosper will be those who make effective use of information technology.

THE INVESTMENT MANAGEMENT ARENA

To say that effective use of a technology is required is to imply that technology may be used ineffectively. Ineffective use is not only possible but occurs frequently in the investment management arena as it exists today. To appreciate the impact of information technology on investment managers, it is necessary to understand the nature of the current environment. This can best be accomplished by examining the origins of the trends which have converged to produce the present state of the investment management industry.

The most important of these trends started with the enactment in 1974 of what can now be seen as a watershed event in the recent history of financial markets. That event was the passage of the Employee Retirement Income Security Act, more commonly known by its acronym - ERISA. This legislation set down strictures for the operation of pension funds both public and private. Included in these regulations were requirements for the levels of funding as well as the nature and prudence of the investment of the funds. Also spelled out was the role of a Master Trustee. A Master Trustee has the responsibility for insuring that a fund's assets are safely held, that they are properly transferred when bought or sold, and that the fund collects all securities and cash to which it is entitled. Furthermore, a Master Trustee must be able to value a portfolio, i.e. the Master Trustee must know what each security is worth at any given time, including such things as accrued interest and pending dividends. There are stringent reporting requirements. This role is generally filled by a bank or trust company. To meet the regulatory requirements of ERISA, pension plan sponsors began to turn to professional investment advisors for assistance. Paralleling these developments was the transformation of the mutual fund industry. Spurred by the popularity of Individual Retirement Accounts (IRA's), growth in mutual funds beginning in the late seventies and continuing until the October 1987 stock market crash, was phenomenal. This growth, the demand for product differentiation and the premium retail investors placed on performance, fueled the expansion of fund management operations which required substantial investments in information technology. The technology was needed to keep pace in the field when it was growing rapidly and to remain profitable when the business began to retrench due to changes in the tax code and later due to investor diffidence in the wake of the October 1987 crash.

These institutions as well as others, such as insurance companies, combined to create a class of investor with a desire to find the most appealing investment opportunities available. This came to include not only the United States and Europe, but also the Pacific Basin, and ultimately "emerging markets" in Latin America, Africa and Asia. These institutions had the resources to apply the best means available for discovering opportunities, making investment decisions and conducting the operations necessary to support these activities. It is no surprise that they turned to information technology to do the job. The job, or more accurately jobs, that needed doing included analyzing investment opportunities, portfolio accounting, evaluating performance of investment and investment managers, and the job with which this article is most concerned, the movement of securities and cash resulting from the trading of investment instruments.

Strictly speaking, the responsibility for securities movement and control lies with the custodian of the assets. In practical terms, the investment advisor initiates and executes securities trades through a broker and instructs the custodian to receive or deliver securities and/or cash to the broker's clearing agent. The timely settlement of these trades is essential to the performance of the investment advisor. She must arrange foreign exchange deals to coincide with trade settlements and must be ready to reinvest cash generated by the sale of securities. The information links between the investment advisor and the custodian are therefore critical to successful execution of any international investment strategy. This "back office" emphasis is not the natural inclination of investment managers. Terence W. Norman, Systems Manager of PanAgora Asset Management Limited says the back office is "...the Cinderella in terms of IT within [an investment management] company." Thomas J. Lucey, Executive Vice President of The Boston Company in charge of the Securities Management Group, is skeptical that investment managers will tackle this aspect of their information technology problems without help. Application of the technology to these links, in his words, "has to be driven by the custodian." The network of links connecting a plan sponsor, the plan's investment advisors, the custodian and the subcustodians (the latter being the custodian's agent in a country in which the custodian is not based) must cover all the countries in which the various advisors wish to trade. Trade settlements vary from market to market and within markets by type of security. In the United States, for example, an equity trade generally settles in five days; a deal involving a U.S. Treasury Bill settles in one day. The amounts of these trades are frequently very large.

It should be clear that the arena in which the investment manager operates is one where the action is fast and furious, the stakes high, and the margin for error slim. More specifically, this translates into some not unusual, but nonetheless important, requirements for the information technology. First, the diversity of national standards and experience with information processing, is huge. This fact puts a premium on the flexibility and adaptability of hardware and software, even of the people using them. Second, the long distances, combined with the short turnaround times for trade settlement, create the need for fast, reliable information processing. Finally, the large amounts of currency and the importance of data in the successful completion of a deal, require a high degree of accuracy, reliability and data security.

International investment management is one of the first service industries to go global (Porter, 1990). The world's three great financial capitals - New York City, London, and Tokyo - compete vigorously for new clients. Winning this competition depends in large part upon the effective use of information technology (Poppel and Goldstein, 1987). The future of global investing belongs more to the computer screen than to the trading floor (Keyes and Miller, 1990). A securities market will be wherever a market-maker has a computer (Bloch, 1989). As a recent book on investment banking put it:

> Today's technological breakthroughs in information exchange have enabled individuals and organizations to comparison shop in different geographic markets in a manner unimaginable only a generation ago. (Hayes and Hubbard, 1990, p. 339)

According to Sir John Quinton, Chairman of Barclays Bank, international banks which do not build advanced information technology distinctive enough to differentiate themselves from their competition, face extinction (London Financial Times, 1990B).

Three-quarters of the money that banks spend on information technology is spent by the big banks. Between 1980 and 1988, U.S. bank investment in information technology rose 300% (Steiner and Teixeira, 1990). Last year, Citicorp spent $1.5 billion on information technology (Economist, 1990A). After Citicorp, the six biggest spenders are BankAmerica, Chase Manhattan, Chemical, Security Pacific, First Interstate, and Manufacturers Hanover (Steiner and Teixeira, 1990). It is predicted that by 1994, worldwide bank spending on information technology will top $14 billion (London Financial Times, 1990B). In 1988, the average information system on Wall Street was 10 years old (Ipsen, 1988); thus, in 1990, we are only beginning to create modern global information technology. Such systems will be a key determinant in America's future success as a world competitor (Malmgren, 1990; Smith, 1989).

World trade in goods and services is estimated at $3 trillion while the amount of money flowing on the London Euro-dollar market is estimated at 25 times that (Kennedy, 1989). On any business day, it is estimated that $1500 billion in financial transactions are on New York City's communication lines (London Financial Times, 1990D). Global block trades of stock portfolios, worth hundreds of millions of dollars, are common (Oxford, 1988). For example, Wells Fargo Nikko's Celebration Fund shifts huge stock portfolios between the Tokyo and New York City stock markets (Wall Street Journal, 1990B). Worldwide foreign exchange trading averages over $300 billion a day (Powers, 1988). Less than 5% of that is done to pay for traded goods (Oppenheim, 1987).

U.S. stock markets are now moving towards around-the-clock trading. The New York Stock Exchange plans to begin after-hours, electronic trading later this year (Wall Street Journal, 1990C). The American Stock Exchange, the Cincinnati Stock Exchange, the Chicago Board Options Exchange, and Reuters Holdings have announced plans to develop an after-hours, electronic trading system. For the OTC market, NASDAQ began after-hours, electronic trading in September (Wall Street Journal, 1990D).

In Europe, spurred on by EEC momentum, European banks are beginning to take the first steps toward creating Pan-European banks. Credit Lyonnais (Fr) bought Credito Bergamasco (Ita). Deutsche Bank (WGer) bought Morgan Grenfell (UK). Banco Santander (Esp) bought 10% of the Royal Bank of Scotland (UK) (London Financial Times, 1990B). Dresdner Bank and Commerzbank (WGer) are actively moving into East Germany while the Bundesbank is making plans to sell German Unity Fund bonds worldwide (London Financial Times, 1990E). As both Eastern Europe countries and the Soviet Union lack convertible currencies, the mark is likely to become the major trading currency for a large part of Europe (Wall Street Journal, 1990G). London, the home of 150 major financial firms, is the bridge between a closing Tokyo market and an opening New York City market (Euromoney, 1987). Design work has begun on the "Pipe" - an electronic network linking the great European stock markets (International Computer Financial News, 1990C). There is an EEC-wide, electronic data interchange (EDI) project called "TEDIS" (International Computer Financial News, 1989C).

The world's eight largest banks by assets are now Japanese banks (Institutional Investor, 1989). Japanese banks have opened over 50 branch offices on the London Euro-market (Intermarket, 1989). In the U.S., Sumitomo

Bank holds 12.5% of Goldman Sachs, and the Industrial Bank of Japan took control of Schroder (London Financial Times, 1990B). Japanese banks are actively expanding their New York City foreign exchange trading desks (Wall Street Journal, 1990F). Large Japanese institutional investors now have such a large presence in the U.S. bond market that they influence U.S. interest rates (Wall Street Journal, 1990E).

TECHNOLOGICAL CHALLENGES FOR CUSTODIANS AND INVESTMENT MANAGERS

If the world economy is an ocean, the international investment management firm is an ocean-front home on pilings. While its occupants are understandably preoccupied with the flow of the tide and the appearance of sudden storms, the undercurrents are quietly wearing away at what the occupants once understood to be the permanent technological underpinnings of their home. In the last decade, these undercurrents have been very strong indeed. Dramatic changes in computer technology, both hardware and software, necessitate a strategic reassessment of how these pilings should be shored-up, or even replaced.

These changes in information technology pose six questions for international investment firms:

(I) What type of computer platform is the right one for each business function?

(II) What is the most universal, reliable, cost-effective method for communicating trades to others?

(III) How can the batch cycle be reduced, or even eliminated, to accommodate around the clock trading?

(IV) How can custody management data be organized more effectively in databases?

(V) How can expert systems assist investment managers?

(VI) To keep pace with rapidly changing market conditions, how should software development teams be organized?

Appropriate Computer Platforms

The large mainframe computer with its myriad of terminals is no longer all there is to real data processing. Although large applications that process significant amounts of data still need the mainframe, many smaller applications run in a more cost effective manner on smaller computers. For example, the Boston Company, while running its custody and accounting systems on an IBM mainframe, uses Intranet software on a VAX minicomputer to send and receive SWIFT messages. Fidelity Investments, while running its brokerage system on an IBM mainframe, uses a Stratus fault-tolerant minicomputer to send trades to the market. Kemper Mutual Funds, while running its mutual fund systems on an IBM mainframe, uses a Teradata database machine to process marketing data. Citicorp uses Teradata database machines for its branch information management system. Competition in the supercomputer market is beginning to produce smaller, more affordable supercomputers. First Boston, Shearson Lehman, and Bankers Trust all rent time on Cray supercomputers to run computer models that predict the impact of changes in the securities portfolios of large customers (Wall Street Journal, 1990A). Nomura Securities and Barr Rosenberg have formed the Nomura Rosenberg Investment Technology Institute to intensively apply computer algorithms to securities portfolio management (International Computer Financial News, 1990G).

Even the minicomputer, flaunted by salesmen as the replacement for the mainframe, is losing ground. The work, that once could only be done by a $50,000 minicomputer, can now be done by a $15,000 RISC-based workstation or by an $8,000, 32-bit personal computer (Zelkowitz, 1985). Intense competition in the workstation market between Sun, HP Apollo, IBM, DEC, Toshiba, NEC, and Hitachi is lowering workstation prices as performance increases through a marriage of fast, reduced instruction set (RISC) chips and the flexible power of the UNIX operating system. The conflict between AT&T on one side, and IBM and DEC's Open Software Foundation on the other side, over the UNIX standard illustrates the huge market at at stake. At Salomon Brothers, more than 500 Sun workstations are used to track stock and bond prices around the world (Wall Street Journal, 1990A). Trading rooms, which typically have over 50 financial information service feeds, are ideal applications for workstations (Bacon, 1989; Murphy, 1989A). Engineering firms, that pioneered workstations for CAD/CAE, are now moving into banking workstations. TRW Financial Systems has a major systems contract with Bankenes Betalingssenthal A/S - the official clearinghouse for Norway's banks (International Computer Financial News, 1988).

Breakthroughs in microcomputer chip technology have created personal computers with tremendous processing power. The Intel 80486 32-bit microprocessor can do up to 15 MIPS (Nadeau, 1990). The Intel i960 CA 32-

bit microprocessor does 66 MIPS while executing two instructions at the same time (International Computer Financial News, 1989B). Workstation technologies have filtered down to personal computers. Yamaichi, Olivetti Japan, and Advanced Technology Corp. have jointly developed a RISC circuit board that can increase a 386 personal computer's speed 800 times (International Computer Financial News, 1990A). Steven Jobs' Next Computer runs the MACH operating system, a variant of UNIX. AT&T is now offering "Business Orchestration Service" to link DOS, OS/2, and UNIX systems together (International Computer Financial News, 1990B). The Japanese are working on still another new personal operating system - TRON. Toshiba has already spent $70M on a TRON microprocessor (International Computer Financial News, 1989A). In investment management, it is not uncommon to find an investment advisor dazzling a potential client with a windowed graphics and text display of an investment strategy on a color-monitored, personal computer. On a 386 PC with 1MB of extended RAM, Microsoft Windows 3.0 allows for up to 16MB of virtual memory (Luhn, 1990). There are, of course, numerous investor software packages for personal computers (Longman, 1983). U.S. banks are beginning to replace "dumb" terminals with personal computers. Nineteen percent of U.S. bank hardware expenditure is now for microcomputers (Steiner and Teixeira, 1990).

Choosing an appropriate computer platform for each business function is no easy task. Jean Tempel, Executive Vice-President of the Boston Company and Chief Operations Officer, cautions that one should be careful not to become overwhelmed by the sheer volume of interesting technology available. Rather, one should focus on the strategic advantage that she is aiming for and pick the appropriate technology for that. One is putting business solutions on a person's desk, not just a particular hardware platform.

Communicating Trades

Choosing an appropriate computer platform is one battle. Finding a universal, reliable, cost-effective method for communicating trades to other banks and clearinghouses is another.

According to Terrence W. Norman, Systems Manager of PanAgora Asset Management Ltd, "The development of interfaces into other systems is proving to be most beneficial, bringing us closer to the ultimate goal of the efficient, paperless back office."

The most common method, which accounts for 80% of the world telecommunication revenues, is POT or "plain old telephone". The advent of the facsimile machine has improved POT somewhat, but the underlying problem remains. POT works, but it is too manual, too time-consuming (Boult, 1989).

What is needed is automated communications whereby one computer can send trades to another. Either the financial institutions involved connect their computers directly to each other, or they connect to an intermediary network. There are two kinds of networks - private and public. A private network is proprietary to the financial institution that created it; whereas, a public network is open to all members of that network. Large financial institutions do not usually create private worldwide networks because the enormous cost is not offset by the benefit. The biggest advantage of using a public network is that its managers have already addressed the colossal headache of dealing with each individual country's telecommunications authority (Murphy, 1988).

There are three main methods to make remote computer-to-computer connections for communicating trades - mainframe batch data movers, PC batch data movers, and SNA LU 6.2 program-to-program communications.

The most popular mainframe batch data mover is Sterling Software's TRACS (Stevens, 1988). TRACS sends, receives, and reblocks computer files in IBM 3780/2780 emulation mode (Sterling Software, 1985). Typically, scheduled TRACS batch jobs are run to send and receive files. Sterling Software has recently come out with SUPERTRACS, BSC and SNA, which dynamically seeks and uses available communication lines with autodial modems (Sterling Software, 1989).

PC batch data movers, such as Crosstalk, Blast, Access, and VTERM, work in a similar manner to their mainframe counterparts, except they are initiated by the PC user (One Point, 1985).

IBM's System Network Architecture Logical Unit 6.2 (SNA LU 6.2) provides a protocol for online, real-time data transfer from one computer to another, using the Advanced Program-to-Program Communications (APPC) verbs (IBM, 1985A, 1985B).

There are various means for communicating trades - Telex, IBM Information System Network, SWIFT, GEISCO, and others.

Telex is the most common, automated, inter-bank communication network with TRT, ITT, MCI, and RCA competing for the business. To take one as an example, TRT has over 2 million subscribers in over 46 countries (TRT, 1988). The common TRT telex device is the Lane 9000. In manual mode, a telex operator sits at the Lane 9000 typing in the trades. In automated mode, an IBM mainframe can build the telex messages and send them to the Lane 9000 (TRT, 1989). As telex messages, aside from standard transmission headers, are essentially free format unless sender and receiver agree upon an enforced standard format, it is almost impossible for a computer program to parse incoming telexes or to deparse trade data into outgoing telex messages. A number of companies have developed telex deparsers that automatically create standard telex messages from trade data.

The IBM Information System Network is a wideband terrestrial network that IBM clients can use to send each other messages and files by using the IBM Information Exchange utility in host computer RJE mode, PC mode, or SNA mode (IBM, 1987).

SWIFT (Society for World-wide Interbank Financial Telecommunications) is used to send over 1 million messages a day by over 2700 financial institutions in more than 67 countries. Even the Soviet Union and China use SWIFT. In the U.S., 80% of all CHIPS payments originate from instructions on SWIFT messages (Steiner and Teixeira, 1990). The current SWIFT system, SWIFT I, developed by Burroughs and Logica, has been running since 1977. It was originally designed to handle a maximum of 300,000 messages a day (Hobson, 1990; Murphy, 1989B; Helm, 1988). SWIFT I runs on large computers at the two main SWIFT operating centers - one in the Netherlands and one in the U.S. Financial institutions connect through SWIFT regional processors over redundant, 9600 BPS, leased, international circuits (SWIFT, 1984A). The SWIFT I communications protocol is Bisynchronous Communication (BSC) (SWIFT, 1984B). A financial institution can either connect to SWIFT I with a SWIFT terminal or through a SWIFT approved computer-to-computer interface. 70% of SWIFT I users type in their SWIFT messages on SWIFT terminals (Helm, 1988). Two SWIFT approved computer-to-computer interfaces are IBM's MERVA/370 and DSNL/370 on MVS/CICS, MVS/IMS, and VSE/CICS (IBM, 1987A and 1987B), and Intranet's VAX VMS interface (Intranet, 1987). Such computer-to-computer interfaces allow computer programs to create SWIFT messages.

There are 11 SWIFT message categories, of which 5 are of primary interest to the international investment manager - "1" (Delivery of Money), "5" (Security Trades, Confirmation of Security Trades, Corporate Actions, Security Trade Reconciliation), "9"(Confirmation of Money Movement, Money Movement Recon), and "n" (Cancels and Free Format). Despite initial appearance, "3" (Foreign Exchange) is not useful because it deals with contract confirmation, not the actual movement of money (SWIFT, 1989A, 1989B). Within the 11 SWIFT message categories, SWIFT and ISO have designed some 775 message types (Hobson, 1990).

SWIFT messages are not easy to automate. SWIFT messages that a bank sends are variable-length up to 2000 bytes; whereas SWIFT messages that a bank receives are variable-length up to 2600 bytes. A SWIFT message has 3 parts - message header, message text, and message trailer. The format of the message header differs depending upon whether or not the message is one sent by a bank or received by a bank. The message trailer contains authenticator keys and other system indicators. The message text consists of mandatory, conditional, and optional data fields prefixed by identifying field tags and suffixed by control characters. Each field can consist of mandatory, conditional, and optional sub-fields of different formats (SWIFT, 1989A). Since the length of a SWIFT message varies depending upon how many optional fields and optional sub-fields are used, and since the order of the fields is not always mandatory, given a random sample of SWIFT messages of one message type, there is no guarantee that any data element will always be at the same relative byte address. Some SWIFT messages have repeating groups within repeating groups with the number of repeats indicator after, rather than before, the repeats.

SWIFT I enforces the rules for each SWIFT message type and field data type, rejecting any messages that are syntactically incorrect, by sending a NAK (non-acknowledgment) with error codes back to the sender. If SWIFT I accepts a message, it returns an ACK (acknowledgment) to the sender, and guarantees that the message will be delivered, assuming any financial liability if it is not. The average cost to send a SWIFT message anywhere in the world is 50 cents (Steiner and Teixeira, 1990). The fact that there are so many optional fields available and that their content is often loosely prescribed has led to many dialects of syntactically correct SWIFT whose semantics vary.

Some companies have created SWIFT parsers to break down SWIFT messages into trade data elements, and SWIFT deparsers to create SWIFT messages from trade data.

To handle the great increase in SWIFT message traffic and to offer new services such as file transfer, SWIFT plans to migrate from SWIFT I to SWIFT II by 1992 or 1993 (Helm, 1988; Murphy, 1989C; SWIFT II, 1989A, 1989B, 1989C). SWIFT II, written in-house with a new Burroughs network language, uses the X.25 communications protocol on the OSI model (Hobson, 1990). Brokerage firms, exchanges, and clearinghouses have been admitted to SWIFT (Hobson, 1990).

Tom Lucey, Executive Vice President of the Security Management Group at the Boston Company, expects that SWIFT will become the standard trade communication format.

Some security depositories in Europe and the U.S. have developed their own methods for communicating trade information. General Electric Information Services (GEISCO) runs the GEISCO Mark III network which financial institutions use to communicate with the two main European clearinghouses - Euro-Clear and CEDEL. The Mark III network's communication protocol is V24 Bisynchronous Communication (BSC) (GEISCO, 1985). Users of the Mark III network can connect via low-speed PC interfaces or high-speed mainframe interfaces. First, one signs on to the network. Second, one signs on to the clearinghouse computer system.

Euro-Clear is the largest European security and bond house. In the last week of May 1990, over $288 million in Euro-bonds were traded on Euro-Clear (Euro-Clear News, June 22, 1990). Euro-Clear, founded by Morgan Guaranty

Trust in 1968, is operated on a leased basis by a Belgian company (Euro-Clear, 1987). Euro-Clear's computer system, known as EUCLID, operates 23 hours a day (Euro-Clear, 1989A). The mainframe batch data mover, TRACS, can be used to connect in high-speed mode to EUCLID.

EUCLID has its own message formats. Security trades are sent as EUCLID instructions. Each instruction is from 1 to 4 lines of 80-byte card image data. The data fields on each line are in a prescribed order and format according to the Euro-Clear rules for that instruction type. Some data fields are mandatory, some conditional, and others optional. There are no data tags (Euro-Clear, 1988A and 1988B).

When a EUCLID instruction is sent, it is validated syntactically, and a brief instruction validation report is sent back (Euro-Clear, 1989A). Once a financial institution's EUCLID instructions are matched against the counterpart's EUCLID instructions, the trades are settled (Euro-Clear, 1988A).

Security trade confirmations and security trade reconciliation messages are sent back as computer-readable reports (Euro-Clear,1989B).

Cash instructions cannot be sent as EUCLID instructions. They must be sent to Euro-Clear as SWIFT messages; and Euro-Clear has its own special SWIFT dialect (Euro-Clear, 1989C).

Some companies have developed Euro-Clear parsers and deparsers. CEDEL, Centrale de Livraison de Valuers Mobilieres, which began operations in 1971, has over 1,800 participants in over 64 countries (CEDEL, 1989). CEDEL is the next largest European security and bond clearinghouse after Euro-Clear. CEDEL is now growing faster than Euro-Clear (London Financial Times, 1990C). Euro-Clear and CEDEL are presently locked in a dispute over the "electronic bridge" that connects them (London Financial Times, 1990A).

The GEISCO Mark III network can be used to connect to CEDEL's computer system - CEDCOM. Both security trades and their associated cash movements can be sent as CEDEL instructions. CEDEL instructions are 80-byte card image records with mandatory, conditional, and optional data fields arranged in a prescribed order according to the CEDEL rules for the instruction type (CEDEL, 1989).

CEDEL instructions can also be mapped to different SWIFT message types sent on SWIFT I. For security trades, the CEDEL security instructions can be literally embedded as text data lines in the SWIFT MT599 message (CEDEL 1988A and 1988B).

CEDEL sends trade confirmations in the form of computer-readable reports (CEDEL, 1989).

Some companies are beginning development of CEDEL parsers and deparsers.

Some other methods of trade communication are Reuter's I.P. Sharp's Instant Link (I.P. Sharp, 1988), Instinet, GEISCO Trade Watch, Fitel Equinet

(Hobson, 1990), Honkong-Shanghai Banking Group's Hexagon (Hexagon, 1986), and Racal Thomson's EFTPOS (Boult, 1989).

Choosing a reliable, universal, cost-effective method of communicating trades is, thus, no easy task. As SWIFT has the most universal acceptance, and as the cost per SWIFT message is quite low, SWIFT seems to be the best choice.

Around the Clock Trading

Almost any business day, at any time, there is someone somewhere around the world trading securities and foreign exchange. While New York City sleeps, Tokyo trades; and London is the bridge between the two. As global trading activity increases, the international investment manager needs global custody management systems that can handle around-the-clock activity. Custodians demand 24 hour trading. As Jean Tempel, Executive Vice-President and Chief Operations Offficer at the Boston Company, puts it, future trade entry systems will have the look and feel of ATM processing. Such a need presents an immediate problem for some online custody management systems. Some were originally written assuming a short business day local to their country and time zone. The rest of the day the online system is down so that a long batch cycle can run, doing system accounting, management reports, and client reports. While the batch cycle works on the files, the online system is unavailable because the files cannot be open for update to both the batch jobs and the online system at the same time. To accommodate around-the-clock trading, such custody management systems need to change, severely reducing, or even eliminating the batch cycle.

On the batch cycle side, reduction can be achieved by a combination of eliminating as many batch jobs as possible and by streamlining the remaining batch jobs to run faster, by improving code flow and by using file buffers better.

On the online side, background online processes can be written to take the place of tasks that were once done by batch jobs. Background online tasks have no problem sharing files with foreground online screen tasks.

There are also new promising software tools available, such as The CICS Connection from Beacon Software International that allows both batch jobs and online systems to update the same files concurrently.

Using Custody Management Data More Effectively

Most older investment management systems were built around a group of indexed files, each having, aside from the primary key, one or two alternate indices. Although this indexed file approach has served the industry well, it is beginning to push up against the limits of that technology.

There is often redundant data in the group of files. Sometimes the redundant data elements have slightly different data formats and are subject to different data entry edits. Redundant data can lead to data integrity and maintenance overhead problems. The relationships between the data elements in different files in the file group are not always clear. The primary key structure, although right for the original use of the file, is not adequate for newer needs. To get around this, new alternate indices are added, or records are sorted in different ways into temporary work files; but, there are limits to this because, if done excessively, it seriously degrades system performance. In many cases, the file records themselves have just gotten too big to be easily manageable. In extreme cases, there is no room for record growth, file growth, or both because the outer limits of indexed file technology have been reached. When users ask for new ways to combine and separate data elements on screens or in reports, there is no easy way to do that (Atre, 1980).

The rise of relational database technology has changed all that, making it possible to replace older indexed file structures with relational tables in a relational database, where records can be selected, projected, and joined to create new combinations of data elements (Date, 1983). The SQL Query Language has opened almost unlimited possibilities for the combination of data elements on query screens and in reports (Date, 1987). The increasing ability of each release of IBM's DB2 to handle high-volume applications is very encouraging (Date, 1988).

Still, one has to recognize that the type of relational database that is best for ad hoc queries made by money managers may not be the best type for getting out client trades fast enough. One also needs to think of databases in terms of business function. The custodian needs a centralized database that guarantees data security and data integrity; whereas, the money manager only needs the ability to download data for query and report manipulation on a local database.

Expert Systems to Assist Investment Managers

Although artificial intelligence research began in the 1950s, because of the time needed to develop specialized AI hardware and AI software tools, commercial AI applications have been very slow in coming (Schutzer, 1987). Starting in the late 1980s, international investment managers began investing in custom AI systems. A 1988 Coopers & Lybrand survey found that 12% of U.S. banks were using AI systems while 31% of U.S. banks were developing them (Kanji, 1988). U.S. bank investment in AI is expected to reach $200M a year by the mid-1990's (Steiner and Teixeira, 1990). The main artificial intelligence programming languages are LISP and PROLOG. Most AI systems use one or more of four different knowledge representation systems - predicate calculus, production rules, frames and scripts, or semantic networks - to create expert systems that mimic human experts in a particular field.

International investment managers now use expert systems for a variety of functions. Canadian Imperial Bank of Commerce uses an AI program trading package from Intelligent Environment City (Kanji, 1988). Colonial Management uses its "quant" system to plan program trades (Clements, 1989). Batterymarch Financial Management uses an expert system that looks for profitable arbitrage opportunities. Paine-Webber used an Integrated Analytics expert system to plan the hedging of block trades. Chemical Bank uses an expert system for foreign exchange trading. Barclays de Zoete Weld, Sun Life, Royal Insurance, Banque Paribas, Credit Suisse, and Morgan Grenfell have invested over 1 million pounds in developing "Taurus" - an expert system that manages large stock portfolios (Friedland, 1988). Citicorp Information Services Services and Cognitive Systems developed an AI system that reads telexes and converts them to SWIFT messages. Wells Fargo and First Wachovia assisted Syntelligence in developing Lending Advisor - an expert system that does loan analysis (Steiner and Teixeira, 1990). Shearson Lehman's bond trading room has a bond inventory system that can understand human speech (Wall Street Journal, 1990A). Authorization clerks at American Express have an expert system assistant, Authorizer's Assistant, that follows some 800 rules to advise them on difficult credit card authorizations (Steiner and Teixeira, 1990). American Express and DEC are working together to develop an expert system that assists fraud investigators. Daiwa Securities has recently begun the construction of a large neural network that will do program trading (International Computer Financial News, 1989C). A promising new area is that of genetic algorithms where principles of Darwinian, Mendelian genetics are applied to computer software, mutating and reproducing code to create new software species that are confronted with software predators in a simulated environment, in order to pre-test the likely fate of new products and services (Ballester, 1990). There are also, of course, numerous generic decision support packages - e.g. EIS, Empire, Express, IFPS, Strategm, Xsim, etc. (Burns and Burrows, 1982).

Information technology can be used not only to provide answers to business problems, but also to help one learn to ask better questions about business problems (Economist, 1990B). In this role, expert systems, that prompt humans with "if this happens, have you thought of ...", are a very useful tool, particularly for stock market watchers, traders, and trade reconcilement staff. Trade reconciliation is particularly important in global investment. Whereas less than 2% of domestic trades fail, only 50% of international trades succeed. Like their mechanical counterparts, expert systems can also serve as "smoke detectors" that alert the systems'occupants to the need to take immediate action. For custodians, expert system "smoke detectors" that sense the occurrence of assets that need assignment, of corporate actions that require fast action, and of proxies that need attention, would be quite useful.

The problem with any expert system is that expert systems, like the human experts they mimic, often disagree on the best method to make the "correct" expert decision; and although one expert system may play the market very well for a period of time, eventually the market changes in such a way that the old approach is no longer successful. Which expert system should watch the expert systems?

Software Paratroopers

Systems used by investment firms and custodial banks are typically divided into "back-office" systems and "front-office" systems. Typical "back-office" systems are custody systems, trade transmission systems, accounting systems, and trade recon systems. Typical "front office" sub-systems are modeling, trade entry, client inquiry, and ad hoc reporting systems.

Custodians focus on "back-office" systems. As Terence Norman, Systems Manager of PanAgora Ltd., puts it, "...the one common area where all these companies strive for the holy grail of total efficiency and a further edge is within their back office operations." The bull markets of the 1980s put a tremendous load on the "back office", increasing pressure on systems staff to make their "back office" sub-systems more powerful, more robust, and faster (Sowton, 1989). Firms have increasingly moved from batch systems to online systems (Hagstrom, 1990).

One interesting new application of optical technology is use of imaging systems to create the "paperless" office (Lewis, 1990). In 1989, 50 U.S. banks had either planned or implemented image processing systems. It is currently estimated that U.S. financial institutions will buy $200 million of image processing equipment in 1990. Image processing systems are used at Bankers Trust for mortgage documents, at US Trust for trust documents, at First Wachovia for corporate account signatures, at Bank of New York for customer correspondence, at Security Pacific for investigation documents, and at American Express for billing (Steiner and Teixeira, 1990). Custodians could use image processing to deal with the growing piles of paper, broker confirms. Ironically, image processing systems create new problems as they solve old ones. A bank check that is stored as a compressed digital image needs 20,000 bytes of storage. A large bank that deals with one million checks would be unable to transmit their digital images in less than 29 hours on a T1 line (Steiner and Teixeira, 1990).

Money managers focus on "front office systems." New personal computer presentation interfaces - windows, icons, graphics, hypertext - have made elaborate, new data displays possible, redefining the human-computer interface (Schneiderman, 1987; Schneiderman and Kearsley, 1989). "Smart" terminals can now do screen format selection, data edits, and user help locally. System developers, who used to divorce word-processing, voice communications, and office publishing from real data processing, need do so no longer. "Front office" users have become so computer literate that they sometimes ask, not for new systems, but for software toolkits to create their own systems (Miller, 1989; The Banker, 1990).

Given the fast moving pace of international investment in a rapidly changing world economy investor demands for new investment products, and changing government regulations, there is tremendous pressure on systems professionals to rapidly alter older information systems and to create new information systems in both the "back office" and the "front office". It is extremely doubtful that the plodding bureaucracy of the traditional MIS department can handle the strain, especially when such departments often have to be reminded that they exist to support the business rather than vice versa. The future, instead, belongs to extremely flexible systems people, with considerable education and training, who understand the business, and who are not afraid to operate in a somewhat entrepreneurial mode (Zuboff, 1988). As Tom Lucey, Executive Vice-President of the Security Management Group at the Boston Company, puts it, software developers need to understand the "culture of the market". What the international investment firm needs is small teams of "software paratroopers" who can be dropped into the "back office" or the "front office" battle zones, quickly spec a new system, prototype it, code it, test it, install it, and escape with an acceptable number of casualties before the competition has time to react. To do this, a fast, simple system development methodology combined with the programming of small, reusable procedures for specific business functions is needed. It is time for investment management systems staff to seriously look at the advantages of the structured coding techniques and structures developed in programming languages like PASCAL, MODULA 2, and ADA.

APPLYING INFORMATION TECHNOLOGY TO SECURITIES PROCESSING

In international investment management, there is currently no simple dichotomy between firms with advanced information technology and those without it. It is true of investment advisors, portfolio owners, custodians and subcustodians that information technology is applied unevenly within organizations and across the various types of firms. Since the processing path of a given securities transaction wends its way through a combination of these organizations, the data may progress quickly along the divided highway of electronic communications and suddenly come upon the unpaved uncertainties of manual processing. An interesting effect of this is that any one firm, only part of the processing, cannot gain overwhelming competitive advantage by investing in advanced information technology unless it is in a position to influence the others as well. Conversely, a relatively unsophisticated participant in this process benefits from being a part of a processing path which includes some technologically advanced organizations.

The value that advanced, effectively utilized information technology holds for international investment managers can best be demonstrated by a detailed analysis of the steps in the processing path of a typical activity conducted by an investment manager: using the proceeds of a sale of securities to make an investment in another asset in a different market, using a different currency. We will trace this activity through two combinations of organizations. For purposes of illustration, we have "stacked the deck" by making the first combination more uniformly unsophisticated in information technology and the second more uniformly technologically advanced than might be the seen in actual circumstances. The institutions described in each of the two cases which follow are, composites put together to demonstrate common practices.

Case One: Just the Fax

Our first investment management firm, which we will call Barchester Associates, is an established firm of excellent reputation. An investment advisor at Barchester has executed a sale of a Japanese equity for one of the portfolios he is managing, the Global Growth Fund. He is impatiently waiting for the trade to settle so that he can reinvest the proceeds. The subcustodian, Tokyo International Bank, has been notified by the custodian, Central Trust, to sell 10,000 shares of Sumitomo Construction Company versus 7,740,304 yen. When the trade settles, i.e. when the agent for the buyer's broker pays Tokyo International, a hand-written paper ticket is hand-carried through the bank to a clerk at a telex machine who types and telexes the settlement to Central Trust. At Central Trust, the account representative for the Global Growth account receives the telex and types a transaction into his custody and accounting system for processing. Since the investment advisor has asked to be kept informed on a daily basis of trade settlements, a report is printed overnight from the accounting system. The Global Growth account representative takes the report to a Xerox machine to reduce it, then sends it, via fax to Barchester Associates.

Since the settlement period of the trade that the investment advisor made is five days, by the time he has been notified of the settlement of the sale of the Sumitomo Construction Company shares, he has already executed the buy of Mannesman AG, a German bond held at a depository in Brussels known as Euro-Clear. He will have timed the settlement of this trade to coincide with the availability of funds. To accomplish this, the advisor will have executed a foreign exchange deal (FX) for settlement on the same day the buy was due to settle, perhaps one day after the sell settled. It is entirely possible therefore that the notification of the settlement of the sell reaches him after the funds are due to be used in the FX transaction. The perils of this arrangement hardly need amplification if one understands even the rudiments of financial dealings. Our advisor's foreign exchange deal was executed by telephone with an FX trader; a confirming letter will follow. Barchester Associates must now notify Central Trust that an FX deal has been executed. This is done via fax. It takes the form of instructions from the investment advisor hand-written on a form provided by Central Trust and completed by the investment advisor. The same procedure will be followed for the purchase of the Mannesman AG bonds.

These two transactions are treated differently at Central Trust. The foreign exchange deal requires two messages to be created. The first is a payment transaction which must be sent to the Japanese subcustodian, Tokyo International Bank, which is instructed to pay 7,740,304 yen to the Japanese agent of the FX trader. The second message must be sent to Central Trust's German subcustodian, Frankfurt Industrial Bank, instructing it to receive 38,040 deutschemarks from the German agent of the FX trader. These messages are created in the form of hand-written, multiple copy, paper tickets. One copy is used to key a transaction into the custody and accounting system, and the other is sent to a telex operator who uses it to type a message. The buy transaction is also converted to a paper ticket and keyed into both the custody/ accounting system and a telex terminal. Once received by Frankfurt Industrial Bank, the telexes for the FX and the Buy of securities are used as input documents for data entry into their custody and banking systems. When each of these deals settles, and if all goes according to plan, Frankfurt Industrial Bank will input the settlement to its internal systems and separately transmit the data via telex to Central Trust. A clerk at Central Trust will pass along the paper documents to the account representative for Global Growth who will arrange for their input into the custody and accounting system and, when a report is available, fax the notification of the trade settlement to Barchester Associates.

Case Two: Integrated Circuit

Upon his arrival at Bernardo Asset Management, our second investment manager logs on to his company's back office accounting system which is linked to a communications and reconciliation system, called Iris, which is itself connected with the custody system of Southwestern Bank and Trust Company and the other custodians with whom investment managers at Bernardo do the bulk of their business. Today he is interested in the settlement of a sale of 15,000 shares of Furukawa Mining Company in Japan on behalf of a client which maintains a World Capital Fund. The settlement which occurred while both Bernardo and Southwestern were closed for business has been recorded by Iris. The sequence of events started with a SWIFT message sent to Southwestern Bank and Trust from Commercial Bank of Tokyo confirming the settlement of the sale of securities. This confirmation message was processed by Southwestern's custody system and matched to a trade. The posting of the settlement on the bank's custody system in turn triggered notification to Iris which matched the settlement to a transaction on Bernardo's accounting system and sent it a response.

Having assured himself of the availability of funds, the Bernardo investment manager can now execute a buy of Bunders republic Deutschland, a German bond held at the Euro-Clear depository. Since he must pay for this security in Deustchmarks, he will also arrange for a foreign exchange deal to settle on the day the security trade is completed. The details of the trade are keyed into the Bernardo accounting system by the investment manager or a clerk in the office. They become part of one of the several transmissions of trade instructions processed by Iris daily. Iris segregates the transactions by custodian and by the locations at which they are due to settle. The FX transaction is also processed by Iris as two separate transactions, instructions to pay yen at one location and to receive deutchemarks at another. All three of these transactions are sent to Southwestern Bank's custody system. At Southwestern, the custody system processes the transactions: the trade details are reviewed in the custody operations area for completeness. Once approved, they are transmitted automatically as EUCLID instructions to Euro-Clear in Brussels at a predetermined time. A similar process is followed for the receipt of deutschemarks which will occur at Hanover Bank. This transaction is sent via SWIFT. The payment of yen must be done by Commercial Bank of Tokyo. This transaction has been labeled with a different location but is otherwise processed in the same manner as the previous transaction. At a predetermined time it is transmitted via SWIFT to Commercial Bank. All of this has occurred by the day after the trade was executed, referred to as trade date plus one. At any point in this process, Southwestern Bank's account representative for the World Capital Fund can inquire into its custody and accounting system, the latter getting its information instantaneously from the former, about the details of any pending trade or FX or any other pertinent information. The representative has the responsibility to insure that the automated processes are working as expected and to recognize, diagnose and see to the correction of any problems.

On settlement date at Commercial Bank, the yen transaction is routed to the accounting system and the payment made via SWIFT to the counterparty contained in the appropriate message field in the SWIFT message. At Southwestern Bank and Trust the confirmation of this payment is received in the form of a SWIFT message. While these events are occurring, Hanover Bank is processing its part of the deal. The deutschemarks are received from the German agent of the FX trader who contracted with the Bernardo investment manager. A confirmation of the receipt of these funds is sent via SWIFT to Southwestern Bank. The securities are booked to Southwestern's account at Euro-Clear. The cash is paid via SWIFT to the agent of the broker who sold them to the Bernardo investment manager. Confirmation of the settlement of the trade is sent via a computer-readable Euro-Clear report to Southwestern Bank.

Each of the confirmations received at Southwestern Bank is automatically processed by the custody system. Since they are recognized as belonging to an account participating in the communications and reconciliation service, they have been routed to the Iris system. Iris has matched them to instructions it received from Bernardo Asset Management and transmitted them to that company's accounting system on the day the confirmations were received which is normally settlement date. If there has been any difficulty in the settlement of the FX contract or the trade, this fact will also be known on the day the deals were due to settle.

CONCLUSION

These two cases clearly demonstrate the benefits of the effective use of global information technology. Several observations can be made about operations at Barchester Associates. First, their operations are prone to human error. Every time human intervention is involved at a transitional point, for example, writing a ticket or keying data into a system, there is potential for error. Authorization and data integrity are dependent on people following prescribed procedures. So much communication by fax machine provides opportunities for data to be lost or tampered with. Movement of millions of dollars in cash and securities warrants much vigilance. Telex offers some protection in this regard if test key procedures are in place and religiously followed. Telex however raises another issue-ineffective use of technology. Telex, as used at Barchester Associates, had the disadvantage of requiring data to be keyed a second time before it can be transmitted; the first time was into an internal system. Another point to be made about this process is that it is inherently slow. Data is written, keyed, copied, faxed; forms are carried, forwarded and filed. Data entry clerks typing meaningless numbers and phrases in an endlessly repetitive pattern, into a terminal, have been shown by Zuboff (1988) to work against productivity and accuracy. The elapsed time for communicating any one message is a function of various vagaries such as an operator's keystroke speed, workload, break schedule and, perhaps, general attitude for that day. These clearly are not factors to instill confidence in one that a complex, time-sensitive and expensive process will be executed efficiently.

In contrast, operations at Bernardo Asset Management illustrate the immediate competitive advantage inherent in the timely processing of information. While the Barchester investment manager in the first case is waiting for information from his custodian, the Bernardo adviser in the second case is free to formulate his next investment without the nagging uncertainty of the disposition of his last deal. Competition does not only mean making the right investments, it also means being efficient. In the words of Terry Norman of PanAgora: "Events such as overdrawn cash positions, the late processing or settlement of trades, which take place on both a local and global basis, can be very costly, not only in terms of interest claims etc, but in reputation." At Bernardo Asset Management, a transaction was keyed once, at its source, where the details were known and comprehended in a meaningful way. The advantages for productivity extended to the custodian as well. The job of reformatting, translating and communicating was left to the hardware and software, which are able to complete it effectively and reliably in a much shorter time than if human involvement was required. The salient information about any activity is communicated to the investment manager virtually simultaneously with its communication to the custodian. This enables a larger volume of transactions to be processed by fewer accounting and clerical personnel.

In William Gibson's provocative science fiction thriller *Neuromancer*, information technology is pervasive and computer "cowboys," whose neurological system can "link in" directly to the computer network, make their living prying information from various databases in ingenious, if somewhat nefarious, ways on behalf of a client. This must seem to more than a few investment managers to be the reductio ad absurdum of trends in their profession which have progressed to a point where clients are as interested in the technological sophistication of an investment advisory firm as they are in its market expertise (Gibson 1984). The rapid changes in the investment arena and the recurring revolutions propelling information technology promise a transformation in the business of investment management as radical as anything any science fiction author can imagine.

References

Atre, S. (1980) *Data Base: Structured Techniques for Design, Performance, and Management.* New York: John Wiley & Sons.

Bacon, P. (May 1989). Feed for Thought. *The Banker*, pp. 71-73.

Ballester, G. (March 1990). Unnatural Selection. *Information Center* , pp. 33-34.

Bloch, E. Inside Investment Banking. Homewood, Illinois: Dow Jones Irwin, 1989.

Boult, R. Networks Add Value. The Banker, December 1989, pp. 75-77.

Burns & Burrows. The Analysis of Competitive Structure in Industrial Service Markets: A Study of the Market for Financial Decision Support Systems (MIT Sloane School MSC Thesis, June 1982).

CEDEL. *Handbook for Participants.* Luxembourg: CEDEL, 1989.

CEDEL. *Communication System Via SWIFT - Cash Instructions.* Luxembourg: CEDEL, 1988.

CEDEL. *Communication System Via SWIFT - Security Instructions.* Luxembourg: CEDEL, 1988.

Clements, J. Calculated Risk. *Forbes,* June 26, 1989.

Date, C. J. *An Introduction to Database Systems* (Vol I and II). Reading, Ma.: Addison-Wesley, 1983.

Date, C.J. *A Guide to SQL.* Reading, MA: Addison-Wesley, 1987.

Date, C.J. *A Guide to DB2.* Reading, MA: Addison-Wesley, 1988.

Economist staff. A Survey of International Banking. *Economist,* April 7, 1990, p. 21.

Economist staff. Information Technology. *Economist,* 16-22 June, 1990, pp. 5-20.

Euro-Clear. *EUCLID User Guide - High Speed.* Brussels: Euro-Clear, 1987.

Euro-Clear. *EUCLID Release -* October 1988. Brussels: Euro-Clear, 1988.

Euro-Clear. *EUCLID October 1988 Release Appendices.* Brussels: Euro-Clear, 1988.

Euro-Clear. *EUCLID User Guide.* Brussels: Euro-Clear, 1989.

Euro-Clear. *EUCLID User Reference Manual.* Brussels: Euro-Clear, 1989.

Euro-Clear. *Operating Procedures of the Euro-Clear System.* Brussels: Euro-Clear, 1987.

Euro-Clear. *Using SWIFT Messages to Send Money Transfer Instructions to the Euro-Clear Operations Center.* Brussels: Euro-Clear, 1989.

Euro-Clear. *Euro-Clear News,* June 22, 1990.

Euromoney staff. World Equity Flows into London. *Euromoney,* April 1987, pp. 54-60.

Friedland, J. The Expert-Systems Revolution. *Institutional Investor,* July 1988, pp. 106-111.

GEISCO. *High-Speed Service Reference Manual.* GEISCO, 1985.

Gibson, W. *Neuromancer.* New York: The Berkley Publishing Group, 1984.

Hagstrom, P. New Information Systems and the Changing Structure of MNCs. In Barlett, Ooz, and Hedlund (Eds.), *Managing the Global Firm.* London: Routledge, 1990, pp. 164-185.

Hayes, S. & Hubbard, P. *Investment Banking - A Tale of Three Cities.* Boston, MA: Harvard Business School Press, 1990.

Helm, S. SWIFT Moves On. *Computers in Banking,* January 1988, pp. 35-41.

HEXAGON. *HEXAGON Customer Guide.* Honkong-Shanghai Bank Group, 1986.

Hobson, D. *SWIFT and Securities: Flight or Fancy.* Global Custodian, March 1990, pp. 49-57.

IBM. *IBM Information Exchange Introduction - Service Users Guide* (GC34-2221-3). June 1987.

IBM. *IBM MERVA/370 Operating* (SH12-5472). 1987.

IBM. *IBM DSNL/370 General Information Manual* (GH12-5274). 1987.

IBM. *IBM SNA Format and Protocol Reference Manual: Architecture Logic for LU Type 6.2* (SC30-3269-31). December 1985.

IBM. IBM SNA *Transaction Programmer's Reference Manual for LU Type 6.2* (GC30-3084-2). November 1985.

Intermarket staff. 1992: Ready or Not?. *Intermarket,* May 1989, pp. 18-21.

Institutional Investor staff. Ranking the World's Largest Banks. *Institutional Investor,* June 1989, pp. 119-132.

International Computer Financial News. Arlington, MA: George Ballester, December 1988.

International Computer Financial News. Arlington, MA: George Ballester, June 1989.

International Computer Financial News. Arlington, MA: George Ballester, October 1989.

International Computer Financial News. Arlington, MA: George Ballester, November 1989.

International Computer Financial News. Arlington, MA: George Ballester, February 1990.

International Computer Financial News. Arlington, MA: George Ballester, April 1990.

International Computer Financial News. Arlington, MA: George Ballester, May 1990.

Intranet. *Intranet Payment Entry Reference Manual.* Newton, MA: Intranet, 1987.

I.P. Sharp. *Instant Link Release 2.2 User Documentation* (09808809E1), Sept. 1988.

Ipsen, E. The Eight Great Myths of Globalization. *Institutional Investor,* April 1988, pp. 82-86.

Kanji, S. When is an Expert Not an Expert? *The Banker,* April 1988, pp. 86-88.

Kennedy, P. *The Rise and Fall of the Great Powers - Economic Change and Military Conflict from 1500 to 2000.* New York: Vintage Books, 1989.

Keyes, T. & Miller, D. *The Global Investor - How to Buy Stocks Around the World.* Chicago: Longman Financial Services Publishing, 1990.

Lewis, V. Capture and Retrieve. *The Banker,* April 1990, pp. 67-68.

Longman. *The Buyer's Guide to Financial Services Software.* Chicago: Longman Financial Services Publishing, 1983.

LFT staff. *London Financial Times,* March 19, 1990.

LFT staff. *International Banking Survey.* London Financial Times, May 9, 1990.

LFT staff. *London Financial Times,* May 18, 1990.

LFT staff. *London Financial Times,* June 6, 1990.

LFT staff. European Finance and Investment - West Germany. *London Financial Times,* June 19, 1990.

Luhn, R. Windows Makes the Grade. *PC World,* July 1990, pp. 75-77.

Malmgren, H. Technology and the Economy. In Brock & Hormats (Eds.), *The Global Economy - America's Role in the Decade Ahead.* New York: W.W. Norton & Co., 1990, pp. 92-119.

Miller, R. Super*Banking: Innovative Management Strategies (That Work).* Homewood, IL: Dow-Jones Irwin, 1989.

Murphy, P. Linking Up. *The Banker,* July 1988.

Murphy, P. The Silent Approach. *The Banker,* March 1989, pp. 75-76.

Murphy, P. A Day in the Life of. *The Banker,* November 1989, pp. 136-137.

Murphy, P. SWIFT II: Long Overdue. *London Financial Times,* November 9, 1989.

Nadeau, M. The Fast Keep Getting Faster. *Byte,* May 1990, pp. 131-132.

Oppenheim, P. *International Banking.* Washington, DC: American Bankers Association, 1987.

One Point. *Communicating Online.* Hasbrouck Heights, NJ: Hayden Book Company, 1985.

Oxford, J. Macho Game. *Global Finance,* September 1988, pp. 46-54.

Poppel, H. & Goldstein, B. *Information Technology - The Trillion-Dollar Opportunity.* New York: McGraw-Hill, 1987.

Porter, M. *The Competitive Advantage of Nations.* New York: The Free Press, 1990.

Powers, J. FX: New Faces, New Places. *Intermarket,* June 1988, pp. 31-37.

Schneiderman, B. *Designing the user interface: Strategies for Effective Human-Computer Interaction.* Reading, MA: Addison-Wesley, 1987.

Schneiderman, B. & Kearsley, G. *Hypertext Hands-on! - An Introduction to a New Way of Organizing and Accessing Information.* Reading, MA: Addison-Wesley, 1989.

Schutzer, D. *Artificial Intelligence - An Applications-Oriented Approach.* New York: Van Nostrand and Reinhold, 1987.

Smith, R. *The Global Bankers.* New York: Truman Talley, 1989.

Sowton, E. Faster, Better and More Profitable. *The Banker,* August 1989, pp. 22-27.

Steiner, T. & Teixeira, D. *Technology in Banking - Creating Value and Destroying Profits,* Homewood, IL: Dow Jones-Irwin, 1990.

Sterling Software. *TRACS Installation/Operation Manual* (OS Version 2.0). Sterling Software, 1985.

Sterling Software. *SUPERTRACS General Information Manual.* Sterling Software, 1989.

Stevens, L. Users Say EDI Cuts Inventory Costs, Speeds Product Delivery. *Computerworld,* May 2, 1988, pp. 53-59.

SWIFT. *SWIFT User Handbook* (Vol 2). Belgium: SWIFT, 1984.

SWIFT. *SWIFT User Handbook* (Vol 4). Belgium: SWIFT, 1984.

SWIFT. *SWIFT User Handbook* (Vol 1). Belgium: SWIFT, 1989.

SWIFT. *SWIFT User Handbook* (Vol 2). Belgium: SWIFT, 1989.

SWIFT. *SWIFT II Planning Guide.* Belgium: SWIFT, 1989.

SWIFT. *SWIFT II Policy Volume.* Belgium: SWIFT, 1989.

SWIFT. *SWIFT II Administration* Volume. Belgium: SWIFT, 1989.

The Banker staff. Whose Hand on the Wheel? *The Banker,* January 1990, pp. 10-14.

TRT. TRT Overview, TRT, 1988.

TRT. TRT Lane 9000, TRT, 1989.

WSJ staff. *Wall Street Journal,* May 25, 1990, p. C1.

WSJ staff. *Wall Street Journal,* June 12, 1990, p. 15.

WSJ staff. *Wall Street Journal,* June 15, 1990, p. A4.

WSJ staff. *Wall Street Journal,* June 18, 1990, p. C1.

WSJ staff. *Wall Street Journal,* June 19, 1990, p. 14.

WSJ staff. *Wall Street Journal,* June 22, 1990, p. C1.

WSJ staff. *Wall Street Journal,* June 25, 1990, p. C1.

Zelkowitz, M. Software Engineering Concepts and Techniques. In Umbaugh, R. (Eds.), *The Handbook of MIS Management.* Pennsauken, NJ: Auerbach, 1985, pp. 219-247.

Zuboff, S. *In the Age of the Smart Machine - The Future of Work and Power.* New York: Basic Books, 1988.

SECTION 4
MULTINATIONAL ISSUES:
TECHNOLOGY TRANSFER, ADOPTION, AND DIFFUSION

The impact of information technology has proliferated to virtually every corner of the world. Its effects are substantial and interest in this phenomenon is increasing every day. Of particular interest more recently is the impact of information technology on developing countries. Since the response to information technology varies substantially from country to country, it is vital to understand the process of adoption or absorption of such technologies. The chapters in this section address this and related issues germane to the proliferation of information technology. The first chapter written by Gordon B. Davis addresses the issue of information technology proliferation directly. He discusses the imperatives for information systems and technology use in developing countries and then examines the efficacy of Nolan's Model and a Stage Model relative to the process of information technology adoption. He also presents the justification of expenditures for information systems in developing countries and how that differs from the justification that may be utilized in developed countries.

The second chapter by A. Lee Gilbert addresses various approaches to the transfer of technology and the necessary planning that must be done for that transfer. He examines the value of expert systems and the impact of the legal system and culture on information technology transfer. The next chapter addresses the effects of information technology as an intrusive phenomenon. Since information technology has the potential to cross national borders with apparent ease, it may create a myriad of problems. This is the subject of the chapter by William B. Carper. A variety of issues, relative to Transborder Data Flow (TBDF) are addressed. Included in the discussion are problems that arise with respect to security, sovereignty, local laws, and the technical aspects of TBDF. This section ends with a chapter that addresses TBDF from a different perspective. George S. Vozikis, Ernie Goss and Timothy Mescon discuss ways of enhancing technology transfer from one country to another.

16

A Model for Adoption and Diffusion of Information Systems in Less Developed Countries

Gordon B. Davis
University of Minnesota

Organizations in less developed countries (LDCs) have many of the same reasons for implementing computerized information systems as organizations in developed countries. There are also fairly unique reasons why they adopt computers.

The traditional model for adoption and diffusion of information systems in the developed countries is the Nolan Stage Model. The basic idea of the Nolan Stage Model can be applied in organizations in LDCs, but the model is modified to emphasize organizational learning as the underlying phenomenon and the necessity for procedural discipline for functions to which computers are applied.

The criterion used for selecting initial applications tends to be different for LDCs. Cost displacement is not a strong condition in developing countries; value added is the most important rationale for initial applications. Especially in the initial applications it is important to not violate or clash with organizational or national culture. Conflict with culture may add difficulties so that the initial applications fail.

While the introduction of computer technology can take place with a rather primitive infrastructure, the organization will be constrained in moving to more sophisticated applications by the lack of a modern technology infrastructure. This will include reliable electrical power source, educated personnel, and general training. If the nation does not provide this infrastructure, the organization must make the investment.

The chapter examines the rationale, processes, and problems of introducing information technology and information systems into organizations in less developed countries (LDCs). It explores the traditional developed country explanations and rationale about the introduction of computers and reasons how they apply to LDCs. Based on the author's experience, factors and considerations that affect the adoption and diffusion of information technology in less developed countries are examined, and relevant concepts are proposed.

INTRODUCTION AND OVERVIEW

Organizations in less developed countries have some of the same reasons for implementing computerized information systems as those in developed countries. There are also fairly unique reasons why organizations in a less developed country adopt computer data processing or enhance existing computer-based information systems.

The traditional model for adoption and diffusion of information systems in the developed countries is the Nolan Stage Model. Closely related to the stage model is the rationale for the application of computers to information processing. The initial rationale for the introduction of computers in the Western countries has been a displacement of existing costs with lower computer data processing costs; only after computers proved effective at displacement of costs were they used for value-added projects and performance enhancement.

The basic idea of the Nolan Stage Model can be applied in organizations in LDCs but the model is modified to emphasize organizational learning as the underlying phenomenon and the necessity for procedural discipline (existence of and willingness to follow procedures and standards for business transactions). The criterion used for selecting initial applications tends to be different for LDCs. Cost displacement is not a strong condition in less developed countries; therefore, value added is the most important rationale for initial applications. The modified stage model plus economic rationale result in two necessary conditions for most initial applications in LDC organizations: existing procedural discipline and value added potential.

Productivity from application of technology is a strong presumption in developed countries, yet economic measurements have not demonstrated productivity improvement. A reason may be that the productivity improvements have been used up in providing more customized, differentiated services and products. Differentiated services and products may be a less important factor in the application of computers in LDCs, so there may be greater measurable productivity gains than in developed countries.

There are some more or less unique conditions and limitations relative to information systems applications and implementation. Special education for applying information technology is assumed by society in developed countries; it may need to be provided by the organization in an LDC. Relative to developed countries in which technology is culturally supported, the computer in LDCs is likely to disturb some important customs and cultural values. Government policies and laws may be significant; for example, an important factor in encouraging the free flow of computer software is for LDCs to provide protection for intellectual property.

IMPERATIVES FOR INFORMATION SYSTEMS/ INFORMATION TECHNOLOGY USE IN LESS DEVELOPED COUNTRIES

There are some distinctive imperatives in less developed countries for the introduction of computer-based information systems and information technology. These are access to capital markets, improved written language communication, reduced distance to markets, improved business support services, and management of cultural change for organizational improvement. Each issue and its relationship to information technology will be surveyed briefly.

Access to Capital Markets

Developed countries are willing to invest in less developed countries. However, investment requires financial reporting to investors and use of generally accepted international standards for the reports. Many LDCs have had family businesses that relied for control upon family members in key positions rather than financial controls and reports. Also, the distinction between invested capital or debt and earnings available for distribution is not an important one for a business owned by a family; it is a fundamental issue for external investors.

The change from a family business to a professionally managed business with access to capital markets therefore requires more sophisticated financial controls and reporting. Although such improvements in accounting can be performed manually, information technology is so well developed in financial reporting that it is imperative to apply it to any growing company in a less developed country that seeks access to capital markets.

Improved Written Language Communication

Less developed countries generally have a much lower volume of written communication than developed countries. When communication volume increases, some LDCs have a disadvantage in using traditional computer technology and coding. The computer standard for coding is the 8-bit code. This is ample for storage and communication of alphabetic, numeric, special and graphics characters. The stored representation is easily converted into output of text and graphics. Retrieval requests can specify unique strings of characters.

A large proportion of the population of LDCs employs character systems or ideograms rather than alphabets. Examples are China, Taiwan, and Japan. Although ideogram character systems can be encoded, they suffer from a relative disadvantage compared to alphabetic coding when simple information technology is applied. The disadvantage is the lack of a simple, unambiguous coding scheme for defining the ideograms. (Note: This lack is not true for modern Korean.) This disadvantage is likely to persist, but some of the relative disadvantage can be removed by more sophisticated technology. A few examples illustrate the power of information technology for improving data entry and written language communication with ideograms.

• The current technology for entering Chinese ideograms requires the operator to enter phonetic codes and then select from the characters that are displayed (since more than one ideogram will have the same phonetic representation). More sophisticated expert systems built into the entry procedure can reduce the selection overhead.

• The facsimile technology is useful in all countries, but it is especially useful in countries with ideogram character systems because part or all of the document can be handwritten.

Reduced Distance to Markets

A characteristic of a typical LDC is that the country itself does not provide sufficient market for goods and services. There must be significant export activity. The distance between the country and its markets in developed countries can present a significant barrier. This is especially so since the trend in developed countries is to reduce the length of the procurement/delivery cycle. This is being done by mechanisms such as EDI (Electronic Data Interchange) which supports computer-to-computer procurement.

There is also a problem with time zones, and even if the time zone constraint is overcome, there may be problems in telephone communication. As an example, the normal work day in New York is entirely nighttime in Taiwan, Korea, or the People's Republic of China.

Information technology aids in overcoming distance difficulties. Examples of the use of technology for this purpose are:

- Voice mail
- Electronic mail
- Facsimile
- Electronic data interchange

Assuming a telephone connection is made, the problem is not the language to be used. The language of worldwide commerce is English, but when English is not the native language there is an increase in the probability of errors in understanding due to the loss of quality in telephone transmission and verbal clues compared to face-to-face communication. The above technologies allow messages to be read and reread (or repeated in case of voice mail) to ensure understanding.

Information Technology Infrastructure and Business Support Services

An essential precondition for business support services is a good telephone system. There is a natural priority with the first being a good international phone system followed by a good national phone system. The international trunk lines are easier to install because they do not entail construction inside cities and the impact on international commerce is immediate. A recognition of these priorities is demonstrated by the 1980s high quality international lines into India and the People's Republic of China and the poorer quality lines inside the countries. Some businesses in India during the late 1980s were reportedly making calls to another city in India by calling a subsidiary in Singapore and having them connect with the other city in India because it was simpler to get a good international line than to call within India.

Good satellite facilities are important business support services both for the transmission of large amounts of data and for video communication.

Business support includes good general education and specialized technical education in information technology. Many LDCs have higher education systems that emphasize traditional educational topics and neglect new technologies.

Management of Cultural Change

In developed countries, information technology has been used to effect changes in organizations. It has been used as a change agent mechanism for centralizing, decentralizing, etc. The same concept is applicable to LDCs, but because these countries have had less time to adapt to technology and large-scale business practices, there may be more opportunities to use computers to effect cultural changes that are necessary in order to have more effective organizations. An example illustrates the use of technology to overcome a deeply entrenched custom.

Example: Airline reservation system and *baksheesh.* Online reservation systems are designed to give instant feedback as to the availability of reservations and to confirm the reservation. Travelers in India had become accustomed to a manual reservation system for trains and planes that provided very few guaranteed reservations. To obtain a reserved seat on the train or plane required the payment of a bribe or gratuity (*baksheesh*). The online reservation system for Indian Airlines removed the uncertainties and problems of *baksheesh* for reservations by confirming seats. When all seats are sold, a computerized wait list is maintained.

THE TRADITIONAL NOLAN MODEL OF ADOPTION AND DIFFUSION

The Nolan Stage Model has been the most popular explanation for the "natural" evolution of computer-based information processing in organizations in developed countries. The model was developed by Nolan based on a few case studies during the early 1970s. The earliest publication of the model was in Communications of the ACM (Nolan, 1973), but the best known explanations and advocacy for the model appeared in two articles in the Harvard Business Review in 1974 and 1979 (Gibson & Nolan, 1974; Nolan, 1979). The 1974 article defined the Stage Model as four stages with four growth processes. The four stages are:

Initiation. Early applications in areas such as accounting with cost displacement as justification

Expansion Contagion. Proliferation of applications with little justification or budgetary control

Formalization Control. Imposition of justification and budgetary controls. Slowing of application growth.

Maturity Integration. Integration of applications and development of databases.

The growth processes associated with each stage of development are:

- Composition of applications portfolio
- Organization of data processing or MIS function
- Planning and control for information systems
- User awareness and accountability

The later article in 1979 described six stages; however, the basic model is four stages, and the six stage variation does not add significantly to the fundamental concept. The six stages are initiation, contagion, control, integration, data administration, and maturity. The inserting of two stages between control and maturity addresses the two types of integration that take place: application integration and data integration.

The influence of the model has been noteworthy. In addition to thousands of organizations that were influenced by the model in their planning and organization, Nolan (1984) noted that over 200 stage studies had been conducted in major corporations by his consulting firm, Nolan and Norton.

The model postulates organization and policy change dynamics built around a changing portfolio of applications. It has been criticized as not being testable in a research sense (Benbasat et al., 1984), but has also been defended as being high in directional explanatory power even though it is low in prescriptive power (King & Kraemer, 1984). In other words, the model is useful in understanding the direction of change but is not very useful in making detailed plans at a given point in time.

A STAGE MODEL ADAPTED TO LESS DEVELOPED COUNTRIES

An organization in a less developed country, seeking to take advantage of the experience of developed countries to close the gap, may question whether or not organizations must progress through the Nolan stages. Could an organization build a mature system without the cost, time, and trauma of the other stages? Nolan's answer is that the stages are necessary. Planning for progression through the stages may result in a smooth transition, but the growth processes are a natural response to the introduction of computers and information systems.

In the early stage model literature, there was some emphasis on the application portfolio and budget as the forces which moved the organization through the stages. In a talk at a Harvard symposium on information systems, Nolan (1984) expressed the idea that the underlying phenomenon driving the changes in the portfolio of applications and changes in the organization was organizational learning. This is a fundamental phenomenon and allows an adaptation of the Nolan stage model to an organization in an LDC.

In the organizational learning view, organizations do not easily adapt to new technology that requires new procedures and makes established experience obsolete. Organizations learn to utilize computers by a few applications well suited for introduction of information technology. They choose applications that require minimal adaptation of procedures and where employees are receptive to training and change. This learning with the initial applications induces new types of applications and new demands for information processing capabilities. The organizational learning and adaptation progresses through the four (or six) stages. This line of reasoning suggests that an organization would not succeed if it implemented an advanced, integrated system without the necessary organizational learning from earlier stages.

The underlying concept in organizational learning is experience and procedural discipline. Experience is an obvious consequence of organizational learning; procedural discipline is perhaps more important but not usually emphasized. Procedures are an important condition for the functioning of organizations. They are a type of corporate memory that incorporates learning.

Procedural discipline is willingness and ability to follow a set of well-defined standard procedures for performing a task. The procedures embody experience in doing the task. The discipline also includes performing activities required for quality assurance. Some organizational functions tend to have good procedural discipline. For example, accountants are trained to follow procedures that minimize the probability of an error. Checking, footing, crossfooting, tracing to control totals are examples of procedural discipline that reduces the error rate in accounting work. The procedural discipline in other functions may be much lower, as for example sales where following procedures is less important than making the sale.

This concept means that the first applications for an organization in a less developed country should be those where the application to be displaced already has a high level of procedural discipline. Accounting and engineering applications usually meet this criteria.

In terms of the model of organizational learning, information processing discipline must be learned by experience and supported by training and procedures. This means that organizations in LDCs must establish a growth and development path which supports rapid organizational learning.

The stage model for less developed countries still has four stages: initiation, contagion, control, and integration. An added element is the use of microcomputers in the early stages of growth. Unlike developed countries, LDCs are likely to begin computer use with microcomputers. In terms of the critical issue of procedural discipline, the stages are defined as follows:

Initiation. Necessary condition for first applications is existing procedural discipline. Initiation can be microcomputers in a few well-disciplined areas of the organization.

Contagion. There is an expansion but only to areas that are willing to accept training that will instill procedural discipline in using computer applications. Minicomputers may expand the hardware configuration.

Control. There is formalization of procedures for performing tasks and for-malization of procedures for evaluation of proposals. Applications that have failed because of lack of adaptation of procedures and lack of training are ei-ther dropped or reintroduced along with organizational changes and new staff-ing. Mainframes may be viable.

Maturity. The procedural discipline for applications in prior stages has focused on applications and databases within functions or functions for which cross-functional needs were well understood and formalized. In the maturity stage, the organizational learning is pervasive enough in the organization to support applications that cross functional boundaries and even applications that cross organizational boundaries. The maturity extends to organization-wide databases. The organizational infrastructure for information technology is not isolated within a single function but includes many persons in each of the functions.

THE TRADITIONAL JUSTIFICATION OF INFORMATION SYSTEM EXPENDITURES

The introduction of information technology in organizations may have a number of motivations. For example, two types of motivation are economic or political. Economic justification is based on performing work at lower cost or performing tasks not possible using other technology. This may include applications for competitive advantage. Political motivations are to keep up with the latest technology, to appear "advanced" by using information technology, or to appear rational by having the information provided by computer technology. The latter point has been noted by Feldman and March (1981).

Western business and government organizations tend to justify all information technology expenditures on an economic basis; if there are political considerations, these tend to be hidden. The discussion will therefore concentrate on the traditional economic justification as a motivation for introducing information technology and for continued expenditures to main-tain it. Economic justification can be divided into cost displacement, competitive advantage or competitive threat, and performance enhancement. There is an implied assumption (rarely examined) in developed countries that investment in information technology will improve productivity.

Cost Displacement Justification

The cost displacement approach to justification dominated the introduction of computers in the developed countries. This is demonstrated by the methodology used by IBM analysts and sales force during the 1960s for analyzing the introduction of computers for data processing. The methodology, called Study Organization Plan, resulted in a proposed processing system for an organization, well documented as to equipment configuration, computer application runs, costs, benefits, etc. (IBM, 1963). The report consisted of five sections:

1. Management abstract
2. The new system in operation (information, flow, equipment, personnel)
3. Implementation
4. Appraisal of system value
5. Appendix of application flowcharts, file and record descriptions, etc.

The Appraisal of System Value used a cost displacement analysis built around the organizational budget. The costs savings were identified by organizational unit for objects of expenditure of equipment, personnel, and supplies. These cost savings were contrasted with the cost of the new computer data processing installation and an overall savings identified.

Much of the success of IBM in capturing a large market share can be associated with the approach to analysis of system value and demonstrating the departments and objects of expenditure that would fund the computer through cost reductions. The savings were "hard savings" rather than "faster" or "better." Faster and better were pluses but not the basic justification. The concept of hard dollar savings as the only basis for justification of computer expenditures is still frequently repeated in the literature.

Competitive Advantage or Competitive Threat

Competitive advantage (and the related idea of competitive threat) as a basis for justification of computer expenditures has been developed during the 1980s. It is based on the business strategy analysis of Michael Porter (1980). In the Porter framework, there are four major competitive threats and two basic competitive strategies (low cost or differentiation) plus a niche strategy that applies one of the two strategies to a part of the market. Its application to information systems was formulated by McFarlan and McKenney and others at Harvard Business School and demonstrated by case studies (McFarlan & McKenney, 1983).

The basic idea is that information systems can be used to provide competitive advantage. Such applications are often termed strategic applications because they fit the concept of a strategy to meet the threat of competition. The analysis for identification of strategic opportunities for competitive advantage looks at ways in which information systems may assist in being a low cost producer or in differentiation. In identifying opportunities, the analysis looks at the company's value chain for ways to reduce costs or to differentiate them. It also examines the interfaces with customers and suppliers (a value system) for ways to add value by reducing costs or improving service at the interfaces.

Most of the literature on justification based on competitive advantage has emphasized the positive aspects of achieving competitive advantage by using information technology. However, information technology is easily duplicated, so the advantage achieved in this way may be transitory as competitors match or improve upon what has been done. The advantage is usually sustainable only if it is part of a broader competitive advantage.

Given that competitors may use information technology to obtain competitive advantage, a justification for technology investment is to match or improve upon the applications of competitors. In fact, the investment may be required to survive. For example, once one competitor airline installed an online reservation system, other airlines had to do so to survive.

Internal Performance Enhancement

In contrast to the "hard" savings or profits that can be matched against expenditures to show a positive return from information technology, many internal expenditures that do not directly impact the value chain are justified on the basis of performance enhancement. There may be no reduction in cost or improvement in profits, but performance is enhanced. For example, using a personal computer may not result in greater productivity in terms of documents produced or analyses performed, but the document quality may be improved and analyses may be more complete.

Internal performance enhancement may have a competitive survival aspect in terms of ability to attract and retain high quality personnel. An organization that is too backward with respect to information technology may not be able to attract or retain high quality personnel who expect to work with state-of-the-art technology.

The Productivity Improvement Assumption

There is a strong presumption in Western culture that technology will improve productivity. The presumption is well supported by dramatic improvements in manufacturing and farm productivity. Traditional economic measurements have demonstrated this productivity improvement. However, in the case of information technology, the economic measurements of productivity fail to show productivity gains.

One reason for failure to show productivity gains from information technology investment is that traditional productivity measurements do not measure significant changes in the way things are done when computers hardware and software are used. Therefore, enhancement of performance may not show up in the statistics.

Another explanation for the apparent lack of productivity from information technology is that the gains have been used to achieve more differentiation, individuation, or customization of processes and services. This is supported by a broad interpretation of industrial trends which suggests three concepts that have motivated the behavior of industrial organizations:

• *Manufacturing efficiency.* This requires standardization. Alternatives must be reduced in order to achieve the benefits of standard processes. Henry Ford's comment that the customer could have any color he wanted as long as it was black is an indicator of this concept.

•*Market efficiency.* This requires the identification of market segments that can be treated as homogeneous for the purposes of production and marketing. Marketing is targeted at market segments, and production is organized around these.

•*Customization.* Marketing and production are organized to provide differentiated or individualized products and services.

In an evolutionary sense, manufacturing efficiency was replaced in many industries by market efficiency, and market efficiency is being replaced in many cases by customization.

One explanation for the lack of productivity improvement from the use of information technology is that traditional economic measures do not take into account its use for achieving differentiated or customized products and services. For example, prior to information technology, all air fares were identical, and airlines kept very little individual information on passengers.

Much of the investment in information technology for the airlines has been devoted to individualized fares to take into account the characteristics of customers. Additional information is maintained about customers such as meal preference, frequent flyer number, etc.

When computer information processing technology is introduced in LDCs, an issue is whether the organization is motivated by manufacturing efficiency, marketing efficiency, or customization. The answer may affect the measurable productivity gain from computerization.

JUSTIFICATION OF INFORMATION SYSTEM EXPENDITURES IN LESS DEVELOPED COUNTRIES

The justification of information system expenditures in less developed countries can be classified into initial expenditures and expenditures after successful introduction.

Justification for Initial Applications

Unlike developed countries, the economic justification for initial applications will not usually be cost displacement because the relative costs of clerical employees versus cost of computer technology makes it unlikely that cost justification based on reducing clerical employees will show a positive return. Also, in countries where there is high unemployment, those who are hired may have strong family or other ties to higher level employees and may not be displaceable. Further, staffing levels may be specified by government agencies.

Example: The Hudang shipyard in Shanghai is a major industry. The shipyard bids on construction of large ships such as container ships. The staffing levels are established by the government. The shipyard obtains a fairly large IBM mainframe. What should be the first application? Although the accounting functions have necessary discipline, the standard bookkeeping functions will not be markedly improved, and bookkeeping personnel displaced by the computer application will not be terminated. The traditional accounting applications should therefore not be the initial applications. The value added criteria suggests an applications in which those using the computer have an existing procedural discipline and the use of the computer will add value to their work rather than simply eliminating employees. This logic leads to computer aided engineering as the initial applications. It adds value to an important activity but does not adversely affect staffing levels. Cost accounting and estimating/bidding are two interrelated applications. They are not good initial applications because cost accounting has not been well developed and the necessary discipline is not established.

Example: China Airlines installs an online reservation system. There are two justifications but neither are cost displacement. The first is that travel agencies outside the People's Republic of China will hesitate to use the airline unless it can respond to reservation requests and can control the reservations made. The second is that the limits of human coordination mean that a manual reservation system can never perform as well as a an online computer system. Even adding unlimited labor to a manual reservation system will not make it equal to an online computer system.

Justification of Subsequent Applications

After the initial set of applications, the growth of applications and diffusion of procedural discipline necessary for implementation of applications may suggest other criteria such as performance enhancement. As long as the organizational learning criterion is met, the full range of justification common to developed countries may be appropriate.

CONDITIONS AND LIMITATIONS FOR ADOPTION AND DIFFUSION

There are a number of conditions and limitations relative to the introduction and use of information technology and information systems in LDCs. Procedural discipline and value added have been described as necessary conditions for initial applications. In addition, there is a need for education and training. Culture is an important difference affecting creating and use of certain applications. A societal condition limiting transfer of software technology is the absence in many LDCs of protection for intellectual property.

Education and Training

In developed countries, the school system provides a substantial part of the general background and procedural discipline for positions dealing with computers. The education will generally involve use of computers for mathematics and word processing. The concept of the computer, stored program, and necessity for procedural discipline by users will have been imparted as computer literacy by the secondary educational system.

LDCs differ widely in delivery of secondary education; in countries where the education system does not include computer literacy and some experience with computers, education of personnel will be necessary. The education must extend beyond the simple requirements of the job; using computers is most effective if there is a suitable mental model or framework to guide decisions and actions.

Many less developed countries view technology as the essential condition for catching up with developed countries. There is frequently an undue emphasis on technology and a failure to recognize the importance of educational infrastructure, work discipline, removal of barriers to change, etc. This is most effectively done as part of the general education but if not, it must be done on the job by organizations introducing computers.

Culture as a Limiting Factor in Computer Use

An observation that is frequently made with respect to computers is that information systems cause change. They alter relationships in organizations, change jobs, affect organizational power, and modify job social interaction. These changes are affected by cultural conditions. Various authors have reasoned that information systems are social systems that use information technology (Hirschheim, 1986; Smithson & Land, 1986). An approach to analysis of such systems is the Kling (1980) web model. In this context, it is sufficient to view culture and social systems within organizations as limiting factors in computer use. There are such a variety of cultural conditions that may have an effect, that it is not possible to analyze them in this chapter. Rather the effect of cultural conditions will be illustrated by examples.

Example: In the example given earlier of change by India to a computerized reservation system eliminated the use of *baksheesh* to obtain reservations. However, customs are difficult to eliminate and so the computerized reservation system was not completely successful in eliminating *baksheesh*. The Western custom of overselling flights was not followed, so the agents at the airport made decisions about standby passengers. An experience recounted by a traveler was that the information system maintained a waitlist and assigned a priority number. This use of information technology was overridden by the agents at the airport who disregarded the waiting list in favor of *baksheesh* for assigning seats made available by no shows.

Example: The computer as a symbol of power and progress. When the People's Republic of China became open to Western technology, many institutions obtained computers. Western visitors often commented on the respect for the technology demonstrated by limited access and use of sandals rather than street shoes. They also commented on the rather low usage at many installations. During that early period, the existence of modern technology was apparently more important than the usage. This same phenomenon has been reported for other LDCs and other technologies.

Example: Hiring family members. In some less developed countries, the loyalty of persons is much more to family, extended family, tribe, etc. than to a larger society. Since most jobs in an undeveloped society can be done without specialized training, there is a tendency to hire within a limited family or extended family. This has some favorable effects in terms of work group cohesion. However, when technology is introduced that requires both general educational qualifications and specialized skills, the family hiring system can be detrimental.

Tendency to Ignore Organizational and Managerial Considerations

There is a tendency in less developed countries to focus on computer technology and to not pay sufficient attention to the organizational and managerial problems of using the technology effectively (Mohan, Belardo & BjQrn-Andersen, 1990). Computer technology, especially at the micro- and mini-computer level, is very easy to transfer to a less developed country. Technical skills such as programming can be easily taught. The difficulty is that information systems interact with organizations and, in general, computers cannot be used effectively without making some organizational changes.

Intellectual Property Rights Protection

Developed countries have well established protection via patents and copyrights for intellectual property. Many LDCs have been slow to adopt such protection. For example, during the late 1980s, Singapore and Taiwan finally adopted copyright protection. The People's Republic of China was delaying implementation of protection. Other LDCs have moved slowly or not at all.

The reason this issue is important for less developed countries and information technology is because computer software and educational materials are copyrighted. A less developed country may wish to encourage pirating of software and books in order to reduce its costs of information technology. However, the lack of protection may inhibit companies from setting up sales and service facilities for the country. For example, the vendor of a leading simulation software package for microcomputers will not sell to the People's Republic of China and has no mechanism for servicing potential customers located there.

SOME COMMENTS ABOUT RESEARCH

The literature on the introduction of computers in LDCs has tended to focus on governmental use. A recent conference provides a broad set of papers related to computers in developing countries.

Bhatnagar, S.C., and BjQrn-Andersen, N. (Editors), Information Technology in Developing Countries, Amsterdam: North-Holland, 1990.

This is a report of the Working Conference sponsored by the International Federation for Information Processing (IFIP) Technical Committees 8 (Information Systems) and 9 (Relationship Between Computers and Society). The Conference, titled "Impact of Information Systems on Developing Countries," was held in New Delhi, India, 24-26 November 1988. The Conference report is useful for those interested in information systems in developing countries. The sections of the report are:

> Section 1: Frameworks for Developing Information Systems in Developing Countries

> Section 2: Country/Regional Reports of Computerisation in Developing Countries

> Section 3: Computerisation in Specific Sectors and Other Related Issues

SYNTHESIS AND SUMMARY

Because cost displacement is not usually a suitable basis for introducing computers into organizations in LDCs, the basis should be value added. This may be value added that aids competitive advantage, meets competition, or improves or enhances procurement, production, marketing, or distribution. A decision criterion of hard savings or benefits and positive rate of return is generally appropriate at the introduction of information technology.

A necessary condition for the initial applications for information systems is a pre-existing procedural discipline that is amenable to computerization. This is usually found in accounting and engineering applications. These initial applications form the basis for organizational learning to diffuse the concept of computer application procedural discipline throughout the organization. The diffusion of procedural discipline by organizational learning is the underlying phenomenon that governs the progression of an organization in a less developed country through the stages of the Nolan Stage Model.

Especially in the initial applications it is important to not violate or clash with organizational or national culture. The reason for this principle with initial applications is that there are already sufficient problems of implementation and the organizational changes and organizational learning associated with it. Conflict with culture may add enough problems that the initial applications fail. Later applications may be able to deal with culture changes; initial ones generally cannot.

While the introduction of computer technology can take place with a rather primitive infrastructure, the organization will be constrained in moving to more sophisticated applications by the lack of a modern technology infrastructure. This will include reliable electrical power source, educated personnel, and general training. If the nation does not provide this infrastructure, the organization must make the investment.

References

Benbasat, I., Dexter, A.S., Drury, D.H., & Goldstein, R.C. (May, 1984). A critique of the 'Stage Hypothesis': Theory and empirical evidence. *Communications of the ACM, 27*(5), 476-485.

Bhatnagar, S.C., & BjQrn-Andersen, N. (Eds.). (1990). *Information Technology in Developing Countries.* Amsterdam: North-Holland.

Feldman, M.S., & March, J.G. (June, 1981). Information in organizations as signal and symbol. *Administrative Science Quarterly, 26,* 171-186.

Gibson, C.F., & Nolan, R.L. (January/February, 1974). Managing the four stages of EDP growth. *Harvard Business Review,* 76-88.

Hirschheim, R.A. (June, 1986). The effect of a priori views on the social implications of computing: The case of office automation. *Computing Surveys, 18*(2), 165-195.

International Business Machines. (1963). *Study Organization Plan Documentation Techniques* (C20-8075-0), International Business Machines Corporation, White Plains, New York.

King, J.L., & Kraemer, K.L. (May, 1984). Evolution and organizational information systems: An assessment of Nolan's stage model. *Communications of the ACM, 27*(5), 466-475.

Kling, R. (1980). Social analyses of computing: Theoretical perspectives in recent empirical research. *Computing Surveys, 12,* 61-110.

McFarlan, F.W., & McKenney, J.L. (1983). *Corporate Information Systems Management: The Issues Facing Senior Executives.* Homewood, IL: Richard D. Irwin, Inc.

Mohan, L., Belardo, S., & BjQrn-Andersen, N. (1990). A contingency approach to managing information technology in developing nations: Benefitting from lessons learned in developing nations. In S.C. Bhatnagar & N. BjQrn-Andersen (Eds.), *Information Technology in Developing Countries.* Amsterdam: North-Holland, 15-22.

Nolan, R.L. (1984). Managing the advanced stages of computer technology: Key research issues.

In F.W. McFarlan (Ed.), *The Information Systems Research Challenge*. Boston: Harvard Business School Press, 195-214.

Nolan, R.L. (March, 1973). Managing the computer resource: A stage hypothesis. *Communications of the ACM, 16*(3), 399-405.

Nolan, R.L. (March/April, 1979). Managing the crisis in data processing. *Harvard Business Review,* 115-126.

Porter, M. (1980). *Competitive Strategy.* New York: The Free Press.

Smithson, S.C., & Land, F.F. (1986). Information systems education for development. *Information Technology for Development, 1*(2), 59-74.

17   A Transaction Costs Model of International Information Technology Transfers: The Dynamics of Intelligence and Control

A. Lee Gilbert
United Nations Economic and Social Commission
for Asia and the Pacific

Successful transfers of information technology require planning, establishing, and managing complex links between internal and external innovation. International transfers require planning and managing an even more complex chain of activities. This chapter links several theoretical models and schools of thought to demonstrate the links between private sector strategy, public policy, and planning. A contingency theory of planning based on this integrative framework is validated via a series of eight case studies.

INTRODUCTION

Successful technology transfers require linking three innovations: acquiring technology (including the knowledge and skills required for use), applying this technology in the organization, and managing the reconfigured activities toward desired goals. While all technology transfers cross legal boundaries, international transfers require that these processes also cross national boundaries. Strategic transfers differ only in that they use the newly acquired technology to alter the power relationships between organizational stakeholders.

Organizational structure is "first, the lines of authority and communication between the different administrative offices and officers, and second, the information and data that flow through these lines of communication and authority" (Chandler, 1988). Information flows, as communication among members of an organization, also determine the adoption of innovations

(Rogers, 1962). But information technology (IT) can be used to redirect communications flows. This inseparability of information technology-based innovation from organizational process has implications for international business strategy and for national development policy. This, according to the visionary American banker, Walter Wriston, is because:

> Knowledge has always conferred power upon those who have it and know how to use it, and the proliferation and dissemination of information to huge numbers of people can be, and more often than not is, a precursor to a shift in the power structure (Wriston, 1989).

This chapter begins with a multi disciplinary overview of the concept of technology and the processes by which it is transferred. A research framework derived from the cybernetic (Ashby, 1956), value chain (Porter & Millar, 1985), and transaction costs models (Williamson, 1985) integrates these diverse perspectives. This framework then provides the base for a contingency model of information technology planning, validated via a series of case studies. The recommendations which follow are based on analysis of the cases in the context of the model.

TECHNOLOGY AND THE TECHNOLOGY TRANSFER PROCESS

Technology is far more than those static objects we see (Tornatzky & Klein, 1982). Technology has been defined as a "package" (Kraemer & King, 1983) which includes the physical object and the knowledge which it represents, plus the social arrangements for their use. From this perspective, the flint arrowhead used by tribal hunters first draws our attention to the process of producing the tool, then to effects from its use on the patterns of a tribe's hunting and defense activities.

Technology interacts with the context in which it is created and used, not merely as a static input to production processes. Further, the social consequences of technology are not neutral, because use transforms the value (not only economic, but social value) of labor and other inputs to production. From a strategic perspective, technology must be defined in terms of the transformations in the relationships between individual or collective users and their economic, social, and physical environment, resulting from its use. This perspective draws attention to the structural effects from the use of bow-and-arrow technology on hunters, warriors, or others within a tribe, to shifts in power between tribes which adopt bow-and-arrow technology versus those using spears or other technologies, to the primary effects of such use on the wildlife population, and to the secondary effects on their habitat.

Technology transfer is human activity related to the innovation process, and requires communication flows between the actors: source, receiver, and those in the environment (Rogers, 1986). The motivation of a source to engage in technology transfer ranges from social justice to commercial gain. Such transfers may not always require assistance from a source, while others take place despite the best efforts of a source to block the diffusion of its technological secrets. The receiver's objective is to bypass delay, mitigate risk, or reduce other costs inherent in the generation of new technological solutions from internal resources. Actors in the environment include the government, whose policy may create incentives or barriers to technology transfer, such as direct or indirect subsidies, the laws creating industrial property rights or otherwise limiting competition, and tax regulations which differentially treat expenses for each of the elements in the transfer process. International transfers involve foreign investment, movements of foreign exchange, flows of technical expertise, and other factors regulated or influenced by national policy.

One model of technology transfer links physical artifacts (devices or products) and "know-how" (data or information) across four elements of the transformation process: technique, knowledge, the organization of production, and the product (Muller, 1981). Technique is the pattern of interaction between production factors (raw material, capital facilities such as machinery or tools, and human abilities or labor) at the process level. Knowledge consists of the applied science, skills, and even intuition inherent in the creation and use of a specific process. Organization of production is structured by technique and knowledge, but also by the economic and social structure of the environment. The product which results mediates between the elements which determine its production and the legal, economic, and social context in which it is distributed and consumed. These four elements (technique, knowledge, organization, and product) interact as a system, in that change in any one element leads to corresponding changes in others (Lorentzen, 1990).

The Technology Transfer Cycle

Technology transfer alters the technological process of a receiver organization through the introduction of one or more of these technology elements from a source. A complete technology transfer cycle consists of three phases:

Acquisition: It is difficult to identify technologies which may provide advantages to an organization because of the wide choice and imperfect information about the availability, performance, adaptability, and life cycle costs for alternative technologies. This phase requires high-level knowledge from external sources (intelligence) regarding the probable implications of known alternatives, such as effects on the product and organization. The primary objective is the transfer of technique, plus the tacit knowledge which will be required for its installation and subsequent utilization. A variety of mechanisms, such as joint ventures, outright purchase, leasing, licensing, and training are available. These usually involve some form of transaction.

Mutual Adaptation: The installation and efficient operation of technology within its design parameters requires organization of the receiver environment to meet the specifications intended by the source. Transfers ending here rarely attain their full performance potential, because optimum performance normally requires mutual adjustments to the technique and the receiver organization. This learning phase is focused on two tasks: adapting the technique to accept local skills and materials inputs, while adapting the receiver's managerial structure and processes to master the still evolving technique.

Initiatives: By the end of a full transfer cycle, the receiver organization should have acquired new technological assets: the technique, knowledge, and organization to enable it to improve installed technology, generate new technology packages based on the abilities gained during transfer, transfer such new packages to similar sites, and create other new or improved products.

The level of technology transfer is reflected in the increased individual and collective abilities which are acquired during a cycle. At the lowest level is the know-how used to operate and maintain a technology, at the next that required to adapt and improve technologies, and only at the highest level those abilities needed to internally generate new technologies surpassing those previously acquired. Potential extrinsic rewards, inherent risks, and resource requirements rise rapidly from one level to another. Therefore, the level to be pursued in a given case should balance the present circumstances and future goals of both the source and receiver organizations.

Strategic Transfer of Information Technology

Information technology (IT) may be used as a strategic tool to transform links between organizations (Barrett & Konsynski, 1982). IT thus provides a means to restructure economic opportunities. Formulating and implementing such information technology-based strategies, and shaping the public policies needed to facilitate their success, requires not only an understanding of information technology as a form of innovation, but as an economic tool for national development.

Information Technology-based Innovations

Innovation as action is the introduction and subsequent first use of technology in a specific context. Diffusion is the process of spreading initial uses to new, but related contexts. The classic model of diffusion has five elements: "diffusion is the process by which (a) an innovation is (b) communicated through (c) certain channels (d) over time, among the (e) members of a social system" (Rogers, 1986). However, the distinctions between the elements of the process become blurred for innovations (including information systems) which require interaction between the source and receiver to adapt the attributes of the technology and behavior in the receiver's system. More recent diffusion research reveals that the attributes of innovations which predict not only an initial adoption, but its long-term success, are those perceived by targeted users as important for their job performance (Tornatzky & Klien, 1982). Perceptions of the value of new systems by end users, which thus determine their innovation response, are heavily influenced by the introduction process (Leonard-Barton & Sviokla 1988).

A concrete example of these concepts emerges from the examination of a specific (if over-publicized) information technology-based innovation. Designed to mimic the reasoning tasks of experts, expert systems may be used to solve problems. Expert systems have two main parts: a shell, and a knowledge base. The shell is a system of computer programs, and includes an "inference engine" to perform symbolic reasoning, a diagnostic tool to trace the logic path used for the solution, and an interface to communicate with users. These components represent current expert systems technique. The knowledge base results from the organization of heuristic knowledge used by an expert to solve well-defined problems in a restricted domain. This knowledge is represented as the information needed to make decisions, and the decisions to be taken based upon this information in some bounded domain. This must be converted to rules, restructured to reduce redundancy and internal conflict, then integrated with a shell. The new system may be used within an organization to improve its performance, and if it is also relevant in external contexts, might be sold to others. But converting an expert systems-based internal application to a product may consume thousands of additional hours of effort (Feigenbaum, et al. 1988).

Information Technology Transfer as an Economic Tool

The value of technology parallels the economics of information. Data become information only by communication. The quality and relevance of the information to a specific context determines its value.

In mathematics, the relationship between the terms in an equation represents structural information, while the values of the terms are parametric information. Structural information determines the potential of an entity to respond and guides the receiver response to parametric information communicated in signals (Langlois, 1983). As in any computer program, the rules in an expert system are structural information. Rules can be structured to initiate actions (e.g., transactions) to alter relationships between entities, based on the values of parametric information (e.g., market prices) acquired at low cost via telecommunications linkages. Data are transformed into information immediately upon receipt, while a deferred investment in structural information results in knowledge.

The value of knowledge is determined partly by the probability of its use in multiple contexts (Gotlieb, 1985). Knowledge with a low probability of use has the economic properties of a public good: efficiency is maximized when barriers to its access are low (Arrow, 1974). This applies to knowledge in library books, stored in computer databases, and imbedded in computer programs, whether as algorithms or the rules used by expert systems.

However, the economic effects of information technologies vary. Data networks provide increasing returns on use for transmitting information. An expert system, by capitalizing parametric information for which the expected value added is high, reduces the future cost of its use. Mainframe computers and databases provide economies of scale which favor large institutions, network technologies offer economies of scope which favor organizations with large membership, while expert systems offer economies of scope to small entities faced with complex tasks. For those entities with specialized skills and access to differentiated markets, the combination of expert systems and networks might be used to minimize costs for negotiating, monitoring, and enforcing transactions (Coase, 1937). To the extent that new forms of cooperation between organizations are enabled, "intelligent networks" provide new sources of competitive advantage.

Entity	Source	Integrator	Local Adopters	End User
Family Planning Methods	Pharmaceutical Maker	International Development Agency	Community Development Agency	Cambodian Refugee
Medical Records Systems	Computer Maker	Custom Software Development Firm	Ministry of Health Hospital	Medical Staff, Public

VALUE ADDED: —ACQUISITION—> —ADAPTATION—> —USE—>
Effects: Technical   Organizational   Developmental

Figure 1: Technology Transfer as Development

Technology Transfer as a Mode of Development

Development can be defined as the new value added to its members by a society. Technology transfer adds value in stages: Acquisition generates technical benefits; Adaptation reconfigures activity in a value chain (Porter, 1990). The path along which value is added extends from a technology source to end users, as portrayed in Figure 1.

Acquisition as a Source of Technical Benefits: Science enables the development of new technologies, which are packaged for use by adopters. Technology is acquired in three steps: Scanning the market for potentially useful technologies, Evaluating the features to identify technical benefits which may add value, and Negotiating with sources to define the terms. More precise information about life cycle costs, technical benefits, and potential value is needed as a receiver's commitment increases (Arrow, 1974). Integrators mediate between sources of technology and the local adopters of technology, narrowing technology choices and adding value for selected types of end users, thus reducing the inherently high transaction costs in this step.

Adaptation as a Source of Organizational Benefits: Use of information technology may be directed toward internal goals such as lowering costs, increasing the value of products or services, or substituting for scarce skills (Porter & Millar, 1985). Such uses may distribute new benefits to some stakeholders and new costs to others: the redistribution is determined by interaction between the problem and the design (Perrolle, 1988). For example, the problems which are likely candidates for expert systems are those which can be clearly described in words, solved in a few hours, and for which the abilities that designate experts are clear (Leonard-Barton & Sviokla, 1988). An expert system may be designed either to increase the productivity of experts for routine tasks, or to enhance the abilities of less experienced workers; dependence on scarce skills may thus be avoided. Problems which an expert system is designed to solve may previously have been ignored, at higher risk; solved by consultants, with loss of learning; or solved by internal experts, who may experience either gains in efficiency or reductions in demand for their expertise. These design decisions allocate costs and benefits to organizational stakeholders.

Potential net benefits may not always be available. Unless technical benefits can be captured and converted to added value through changes in decision making, new information systems merely add to costs. Changes in information flows shift economic and social costs between employees and other stakeholders. Flexibility in job content and organizational structure is a critical success factor; when these factors are difficult to alter, the potential benefits are limited.

Strategic Initiatives as End Use: Information Technology Initiatives are uses which alter strategic relationships with buyers (e.g., American Hospital Supply's *ASAP Express*), clients (e.g., American Express's *Credit Authorizer's Assistant*), or other stakeholders (Gilbert & Vitale, 1988).

Information Technology Initiatives may be intended to alter transaction costs (those for negotiating, monitoring and enforcing agreements) in specific markets (Williamson, 1985). A network of cooperating firms is an alternative to markets or hierarchies if transaction costs can be reduced for participants (Jarillo, 1988). The market position and scale of many locally owned enterprises in the third world is appropriate to a network strategy, which could take full advantage of the combined economic effect of expert systems and telecommunications. However, the inherent flexibility of information technology endows such a strategy with downside risks. Failure may be triggered either by internal effects of, or an environmental response to, the use of information technology when it plays a structural role in an organization or industry (Vitale, 1986; Johnston & Vitale, 1988). As the external effects of strategic innovations cannot be completely predicted, strategic planning is one means to mitigate the risks inherent in their use.

Linking Technology Transfer Policy, Strategy, and Planning

Information technology policy and strategy are linked. Information processing is now the world's major economic activity, while organizations are the primary focus of economic development. The public thus has an interest in improving the information processing productivity of private organizations. Strategic uses of technology may also affect individuals, group and institutional relationships, and even societal values (Laudon, 1986). National policy determines the competitiveness of organizations within its borders by easing or hampering automated interconnections between enterprises. These have become a prerequisite for suppliers in certain industries (Barrett & Konsynski, 1982).

Interconnections are influenced by policy in three ways: by defining standards and infrastructure determining efficient organizational boundaries for networks; governing access to and ownership of networks; and regulating market structure for these services (Estrin, 1987). For industries based on long-distance networks, such as shipping, air transport, and telecommunications, the strategic forces are transnational. Also, major information technology decisions require heavy investments which will generate benefits only over a long cycle of use. Such commitments are not easily reversible, and influence other decisions such as the location of facilities and the creation of employment.

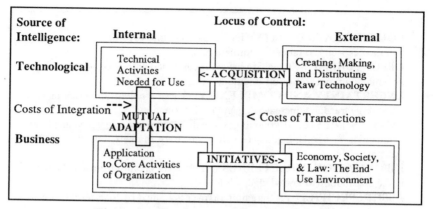

Figure 2: The Control-Intelligence Model

While the need for policy is very clear, no current approach to planning reliably pinpoints and mitigates the risks inherent in growing dependence on the widespread use of information technology (Vitale, 1986).

TECHNOLOGY TRANSFER PLANNING: A TRANSACTION COSTS MODEL

Technology transfer, a form of innovation, is the process of introducing into a new context a "package" of technique, knowledge, organization and product (Muller, 1981). Long-term studies by Kenneth Kraemer and John King (1983) of computer use by public sector organizations in North America and Europe examined relationships between innovation activities according to their locus: either external or internal to the receiver organization, and within its technical infrastructure or its core activities. Their research showed that economic and political forces (not technology) were the driving forces for information technology adoption and organizational change. The Control-Intelligence (C-I) model redefines the Kraemer and King model's activity boundaries as the locus of control (whether an activity is controlled within or external to the receiving organization), and the source of intelligence (whether information is derived from business or technological activity) (Gilbert & Vitale, 1988). The C-I model defines four static and three dynamic types of adoption activities for information technology-based innovations, and examines the linkages between them:

The C-I model (Figure 2) differentiates between static and dynamic activities. Static activity, represented within a single cell in the model, (e.g., computer operations in cell 2, or manufacturing in cell 3), influences perform-

---

BOUNDED RATIONALITY: Individuals and thus organizations have only a limited capacity to process information;

OPPORTUNISM: Self-seeking behavior combined with guile deprives decision making processes of information;

UNCERTAINTY AND COMPLEXITY: These problems, inherent in technology transfers, increase demand for information;

SMALL NUMBERS: Bargaining power distributed to a select few, and large inequalities in bargaining power distort not only markets, but entire value systems;

INFORMATION IMPACTEDNESS: Inefficiency results from asymmetries in the distribution of knowledge; while

ASSET SPECIFICITY: Bargaining power is limited by long-term commitments to a specific type of transaction.

Figure 3: Sources of Transaction Costs

ance, but not the overall pattern of activity. Dynamic activity, represented as a path between cells, is the means by which new technologies and other forms of change are introduced. *ACQUISITION* (technology scanning, selection and transfer, between cells 1 and 2) normally involves a transaction between a source and receiver. The design and use of an information system requires *MUTUAL ADAPTATION* (Levinson, 1985; Leonard-Barton & Sviokla, 1988) between technological (cell 2) and core business (cell 3) activities. A use which purposefully shifts relationships with external entities such as customers or clients (Barrett & Konsynski, 1982) is an information technology-based *INITIATIVE*, and involves transactions between cells 3 and 4. Cross-domain activities thus generate costs for transactions with external entities (Williamson, 1985) or internal costs for integration activity (Lawrence & Lorsch, 1967). These costs, sources of which are listed in Figure 3, are influenced by access to and the capacity to process information (Jones & Hill, 1988).

Four Generic Approaches to Technology Transfer Planning

The C-I model views information technology transfer as an interactive process between actors trained in multiple disciplines with varying organizational interests. Planning activity mediates between these perspectives and facilitates integration between activities. Although many methodologies for planning such transfers have been developed, the choice of an effective approach in a given situation is a practical problem which has yet to be resolved.

This can be viewed as a more general problem related to decision making in organizations. Allison (1971) identified three competing decision paradigms (information processing, rational action, and political negotiation).

Four generic approaches (Top-Down, Middle-Out, Integrated, and Learn-by-Doing) to technology transfer planning can be derived from these. A Top-Down (information processing) model relies on structural mechanisms to contain uncertainty and to shape its environment (Galbraith, 1973; Allaire & Firsirotu, 1989). Such strategic management (McFarlan, 1984) or executive (Kraemer, et al 1989) approaches assume that internal conflict (and integration costs) can be contained. The Middle-Out (or rational action) approach (IBM, 1975; Henderson & Sifonis, 1988) assumes that technologists have implementation capacity and sufficient credibility to link information technology to strategic plans. However, such "predict and prepare" models are blind to the transaction costs flowing from environmental instability. An Integrated (political) approach requires top management participation, as decisions result from negotiation (Wiseman, 1985). It assumes that technical leaders have full access to strategic planning processes (Galliers, 1988). The default is to Learn by Doing, by allocating slack resources to a continuous ad-hoc planning process. This approach assumes that lessons gained from the use of technology are captured at the bottom and transmitted to the top of the organization.

Research Proposition. *PLANNING OUTCOMES CAN BE PREDICTED BY THE "FIT" BETWEEN A GIVEN INFORMATION TECHNOLOGY PLANNING APPROACH AND ITS STRATEGIC CONTEXT.* A specific approach to technology transfer planning is a decision making system, which is differentiated by technical and other features determining its performance in a specific situation. The management problem is to select a system which fits the specific situation. A contingency model for selecting a planning approach can be defined in terms of the interaction between the organization and its environment. The key factors are operationalized as environmental turbulence, factors which generate uncertainty (Simon, 1957) and increase organizational demand for services from its information technology function; and *Information Technology Heritage*, a supply of resources needed to plan and implement information technology-based solutions (Feeney, 1986). The theory is simple. Limited communication between information technology and business functions is needed to meet low demand with a weak supply of information technology resources. The interaction required for effective planning increases with these factors, so that planning processes should become more integrated as they increase. When one factor is dominant, the flow of planning communications will be unidirectional.

Hypothesis 1: RATIONAL DECISION MAKING PROCESSES WILL BE UNSUITABLE, GIVEN HIGH ENVIRONMENTAL TURBULENCE. This construct represents high demand for information, as a function of uncertainty and variety in the forces which organize markets (Porter, 1990), and in the political, social, and legal issues shaping the mission (Chandler, 1990). In theory, speedy decision making is needed when environmental turbulence is high, so organizational performance improves with processes which trigger action and with the decentralization of power to functional managers (Bourgeois & Eisenhardt, 1988).

Hypothesis 2: **TOP-DOWN DECISION MAKING PROCESSES WILL BE UNSUITABLE, GIVEN A STRONG I.T. HERITAGE.** The "Information Technology Heritage" is the supply (at a given point in time) of an internal capacity to use information technology to respond to organizational changes in the demand for information. The Information Technology Heritage includes technique (hardware and software), access to knowledge, architecture and the organization of resources. Knowledge is the quality of management, user, and technical skills for the assimilation and use of information technology; the flexibility and end user-orientation of arrangements for Information Technology use; and the credibility of key information technology personnel. Architecture is a term used to characterizes structural relationships between the various information technologies and applications within an organization. With a strong I.T. heritage, strategic and executive approaches are not very effective.

Hypothesis 3: **THE FIT BETWEEN AN APPROACH TO IN-FORMATION TECHNOLOGY PLANNING AND THE ORGANIZA-TIONAL CONTEXT IS ADEQUATELY DESCRIBED AS AN INTER-ACTION BETWEEN SUPPLY AND DEMAND FORCES.** Environmental Turbulence and the IT Heritage represent the demand for and supply of information technology. Transaction and integration costs influence these supply and demand factors. New planning systems are management innovations (Rogers, 1986) which govern the allocation of information technology resources. A poor fit between a planning approach and its context (Weill & Olsen, 1989) results in poor performance. For example, a given methodology

strong		
	MIDDLE-OUT • style is rational • data-intensive • high complexity • uncontained risk	INTEGRATED • style is negotiation • time-intensive • low certainty • very high risk
	• style is mixed • low communications • low stakes • low complexity LEARN BY DOING	• style is learning • information-intensive • high stakes • contained risk TOP-DOWN
weak		
	low	high
	ENVIRONMENTAL TURBULENCE	

Figure 4: A Theory of IT Planning

may require inputs which are unavailable in a specific situation (e.g., top management participation and explicit strategies), produce outputs which inhibit control, or which are unusable in the later steps (Brancheau & Wetherbe, 1986). Figure 4 portrays the hypothetical relationship between the four generic approaches and the environmental context:

THE RESEARCH PROGRAM

A field research program was initiated in 1986 to explore these hypotheses. The first step was to acquire a database of information technology planning cases which represented a range of contexts: the public and private sectors, high-growth and mature industries, and ranging from North America to the developing world. Many of these cases were developed while the author was a Fellow of the Future Information Systems Faculty at the Harvard Business School; some are drawn from well-documented published cases, and the remainder were derived by participant-observer methods while the author was a practicing information systems manager and consultant in the US and Asia.

As the next step, an independent rating exercise was conducted to validate the contingency variables. A written description of the Environmental Turbulence and Information Technology Heritage constructs was provided to an expert, who was asked to rate these factors on a three-interval scale for twenty cases which had previously been rated by the author. The expert was unable to rate two cases from the information provided. The correlation between the ratings of the author and the expert for the remaining cases exceeded .90 for both constructs. The long-term objective is to validate the model as a diagnostic instrument for use by practitioners. The section following reports the status of the current research.

Case Selection

As an initial test of the model, a sample of eight North American and international cases was selected from the database to represent the full range of planning approaches, and to portray both successes and failures, either in planning or implementation. These cases (many of which are published elsewhere) are briefly abstracted below:

INTERNATIONAL AIRLINE: Singapore Airlines

LOCATION: Southeast Asia
ENVIRONMENTAL TURBULENCE: High

I.T. HERITAGE(relative):	Intermediate
PLANNING STYLE:	TOP-DOWN
OUTCOME OF PLAN:	Fully Implemented

A rapidly growing Asian merchant airline with a market image based on its cabin service quality began expert systems use by designing and implementing a system to aid three executive chefs (two were expatriates) in preparing menus for in-flight meals. This complex and exacting task required frequent updates (as flights were often rescheduled or added) and quarterly revisions. Several hundred rules were required for this small system, which was not used to make decisions, but to respond to tentative choices made by a chef, to present alternatives, and to print the final plan.

Strategy: This simple application was credited by management with helping to avoid a loss in quality while new routes were being added, thus supporting an aggressive growth strategy. Planning was directed by top management, and a consultant was engaged to insure that the information systems staff gained experience with the new technology for use in improving its future cabin crew scheduling practices (Gilbert, 1988).

FINANCIAL SERVICES: Financial Designs

LOCATION:	US
ENVIRONMENTAL TURBULENCE:	High
I. T. HERITAGE:	Low
PLANNING STYLE:	ISOLATED
OUTCOME OF PLAN:	Implemented, later abandoned

Preparing personalized investment plans for wealthy clients is not a well-structured task, and the financial services industry is extremely competitive. A highly specialized investment planning firm sought to expand its capacity by adopting an expert system to support its small group of professionals.

Strategy: Led into the system by a technology enthusiast, the firm had no clear idea of what the benefits and costs would be, or how the system might affect relationships with its clients. It became clear only with use that the system was incompatible with the current structure and strategy of the firm, and it was eventually abandoned (Sviokla, 1985).

FUEL DISTRIBUTOR: Pacific Pride

| LOCATION: | US |
| ENVIRONMENTAL TURBULENCE: | High |

I. T. HERITAGE: Weak
PLANNING STYLE: TOP-DOWN
OUTCOME OF PLAN: Fully Implemented

A commercial Pacific Northwest fuel vendor developed a regional network of unmanned computer-controlled service stations for use by corporate fleets. The concept was to report fuel use by vehicle and driver, based on data collected at the time of fuel purchase, thus assisting fleet operators with their internal vehicle management and loss control processes. Fleet owners saw this information as value added to fuel: the vendor received a premium price by altering the terms of trade in a commodity market.

Strategy: Had the system failed to provide buyers with the desired level of control, the concept of an unmanned station selling fuel at a premium price might not have been viable. Selection of a simple, proven technology package minimized transaction costs in the acquisition step. The small scale of the young firm facilitated adaptation and minimized integration costs. These factors allowed information technology planning to be directed from the top level of the firm, until the growth of the enterprise required the task to be delegated to an MIS manager (Vitale, 1988).

IMPORTED AUTOMOBILE DISTRIBUTOR: Volvo NA

LOCATION: North America
ENVIRONMENTAL TURBULENCE: High
I.T.. HERITAGE: Weak
PLANNING STYLE: MIDDLE-OUT, then
                                   INTEGRATED
OUTCOME OF PLAN: Implemented but abandoned

New Japanese products were targeted directly at the market niche occupied by this U.S. distributor of quality European cars. A new vehicle distribution system was needed to improve product allocation, but rigid cost controls limited information technology development capacity. Three years were lost when MIS-led planning efforts ("we're good at construction, and if we get good specifications, we can build it") resulted in a technically sound new system, but with inappropriate features from the business perspective.

Strategy: Marketing engaged an experienced consulting firm, then transferred from one of its field offices a project leader who had previously worked for a leader in the use of information technology (a competitor). The Marketing VP, facing stiff internal opposition to a $2.5 million project budget (the largest in the firm's history), identified the project as the cost of correct product distribution. This clarified the required features and led to a new distribution system which successfully decentralized access to vehicle availability data for Volvo's regional marketing staff and reconfigured the distribution value chain (Gilbert, 1987).

OIL FIELD SUPPLIER: Baroid

LOCATION:	International
ENVIRONMENTAL TURBULENCE:	High
I.T. HERITAGE:	Strong
PLANNING STYLE:	INTEGRATED
OUTCOME OF PLAN:	Fully Implemented

In an oil field in the developing world, the use of experienced expatriates to monitor offshore drilling often conflicts with government policy to nationalize employment in the industry. But task performance is critical, as the daily operating cost of a drilling rig can exceed $500,000, and an error may stop work for days or weeks. When trained (but inexperienced) local workers were assigned to this task, they had difficulty interpreting the 20-plus parameters from the well logs, managing the many variables in the makeup of the drilling fluid, and writing required reports (Sviokla, 1985).

Strategy: The use of MUDMAN (an expert system designed for these tasks) was proposed by top management. This gave local workers access to the experience of experts who designed the rule base and reduced total labor costs, but also decreased the demand for expatriate skills during a slack exploration period. After negotiations between management and offshore workers, the system was fully implemented (Gilbert, 1988).

TOY RETAILER: Child World

LOCATION:	US
ENVIRONMENTAL TURBULENCE:	Medium High
I.T. HERITAGE:	Intermediate
PLANNING STYLE:	MIDDLE-OUT, then INTEGRATED
OUTCOME OF PLAN:	Partly Implemented

The sales reporting and distribution system used by this toy retailer to sustain its rapid growth acquired data from a point-of-sale (POS) network, which was not integrated with its aging distribution and accounting systems. Failure of its POS system could cripple the "retail machine" strategy articulated by the CEO. The MIS group had experienced difficulty with both implementation and operation of their plans, which were based on use of the IBM BSP methodology.

Strategy: The new MIS VP asked the telecommunications vendor to design and conduct a strategic IT planning process. The resulting plan proposed heavy investments in technology and infrastructure to improve the reliability and availability of the firm's data before initiating automated links with its key suppliers to share POS-originated data (Vitale & Gilbert, 1987). Several minor recommendations contained in the plan were implemented, but the MIS manager was unable to gain support for allocation of the resources needed to implement the full plan, and later resigned.

EMERGING AIRLINE: Malaysian Airlines

LOCATION:	Southeast Asia
ENVIRONMENTAL TURBULENCE:	High
I.T. HERITAGE:	Weak
PLANNING STYLE:	ISOLATED
OUTCOME OF PLAN:	Implemented, later revised

This publicly owned international airline was in transition from a focus on its internal markets to long-haul traffic, and had adapted or developed new information technology systems to support its major core business processes. As the airline's management and technical skills evolved, expatriate employees were rapidly displaced by local staff to support national development policy. Limited information technology development resources were committed to an ambitious long-range plan including a major revision of its computerized reservations system (CRS) (Cash & Gilbert, 1988). Shortly after implementation of this updated CRS, powerful competitors invaded these same markets with technology which offered travel agents desirable system functions which could have been, but were not, installed by the carrier.

Strategy: Although all information technology planning was approved by a top level steering committee, communication between the senior manager of marketing and the relatively inexperienced MIS manager did not identify this critical gap (Interview, 1989).

PUBLIC AGENCY: Ministry of Health

LOCATION:	Asia
ENVIRONMENTAL TURBULENCE:	Medium
I.T. HERITAGE:	Weak
PLANNING STYLE:	MIDDLE-OUT
OUTCOME OF PLAN:	Not Fully Implemented

The Ministry of Health had provided subsidized care to the majority of the population for many years. Supported by the computer services arm of the national government and its computer vendor, its Computer Services Department (CSD) used the IBM Business Systems Planning methodology in an effort to align its plans with government strategy. But these plans committed the Ministry to develop and maintain centralized systems far beyond its technical and managerial capacity, while fierce competition for manpower between the public and private sector increased turnover of its technical staff.

Strategy: A high-level technical team developed a new long-range plan. Orders were placed for mainframe computers and software packages, and the computer vendor was engaged to tailor the features of imported applications to the needs of the Ministry. But by the time these applications were developed and in use, public policy had shifted toward privatisation of the national hospital system, and the emphasis for many systems shifted from resource optimization to revenue collection. (Interview, January 1990).

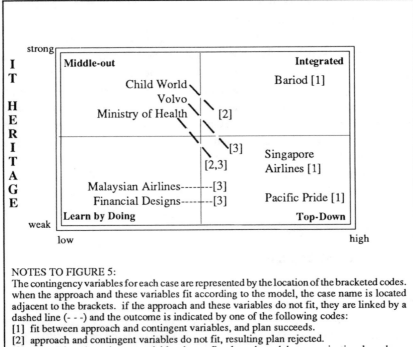

NOTES TO FIGURE 5:
The contingency variables for each case are represented by the location of the bracketed codes. when the approach and these variables fit according to the model, the case name is located adjacent to the brackets. if the approach and these variables do not fit, they are linked by a dashed line (- - -) and the outcome is indicated by one of the following codes:
[1] fit between approach and contingent variables, and plan succeeds.
[2] approach and contingent variables do not fit, resulting plan rejected.
[3] approach and contingent variables do not fit, plan adopted, but organizational needs
    were not met by the resulting systems.

Figure 5: Approaches vs. Outcomes

Case Analysis

The cases generally support the hypotheses derived from the model. For three of the eight cases in the sample, the planning approach matched that indicated by the model, and the plan was adopted and implemented with favorable results. While in the other five cases, the approach varied from that predicted by the model, the results were also unfavorable. In one, the resulting plan was never adopted. In three others, the plan was implemented but led to undesirable outcomes. All four generic planning approaches are represented in the sample, but only one case in the sample portrayed a strong information technology heritage, and none portrayed low environmental turbulence. The cases are mapped to the model in Figure 5 according to the approach (as described above) used to develop the plan.

The Control-Intelligence model has been used mainly as a lens to focus research. It also provides the theoretical basis for the contingency planning model, intended as a diagnostic tool for field use by practitioners, as discussed in the following section.

Evaluating the Control-Intelligence Model

The C-I model is an alternative to the classic innovation model, which views the effects of a technology transfer only at the final step. Actually, the participants within each entity may also experience private and other effects: changes in employment conditions, role status, and in the norms governing their contribution to the value of a product or service. These are reflected in the mediation processes which occur at each boundary in the C-I model.

The primary theoretical value of the C-I model is in representing technology transfers as a series of linked transactions of three different types, and thus isolating the asymmetries in access to information and conflicts in values which determine transaction and integration costs. It may also be useful as a practical tool for diagnosing the risks inherent in a given technology transfer, but its value for this application has not yet been demonstrated.

Evaluating the Proposed Contingency Theory

These early findings are suggestive. Even from this small sample, it seems clear that a Learn-by-Doing approach is inherently risky, and that when environmental turbulence is, or is expected to be, high, Middle-Out (technological) approaches to planning are risky. The analysis indicates that a Top-Down (or executive) approach to planning becomes less useful as the firm builds its information technology Heritage. However, an Integrated approach to planning may also be inherently risky. Technology transfer planning requires the use of multiple techniques at several levels of analysis. The environmental forces which shape the strategy of the enterprise must be evaluated. At another level, the focus is on production system economics (e.g., global costs in the value chain), including the relationships between physical activities and information flows (Porter & Millar, 1985). This information must be accurately communicated between individual tasks within the system of planning, and thus between individuals with very diverse professional training and organizational viewpoints for technology planning to support strategy. Based on these factors, planning tasks will become more complex as the Information Technology Heritage becomes stronger.

In theory, planning tasks should also become more tightly coupled under conditions of high turbulence. Coupling enables activities to be integrated over a broad range of disciplines, and facilitates a rapid response to the changing environmental conditions which shape strategic forces. But systems which are both complex and tightly coupled are prone to failure (Perrow, 1984). Because the sources of risk in tightly coupled systems are serial, the inherent risk of a fully integrated approach to planning will be high unless the structure and flow of planning activities can be configured to decouple time-critical tasks.

RECOMMENDATIONS AND CONCLUSIONS

Creating a policy climate which nurtures international transfers of information technology is particularly relevant to policymakers in developing nations: First, unless organizations are able to use IT to improve their performance, new IT simply results in new expense. Second, the global diffusion of IT means that enterprises in the region will confront strategic issues in planning major IT transfers. Third, the approach selected for planning such transfers may lead either toward failure, dependence, or self-sufficiency.

The successful transfer and use of information technology by local organizations will be a factor in national development, especially for the more information-intensive export-oriented segments of a nation's industrial structure. Until recently, the skills differentiation, specialization, and complexity associated with new technologies favored larger organizations based in high-margin markets. New technologies merely tended to widen the gaps between firms based in industrialized and developing nations. But as information technology is rapidly becoming a commodity, and as globalization of the marketplace becomes a reality, new opportunities are emerging. Even in a global economy, products, services, and activities must still be differentiated to local contexts, where legal practices may vary and where culture is a critical factor. Information technology can be used to add the value of local information to products jointly produced by networks of specialized small firms. And as information reduces transaction costs, it provides such networks with the economies of scope needed to compete with larger firms.

In planning technology policy and strategy, the social and legal effects of information technology transfer on individuals must also be considered. The heavy investments needed to supply technical skills, and the capital required to maintain the telecommunications infrastructure at the international standard, may conflict with economic, political or social needs. At an institutional level, legal and procedural constraints intended to protect local enterprises from competition may be a barrier to the changes required for the adoption of international networks, or inertia may prevent the erection of barriers to loss of individual freedom resulting from increased institutional access to information. At an individual level, unless agreements for technology transfer explicitly address manpower development issues, and local educational institutions are included in the planning process, local professionals will lack the current skills and experience required to participate and contribute. These, like all policy issues, will require discussion and mediation between stakeholders. But the stakes are higher for IT than for other technologies, because the resulting policy decisions also determine the collective growth rate for the IT Heritage. This represents a nation's capacity to initiate or respond to structural changes in its strategic industries.

The primary message of this chapter is that the choice of information technology transfer planning methodologies is not a search for "one optimal way," but for a reasonable fit between an approach to decision making and the specific context in which it will be used. Nations planning to use information technology as a development tool face two strategic tasks: upgrading the policy climate in which technology transfer takes place, and accelerating the acquisition of planning methods and skills by locally based organizations. The C-I model provides both theoretical and practical insights into these two challenges.

References

Allaire, J., and Firsirotu, (Spring, 1989). Coping with Strategic Uncertainty. *Sloan Management Review,* 7-16.

Allison, G. (1971). *Essence of Decision: Explaining the Cuban Missile Crises.* Boston, MA: LIttle, Brown.

Arrow, K. (1974). *The Limits of Organization.* New York, NY: Norton.

Ashby, W. (1956). *An Introduction to Cybernetics.* New York, NY: Wiley Science Editions.

Barrett, S., and Konsynski. (1982). Interorganization Information Sharing Systems. *MIS Quarterly,* Special Issues, 93-105.

Bourgeois, L., and Eisenhardt. (1988). Strategic Decision Processes in High Velocity Environments. *Management Science, 34*(7), 816-842.

Brancheau, J., and Wetherbe. (1986). Information Architecture: Methods and Practices. Working Paper, University of Minnesota School of Management.

Cash, J., and Gilbert. (1988). *Malaysian Airlines Systems*. Boston, MA: Harvard Business School Case Services.

Chandler, A. (1988). Introduction to Strategy and Structure. *In The Essential Alfred Chandler*. Boston, MA: Harvard Business School Press.

Chandler, A. *Scale and Scope: The Dynamics of Industrial Capitalism*. Cambridge, MA: Harvard University Press.

Coase, R. (1937). The Nature of the Firm. *Economica*, n.s., 4.

Estrin, D. (September, 1987). Interconnection of Private Networks. *Telecommunications Policy*.

Feeney, D. (1986). Competition in the Era of Interactive Network Services. Unpublished thesis, Templeton College, Oxford.

Feigenbaum, E., McCorduck, and Nu. (1988). *The Rise of the Expert Company*. New York, NY: Times Books.

Galbraith, J. (1973). *Designing Complex Organizations*. Reading, MA: Addison Wesley.

Galliers, R. (1988). Information Technology Strategies Today: The UK Experience. In Earl, M. *Information Management*, Oxford: Clarendon Press.

Gilbert, L. (1987). *Volvo North America*. Boston, MA: Harvard Business School Case Services.

Gilbert, L. (1988). Information Technology Initiatives in the 1990s. *Proceedings of the Singapore Computer Society*, Singapore.

Gilbert, L., and Vitale. (1988). Containing Strategic Information Systems Risk: Intelligence and Control. *IEEE Proceedings of HICSS-21*, Kona, Hawaii.

Gotlieb, C. (1985). *The Economics of Computers*. Englewood Cliffs, NJ: Prentice Hall.

Henderson, J., and Sifonis. (1988). The Value of Strategic IS Planning. *MIS Quarterly, 12*(2).

IBM, (1975). *Information systems Planning Guide: Business Systems Planning*. IBM Corporation, New York.

Interview (by author) (December, 1989, January, 1990). Discussions with government offices. Kuala Lumpur, Malaysia, and Singapore.

Jarillo, J-C. (1988). On strategic Networks. *Strategic Management Journal, 9*, 31-41.

Johnston, R., and Vitale. (June, 1988). Creating Competitive Advantage with Interorganizational Information Systems. *MIS Quarterly*, 153.

Jones, G., and Hill. (1988). Transaction Cost Analysis of Strategy-Structure Choice. *Strategic Management Journal, 9,* 159-172.

Kraemer, K., and King. (1983). The Dynamics and Evolution of Computing. Working paper for the Conference on Critical Issues for National Computerization Policy, Honolulu, HI.

Kraemer, K. et al. (1989). *Management Information Systems.* San Francisco, CA: Jossey-Bass.

Langlois, R. (1983). System Theory, Knowledge, and the Social Sciences. In Machlup, *The Study of Information,* New York: Wiley.

Laudon, K. (1986). *Dossier Society.* New York: Columbia University Press.

Lawrence, P., and Lorsch. (1967). *Organization and Environment.* Boston, MA: Harvard Business School Press.

Leonard-Barton, D., and Sviokla. (March-April, 1988). Putting Expert Systems to Work. *Harvard Business Review.*

Levinson, E. (1985). Turning Cases into Data: Implementation Path Analysis. *Office: Technology and People, 2,* 287-304.

Lorentzen, A. (1990). Division of Labor and Infrastructure in Technology Transfers. In Chatterji, *Technology Transfer in Developing Countries,* London: Macmillan.

McFarlan, F.W. (March-April, 1984). Information Technology changes the Way You Compete. *Harvard Business Review,* 98-103.

Muller, J. (1981). *Liquidation or Consolidation of Indigenous Technology.* Aalborg: Aalborg University Press.

Perrolle, J. (1988). Artificial Intelligence in the Workplace. In *Social Implications of Artificial Intelligence,* IEEE Professional Program Session Record of Electro/88, Boston, MA.

Perrow, C. (1984). *Normal Accidents: Living with High-Risk Technologies.* New York: Basic Books.

Porter, M. (1990). *The Competitive Advantage of Nations.* Glencoe, IL: Free Press.

Porter, M., and Millar. (1985). How Information Gives You Competitive Advantage. *Harvard Business Review, 63*(4).

Rogers, E. (1962). *Diffusion of Innovations.* New York: Free Press.

Rogers, E. (1986). *Communications Technology.* New York: Free Press.

Simon, H. (1957). *Models of Man, Social and Rational.* New York: Wiley.

Sviokla, J. (1985). *Planpower, XCON and Mudman.* Unpublished DBA Dissertation. Boston, MA: Harvard Business School.

Teece, D. (1977). Technology Transfer by Multinational Firms: The Resource Cost of Transferring Technological Knowhow. *The Economic Journal, 87,* 242-261.

Tornatzky, L., and Klein. (1982).   Innovation Characteristics and Innovation Adoption-Implementation. *IEEE Transactions on Engineering Management, EM-29*(1), 28-45.

Vitale, M. (December, 1986).   The Growing Risks of Information Systems Success. *MIS Quarterly.*

Vitale, M. (1988). *Pacific Pride.* Boston, MA: Harvard Business School Case Services.

Vitale, M., and Gilbert, L. (1987). *Child World Information Systems Planning.* Boston, MA: Harvard Business School Case Services.

Weill, P., and Olsen. (1989).   An Assessment of the Contingency Theory of Management Information Systems. *Journal of Management Information Systems, 6*(1), 59-86.

Williamson, O. (1985). *The Economic Institution of Capitalism.* New York: Free Press.

Wiseman, C. (1985). *Strategy and Computers.* Homewood, IL: Dow Jones-Irwin.

Wriston, W. (Winter, 1988/89). Technology and Sovereignty. *Foreign Affairs,* 63-75.

18 Societal Impacts and Consequences of Transborder Data Flows*

William B. Carper
Georgia Southern University

The information age is here and one of the more important aspects of this new age is that information has become a commodity which has value and which, like any other good, can be bought and sold. Unlike virtually any other product, however, information can be transmitted or shipped from one location to another without ever having to physically move the original data. When this transmission takes place across national boundaries, transborder data flows (TBDFs) are created.

The following chapter examines the general topic of TBDFs by looking at a number of specific problems which result from these international transmissions. The specific problems discussed here are grouped under the headings of Security Issues, Sovereignty Issues, Technical Issues, and Developing Issues. Finding ways of dealing with these issues and their potential consequences for society will be one of the major tasks facing individuals, organizations, and governments as we move into the 21st century.

INTRODUCTION

More than 25 years ago, Marshall McLuhan (1964) coined the term "global village" to characterize the shrinking of the world as a result of the increased speed of communications and information flows created by the electronic age. The creation of the global village meant that the earth had been

*Portions of this chapter were previously published as: "Transborder Data Flows in the Information Age: Implications for International Management" by this author which appeared in the *International Journal of Management*, 4(4), December 1989, 418-425.Societal Impacts and Consequences of Transborder Data Flows

effectively shrunk to the point where distance was irrelevant to the almost instantaneous transmission of information from one place to another.

Twenty years ago, Alvin Toffler (1970, p. 11) spoke of "future shock" as being the "dizzying disorientation brought on by the premature arrival of the future." This premature arrival and accelerated pace of change was fueled by the increasing speed of communications and access to information. In earlier periods, knowledge of events either remained confined to a limited geographic area or took so long to reach others that its impact had been rendered less important by the very passage of the time involved in the transmission. By the 1970s, however, national boundaries and geographic barriers were no longer obstacles to the almost immediate transfer of information.

Eight years ago, John Naisbitt (1982) presented a discussion of the information society as his first "megatrend" and proclaimed that the "industrial era is over." Basing his argument on the fundamental change which occurred in 1956 when more Americans became employed in information oriented jobs than in production oriented ones and on the launching of Sputnik in 1957, Naisbitt believes that global satellite communications, which allow virtually instantaneous access to information stored anywhere in the world from anywhere in the world, will provide the foundation for the society of the 21st century. Since information is a commodity which has value because of its strategic importance to people, there is an increasing need to have it immediately available with "the net effect [being] a faster flow of information through the information channel, bringing sender and receiver closer together."

Today, as the world sees nightly news reports of democratic changes in Eastern Europe, South Africa, mainland China, and even the Soviet Union, the writings of authors such as those cited above come into stark reality with regard to the role of information flows in the global society in which we live. Unlike past generations when messengers could be stopped at borders and executed or printing presses and radio stations could be destroyed to stop the flow of information, back pack satellite transmitters and smuggled video tapes mean that no place in the world can conduct its business in a vacuum.

Clearly, the vivid television pictures of the events in Tiananmen Square during June of 1989, or of the tearing down of the Berlin Wall in February of 1990, or of the freeing of Nelson Mandela in May of 1990 have shown the power of the electronic age and the relative smallness of the global village. There is no longer any doubt that such a society exists. The only uncertainty is how to best take advantage of it. Because of events such as these, a consideration of transborder data flows (TBDFs) is central to any discussion of the global issues associated with information technology management.

SETTING THE STAGE

As we move into the latter years of the twentieth century, a plethora of new, although not totally unforeseen, forces are impacting upon the established world order in general and the business sector in particular. Advances in computer technologies, manufacturing processes, agricultural methods, and service needs have combined to force business organizations of all types to rethink the ways in which they conduct their operations in what has quickly emerged as a true global economic system. Because of these changes, survival for an increasing number of business organizations will depend on their ability to acquire, analyze, and use appropriate information about their various environments.

The computer is at the very center of this headlong dash into the information age and as such it simultaneously represents both a cause of the new age as well as a necessary result of it. As a result of the creation of our contemporary worldwide information society, accurate and timely information has become of enormous value to a wide range of "information consumers." Increasingly, today's business, government, and service organizations are dependent upon access to a myriad of data sources and increasingly this access is via computer linkages. At the same time, the accelerating pace of international commerce has caused traditional methods for data and information transmittal to be no longer adequate and direct computer-to-computer networks (e.g., BITNET, INTERNET, TELENET, SWIFT, EURONET, or COMSHARE) have emerged as the evolutionary successors. The ability of these computer networks to transmit virtually unlimited amounts of computer resident data anywhere in the world in just a few seconds presents a host of new opportunities as well as threats for businesses, governments, and society in general.

EVOLUTION AND DEFINITION

The transmittal of information (i.e., data) between individuals and/or organizations is as old as recorded history, which is itself the transmittal of information about people and events which occurred at one point in time to those who are or will be living in another. In earlier times, the transmission of information was accomplished first by cave drawings and later by travelers and/or couriers who carried oral or written data from place to place. This personal delivery system lasted for thousands of years in one form or another until the 1800s when the invention of the telegraph made it possible to transfer data from one site to another without having to physically move it or a copy of it. The telegraph thus significantly decreased the time required to access the data and greatly increased the ability to make timely use of them. Although transoceanic cables and high frequency radios later provided direct links between the continents, it has only been in the last 30 years that true worldwide communications have been possible through the use of satellites, thus creating the contemporary global village (for a more detailed history, see Glatzer, 1983).

Just as the ability to transmit data evolved from messengers to satellites, the media used to store and access data have changed from carved stones, painted cave walls, or handwritten scrolls to computer based systems. The quantum advances in computer technology which have taken place in the last three decades are largely responsible for the establishment of the contemporary information society in which data has become a commodity that has enormous value.

Because of the recent changes in the way that data are stored, processed, and transmitted via computers, the term "transborder data flows" (TBDFs) has been created to refer to the particular type of data transmission which takes place between computers across international boundaries using some type of telecommunications circuit (Pipe, 1984). The variation of these TBDFs is quite large and may: (1) involve the use of mainframe, mini, or increasingly microcomputers; (2) cross borders as close as next door or as distant as half way around the globe; and/or (3) use telecommunication circuits as simple as modems and public telephone lines or as sophisticated and expensive as direct broadcast transmissions using fiber optics, lasers, and satellites. A major reason why the issue of TBDFs has been gaining an increasing amount of international attention recently is that, given the current cost of the technology, it is possible for virtually anyone to acquire the equipment needed to access any database in the world from anywhere in the world (Gross, 1985). Simply stated, TBDFs simultaneously represent both a promise for the future of the information society and a Pandora's box of potential trouble for the international community as it moves into the 21st century.

TBDF OPPORTUNITIES

The opportunities which TBDFs can provide for business organizations of all sizes and types are many. For example, in terms of direct uses, TBDFs make it possible for a manufacturer in the Far East to obtain up-to-the minute revisions of design specifications from its R&D office in another country. Retail operations can use electronic funds transfers to eliminate float on their accounts receivables and thereby increase their cash flows. Franchise operators can transmit sales and inventory data directly to the franchiser's headquarters. Or consultants may use TBDF procedures to access virtually any type of on-line database to obtain information needed to better serve their clients.

An example of how these data flows can be used occurred during the 1987 America's Cup races in Australia. According to a published report, "Dennis Conner's Stars and Stripes syndicate used a General Electric Information Services electronic-mail system to instantly transfer design data, parts orders, race statistics, and fund-raising updates between Freemantle, Australia, and the yacht's home base in San Diego" ("PC Transportation Technology . . .," 1987, p. 34). Whether these TBDFs were the deciding factor in the outcome of the America's Cup races or not, it is clear that mere geographic distance is no longer a practical barrier to the instantaneous transfer of data from one party to another.

On the supply side of these TBDFs, businesses will be able to manufacture, distribute, install, and service the equipment needed to physically conduct the information flows as well as serve as information brokers by writing, maintaining, and searching various databases for their customers. The coming information age coupled with the need to adopt a user orientation will force both business organizations and governments to focus on these opportunities.

One of the biggest opportunities for businesses in the United States in the next few years will come as a result of President Reagan's 1984 decision to allow separate commercial satellite systems to be placed into orbit and thereby directly compete with INTELSAT. Given that the annual cost of leasing a circuit on INTELSAT has decreased from $22,800 when the first generation satellite was launched in 1965 to a projected $80 or less for the next generation which is about to be launched, the demand for TBDFs by all types of organizations, and even by individuals, will certainly increase dramatically in the coming years (Rosner, 1982). Similarly, the size and cost of earth stations have shrunk to the point where they are available to virtually everyone. For example, a subsidiary of COMSAT began marketing a complete, portable earth station that weighed only 110 pounds and could be carried in two suitcases in 1985. At that time, the unit cost $38,000 while the cost of voice transmissions was $10 per minute and telex was only $4 per minute. The firm's Vice President estimated that the market for these portable earth stations would be around 100 units per year with half of the sales going overseas (Gross, 1985).

The rapidly declining cost structure for all types of telecommunications equipment will further hasten the arrival of the information age and the global village. Along with this will come an increased demand for the equipment, personnel, and software which will be needed to support the resulting TBDFs. Those organizations which are willing to take the lead in what Toffler (1980) called the "third wave" stand to be at the forefront of the post industrial society of the 21st century.

AUTHOR	ISSUES CITED
Chandran, Phatak, & Sambharya (1987)	1. Economic Issues 2. Privacy Issues 3. Political Issues 4. National Sovereignty (Cultural Imperialism) Issues
Tsanacas (1985)	1. Unemployment Issues 2. Cultural Infringement Issues 3. Access to Data (Security and Privacy Issues) 4. Vulnerability of Society (Cultural Imperialism) 5. Balance of Payments Issues
Sauvant (1984)	1. Impact on the Competitive Positions of Enterprises in Developing Countries 2. Personal Privacy Issues 3. Technical Matters 4. Legal Issues 5. Sovereignty Issues 6. Cultural Identity Issues 7. Data Vulnerability Issues 8. TBDF Regulations Which Create Barriers 9. Economic Issues 10. National Security Issues 11. Third World Development Issues
Buss (1984)	1. Lack of Uniform TBDF Laws and Reciprocal Legislation 2. Privacy Issues 3. Cultural Sovereignty Issues 4. Economic Issues 5. Lack of an Identifiable Person in Most Companies to Deal with TBDF Concerns 6. Lack of an Accepted International Policy Making Body
Butler, P. (1983)	1. Privacy Issues 2. National Sovereignty Issues 3. Cultural Identity Issues 4. Economic Growth Issues
Basche (1983)	1. Political Issues 2. Privacy Issues 3. Economic Issues 4. Third World Development Issues 5. Technical Issues

Table 1: A Sampling of TBDF Issues Cited By Various Authors

ACTUAL AND POTENTIAL PROBLEMS

While the advantages of instantaneous access to information regardless of where either it or the seeker is located are fairly obvious, many of the problems associated with TBDFs are only now beginning to be seriously discussed (Briat, 1984; Leeson, 1984; Mason, 1986; Pipe, 1984; Sandler, 1985a, 1985b, 1985c,; Stabler, 1984; "Study . . .," 1984; Willard, 1984). A sampling of the type of problems which are relevant to this discussion is contained in Table 1.

Using the issues presented in this Table as a foundation, it is possible to categorize TBDF concerns as coming under one of the four general headings shown in Figure 1. Restructured somewhat, these important TBDF issues in turn yield the 12 sub-issues depicted in Table 2. While there is obviously some amount of overlap among these groupings, they still represent the major topics of discussion in the literature and will serve as the basis for the discussion which follows.

Before presenting a brief analysis of each of these issues, it is necessary to acknowledge that for all of them the overriding area of concern is that of control. No nation, organization, or individual wants to relinquish its dominion over such an important commodity as information, and given the ease with which the technology and skills for conducting TBDFs can be acquired, it is of paramount importance that only bona fide users be able to gain access to any computer resident database. While the topic of data security per se is beyond the scope and intent of this paper, it obviously is something that all information system managers must constantly seek to maintain and for which no ultimate solution has yet been devised.

SECURITY ISSUES

National Security

In the past, it was fairly easy for a government to control the physical flow of data leaving its territory by controlling the media used for transmission or by searching people and vehicles crossing its borders. Such methods are hardly as useful when the data is resident in computers that can be directly linked to each other via a telecommunication circuit which allows for the quick and often unmonitored transfer of files. Should the data banks contain classified information relevant to the national defense of a particular nation state, illegal or unauthorized access to them could obviously jeopardize that country's national security or even the overall security of the world.

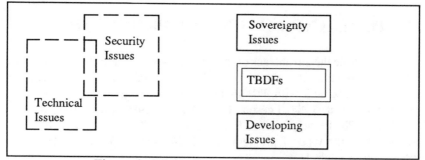

Figure 1: Major Issues Affecting TBDFs

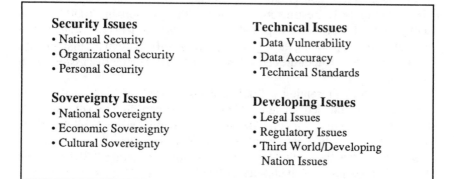

Security Issues
- National Security
- Organizational Security
- Personal Security

Sovereignty Issues
- National Sovereignty
- Economic Sovereignty
- Cultural Sovereignty

Technical Issues
- Data Vulnerability
- Data Accuracy
- Technical Standards

Developing Issues
- Legal Issues
- Regulatory Issues
- Third World/Developing
  Nation Issues

Table 2: TBDF Issues

While this type of situation was the theme of the 1983 fictional movie "WarGames," it became reality and front page news soon after the movie's debut when a group of teenage "hackers," using a microcomputer, a random number generator, and a modem, broke into the Los Alamos (New Mexico) National Laboratories' computers which contain nuclear weapons information (Krucoff, 1983; "'WarGames' Comes to Life . . .," 1983). Although the government's official statement claimed that no classified information was compromised in the Los Alamos incident, steps were subsequently taken to reduce the possibility of similar future "break ins" (Schrage, 1983). In cases like this, however, the implementation of new security measures hardly means that the computers have been made invulnerable to unauthorized access; rather, given the contemporary reality, it is only a matter of time before someone finds a way to get around these new locks as well.

In addition to trying to find ways to minimize these risks domestically, the Reagan Administration also attempted to control the sale of high technology hardware and software to foreign companies and governments through legislation and the refusal to grant export permits in an effort to limit this potential overseas (Rovit, 1984; Willard, 1984). Other countries, such as Canada, Taiwan, and West Germany, share this concern and are also actively seeking ways to protect their national security in the information age ("Study Notes . . .," 1984). At this point, however, no one has been able to devise an appropriate solution.

Another example of the impact which unauthorized access to governmental data flows can have on national security occurred in early 1987 when the issue of security at the new United States embassy in Moscow became public (Lee, 1987; Ottaway, 1987b). In addition to the discussions about KGB agents and listening devices being found in the embassy, one of the Soviet activities that received a good deal of attention was their interception of open air data transmissions between the embassy and the United States State Department in Washington. A similar discussion emerged domestically in reports that personnel in the Soviet embassy in Washington are able to intercept voice and data transmissions emanating from such sensitive areas as the White House, the Pentagon, the State Department, and the Central Intelligence Agency (Ottaway, 1987a). Clearly, if the United States government is having difficulty protecting its diplomatic, military, and intelligence transmissions from this type of unauthorized access, there is cause for concern on the part of businesses and others who might engage in similar types of TBDFs.

Organizational Security

As has been discussed above, information is a commodity which may have enormous value to any number of individuals, organizations, and/or governments. Just as a nation's security may be jeopardized by the unauthorized access to or alteration of its databases, so too can an organization's security. The news media has for years been reporting about "hackers" who break into an organization's data banks and play with market research data, sales forecasts, or even the grades on a university's computer. Clearly if proprietary information held by one organization is accessed or altered by its competitors, then the former may well end up in a weaker competitive position vis a vis the latter. While this problem is obviously more critical for organizations engaged in highly dynamic and competitive environments, banks and other financial institutions, and firms which do work for a governmental unit, it will become increasingly important for all organizations in the future (Budiansky, 1987).

Another side of the organizational security issue relates to the impact of various TBDF laws on both domestic and multinational operations. For example, France requires that every database maintained in that country be registered with the government. As of 1984, more than 140,000 databases had been registered (Mills, 1984). Similarly, the 1980 Canadian Banking Act requires that all processing of records on Canadian citizens be done in Canada and be subject to governmental scrutiny (Buss, 1984). And in Taiwan, all data transmissions are monitored by the government for the stated purpose of making sure that no information affecting the country's national security is exported (Turbett, 1985).

All of these intrusions into the files of an organization mean that the chance of corporate data being compromised increases almost exponentially. When databases have to be registered, then they become matters of public record, especially in countries such as France and Sweden which define privacy protection as applying to both physical persons and legal persons (i.e., corporations). When a government monitors data transmissions under the guise of national security, it creates the potential for abuse. In each instance, the organization must weigh the value of doing business in a given country versus the possible harm that might take place by complying with the regulations. As more and more countries respond to fears about TBDFs by enacting restrictive legislation, this issue will become even more critical.

Personal Security

Governments and organizations maintain extensive records of one type or another on virtually every member of society. This is especially true in the industrialized nations of the West and increasingly these data are being kept on computers. Since this information may cover everything from the titles of books checked out of a public library to sensitive bank and tax records, individuals are becoming more and more concerned about who has, or may have, access to these data and how they may be used or even more importantly, misused.

A recent outgrowth of the proliferation of databases has been the increased sharing of them by organizations and government agencies, generally without the authorization or consent of the people whose data is being exchanged. Anyone who has had his or her name mysteriously appear on the mailing list of an organization and wondered how it was obtained has been a victim of this type of data "sharing." At the federal level in the United States, the Internal Revenue Service recently announced plans to buy demographic market research data from private companies which contain income statistics and zip codes and then compare it with the tax returns of individuals who live in those areas in order to check on whether or not people are filing accurate tax returns. Since access to computerized databases is becoming easier for more and more people as computer literacy increases and associated costs decrease, the potential impact on personal privacy is truly becoming a major issue for the information age.

In the international arena, Sweden was one of the first nations to adopt strict privacy laws with regard to personal data in the early 1970s (Turbett, 1985). Other nations have followed suit since, with Canada, France, Brazil, and West Germany leading the way. Basic tenets of these privacy laws require that the database must reside within the native country and that access is controlled through some type of governmental licensing body or authority.

While the desire to maintain the personal privacy of individuals is laudable, the problem is that there is little similarity or agreement in terms of how this is to be accomplished. Consequently, the laws of one nation are often in conflict with those of another thus creating confusion and expensive redundancy. Buss (1984) relates the predicament of a European bank which sought to establish a data processing center in France which would handle both French and West German accounts only to be told by the German government that French laws did not provide enough protection for the data on German nationals and thus the bank was forced to establish a second data processing center in West Germany just to handle the German accounts. One of the hopes for the Europe 1992 movement is that situations such as this will cease to occur as the governments seek ways to remove barriers and increase cooperation.

SOVEREIGNTY ISSUES

National Sovereignty

The fact that the United States is the dominant provider of computer hardware and software as well as the main processor of information has caused many nations in both the developed and the developing world to fear for their very national sovereignty. Given the increasing importance ascribed to all types of data, if a foreign nation is totally reliant on the U.S. for its data processing equipment and service, then it runs the risk, however remote, that those products and services can be cut off or restricted. In the absence of a local data/information industry, this could be viewed as tantamount to a siege. Many nations have responded to this type of informational colonialism by enacting very restrictive data processing legislation. At this point in time, it is still uncertain if this approach will bring the benefits sought or if it will have the opposite effect.

Economic Sovereignty

TBDFs are also seen as a potential economic problem in a number of countries including Brazil and France (Pipe, 1984). A recent French report on the potential economic impact of TBDFs concludes that their unregulated use could seriously affect the country's balance of payments by, among other things, allowing information to leave the country which could be taxed, or by electronically transferring funds to avoid taxation (Pipe, 1984). In Brazil, the argument is more in terms of protectionism. The Brazilian government, fearing a kind of information colonialism, has enacted some of the world's most restrictive telecommunications and computer use laws in an effort to keep foreign products out of the market and thereby encourage the development of domestic electronics, computer, and telecommunications industries. Again, it is too early to tell if these laws will have the desired effect, but preliminary indications are that they will not, especially since many business organizations view them as being overly restrictive and some have even chosen not to do business in Brazil because of its laws.

Another economic concern relates to the ancillary employment that is associated with the data processing industry. If manufacturing and processing take place off shore, then a ripple effect is seen in the general unemployment rates and local citizens who might have found employment in a domestic information sector are denied that opportunity.

There is still another side to the concern over economic issues and that is how the actions of the various nations which have enacted restrictive legislation have impacted multinational corporations (MNCs). Many MNCs, including IBM, are selective in terms of deciding to do business in a given country. In the case of IBM, it chose to stay and do business in Brazil despite having to live with some of the world's most restrictive data laws while at the same time withdrawing from India (Moore, 1984). Since MNCs, regardless of their line of business, require large amounts of data to be transmitted across borders in order for them to operate, any TBDF restrictions add a significant increase to the cost of doing business. When that increased cost outweighs the potential revenue gains of doing business in a particular country, then the MNC will opt to leave. In the end, it is the host country which will most likely suffer more than the MNC.

Since virtually every threat can also be viewed as an opportunity, the opportunity resulting from having various nations enact restrictive data laws is that other nations will choose to become what have been called "data havens" where MNCs can do their data processing operations without as many controls (Chandran, Phatak, & Sambharya, 1987). Similar "havens" have resulted when nations have enacted onerous tax laws, bank reporting laws, ship licensing laws, and corporate chartering laws. It is just a matter of time before the same thing happens in the information sector.

Cultural Sovereignty

Another of the concerns expressed by many nations relates to their desire to maintain their cultural identity in the face of an increasingly rapid rate of world change (Buss, 1984; Butler, 1983; Chandran, Phatak, & Sambharya, 1987; Sauvant, 1984; Tsanacas, 1985). Fearing a new type of "Ugly American," these countries worry that unless they are in control of their own information industries, they will be relegated to very subordinate roles in the new world order by such American based firms as IBM, UNISYS, or TRW. This fear was well stated by Eger (1978) who wrote:

> What many countries fear is cultural inundation or annihilation. They are resisting what they call "electronic colonialism" or "electronic imperialism." They do not want their minds, banks, governments, news, literature, music, or any other aspect of their lives to be Americanized. Neither do they want to be Anglicized, Sovietized, otherwise victimized by advanced technology and information that freely flows across their borders, thus possibly causing their own identities to become extinct (page 51).

Regardless of whether the mind set described above by Eger is considered to be paranoid or just pragmatic, the fact remains that it is shared by a sizable group of nations representing both the developed and undeveloped classifications. The knee jerk reaction to this fear has again been the promulgation of restrictive laws which in the long run may do more to inhibit the economic, social, and cultural development of these nations than they will do to encourage it.

TECHNICAL ISSUES

Data Vulnerability and Accuracy

If computer data banks can be accessed, either legally or illegally, then the possibility that their data will not just be accessed but that they will be altered becomes a major concern. Any database is only useful as long as the data in it remain valid. One of the most insidious ways for a competitor or a foreign enemy to gain an advantage is to sabotage an organization's or a country's databases in a subtle way so that the data continue to appear valid while the use of the altered data causes the user to make the wrong decisions. The search for ways to authenticate data, identify who has had access to it, and determine whether or not it has been altered is a never ending task for both organizations and governments.

A recent, non-fiction account of one such successful search has been presented by Stoll (1989) who details how he broke an international spy ring that had gained illegal access into a number of America's more sensitive computer networks. While Stoll's book makes for captivating and entertaining reading, it leaves the reader wondering how many similar situations may have gone undetected over the years and how many may be still in progress.

Accuracy also means that ways must be established to make sure that the information entered into data banks is complete and verified. Mason (1986) recounts incidents in which one individual almost lost his home because of an entry error in the mortgage holder's computer and another in which a ship's crew member lost his life because the captain depended on a computer generated weather forecast which was based upon incomplete observation data. Were these isolated incidents, they might be looked at as part of an acceptable error margin. The problem is that they are not isolated and similar events occur all too often.

Technical Standards

The fact that there is as yet no global information policy or body to establish standards means that by default there are also no global technical standards. While some organizations such as the International Telecommunication Union (ITU) have proposed certain technical protocols, adoption of them is voluntary even among ITU members and not all countries are members of the ITU. The lack of technical standards thus presents another barrier to the free flow of information.

In many cases, even countries or organizations which wish to transmit data are not able to do so because of incompatible systems or because no telecommunication infrastructure exists. According to Richard Butler (1983), there were approximately 565 million telephones in the world in 1983 with 90 percent of them being in 15 percent of the countries. More revealing is that only seven percent of them were in the 117 developing countries which account for 70 percent of the world's population. Obviously, before it will be possible for these nations to engage in TBDFs, they will have to establish a telecommunications infrastructure literally from the ground up.

There are also other, and perhaps less obvious, technical issues that must be addressed. For instance, since global communications now rely largely on satellites, and since not all nations have the money or technology to launch satellites, how should transponder channels be allocated and what orbits should be assigned to which satellites? What about the issue of data encryption? What about the allocation of broadcast channels? In the future, pragmatic questions such as these will out of necessity begin to dominate discussions of TBDFs.

DEVELOPING ISSUES

Legal and Regulatory Issues

Legal issues that relate to TBDFs cover a wide range of topics. At the global level, the basic matter of jurisdiction (i.e., which country's laws will be applied when data transmissions cross international borders) is of growing concern. Still, less than two dozen of the world's nations have any laws regulating the use of TBDFs and there are as yet no international treaties which specifically address this issue. A plethora of "alphabet soup" organizations and agencies such as the EEC, OECD, CEPT, ITU, UNESCO, and FCC have emerged claiming the right to determine global information policy (Buss, 1985). The problem is that none of these groups has as yet been able to accomplish the feat with the result being that each nation has been left on its own to enact whatever regulations it deems appropriate without regard to the conflicts they might cause. Table 3 shows how a few selected countries have chosen to respond to various fears about TBDFs.

At a more personal level, what recourse is available to the individual who feels his or her privacy has been compromised by the unauthorized use or misuse of transmitted data? In the United States, Congress has enacted a Fair Credit Reporting Act which allows individuals the right to see and challenge a credit report which contains false or inaccurate information about themselves. However, before the challenge can take place, the individual must first know that an inaccurate report exists and then he or she must pay a fee to obtain a copy of that report.

The fact that TRW and Equifax, the two largest credit reporting companies, generate considerable revenues from issuing reports that the subject individual has never authorized or been made aware of makes this problem even more difficult to resolve. Think about this the next time you receive an unsolicited application for a credit card from a bank you have never heard of that says you are being offered a pre-approved line of credit because of your excellent credit history. The ease with which such information sharing takes place in the U.S. causes many foreign governments to feel that American laws do not provide for enough data protection and thus they do not want information on their citizens exported to America for processing and possible compromise (Tsanacas, 1985).

Finally, a whole new area of law is being developed around the issue of intellectual property and how such things as copyrights, patents, licenses, and software can be protected in the information age (Sauvant, 1984). Perhaps this problem of intellectual property rights is seen most clearly as it relates to microcomputer software. Were microcomputer users to be surveyed, most would probably say that they "own" the software they use and that they can therefore do as they please with it. The truth of the matter is, however, that what they in fact "own" is a limited license from the publisher to use the software in certain proscribed ways for a given period of time and that if they are found to ever be in violation of the license agreement, the licensor can terminate the license, reclaim the software, and take legal action against the licensee. Although most software disks are shipped in packages sealed with a sticker that says something to the effect of "By opening this package, you indicate your acceptance of our license agreement . . . ," the average user either does not read or understand what the publisher is saying about the actual ownership of the intellectual property contained in the envelope. While some software publishers such as Lotus Development have taken an aggressive stance in prosecuting individuals and corporations who have violated their licensing agreements, the issue of intellectual property rights is only beginning to emerge as a major issue for the information age.

Third World/Developing Nation Issues

Numerically there are more nations in the world today that can be classified as developing than can be as developed. While many of the issues presented above have alluded to various TBDF impacts on the developing nations, this area has the potential to be the most explosive one in the next 10 to 20 years. The likelihood for conflict between the technological haves and have nots of the world is high indeed. One of the consequences of having created the global village is that no people or country is completely isolated and ignorant of what is going on in the rest of the world. The old saying about ignorance being bliss has been replaced with a demand to be treated as equal members of the contemporary economic, technological, and social order.

Perhaps the most significant future TBDF arena will be in those countries of Eastern Europe which are currently asserting their independence from the Communist bloc. Although these nations may appear to be more closely akin to various third world states in their present levels of economic development, they are clearly at a take-off stage from where, given very little stimulation, they will be able to achieve a great deal in a short period of time.

When this chapter was first being prepared, the recent events in Eastern Europe which have propelled many former Communist bloc countries headlong toward democracy were still just so much idle chatter. By the time the first revision of the manuscript was submitted, things were well under way and the reunification of East and West Germany seemed to be a future possibility. Today, less than a year from the time of the initial draft, that unification has actually taken place and the Soviets are now saying that they want to have a market based economy in place within the next five years. This

COUNTRY	PRESUMED FEAR	ACTUAL RESPONSE
Brazil	Information colonialism and a lack of development of a domestic information industry.	All companies must maintain copies of all databases physically within the country, offshore processing is prohibited, and requires the purchase of Brazilian made hardware and software when available (Barovick, 1983). Requires government approval prior to installing or purchasing any data processing system (Basche, 1983; Buss, 1984; Turbett, 1985). Microcomputer operating systems must be developed locally (Mills, 1984).
Canada	Exportation of corporate information to headquarters in other countries (especially the U.S.). Abuses of the personal privacy of its citizens. Loss of cultural and national sovereignty.	1980 Banking Act prohibits processing data transactions outside of the country unless approved by the government (Barovick, 1983; Basche, 1983; Buss, 1984). Limitations on the number of direct access links for international data transmission and limitations on satellite usage (Turbett, 1985).
France	Basically the same as Canada.	Imposition of taxes on and duties on computer equipment and software and on information and information transfers (Barovick, 1983; Basche, 1983). Requires every database maintained in France to be registered with the government (Mills, 1984).
Sweden	Abuses of privacy. Domestic economic data may not be accessible if stored abroad.	Has a data protection law and a commission to license and approve all data systems (Turbett, 1985). Prohibits offshore processing and storage of data (Chandran, Phatak, & Sambharya, 1987).
Taiwan	National and economic security.	Government monitoring of data transmissions (Turbett, 1985).
United States	National security.	Refusal to grant export permits for certain hardware and software (Rovit, 1984; Willard, 1984).
West Germany	A lack of development of a domestic information industry. Abuses of personal privacy.	Protectionist regulations which favor the domestic information industry and control of private leased telecommunication lines which connect to public communications networks (Barovick, 1983; Turbett, 1985). Data records on German nationals must be kept in Germany (Buss, 1984; Chandran, Phatak, & Sambharya, 1987).

Table 3: How Specific Countries Have Responded to TBDF Fears

is the pace of the world in which we live and much of what has happened in the last few months can be traced directly to the flow of information.

While there are many factors working in favor of a reunified Germany, one which is holding up even more progress is the lack of a modern communication system in East Germany. Early in the talks which were held after the destruction of the symbolic Berlin Wall, both sides realized the limitations which this lack of a shared telecommunications system posed for reunification and the reindustrialization of East Germany. Among the first groups to visit in the Eastern sectors were representatives of AT&T and General Electric who were brought in to assess the status of what needed to be done in this critical area.

Hardly surprising was the conclusion that East Germany's telecommunications systems was much the same as it had been under Hitler, some 50 years ago. Lines were old and in poor repair. Switching equipment was found to be incompatible with modern digital and computer controlled systems. And even the areas served by the telecommunications system were limited to the major populated cities with many rural areas lacking service of any kind.

All of this means that before any real economic development and improvement in the East German standard of living is going to take place, a new and complete communications infrastructure must be put into place which will allow East Germany to be networked with both West Germany and the rest of the world. The same holds true for the other countries which are emerging or trying to emerge from behind the Iron Curtain.

This problem is not limited to Eastern Europe however. Many third world nations harbor fears and misgivings about what the information society will mean for them. As indicated above, these fears may well fuel the fires of social and political unrest during the next generation.

DISCUSSION AND CONCLUSION

As with any complex issue, there are no easy solutions for dealing with the problems associated with TBDFs. While perhaps most of the areas discussed above could be aided by finding better ways to safeguard, protect, and control access to the data which are being transmitted, this is largely easier said than done and it is certainly beyond the scope of this analysis to propose specifically how it might be accomplished. It is an accepted fact that as long as people devise protection schemes, people will also seek to devise ways around those schemes. In some cases, the cost of the protection may make the data too expensive to use. In others, the technology needed to secure the data may be so cumbersome that it will not be practical to use (Budiansky, 1987). There is clearly a "Catch 22" type of situation here in that while one of the main benefits to be derived from the information age is that of making access to the information as easy or user friendly as possible, there is a simultaneous need to make sure that the data are not compromised or accessed by unauthorized people. To balance these conflicting needs of privacy and protection, governments will surely have to reach a number of compromises and those compromises will just as surely create more problems.

While a small number of countries have adopted some very restrictive and even protectionistic laws about data flows, most seem to feel that such an approach is myopic and counter productive to the long term development of a nation's economy and at least one (i.e., West Germany) has reconsidered its position (Wilkins, 1985). Clearly the tax revenues which might be generated from some of the French laws will never become a major source of income for the country and the restrictive import/export laws enacted by Brazil have had anything but the desired effect with regard to its international financial condition. These types of responses do not really address the underlying issues relating to TBDFs and indicate that the governments of these countries do not understand the long term harm that such measures will cause. Since these types of responses are also politically motivated, the best hope is that future governments will be more educated to the long term consequences of such policies and will repeal them.

There is still a very definite need to have a concerted international effort to resolve jurisdictional issues and provide for the redress of grievances which arise because of TBDFs. While initial attempts have been made to establish an international information policy through such organizations as the United Nations, the Organization for Economic Cooperation and Development, and the Council of Europe, among others, there has been little real progress (Buss, 1984; Pipe, 1984). In the future, as the TBDF issues examined here continue to receive more attention, the need to establish an international agreement specifying basic ground rules for the use and protection of TBDFs will force the major world powers to act. As in many other areas where global level action has been required to deal with an issue however, it will most likely take a major international incident of some type to generate the momentum necessary for this undertaking.

While there has been a great deal of discussion (e.g., Weihrich, 1990; Yon, 1990) concerning the removal of trade barriers among the 12 member nations of the European Community and the potential impact that the "United States of Europe" will have on world trade, there has been relatively little consideration of how Europe 1992 will affect TBDFs. The overall restructuring of both Western and Eastern Europe make it even more imperative that international standards governing TBDFs be established as quickly as possible.

While issues such as those dealing with the establishment of technical standards may be easier to address because they are more tangible, it is the psychologically based fears relating to concerns over a potential loss of national or cultural sovereignty that will perhaps create the most turmoil whether one is dealing with Western Europe or some underdeveloped nation. As long as nations are suspicious about the motives of others, there will be a basis for conflict. The "Ugly American" syndrome and charges of economic and/or cultural colonialism have been used for years to justify defensive postures by various nations against the United States. The only difference at this point is that information has become the focus of attention and not foreign aid or military activities. Perceptions become the reality for those who hold them and it is a lot easier to create a perception than to change it. In the future, these negative perceptions will have to be addressed or else many countries will continue to seek protectionistic responses which will only end up hurting them more than they will those against whom the protection is sought.

Finally, the impact of TBDFs on the third world and the emerging democracies has yet to be fully explored. TBDFs offer a potential avenue for these countries to use to improve their economic and social conditions. However, until at least basic, modern telecommunication networks are established in many parts of the world, very little practical benefit will be possible. Once those networks are available and an information infrastructure is in place, these countries will have to be guided by the promise of the future and not the paranoia of the past in terms of how they relate to the information age. This will most likely be where the challenge for the next generation will be found.

As can be seen from the above discussion, TBDFs represent both opportunities and threats to individuals, organizations, governments, and society in general in the latter years of the twentieth century. Although a number of these issues have been considered here, many more arise every day as the use of TBDFs increases. At least for the near term, the most worrisome TBDF problem will continue to be that of developing ways to maintain control over the access to and use of the data that may be transmitted internationally using direct computer to computer linkages and some type of telecommunications circuit. Given the diffuse nature of these data flows and the increasing ease with which they can be accomplished, this task will be both a major challenge and an obvious necessity for all sectors of the global society in the information age.

There is much that remains to be done before all nations of the world are able to fully participate in the benefits which can accrue from the free flow of information across national borders. There are at least three key actors who should be involved in determining the future of the global village. First, because it is the home of many of the world's leading information companies and because of its premier position in satellite technology, the United States should take the lead in seeking ways to promote the creation of a global telecommunication policy and in working to remove barriers to TBDFs.

Second, Western Europe, as it moves toward the reality of Europe 1992, needs to find ways to break down the barriers to information transfer which exist in that important area. Finally, the third world and the emerging democracies, because of the sheer numbers they represent, need to be brought into the discussions at the earliest stages. Working together, these three groups should be able to establish a foundation for cooperation which has been lacking to this point. Clearly, it is time to begin.

References

Barovick, R.L. (1983). Study Points Up Stumbling Blocks to Global Data Flow. *Public Relations Journal, 38*(6), 6.

Basche, J. (September, 1983). Information Protectionism. *Across the Board, 20*, 38-44.

Briat, M. (November, 1984). Transborder Data Flows—The Legal Issues. *The OECD Observer, 131*, 15-16.

Budiansky, S. (May 18, 1987). Cheaper Electronics Make It A Snap To Snoop. *U.S. News & World Report*, 54-56.

Buss, M.D.J. (1984). Legislative Threat To Transborder Data Flow. *Harvard Business Review, 62*(3), 111-118.

Butler, P.F. (November 14, 1983). Countries Move to Control Foreign, Domestic Data Flow. *Business Insurance*, pp. 49, 52.

Butler, R.E. (August 22, 1983). The ITU's Role in World Telecom Development and Information Transfer. *Telephony, 203*, 80-86.

Chandran, R., Phatak, A., & Sambharya, R. (1987). Transborder Data Flows: Implications for Multinational Corporations. *Business Horizons, 30*(6), 74-82.

Eger, J. (November, 1978). Transborder Data Flow. *Datamation*, 50-54.

Glatzer, H. (January, 1983). Telecommunications Past, Present, and Future. *PC Magazine*, 68-72.

Gross, B. (September 23, 1985). Satellite Earth Stations Small Enough to Travel Light. *Washington Business*, pp. 17, 25.

Krucoff, C. (August 13, 1983). Code War: 'Curious' Youths Raid Weapons Lab Computer. *The Washington Post*, pp. C1, C4.

Lee, G. (April 8, 1987). U.S. Might Demolish Embassy in Moscow: Probers Say Repairs May Take Five Years. *The Washington Post*, pp. A1, A14.

Leeson, K.W. (1984). Information Policy: National Strategies, International Effects. *Telematics and Informatics, 1*(4), 395-408.

Mason, R.O. (1986). Four Ethical Issues of the Information Age. *MIS Quarterly, 10,* 486-498.

McLuhan, M. (1964). *Understanding Media: The Extensions of Man.* New York: McGraw-Hill.

Mills, L. (April, 1984). DP Industry Struggles to Survive Overseas, In the Face of Mounting Obstacles. *Data Management, 22,* 28-30.

Moore, S. (June 6, 1984). Global Information Policies. *Computerworld, 18,* 49-51.

Naisbitt, J. (1982). *Megatrends.* New York: Warner Books.

Ottaway, D.B. (April 6, 1987a). Security Probes Reported at 10 More U.S. Missions: State Dept., Envoy Resisted Changes. *The Washington Post,* pp. A1, A21.

Ottaway, D.B. (April 3, 1987b). Top Security Aide in Moscow Recalled As State Dept. Widens Embassy Probe. *The Washington Post,* p. A32.

PC Transportation Technology Leaps Into Wild Blue Yonder. (February 10, 1987). *PC Week,* p. 34.

Pipe, G.R. (1984). International Information Policy: Evolution of Transborder Data Flow Issues. *Telematics and Informatics, 1*(4), 409-418.

Rosner, R.D. (1982). *Distributed Telecommunications Network via Satellites and Packet Switching.* Belmont, CA: Lifetime Learning Publications.

Rovit, S. (September, 1984). Report: Washington, DC—Which Government Office has Jurisdiction Over International Communications Policy. *Telecommunications, 18,* 37-40.

Sandler, C. (June 4, 1985a). Tuning in Data With Direct PC Broadcasts. *PC Week,* p. 33.

Sandler, C. (June 11, 1985b). VBI Technology Fertile Ground In TV Wasteland. *PC Week,* p. 37.

Sandler, C. (June 18, 1985c). Beaming Up a Satellite Transmission Solution. *PC Week,* p. 34.

Sauvant, K.P. (June 25, 1990). The Growing Dependence on Transborder Data Flows. *Computerworld, 18,* ID19-ID24.

Schrage, M. (October 4, 1983). Big Computer Network Split By Pentagon. *The Washington Post,* pp. D7, D17.

Stabler, C.N. (December 17, 1984). World Trade Grows In Bits and Bytes. *The Wall Street Journal,* p. 1.

Stoll, C. (1989). *The Cuckoo's Egg: Tacking a Spy Through the Maze of Computer Espionage.* New York: Doubleday.

Study Notes Growing Concern About Data-Transmission Laws. (November 9, 1984). *Marketing News,* p. 48.

Toffler, A. (1970). *Future Shock.* New York: Random House.

Toffler, A. (1980). *The Third Wave.* New York: Morrow.

Tsanacas, D. (1985). The Transborder Data Flow in the Now World Information Order: Privacy or Control. *Review of Social Economy, 43*(3), 357-370.

Turbett, P. (February 4, 1985). Banks Keep the Barrier Watch to Maintain Global Data Flows. *American Banker, 150*, 12, 21-22.

'WarGames' Comes to Life at Nuclear Arms Lab. (August 12, 1983). *The Washington Post*, p. A7.

Weihrich, H. (1990). Europe 1992: What the Future May Hold. *The Academy of Management Executive, 4*(2), 7-18.

Wilkins, B. (December 16, 1985). West Germany Reexamines Private-line Data Regulations. *Computerworld, 19*, 15.

Willard, R.S. (1984). Beyond Transborder Data Flows. *Telematics and Informatics, 1*(4), 419-426.

Yon, E.T. (1990). Corporate Strategy and the New Europe. *The Academy of Management Executive, 4*(3), 61-65.

Technical Factors Affecting International Information and Technology Transfer

George S. Vozikis   Timothy S. Mescon
The Citadel   Kennesaw State College

Ernie Goss
University of Southern Mississippi

The purpose of this chapter is to discuss the technical factors that affect the international information and technology transfer process and identify data storage technologies that could enhance the capability to transfer technology from Developed Countries to Less Developed Countries. It is the contention of the authors that expensive on-line search methods, combined with complex software interfaces, have impeded international information and technology transfer. In contrast, CD-ROM storage techniques combined with powerful microprocessors allow technology information to be distributed locally with unlimited use to technology research users. Alternative storage media in terms of media cost, drive cost, capacity, access time, and data rate are compared, recommendations for the CD-ROM methodology are advanced, and some disadvantages of the CD-ROM approach are discussed.

INTRODUCTION

Little is known about the nature of international trade in services or international telecommunications, and it is ironic that we are moving into an international information economy about which we are basically naive. The major implication of competition and liberalization in these services, though, is that costs will diminish and international technology transfer as well as integration of international locations will be much more feasible. Additionally, a shift toward an international information economy will surely necessitate coalitions between countries and large companies (Langdale, 1989).

The new international economic order between Developed nations of the "First World" and Less Developed nations of the "Third World" implies among other things, the restructuring of the technology transfer process from the developed countries (DCs) to the less developed countries (LDCs). The pivotal issues are the increase of both the amount of the information technology transfer, as well as the facilitation of the process, so the poorer countries can take immediate advantage of the technical know-how and apply it effectively and efficiently toward Research and Development (R & D) and economic growth.

A historical tracing of the economic development of nations seems to suggest a strong association between technology and economic progress (Rothwell & Zegveld, 1985; Tuma, 1987). By extension, it has been advanced that effective transfer of technology from technologically advanced countries to the less developed countries is a critical factor in stimulating entrepreneurship (Samli, et al., 1985) and economic development (Baranson, 1969; Balasubramanyam, 1973; Tuma, 1987).

The basic argument is that some developing countries have adequate supply of certain components of technology, although their meager Gross National Product (GNP) per capita might make them to be conventionally classified as less developed countries. For example, India has adequate pool of technical and skilled human resources although it may lack the necessary venture capital, and machinery and equipment due to its very low GNP/capital (Stoever, 1985). On the other hand, the oil-rich middle eastern countries have the requisite incomes to purchase the hardware component of the technology, but may lack the indigenous human capital to make the imported technology operational and sustainable (Tuma, 1987). The alternative is for them to import skills and talents at exorbitant costs to complement the technology (Lado, 1990).

The purpose of this chapter is to discuss the technical factors that affect the international information and technology transfer process and identify data storage technologies that could enhance the capability to transfer technology from Developed Countries to Less Developed Countries. It is the contention of the authors that expensive on-line search methods, combined with complex software interfaces, have impeded international information and technology transfer.

TECHNOLOGY AND ITS TRANSFER

Technology is a new variable in the equation of economic relations. Traditional economic theory assumes that all nations have equal access to technology, and therefore, there is no need to transfer technology from one country to another. However, it is precisely technological differences that constitute a primary cause of international inequalities in economic development. To reduce these inequalities, technological capabilities of the LDCs must be strengthened. The quickest way to accomplish this is by transfering technology from the developed to the developing nations. How to bring about the necessary international technology transfers is an urgent and complex problem. There is no acceptable formula or body of literature on the subject, despite massive amounts of research in recent years, mainly because technology per se is an elusive subject. For example, Tepstra and David (1985: 148) define technology as "a cultural system concerned with the relationships between humans and their environment." In its narrowest sense, technology is any device or process used for productive purposes. In its broadest sense, it is the sum of the ways in which a given group provides itself with goods and services, the group being a nation, an industry, or a single firm. Narrow definitions are not meaningful, given the breadth of the technology concept, while broad definitions are not easily subject to analysis (Kolde, 1985).

Technology transfer has been defined as "the transmission of know-how to suit local conditions, with effective absorption and diffusion both within and from one country to another" (Kaynak, 1985: 155-156). Hall and Johnson (1970) use a classification scheme that defines a technology system as consisting of three components: product-embodied, process-embodied, and person-embodied.

In the case of product-embodied technology transfers, one transfers the physical product itself, while in process-embodied transfers, blueprints, patent rights, or the actual scientific processes and engineering know-how are transferred. Finally, with the person-embodied technology transfers, the success of the transfer depends on the development of a sophisticated technical core to implement and diffuse the knowledge.

However, as Kedia & Bhagat (1988) pointed out, process- or person-embodied technologies are much more difficult to transfer across nations compared with product-embodied technology, primarily because of societal/culture-based differences.

Perhaps a more concise and comprehensive definition is that offered by Afriyie (1988). Utilizing a system's perspective, Afriyie defines technology transfer in terms of a spectrum of capabilities consisting of essentially three subsystems: (1) the basic knowledge subsystem, (2) the technical support system ("software"), and (3) the capital-embodied technology ("hardware").

The system's perspective to technology transfer recognizes the need to identify the different elements of a particular country's technology that are complementary and mutually reinforcing (Afriyie, 1988). Afriyie (1988) discusses several sets of generic technological elements and functional capabilities within the broad classification of the basic knowledge, software and hardware subsystems. The scientific subsystem comprises the existing and future stock of theoretical and applied knowledge by the country's educational and research institutions. The software subsystem consists of production methods, techniques, and technical and administrative support systems. The hardware subsystem includes finished goods and services, raw materials and goods-in-process, and machinery and equipment.

Finally, technology transfer refers to the use of technology in a setting other than the one in which the research and development (R & D) was originally performed. It involves the conversion of research results into commercial products, processes, or services covered by patents or license arrangements, enabling the recipient firm, industry, or nation to benefit from technology developed elsewhere. Exhibit 1 provides an overview of the sources, subjects, and methods of technology transfer.

INTERNATIONAL INFORMATION AND TECHNOLOGY TRANSFER

Technology is not a free good, contrary to classical assumptions, but instead it is a valuable property that requires a carefully planned process in

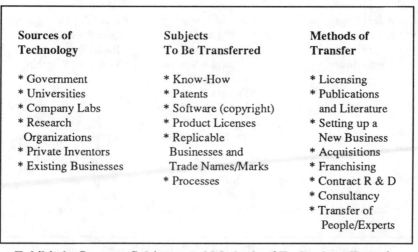

Sources of Technology	Subjects To Be Transferred	Methods of Transfer
* Government	* Know-How	* Licensing
* Universities	* Patents	* Publications
* Company Labs	* Software (copyright)	and Literature
* Research	* Product Licenses	* Setting up a
Organizations	* Replicable	New Business
* Private Inventors	Businesses and	* Acquisitions
* Existing Businesses	Trade Names/Marks	* Franchising
	* Processes	* Contract R & D
		* Consultancy
		* Transfer of
		People/Experts

Exhibit 1: Sources, Subjects, and Methods of Technology Transfer

order to be distributed around the globe. The demand for rapid information and technology transfer has evolved out of the expansion of international production by multinational firms. At the same time, advances in technology and increasing competition in telecommunications and other information technologies have lowered the costs of electronic information transfer. It cannot be assumed that this is an unimpeded process, however, because of the political, financial, market, and other factors that come into play. Since the degree of favorableness of these factors differs from country to country, the supply of technology and its transfer process also differs widely. It should also be noted that technology transfer is not based on a single investment decision as an immediate response to purely financial considerations, but rather it is a result of the perception of the creation of a long-term advantage for the investor generated by the transferred technology. Whether technology will be transferred, therefore, depends on the gradual evolution of a two-way process in which the technological capabilities of the investor and the condition of the technology-seeking host economy interact. The former seeks to exploit its own push factors of strength, while the latter uses pull factors, such as material resources, special incentives, etc., that may form the basis for the technology transfer decision. At the heart of this push-pull process lie the technical factors that will impede or facilitate the technology transfer mechanism (Exhibit 2).

Technology researchers, therefore, have the very complex job of assessing the opportunities as well as the obstacles in achieving data transfer. Researchers will also have an advantage in knowing what leverage they have

Financial Factors	Market Factors	Technical Factors
* R & D Expenditures	* Size of Market	* Available Data Storage
* Return on Investment	* Strength of	* User Friendly Interface
* Source of Finance	Competitors	* Rapid Retrieval
* Special Incentives	* Particular Material	* Low Cost Searching
	Resources	
	* Product Standards	
	* Location Advantages	
Behavioral and Cultural Factors	**Intangible Factors**	**Government Factors**
	* Experience Curve	* Intellectual Property
* Management Philosophy	* Quality of Labor	Protection
* Cultural Mores	Force	* Tax Policy
* Values and Attitudes	* Government Support	* Regulations

Exhibit 2: Factors Affecting the International Technology Transfer Process

in ensuring economic and secure data dissemination for technology transfer purposes.

Technical Barriers to International Information and Technology Transfer

Most LDCs do not take full advantage of the emerging technology, not only because of the rapid rate of change and complex nature of science and technology, but also because of the absence of an effective technology transfer process. This process has been slowed even further by data storage technology that has not been able to support large narrative databases on microcomputers until very recently. As a result, since most technology transfer systems are designed around online access to centralized databases residing in mainframe computers, the technology transfer process from DCs to LDCs has been almost nonexistent. The centralized database/mainframe computer technology transfer methodology presents several problems to the potential LDC user wishing to browse or search the technology database:

1. High telecommunications charges due to inefficient searching or browsing. Blair & Maron (1985) found that even experienced searchers familiar with the subject area retrieved only 20 percent of the relevant documents. By the time a user develops a list of terms restrictive enough to exclude the irrelevant, more than half of the desired documents have been excluded as well.

2. A complex computer/user interface that is sometimes unintelligible to the user.

3. Less flexibility since users are often not able to alter the search strategy and customize the search according to their needs.

As a consequence of these problems, efforts to promote the transfer of technology developed by DC firms to LDC firms have failed in a dismal manner. This failure is primarily a result of a bankrupt notion, that technology is a "reservoir of knowledge" with significant economic value readily available to interested parties. This false "reservoir" concept coupled with expensive and complex online date access methods, as well as lack of real incentives have caused technology transfer efforts to be limited in their effectiveness. The system recommended below circumvents most of these problems and greatly enhances the ability of LDC users to benefit from technological breakthroughs at DC firms and labs.

RECOMMENDED DELIVERY SYSTEM

Searching has been the most common mechanism to support the transfer of technology from DC firms and labs to LDC businesses. Until recently, retrieval has been primarily "online". Traditionally online information vendors have charged for the use of their databases by monitoring connect-time and search activity. It has therefore been limited by the slow data transfer rates available over telephone lines. Slow transfer rates, high telephone charges, and very complex computer/user interfaces have limited the effectiveness of technology transfer programs.

CD-ROM storage techniques combined with powerful microprocessors (e.g. 80386, 80486) allow technology information to be distributed locally with unlimited use to customers who, in the past, paid instead for the length of search. The database owners can still earn the same subscriptions fees as in the past. The real loser is the telephone company.

A CD-ROM system can connect a large database directly to a personal computer. A document collection on CD-ROM coupled with a personal computer greatly expands the interaction between technology researchers and technology transfer applications. It can search through the entire document or an index of the document and allows the researcher to alter his/her search strategy as the search progresses. CD-ROM offers the following advantages:

1. High density storage. Capacity = 660 megabytes (MB) contains over 20,000 compressed images or equivalently 10 times the storage capacity of microfiche.

2. Virtual indestructibility of the discs in an environment where careful handling of media is impractical.

3. Low-cost hardware to support media.

4. High consumer acceptance. Most users are familiar with audio CDs.

The CD-ROM physical format was created by Philips and Sony and an agreed upon standard exists. Physical compatibility is a significant achievement since video disc and optical media do not possess a single format. Given the many users for which this technology must be distributed, compatibility is an important attribute that cannot be overlooked. Exhibit 3 compares various alternative storage media including the technology currently used by NASA (large Winchester Drive).

Media	Small Winchester Disk	Large Optical ROM	Floppy Disk	Magnetic Tape	Large Winchester Drive	CD-ROM
Media Cost/MB	$5-10	$.006	$1-5	$.05-.1	$10-20	$.006
Drive Cost	500-3000	7000-100,000	200-1500	3000-15,000	10,000-150,000	500-2500
Capacity (MB)	5-80	1000-4000	.36-1.2	30-300	50-4000	550-680
Access Time (sec.)	.03-.3	.03-.40	.03-.05	1-40	.01-.08	.40-1
Data Rate (KB/sec)	625	300	31	500	2500	150

Source: Vozikis, Goss, and Grantham, 1990, p. 699

Exhibit 3: Comparison of Alternative Storage Media

The methodology advanced here consists of the DC firm or lab distributing to the LDC business or lab contact point monthly CDs with the latest data on patents, technology, etc.

The delivery system proposed here consists of:

1. A drive, which reads the digital data stored on CD-ROM disc.

2. A controller, which gives directions to the drive.

3. A search engine, which consists of a microprocessor, memory, and software.

This system interprets the user's requests and responses and generates instructions for the controller. A scheme for indexing and organizing information on the CD-ROM disc needs to be developed during premastering by the DC firm or lab. Additionally, the search engine includes the software that interprets queries and generates citations (listings of where relevant information can be found on the disc) and the processor (preferably Intel 80386 or more powerful), which runs the software, receives queries from input device and sends requests to the CD-ROM drive device interface. It also processes the information as needed, and sends the information to the output device.

4. An input device (mouse or keyboard), which receives the user's requests and responses.

5. An output device (laser printer), which displays information taken from the disc for the user.

Such systems can be part of larger systems which include other microcomputer applications such as word processing, etc. The microcomputer is the most frequently used host for CD-ROM technology. CD-ROM drives contain most of the functions associated with magnetic disk controller, including data separation, error correction, and simple data buffering. As opposed to magnetic fixed disk technology, CD-ROM is a low-cost medium of data exchange.

Encoding the Data on CD: Some Comments

Documents as well as record-based data can be stored on CD-ROMs. Document retrieval systems answer inquiries less directly than do data retrieval systems. A data retrieval system returns precise data, while a document retrieval system returns a list of documents most likely to contain the data. In a sense, document retrieval systems are probabilistic while data retrieval systems are deterministic. As a result, the design and evaluation of document retrieval systems are more challenging since they involve making judgments under uncertain conditions.

To aid searching in document retrieval systems, generally abstracts and indexes are created for the documents. One can then package the abstract and the index with digitized images of the articles it references. It is easy to see that searching through an index (or abstract) is much more efficient than searching the entire document.

Some other recommendations/features for capturing data on CD-ROM are:

1. Electronic documents may or may not contain codes that mark the different structural elements, so embedding codes that are intelligible to the indexing software in appropriate places throughout a document may be desirable. This would be a feature in the text preparation software.

2. The indexing process goes over the document to prepare the necessary indexes. To turn off the indexing so that it skips over a section of text, special non-displayable codes are inserted at the beginning and end of the section.

3. Restrict indexing to terms extracted from titles and abstracts.

4. Store only the roots of keywords, e.g., factor versus factoring or factored. Some successful CD-ROM Data Search and Storage Systems that can be used as models for international technology transfer include:

Army Corps of Engineers. Contracted with Reference Technology, Inc. to take about 17,000 pages of technical engineering material previously stored in binders and transfer them to CD-ROM for dissemination to engineers at sites throughout the country.

U. S. Patent and Trademark Office. Another major government-sponsored CD-ROM project was recently initiated by the U. S. Patent and Trademark Office (PTO). By the end of the year, PTO plans to replace its current online system for disseminating patent information with a CD-ROM information retrieval system at each of 62 patent depository libraries. Using Dataware Technologies' CD Author development system, PTO will publish updated disks every two months containing a 5 million record database. The full text approximates 120,000 titles in the U. S. Patent Classification Manual, a file of about 100,000 corporations holding patents.

Disadvantages of the CD-ROM Approach

Frequency of access is a concern because access and transfer are slow. Because of the mechanical characteristics of a CD-ROM drive, the access time from one edge of a disc to the other is comparatively slow. For example, at the standard CD-ROM transfer rate of 150 KB/sec, reading 300 MB of text would require 2000 seconds, or more than half an hour. Therefore, it is important for a retrieval system to avoid unnecessary accesses. Thus the transfer agents, in some cases, may require that the user develop a rather restrictive list of search terms.

Moreover, in the context of technology sharing, a CD-ROM drive among several users is difficult and frustrating. Even in a shared or network environment, it is wise to have multiple CD-ROM drives to avoid contention. Multiple CD-ROM drives could increase costs to unacceptable levels. Finally, with the CD-ROM methodology, new discs would have to be created frequently so that each contact point would possess the most up-to-date databases.

Despite these disadvantages, CD-ROM data storage offers DC firms and labs a technique that would greatly facilitate technology transfer in the U.S. and among nations.

CONCLUSIONS

The need to improve technology transfer from the Developed Countries to the Less Developed Countries has been underscored numerous times as a *sine qua non* condition for economic development. The issue is the following: Is an LDC likely to develop faster by importing technology from the industrial world or by allocating its limited resources to "reinventing" that technology? The best investments for LDCs would seem to be reverse engineering and adaptation of existing technologies to problems peculiar and customized to their economies. The primary reason that technology transfer efforts from DCs to LDCs have been, and continue to be, ineffective is that policies governing the technology transfer process of such programs have been slow in recognizing the importance of up-to-date storage and retrieval methods, while mainframe searching methods of the past have thwarted technology transfer by making it both expensive and difficult.

The transfer and use of information carries some of the same complex social and political implications that affect relationships between the Multinational Corporation, home country, and host country, as the world moves toward globalization. Information is a double-edged sword. It is a resource that, if not properly used, can contribute to harmful relationships among individuals, firms, or nations, or it can actually foster economic development and enhance international trade. It is not surprising that some nations have concern about their sovereignty, about the influence of foreign countries who provide information services, and see the need to regulate transborder data flow. Until multinational firms and host nations come to trust each other a great deal more, and until there is easier access to information databases between nations, there will always be obstacles to free information flow and technology transfer.

The problem faced in international technology transfer is as Ralph Gomory, Vice President and Director of R & D for IBM put it, "Simple things are hard to keep secret, and complex things like technology are hard to give away." (1983).

References

Afriyie, K. (1988). A technology-transfer methodology for developing joint production strategies in varying systems. In F.J. Contractor & P. Lorange (Eds.), *Cooperative Strategies in International Business:* 81-95. Lexington, MA: Lexington Books.

Alic, J.A., (1988). The federal role in commercial technology development. *Technovation,* (Netherlands), 4, pp. 253-267.

Balasubramanyam, V. (1973). *International transfer of technology to India.* New York: Praeger Scientific Press.

Ball, D.A. & McCulloh, W.H. (1990). *International Business* (4th ed.). Homewood, IL: Irwin.

Baranson, J. (1969). Industrial technologies for developing countries. New York: Frederick A. Praeger.

Bhaneja, B., Lyrette, J., Davies, T.W., & Dohoo, R.M. Technology transfer from government laboratories to industry: Canadian experience in the communications sector. R & D Management, (UK), 12, 53-59.

Blair, D.C. & Maron, M.E. (1985). An evaluation of retrieval effectiveness for a full-text document retrieval system, Communications of the ACM, 28(3), 289-299.

Bremer, H.W. (Fall, 1985). *Journal of the Society of Research Administrators, 17,* 53-65.

Charpie, R.A., Desimone, D.V., Apsey, J.F., Costelloe, J.F., Dessauer, J.F., Fisher, J.M., Gellman, A.J., Goldmark, P.C., Kintner, E.W., Massel, M.S., Morse, R.S., Peterson, P.G., Roberts, S.I., Stedman, J.C., Smith, D.T., & Woodward, W.R., (1967). *Technology innovation: Its environment and management.* Washington, DC: U.S. Government Printing Office.

Congressional Budget Office, (1984). *Federal support for R & D and innovation.* Washington, DC: U.S. Government Printing Office.

Doctors, S. (1968). *Role of federal agencies in technology transfer.* Cambridge: MIT Press.

Finegan, J. (February 1987). Uncle Sam research director, *Inc., 9,* 23-26.

Gomory, R.E., (1983). Technology development. *Science, 220,* 576-580.

Hale, G. & Johnson, R. (1970). Transfer of United States aerospace technology from Japan. In R. Vernon (ed.) *The technology factor in international trade.* New York: Columbia University Press, 305-358.

Heaton, G.R., Hollomon, J., Horbert, (1984). Technological diffusion and national policy. *Research Management, 27,* 21-24.

Herrman, J.F., (1983). Redefining the federal government's role in technology transfer. *Research Management, 26,* 21-24.

Hetzner, W.A., Tornatsky, L.G., & Klein, K., (1983). Technology in the 1980's: A survey of federal programs and practices. *Management Science, 29,* 951-961.

Kaynak, E. (1985). Transfer of technology from developed to developing countries: Some insights from Turkey. In A.C. Samli (Ed.), *Technology transfer: geographic, economic, cultural, and technical dimensions.* Westport: Quorum Books, 155-176.

Kedia, B.L., & Bhagat, R.S., (1988). Cultural constraints on transfer of technology across nations: Implications for research in international and comparative management. *Academy of Management Review, 13*(4), 411-432.

Kolde, J.E. (1985). *Environment of international business.* Boston: PWS Kent Publishing.

Lado, A.A. (1990). Cultivation of entrepreneurship in developing countries: The role of technology transfer. Unpublished manuscript.

Langdale, J.V., (September, 1989). International communications and trade in services. *Telecommunications Policy,* 203-221.

Mansfield, E., (1968). *The economics of technological change.* New York: W.W. Norton.

Mansfield, E., Romeo, A., Schwartz, M., Teece, D., Wagner, S., & Brach, P., (1982). *Technology transfer, productivity, and economic policy.* New York: W.W. Norton.

McDermott, K. (1985). Government R & D: A wealth of new product ideas. *D & B Reports, 33,* 41-42.

National Governors' Association (1983). *Technology and growth: State initiatives in technological innovation.* National Governors' Association, Washington, D.C.

Nelson, R.R. (Ed.) (1982). *Government and technical progress.* New York: Pergammon Press.

Rothwell, R., & Zegveld, W. (1985). *Reindustrialization and technology.* New York: Longmans.

Samli, A.C., & Gimpl, M.L., (1981). Transferring technology to generate effective entrepreneurs in less developed countries. In A.C. Samli (Ed.), *Technology transfer: geographic, economic, cultural, and technical dimensions.* Westport: Quorum Books.

Schmitt, R.W. (1985). Technology transfer - Lessons from the industry. Lecture delivered at the Director's Special Colloquium, Argonne National Laboratory, R.A. Valentin, (Ed.), 33-35.

Sobczak, T.W. Technology transfer: Who, what, where, and how (Part III). *Manufacturing Systems, 4,* 48-49.

Soderstrom, E.J., Carpenter, W.W., and Postma, H. (1987). New initiatives in technology transfer: Introducing the "Profit Motive". Monograph, Oak Ridge National Laboratory.

Spotts, P.N. (January, 1988). Government money buoys U.S. Spending on new technology. *The Christian Science Monitor, 3.*

Stoever, W.A. (1985). The stages of developing countries policy toward foreign investment. *Columbia Journal of World Business, 20,* 3-11.

Tepstra, V., & David, K., (1985). *The cultural environment of international business* (2nd edition). Cincinnati: Southwestern Publishing.

Tuma, E.H. (1987). Technology transfer and economic development: Lessons of history. *The Journal of Developing Areas, 21,* 403-428.

U.S. Department of Commerce, (1983). *Information and steps necessary to form research and development limited partnerships.* Washington, DC: U.S. Government Printing Office.

Vozikis, G., Goss, E.P., & Grantham, J., (1990). Technology transfer and data storage methodology. *Journal of Economics and Finance.* Papers and proceedings, 693-703.

SECTION 5
NEW CHALLENGES FOR THE CIO

In the previous section, the focus was information technology transfer, adoption, and diffusion between and among countries and multinational corporations. The chapters in this section address the added responsibilities and challenges of the Chief Information Officer (CIO) promulgated, in part, by those changes discussed previously.

The first chapter, written by Jerry Kanter and Richard Kesner, reflects the effects of technology transfer, adoption, and diffusion by suggesting that the title of Chief Information Officer be changed to Global Information Officer (GIO). This new title, they argue, more accurately describes the role and responsibilities of the organizational information officer. Today, this individual needs a broad, global, and flexible vision in providing and using information technology resources for the multinational organization—especially the organization with operations (not just markets) in several countries. On the basis of an adroit analysis of various problems and challenges faced by CIOs in four real business scenarios, the author describe six critical success factors for the GIO.

The second chapter is written by Warren McFarlan of the Harvard Business School. He describes how information technology facilitates the geographic transfer of work, global networking, improved service levels, faster response times, and cost reduction. In addition, Dr. McFarlan addresses some special issues faced by the multinational CIO, for example, the complexities of network integration, uneven local technical support language barriers, great physical distance, irregular needs for systems development staff, and the wide differences in labor costs between countries. The chapter concludes with a list of six crucial activities that the multinational CIO must focus on, specifically: guidance on architecture, awareness of technology, corporate training and prodding, centers of excellence, human resource development, and advisory committee.

	The CIO/GIO as Catalyst

20

The CIO/GIO as Catalyst and Facilitator: Building the Information Utility to Meet Global Challenges

Jerry Kanter
Babson College

Richard Kesner
Babson College

This chapter opens with a definition of three types of business corporations - the domestic, the multi-national, and the global. The traditionally defined role of the Chief Information Officer (CIO) is next reviewed in light of the changes in this position brought on by the global nature of business. The reader is then offered four company scenarios, each describing a different set of global issues and challenges. This analysis leads to the redefinition of the CIO as GIO (Global Information Officer). As part of the GIO profile, the authors provide six critical success factors for the reader's consideration. The point is made that the GIO is not just a perfunctory job title change. The emerging global business environment makes it mandatory for enterprises to re-engineer their information management functions if these organizations are to remain viable and competitive.

INTRODUCTION

As organizations grow beyond national boundaries, their communications and information management networks have become increasingly vital to their operations. The global dimension to these networks has rendered them complex, costly, and at times unresponsive to the needs of those they have been designed to serve. The technologies themselves, from telecommunications and satellite networks to lap-top computers and distributed processors, to relational databases, icon-driven interfaces, and desk-top publishing, have proliferated and in many instances have exceeded the user's capabilities to comprehend and therefore exploit their full potential.

To realize the full benefit of recent developments in information technology (IT), the managers of these systems must define their roles in the context of the larger, global organization. More specifically, the organization's Chief Information Officer (CIO) must look upon him/herself as the catalyst and facilitator of a process involving trans-national teams of IT systems designers and implementors, working under the aegis of a set of unified strategic objectives. The end product of their effort must be the establishment of a user-driven "information utility" that can respond quickly to shifts in the environment and to the business strategies of the parent organization.

Implicit in this definition of the corporate CIO is a skill base that encompasses an understanding of the organization's businesses and customers as well as a comprehensive knowledge of available IT options. Even with this base of information, the CIO cannot succeed without a highly proactive approach to his/her efforts and a commitment to "total quality." What is more, the CIO must ensure that this same energy and direction pervades the culture of his/her IT team. Ultimately, success will come to those who can bring this mix of skills, perspectives, and attitudes to bear on the practical needs of the greater organization's user community.

Taking this synthesis one step further, the operational requirements of a truly global organization significantly increase the difficulties faced by the CIO. As a Global Information Officer (GIO), this person's responsibilities and performance expectations are magnified - both quantitatively and qualitatively.[1] It is the purpose of this chapter to explore the salient differences between the role of the CIO and GIO as well as to review the common characteristics and underpinnings of both positions. To achieve this end, the authors have developed a series of simple, illustrative scenarios based upon their own experiences as information services managers, consultants, and educators. Through these examples, they will articulate the challenges faced by the Global Information Officer in the execution of his/her assignments. In light of these observations, the authors will conclude with a list of what they believe to be the critical success factors for the realization of the CIO/GIO's objectives.

DOMESTIC, MULTI-NATIONAL, AND GLOBAL ORGANIZATIONS

If one peruses the professional literature, it will become immediately apparent that globalization is a topic of considerable interest. John Naisbitt's

Megatrends 2000, for example, opens with a chapter describing the global economic boom of the 1990's.[2] Lester Thurow of MIT's Sloan School has pointed to "Europe 1992" as the seminal economic and political event of this decade.[3] While Naisbitt may share this view, he has also rightly suggested that the changes overtaking Communist Eastern Europe will have a significant impact on the formation of the emerging global economy.[4]

In response to these developments, many business school educators have argued that we must rethink the criteria by which we measure the adequacy of executive training and subsequent performance. Both Harold Leavitt of Stanford University[5] and Noel Tichy of the University of Michigan[6] argue that we need to provide our students with a global perspective, and a knowledge of foreign languages and cultures. We must also make them problem solvers, change managers, innovators, intra/entrepreneurs, versatile communicators, and technologically literate. Indeed, the annual survey of top corporate CEOs, published in *Management Practice Quarterly,* clearly substantiates these points by indicating that to succeed in the business world, future MBA's will need to be multi-cultural in their sensibilities and highly flexible in their approach to management.[7]

All of this scholarly attention merely emphasizes the obvious: organizations in both the public and private sectors are migrating from domestic (national) to global entities. In the context of our discussion, it is essential that we differentiate between these operational environments as they affect the responsibilities of the CIO/GIO.

A "domestic" business operates locally, regionally, and/or nationally within a single set of national boundaries. It may obtain materials from a foreign country, outsource production, or sell abroad but the domestic organization remains rooted in its home country and does not therefore have significant operational requirements in other nations. For that matter, it tends to be managed by and recruits from the domestic market for its executive leadership.

By contrast, multi-national corporations have one or more operations of their own in foreign locations. These overseas entities either evolve from start-up operations or come into being as the result of the merge/acquisition process. Typically, the overseas components of a multi-national corporation function as semi-autonomous enterprises with their own management, sales, production, and information technology teams. They may operate under the same banner but as business enterprises, they are often quite different in terms of what they do and how they do it. Business organizations along these lines have been in existence for decades. Indeed, one finds examples of French, British, and U.S. multi-national corporations as early as the middle to late-nineteenth century. [8]

Today's "global" corporation may be distinguished from its multinational predecessors in that it makes every effort to integrate its foreign and domestic operations into a unified enterprise. Typically, such an organization functions under the aegis of a common strategic plan, draws its leadership from all over the world, rotates its management team among its various locations, and strives to meld its common corporate identity with those of its host cultures. Thus, a global company balances its need for centralized control with its desire to adopt a "domestic" image and exploit competitive advantage in respective national customer bases.[9]

The realization of a global approach to business has developed largely as a result of advances in information and telecommunication technology. With these tools, executives possess the means to communicate with and direct widely dispersed operations. For example, in addition to improving the speed and quality of information exchange, modern voice, facsimile transmission, and teleconferencing systems allow a greater degree of interaction over considerable distances. Similarly executive support systems and other data-base/artificial intelligence-driven tools create pathways through the morass of data generated by large corporations. These types of systems facilitate decentralized control without sacrificing centralized management of quality and standards.[10]

THE EVOLUTION OF THE CHIEF INFORMATION OFFICER

To administer this complex array of technologies, many organizations have appointed Chief Information Officers. These executives are typically responsible for all of the information technology-related functions of the corporation, including data processing, voice/data communications, network services, records management, and end-user computer training. However, unlike his/her Director of Management Information Systems (MIS) predecessors, today's CIO carries a broadly defined mandate. First, the CIO enjoys a more senior status, often reporting directly to the Chief Executive Officer (CEO) of the organization. He/she operates as an equal to other senior managers and regularly participates in key policy and business decisions.

Most importantly, the CIO serves as the corporate advocate of information technologies. He/she moves proactively to study, evaluate, and eventually deploy new computer and telecommunications applications as these become available. The CIO also looks for ways to maximize the benefits of the organization's installed base of systems and procedures. By promoting the creative use of technologies, the CIO function has transformed the service-bureau mentality of the old MIS model to one that raises IT to partnership status with that of the other operating units of the corporation. As we shall see, the

Global Information Officer (GIO) takes these developments a number of steps further by serving as a unifying force within a highly diversified and disbursed organization.

If the organizational response to the challenges of corporate information management is the office of the CIO/GIO, the tangible manifestation of his/her efforts is the so-called information "utility." This useful expression encompasses all information systems, facilities, and services provided by the corporation to its end users. The significance of the term has less to do with what it includes and much more to do with the image of accessibility that it projects. Like any public "utility" the expression "information utility" suggests easy access, the simplest of user interfaces, and a universal set of standards.

To achieve "utility" functionality is no mean task. At the same time, within the context of a global organization, the benefits associated with the delivery of such capabilities should be obvious. From the end user's perspective, information services are always there, relatively easy to access and employ, and suited to the multitude of applications typical of a complex enterprise. It is the CIO/GIO's responsibility to manage the utility of his/her organization and to ensure that new applications are developed centrally or by operating areas of the company as required by the company's user constituencies. As the reader will soon see, this is an extraordinarily difficult assignment that calls for special technical and management characteristics on the part of both the organization and the CIO/GIO if it is to succeed.

THE CHALLENGE OF GLOBAL IT MANAGEMENT

The following four vignettes illustrate different aspects of the Global Information Officer's duties and concerns. Their purpose is to serve as a vehicle for the exploration of the challenges confronted by any senior IS professional operating in a global context. In sifting through these examples, we will establish the basic job description and profile for a CIO/GIO.

Scenario I:

The Barkely Company is a manufacturer and distributor of cosmetics and toiletries in the United States. They have developed a multi-billion dollar business and have one of the top names in the industry. But now they have acquired a company, Chateau, Inc., headquartered in Brussels, a firm that manufactures a similar line of products for the European market. Chateau had been planning to exploit the EEC in 1992 and also plans to expand into Asia and other parts of the world.

Tom Brooks is the CIO of Barkley and has been responsible for the operation of the Information Technology Group within Barkley for five years. In one stroke of the pen, he has become a GIO. He must now bring Chateau, expansions and all, under the Barkely IT umbrella.

Scenario II:

Ralph Jones is the Vice President of Information Systems for the Global Banking Corporation headquartered in New York. He has domestic and international responsibilities for the management of multiple information system development and implementation activities in ten countries throughout Europe, Asia, and Australia. He oversees the systems development and the operation of ten field data centers in London, Rio, Paris, Brussels, Madrid, Tokyo, Rome, Sidney, Singapore, and Manila.

He recently installed a new communications system to ensure that all data centers are current as to one another's activities, maintain systems standards, employ the most recent releases of commercial software packages, and develop applications in concert. Ralph is also responsible for the development of a strategic plan for the Bank's use of IT on a global basis.

Scenario III:

In 1975, Jeans, Inc., an outdoor/casual clothing retailing company, opened its doors in Toronto. Since that date, its growth has been meteoric with over seven hundred sales outlets throughout Canada and the United States. Now Jeans, Inc. is preparing to enter the European and Far East markets in a big way. A marketing team has identified eighty new store locations overseas while operations has geared up to deliver product in accordance with customer needs.

As the CIO for Jeans, Inc., Terri Schwartz must install point-of-sales and inventory control systems in each new store. She must also engineer the adaptation of the corporation's centralized financial control system to accommodate a multitude of different currencies, tax laws, and home-country reporting requirements. In addition, Jean Inc.'s Europe and Far East management teams want their own customized executive support systems and enhanced voice/data communications.

Scenario IV:

Travel Unlimited is a highly successful, world-wide travel services organization headquartered in Chicago. The firm has decided to enter the recently opened Eastern European market. Since entry into Eastern Block economies is difficult, Travel Unlimited has established strategic alliances with domestic travel services in Czechoslovakia, East Germany, Hungary, Poland and Rumania.

While Jack Czaja, Travel's CIO, has built a global communications network over the years, the problems associated with this new assignment are quite unique. In the first place, some of the necessary computer and telecommunications technologies are not immediately available. Second, communication services are unreliable. Third, electronic currency exchange, transborder data flow, and even multi-national partnerships raise questions that Eastern European host countries have yet to address.

A Summary Analysis of Scenarios

The first of our case studies identifies what is becoming an almost commonplace occurrence, namely the expansion of an organization overseas through the acquisition of a foreign firm. The Barkely Company buys Chateau, Inc. In a typical multi-national business plan scenario, Barkely could have run Chateau as a separate entity, skimming off profits and possibly cross-selling products. However, the strategy of the parent company is global in nature; that is, the Chateau acquisition is viewed as an entry to Europe 1992. To fulfill its objectives, Barkely must integrate Chateau into its U.S.-based marketing, sales, manufacturing, and distribution programs. It must also adapt its own practices to complement those of Chateau.

These business needs in turn drive the development of Tom Brooks' IT efforts. In the first place, the CIO (now GIO) must establish a common basis for the communication of vital financial and operational data between the U.S.-based parent and its European-based acquisition. He must raise questions about the design, functionality, and communications standards employed by the existing voice/data networks within both organizations. In this process, he and his MIS team will access the merits of the company's newly-expanded base of installed software and hardware, and make changes as necessary. When settling on a common global strategy for IT, the CIO/GIO will need to establish more rigorous criteria for system selection and design so as to accommodate the business requirements of the European as well as the U.S. market place.

Furthermore, to avoid confusion, redundancy, and wasteful conversion costs, he must participate more directly in the key decision-making processes of the corporation. In brief, the CIO/GIO can no longer sit back and concern him exclusively with computer and telecommunications-related issues. More than ever, his organization's sales, operations, and distribution strategies will drive his team's priorities and limit its options. The additional burden of coping with the IS complexities brought on by the acquisition of Chateau compounds these difficulties, underlining the importance of CIO/GIO access to and participation in the highest levels of corporate planning.

To those who would object to the participation of a technologist in the formulation of corporate business strategies, we would offer two lines of response. First, the CIO/GIO manages a set of vital and expensive services. To ensure the best use of these resources, he/she must have a thorough knowledge of and input to the highest levels of decision making within the organization. For example, if the parent company intends to impose its management "culture," sales and inventory control methods, and reporting requirements on its acquisition, these decisions have clear implications for the types of information systems to be installed as well as for the prioritization of projects by the IT Group.

Second, as senior management articulates its plans, it does so with certain assumptions as what the IT Group can deliver. For example, plans may have to be altered in light of technological and/or human resource constraints. The only person within the organization who can present these and like issues with any authority will be the CIO/GIO. Thus, as an enterprise moves into the global market place, the relative importance of its IT function grows, elevating the office of the CIO/GIO into the senior ranks of management.

Clearly in the case of our second scenario, the Global Banking Corporation of New York, this type of organizational structure is already in place. Ralph Jones manages world-wide information technology operations, oversees standards, and prepares global IT strategic plans for his company. In this regard, his position is certainly helped by the industry within which he works. Traditionally, financial services institutions, including banks, insurance companies, and brokerage firms, have been at the leading edge of IT systems development and deployment. Indeed, these businesses are driven largely by the vast amounts of sensitive data that they must collect, store, process, and communicate on a daily (even minute-by-minute) basis. They therefore spend heavily on high-tech delivery systems and associated products, but for this investment, they expect rapid response times, fault tolerant computer systems, and a high level of data integrity.

For his part, Ralph Jones must manage ten data centers around the globe to performance standards set by his bosses, Global's CEO and Executive Committee. As key elements of this assignment, the corporation expects the CIO/GIO to ensure that all of its data centers run current versions of the corporation's software, that all security, auditing, and back-up/contingency planning systems are in place and fully operational, and that communication standards and procedures are followed at all times. Because a particular locale might impose special operating considerations on a data center operating in that country, the CIO/GIO needs to be sensitive to cultural differences and environmental conditions. Finally, he must keep an eye on developments within the information industry and among his competitors so that his company can maintain a competitive edge in IT.[10]

In developing a profile of the GIO, the experiences of Ralph Jones at the Global Banking Corporation are illustrative in a number of respects. First and foremost, while Mr. Jones enjoys access to the top, this in and of itself may not prove sufficient to ensure his success. To manage effectively, he also requires local knowledge of each of his operating units. He works to position the IT function strategically within the corporation and to ensure that his group's plans evolve in concert with those of the parent company. But he must also balance stability and reliability with flexibility because both he and his superiors recognize the need to respond rapidly to changes in the external environment.

Perhaps most important of all, the CIO/GIO recognizes an ongoing need to scan the technological horizon in search of new hardware, systems, and services. His approach in this regard might be three-fold. In the first place, he could encourage and evaluate home-grown IT solutions from any of his own operating sites for deployment throughout the global organization. Second, he could look for applications elsewhere in the banking industry or in some allied business for use at Global.

Finally, he might establish his own IT review office. The purpose of this small core group would be to acquire and experiment with the latest in computer and telecommunications technologies, such as advanced work stations, CD-ROM utilities, and imaging systems. Through a modest investment in personnel and facilities, the CIO/GIO could even establish a think tank within his organization devoted to innovation and change. As new IS solutions emerge within the technology review unit, they will be assigned to systems operations for full development and deployment. Whatever course the CIO/GIO selects for the Global Banking Corporation, his ultimate goal is to run his global corporation's information utility efficiently and economically, and to ensure that the IT group has the means to freshen and rejuvenate itself in line with shifts in the business.

By contrast the challenges faced by the CIO of Jeans, Inc. are quite different from those of Mutual or Barkely. Mutual is already an established global player; Barkely purchased an existing European network to become a global organization. Neither firm confronted the difficulties of starting de nouveau. As a young upstart, Jeans must create an infrastructure and related delivery systems in keeping with its expansion plans. To achieve these objectives, executive management at Jeans appointed two independent development teams - one for Europe and one for the Far East.

Each of these teams is headed by a senior sales person and has been allotted a budget with which to acquire sales and distribution locations, identify key markets, and define product lines and sales strategies. In addition to the team leader, each team includes operations, financial, marketing, and legal specialists. However, neither team includes an equally senior IT expert. Instead, the CIO is an ex officio member of both teams. This was done by senior management because they recognized the importance of voice/data communications standards and well integrated IT solutions. They have decided, therefore, to keep the responsibility for these functions in one set of hands.

While the reasoning behind this decision is perhaps laudable, it places Terri Schwartz in a difficult position. She must establish and maintain a close working relationship with both teams. At the same time, she must balance their demands and expectations with those of the parent company, operating in the U.S. Unlike the team leaders who are understandably caught up in the excitement of their respective assignments, Ms. Schwartz recognizes the many difficulties, potentially high costs, and considerable risks that she and her IT group will face in addressing the expectations of Jeans, Inc.'s expansion teams.

In this instance, the CIO must balance competing demands for her group's limited resources. This situation is further complicated by the fact that the decision-making and priority setting context is clouded with uncertainties. Simply put, Jeans, Inc. has never ventured overseas before. Yet, rather than building strategic alliances with businesses already operating in the firm's targeted geographic locations, Jeans management have decided to go it alone. To mitigate the dangers inherent to the plan, the CIO must marshall her team to limit the uncertainties. In particular, she will need to prototype and test the company's expanded financial and inventory control systems prior to their formal implementation. She must build consensus around networking and reporting standards both at headquarters and at the global periphery. Furthermore, she must ensure that the systems so deployed meet the multi-currency, multi-lingual, and diverse regulatory environment as identified by the two business development teams. The ultimate success of the enterprise depicted in Scenario III will depend largely upon the CIO's ability to win general support for a unified IT strategy in light of these factors.

This particular set of circumstances demonstrates the importance of clearly articulating the IT strategic vision and of building a consensus around a single operational plan. For Jeans, expansion comes at a high cost and to misstep initially could doom the long-term effort. Given these circumstances, the technical expertise of the CIO is less a factor in making the right decision than is Ms. Schwartz's thorough understanding of the business and the market place. She must also be sensitive to the operational needs of those who manage Jeans Inc.'s sales outlets. With this knowledge and the support of both development teams and corporate leadership, she can fashion practical solutions, employing proven information technologies.

Our last example, Scenario IV, takes a different strategic approach to global expansion. In the case of Travel Unlimited, a globally diversified travel-services company wants to enter the Eastern European market where it has never had a presence. The firm's executive management recognizes its limitations from the outset and therefore decides to link up with appropriate domestic travel-service providers in the targeted host companies. In Poland and Hungary, the partners in question are newly created corporations run by private citizens. But in Czechoslovakia, East Germany, and Rumania the travel business is still managed by state agencies. Here partnerships will require the establishment of a liaison function administered by local entrepreneurs.

Once the company's East European Task Force has developed these linkages, Jack Czaja, Travel Unlimited's CIO, enters the picture. Of Eastern European ancestry himself, Mr. Czaja is conversant in both Polish and German. He will find his knowledge of East European languages and culture extremely useful as he moves to solidify the agreements struck between his company and those organizations/government agencies with which Travel Unlimited has built alliances. While the terms of each protocol identify the nature of these business relationships, they do not suggest how either the host country or Travel will deliver services to the customer.

These operational considerations are the CIO's primary concern. First, he must familiarize himself with the IT infrastructure of each host country, including its telecommunications capabilities, the computer and telecommunications vendors selling and supporting products in that region, restrictions concerning the trans-border flow of data, and so forth. Next, he must determine which if any of these resources/barriers will play a role in the development of his plans. For example, will he rely on existing phone services or will he bypass them in favor or microwave or satellite communication systems? Will he rely on local suppliers for equipment and maintenance or will he work with his new business partners to develop in-house servicing capabilities?

As part of the business relationship, Travel Unlimited and its Eastern European partners will agree to terms regarding order processing, service fees and commissions, and management reporting. At least a few of these mechanisms will be new to the participants. Mr. Czaja must win their agreement to certain standards and controls. From his point of view, the CIO would like to build consensus around a single set of such procedures. However, in light of all the variables that enter into a global business strategy, a single approach to IT may not be a realistic objective. Solutions must be flexible, taking into account the unique characteristics of the host country.

As the CIO of Travel Unlimited learned through his experience in Eastern Europe, the choice of appropriate information technologies may be limited by cultural, operational, or even maintenance considerations that were unforeseen during the initial negotiations and planning process. Resource limitations aside, the best fit in IT may depend largely on what makes sense for the alliance of parties rather than what is available in the West. Like his colleague at Jeans, Inc., Mr. Czaja must strike a balance in his design and development efforts between what is optimal and what is "realizable." He must communicate these realities to executive management and win them over to his point of view. Throughout this process, he will be well served by his understanding of local conditions and restrictions as well as by a comprehensive knowledge of the parent corporations business/operational requirements.

ATTRIBUTES OF THE CIO/GIO

Now that we have reviewed four possible IT globalization scenarios, we are in a position to ask what these examples suggest about the role of the CIO/GIO. From the outset, let us set aside as given those capabilities that one would expect to find in any CIO regardless of the global scope of his/her responsibilities. Chief among these would be a broad understanding of and fluency with information technologies, computer and phone systems, and voice/data networking strategies. In terms of operating environments, the CIO ought to have a working knowledge of both centralized and distributed data processing services, a familiarity with personal computers, intelligent work stations, and hardware peripherals, and experience in managing the personnel who run these machines, systems, and services.

However, the CIO need not be a technologist in the strict sense of that term. Rather, he/she should know how to exploit IT resources, cope with the issue of standards, and plan in a constantly evolving IS environment. More than anything else the CIO must be strategic in the way he/she manages the parent organization's information utility. It is also essential that the CIO be user driven and as informed about the business and operational requirements of the firm as he/she is about the application of IT. Indeed, it is quite common for a CEO to select an experienced line manager as his/her CIO, allowing the appointee to develop the necessary technical expertise on the job.

Last but not least, the CIO requires the capacity to administer complex, multi-faceted projects effectively and through consensus. Here staff development and delegation are the keys to success. The CIO cannot afford to be "hands on" all of the time; he/she must rely upon trusted lieutenants to implement programs that emerge out of the planning process.

All of the aforementioned characteristics are necessary to the making of a CIO or a GIO. What distinguishes the global player interestingly enough is not that person's level of technical expertise. Rather it is the GIO's capacity to place the information technology requirements of his/her organization in the proper context and to exploit highly disbursed resources to get the job done.

In each of the scenarios presented above, the CIO/GIO's first assignment in line with the corporation's global expansion had two primary focuses. On the one hand, he/she focused internally to review and value the operational requirements of the organization as driven by its strategic plan and the resources available - both from within the parent company and its acquisition(s) - to address these needs. Like any other executive manager the CIO/GIO must master these issues if he/she is to perform adequately.

On the other hand, each of these representative information officers also treated the external environment as a key element in his/her planning efforts. To the extent possible, they addressed the cultural differences, language issues, infrastructural and business practice variations, and technology limitations prevalent in each of the host countries where they operated. They were sensitive to the nuances of multi-national/cultural IT systems development and exploited this diversity in formulating responses to the challenges posed by corporate management.

Influence Without Authority

In moving from planning to action, the GIO must be a team leader first and foremost. He/she may maintain a core group at headquarters to operate the world-wide voice/data network, monitor standards compliance, and scan the technology horizon for new opportunities. However, the bulk of the systems development and implementation work will be done in the field. Indeed, most applications will require the participation of IS personnel from various global locations.

As systems teams become international, it will be incumbent upon the GIO to ensure player compatibility and overall team productivity. Here again the GIO's understanding of both end user requirements and the cultural context within which the customer and the IT support team operate is essential to his/her effectiveness. Implicit in this statement is the less tangible but vital ability to balance the interests of competing corporate factions and get them to buy into a common approach to IT deployment.

There is no question that both technical and managerial capabilities are essential for the successful GIO. There is also no question that senior management credibility and rapport are requisites in the job. Furthermore, it is essential that this new IS executive adapts to the role of consultant, advisor, director, and guide in an evolving global structure. But it is no longer a case of exercising power through the direct control of budgets and people. To many who have grown up in the hierarchical, domestic business environments of the 1970s and 1980s, this approach is completely antithetical to their style and way of managing. Yet, if they are to succeed in the context of global IS management, they must change their style and adapt new methods.

Successful adaptation will come from an almost complete role reversal. As Allan Cohen (Babson College) and David Bradford (Stanford University) emphasize in their recent work,[11] the modern manager must rely more heavily on social psychology and such concepts as "mutual benefit," "reciprocity," and "personal exchange." Here the emphasis is on the anticipation of mutual gain by the participants in a specific event or transaction. In theory, this type of exchange should occur even in hierarchical organizations. However, the presence of a "boss" within this structure serves as an impediment to consensus building because he/she can act as a tie breaker, favoring one party over another. In the decentralized global organization, this type of leverage is not available. It is therefore necessary for people to rely on processes fostered by mutual benefit rather than personal gain.

Expanding on this point, Cohen and Bradford have argued that a solid foundation of trust within the global corporation also requires reciprocity and exchange. For example, the authors refer to mutual debts and phrases like "you owe me one" and "accumulating chits." Successful corporate players understand this trading concept as well as the "currencies" (e.g. recognition, reputation, visibility to superiors, ownership/involvement, money, and so forth) with which deals may be struck. To get results, participants must also be cognizant of the fact that they may often find themselves dealing in "foreign currencies," that is, cultures other than their own where an entirely different motivational system may be in place.

Like any other executive who must manage under these circumstances, the GIO should take the message of *Influence Without Authority* seriously. In a global context, he/she does not have the budgetary or hire/fire control over operating units and personnel to get the job done through sheer force of will. Instead the GIO must rely upon mutual respect and an accompanying new style of management. At the heart of this change in approach, the GIO must do his/her homework, understand the culture of each and every host country where corporate IS operations reside, and learn to deal on a peer level with IS people spread throughout the organization worldwide.

THE GIO: CRITICAL SUCCESS FACTORS

In summary, the Global Information Officer is very much a Renaissance man or woman whose skills as a manager, facilitator, and catalyst for change far outweigh in importance his/her need for technical expertise. He/she is a strategic thinker but one who can move beyond theory to the practical issues of how to get the job done. The challenges are great, and without the presence of a number of key critical success factors, perhaps insurmountable. The concluding section of this essay therefore identifies six essential components that will facilitate the GIO's winning performance.

1. Management Style and Leadership
Throughout this essay the authors have emphasized the leadership qualities

vital to the success of a GIO. These include: (a) a strategic focus, (b) flexibility in addressing tactical issues, (c) a people- as well as a task-oriented project management style, (d) the ability to delegate and manage through others, (e) ruling through consensus, and (f) a team approach to problem solving. No doubt the GIO needs a strong ego but he/she must subordinate personal ambition to the total team effort. As already mentioned, an understanding of the peoples and cultures that comprise the global IS organization and its users are essential ingredients to success. At the same time, the GIO must accept the fact that there is a degree of risk associated with his/her assignment. It is more important to contain the damage from efforts that fail than to avoid risk entirely.

2. Organization and Structure of the IT Function
The GIO will never be effective unless he/she and the IT group are appropriately positioned within the larger organization. First and foremost this means that the GIO reports to the senior executive officer of the corporation, usually the CEO and that he/she sits as a peer on the organization's senior executive council. The core IT group reporting to the GIO should include centralized MIS services, network management, a standards committee, and a technology review team. Applications support could report to the GIO but more likely to the respective operational heads who employ these systems. This would depend on the criticality of the applications, the culture of the corporation, and the personalities of those involved. Frankly, the authors prefer a decentralized approach to systems development and implementation as long as this process operates within a well defined set of corporate guidelines and procedures.[12]

3. Skill Base: Individual and Team
As has already been stated, the GIO need not be a technologist but he/she must be conversant in computer and telecommunications technologies. More importantly, the GIO must have the vision to appreciate the potential uses of emerging IT and how they may benefit his/her organization. The GIO must have a comprehensive knowledge of the corporation, its product lines/services, and its functional requirements. To as great an extent as possible, the GIO should also have an understanding of the countries and cultures in which his/ her organization operates. Knowing what motivates people and the work ethics of different nationalities is essential for optimizing global IS projects. Fluency in one or more foreign languages is a definite plus in this regard. At the same time, the authors acknowledge that there is a reasonable limit to human capacity. The GIO therefore must build the IT team to complement his/her own strengths. Indeed, the effective development and use of team players makes for a much stronger performance of the entire IT function than leaving the bulk of responsibility in the hands of a limited set of individuals.

4. Total Quality Project Management

The GIO must implement and enforce a total quality program within the IT organization. The concept of "total quality" has been discussed in detail elsewhere,[13] but at its heart lies a focus on excellence in individual and team performance. To complement this effort, the entire culture of the IT organization must become team oriented usually implying an overall reduction in reporting levels, flexibility in project assignments, and rotating team leadership. This approach will foster a sense of ownership and commitment among IT team players that will lead to improved end products.

5. The Environment

Rather than viewing the environment as an obstacle to success, the GIO should treat it as an ever expanding reservoir of opportunities. In this context, the GIO should turn to resources outside his own organization for guidance and support. For example, he/she should develop strategic alliances with institutions of higher education, research centers, and/or professional associations whose interests parallel those of the corporation's IT program. Instead of relying entirely upon home-grown solutions, the GIO might rely more heavily on outsourcing for specific expertise or on the cooperation of hardware and software vendors. Admittedly there are costs (and risks) associated with the development and nurturing of these and similar alliances. However, in the long run, such an approach will establish a reliable - albeit more eclectic - support network for the corporate IT function.

6. Technology Transfer and Change Implementation

In the area of technology transfer, the GIO needs to become more creative in his/her exploitation of established, standard products. He/she need not develop all of the organization's systems in house. Indeed, in today's fast paced high-tech environment, it is in most cases economically unfeasible to develop, maintain, and support home-grown IT products. Instead, the GIO should rely more heavily upon the work of his/her technology scanning team to bring new hardware, software, and applications to the attention of the IT group. The challenge then becomes one of refocusing these products for effective deployment.

Perhaps the most critical success factor of all, the GIO must become the agent/prophet of change within his/her organization. It is not sufficient to merely select and install the best in information technologies. If these efforts are to justify the cost of their development and implementation, people must use them. The GIO (along with the CEO and other senior managers) needs to build a corporate culture that is receptive to change and a work force that is willing to forego old work habits in light of technological innovations. To achieve these ends, IT tools must be user friendly and well focused on the business requirements of the application. Beyond this, they need an advocate in the person of the GIO and his/her team if they are to be received by the rank and file and to serve well.

As a closing thought to this section, the authors would like to share with their readers another important precept as stated by Massachusetts Institute of Technology's Scott Morton. "All the effort and money spent on installing new hardware, software, or networks won't get you anywhere unless you also invest equal of greater amounts in training, work redesign, new reward structures, and whatever else it takes to effect a substantive change in the corporate mindset."[14]

CONCLUSION

It is quite clear that a lead item on every pundit's trend list today is that business is going global and that successful enterprises will be those that know how to operate in a global environment. This essay began by differentiating three types of companies (domestic, multi-national, and global) and four scenarios for business expansion into the global market place. The Barkley Company found itself in the global market when it acquired a European manufacturer. The Global Banking Corporation evolved into a truly global enterprise as an outgrowth of the very nature of the services that it was delivering to its customers. As relatively new players, Jeans, Inc. expanded overseas with a series of start-up operations and sales outlets, while Travel Unlimited achieved similar ends through overseas alliances and partnerships.

The experiences of these companies was employed by the authors as a backdrop to discuss the changing role of the CIO/GIO. We focused on the job attributes and management style necessary to succeed in this new environment. Our discussion culminated in the identification of six critical success factors for the GIO.

The IS professional has been accused of reacting to changing times and travail by merely altering his/her identity. For example, the electronic data processing manager of the 1960s evolved into the management information systems director of the 1970s and from there to the information resource manager of the 1980s. Today the titles of chief and global information officer are receiving greater play. If we fixate on the title rather than the substantive changes that underpin it, we will miss the boat. Throughout this chapter, the authors have emphasized not just the name change to GIO but also an entirely new way of doing business. Title the position whatever you like. The really important issue is to recognize the true scope of the assignment, the critical factors for success, and the knowledge-base implications that go along with the global management of world-wide information system enterprises.

Notes

[1] From a survey of the literature, it would appear that Dr. William H. Gruber first coined the expression "Global Information Officer" (GIO). Others, most notably Robert H. Reck, have expanded upon this concept in their writings. See William H. Gruber, "Global Information Officer: The CIO Grows Up," Global Magazine (March 1990); Robert H. Reck, "The Shock of Going Global," Datamation (August 2, 1989) p.67; and Patricia Burnson, "The Perils of Going Global," Infoworld (August 14, 1990) p.39. For a complementary article on the CIO, see "Management's Newest Star: The Chief Information Officer," Business Week 2968 (October 16, 1986).

[2] John Naisbitt and Patricia Aburdene Megatrends 2000 (New York: William Morrow, 1990).

[3] Lester Thurow, from a speech at Babson College, October 20, 1989.

[4] John Nasbitt, ibid., p.107.

[5] Harold Leavitt as cited in the Johnson, Smith & Knisely, Inc. study Management Practice Quarterly (Spring 1989) p. 3.

[6] Noel Tichy, as cited in the Johnson, Smith & Knisely, Inc. study Management Practice Quarterly (Spring 1989) p. 3.

[7] Management Practice Quarterly (Summer/Fall, 1989) p. 96. See also the Johnson, Smith & Knisely, Inc. study Executive Search/Europe 1992 (New York: Johnson, Smith & Knisely, 1989). For that matter, Babson College, an undergraduate/graduate school of business education, recently completed a "21st Century Committee Study" that identified innovation/change management, globalization, and information technology as the hall marks for all future training in the field. See Babson College Excel Committee on Management Education in the 21st Century, "Management Education in the 21st Century," (Wellesley, MA: Babson College, 1990).

[8] For example, see David K. Fieldhouse, Unilever Overseas: The Anatomy of a Multinational, 1985-1965 (Oxford: University of Oxford Press, 1968), and Richard M. Kesner Economic Control and Colonial Development (Westport, CT: Greenwood Press, 1981).

[9] Charles R. Morris, The Coming Global Boom (New York: Bantam Books, 1990); and The Index Group, "Europe in 1992, Winning Through Technology" Indications (Fall 1988).

[10] "Employ information technologies to achieve strategic advantage" has emerged as a subject of considerable interest among specialists in the field. See James C. Emery, The Strategic Imperative (Oxford: Oxford University Press, 1987); F. Warren McFarlan and James L. McKenney, Corporate Information Systems Management (Homewood, IL: Irwin, 1983); Charles Wiseman, Strategic Information Systems (Homewood, IL: Irwin, 1988); and Richard M. Kesner, Information Systems: A Strategic Approach to Planning and Implementation (Chicago: American Library Association, 1988).

[11] The authors have borrowed this subtitle and the meaning behind the term from their distinguished colleague, Allan Cohen. See Allan R. Cohen and David L. Bradford, Influence Without Authority (New York: John Wiley, 1990).

[12] For an example of how distributed application systems development works within a single industry, see Richard M. Kesner, "Strategic Planning for MIS," The Bankers Magazine (July/August 1989): 40-44.

[13] Peter Linkow, "Is Your Culture Ready for Total Quality?" Quality Progress (November 1989) pp. 12-4; David A. Garvin, "Competing on the Eight Dimensions of Quality," Harvard Business Review (November/December 1987) pp. 101-9. See also Tom Peters, Thriving on Chaos (New York: Knopf, 1987) pp. 65-87.

[14] Computerworld (June 25, 1990) p. 67.

References

Burnson, P. (August 14, 1990). The Perils of Going Global," *Infoworld.*

Cohen, A.R., and Bradford, D.B. (1990). *Influence Without Authority.* New York: John Wiley.

Emery, J.C. (1987). *The Strategic Imperative.* Oxford: Oxford University Press.

Fieldhouse, D.K. (1968). *Unilever Overseas: The Anatomy of a Multinational, 1985-1965.* Oxford: University of Oxford Press.

Garvin, D.A. (November/December, 1987). Competing on the Eight Dimensions of Quality. *Harvard Business Review,* 101-9.

Gruber, W.H. (March, 1990). Global Information Officer: The CIO Grows Up. *Global Magazine.*

The Index Group. (Fall, 1988). Europe in 1992, Winning Through Technology. *Indications.*

Kesner, R.M. (1981). *Economic Control and Colonial Development.* Westport, CT: Greenwood Press.

Kesner, R.M. (1988). *Information Systems: A Strategic Approach to Planning and Implementation.* Chicago: American Library Association.

Kesner, R.M. (July/August, 1989). Strategic Planning for MIS. *The Bankers Magazine,* 40-44.

Lonkow, P. (November, 1989). *Is Your Culture Ready for Total Quality.* Quality Progress.

McFarlan, F.W., and McKenney, J.L. (1983). *Corporate Information Systems Management.* Homewood, IL: Irwin.

Morris, C.R. (1990). *The Coming Global Boom.* New York: Bantam Books.

Naisbitt, J., and Aburdene, P. (1990). *Megatrends 2000.* New York: William Morrow.

Peters, T. (1987). *Thriving on Chaos.* New York: Knopf.

Reck, R.H. (August 2, 1989). The Shock of Going Global. *Datamation.*

Wiseman, C. (1988). *Strategic Information Systems.* Homewood, IL: Irwin.

21

Multinational CIO Challenge for the 1990s

F. Warren McFarlan
Harvard Business School

Over the past decade, as information technology (IT) has penetrated to the heart of a firm's operations, the term CIO has been coined to describe the job of the key leader of the effort. To date a large body of both formal and informal research has been published concerning the nature of the job, the different ways it can be executed and its various challenges. This research has had an almost total domestic orientation. It is either assumed the CIO is operating exclusively within the confines of one country or, alternatively, that no additional complexities are introduced by the transnational firm. The reality is, of course, quite different. IT support coordination issues for international operations are vastly more complex than purely domestic ones, involving all the domestic issues plus many additional difficulties as described below. During the coming decade, managing these issues will become more rather than less important. Europe 1992, the opening of eastern Europe to private enterprises, the need to share technologies within a firm for common problems around the globe, the continued evolution of transnational firms in both products and structure all make this topic even more important for a larger number of CIO's. The cross-border flows of goods and materials are accelerating, requiring new and complex information infrastructures. Financial and human resources for global operations require much more coordinated management. Many firms are growing pools of staff which require extensive global coordination and development and their electronic support. Finally, technology skills, expertise and intelligence all require much tighter coordination. Information technology is central to accomplishing this.

Additional complexity is added to this topic by the wide differences in culture, labor/technology costs, products, and need/viability of IT support in different areas of the world. A subsidiary in India, for example, with its cheap labor and marginal telecommunications, realistically poses fundamentally different integration issues than one in Singapore with its high cost labor, high quality telecommunications, and small geography. Additionally, recent technology advances have impacted the overall organization structure of the firm, permitting the moving of tasks around the globe, opening the possibility of maintaining much tighter management control over far-flung operations, as well as facilitating new ways of defining and doing work. To deal effectively with these items, transnational CIOs need both intellectual and visceral sensitivity to these issues. There is no substitute for substantial personal international assignment in gaining this experience . Indeed, in a recent interview, the CIO of a large chemical company noted a key requirement for his successor is that he have had substantial international experience, including a period of overseas residency.

TECHNOLOGY IMPACT ON FIRMS

The new technologies in the past decade have not only shaken the ways and places where firms do work, but their impact will be even greater in the coming decade, as the technologies evolve and firms gain experience in implementing the changes enabled by the technologies. Organization structures, control procedures, and the nature of tasks are being altered, albeit with great effort and expense. For example:

Geographic transfer of work
The new technologies have facilitated the physical movement of work from high-cost labor pools to labor pools which are both high quality and low cost. In the domestic USA setting, this was a driving force behind Citibank moving their credit card operation from high cost New York City to Sioux Falls, South Dakota, (achieving enormous savings). In the same vein, American Airlines has moved a significant amount of its data entry work from Dallas, Texas to Barbados, where the documents are keyed in and the resulting outputs transmitted electronically back to Dallas. A major U.S. insurance company, several years ago, developed a significant systems development and programming unit in Ireland. This allowed them to access the much cheaper high-quality Irish labor pool effecting important savings. An added bonus was that the firm was able to use the third shift of the domestic computer operations for debugging because of the 5 hour time difference between Ireland and the USA. Similarly, a number of programming organizations have developed in the "free trade" zones of India which compete cost effectively with western Europe and American systems development activities particularly for highly structured

tasks. In a world where a bigger piece of the economy is becoming service oriented and where telecommunications costs continue to drop, these trends will accelerate in number. In this new transportable world local tax authorities must be careful not to be too greedy or big pieces of economy can geographically disappear overnight . Clerical and knowledge-based work is much more movable than office buildings and factories.

Global networking and expertise sharing

Firms like IBM and DEC have developed very sophisticated international electronic mail and conferencing procedures. Tens of thousands of professional support staff around the globe now have direct electronic access to each other. Global sources of knowledge can be quickly tapped into and the barriers of time zones swept away and the overall response *time* to problems sharply altered. I watched in fascination two years ago, as an IBM marketing representative, in 48 hours assembled electronic documentation from around the globe from 8 people he had never met to prepare a 200-page, multi-million dollar project proposal for a newly emerged opportunity (which he ultimately won). As overseas' markets, manufacturing facilities and research facilities proliferate, these coordinating mechanisms become vitally important in a world of time-based competition. Cheap, broad-band, global communication provides important opportunities to share and manage both designs, manufacturing schedules and text. The identification of expertise and its global sharing is one of the major competitive levers that a transnational firm will use to differentiate itself in the 1990's. The new capabilities made possible by optical fibre will only accelerate these possibilities.

Global service levels

The standards of what constitutes world-class service are sharply increasing. For example, a major U.S. trucking company, two years ago, could tell you where every one of their trucks were and what was on it. That is, they could tell you the truck had left the depot in Kansas City and was on the way to San Francisco and should arrive in 36 hours. Where the truck was on the road of course, was unknown and there was no way to divert it to cities in between for emergency pickups. (This was as good as any of their competitors could do.) Today, the company has installed small satellite dishes on top of each truck which has a computer in it. The firm now knows up to the minute where their trucks are (within a city) and at any minute can send instructions to the driver to alter their routes as new customers needs emerge and old customer plans are suddenly modified. In the overseas' transportation business, these kinds of global information-edge links have been the key to American carriers such as American President Lines being able to survive in a world dominated by low-cost competitors. For more than a decade they have used IT to provide a highly customized and differentiated electronic-based service for their global customers. In so doing they have neutralized the significant labor cost advantage of their competitors by providing a highly valuable customer service. This service includes up-to-the minute cargo locations, reliable delivery promises and flexibility in handling emergencies. Such advantages, of course, do not endure forever and there is constant pressure to innovate to maintain this edge.

Time based competition

Whether one likes it or not, the required response time in the global community is dramatically shrinking. For industries such as automobile and large construction projects, firms have been able to shave months and years off the design cycle as local computer assisted design equipment is hooked internationally to CAD equipment owned by them, their suppliers or customers. At the other extreme in financial services, repeatedly the question arises "is two-second response time enough or are we at a significant competitive disadvantage?" I have listened to foreign exchange traders wax eloquently about the remarkable things they could do for their company if they could get a one-second or two-second information edge on their competitors on foreign exchange quotes. In between these polar extremes, of course, are situations where we talk about taking weeks off order entry, order confirmation and manufacturing cycles. We recently completed a research project in a UK chemicals company where a combined $30 million investment in manufacturing and information technology transformed what had been a 10-week order entry and manufacturing cycle to one of two days. Needless to say, this transformed the rules of competition in the industry and put unbearable pressure on their less responsive competitors. To coin the words of one of my colleagues, "This is not done by speeding up the mess but by enabling the construction of very different infrastructures which challenge every aspect of the firm's procedures." Global information-based time competition will be a major item in the next decade.

Cost reduction

The much tighter information links between overseas' operations, its customers and suppliers allows a firm to squeeze significant slack out of their manufacturing systems. This has resulted in significant reductions of buffer inventories, staffing levels and a general acceleration of the level of asset utilization. At the extreme it enables the creation of the hollow global corporation like Benetton which owns virtually nothing but a sophisticated global information system which links the activities of their franchises to their suppliers.

The sum of these observations is that the very structure of a transnational organization, the type of work it does and where it is done, has been already transformed by IT. More importantly, the new technologies suggest continued evolution in this impact. The dark side of this, of course, is a huge increase in the operational dependence by the firm on its networks, central processors, etc. This has forced them to build high levels of redundancy into their networks creating alternative paths of information flows to back up computing centers, etc. A firm like Reuters, for example, provides more than a dozen electronic information paths from one part of the world to the other. The end impact of this is that for a number of firms, these issues are so fundamental and of such potential impact that the CIO has been positioned near the top of the firm at extraordinary compensation levels and become intimately involved in all of the firm's detailed strategic planning activities, to ensure a fit between IT and the firm's strategic plans.

IT DEVELOPMENT

A critical topic which must be addressed if the IT potential for the firm is to be realized is resolution of the issues relating to the deployment of IT resources. At a minimum, the critical issues which demand central coordination are those which involve networking and data architecture. Networking allows information to be cost effective and virtually instantaneously passed from one corner of the globe to another. Data architecture on the other hand is the critical glue which ensures that information is easily accessible to all within the firm who have a legitimate need to access it.

Data architecture, although easy to describe, is an extraordinarily tortuous and drawn-out activity to execute. Old applications have to be completely redone to disengage data files from their old formats and recast into relational form. As a practical matter the job is so complex this is not a one-time move but rather a long-term evolutionary process as new technologies allow different parts of the problem to be economically addressed. Most other issues relating to the deployment of IT resources globally are negotiable. For example, it is theoretically desirable to have common PC and minicomputer standards around the globe. The practicality, however, is that the level of support, local service issues and national relationships vary so widely as to make even this ostensibly straightforward issue a very complex area. Similarly, it may be overwhelmingly attractive for government relations reasons to source hardware from a local plant in a country regardless of the global systems integration problems which this may cause. On another topic it is desirable in general to have development staff located physically close to end-users but the huge disparity between salaries in India and Ireland, for example, vis-a-vis the U.S. may make it overwhelmingly attractive to push portions of major development jobs overseas and accent the risks of poor coordination. The more defined and structured the outputs of the task, the easier it is to move it overseas. The more ambiguous and evolutionary the outputs are, the harder it is to move. For example, a highly defined payroll system is much easier to have developed overseas, than a new marketing information system, portions of whose specifications will unfold over time through close user discussions. The frictional coordination problems associated with the marketing information systems create such problems as to more than offset the labor costs savings.

A complex related issue in thinking through the deployment of IT resources is that of subcritical mass. Development staff does work on balance more effectively in clusters of individuals. These clusters facilitate idea sharing, building team morale, as well as work load leveling. The physical distance from a local culture, the need for strong relationships to make a tool work, etc. all make remote development of decision support systems very difficult to accomplish. Transaction processing systems, however, are an entirely different story. There is a real possibility for significant amounts of this work to be subcontracted to third party vendors.

An issue of great importance for the transnational IT organization is creation of redundancy in data transmission paths, location of data, and so forth. As day-to-day operations which depend on the smooth, reliable operation of the networks become more critical, it is essential that failure of one node not bring the entire global system down. Whenever possible the data bases should be dispersed and multiple electronic paths to those data bases be developed. The Reuters network is a good example of this with data nodes and multiple communications paths to them installed around the globe. The failure of any node or path will cause the system to degrade, but not utterly fail.

Finally, an issue which relates to the deployment of IT resources is that of computer privacy and what files can be legally and ethically shared around the globe. A relatively benign topic in the 80's, it will rear its head much more vigorously in the 1990's. The use of personal data generates a wide range of sensitivities in different societies. In general it is of most concern in Western Europe today (particularly Scandinavia) and is of lesser interest in the U.S. Existing legislation and practice is extraordinarily fragmented within countries as well as the criteria used to resolve these issues. The current apparent lack of interest in these issues in many societies should not lull anyone to sleep. The issues are deep and emotional and the spotlight will surely make this a burning issue in the 1990s. What in one environment is seen as a sharp consumer micro-marketing implementation in another may be seen as deeply intrusive and immoral. The word Orwellian is being increasingly used in regard to some of the newer IT applications using personal data.

SPECIAL TRANSNATIONAL PROBLEMS

Beyond the issues relating to new applications and the redeployment of IT development and data resources around the globe, another series of important issues remains for the multinational CIO.

1. Planning and execution of networks is excruciatingly time consuming. In some countries, installation of new telephones and lines still require lead times of two to three years. Cellular networks have helped but not completely resolved these problems. Availability and cost of network infrastructure varies widely around the globe.

2. Great unevenness in local technical support exists from one country to another. While communications and software standards are steadily evolving, the incapabilities that stem from this service support problem will endure for the foreseeable future.

3. Unglamorous but basic are the simple problems of language. Global systems must be designed to support people speaking dozens of different languages and deal with many alphabets other than our familiar 26-letter alphabet.

4. Sheer physical distance remains a major challenge. When hardware/software problems occur, it is often very difficult to get specialists to the geographic area where the problem is occurring. Additionally, cultural/family issues often make moves of competent staff very complex to execute. No matter how much you need your top telecommunications specialists to take up a year's residence in Bangladesh, it is very difficult to make this happen.

5. Small local country operations have episodic needs for systems development but frequently don't have high enough sustained needs to provide employment continuity for a group of specialists. They lack the scope of work to justify full-time employment of this expertise, consequently they also are unable to identify and scan the emerging technologies that might impact their operations. Acquiring this skill involves either relying on local third party vendors or providing support from corporate headquarters.

6. Scattered across the 24 time zones, the problems of finding hours of the day to communicate between the different operations are difficult. For example, the Hong Kong Shanghai Bank built their second data center in Vancouver rather than Toronto primarily so that the end of the day in Vancouver would overlap the beginning of the next day in Hong Kong and a

two-hour window would exist for joint work. The FAX machine and e-mail have made a contribution to diminishing this problem but certainly are incapable of fully solving it.

7.Sharply different labor technology cost tradeoffs exist in various regions suggesting common approaches to systems design issues may be impractical.

THE ROLE OF THE TRANSNATIONAL CIO

The earlier discussion suggests this is an extraordinarily challenging and difficult job. The key roles the CIO must play and areas of emphasis are discussed below. These roles and tasks vary widely among different organizations depending on their size, breadth of transnational activities, and the firm's current state of IT sophistication.

1. **Guidance on Architecture** - The most important CIO role is to facilitate the development and implementation of a view on appropriate telecommunications architecture and database standards. He must pragmatically move to ensure that these standards are installed across the firm. There is no substitute in this part of the task for travel, pragmatism and the ability to listen. Ideas that make perfect sense in Detroit often need selective fine tuning in Thailand, if indeed they are even viable there.

2. **Awareness of Technology** - The second critical function of the CIO is to facilitate the discovery of appropriate new technologies, fund pilot projects with these technologies, and for those which look promising, help facilitate their movement around the globe. The exact way in which this function is executed depends on the firm's size, the number of large international IT units in the firm, whether the company is fundamentally a technology-based company, etc. An important facilitating tool in this effort is the establishment of international IT conferences where key staff from around the world can get together to share their thoughts. These conferences are usefully broken apart between those, for example, from the large, relatively sophisticated units vs. those from very small units from often very technologically unsophisticated countries. These two groups have little in common. Several of our major pharmaceutical companies have executed this approach.

3. **Corporate Training and Prodding** - One of our largest chemical companies has literally a one-person CIO department. He continuously travels the globe helping to facilitate the education and training sessions in the local countries, identifying both topics and sources of expertise for the local

countries to grab a hold of. This individual is a member of the most senior general management of the firm and he clearly adds substantial value. General management and middle management staff awareness programs remain a central 1990's challenge.

4. **Centers of Excellence** - Helping to facilitate the development of centers of systems expertise around the globe is another important role. It is not immediately obvious why a single system unit in the parent company's home country is the right way to operate. Many jobs can be usefully split over three or four development centers. One of our large entertainment companies recently took big pieces of financial systems, marketing systems and production systems and assigned them respectively to their U.K., German and French development units. While each unit was enthusiastic about leading their piece of the effort, they also knew that if they didn't cooperate with the other units, they would not receive the necessary cooperation to assure their units output would be successful. This approach tapped new sources of expertise, and was successful because of the *shared* interdependencies of *leadership* and innovation.

5. **Human Resource Development** - Another critical role of the CIO is identification of IT human resources in the company and helping to facilitate their technical and managerial development. Aspiring future overseas managers need to be identified early in their career and encouraged to spend several years at corporate headquarters, not so much to brush up on their technical skills, as spending time to develop the network of personal relationships and absorption of corporate culture which will allow them to reliably perform for the rest of their careers in their local settings. In this regard stability in the corporate staff is not so much a virtue as a liability. It is very important that new people be continuously coming in while others leave. Similarly, upwardly mobile staff from corporate headquarters needs to spend substantial blocks of overseas time early in their careers — 2-3 year moves should dominate the alternative of flying trips from a headquarters home base. Full time residence in a foreign environment gives a feel for the complexity and subtlety of global business that cannot be replaced by trips.

6. **Advisory Committee** - The notion of an external advisory committee of other CIOs and figures in the field has proven to be a useful way both to get directional outputs from outside sources and also give additional credibility to senior management of the CIO's recommendations.

The bottom line is that the international CIO job is an extraordinarily complex one. One has maximum responsibility but often practically little (limited) authority over distant staff and technologies. Persuasion and cajoling plus simply being better informed on new technologies and the nuances of corporate culture are the ways that one leads in this field. The job requires very high visibility and reporting structure inside the firm. This is particularly important because of the need to lead through relationships. The CIO must be in the network at the top of the firm where acquisition, divestiture and other important components of changing corporate strategy are developed. The CIO's effectiveness crucially depends on being in on this communications stream. Further, the job varies widely by industry, global reach and size of firm. An airline, by the nature of its business, requires a large central hub which provides a record of the status of every seat on every plane for the next year for global access. The CIO's job in this industry consequently has a very strong line management component. The earlier described chemical company's operations, however, were largely contained inside individual countries with relatively autonomous activities, and hence an entirely different structure of the CIO's role was appropriate. The role involved little line responsibility but high placed coordination.

There is also huge personal vulnerability in this position as normal changes occur in both staffing and corporate strategy at the top of the firm. The requisite skills demanded from a CIO will often change markedly in these settings. A significant element of adroitness is needed to grasp and move on the new agenda.

In closing, I should note that throughout this discussion, the actual running of networks, data centers, etc. have not been referred to. Those jobs, while important, can be safely delegated to others. The primary role of a CIO is as a planner, initiator and a generalist. Most emphatically, one does not ordinarily need an army of a thousand people reporting to him in a solid line to be effective.

SECTION 6
ISSUES FOR THE MULTINATIONAL ORGANIZATION

Section 5 delineated the added responsibilities of the CIO/GIO in the new setting of a global corporation. This section goes deeper into the specific issues faced by multinational corporations suggesting some frameworks for studying these issues. The first chapter by Maryam Alavi and Greggry Young provides a very useful framework for aligning a firm's international business with its information technology strategies. The authors develop and discuss this integrated approach to corporate strategy utilizing a 4 x 3 matrix showing two dimensions of information technology. The next chapter by Vikram Sethi and Josephine Olson provides an exhaustive list and description of several perspectives drawn from past research, followed by a proposed integrative framework for information technology in the transnational environment.

The third chapter in this section by Shailendra Palvia and Satya Prakash Saraswat is based upon an exhaustive literature search and identifies eight categories of issues in information technology relevant to multinational corporations. These issues are: information technology transfer, cultural differences, international standards, information infrastructure, global information technology applications, global information technology policy, global information techology marketing and transborder data flows.

Next, Peter Keen provides several practical strategies for information technology planning and utilization for the transnational firm. This chapter highlights management concerns, emphasizes the need for building a dialogue at the top of the organization, and proposes an economic model for information technology.

A.G. Kefalas offers a framework for the design and management of a Global Information System, emphasizing the statutory, tactical and strategic requirements of both the external and internal GIS. And in the last chapter, Edward M. Roche, through seven representative and instructive case studies, highlights the major problems and challenges facing today's multinational corporation.

22 Information Technology in an International Enterprise: An Organizing Framework

Maryam Alavi and Greggry Young
University of Maryland at College Park

This chapter provides a structured framework for aligning a firm's business and information technology strategies when the headquarters and subsidiary units are separated by national borders. The multinational, global, and transnational forms of international business strategy are defined and are shown to differ in organizational structure, strategic objective, transaction scope, and locus of management. These three international business strategies are integrated with the dimensions of information technology, including the technology architecture, data architecture, telecommunication architecture, and information technology management. The integration shows systematic differences in fit. Propositions derived from this integration are examined and practical approaches for managers as well as a research agenda for scholars are derived from these propositions.

INTRODUCTION

Scholars and practitioners believe that competitive forces are pushing all major firms to become international businesses and compete in multiple countries (Carlyle, 1990a). In a recent survey, half of the information technology (IT) professionals reported that their firms compete globally (Carlyle, 1989). This trend toward international enterprise makes it imperative that information technology managers understand the underlying dynamics of international business strategy and the impacts on the information technology function. This chapter presents a conceptual framework that systematically differentiates the form and function of information technology in international business.

International business is based on information networks that cross borders (Wiggin, 1987). In fact, information systems permit firms to coordinate their activities in distant countries (Porter & Millar, 1985). Therefore, information technology managers must be able to manage multinational networks in order to successfully support their firm's strategy (Carlyle, 1990b). However, the management approaches appropriate for international information technology are not inconsequential. Consider these examples:

Centralized Consumer Products Company
In the 1970s, Kao, a leading Japanese consumer goods company, was a centralized international firm with strong headquarters (HQ) control over its subsidiaries. An online information system provided the functional managers at the HQ direct access to the databases of the international subsidiaries.

In the 1980's, Kao's top management established more autonomous regional HQs in several countries to increase the firm's responsiveness to local market conditions. However, the central HQ used the established information link with the subsidiaries' operating units to bypass the newly-formed regional HQ divisions (Bartlett & Ghoshal, 1989).

Decentralized Consumer Products Company
The international division of a $1.7 billion U.S.-based consumer products company used information technology to produce monthly management reports that compared operating results and product margins. However, these reports were almost always late and the delay seriously hindered the division's foreign currency positions.

Although the division's financial requirements were uniform worldwide, regional offices had developed different data processing architectures, including different computers, software, data definitions, and telecommunication configuration. The different architectures made automated consolidation of regional data impossible (Buss, 1982).

These cases demonstrate that although information technology is an important ingredient of a firm's international business strategy, there is no well-defined methodology for the successful integration of information technology with an international business strategy. At Kao, centralized information technology provided a management tool that counteracted the firm's intended multinational strategy. Conversely, the information technology approach at Decentralized Consumer Products Company made integrated management of global operations difficult.

Moreover, despite the critical importance of the role of IT, there has been little systematic examination of the linkage between the firm's international business strategy and the international information technology strategy. International information technology is a major, but largely unstudied phenomenon (Cash, McFarlan, McKenney, & Vitale, 1988).

The objective of this chapter is to provide an integrated framework for aligning a firm's international business and information technology strategies. To do this, models of three different forms of international business strategy are defined. These three models focus on the HQ-subsidiary relationship in multinational, global, and transnational businesses. Next, the components of international information technology strategies are defined. The models of international business strategies and the dimensions of international information technology strategies are then integrated. Finally, propositions derived from this integration are discussed. Practical approaches for managers as well as a research agenda for scholars of the linkages between the international business and information technology strategies are derived from these propositions.

INTERNATIONAL BUSINESS STRATEGIES: OVERVIEW AND DEFINITIONS

> Multinationals develop products in each market for each market. Global companies start by looking at the marketplace as a whole and finding what is common. They then find ways to address the needs of individual markets with a global product. Ford is working toward the global model. Director of North American Systems Group, Ford Motor Co. (Carlyle, 1990a).

> In Bechtel, each project team is electronically linked to the product line and capabilities of the entire company. In that way, the client has access to the resources of the entire company wherever they are located. Chief Telecommunications Engineer, Bechtel Corporation.

These two perspectives highlight an often overlooked aspect of international business strategy. That is, there are distinctive objectives and approaches to international business which differ from one another and, therefore, assign different requirements to the organization and its managers.

This section examines these differences and categorizes the critical dimensions of organization and management.

In its broadest sense, international business refers to any organization that has one or more activities that cross international borders. For example, a firm that is entirely located in one country, but has suppliers or customers in another country, is an international business. However, the study of international business in the strategy literature most often examines the relationship between a headquarters (HQ) unit and a subsidiary that are separated by an international border (Bartlett & Ghoshal, 1989; Gupta & Govindarajan, 1989; Porter, 1986a). This chapter presents the implications of this strategy research for information technology in international business. Therefore, the focus here is not on an international marketplace in which a firm in one country has suppliers and buyers in another. Rather, this chapter examines the implications for the information technology function when a corporate HQ and its subsidiaries are separated by national borders.

While many forms of international HQ-subsidiary relationships have been studied and labeled, it is interesting that there is no standard typology of international business structures (Fayerweather, 1982). This deficiency of standard terminology leads to confusion in discourse and inhibits the development of precise analytical tools. Therefore, this chapter adopts the terminology that is coalescing in the business strategy literature (Bartlett, 1986; Gupta & Govindarajan, 1989; Porter, 1986b):

> 1. **Multinational enterprise:** any HQ organization that has an equity investment in one or more autonomous subsidiaries in a foreign country.
> 2. **Global enterprise:** any organization that centrally controls its foreign subsidiaries' activities from its HQ so that the entire business enterprise achieves economies of scale and cost efficiencies.
> 3. **Transnational enterprise:** any enterprise that transfers product, capital, and knowledge between its central organization and foreign subsidiaries, and facilitates such transfers among the subsidiaries, to create competitive advantage in any of its markets from any combination of resources in the enterprise system.

The development of an international business strategy which is successful over time corresponds to a transition from the multinational, to the global, and then to a transnational form (Bartlett & Ghoshal, 1988). This is a transition from a relatively simple organization structure with relatively few intraorganizational linkages to a more complex structure with many more such linkages.

The underlying assumption is that this transition of strategy and

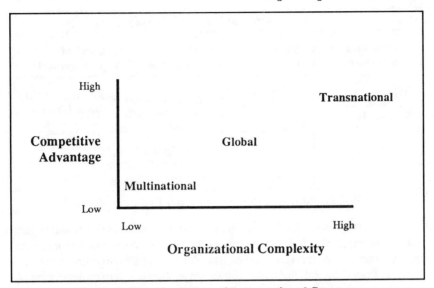

Figure 1: The Evolution of International Strategy

structure, if successfully implemented and managed, offers more competitive advantage. Competitive advantage is evident in superior market share, sales growth, or financial performance relative to competitors. The relationship between complexity of structure, competitive advantage, and international business strategy is depicted in Figure 1.

The **multinational strategy** requires the least complex organizational structure, and, therefore, is an early stage of international business. In the multinational organization the subsidiary retains its operational autonomy while the HQ gets the rights and benefits of its equity position. The strategic objective of the HQ organization which has adopted a multinational strategy is to realize its goals for returns on the investment in the foreign subsidiary. Therefore, the business mechanisms that operationalize the HQ-subsidiary link in this strategy are largely financial in nature and the relationship between the HQ and subsidiary is analogous to that between an investor and a venture.

Since the HQ-subsidiary link is limited in scope, the transactions that support this link are also limited. The bulk of the transactions processed within each business unit, instead of supporting the HQ-subsidiary relationship, support that unit rather than the link between it and the HQ. Table 1 summarizes this strategy.

Dimensions of Business Strategy			
Organization Structure	Strategic Objective	Scope of Transactions	Locus of Management
HQ and Autonomous Subsidiaries	HQ: Return on Investment. Subsidiary: Serve Local Market.	Bulk of Transactions are Local; but Well-Defined Financial Transactions Between HQ and Subsidiary	Subsidiary Gives Direction and Control with Minimal Influence from HQ.

Table 1: Summary of Multinational Business Strategy

A more complex form of international business is the global organization. In the **global business strategy** the HQ exercises much more operational control over the subsidiaries in order to build a large enterprise that benefits from economies of scale. The strategic objective is to achieve competitive advantages derived from efficient and low cost production.

Centralized coordination, communications, and control are the mechanisms to achieve the advantages of global size. Therefore, the autonomy of the subsidiary is constrained by the chain of command that links it to its HQ. The HQ, in order to serve this controlling function, needs a great deal of information concerning the local operations of its subsidiaries. However, the local transactions of the subsidiaries need to be aggregated for reporting purposes in order to avoid overloading the HQ management with information. Table 2 summarizes this strategy.

The most complex form of international business is based on a **transnational strategy.** This strategy applies flexibility, rapid multilateral

Dimensions of Business Strategy			
Organization Structure	Strategic Objective	Scope of Transactions	Locus of Management
Centralized Chain of Command from HQ to Subsidiaries	Economies of Scale and Efficiency.	Aggregated Transactions from Local to Global Level.	Subsidiary IS Centrally Coordinated and Controlled from HQ.

Table 2: Summary of Global Business Strategy

Dimensions of Business Strategy			
Organization Structure	**Strategic Objective**	**Scope of Transactions**	**Locus of Management**
Interdependent HQ and Subsidiaries	Flexibility to Respond to changing Opportunities.	Rapidly Changing and Distributed.	Shared Responsibility and Authority for Management, Team Orientation.

Table 3: Summary of Transnational Business Strategy

communication, and portability of resources to achieve competitive advantage. The objective is to identify and communicate business opportunities in the "system" of HQ and subsidiaries and rapidly shift resources to optimize the business advantage for the exploitation of those opportunities. The success of a transnational strategy depends on the responsiveness of the entire enterprise and the ability to draw upon the organization as required. The critical capability, then, is rapid and dynamic formation of teams whose members are linked together with the resources appropriate for the job at hand. Table 3 summarizes this strategy.

This review has shown that not only do the three business strategies differ in their objectives, but they also are uniquely implemented in organizational structure, management relationships, and scope of operational transactions. It is widely accepted that the development of an information technology strategy should be based on the firm's business strategy (Ives & Jarvenpaa, 1989; Keen, 1986; King & Premkumar, 1989). Therefore, the information technology strategy in an international business must respond to these unique requirements of multinational, global, or transnational strategy. Moreover, the information technology strategy affects the development of the business strategy (Doz & Prahalad, 1981). The information technology manager in an international enterprise, then, should anticipate the changing requirements and objectives of the business as the strategy evolves so that the information technology organization enables rather than hinders accomplishment of critical strategy dimensions. The fundamental challenge is to manipulate the activities of the information technology organization to define, within economic and organizational constraints, activities and technologies that are the most responsive to the requirements of the business strategy and the unique characteristics of the international environment.

The next section of this chapter examines the components of international information technology to distinguish areas of fit, or alignment, with the dimensions of the business strategy.

TYPOLOGY OF INTERNATIONAL INFORMATION TECHNOLOGY

Mandel and Grub (1979) have proposed that information technology in international business can be compared, analyzed, and classified according to the information system configuration and the organizational structure of the firm. They have shown that the relationship between the headquarters and subsidiary in an international firm can be modeled as a function of the information technology architecture, the data architecture, the telecommunications architecture, and the organizational structure. The usefulness of this perspective has been demonstrated by the valuable insight derived from the examination of these aspects of information technology in the organization (Keen, 1987; King & Sethi, 1990; Reck, 1990) and is embraced here. In this chapter, technology architecture refers to the configuration, or location, of the information systems hardware and software. The data architecture is the design and relationship among the organization's databases. The discussion of the telecommunications architecture focuses on the nature of the communication links between the headquarters and subsidiary units. Finally, the organizational structure is described here by the locus of information technology management (that is, the relative power exercised by information technology management in the headquarters and subsidiary organizations).

Integration Of International Business Strategy and Information Technology

The three forms of international business (multinational, global, and transnational) can be consolidated with the dimensions of international information technology defined in the previous section to provide the framework for the integration of the business and information technology strategies. This framework, presented in Table 4: International Business and Information Technology Strategy Alignment, provides the conceptual structure with which information technology issues are examined in this section.

The three columns in Table 4 represent the three forms of international business strategies discussed in the previous section: multinational, global, and transnational enterprise. The rows are the dimensions of information technology relevant for international business. Table 4, then, can be read in two

Dimension of IT Strategy:	Business Strategy		
	Multinational	**Global**	**Transnational**
Technology Architecture	Independent/Local IT Facilities at HQ & Subsidiaries	Central, Shared IT Facilities at HQs. Some IT Support at Subsidiaries.	Interdependent IT Facilities at HQ & Subsidiaries.
Data Architecture	Low Level of Integration Among Independent Databases at HQ & Subsidiaries.	Large, Central Shared Databases, some Small Special Databases at Subsidiaries.	Distributed Database.
Telecommunication Architecture	Direct, Simple Communication Link Between HQ & Subs for Transfer of Financial/Legal Data	Multiple Regional Nodal Networks Connecting HQ-Sub for Global Application Systems	Global Networks to Provide High Degree of Enterprise-Wide Connectivity.
Locus of IT Management	Local/Subsidiary Level, Minimal HQ Influence and Control	Centrally Coordianted & Managed IT Activities, Moderate Local Subsidiary Control.	Shared Responsibility & Authority for IT management; Team Orientation.

Table 4: International Business and Information Technology Strategy Alignment

ways: down the columns to define the information technology dimensions of a particular form of international business; or across the rows to examine the effect of changes in business strategy on information technology requirements. First the column, or international business perspective, will be described. Then, the row-wise, or evolutionary perspective of international information technology will be examined.

Since the **multinational enterprise** is formed by the financial investment of a HQ in a set of existing organizations which become its subsidiaries, the technology architecture of the multinational consists of those developed independently by the HQ unit and the subsidiaries. This autonomy is also reflected in the management of the information technology function. Both the HQ and its subsidiaries retain the control of their respective information technology subunits. In addition, because the subsidiaries operate autonomously, a low level of data integration is expected. However, financial data is an exception: since the strategic objective of the HQ (which formed the multinational by its investment) is return on investment, the HQ will typically demand access to the financial data of the subsidiary. Therefore, the information technology staff of the subsidiary can expect to provide financial reporting capability to the headquarters. Since the reporting is periodic and typically consists of summarized information, the information technology requirement will entail the establishment of simple, low capacity data telecommunication links. Consider the following example of a multinational firm's information technology strategy:

> *Trafalgar House PLC* (a commercial and residential property development conglomerate based in London): There is no overall information systems (IS) strategy. The IS divisions are decentralized at the divisional level and the central IS group acts in an advisory capacity. Integration is achieved, if at all, by the contagion across divisions of a successful system (Runyan, 1989).

The **global enterprise** is centrally coordinated from the HQ in order to achieve economies of scale and efficiency. Therefore, we expect to find most of the information technology to be centralized and information technology services from the HQ provided to the subsidiaries. The centralization and sharing extends to the data architecture as well, therefore, the information technology organization will be expected to maintain large enterprise-wide databases. Only specialized data of a local nature will be maintained at the subsidiary level. Since the enterprise-wide data must be collected on a global scale, and assuming a data aggregation scheme that minimizes bottlenecks on the central HQ system, the telecommunication architecture will be a vertical hierarchy. In other words, the subsidiaries connect to their regions where data is aggregated, and then the regions transmit summarized information to the HQ. Consider the following example of an information technology strategy in a global firm:

> *Klockner & Co. AG* (a German transportation carrier with worldwide operations): Information systems standards enable information technology to be deployed across the global operations of this transportation carrier. Central planning of information technology encourages standardization and lowers costs (Runyan, 1989).

The **transnational business** is a flexible enterprise with functionality distributed throughout the organization. Since the strategy is based on rapid organization-wide response to local market opportunities, the critical information technology capability is portability of information. Therefore, data architecture is distributed and there is a high degree of connectivity between HQ and all subsidiaries, as well as among all the subsidiaries. The connectivity supports managerial input from the subsidiaries, which is essential for knowledgeable response to local opportunities and the application of the resources distributed throughout the organization. This team orientation extends to the information technology management, which must share technology resources with the responsible unit in order to support the information system that is most responsive to the business requirement. Consider the following example of a transnational information technology strategy:

> *Federal Express Corporation* (a U.S. international delivery services business): The senior information officer maintains a five-year world-wide IS plan which is updated every six months. The plan covers technology architecture (hardware, software, applications); and telecommunication architecture (communications network). Distributed relational database (data architecture) technology allows remote users to customize information for their own needs while providing a standardized corporate information base. Key applications are developed according to operating standards, customized to respond to local needs, and then integrated across geographic regions and architectures (Runyan, 1989).

Another look at Table 4 demonstrates the evolutionary demands on information technology as the business strategy evolves from multinational, to global, and finally to transnational forms. Clearly, the transition is from less complexity to more; the multinational is the least complex and the transnational form is the most (recall Figure 1). It is reasonable to see this increased complexity reflected in the requirements placed on IT.

As the organization evolves from the multinational form to the global, the information technology management will be required to centralize technology and provide service to the entire organization. This will be challenging on many levels (budgetary, political, and technical) because the starting point is the multinational information technology context of autonomy and independence (and incompatibility!). This conceptual analysis is supported by events (Carlyle, 1990b; Runyan, 1989). Consider the following example of a firm evolving from the multinational to the global form:

> *Grand Metropolitan PLC* (an international retailer and food and beverage conglomerate with headquarters in London): Operating companies control their own IS plans. Regional data centers support distributed operations. Now that data centers have been established, senior systems management perceives a need to emphasize standards and application development. Group Systems Planning Director notes that "Not enough companies push for commonality". However, standards need to be endorsed by each of its subsidiary companies (Runyan, 1989).

Perhaps the more challenging task concerning technology and data architectures comes with the shift from the global to the transnational form. Information technology managers will be required to distribute the architecture they just centralized! While distribution is facilitated by the standardization imposed during the consolidation of information technology to support the global form, the transnational form requires that the standard architectures support the unique needs of the subsidiaries. This calls for a combination of central control and shared information technology management in an international environment. The discussion below in the section on the configuration of information technology in international business discusses the dimensions of the tradeoffs between consolidation and decentralization of information technology resources.

The evolution of telecommunication architecture can be viewed as an engineering problem of providing enough connectivity infrastructure to carry increasing traffic as the business demand grows. However, the management of the telecommunication service becomes more complex as the transition is made from direct simple links (in the multinational enterprise), to the central coordination of multiple links (to support a global strategy), and finally to enterprise-wide connectivity (the transnational form). Issues concerning security, architecture standardization, transborder data flow restrictions, economic justification and internal costing become more complex. Consider the following example:

> *Rhone-Poulenc* (a worldwide chemical company headquartered in Paris): A centralized IS department operates worldwide telecommunications and IS facilities. Subsidiaries maintain their own IS capability under the central unit's guidance and coordination. The Deputy Manager of Organization and Systems notes that "Information technology forms part of the internationalization of the group and accompanies its evolution" (Runyan, 1989).

Many of these issues can not be resolved by information technology management alone. A survey of 550 senior information technology managers found that 23% of their time is spent working with managers from outside the information technology organization (Carlyle, 1989).

The introduction to this chapter noted examples in which there were mismatches between the firm's information technology infrastructure and the requirements of the international business strategy. The previous section identified three models of international business and examined how the components of information technology are coordinated in each. This discussion has presented a framework for the integration of international business strategy with information technology. The next section examines the implications of the integrated framework for the physical configuration of information technology in international business.

Configuration of Information Technology in International Business *drivers*

In an international business it is possible for each component activity to be dispersed in several countries or consolidated in one. For example, data centers can be dispersed over many locations or consolidated into fewer and larger centers. Issues concerning the physical distribution of information technology often have been framed in terms of cost efficiencies (Carlyle, 1990b). However, a narrow economic perspective ignores both the strategic component and the value that information technology adds to other business activities (Parker & Benson, 1987). A managerial perspective that integrates information technology planning with the unique requirements of the business strategy provides a richer analytical approach.

Generally, the location of information technology activities will be driven by both economic considerations and the larger business strategy. More specifically, the decision embraces the following considerations (Carlyle 1990b; Porter 1986a):

1. The potential to realize **cost economies** from fewer and larger facilities. For example, capacity utilization may be improved and cost efficiencies obtained from the aggregation of similar transactions which can be run on more powerful and efficient hardware. Non-compatible architectures and redundant activities can be eliminated during the aggregation and consolidation process. In addition, the fixed costs (e.g. rent) associated with information technology facilities are generally less for fewer sites.

2. The ease of **transferring knowledge** among multiple sites. If information technology activities are dispersed, it may be difficult to provide the appropriate information technology skills where and when they are most needed. Restrictions on transborder data flows, cultural and political differences among information technology staff, and nonstandard architectures may hinder the transfer of skills to support primary activities.

3. The **local conditions** that favor an activity. While some countries may have regulations that restrict IT, others may encourage it. Some countries may be rich in highly skilled information systems profes-

sionals, or have a well-developed infrastructure (e.g., telecommunications capability, or information technology vendors to supply technology equipment and service) to support information technology activities.

4. Linked activities located in proximity with each other may be more effective and efficient. An important business activity with unique requirements may not be well-served by the uniform services of a consolidated information technology infrastructure. In this case, information technology activities may need to be co-located with the business activity it serves.

Management decisions to locate information technology facilities need to consider tradeoffs in these four factors. These tradeoffs have business performance implications, but they also should be linked to the requirements of the international business strategy (Parker & Benson, 1987; Keen, 1986; King & Premkumar, 1989). Therefore, tradeoffs should be evaluated in two ways: (1) an assessment of the efficiency and costs with which the information technology activities are conducted; and (2) an appraisal of the value added to the activities of the larger organization. The first is an economic evaluation; the second is part of a larger information technology strategic assessment. These two approaches are complementary. That is, an economic evaluation assesses the cost and benefit characteristics of a configuration. The strategic assessment incorporates the relative importance of the above four factors in the information technology planning process. The application of this complementary perspective is discussed below.

In the multinational enterprise, the primary and infrastructure activities of one subsidiary are consolidated in one country, with different autonomous subsidiaries in different countries. Therefore, following Consideration 4: Linked activities located in proximity, the enterprise-level information technology configuration will be decentralized in order to co-locate with the subsidiary it serves. For example, Trafalgar House PLC decentralized its information systems activities to pursue a multinational strategy.

In the global form, the organization locates each activity in whatever country offers the greatest potential economies of scale. Consideration 1: Cost economies, is dominant. The information technology configuration is centralized, but local conditions (the third consideration) and restrictions on transferring knowledge (the second consideration) determine the preferred location. Klochner & Company's focus on lower costs and standardized operations is typical of the global strategy.

In the transnational form, the firm locates activities in order to realize enhanced coordination of the inter-activity linkages while simultaneously responding to local markets. Consideration 2: Transferring knowledge is dominant. Information technology activities are configured in a distributed typology (standardization of communications, data and technology architectures; decentralized management) to maximize connectivity among subsidiaries. For example, The Federal Express Corporation uses a relational database and standards that allow for customization across geographic regions.

In an international business it is possible for business activities to be dispersed in several countries or consolidated in one. The choice of location should reflect the costs and benefits associated with each site as well as the contribution to strategic objectives. The idea that the information technology organization should support the business strategy is neither new nor unique to the domain of international business. However, the models developed in this chapter provide a substantive and structured framework with which to integrate the information technology and business strategies when operations are distributed across national borders. The next section applies these models to critical issues of information technology in international business.

IMPLEMENTING INTERNATIONAL INFORMATION TECHNOLOGY STRATEGIES

A review of the emerging literature in the area of international information technology management (Buss 1982; Cash, McFarlan, McKenney, & Vitale, 1988; Ives & Jarvenpaa, 1989; Keen, 1987) reveals a small number of factors that are necessary for success of the international information technology strategies. These factors consist of senior management awareness and involvement, effective organizational communication between the headquarters and subsidiary information technology units, standardization, and an integrated and flexible technology infrastructure.

In this section the information technology activities associated with

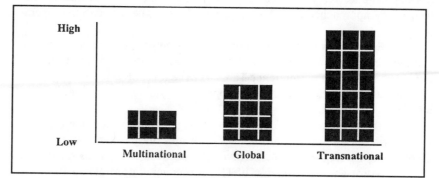

Figure 5. Significance of Critical Implementation Issues

these critical factors are linked to the dimensions of strategy. In this way, the organizing framework is operationalized. Furthermore, it is shown that the significance of these critical implementation issues varies systematically with the form of international business strategy. This relationship is summarized in Figure 5 and discussed in this section.

Senior Management Awareness And Action

A U.S. based oil firm has 40 telecommunication centers, each of which is authorized to approve expenditures of up to a million dollars. Senior management, failing to establish the link between the corporate and information technology strategies, is frustrated by the inability to connect its main divisions with its subsidiaries in support of their global business activities (Keen, 1987).

An international information technology strategy can not be conceived of as a simple aggregation of separate domestic information technology strategies. It should be driven by international business priorities (e.g., global product and customer basis) as determined by the senior management. Only the senior management has the perspective and influence required to establish the link between the international business and information technology strategies. Keen (1987) states that "It is absurd that so many international firms have global business strategies but no corresponding international information technology strategy."

The international business strategy as articulated by senior management defines the business terms against which the value of a coordinated information technology strategy is evaluated. In addition, senior management must allocate the resources for the appropriate information technology infrastructure. Delegation and separation of business and technology strategy development leads to disjointed, uncoordinated and regional information technology approaches unfit for supporting large scale international operations.

Earlier, this chapter observed that the requirement for coordination and the locus of management systematically varies with the form of international business strategy (reference Table 4). The level of senior management involvement with information technology strategy, then, is expected to vary with the type of strategy.

The involvement of HQ senior management is least in the multinational form because the management of each subsidiary is autonomous. The global strategy requires more involvement because it is characterized by central control and coordination of IT. Moreover, in the global form the organization's information technology budgets become more visible and investment in information technology is more critical for the entire enterprise. The transnational form is expected to require even more senior management involvement than the global form. The investment in global connectivity is substantial.

The shared responsibility of the team orientation allocates management responsibility horizontally rather than vertically, which alleviates some of the burden on top managers. Nevertheless, additional senior management attention is required to ensure that critical information technology projects are appropriately funded and managed. Senior business management, both at the headquarters and subsidiaries, should become aware and understand their role in applying information technology in support of international business strategies.

Organizational Communication

It takes five to ten times longer for an information technology project team to reach an understanding and agreement on system requirements and deliverables when team members are located in different countries (Ives & Jarvenpaa, 1989).

Effective organizational communication between headquarter, subsidiary information technology units, and remote users is a major factor in the successful development of international information technology strategies. Cultural differences, differences in personnel skill and training, and technical limitations, make effective communication a major challenge.

Mechanisms for enhancing communication among the remote information technology units in an international firm include regular international meetings and visits, educational programs, newsletters and planned staff rotations. Frequent communication among the headquarter and subsidiary information technology units increases the awareness of the units of the different levels of technology resources and vendor support at various geographical areas as well as the variations in the skill levels and special competency levels of the remote information technology staff. Communication that effectively alleviates cultural and language barriers and enhances cooperation is vital to successful implementation of an international information technology strategy. However, the communication requirements are expected to be a function of the international business strategy.

For example, the success of a transnational strategy depends on collaboration and teamwork between business units that cross national boundaries. This places an extremely heavy burden on organizational communication and connectivity. Conversely, the multinational firm assigns far fewer requirements on the communication technology infrastructure of the firm because each subsidiary operates autonomously. The global firm has more moderate communication requirements. The consolidated information technology activities are stable and uniform, but each subsidiary needs to be connected to the centralized information technology facility.

Business And Technology Standards

Evolving standards will help us more than any specific technology. Senior Vice President of Information Systems and telecommunications, Federal Express Corp. (Runyan, 1989).

We would like to have an open architecture so that we could take advantage of a single operating system and a single telecommunications protocol around the world. Vice President of Information Systems, DuPont (Carlyle, 1990b).

Public and private technology standards determine what is practical in an international information technology environment (Keen, 1987). A prerequisite to success of international information technology strategies is selecting a number of key standards for hardware, software, and telecommunications that are consistent with the regulatory constraints and supply of technology in different geographical regions. Standards are important because they impact the degree of interconnectivity of computer and communication equipment as well as operating systems, application software and databases across national boundaries.

Standards in the international information technology arena can emerge from three sources: regulatory institutions (such as the Consultative Committee of the International Telecommunication and Telegraph), industry cooperation (such as the Society for World-wide International Funds Transfer), and de facto market conditions (such as the influence of IBM, a dominant vendor). In addition, a firm can work to achieve internal standardization of its information technology infrastructure. For example, standardization of data enables the creation, transfer and use of organizational information in the form of dictionaries and repositories (Carlyle, 1990b).

Regardless of the source of standards, they are a critical prerequisite for an international information technology strategy. In fact, the entire international technical plan depends on assumptions about progress in implementation and availability of international standards. International firms should monitor the trends in business and technical standards and international vendor products to keep abreast of emerging standards. International companies can also influence the standard setting process by getting involved in the international committees and forming consortia for developing business standards.

The value of information technology standards to a business is expected to vary with the type of international strategy it pursues. A multinational business would value international standards the least because its subsidiaries are autonomous with few intra-organizational linkages. The global business, which seeks to achieve economies by aggregation of similar transactions and provision of common services, should value information technology standards much more. The transnational firm should value information technology standards the most because it is expected to share information resources and responsibility among the central HQ information technology organization and those of the subsidiaries. Since the information technology activities are so dispersed in the transnational, standards become critical to ensure commonality and transferability.

Technology Platform

A U.S. based international firm operates a large telecommunication network interconnecting 3 million devices (including burglar alarms, workstations, and processors). Every hour five thousand lines of text (equivalent to Shakespeare's *Hamlet*) describing the active states of the network are displayed at the operator console.

An information technology strategy is a framework for development of a technology platform consisting of appropriate databases, computing, and data communication capabilities and architecture. Global and transnational information technology strategies lead to more complex — and more expensive — telecommunication networks than those required by multinational firms. In this context, the international coordination of very distributed data resources across massive telecommunication networks will be a major technical and organizational challenge.

The data architectures to support transnational businesses are the most complex. For example, COVIA (a subsidiary of United Airlines) operates an airline reservation system that processes about 1,400 transactions per second. Future expansion plans for the system include addition of travel related services and linking to other airline systems, hotel and car rental services (Keen, 1989). A short-term forecast estimates the level of the traffic over the network at 2,000 transactions per second. COVIA exemplifies the data communication and capacity demands, coordination and security requirements of an extremely complex information technology application that is supporting a transnational enterprise.

Implementation of transnational information technology strategies also requires the largest degree of discipline and coordination in enterprise-wide data management. Coherent and compatible data definitions, data structures, and data organization are key determinants of success in implementation of the transnational information technology strategy.

Developing technology platforms for support of international business strategies requires an extraordinary amount of planning and coordination. An international technology platform evolves over time, guided by business priorities and requirements.

CONCLUSIONS

This chapter has described the role of information technology in support of international business and the evolution of this role as the organization changes from one form of international business to another. It has shown that the issues and requirements that information technology is called on to resolve can be anticipated by examining the implications of the international business strategy for the HQ-subsidiary relationship.

While there is minimal interaction of information technology management in the multinational form of enterprise, there will be strong pressure to centralize the information technology function when the organization develops into a global business. However, these pressures will be reversed as the business strategy evolves into a transnational orientation.

While the framework outlined in this chapter is broadly defined, it is extremely useful because it specifies the interface between business and information technology strategy. Moreover, it identifies extremely difficult challenges to the information technology function that go beyond the typical perspectives of life cycle analysis, systems analysis and design, operations management, and data communications. The evolution of an international business strategy from multinational, to global, and then to transnational places discontinuous demands on IT.

In 1986, Jack Evans, Vice Chairman and Director of Manufacturers Hanover's world-wide Geonet, observed that the business strategy will beget the information technology structure, but the two must be linked. It is precisely in those areas of interface identified in this chapter that the information technology strategy must demonstrate responsiveness and alignment if it is not to fail its fiduciary responsibility to the enterprise. The framework presented in this chapter, then, identifies the **critical factors**, and their expected values in three forms of international business, that must be addressed in order to align information technology and international business strategy. The organizational responses to these factors are expected to correlate with the success of the integrated strategy.

References

Ahituv, N., & Neumann, S. (1986). *Principles of information systems for management.* Iowa: Wm. C. Brown, Pub.

Bartlett, C.A. (1986). Building and managing the transnational: The new organizational challenge. In M.E. Porter (Ed.) *Competition in global industries.* Boston, MA: Harvard Business School Press.

Bartlett, C.A., & Ghoshal, S. (1989). *Managing across borders: The transnational solution.* Boston, MA: Harvard Business School Press.

Bartlett, C.A., & Ghoshal, S. (Fall, 1988). Organizing for worldwide effectiveness: The transnational solution. *California Management Review, 31*(1), 54-74.

Buss, M.D.J. (September-October, 1982). Managing international information systems. *Harvard Business Review, 60*(5), 153-162.

Carlyle, R.E. (August 15, 1989). Careers in crisis. *Datamation, 35*(16), 12-16.

Carlyle, R. (February 1, 1990a). The tomorrow organization. *Datamation, 36*(3), 22-29.

Carlyle, R. (April 15, 1990b). Why consolidation makes sense. *Datamation, 36*(8), 24-29.

Cash, Jr., J.I., McFarlan, F.W., McKenney, J.L., & Vitale, M.R. (1988). *Corporate information systems management: Text and cases* (2nd Ed.). Illinois: Richard D. Irwin, Inc.

Caves, R.E. (1982). The multinational enterprise as an economic organization. Ch. 1 in the author's *Multinational enterprise and economic analysis.* Cambridge, UK: Cambridge University Press.

Egelhoff, W.G. (1988). *Organizing the multinational enterprise: An information processing perspective.* MA: Ballinger Publishing Co.

Fayerweather, J.F. (1982). *International business strategy and administration.* MA: Ballinger Publishing Co.

Galbraith, J.R. (1973). *Designing complex organizations.* MA: Addison-Wesley.

Ghoshal, S. (1987). Global strategy: An organizing framework. *Strategic Management Journal, 8*(5), 8:425-440.

Gupta, A.K., & Govindarajan, V. (1989). Knowledge flows and the structure of control within multinational corporations. Working paper, The University of Maryland.

Ives, B., & Jarvenpaa, S.L. (1989). Global information technology: Building Bridges for the third millennium. Southern Methodist University: Unpublished manuscript.

Keen, P.G.W. (1987). An international perspective on managing information technologies. The International Center for Information Technologies: Briefing paper. Washington, D.C.

Keen, P.G.W. (1989). Information technology and organizational advantage: The next agenda for research. The International Center for Information Technologies: Briefing paper. Washington,

D.C.

King, W.R., & Sethi, V. (1990). The transnational context of information systems and technology: The transnational system. The Joseph M. Katz Graduate School of Business, University of Pittsburgh. Working Paper.

King, W.R., & Premkumar, G. (1989). Key issues in telecommunications planning. *Information and Management, 17,* 255-265.

Kogut, B. (1989). Research notes and communications: A note on global strategies. *Strategic Management Journal, 10*(4), 383-389.

Malone, T. (1988). What is coordination theory? Sloan School of Management, Massachusetts Institute of Technology. Working Paper No. Sloan WP No. 2051-88.

Mandell, S.L., & Grub, P.D. (1979). Survey of multinational corporate computer-based information systems. *European Journal of Operational Research, 3,* 359-367.

Pantages, A. (August 15, 1989). The right IS chemistry. *Datamation, 35*(16), 61-62.

Parker. M.M., & Benson, R.J. (December 1, 1987. Information economics: An introduction. *Datamation, 33*(23), 86-96.

Porter, M.E. (Winter, 1986a). Changing patterns of international competition. *California Management Review, 28*(2), 9-40.

Porter, M.E. (1986b). Competition in global industries: A conceptual framework. In the author's *Competition in global industries.* Boston, MA: Harvard Business School Press.

Porter, M.E., & Millar V.E. (July-August, 1985). How information gives you competitive advantage. *Harvard Business Review,* 149-160.

Reck, R.H. (August 1, 1989). The shock of going global. *Datamation, 35*(15), 67-69.

Runyan, L. (December 1, 1989). Global IS strategies. *Datamation, 35*(23), 71-78.

Snapp, C.D. (March 1, 1990). EDI aims high for global growth. *Datamation, 36*(5), 77-80.

Wiggin, G. (October 1, 1987). The golden rules of global networking. *Datamation, 33*(19), 68-73.

23

An Integrating Framework for Information Technology Issues in a Transnational Environment

Vikram Sethi and Josephine E. Olson
University of Pittsburgh

Information Technology (IT) has substantially altered societies, economies, and polities, and in the process has transcended state boundaries to form a global environment. This chapter examines the character of IT in a transnational environment and its effects on different societal units in order to understand the manner in which issues pertaining to IT arise and are resolved by national and international policy. The chapter explicates three dimensions of IT. The first, the characteristics dimension, refers to the salient characteristics of IT, which are convergence of technologies, transnationality and market concentration. The second, the effects dimension, considers the impact of IT on the individual, the transnational firm, and the state. The interaction of the above two dimensions creates issue areas and a demand for regulation and public policy—the third dimension. Harmonizing these differences in national policies is accomplished through bilateral, regional, or multilateral negotiations. The major emphasis of this chapter is the identification of variables related to the transnational use of IT and their interaction.

Burgeoning cross-border capital flows. Expanding international trade. The telecommunications revolution. These are the forces that drive finance worldwide. (Deutsche Bank Group, 1990)

[A global data communications network] from Northern Telecom has made every time zone in the world more accessible for Bankers Trust. (Northern Telecom, 1990)

With offices in 74 countries, BNP monitors major world markets 24 hours a day, gathering and analysing up-to-the-minute data in the service of its clients" (BNP, 1989)

As the above examples point out, more and more transnational firms are adopting Information Technology (IT) as a tool to manage global operations. For example, "global networking" serves to knit together the manufacturing plants of ICI, spread over 40 countries, and its distribution outlets in 150 countries; the 35 plants of Sharp (Bradshaw, 1990); and Texas Instrument's 43 IBM mainframes in 20 data centers around the world (Pantages, 1989). Instantaneous global communications capability is fast becoming a prerequisite for competitive survival in the international marketplace.

Network globalization has been classified as the final phase of corporate evolution when corporate networks become "geographically blind" (Irwin & Merenda, 1989). This trend can be seen in firms such as Federal Express, Merrill Lynch, Nissan, General Electric and Citicorp, and occurs in several functional areas including finance, retailing, printing and office support services.

With the increasing globalization of business, IT has transcended state boundaries and the results have been increased services to buyers, increased competitive advantage to sellers, and increased economic advantages to the nations of the buyers and sellers. Accompanying the benefits of IT are changes which have required adjustments from all constituents affected by IT: individuals, firms, and states. This readjustment has required new forms of national regulation and international policy harmonization.

This chapter deals with the above issues and undertakes the following tasks:

• Examines the role of IT in a transnational environment and the manner in which it has altered the roles of states, firms, and individuals;

• Discusses various issues which arise due to the utilization of IT for global communication;

• Identifies the means available for harmonization of IT-related issues and the appropriate fora at which such actions have been undertaken.

THE IMPACT OF THE GROWTH IN TRANSNATIONAL INFORMATION FLOWS

Numerous studies show that transnational communication is increasing. Within the United States, revenues from overseas communication services increased by 40 percent in the years 1980 to 1987[1]. Increases for the years 1960-1970 and 1970-1980 were 495 percent and 513 percent, respectively. INTELSAT (International Telecommunications Satellite Organization), which has 13 satellites providing trans-oceanic video, facsimile, data and telex services, today services 173 countries compared to 15 in 1965; it provides 116,353 full-time channels versus 150 in 1965 and 68,658 television channel hours versus 80 (Burch, 1989). A recent study of electronic mailboxes ("Strong Growth," 1990) projected annual growth rates in Europe and North America ranging from 20 percent for Sweden to 80 percent for Germany.

Value added services, such as Electronic Data Interchange (EDI), have also increased as firms attempt to improve efficiency and compete more effectively (Taylor, 1990). These services, which totaled 3,215 million ECU in the European Community in 1989, are projected to be 12,550 million ECU in 1994. Telecommunications equipment expenditures are also increasing. The Financial Times ("Survey on," 1990) projected forecasts for the period 1990-2005 of approximately 125 percent for transmission equipment expenditures and 175 percent for world public switching expenditures. It is therefore highly likely that worldwide communications will maintain its explosive growth.

This growth has altered, and will continue to alter, international relationships at both intergovernmental and transnational levels. This leads to the question: Are global information transactions conceptually different from those which occur within national boundaries?

From a theoretical perspective, the major characteristic of international information flows is that they cross national boundaries and cut across two or more political, economic, and socio-cultural systems. The study of international information flows therefore hinges on the reciprocal relationship in which: information flows affect different environmental systems; and different environmental systems affect and modify international information flows.

The international political system is based on the principle of state sovereignty. Each national government has exclusive jurisdiction over the territory of its state, monopoly over the use of physical force and over the enactment of laws governing individuals and organizations within its jurisdiction, and control over its legal residents and their operations. This concept of sovereignty has raised various problems for the multinational firm such as dual allegiance, double taxation, expropriation, and legal rights and remedies (Root, 1988). The same principle has also affected international information flows. Information technology has resulted in the global dissemination of knowledge, information, ideas, and intellectual creations which governments have found difficult to tax, censor, monitor, and generally control. Of primary concern have been the state's claim to ownership of information and an individual's right to communicate freely across frontiers. Information technology has made ownership and control of information difficult while facilitating cross-border communications. Moreover, IT has made it possible to exercise control over long distances, for example, through a centralized network located in another nation and by remote sensing.

Although it is not evident that the use of IT has yet challenged the state as a sovereign political institution, concern has been expressed as to whether IT has enabled economically powerful states to extend their influence over weaker states. The majority of information networks are predominantly under the control of a few West European and North American countries (Vinogradov et al., 1984). Given this imbalance, developing countries have taken measures to protect their indigenous IT sectors by actions such as limiting transborder data flows and controlling trade and foreign direct investments in IT-related goods and services. In turn, developed countries have focused on liberalizing trade in services, including IT, in negotiations such as those under the General Agreement on Tariffs and Trade (GATT). The international economic system, consisting of the flow of goods, services, money, capital, technologies, and skills, has therefore been directly influenced by international information flows.

The international socio-cultural system is another subsystem affected by international information flows. To Masmoudi (1984), the North-South[2] disparity in IT, news media ownership, and control over media content is akin to a *de facto* information hegemony fueled by a will to dominate on the part of the North. Similar statements were endorsed in the past by the New International Information Order Summit in Algiers (1973) and the Colombo Summit (1976)[3]. A recent debate in Europe concerning cross-border information flows and cultural issues has been over the international regulation of transborder television services. France stressed that a European television program must be backed by cultural safeguards in order to prevent an inundation of "cheap programs of low cultural interest marketed mainly by American producers" (Hondius, 1989, p. 19). Similar concerns over the content of media and information have been voiced in the past by countries such as Canada and Sweden (Blatherwick, 1987).

International information flows, therefore, affect these three environmental subsystems, which in turn influence the content and method of information flows. These issues are developed in greater detail in the next sections.

PERSPECTIVES IN PAST RESEARCH

Literature pertaining to international information flows and transnational IT is dispersed over several theoretical areas: international politics, economics, law, and telecommunications. Although the literature offers important insights for the development of theoretical perspectives, few studies have directly dealt with transnational IT issues or have attempted to integrate past literature.

At a general level, the literature related to transnational IT has usually adopted one of two perspectives: a focus on transborder data flow (TBDF) policy; or IT in the context of trade in services.

Studies in the period 1975-1985 primarily adopted the first perspective. Since 1985, focus has shifted to issues of trade in services and the role of IT in them. However, both research streams deal with the same conceptual issues, albeit adopting different interpretive viewpoints.

The focus of TBDF studies has been on the development of an understanding of international data flows and their impact on nations and multinational firms. A representative study by Hamelink (1984) considers: the impact international data flows have on the imbalances in the information capacities of developed and developing countries, and the impact transnational data flows have on the informational advantage and social impact of transnational corporations. Issues under the TBDF research stream include the effect of international data flows on employment, privacy, national sovereignty, free flow of information, and international telecommunications policies. For example, the OECD in 1980 issued its Privacy Guidelines (Organization for Economic Cooperation and Development [OECD], 1981a) related to the international transfer of name-linked data and in the period 1980-1985 focused on the aspects of data protection, economic data, and operations of transnational corporations.

A significant outcome of studies in the TBDF period was the recognition of the imbalances in information and IT capabilities among nations. Although this was especially true for programs of UN agencies such as UNESCO (United Nations Educational, Scientific and Cultural Organization), other institutions such as the Intergovernmental Bureau of Informatics (IBI) also organized several conferences on this issue. In addition to the debate in UNESCO, issues of global information flows were adopted as major programs at several meetings of the non-aligned countries. Although these programs were helpful in bringing global information issues into prominence, they also resulted in the withdrawal of support by the developed countries from research programs and international agencies. The withdrawal of the U.S. from UNESCO is a case in point. The U.S. viewed NWICO[4] (the New World Information and Communication Order) as promoting "statist, restrictive, nondemocratic concepts" (Bolton, 1989) since, by calling for balanced information flows, it invited government regulation of media. The fundamental issues raised were: Who decides whether there is a balance and how it is achieved? Is balance to be achieved by vesting authority in governments to restrict the flow of information into a country? Under such a proposition, freedom of information and communications is seriously curtailed. As McDowell (1989) points out, nations with strong data resources and IT producers and users have no interest in having their use of these resources limited by ascribing to strong information rights of states. Neither would these nations be expected to develop rigorous programs to achieve worldwide equality in the ownership and use of information resources. Understandably, support for programs which accentuated the unevenness of global information markets declined, and the work by IBI and the United Nations Center for Transnational Corporations (UNCTC) was limited.

In order to discuss how communications issues have resurfaced under the label "trade-in-services," we need to note the growing role of services in international trade. Services have become a significant component of world trade and a large net contributor to the GNP of most nations. As the largest service exporter, the United States has emphasized the need for an open trade environment in services. The Trade Act of 1974, which laid down the negotiating terms for the Tokyo Round of trade talks, represented the first time the United States raised the issue of including services in the concept of international trade. Its efforts culminated in the inclusion of services in the Uruguay Round of the GATT talks begun in 1986.

This emphasis on services trade has shifted the focus of global communications to primarily trade issues. Data services, which are comprised of data processing, information storage and retrieval, software and telecommunications services, are the focus of attention because they increasingly enter international trade and also increase the tradeability of other services. Data services permit transnational communications and enhance other services such as banking, financial management, and inventory control. However, as Sauvant (1989) notes, the potential of data services can only be fully realized in an international environment which is relatively free from restrictions on their flow. Thus, information and IT-related issues find their place in the context of data services and in the broader framework of trade-in-services. The central question is that of identifying and eliminating market barriers and restrictions on services. As McDowell (1989) notes, the emphasis is on mutual benefits from free trade as opposed to reduction of inequalities in global communications (the TBDF focus). Other concerns of the TBDF approach now appear as barriers to trade-in-services. For example, the issues of state sovereignty and cultural domination which were dealt with directly under the TBDF perspective now appear as factors restricting trade in data services.

A MODEL FOR IT IN A TRANSNATIONAL ENVIRONMENT

The changing perspectives of past research have been particularly useful in developing alternate views of global information issues. Another contribution has been the understanding that technology change (e.g., telecommunications services) necessitates different formulations of concepts (e.g., data flow as services trade). Despite these contributions towards understanding global information issues and problems, formulation of a concrete agenda as a basis for further discussion is still lacking. What are some invariant properties or theoretical constructs across the two research streams? This section presents various dimensions of IT in order to answer this question. The identification of these characteristics will enable a means for classifying research as well as for explaining and developing information and IT-related issues.

Three dimensions of IT emerge from the existing literature. These are: the characteristics dimension; the effects dimension; and the issue area and policy dimension.

The first dimension, the Characteristics Dimension, is based on properties of IT pertinent to the transnational environment. Here we distinguish properties of IT which affect the role or functioning of the nation, firm, or individual. IT is a collaborative enterprise of telecommunications and computer technology, and thus its first characteristic is converging technologies. A second characteristic, transnationalism, pertains more to information and applies to IT since, by facilitating the cross-border movement of information, IT enhances the public goods nature of information and information products. Thirdly, the distribution of IT is uneven across the nations of the world, leading to market concentration.

These characteristics are particularly important to the transnational environment because most of the issues associated with global information flows are directly linked to them. For example, the issue of privacy has occurred because transnational networks are capable of carrying large volumes of data. This has occurred due to converging technologies. Similarly, the emergence of movements such as NWICO are due to the characteristic of market concentration or an imbalance of IT resources.

Most studies have focused on the impact of IT characteristics on the state, the transnational firm, or the individual. This classification represents the second dimension, termed the Effects Dimension. The state is affected, for example, by principles of sovereignty; the firm, by using IT to manage its operations; and the individual, by changing work and home environments and the impact of IT on culture.

Dimensions such as those above may not be collectively exhaustive, but do appear regularly in past research. Table 1 lists several studies and the main units of analysis adopted. Also included are the major characteristics of IT discussed by each study. It should, however, be recognized that this classification presents the major focus of each study and <u>not</u> the only one. For example, a study discussing the economic impact of IT on the MNC must necessarily discuss the environment of information and telecommunications policies of the nations in which it operates.

Figure 1 presents the complete model for IT in a transnational environment. It shows the three characteristics of IT which influence different societal units. This interaction results in the third dimension, the Issue Area and Policy Dimension.

Privacy is an issue area and so is economic dependence for information resources. Since national policies differ, regulation adopted in different countries to deal with these issues can vary substantially. In order to avoid the restrictive aspects of national policy there must be harmonization at an international level. This is shown in the oval at the bottom of Figure 1. For example, legal systems vary a great deal across countries. However, some common ground and understanding is required in order for data flows to occur among nations.

Figure 2 presents the three dimensions in matrix form and outlines the major issues arising out of the interaction of the effects and characteristics dimensions. These dimensions and the literature on them are discussed in detail below. Finally, international harmonization, through international arrangements, pertains to the characteristic-effect interactions and is discussed in a later section.

The Characteristics Dimension

As can be seen from Table 1, three main characteristics of IT have been noted in literature. These are: Converging technologies, Transnationality, and Market concentration.

Converging Technologies: Converging technologies refers to the integration of communication and computer technology. This is seen in the development of very large scale integrated circuits, parallel processing and expert systems together with the use of fibre optics, private satellites, and integrated service digital networks in the communications sector.

The primary impact of the merger of computers and communications has been the introduction of intelligence into the telecommunications network. A whole range of network-based services are now available—enhanced telephony, facsimile, videotext, electronic messages, and videoconferencing. Because of its increased intelligence, functions which were primarily outside the telecommunications network are now incorporated within it. This incorporation of external functions is manifested in the growth of integrated informa-

Author	Unit of Analysis	Characteristic Area
OECD (1979a)	MNC	Market Concentration
	State	Transnationality
Bartnick (1983)	State	Market Concentration
		Converging Technologies
Gray (1983)	State	Market Concentration
OECD (1983)	Individual	Converging Technologies
	State	Transnationality
	MNC	Market Concentration
Sweeney (1983)	State	Market Concentration
White & McDonnell (1983)	State	Market Concentration
Cole (1986)	State	Market Concentration
OECD (1986a)	State	Market Concentration
OECD (1986b)	State	Converging Technologies
		Transnationality
Berman (1987)	State	Transnationality
Cleveland (1987)	Individual	Transnationality
	State	Converging Technologies
Huber (1987)	State	Converging Technologies
Lanvin (1987a)	State	Market Concentration
	MNC	Converging Technologies
		Transnationality
Lanvin (1987b)	State	Market Concentration
	MNC	Converging Technologies
		Transnationality
Oman (1987)	MNC	Converging Technologies
Weingarten (1988)	Individual	Converging Technologies
Fauvet (1989)	Individual	Converging Technologies
	State	
Gallagher (1989)	State	Market Concentration
		Transnationality
Gassmann (1989)	Individual	Converging Technologies
	MNC	
Hepworth (1989)	MNC	Market Concentration
Hustinx (1989)	Individual	Transnationality
Lamborghini (1989) MNC		Transnationality
Lanvin (1989a)	State	Market Concentration
	MNC	Converging Technologies
		Transnationality
Lanvin (1989b)	State	Market Concentration
	MNC	Converging Technologies
		Transnationality
Monk (1989)	Individual	Converging Technologies
	State	Transnationality
	MNC	Market Concentration
Matta &		
Boutros (1989)	State	Market Concentration
OECD (1989)	State	Converging Technologies
	MNC	
Simitis (1989)	State	Transnationality
"Comissioners"		
(1989)	Individual	Converging Technologies
	State	Transnationality
Snapp (1990)	MNC	Converging Technologies
Palvia & Palvia		
(1990)	MNC	Transnationality

Table 1: Past Studies on IT in a Transnational Environment

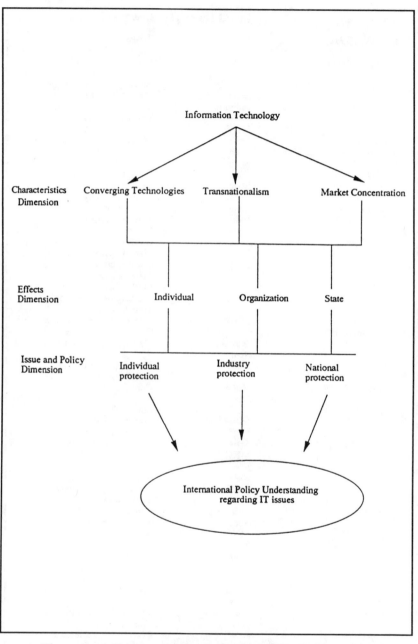

**Figure 1: A Framework for Information Technology in a
Transnational Environment**

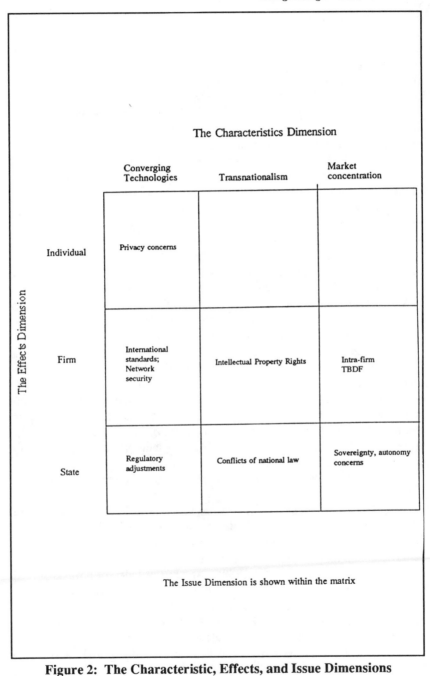

Figure 2: The Characteristic, Effects, and Issue Dimensions

tion systems technology, for example, the integrated services digital network (ISDN) systems and services.

Convergence does not imply that all systems are or will be integrated. Non-integrated technology and systems still exist. However, much of the impact in the transnational environment, for example, growth of telecommunication services and their trade, can be attributed to converging technologies. The capability of integrated networks to store, process, and communicate information has allowed an expansion of the capacity of non-integrated systems. This is possible since information resources can now not only be carried as network traffic but also be economically transformed.

There is increasing agreement among countries, especially OECD members, that common network services across states are necessary for the development of international business. However, given the differences in national policies and priorities among countries, differences in development of services arise and these are considered in the Issue Area and Policy Dimension.

Transnationality: Information, the products of information, and the costs and benefits resulting from information are becoming increasingly transnational[5]. Although one can argue that converging technology has increased the transnationality of IT, the attribute of transnationality results from a variety of events, particularly the growth of the MNC and has in turn fostered the growth of the transnational enterprise.

Conceptually, the attribute of transnationality can be associated with IT in several possible ways by demonstrating: that IT has promoted transnational interactions; that the use of IT has precipitated a growth of transnational organizations; that IT-promoted interactions have required transnational regulation and increased intergovernmental cooperation; that IT has required an alternate theoretical formulation of the concept of the "state"; and that the application of IT has resulted in tangible or intangible products that defy classical state ownership doctrines.

Several of these ideas will be used below to show that transnationality is a valid property of IT.

The world financial markets are prime examples of the growth of computer-mediated transnational interactions. The Eurodollar market had a daily turnover of $300 billion per day in 1986. This figure is larger than the value of annual trade and about twice the value of the rapidly growing trading in foreign currency (Estabrook, 1988). Another instance of a transnational system, the SWIFT (Society for Worldwide Interbank Financial Telecommunication) System, is a financial community in its own right, processing more than one trillion dollars on a daily basis. The system is operated by a Belgian cooperative society owned and managed by 1,460 financial institutions worldwide. While banking systems in the U.S., e.g., Fedwire and CHIPS (the Clearing House Interbank Payments System), are subject to examination by the

Federal Reserve System, the SWIFT system is not; there does not seem to be any regulation for this transnational society (U.S. General Accounting Office [GAO], 1989b). It seems likely that transnational communities such as SWIFT proliferate with no geographic boundaries, and much of this spread can be associated with IT.

IT products also exhibit characteristics of transnationality. The products of IT are information commodities, and the producers of these are affected by the public goods nature of information. Information technology enhances the public nature of information commodities by ease of duplication and transference. Consider an original copyrighted work in a database to be accessed by specified users. Since sharing is extremely easy, the private nature of the commodity is soon destroyed. To complicate matters, international transfers of information are just as easy as those within the country and are difficult for the state to control. What government can control or regulate the content of a network, much less how and where data are moving?

Monk (1989) contends that the viability of any information commodity depends upon the protection afforded by copyright, patent or property rights. However, few national or international intellectual property or copyright conventions have been able to come to terms with international information transfers.

Perhaps a more important question is that of information ownership and territoriality. Classical issues of patent, trademark, trade secret, and copyright are based on the principle of territoriality (Mestmacker, 1989) and maintained through agreements promulgated bilaterally. These principles are mostly ineffective when dealing with information and information products. Since information can travel across states, what of its ownership? And once the issue of ownership is in question, it is debatable whether appropriate measures based on territoriality can be advocated to protect information commodities.

A more abstract conceptualization of transnationality is that of the impact of IT on the classical principles of the "state." Smith (1980) provides one example of the manner in which the concept of the "state" has suffered infringement through IT. In a case before the House of Lords in London in 1977, a U.S. prosecutor wanted to take evidence in Britain from an official of a Crown Corporation which was before an American court on charges relating to financial management. The Lords confirmed the decision of lower courts that questioning British subjects on British territory by agents of a foreign government would constitute an infringement of sovereignty. One of the issues pondered in this case was whether this sovereignty could have been protected if the information concerned had been stored in a computer under American control. Any information stored within the U.S. falls under American jurisdiction and can be subpoenaed by an American court. The same principles apply to data bounced off an American satellite. Again, territoriality which defines the boundaries of a state is little respected by data or information flows.

Pipe (1984) refers to another example of the impact of IT on the state. A basic tenet of the nation-state is independence in formulating policies for the use of its resources, including information. A state must be allowed the right to plan its information resources and evaluate its social allocation and control in the wider context of society's specific interests. This principle is in direct conflict with the available technology. Insofar as IT is instituted within a transnational society, the interest is on the right to communicate across national boundaries. Information technology, by enabling information flows across borders, threatens a nation's sense of its own independence and sovereignty.

Traditionally, national boundaries not only mark the territorial limits of the state, they also serve as the location at which a nation exercises its sovereignty. Movements of goods and people are controlled at the frontier or at locations of first landing. If a nation-state so desires, it can exercise its ability to monitor and/or control the flow of goods across its borders. A state exercises its sovereignty in these matters through customs and immigration checkpoints, landing and berthing rights, import or export restrictions, tariffs, etc. However, what are the physical boundaries for information? The "boundaries" of a computer network are defined by all the locations from which its users access the system. If a state wishes to create electronic boundaries to coincide with physical boundaries, it would be required to make enforcement decisions of a much different nature than those which currently apply to the movement of people and physical products. These decisions would relate to the feasibility of information boundaries, surveillance and control of information, and methods of evaluation and taxation of information. All these issues are complex due to the intangible nature of information.

Information technology substantially challenges a state's rights of: exercise of jurisdiction; control of economic resources; trade; and supervision of social and cultural matters within its borders. Although this by itself is not sufficient to characterize IT by the property of transnationalism, IT alters the state-centric paradigm of international relations, giving prominence to the non-government actors in a world society. Insofar as this society forms across state boundaries and necessitates adjustments on the part of the state, IT endorses transnationality.

Market concentration: Lamberton (1989) treats information imbalances in a simple fashion: A knows and B does not know. Since imbalances are a consequence of differential capabilities, we modify this premise as follows: A has the capability to know and B does not. Where this capability refers to the availability of IT and the knowledge of its use, we refer to this as IT imbalances and it forms the basis of international market concentration.

Information technology and expertise in its use are concentrated within a few states. This concentration, while highly visible between the developed and the developing countries, is also present among the developed countries. Within the OECD, Mansell & Ypsilanti (1987) describe the following differences in telecommunications infrastructure. The 24 OECD countries have 79% of the telephones and 78% of the main lines despite only 65% of the world's GNP and 17% of the population. However, within the OECD, the United States, Japan and the ten oldest members of the European Community account for 85% of OECD main lines. There are also significant differences in the OECD countries in terms of per capita telecommunications service income and its growth.

In another analysis, Staple & Mullins (1989) suggest that international telecommunications traffic, measured in "minutes of telecommunications traffic (MiTT)," is an accurate way of tracking business activity, particularly in the service sector of the economy. Their study analyzed MiTT data in three countries and found that U.S. telecommunications traffic is directed to a relatively few countries, and this concentration appears to be growing over time. Thus, services trade appears to be concentrated among a few countries.

As noted above, inequalities are even more pronounced between the developed and the developing countries. One of the earliest and most comprehensive reports covering communication problems was the McBride Report commissioned by the United Nations Educational, Scientific, and Cultural Organization (UNESCO, 1980). That report, while describing the international imbalance in news circulation in the world, noted that the imbalance not only affects news flows but the collection of data for scientific, commercial, military and other purposes; thus there is also "an imbalance regarding strategic information for political and economic decision making" (1980, p. 36).

Yet another report described the gap in IT infrastructure between the developed and developing countries. The Nairobi Plenipotentiary of the ITU created a Commission for World-Wide Telecommunications Development in order to examine methods for stimulating telecommunications development in the developing world. That Commission—dubbed the Maitland Commission (1984)—estimated that $12 billion would be needed to bring the developing countries up to an acceptable level of development.

It is for the same reasons that the "New World Information and Communication Order" (NWICO) was founded at the 1978 General Conference of UNESCO and the General Assembly of the United Nations. The greatest contribution of NWICO is that it focused attention on the inequality in the distribution of communication resources among states.

While the above evidence points to "information gaps" among the nations, a number of arguments suggest that the trend towards regional inequality will continue. Gillespie & Robins (1989) contend that most global systems are formed by transnational corporations in support of their functions—distribution, marketing, and management controls. Also, most global telecommunications systems are private networks available only to a closed community of end users. Digital networks, therefore, support existing monopolies and empires by creating "private systems of communications" (p. 13). In further support of their argument, they cite conclusions from two studies undertaken for the Commission of the European Communities that advanced communications technologies display a bias for core regions. Without policy intervention, the considerable economic benefits associated with IT will be reaped by the core regions, which will further polarize the developed and the under-developed regions. It is possible to argue that organizations in the peripheral regions can use IT to overcome their remoteness from the core. However, these peripheral organizations tend to be "central outposts" (p. 13) of the core firms.

Diffusion of IT into the peripheral and the less-developed areas is not a solution to the problem. Diffusion is likely to increase access by the core firms to the peripheral areas giving them competitive advantage over firms which do not have access to the periphery or from the periphery to the core. Information technology, according to Gillespie and Robins, is not neutral but a reinforcer of structures, providing new forms of global subordination and domination.

Although opportunities may exist for some of the Newly Industrializing Countries, Ernst & O'Connor (1989) note two main barriers for NIC's. The first is a formidable threshold level of R&D outlays, production facilities and access to networks. Second, other factors such as the "lock out" effect of dominant standards limit the scope for latecomers and new entrants. Standards are set either de facto by dominant suppliers or *de jure* by international organizations or by a combination of the two. Even when this task is performed by international organizations, the influence of the dominant nation is extensive.

The Effects Dimension

Although earlier studies have adopted different perspectives, they have generally focused on the impact of IT on the nation, the transnational firm, and/or the individual.

State: Studies that have focused on the impact of IT on the state have mostly arisen in the domain of Information Economics.

According to Monk (1989), there are two general themes in information economics. The first theme, represented by studies such as those by Bell (1973) and Stonier (1983), focuses on the development and transition of economies from one dominant mode to another; from the predominantly agricultural to the industrial mode and now to the "post-industrial" mode based on IT.

The second theme has addressed the question of what constitutes the information economy and what methods are available for its analysis. Seminal studies by Machlup (1962) and Porat (1977) and their extensions, OECD (1981b) and Karunaratne (1986), are representative of this approach. Both Machlup and Porat attempt to measure the contribution of the "information industries" to GNP in the United States. According to them, information activities in the economy now account for between a quarter and a half of gross domestic product (GDP). In addition, information technologies which drive information activities continue to grow at an increasing rate and require the treatment of information as an economic phenomenon.

Firm: At the level of the firm, two broad streams of research can also be identified. At a macro level, studies have discussed the impact of IT on the structure and form of the Multinational Corporation (MNC) while studies with a micro-level focus have examined specific technologies such as EDI and their impact on the operations of the MNC.

Under the macro theme are works such as those by Hepworth (1989), who argues that the employment of information and IT by firms is a response to environmental uncertainty. One impact of the utilization of IT to reduce uncertainty has been the rise of the "networked organization." A networked organization consists of a nucleus, or hub, and interorganizational and international relations which are "connected through communicating workstations" (Kilmann, 1990, p. 23). The hub of a network organization is a small centralized staff concerned with ownership of assets. The extended network is decentralized, global, concerned with control of resources, and designed for the multiple functions others perform better than the hub itself.

A second impact of the use of IT to reduce uncertainty has been the adoption of flexible systems by firms—flexible production, consumption, and acquisition. Computer network technologies contribute to this flexibility by allowing centralized and decentralized spatial arrangements of both office and manufacturing production activities on a larger geographical scale.

Under the more micro-level perspective, we include studies such as those by Grant (1989) and Snapp (1990). Grant explains issues surrounding information services from the perspective of a corporation involved in the trading of services—the Royal Bank of Canada. He reviews various international services offered by the bank through the use of IT and notes the revolutionizing contribution of EDI to trade and commerce of all goods and services. Snapp also concludes that global EDI has the obvious advantages of greater efficiency and accuracy in the conduct of international trade through the timely processing of information. In fact, the far reaching effects of IT on the firm and the trade of goods and services prompted Grant to label the present economic era as the "New International Electronic Order" (p. 112).

Individual: Few studies have directly discussed the impact of transnational IT on the individual. Richter (1989) focuses on the differential capabilities among states in utilizing IT for education and professional training. Pogorel (1989) addresses the internationalization of cultures due to information media and questions its impact on international awareness. He asks the question: "do people in various countries feel a stronger solidarity when they read the same news, [or] watch the same TV programs..?" (p. 208). He concludes that the growing gap among states in the use of IT needs to be considered seriously in order to avoid social fractures. The social impact studies are best summarized by Tehranian (1989). He writes that IT can have positive effects by eliminating routine tasks, by creating greater leisure, and by extending a variety of social services to remote and deprived sectors of the population. However, IT can also serve as an instrument of a new totalitarianism by creating greater powers of surveillance, by widening the information gap between rich and poor, and by creating greater unemployment through automation.

A second set of studies regarding the impact of IT on the individual relates to the question of personal privacy and abuse. A review of this literature is deferred to a later section.

Issue Area and Policy Dimensions

In the prior sections we noted the three characteristics of IT pertinent to the international environment: the covergence of computers and communications, transnationality and market concentration; and the three effects: individual, organization and state The interaction of the characteristics and effects dimensions in turn creates issue areas and a demand for regulation and public policy. Some of these issues are shown in Figure 2 and are discussed below in terms of the effects dimension.

Individual Issues: The main issue of importance at the individual level is that of privacy protection. The dominant privacy theme has been in the context of record-keeping processes and the concern has been with IT used to make decisions regarding an individual. As the OECD (1983) study on legal issues in IT has noted, the concern for privacy has been initiated by the convergence of computer and communication technology.

In the U.S., much of the privacy debate has focused on how information about people is handled, what is collected by whom, and for what purpose. The U.S. Department of Health, Education, and Welfare Report (1973) and the Privacy Protection Commission Study Report (1977) are two extensive studies on the subject. The Privacy Act of 1974 was a significant effort to protect personal information collected by federal agencies.

With an increase in the use of IT, privacy laws have been affected in three significant areas: wiretapping, monitoring, and technological protection

(Weingarten, 1988). Title III of the Omnibus Crime Control and Safe Streets Act of 1978; the Foreign Intelligence Surveillance Act of 1978; and the Electronic Communications Privacy Act (ECPA) of 1986 all have provisions dealing with wiretapping and unauthorized interception. Actions dealing with employee surveillance have been few and have been considered by Congress on a piecemeal basis. Technological protection deals with the role of the federal government in providing technology for secure communications to users in the private and public sector.

The ECPA has been a first major step towards dealing with electronic media; it requires privacy protection for electronic communications. The Computer Matching and Privacy Protection Act of 1988, enacted to amend the Privacy Protection Act of 1974, requires government agencies using computer matching of databases on individuals: to develop computer matching agreements prior to exchange of any personal information; to provide notice to individuals identified in its records; and to establish Data Integrity Boards within every federal agency that engages in computer matching. According to a recent report ("Status of Data," 1988) most countries have either adopted or have under consideration similar legislation dealing with privacy and data protection.

The value of information is enhanced by the use of IT since it can be used, copied, further processed and spread widely. However, this attribute of uncontrolled dissemination of information constitutes a primary threat to privacy. The emergence of new technologies such as digital display of phone numbers on incoming calls, data available to management, and the issuance of smart cards by hospitals are an increasing threat to privacy ("Commissioners Stress," 1989), especially since IT facilitates easy transference of information internationally.

Firm Issues: As shown in Figure 2, the major firm-level issue resulting from the characteristic of converging technologies is the need for international standardization. Transnationalism results in the issue of intellectual property concerns. Market concentration leads to the issue of intra-firm transborder flows.

As noted earlier, the benefits accruing to organizations from the transnational use of IT are due to the rationalization of their operations and the exploitation of sources of competitive advantage. This presupposes uninhibited application of IT by the firm and is further based on the assumption that standards across states exhibit a certain degree of similarity.

EDI, as noted above, is in use by several MNCs. Yet, EDI standards differ markedly across states (Purton, 1989). West Germany's Teletex, U.K.'s GTDI and the rest of Europe's EDIFACT show several differences. A Datamation Report ("International Users," 1988) noted that international standards are far from being available in information products.

A second organizational issue pertinent to converging technologies is the issue of network security. The November 1988 computer virus on the Internet in the U.S. prompted Congressional interest in the matter. A GAO (1989a, p. 3) report noted the high vulnerabilities of computer networks.

In a transnational environment, the development of data bank inter-connections via international telecommunications networks brings an international dimension to security. Several such questions were raised by an OECD (1986b) report on computer-related crime. For example, suppose a person at a terminal in country A manipulates a program or accesses computer memory in country B and in this way affects the interests of a person in country C. Which courts would have jurisdiction and which country's legislation would apply?

The characteristic of transnationality creates issues of intellectual property concerns and piracy. Martin (1989) reported that U.S. software firms have undertaken widespread campaigns against software piracy in Europe with raids on major Italian corporations. As noted earlier, most IT products are transnational and so is their use. Intellectual works are simultaneously available to many individuals who may access them from a central database. Identification of authorship, repackaging of information, and reprocessibility are some problems associated with the protection of IT products.

The third characteristic of IT, market concentration, has led to issues in intra-firm transborder data flows. As noted earlier, MNC operations are greatly affected by the use of IT. As "market concentration" implies, capabilities in the use of IT are concentrated in a few countries. This results in the increasing significance of intra-firm flow of data as MNC subsidiaries rely on their parent firms for data processing and IT-related functions. The dependence of the worldwide subsidiary on its parent and home country is often viewed as a loss of economic opportunity by states (OECD, 1979b). As a result, developing countries have often sought to limit, directly or indirectly, TBDF under the argument that the ability to store and process certain types of data may give one country or company political and technological advantages over others.

Another example of a loss of economic opportunity, as noted by Fishman (1980), arises when corporations from developing countries participate in closed user-group transnational computer communication systems whose principal switching centers are located in developed countries. This does not imply that developing countries do not participate in the international data market, but it does define the nature of the participation (United Nations Center for Transnational Corporations [UNCTC], 1982).

State Issues: A major issue for states has been the regulatory readjustment required by converging technologies.

Basic to the review of regulation and policies is the problem associated with the distinction between telecommunication and information services. In the U.S., the FCC created this distinction by its Computer I and II decisions. In the U.K., the concept of "value added" services as opposed to "basic services" provides the same differentiation. Japan has established Type I and II categories of services based on facilities used.

Much of this concern with differentiation between services is due to the process of liberalization of telecommunications. In the past, telecommunications was structured as a monopoly in most states. Since the breakup of AT&T in the U.S., the telecommunications sectors in Europe and Japan have been liberalized to some extent. In order to specify the terms of competition and demarcate the border between the telecommunications monopoly and the unregulated information sector, policymakers have had to contend with the fusion of telecommunications and computer technology.

The second characteristic of IT, transnationality, has created issues such as conflict of law. As noted previously, data and telecommunications networks make the principle of territoriality difficult to administer.

A third set of issues relates to market concentration. As noted earlier, this often results in concerns of sovereignty and autonomy of a state. The fear of exportation of decision making capability, the desire to develop and protect the indigenous industry, and the loss of control of information are some added concerns for the state.

Brazil's former Informatics Policy is a case in point. In 1976, computers and related products were Brazil's third largest import and much of this was from the U.S. In the same year, the then Brazilian Commission for Coordination of Electronic Activities (CAPRE) developed a master plan for the Brazilian domestic informatics industry. This initiated a policy of reserving to the domestic sector the production of minicomputers, microcomputers, and peripheral devices. These policies were instituted to "protect the infant Brazilian producers until such time that international competition becomes possible" (Gallagher, 1989).

Whereas the above applies to protection of domestic industry, barriers to trade in services have often been a result of concerns about exploitation by MNCs. As Balasubramanyam (1989) argues, the dominance of the developed countries in all segments of the information industry often results in data-processing facilities being located at the headquarters of the MNCs with their foreign affiliates linked to the central system. Most developing countries consider this a threat to their political sovereignty and national economic objectives (UNCTC, 1982).

Whereas the above sections have noted the several issues that emerge due to the interaction of the characteristics and the effects dimensions, it also must be noted that several international arrangements exist which function to regulate these issues and harmonize the differences in national policies due to these issues. As is shown in figure 1 and discussed below, this harmonization occurs to facilitate the transnational use of IT.

INTERNATIONAL HARMONIZATION

A state's response to issues is guided by its position on domestic and international affairs, its development plans, and its trade policies. It is, therefore, not surprising that laws and regulations are very different across nations. However, some degree of harmonization is necessary in order to promote international flows of data and information. One obvious and impractical solution is for nations to have the same laws and regulations. A more realistic situation is that of having international institutions and arrangements (bilateral, regional and multilateral) which focus on the attainment of similarity among national policies in areas of international interest. Several of these arrangements are shown in Figure 3.

Before discussing the focus and functioning of these arrangements, we need to review the concept of international regimes.

Haas (1983, p. 26) writes "regimes are man-made arrangements (social institutions) for managing conflict in a setting of interdependence." In general, regimes arise to manage a specific issue area of common interest and for common benefit. Regimes operate through common principles and by means of agreements that are negotiated. International regimes are those which pertain to activities of interest to members of the international system.

An examination of figure 2 reveals that IT-related issues have been shaped by three international cooperative arrangements and norms. For example, privacy concerns have been debated in the OECD and Council of Europe and much of this debate has derived from the more global Human Rights Regime. Similarly, issues of international standards and regulatory adjustments are the domain of the ITU and the telecommunications regime, while trade issues are a domain of the trade regime centered in the GATT. Thus, three regimes are shown in figure 4 to be applicable to IT. These are: the Privacy and Human Rights Regime; the Telecommunications Regime; and the Trade Regime.

The Privacy and Human Rights Regime

The privacy and human rights regime is based in the United Nations and derives its norms from the Universal Declaration of Human Rights proclaimed in 1949. The Declaration, although not a binding treaty, is often seen as a customary international law. The International Covenant of Civil and Political Rights (ICCPR) is the second main source of regime norms. The

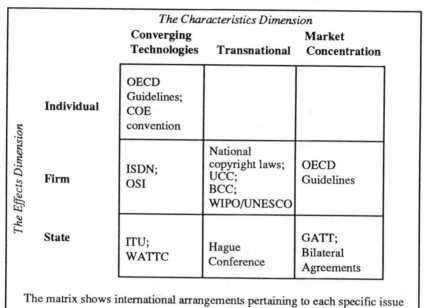

	The Characteristics Dimension		
	Converging Technologies	Transnational	Market Concentration
Individual	OECD Guidelines; COE convention		
Firm	ISDN; OSI	National copyright laws; UCC; BCC; WIPO/UNESCO	OECD Guidelines
State	ITU; WATTC	Hague Conference	GATT; Bilateral Agreements

The matrix shows international arrangements pertaining to each specific issue

Figure 3: The International Harmonization of Issues

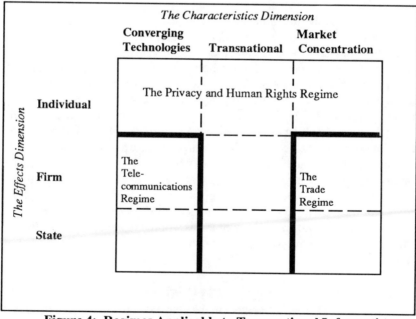

Figure 4: Regimes Applicable to Transnational Information Technology

ICCPR came into force in 1976 and at the end of 1987 had been ratified by 86 countries.

The Universal Declaration and the ICCPR establish the norms for the regime. These are primarily:

> Article 19 of the Declaration: "Everyone has the right to freedom of opinion and expression; this right includes freedom to hold opinions without interference and to seek, receive, and impart information and ideas through any media regardless of frontiers."

> Article 19 of the ICCPR is similar to Article 19 of the Declaration.

There are several other resolutions and draft conventions dealing with the freedom of information. The General Assembly Resolution 59(I), 1966, recognized freedom of information as a fundamental human right. The Draft Convention on the Gathering and International Transmission of News, submitted by the Economic and Social Council (ECOSOC) in 1948, dealt with the free movement and operations of correspondents (Article 2). The General Assembly Resolution 424(V), 1950, noted that deliberate interference by duly authorized radio operating agencies of radio signals originating beyond their territory constitutes a violation of the accepted principle of Freedom of Information.

Most of the instruments that establish basic human rights include some form of privacy protection. For example, Article 12 of the Universal Declaration of Human Rights states that "no one shall be subjected to arbitrary interference with his privacy, family, home or correspondence, nor to attacks upon his honor and reputation." This declaration of "privacy" was based on the concept of "liberty" as in protection of private life and the inviolability of the home (Freedman, 1987). The "right to privacy" was directly addressed by the General Assembly of the United Nations in December, 1968, when it adopted a resolution urging the Secretary-General to undertake a study of the problems in connection with human rights arising from developments in science and technology. A 1976 report by the Secretary General of the United Nations[6] called on states to update existing legislation to provide protection for the privacy of the individual against invasions by modern technological devices.

Thus the human rights regime has worked to stress both freedom of information and the free flow of information across borders, and the right of individual privacy in the age of IT.

The Trade Regime

The Trade Regime centers in the General Agreement on Tariffs and Trade (GATT), which came into effect in 1948. GATT is a basic framework of rules and procedures governing international trade and trade relations between member countries. It has historically only applied to trade in goods.

The trade regime is involved in the discussion of the transnational use of IT primarily because of the call for the inclusion of services in the GATT framework. The share of services in world trade has not expanded as rapidly as its share in the domestic economy. A principal reason assigned for this is the absence of a stable, predictable and transparent framework for trade in services and the existence of trade-restricting national regulations (Sauvant, 1989).

There are several ways in which IT-based services enter international trade:

> Services which were intra-corporate are becoming international; e.g., SWIFT and SITA.

> Services that were normally non-tradeable are now tradeable and take over functions that are initially served by affiliates; e.g., information-intensive industries.

> IT-based services are becoming a part of the infrastructure for trade in goods; e.g., their use in inventory control. These are thus becoming "basic services."

As mentioned in an earlier section, the idea of including services in the GATT framework was first raised by the United States in the Trade Act of 1974. The U.S. campaign in 1982 for the inclusion of services was strongly opposed by developing countries. However, the Ministerial Meeting in Punta del Este, Uruguay, in September, 1986, agreed to establish a "parallel-track" negotiation on trade-in-services in the current Uruguay Round. The objectives of these negotiations were "to establish a multilateral framework of principles and rules for trade in services." In addition, the framework should "respect the policy objectives of national laws and regulations applying to services". (GATT, 1986).

Lanvin (1989c) assesses the applicability of the GATT to telecommunications and data services specifically. His extensive analysis considers three GATT "safeguards": balance of payment provisions; preferential treatment; and restrictive business practices.

With respect to safeguards for the balance of payments, GATT has two provisions (Articles XII and XVIII) that allow the contracting parties to restrict imports for balance of payments reasons. International trade in services are generally in deficit for developing countries. However, this service deficit is likely to be compensated by the indirect effects of increasing the competitiveness of national industry and of developing infrastructure to attract foreign direct investment (FDI).

Regarding the second safeguard, preferential treatment, a doctrine was developed in the 1960s which postulated a link between trade and economic development and stressed differential treatment of developing countries; it culminated in the New International Economic Order of 1974. However, it was contingent on two factors: that preferential treatment will not interfere with trade among developed countries; and that differential treatment is a means to development and not an end in itself. Part IV was added in 1966 to GATT and formalized the non-reciprocity of concessions for developing countries. In 1979, an "enabling clause" was adopted under the Tokyo Round Agreement which permitted "differential and more favorable treatment, reciprocity and fuller participation of developing countries."

Given preferential treatment for developing countries and the striking imbalances in the "information economy", Lanvin (1989c) notes that the following needs of developing countries should be considered:

> The right to selectivity—right of an individual country to select its parties and commitments in the areas of FDI and transborder data flows (TBDF).

> Market access and user access—access to networks in a country and the country's access to global networks.

> Institutional framework—developing countries might be reluctant to participate fully in a non-universal forum like GATT or in a forum like the ITU (International Telecommunications Union) where they would find it more difficult to relate technical issues to the broader context of their development policy.

The third safeguard discussed by Lanvin, Restrictive Business Practices (RBP's), are non-governmental measures taken by individuals or several enterprises jointly in order to acquire, protect or strengthen a dominant position in the market. Inherently, this implies the intent or the actual distortion of the rules of normal competition. Although these practices are not dealt with under GATT, instruments such as the "Set of Multilaterally Agreed Equitable Principles and Rules for the Control of Restrictive Business Practicies" have been adopted by the UN and instituted in the United Nations Conference on Trade and Development (UNCTAD). This is especially important in the case of data services since the IT environment often has national PTTs which are monopolies for the provision of services and monopsonies in terms of service purchases. Since the IT environment is characterized by global networks, this by itself may be construed as an RBP. Finally, vertical groups seem to be the norm in the information industry and thus may be incompatible with the national objectives of LDCs.

To summarize, we note that the trade regime has affected many information sectors. Whether the specifics of the trade regime are applied directly to transnational IT will become clear only when the services negotiations mature.

The Telecommunications Regime

The telecommunications regime is centered in the ITU (International Telecommunications Union), a specialized agency of the UN. The ITU was formed as the International Telegraph Union 1865 and currently has 166 members. In no other field is the need for international cooperation so obvious and necessary as in telecommunications. This largely explains the long history of the ITU.

The international law developed by the ITU emanates from treaties which are either formulated as sets of general rules or specific technical provisions. The ITU aims to "maintain and extend international cooperation ... for the improvement and national use of telecommunications of all kinds ... and the development of technical facilities and their most efficient operations...." (International Telecommunications Union [ITU], 1982). At the Nice Plenipotentiary in 1989, two additions to the purposes of the Union were made:

> To facilitate the worldwide standardization of telecommunications, with a satisfactory quality of service, and

> To promote, with international financial organizations, the establishment of preferential and favorable lines of credit to be used for the development of special projects aimed at extending telecommunications services to the most isolated area in countries.

The regulations affecting telecommunications that were in effect since 1972 were superseded by the new "International Telecommunications Regulation" on July 1, 1990. These new regulations were finalized at the World Administrative Telephone and Telegraph Conference in Melbourne, Australia, in December 1988. The changes were largely brought about by the new information technologies. Problems had evolved because of the distinction between the regulated telecommunications sector and the unregulated information industry.

Some issues pertained to the scope of ITU's jurisdiction. For example, what and who should be regulated? The "Melbourne Package" recognizes the rights of private operating agencies offering international services to the public and includes a resolution explaining how member countries should cooperate in implementing the regulations.

The ITU has coordinated national telecommunications systems by means of its regulations, which convey the status of international treaty law. Much of ITU's role has been in the provision of compatibility across national networks and their interconnectivity. However, several new and important functions have been taken on by the ITU. The Telecommunications Development Bureau (TDB) was recently created to serve as an executive agency to assist in the UN's telecommunications development programs by offering, organizing and coordinating technical cooperation and assistance activities. ITU further assists programs such as UNESCO's International Program for the Development of Communications (IPDC).

Other International Arrangements

While the above three regimes are well established both in the literature and practice, several other cooperative attempts have been made at the international level and have been adopted in the past to facilitate this cooperation. These include the NWICO and its associated texts, and some portions of the international legal regime. Although a regime analysis is probably not applicable to these areas, several of the issues embodied in them are discussed in this section.

There is a clear relationship between UNCTAD's NIEO—New International Economic Order of 1974—and the New World Information Order of 1976. According to Meyer (1982), the NIEO was first demanded by less developed countries to address the following:

- LDCs were to be given absolute sovereignty over their natural resources.

- Preferential treatment was to be given to third world goods in Western markets. Prices for third world goods were to be increased and then linked to the prices of goods imported into the LDCs. Producer controls were also encouraged.

- Transfers of advanced technologies from the West to the third world were to be vastly increased and funded by the wealthy industrialized nations.

- New controls were to be placed on multinational corporations (MNCs) which operate in the third world.

The provisions of NWICO echo the above:

- Absolute sovereignty for LDCs over all of their "information resources."

- Preferential treatment for third world news in Western markets. The percentage of news about LDCs was to be increased in the Western press. "Horizontal communication" (that which is exchanged between LDCs) was to be promoted and "vertical communication" (that which is exchanged between developed and developing nations) was to become less pervasive.

- Direct grants and other gifts of advanced communication technologies from the West to the third world.

- The breakup of the Western transnational news agencies (TNNAS, Agence France Presse, Associated Press, Reuters, and United Press International). These MNCs of communication were to be closely regulated when operating within third world nations.

Although the official withdrawal of the United States from UNESCO was a serious setback to the philosophy of the NWICO, the underpinnings of it are still the same.

Yet another aspect of information cooperation is seen in the issues of conflict of law. As noted earlier, the characteristic of transnationality of information forms the basis of such conflicts. A regime to deal with such issues does not exist but the Hague Conference on Private International Law has been considered as a possible body to deal with them. Although the Hague Convention typically applies to the international sale of goods (OECD, 1983), its applicability to services is unclear. Similar work has also been undertaken at the UNCITRAL, the United Nations Commission on International Trade Law.

Several issues related to IT have been under consideration with UNCITRAL. These were first brought to the Commission by the impact of electronic funds transfers[7]. A report to the Secretary General (A/CN. 9/221) noted that EFT has developed in a legal vacuum and, in the case of international transfers, an adequate legal framework for settlement of disputes does not exist. Other aspects of IT-related activities are also noted. These include the problems associated with the legal value of computer records (A/40/17) in all aspects of international trade. A report to the Secretary General (A/CN. 9/265) concluded that the existence of traditional differences among systems of adjudication did not allow for a single approach, and recommended to governments and to international organizations that they elaborate legal texts to rationalize the use of automatic data processing in international trade.

The Utility of Regimes and Regime Analysis

Having discussed the relevant regimes for transnational IT, we now summarize the issues presented above and discuss the utility of the analysis.

Interdependence means an erasure between domestic and international issues. Increasing interdependence, then, implies a greater overlap between policies enacted at the national and international levels. There is, therefore, an increasing need to link the two areas (Haggard & Simmons, 1987). Regimes can be construed to be one way of achieving this linkage.

In the case of IT, we can discuss several changes and analyze noticeable regime effects. The privacy and human rights regime has been noted to be strongly declaratory. This is so because each state retains almost complete autonomy in implementing norms at the national level; regime norms are fully internationalized, but decision making remains national. Yet, in the case of IT, there are strong pressures to adhere to the international norms. For example, the Data Protection Act, enacted by the United Kingdom in 1984 to provide rights to individuals regarding information stored about them on a computer, also allowed that country to ratify the Council of Europe Convention on Data Protection and ensured that data could flow freely between the UK and other European countries with similar laws (*Data Protection Register*, 1989, p. 3). Simitis (1989) notes a gradual normalization of other national data protection laws.

Thus we see that there is a degree of pressure to conform to regime norms, principles, and standards. Similar conclusions can be drawn in the telecommunications and trade regimes.

Another characteristic of regimes considered is their evolving status. All the regimes considered above have undergone changes due to the nature of IT. Privacy concerns have been altered considerably by the introduction of IT and so has the regime. A change in scope can also be seen in trade regime by the addition of services. Similarly, the new World Administrative Telegraph and Telephone Conference (WATTC) regulations have broadened the scope of the telecommunications regime. As noted earlier, the degree of intervention by states and pressures to conform have also increased due to heightened interdependence by the use of IT. Finally, allocation modes have shown a trend towards market allocation as noted by the changes in the ITU.

CONCLUSION

Marshall McLuhan (1964, p19), in his introduction to the book *Understanding Media: The Extensions of Man* quotes James Reston from *The*

New York Times of July 7, 1957:

> "A health director ... reported this week that a small mouse, which presumably had been watching television, attacked a little girl and her full-grown cat ... Both mouse and cat survived, and the incident is recorded here as a reminder that things seem to be changing."

Certainly, change is occurring at multiple levels—in the operations of the firm, in the environment of individuals, and among nation states. The European Community typifies what is happening in the larger global context. Increased cooperation in the South, between the North and the South, and the opening of the closed economies of the world mark a trend away from regionalism and towards a more open global society. Within this movement, the mandate for IT has also changed. From being an instrument of intergovernmental coordination, IT has developed to be a source of competitive advantage—not only of firms but of nations as well. Within the transnational community, IT has moved from being a source of mass communication to a provider of international services.

As the role of IT in global interaction has increased so has international cooperation to facilitate its use. This cooperation has come in the form of international technical standards, privacy regulations, trade negotiations, and intellectual property agreements. However, instances such as Radio and TV Marti serve as reminders that IT can also be a promoter of international discontent and mistrust. The debate between freedom of information and infringement of national sovereignty is far from over. While the issues of economic dependence, privacy, and infant industry protection still reign strong in the international arena, the newer issues of regulation of telecommunications—monopolization versus liberalization and of trade-in-services—add to the complexity of the international information issues.

Although it is widely recognized that the above problems exist, what is more important is the growing understanding that increased international cooperation will provide radically expanding opportunities for wealth creation and thus for improving social welfare. Nevertheless, research in this area has been dispersed and sporadic. Studies for this chapter have been drawn from the areas of information economics, law, telecommunications, economics, public policy, international politics, and international business. The primary purpose for the aggregation has been to present a unified model to depict the nature and role of transnational IT. A critical evaluation of this presentation would certainly find it wanting in the creation of new theory. Yet the identification of current variables is a necessary first step in the development of theoretical studies, and such a specification has been one goal of this chapter.

Endnotes

[1]Derived from U. S. Federal Communications Commission (1987).

[2]This term is used to refer to relations between developed (North) and developing (South) countries.

[3]These aspects are covered in detail later. Some summary reviews are in Nordensberg (1984).

[4]The NWICO was discussed primarily in the UNESCO. The Mass Media Declaration and the MacBride Commission Report led to the formulation of the eleven principles of NWICO at the 21st General Conference of UNESCO, 1980. See, for example, Kleinwachter, 1986.

[5] In order to clarify the term "transnational", we refer to a framework developed by Keohane & Nie (1972). Transnational interactions are "the movement of tangible or intangible items across state boundaries when at least one actor is not an agent of a government or an international organization" (p. xii). We refer to the use of IT by transnational actors in the support of transnational interactions as the transnational use of IT. This phenomenon is referred to as "transnationalism" and is of special importance in the context of IT.

[6] E/CN.4/1116, 1976.

[7]*Official Records of the General Assembly,* Twenty-seventh session, Supplement No. 17 (A/8717).

References

Balasubramanyam, V.N. (1989). The issue of market presence and right of establishment. In P. Robinson, K. P. Sauvant & V. P. Govitrikar (Eds.), *Electronic highways for world trade* (pp. 131-153). Boulder, CO: Westview Press.

Bartnick, J. (1983). Information technology and the developing world: Opportunities and obstacles. *The Information Society, 2,* 157-170.

Bell, D. (1973). *The coming of post-industrial society.* New York: Basic Books.

Berman, J. (1987). National security vs. access to computer databases: A new threat to freedom of information. *Software Law Journal, 2,* 1-15.

Blatherwick, D.E.S. (1987). *The international politics of telecommunications.* Berkeley: University of California Research Series Number 68.

BNP. (1989, June 24-30). Advertisement. *The Economist.* p. 78.

Bolton, J.R. (1989, October). The United States and UNESCO: 1989. *Current Policy No. 1214.* Washington: U.S. Department of State.

Bradshaw, D. (1990, April 19). A direct line to international management. *Financial Times,* Section III, p. X.

Burch, D. (1989, October). INTELSAT's Future. *Transborder Data & Communications Reports, 12*(8), 5-6.

Cleveland, H. (1987). The twilight of hierarchy: Speculations on the global information society. *The Journal of Technology Management, 2,* 45-66.

Cole, S. (1986). The global impact of IT. *World Development, 14,* 1277-1292.

Commissioners stress TDF risks. (1989, November). *Transborder Data & Communications Reports*, pp. 5-16.

Data Protection Register. (1989, February). Guideline 1 - Data Protection Act, 1984. Wilmslow, England: Springfield House.

Deutsche Bank Group. (1990, March 12). Advertisement, *Fortune*, p. 65.

Ernst, D. & O'Connor, D. (1989). *Technology and global competition*. Paris: OECD.

Estabrook, M. (1988). *Programmed capitalism: A computer-mediated global society*. London: M. E. Sharpe.

Fauvet, J. (1989, November). Privacy in the new Europe. *Transborder Data & Communications Reports, 12*, 17-18.

Fishman, W.L. (1980, Summer). Introduction to transborder data flows. *Stanford Journal of International Law, 16*, 8-18.

Freedman, W. (1987). *The right of privacy in the computer age*. New York: Quorum Books.

Gallagher, J.J. (1989). The United States-Brazilian informatics dispute. *The International Lawyer, 23*, 505-522.

Gassmann, Hans-Peter. (1989, November). Privacy protection and computer networks. *Transborder Data & Communications Reports*.

GATT Focus. (1986, October). *41*, 1-6.

Gillespie, A. & Robins, K. (1989). Geographical inequalities: The spatial bias of the new communications technologies. In G. Gerbner & M. Siefert (Eds.), *The information gap* (pp. 7-18). New York: Oxford University Press.

Grant, J.C. (1989). Global trade in services. In P. Robinson, K.P. Sauvant & V. Govitrikar (Eds.), *Electronic highways for world trade: Issues in telecommunications and data services* (pp. 101-120), Boulder, CO: Westview Press.

Gray, J.C. (1983). Information-policy problems in developing countries. *The Information Society Journal, 2*(1), 81-89.

Haas, E.B. (1983). Words can hurt you; or, who said what to whom about regimes. In S.D. Krasner (Ed.), *International Regimes*, Ithaca: Cornell University Press.

Haggard, S. & Simmons, B.A. (1987). Theories of international regimes. *International Organization, 41*, 491-517.

Hamelink, C.J. (1984). *Transnational data flows in the information age*, Lund, Sweden: Studentlitteratur AB.

Hepworth, M.E. (1989). Geographical advantages in the information economy. In E. Punset & G. Sweeney (Eds.), *Information resources and corporate growth* (pp. 26-35). London: Pinter Publishers.

Hondius, F.W. (1989, December). European TV: Across or without frontiers? *Transborder Data & Communications Reports*, pp. 17-20.

Huber, R. (1987). The role of information technology and telecommunications in promoting economic development in the European Community. *International Journal of Technology Management, 2*, 501-513.

Hustinx, P.J. (1989, November). COE and data protection: What has been achieved? *Transborder Data and Communications Reports*, pp. 21-22.

International users: What the world needs now. (1988, May 1). *Datamation*, 1-4.

International Telecommunications Union (1982). Convention, Nairobi: ITU.

Irwin, M.R. & Merenda, M.J. (1989, December). Corporate networks, privatization and state sovereignty; Pending issues for the 1990s. *Telecommunications Policy*, pp. 329-335.

Karunaratne, N.D. (1986). Issues in measuring the information economy, *Journal of Economic Studies, 13*(3), 51-68.

Keohane, R.O. & Nye, J.S., Jr. (1972). *Transnational relations and world politics*. Cambridge, MA: Harvard Business School Press.

Kilmann, R.M. (1990). A networked company that embraces the world. *Information Strategy: The Executives Journal, 6*, 23-26.

Kleinwachter, W. (1986). Freedom or responsibility versus freedom and responsibility. In J. Becker, G. Hedikro & L. Poldan (Eds.), *Communication and domination: Essays to honor Herbert I. Schiller* (pp. 133-142). Norwood, NJ: Ablex Publishing Corporation.

Lamberton, D.M. (1989). The regional information economy: Its measurement and significance. In E. Punset & G.P. Sweeney (Eds.), *Information resources and corporate growth* (pp. 16-25). London: Pinter.

Lamborghini, B. (1989). The impact of information and IT on the structure of the firm. In E. Punset & G. Sweeney (Eds.), *Information resources and corporate growth* (pp. 26-35). London: Pinter.

Lanvin, B. (1989a, October 25-29). *The development imperative in the age of pervasive information technologies*. Guelph, Ontario: University of Guelph Workshop #4.

Lanvin, B. (1989b, October 24-26). Economic development in global networks. *Fourth Meeting of the Think Net Commission*. Atlanta: TNC.

Lanvin, B. (1989c). Participation of developing countries in a telecommunications and data services agreement: Some elements for consideration. In P. Robinson, K. P. Sauvant & V.P. Govitrikar (Eds.), *Electronic highways for world trade: Issues in telecommunications and data services* (pp. 71-100). Boulder, CO: Westview Press.

Lanvin, B. (1987a). *Information services and development*, UNCTAD Discussion Paper No. 23. Geneva: UNCTAD.

Lanvin, B. (1987b). *Information technology and competitiveness in the service industry,* UNC-TAD Discussion Paper No. 119. Geneva: UNCTAD.

Machlup, F. (1962). *The production and distribution of knowledge in the United States,* Princeton: Princeton University Press.

Mansell, R.E. & Ypsilanti, D. (1987). The economic role of telecommunications and information services: Development changes in OECD countries (Forum 87, IV(I), DM: 19751). Paris: OECD.

Martin, J. (1989, August 1). Pursuing pirates. *Datamation,* pp. 41-42.

Masmoudi, M. (1984). The new world information order. In G. Gerbner, & M. Siefert (Eds.), *World communications: A handbook.* New York: Longman.

Matta, K.F. & Boutros, N.E. (1989). Barriers to electronic mail systems in developing countries. *The Information Society, 6,* 59-68.

McDowell, S.D. (1989, May). The shaping of TDF policy. *Transborder Data & Communications Reports,* pp. 19-23.

McLuhan, M. (1964). *Understanding media: The extensions of man.* New York: Signet Books.

Mestmacker, F.S. (1989, February). Towards a new international telecommunications regime. *Transborder Data & Communication Reports,* pp. 11-16.

Meyer, W.H. (1982). *Transnational media and third world development: The structure and impact of imperialism.* Westport, CT: Greenwood Press.

Monk, P. (1989). *Technological change in the information economy.* London: Pinter.

Nordensberg, H. (1984). Defining the new international information order. In G. Gerbner & M. Siefert (Eds.), *World communications: A handbook* (pp. 28-36). New York: Longman.

Northern Telecom. (1990, March 12). Advertisement, *Fortune,* p. 85.

Oman, J. (1987). The new technologies. Network Planning Paper No. 16. *Proceedings of the Library of Congress Network Advisory Committee Meeting.* Washington: Library of Congress.

Organization for Economic Cooperation and Development. (1989). *Telecommunications network-based services,* Paris: OECD.

Organization for Economic Cooperation and Development. (1986a). *Trends in the information economy,* Paris: OECD.

Organization for Economic Cooperation and Development. (1986b). *Computer-related crime.* Paris: OECD.

Organization for Economic Cooperation and Development. (1983). *An exploration of legal issues in information and communication technologies.* Paris: OECD.

Organization for Economic Cooperation and Development. (1981a). *Guidelines on the protection of privacy and transborder flows of personal data.* Paris: OECD.

Organization for Economic Cooperation and Development. (1981b). *Information activities, electronics and telecommunications Activities* (ICCP Report No. 6) Paris: OECD.

Organization for Economic Cooperation and Development. (1979a). *Usage of international data networks in Europe.* Paris: OECD.

Organization for Economic Cooperation and Development. (1979b). *Transborder data flows and the protection of privacy.* Paris: OECD.

Palvia, P. & Palvia, S. (1990). Information systems issues in a global society: A comparison between the U.S. and India. *Proceedings of the Hawaii International Conference on Systems Sciences.*

Pantages, A. (1989, August 15). The right IS chemistry. *Datamation,* pp. 61-62.

Pipe, G.R. (1984). Transborder data flows: Main issues, trends and impacts on international business. In J.F. Rada, & G.R. Pipe (Eds.), *Communication regulation and international business* (pp. 23-38). Amsterdam: Elsevier Science.

Pogorel, G. (1989). Information technology from social impact to social input: A European perspective. In M. Jussawalla, T. Okuma & T. Araki (Eds.), *Information technology and global interdependence* (pp.205-211). Westport, CT: Greenwood Press.

Porat, M. (1977). *The information economy.* Washington: U.S. Dept. of Commerce.

Privacy Protection Study Commission. (1977, July). *Personal Privacy in an information society.* Washington: U.S. Government Printing Office.

Purton, P. (1989, March 1). Europe's electronic trading bloc. *Datamation,* pp. 76:13-14.

Richter, W. (1989). Impact of IT on education, training, and employment European OECD countries. In M. Jussawalla, T. Okuma & T. Araki (Eds.), *Information technology and global interdependence* (pp. 199-204). Westport, CT: Greenwood Press.

Robinson, P. (1990, February). TDF issues: Hard choices for governments. *Telecommunications Policy,* pp. 64-67.

Robinson, P. (1985, December). Telecommunications, trade and TDF. *Telecommunications Policy,* pp. 310-318.

Root, F.R. (1988). A conceptual approach to international business. In J.C. Baker, J. K. Ryans & D.G. Howard (Eds.), *International Business Classics* (pp. 3-17). Lexington, MA: Lexington Books.

Sauvant, K.P. (1989). Services and data services: Introduction. In P. Robinson, K.P. Sauvant & V. Govitrikar (Eds.), *Electronic highways for world trade: Issues in telecommunications and data services* (pp. 3-14). Boulder, CO: Westview Press.

Simitis, S. (1989, November). Data protection: Transcending the national approach. pp. 23-28.

Smith, A. (1980). *The geopolitics of information.* New York: Oxford University Press.

Snapp, C.D. (1990, March 1). EDI aims high for global growth. *Datamation,* pp. 77-90.

Staple, G.C. & Mullins, M. (1989, June). Telecommunications traffic statistics - MiTT matter. *Telecommunications Policy*, pp. 105-128.

Stonier, T. (1983). *The wealth of information*. London: Methuen.

Strong growth of electronic mail in Europe. (1990, February). *Transborder Data & Communications Report*, p. 4.

Survey on international telecommunications. (1990, April 19). *Financial Times*. Section III.

Sweeney, G. (1983). Information, technology, and development. *The Information Society Journal*, 2(1), 1-3.

Taylor, P. (1990, April 19). The age of electronic trading. *Financial Times*, Section III, p. XI.

Tehranian, M. (1989). Information society and democratic prospects. In M. Jussawalla, T. Okuma, and T. Araki (Eds.), *Information technology and global interdependence* (pp.212-221). Westport, CT: Greenwood Press.

Status of data protection/privacy protection. (March, 1988). *Transborder Data & Communications Reports*, p. 16.

United Nations Center for Transnational Corporations. (1982). *Transnational corporation and transborder data flows*. New York: United Nations.

United Nations Educational, Scientific and Cultural Organization. (1980). *Many voices, one world*. New York: Anchor Press.

U.S. Department of Health, Education, and Welfare, *Records, computers, and the rights of citizens*. (1973, July). Washington: U.S. Government Printing Office.

U.S. Federal Communications Commission. (1987). *Statistics of communications common carriers*. Washington: FCC.

U.S. General Accounting Office. (1989a, June). *Computer Security* (GAO/IMTEC-89-57), Washington: GAO.

U.S. General Accounting Office. (1989b, February). *Electronic Funds Transfer* (GAO/IMTEC-89-25BR), Washington: GAO.

Vinogradov, V.A., Kiouzadjan, L.S., Andrianova, J.V., Vilenskaya, S.K., Kossov, G.B., Kulkin, A.M., Mdivani, R.R., Rakitov, I.E., Khisamutdinov, V.R., & Shemberko, L.V. (1984). Information exchange between developing and industrial countries. In G. Gerbner & M. Siefert (Eds.), *World communications: A handbook* (pp. 49-55). New York: Longman.

Weingarten, F.W. (1988). Communications technology: New challenges to privacy. *The John Marshall Law Review, 21*, 735-753.

White, R.A. & McDonnell, J.M. (1983). Priorities for national communication policy in the third world. *The Journal of Technology Management, 2*, 5-33.

Information Technology and the Transnational Corporation: The Emerging Multinational Issues

24

Shailendra Palvia
Babson College

Satyaprakash Saraswat
Bentley College

Unprecedented political and economic changes taking place in Western Europe, Eastern Europe, the Soviet Union and other regions of the world are creating immense opportunities for the exchange of technology and ideas across national boundaries. These changes have given rise to several issues in the area of Information Technology (IT) management with tremendous implications for national governments, regional and international organizations, and multinational corporations (MNCs). This chapter focuses on IT management issues from the perspective of multinational corporations.

Based on the structured content analysis of articles published in journals and conference proceedings, this chapter identifies eight categories of issues in information technology which are relevant to multinational corporations. These categories are: IT Transfer; Cultural Differences; International Standards; IT Infrastructure; Global IT Applications; Global IT Policy; Global IT Marketing; and Transborder Data Flows (TBDF).

An exploratory survey has been conducted to understand the importance and current status of the above issues from the perspective of the senior management of Fortune 500 companies. The results suggest that 1) the most significant issues on the importance criterion are: TBDF and International Standards; and 2) the most unsatisfactory issues based on the current status are: International Standards, Global IT Marketing, and IT Infrastructure.

INTRODUCTION

Unprecedented political and economic changes have been taking place throughout the world at a tremendous pace in recent years. These changes warrant a serious reassessment of how national governments, regional organizations, international organizations, and multinational corporations use information technology (IT) to cooperate and compete in the new global marketplace. This paper explores systematically the issues of global IT management from the perspective of multinational corporations (MNCs).

About 25 years ago, an obscure scholar from the University of Toronto, Marshall McLuhan, in a treatise called Understanding Media, made a prophesy that there would be a worldwide coalescence of human awareness into a single community which can be called "the global village" (Wright, 1990). How true was his prophecy! In addition to the political and economic changes, IT has played an important role in the realization of the prophesy of this "global village." Some examples of this role of IT include the:

1) Increased use of electronic trading in financial markets which has created opportunities for creative and informed investing throughout the world, (e.g., the October 19, 1987 Black Monday stock crash at the Wall Street induced an immediate domino effect in the London, Tokyo, Singapore, Sydney and other stock exchanges of the world).

2) Increased use of facsimile machines (an effective and efficient means to communicate with the outside world) which helped the Tiananmen Square revolution for democratic reforms in China.

3) Increased worldwide use of video-conferencing which has sharply reduced business travel and the revenues of the transportation industry.

4) Proliferation of the worldwide use of electronic mail services which has tremendously increased the opportunities for collaborative and productive work in diverse areas.

5) Growing use of standardized forms of information exchange (such as Electronic Data Interchange) which has improved the efficiency of business information processing.

Tremendous advances in IT have resulted in round-the-clock electronic transactions among markets, nations, continents, and time zones. Investments in IT during the last five years have been phenomenal and this trend shows every sign of continuing. Industry leaders and CEOs have clearly recognized that IT is crucial and critical to the survival of their companies. American Express, American Airlines and Citicorp have survived because they aligned their business vision with IT investment at the right time. Multinational corporations must recognize the role of IT in selling their products and services in the global marketplace.

According to Tony Brewer (1990), increasingly successful MNCs are those that treat the world as a single market. They design and develop their products and services wherever the skills are available, they buy raw materials and labor wherever they are the least expensive, they manufacture wherever they can achieve the lowest cost, and they sell everywhere. The task of managing these diverse and complex operations of MNCs requires the adroit and vigilant application of IT. This can be accomplished by understanding the issues relevant to the use of IT in managing these operations.

The following section describes the methodology employed to identify and rank order the important issues faced by MNCs in the area of global IT management.

METHODOLOGY

The research methodology used in the investigation of the issues in this paper is two-phased: 1) Structured Content Analysis of published material to identify the most important issues facing MNCs, and 2) Questionnaire Survey of the senior management of U.S.A. Fortune 500 companies to assess the importance and status of these issues.

Phase-1: Identification of Issues

The most important objective of content analysis is to draw inferences by observing and analyzing the contents of a medium of expression using a clearly defined step by step procedure which can be easily replicated and controlled (Jausch, 1980; Stampel, 1981). The medium of expression can be any source of information including written documents, oral communications, or audio-visual presentations. The academic disciplines in which this methodology has been frequently used are journalism, anthropology and history. Through several research studies in these disciplines, it has been demonstrated that this approach provides the analysts the flexibility of interpretation of the meaning of an information source while maintaining the objectivity of analysis (Baxter, 1985; Carrol, 1985; Estep, 1985; Larsen, 1986).

In recent years, Structured Content Analysis has been applied to those problem areas where other empirical methods are difficult to apply due to time constraints, environmental complexity, financial limitations or measurement problems (Roberts, 1970; Albaum & Peterson, 1984). In addition, the use of this methodology has been suggested by many authors to complement other approaches for business and organizational research (Jausch, 1980).

About one hundred and fifty papers were reviewed from various sources for the purpose of Structured Content Analysis. The following journals published during 1981-86 period were selected for review: *Developing Economies, International Economic Review, International Labor Review, International Organization, International Political Science Review, and World Development. The following journals published during 1985-90 period were also included: Management Science, Harvard Business Review, Sloan Management Review, Journal of International Business Studies, Journal of Information Systems Management, Journal of Management Information Systems, Journal of Information Systems, Journal of Information Resource Management, International Journal of Information Management, MIS Quarterly, Communications of the ACM, California Management Review, Information & Management, Columbia Journal of World Business,* and *TIMS/ORSA Interfaces.* For the same period (1985-90), papers published in the proceedings of *International Federation of Information Processing Societies (IFIPS)* and *International Conference on Information Systems (ICIS)* were also reviewed. A content analysis schedule was prepared to obtain information on the subject of "multinational issues in IT" in three categories from these sources: (1) identification of the publication in terms of its author, author's affiliation and the source of publication, (2) identification of the central idea addressed in the publication, and (3) analysis and interpretation of the central idea presented. The primary question to be answered from this analysis and interpretation was whether the author views a particular information technology issue as relevant to the MNCs. The overall content of the publication was searched to capture the central idea of the issue. Subsequently, any statistical data provided in the publication to substantiate the central idea was closely examined. Each article was analyzed by two reviewers and the consensus approach was used to reconcile the difference between the perceptions. This approach provided a sufficient degree of reliability of analysis.

Phase-2: Survey of Issues

The key MIS issues facing U.S. organizations in the past have been identified by several researchers using the methodology of surveying and iterative surveying also called the Delphi approach (Ball et al, 1982; Brancheau et al, 1986; Dickson et al, 1984; Hartog et al, 1986; Martin, 1983; Moon, 1989). Some researchers have also presented comparative studies of the importance of MIS issues for the U.S.A. and Western Europe (Buday, 1988; Wilder, 1989.) A recent study has even compared such MIS issues for the U.S.A., Western Europe and India (Palvia & Palvia, 1990). We decided to use similar approach with certain improvements. First, there was no need to use Delphi approach to determine the top most important issues — we already did this systematically with the structured content analysis approach. Secondly, we concentrated on two aspects of the issues facing senior management of the MNCs—importance of the issues and the status of the issues. Accordingly, the questionnaire is divided into two sections. The first section seeks to determine the importance of different issues from the perspective of senior management. The second section aims at finding out the perceptions of senior management about how well the issues mentioned in the first section are being currently addressed by the appropriate responsible authorities.

GLOBAL IT MANAGEMENT ISSUES: A TAXONOMY

The analysis is presented in two sections. The first section contains a taxonomy of the important issues that emerged from the structured content analysis. In this section, issues have also been interpreted and their implications for MNCs discussed. In the second section, the results of the questionnaire survey are presented.

An acceptable taxonomy of issues should meet the effectiveness test on five dimensions: comprehensiveness, brevity, mutual-exclusiveness, completeness, and usefulness (some ideas are from Vogel & Wetherbe, 1984). A taxonomy must represent as complete a spectrum of the issues under consideration as possible, and the number of categories suggested in the taxonomy should be manageable (Miller, 1956).

With the above criteria in mind, the global IT management issues identified from the structured content analysis are grouped into the following eight categories:

(1) IT Transfer
(2) Cultural Differences
(3) International Standards
(4) IT Infrastructure
(5) Global IT Applications
(6) Global IT Policy
(7) Global IT Marketing
(8) Trans-Border Data Flow

A detailed discussion of these issues follows.

(1) IT Transfer. The transfer of IT from industrialized countries to less developed countries (LDCs) has been the most frequently addressed issue in the past three decades (Saraswat, 1989). A global necessity for the transfer of technology, determination of suitable channels and approaches for the transfer, and the long term benefits of such a transfer to the countries involved in this exchange have been emphasized by several experts (Derakhshani, 1984; UNESCO, 1980; Von Weizsacker, 1984). The debate has generally focused on the transfer of IT from the United States to LDCs largely due to the fact that the U.S. computer and electronics industry has dominated the world market.

However, the issue of IT transfer has now become multidirectional. The IT industries of Japan and Western Europe have become major competitors, largely due to improved worker productivity and substantial IT investments, of the United States in the area of IT exchange. Tremendous opportunities for the transfer of IT to the Soviet Union and Eastern block countries are being created by the economic and political changes taking place in these countries. MNCs are, therefore, positioning themselves to take advantage of these opportunities. In this changed economic climate, MNCs from USA will be competing with the MNCs from Japan and Western Europe. The technology transfer from the U.S.A. to Japan, Korea, Hong Kong, Singapore and Taiwan in the 1950s and 1960s has enabled these countries to become major competitors of the U.S. in many industries such as electronics and automobile. In view of this experience, the long term implications of information technology transfer to Eastern Europe and other countries will also have to be closely examined by U.S.A.

(2) Cultural Differences. The effect of cultural differences on the development and implementation of IT has been recognized and documented in several studies, (e.g., Palvia & Palvia, 1990). In recent years, the emphasis by LDCs on "appropriate information technology" has become a very important issue. Appropriate IT is the technology that is more properly attuned to the cultural values and social needs of a country. Experts have argued in international forums against the acquisition of existing off-the-shelf technology from advanced countries (Hoffman, 1985; Kalman, 1979; Lautsch, 1983). Experts from countries with limited experience with IT have also emphasized the need for developing indigenous information technology (Burnell, 1985; Evans, 1985; Fabio, 1985; Grieco, 1982). Rapid growth of indigenous information technology in the newly industrializing countries of the Pacific Rim supports the viability of this approach.

Some recent empirical studies of the system design and development process conducted in a multinational setting have demonstrated that regional differences influence not only the application and development of computer and electronic technology but also the development of software systems for industrial and social applications. A study of 132 Canadian and 72 Danish system designers in 21 Canadian and Danish organizations found that Danish designers emphasize socio-political concerns as much as the technical and economic concerns, while Canadian designers place relatively more emphasis on the technical and economic concerns (Kumar & Bjorn-Anderson, 1990).

(3) International Standards. The need for consistent international standards has been evident ever since the beginning of the computer industry. Recently, this need has been amplified by the requirements of connectivity and compatibility between diverse computer systems utilized by MNCs throughout the world. While most standardization activity in the U.S. is dominated by voluntary organizations or individual companies, governments are heavily involved in making standards in Western European countries and Japan. European Economic Community is currently involved in the standardization of telecommunications and electronic technology industries through an agency named CEN (Committee European de Normalization). U.S. based MNCs and government agencies are concerned about the possibility of these standards not conforming to the existing standards. Multinational corporations are concerned because (a) incompatible standards can create non-tariff barriers to trade, and (b) U.S. government has no regional representation in CEN even though U.S. is the largest supplier of electronic equipment to the European countries. MNCs have, therefore, tried to install their own representatives in strategic positions within national organizations of the European Community, with some success, although it is costing them millions of dollars. Block voting by European organizations in the International Standards organizations is also creating problems for the U.S. multinationals. The European Community is against official U.S. representation but the U.S. companies are optimistic about the eventual outcome (Frankel, 1990).

(4) IT Infrastructure. The creation of an IT infrastructure is an important theme emerging from the countries which lack information technology, and also those that provide this technology (Ives, 1990). Countries lacking IT infrastructure are: most countries of Asia, Africa and Latin America; some countries of Eastern Europe; and the Soviet Union. Telecommunications and technical education are the two industries which will provide the infrastructure for information technology development (Agarwal, 1985; Bessant, 1984; Evans, 1986; Fabio 1985; Hoffman, 1985; Kalman, 1979; Lautsch, 1983).

Technical education in IT is one area where experts from OECD (Organization for Economic Cooperation and Development) countries have accumulated considerable experience with supplying consulting services and training to LDCs (Alfthan, 1985; OECD, 1981; Smith & Jaysiri, 1983). This accumulated experience can now be successfully utilized to improve the technical education and training facilities in the emerging democracies of Eastern Europe, the Soviet Union and other regions of the world.

Building a strong IT infrastructure for the growth of the Soviet economy has been given a very high priority under the policy of "glasnost" and "perestroika" initiated by Gorbachev. Currently, there are about 300,000 microcomputers in the Soviet Union. However, it is estimated that by the turn of the 21st century, there will be about 28 million microcomputers in the U.S.S.R. Current investment in the telecommunications network is about $13 billion. This investment is expected to double by the year 2000. The Soviet Union, in an effort to boost computer literacy for the next generation, has made computer education compulsory in high schools.

A study comparing MIS issues in the U.S.A. and India (Palvia & Palvia, 1990) found one of the pressing issues to be the lack of trained computer professionals. It also discovered a terrible scarcity of effective and reliable telecommunication networks in India. Recently, a high priority has been assigned by the government to the development of IT infrastructure so that IT can be developed and implemented on a larger scale for the diverse public and private industries.

The Peoples Republic of China is another country which has been very concerned about the IT infrastructure. An ACM delegation to China in 1982 (Wilson, 1988) indicated that the lack of teachers, facilities, equipment and incentives was responsible for the poor quality of computer science education in China. Official recognition of computer science as a discipline and the formation of the Chinese Computer Federation in the middle 1980s has helped the advancement of computer science in China. Computer concepts are being included at the high school level, women are being encouraged to join the computer profession and impressive gains have been made in the advancement of computer science education in recent years (Wilson, 1988).

(5) Global IT Applications. Information technology has been traditionally utilized by private corporations for improving the operational efficiency, productivity and competitive advantage within the confines of local economies. However, now the time is ripe to start thinking in terms of a global economy. The positive economic and political climate across the world is a tremendous boost toward this goal. One negative side of all these developments is that environmental conditions have been deteriorating across national boundaries. These positive as well as negative changes require a redefinition of the role of information technology in the global context. In the 1990s, the areas of global applications of information technology will be: improvement of social conditions and public administration in LDCs and emerging democracies, control and prevention of environmental pollution throughout the world, and the effective management of multinational corporations.

(6) Global IT Policy. Global IT policy should address the issues important from the point of view of five major IT players in the world: the United States, Western Europe, Eastern Europe and the Soviet Union, Japan,

and less developed countries (LDCs). Western Europe has a $90 billion market in information technology and only 20% of it is controlled by indigenous companies. The United States and Japanese companies control the rest of the market. Mergers, acquisitions and reorganizations taking place in companies like NV Phillips of Netherlands and Siemens of Germany in preparation for the 1992 unification will create a formidable challenge to U.S. and Japanese companies. Computer and telecommunications industries are being restructured by European governments to strengthen them in preparation for 1992. Under a program called IMPACT (Information Market Policy Actions), governments will provide up to 25% of the cost of innovative information services to be offered by private companies. These services include ISDN and CD-ROM products. United States companies registered in Europe will be treated on an equal basis in this program with domestic companies, and will thus be allowed to compete for government funds (Frankel, 1989).

The U.S. and Japan are concerned about the prospect of the diminishing influence of their MNCs due to the European integration in 1992. However, these fears are unfounded because DEC, AT&T and IBM are participating as equals of the European companies in programs heavily subsidized by European governments. Businesses have to think globally to recognize these opportunities and become active participants in the formulation of these policies (Jeelof, 1990). Japan's view of the impending European integration is also changing from "Euro-pessimism" to "Euro-optimism" (Eiichi, 1990).

While trade and investment issues are important from the perspective of advanced countries, LDCs have different objectives for a global IT policy. Several experts have raised concern over the possibility of IT being used by the industrialized countries or MNCs as an instrument of economic domination in LDCs (Adler, 1986; Burnell, 1985; Evans, 1986; Evans, 1985; Grieco, 1982; Kleine, 1985; Radice, 1975; Sikkink, 1986). An unbalanced development of IT in different parts of the world may divide the world into two antagonistic groups of "information have" and "information have not" countries. A rapid development of IT in advanced countries and the inability of other countries to keep pace could reduce them to the role of suppliers of raw data, and assemblers of microchips for the advanced countries. The dangers of this industrial restructuring on a global scale will extend beyond economic horizons (Bessant, 1984; Cole, 1986; Ernst, 1985).

(7) Global IT Marketing. There is a growing recognition of increased opportunities for international trade created by information technology. In today's global marketplace, LDCs, the Soviet Union and Eastern Europe are fertile areas for IT export. Information Technology is critical to provide a boost to the sagging economies of these regions. However, there is competition among countries like West Europe, Japan, the U.S.A., and the Four Tigers (Taiwan, Hong Kong, South Korea, Singapore) in Asia to market IT to these

regions. To succeed, one must be aggressive and creative in IT marketing, (e.g., coming up with innovative options for financing and willingness to invest in building the IT infrastructure of the host countries).

The export of software is consistently emphasized as an area where LDCs can obtain favorable terms of trade and such exports are already making an important contribution to the balance of trade of many countries such as India, Israel, Brazil, and the Soviet Union. The processing of microchips, the assembly of circuit boards, and large scale data entry have already become predominant information technology oriented activities in LDCs (Cole, 1986; Hoffman, 1985; Ives, 1990; Rammurthi, 1985; Richie, 1983).

Europe imports 49% of its needs in semiconductors and integrated circuits from several suppliers, especially the U.S.A. IT exports from the United States of approximately $900M are twice as much as Japanese exports. However, Japanese companies are now installing fabrication facilities in Europe to compete more successfully after 1992. The assembly of parts in the European Community countries adds about 45% to the value of the products. For Japan, this added value will meet the minimum local content requirement thus exempting them from additional customs and duties. United States companies will feel pressure from Japanese competitors as a result of these developments (Chiarodo, 1990).

(8) Transborder Data Flows. TBDF is the flow of data across national boundaries on telecommunications networks. There is an unprecedented growth in TBDF primarily created by the rapid convergence of data processing and data communications technologies in the past two decades. Multinational Corporations in the airline, banking, hospitality and insurance industries have become the most important users of TBDF in recent years (Werner, 1986). The challenges faced by MNCs in TBDF are: (1) It is virtually impossible to define "trading of electronic data" under the common rules of the General Agreement on Trade and Tariffs (GATT), because of the abstract nature of the commodity, and (2) measurement and quantification of the value of data for regulatory purposes is problematic due to a lack of commonly accepted measures and standards. The TBDF concerns commonly expressed by MNC managers are related to: the implementation of restrictive laws in many countries, unfair pricing of communications channels in some countries, and the lack of security of international telecommunications networks used for TBDF.

During the 1970s and 1980s, there was a growing trend among countries towards passing restrictive laws for the control of TBDF (Palmer, 1986). Many of these laws were based on the Privacy Act of 1974 enacted in the United States. Other countries, however, made these regulations even stricter, superimposing economic and social factors also. The potential for difficulties in this area remains because, following the lead of Europe, Third

World Countries are now passing restrictive laws to create a "New Information Order" (Barna, 1978). These restrictive regulations are intended to safeguard their national sovereignty and conserve their cultural heritage. Recently, however, there is a tendency toward a more open exchange of information among countries and many U.S. multinationals do not consider the current TBDF regulatory environment a matter of great concern (Kane, 1988).

Another major barrier to TBDF is the lack of availability of communications channels for data transfer in competitive markets outside of the United States (Martin, 1984). Communications channels are provided as a regulated monopoly service of Post and Telegraphs departments in most European and Asian countries. Multinational Corporations, as compared to domestic corporations, are often charged higher rates by these Post and Telegraph departments for telecommunications Services. The implementation of private networks based on channels leased from international common carriers can diminish the reliance on local public channels and also be more cost effective. Citicorp implemented a private data network with nodes in more than 75 countries at a cost of approximately $15M in 1983 and savings of 30% in the cost of data flow have been reported for this network (Stix, 1987). General Electric and some other companies have implemented similar networks.

The security of TBDF networks, in recent years, has become a major concern since data transmission is recognized as the most insecure operation among different computer based information processing operations (Davies, 1989). The problem of network security has been aggravated by the increasing complexity of networking technology and the sophistication of hackers. Data encryption and other standard techniques of network security may not be adequate. Multinational Corporations may have to use proprietary techniques for telecommunication network security, thus increasing the cost. The largest commercial global communication network, spanning 75 cities in 30 countries, is operated by General Electric Information Services. It supports 500 computers with 7500 access ports, and transmits 400 million characters per hour through satellite links (Shain, 1989). The network security in this system is based on a scheme which is a combination of the Data Encryption and ANSI Encryption Standards. Multinational Corporations require advanced cryptographic techniques and a high degree of vigilance by personnel to ensure the security of TBDF operations.

ANALYSIS OF THE SURVEY RESULTS

A questionnaire containing several questions to cover the domain of each of the eight issues delineated above was prepared. It was pretested by two senior MIS executives and two MIS Professors. Survey questionnaires were mailed to the CEOs of Fortune 500 companies in June, 1990. Twenty seven responses from the senior management of these Fortune 500 companies were received by the end of July, 1990. Before presenting the analysis of responses to the issues, the respondents' profile is examined in the next section.

Research Participants' Profile

The participating organizations were diverse and the respondents had rich experience in their industry and also in IT. The median ranking of the responding Fortune 500 companies was 188. The rankings ranged from 3 to 470. The industries of participating companies ranged from Manufacturing, Transportation, and Retailing to Energy, Pharmaceuticals, and Consulting. The mean number of years of experience of the respondents in their respective industries was 20 years and the mean number of years of experience in information technology was 18.5 years.

The following section provides an analysis of the issues according to the criteria of importance and current status.

Analysis of Issues According to Importance and Status

Table-1 provides the mean scores of the eight issues. Each of these issues, in turn, consisted of two or more subissues. The importance and current status of each subissue was assigned by each respondent on a 5-point Likert scale. The first column lists the issues, the second column the scores based on perceived importance of the issues, and the third column the average scores representing current status of these issues in terms of the extent to which these issues are being currently addressed by appropriate organizations. In Table 2 these scores have been replaced by corresponding ranks. Higher scores in the

	Importance Score	Status Score
(1) IT Transfer	3.03	2.79
(2) Cultural Differences	3.17	3.39
(3) International Standards	3.61	2.01
(4) IT Infrastructure	2.82	2.51
(5) Global IT Applications	3.15	2.97
(6) Global IT Policy	2.94	3.08
(7) Global IT Marketing	2.52	2.44
(8) Trans Border Data Flow	4.11	2.93

Table 1: Mean Importance and Status Scores for the Eight Issues

	Importance Score	Status Score
(1) IT Transfer	5	5
(2) Cultural Differences	3	1
(3) International Standards	2	8
(4) IT Infrastructure	7	6
(5) Global IT Applications	3	3
(6) Global IT Policy	6	2
(7) Global IT Marketing	8	7
(8) Trans Border Data Flow	1	3

Table 2: Issue Rankings based on Importance and Status Scores

second column (and also higher ranks) represent greater importance assigned to the issues by the CEOs or their designees. Higher scores in the third column (and also high ranks) convey a greater level of satisfaction with respect to the extent to which these issues are being addressed by appropriate authorities (based on the perceptions and experiences of the respondents).

Following is a discussion of the issues based on their relative significance to the senior management of the Fortune 500 companies. The significance of an issue is primarily determined by its relative ranking on the importance scores. However, rankings based on status scores (high status score implies a relatively high level of satisfaction regarding the extent to which an issue is currently being addressed by appropriate authorities or organizations) are also referred to wherever appropriate.

Issue-One: Transborder Data Flows: Three questions, pertaining to 1) the unrestricted flow of data across national boundaries, 2) security of transborder data flows, and 3) the indispensable role of telecommunications networks in the management of MNCs, were included in the questionnaire to cover this issue.

It is no surprise that this issue came out number one on the importance score ranking and number three on the status score ranking. In three independent surveys — CIO, 1989; CIMS, 1989; and Palvia and Palvia, 1990 — Data Security ranked five, twelve, and nine respectively on the list of important issues. Furthermore, the data security issue assumes even greater importance in the context of an increasing international movement of data through microwave and satellite networks.

Furthermore, the issues of piracy and intellectual property concerns must also be addressed. As mentioned in Sethi and Olson (1991), U.S. software firms have undertaken widespread campaigns against software piracy in Europe. Since intellectual works are simultaneously available to many individuals who may access them from a central database, the identification of authorship, repackaging of information (in terms of encryption etc.); and reprocessibility (in terms of decryption etc.) are the other important issues that need to be addressed with TBDF.

There is a higher susceptibility to violation of integrity and privacy of data due to the greater geographical distances and increased sophistication of hackers. To avoid these problems, more effective methods of control and management of TBDF will have to be developed and implemented.

Issue Two: International Standards: The issue of common international standards has become extremely important in recent years, especially due to the impending unification of the European Economic Community (EEC). The need for uniform international standards for (a) telecommunications networks to facilitate exchange of data, (b) software development to increase trade in software and consulting services, and (c) computer systems architecture to guarantee the compatibility of hardware manufactured in different countries is becoming increasingly evident. Questions on these three issues were included in the questionnaire.

This issue assumes all the more importance when we look at the abysmally low average score on its current status — this issue ranks last (eight) in terms of its current status. The problems of hardware and software standards in the United States alone are many. The problem is magnified substantially when a MNC is dealing with hardware and software developed in several nations. The mixed vendor shop is commonplace in developing nations, (Palvia & Palvia, 1990). There is generally a tremendous lack of international standards thereby making the task of developing, implementing and using global IT applications a nightmare for MNCs. For example, Electronic Data Interchange (EDI), an important global IT application, currently has many different standards across the globe (Purton, 1989).

The need for international standards is extremely important in today's shrinking global marketplace. This task can no more be left in the hands of private organizations. Governments and international public organizations must step in to address this very important issue.

Issue Three: Global IT Applications: Three questions on this issue were asked in the survey: the use of IT for government administration in LDCs, global IT cooperation for environmental improvement, and the use of effective information systems for the management of MNCs.

This issue is perceived as neither important nor unimportant — almost matching its current status. On examining the subissues comprising this issue, it was revealed that:

1) Developing effective information systems for the management of MNCs is perceived as very important and that more measures can be undertaken to improve the current status on this dimension.

2) Global IT cooperation for environmental improvement was perceived as neither important nor unimportant — and its current status is perceived as neither satisfactory nor unsatisfactory.

3) Using IT to improve government administration in LDCs, relatively speaking, was not considered important and its current status is also considered inadequate.

Issue Three (tied): Cultural/Regional differences: Understanding the influence of differences in linguistic and cultural values, social and economic environments, and legal and ethical standards on the development, promotion and implementation of IT in a host country were considered important for this study. Three questions pertaining to these differences were included in the questionnaire.

The average importance score indicates that moderate importance is accorded to this issue by the respondents. Furthermore, the respondents perceive the current status on this issue to be moderately satisfactory. This is approximately true for all the three subissues addressed in this category.

Issue Five: IT Transfer: To analyze the importance and status of this issue, ten questions were included in the survey questionnaire. These are related to IT transfer between the United States and Western Europe, between the United States and Eastern Europe including the Soviet Union, between the United States and Japan, and finally between the United States and LDCs. Additional questions were included to address the role of the U.S. government and computer industry in promoting IT transfer.

Even though the importance of this issue is not the highest, it is heartening to note that the respondents were most satisfied with the current status of this issue as compared to that of all other issues. On examining the subissues that comprise this issue, it is clear that:

1) Unrestricted IT transfer between the U.S.A. and Western Europe and between the U.S.A. and Japan are perceived as very important. Furthermore the current status on this subissue is perceived to be at a satisfactory level.

2) The issue of IT transfer between the U.S.A. and Japan was rated as very important but the status was rated as only moderately satisfactory.

3) The issue of IT transfer between the U.S.A. and the U.S.S.R. (including the Eastern European countries) was rated as relatively less important, but the current status on this issue was perceived as far from satisfactory.

4) The issue of IT transfer from the U.S.A. to the LDCs is perceived as relatively unimportant and its current status is also considered inadequate.

5) A more active role of the U.S. government in promoting IT transfer was rated as modestly important, but its current status suggested substantial room for improvement.

6) In relation to its importance (neither important nor unimportant), the computer industry in the U.S. was perceived as doing an adequate job in pro-

moting IT transfer.

Issue Six: Global IT Policy: Seven questions in the survey addressed the following dimensions of this issue: (a) the role of regional cooperation blocks such as the European Community, in formulating global IT policy, (b) the role of international organizations in policy formulation, (c) the role of computer industry MNCs, such as IBM and DEC in influencing global IT policy, (d) implications for LDCs of possible domination of computer industries in LDCs by the computer industry in advanced countries, (e) implications of such domination for the advanced countries, (f) implications of growing IT gap between "information have" and "information have-not" countries, and (g) the need for national IT planning not only in LDCs but also advanced countries such as the United States.

The overall scores suggest that for this issue, the importance as well as the current status are on the borderline. However, a close examination of the seven subissues provides some insights. First, regional cooperation blocks and MNCs in the computer industry have an important role to play in shaping the IT policy — and at this time they are not doing enough. Second, the current status on all subissues appears to be satisfactory except, 1) the role of international organizations in policy formulation — international organizations like the United Nations can play a vital role in formulating and implementing an IT policy, and 2) the implication of possible domination of LDCs by the governments of advanced countries through the use of IT — the message is that the LDCs can potentially be manipulated by exploiting IT.

Issue Seven: IT Infrastructure: Four questions were considered important for IT infrastructure. The first question applies to the creation of a service industry in LDCs to promote global economic development. The contribution of information technology in the growth of a service sector and the resultant creation of vast employment opportunities has been widely recognized in the advanced countries. This experience has transformed the perspective of experts who have traditionally viewed computers as mere labor substitution devices. The second question relates to the creation of regional agricultural, industrial and demographic data bases to promote global economic cooperation. The development of technical education and telecommunications and other basic infrastructural components in LDCs is the third question. Traditionally, most LDCs have obtained foreign assistance from advanced countries or international organizations for the development of an industrial infrastructure. With the declining aid from these sources, and inadequate indigenous resources, host countries have to increasingly rely on MNCs to develop an IT infrastructure in host countries. The fourth question elicits the opinions of the respondents concerning the assistance MNCs can provide to LDCs for creating a suitable IT infrastructure.

The importance and current performance on this issue were less important (relatively unimportant) and less satisfactory (relatively unsatisfactory) respectively. However, one issue stands out when the subissues are closely examined. Developing an IT infrastructure in LDCs was considered important but its current status was definitely less than satisfactory. This is one area where the governments and the computer industry of advanced nations can help by not only providing regional databases, technical know-how, but also providing human and financial resources to help build the IT infra-structure.

Issue Eight: Global IT Marketing: Six questions in the survey solicited the opinions of chief executives on three dimensions of this issue: (a) host country foreign investment policies, (b) export of software, computer technology personnel and raw data from LDCs, and (c) creation of R&D facilities in LDCs.

This issue is not important at this point. However, one of the subissues — utilizing computer experts from other countries in the United States is perceived as important and the current status is perceives as less-than-satisfactory. Another issue worth mentioning is liberal foreign investment by the computer industry in the host country. On the importance criterion, this issue is perceived as being on the borderline between important and not important, but the current status is much-less-than-satisfactory.

CONCLUSIONS

The issues discussed in this chapter and the methodology employed to identify the issues both have important implications for the managers of MNCs at all levels. Traditionally, the important issues for the assimilation of information technology in the corporate culture of an organization have been: operational efficiency, productivity improvement, competitive advantage, organizational restructuring, and protection of individual privacy. However, in today's era, due to the increased interdependence of economic activity in different nations, it has become imperative for multinational corporations to have an international outlook to compete successfully. In today's global marketplace, unprecedented trade and investment opportunities exist for multinational corporations. In this context, it is important to properly identify and understand the issues that aid in the coordination of transnational activities of MNCs; and creation of strong and sustainable relationships among concerned national governments. This chapter has identified and analyzed several of these issues. These issues have an important influence on the flow of trade, capital and technology throughout the world. The challenge of successfully aligning and integrating information technology with the organizational structure of an MNC can be achieved only after a proper understanding of these issues by the MNC managers.

Two issues of utmost concern identified in this research are: lack of

International Standards (telecommunication, software development, and computer system architecture standards) and problems faced in Transborder Data Flows (restrictions on flow of data, lack of security of TBDF, and lack of telecommunications in the management of MNCs). Both these issues are considered very high in importance, but are perceived to be ignored by the appropriate organizations. Appropriate national, regional, and international organizations must immediately work together to develop globally acceptable standards and also to take steps to reduce or eliminate the impediments to effective TBDF. Further research to identify any relationships between the size, industry, and other characteristics of a MNC and importance given to an issue should be conducted to help in alleviating MNC-specific problems.

From the standpoint of research methodology, the paper broadens the horizons of MIS research. The lopsided growth of technical knowledge in the field of MIS occurring in the past three decades runs counter to the growing recognition that MIS is inherently a multidisciplinary field requiring a study of both social and technical dimensions. For this reason, methodologies prevalent in social disciplines should be employed to answer some epistemological questions. Structured Content Analysis, used in this research, is a research methodology that can be used as a bridge between the scientific empiricism prevailing in MIS research and the phenomenological subjectivism of history, philosophy and social sciences. It can be used as a complementary method for MIS research to provide the researcher sufficient flexibility in analyzing the meaning of the communication without losing its empirical content or broader context, in a relatively short time.

References

Adler, E. (1986). Ideological 'Guerrillas' and the Quest for Technological Autonomy: Brazil's Domestic Computer Industry. *International Organization, 40*(3), 673-705.

Agarwal, S.M. (1985). Electronics in India: Past Strategies and Future Possibilities. *World Development, 13*(3), 273-286.

Albaum, G., and Peterson, R.A.(Spring/Summer, 1984). Empirical Research in International Marketing: 1976-1982. *Journal of International Business Studies,* 161-173.

Alfthan, T. (1985). Developing Skills for Technological Change: Some Policy Issues. *International Labor Review, 124*(5), 517-529.

Ball, L., and Harris, R. (March, 1982). SMIS Member: A Membership Analysis. *MIS Quarterly, 6*(1), 19-38.

Barna, B. (August, 1978). A New Threat to Multinationals. *Computer Decisions,* 34-38.

Baxter, R.L, et. al. (Summer, 1985). A Content Analysis of Music Videos. *Journal of Broadcasting and Electronic Media, 29*(3), 323-331.

Bessant, J. (1984). Technology and Market Trends in the Production and Application of Information Technology. *Micro Electronics Monitor,* (8), UNIDO.

Brancheau, J., and Wetherbe, J. (1986). Key Issues in Information Systems Management - A Delphi Study of IS Executives and General Managers. MISRC Working Paper, University of Minnesota.

Brewer, A. (1990). The Impact of Globalisation on Information Systems Management. *Computer World.*

Buday, R.S. (1988). *Critical Issues of Information Systems Management.* Index Group Report.

Burnell, P. (1985). *Economic Nationalism in the Third World.* Boulder, Colorado: Westview Press.

Carrol, R.L. (Winter, 1985). Content Values in Television News Programs in Small and Large Markets. *Journalism Quarterly, 62*(4), 877-882.

Chiarodo, R., and Mussehl, J. (April, 1990). The Semiconductor Market in European Community. *Communications of the ACM,* 1990.

Cole, S. (1986). The Global Impact of Information Technology. *World Development, 14*(10/11), 1277-1292.

Davies, D.W., and Price, W.L. (1989). *Security for Computer Networks,* (2nd Edition). New York: John Wiley & Sons.

Derakhshani, S. (1984). Factors Affecting Success in International Transfer of Technology. *Developing Economies, 22*(1), 27-40.

Dickson, G.W., Leitheiser, R.L., Wetherbe, J.C., and Nechis, M. (September, 1984). Key Information System Issues for the 1980's. *MIS Quarterly, 8*(3), 135-159.

Eiichi, O. (April, 1990). Japan's View of EC '92. *Communications of the ACM,* 412-416.

Ernst, D. (1985). Automation and the Worldwide Restructuring of the Electronics Industry: Strategic Implications for Developing Countries. *World Development, 13*(3), 333-352.

Estep, R., and Mcdonald, P.T. (Summer, 1985). Crime in the Afternoon: Murder and Robbery in Soap Operas. *Journal of Broadcasting and Electronic Media, 29*(3), 323-331.

Evans, P.B. (1985). Varieties of Nationalism: The Politics of the Brazilian Computer Industry. In A. Botelho and P. Smith (eds.) *The Computer Question in Brazil: High Technology in a Developing Society,* Cambridge, Mass.: MIT Press.

Evans, P.B. (1986). State Capital and Transformation of Dependence: The Brazilian Computer Case. *World Development, 14*(7), 791-808.

Fabio, E. (1985). The Development of the Electronics Complex and Government Policies in Brazil. *World Development, 13*(3), 293-309.

Frankel, K. (November, 1989). HDTV and the Computer Industry. *Communications of the ACM, 32*(11), 1300-1312.

Grieco, J.M. (1982). Between Dependency and Autonomy: India's Experience with International Computer Industry. *International Organization, 36*(3), 609-632.

Hartog, C., and Herbert, M. (December, 1986). 1985 Opinion Survey of MIS Managers: Key Issues. *MIS Quarterly, 10*(4), 351-361.

Hoffman, K. (1985). Microelectronics, International Competition and Development Strategies:

The Unavoidable Issues. *World Development, 13*(3), 23-55.

Ives, B. (1990). Global Information Technology: Some Conjectures for Future Research. *Proceedings, 23rd Annual Hawaii Conference on System Sciences,* 127-136.

Jausch, L.R., Osborn, R.N., and Martin, T.N. (1980). Structured Content Analysis of Cases: A Complementary Method for Organizational Research. *Academy of Management Review, 5*(4), 517-525.

Jeelof, G. (April, 1990). Europe 1992 - Fraternity or Fortress. *Communications of the ACM,* 412-416.

Kalman, R.E. (1979). *Effective Information Technology: Criteria for Selecting Appropriate Technologies under Different Cultural, Social and Technical Conditions.* Milan: IFAC Symposium, Italy.

Kane, M.J., and Ricks, D.J. (Fall, 1988). Is Transborder Data Flow Regulation a Problem. *Journal of International Business Studies,* 477-482.

Kleine, J.M. (1985). *International Codes and Multinational Business: Setting Guidelines for International Business Operations.* Westport, Connecticut: Quorum Books.

Kumar, K., and Bjorn-Anderson, N. (May, 1990). A Cross Cultural Comparison of IS Designer Values. *Communications of the ACM,* 528-538.

Larsen, J.F., McAnany, E.G., and Storey, J.D. (June, 1986). News of Latin America on Network Television, 1972-1981: A Northern Perspective on the Southern Hemisphere. *Critical Studies in Mass Communications, 3*(2), e169-183.

Lautsch, J.C. (1983). Computer Communications and the Wealth of Nations: Some Theoretical and Policy Considerations about an Information Economy. *Computer Law Journal, IV*(1), 101-132.

Martin, E.W. (September, 1983). Information Needs of Top MIS Managers. *MIS Quarterly, 7*(3), 1-11.

Martin, J.L. (1984). *Private Leased Telecommunications Lines: Threat to Continued International Availability.* Michigan Yearbook of International Legal Studies. New York: Clark Boardman Company, 219-239.

McLuhan M. (1964). *Understanding Media: The Extensions of Man.* New York: McGraw-Hill.

Miller, G.A. (March, 1956). The Magical Number Seven, Plus or Minus Two: Some Limits on Our Capacity for Processing. *The Psychological Review, 63*(2), 81-97.

Moon, D.V. (Andersen Consulting - 312-507-2375) (May, 1989). Trendlines: A Sweeping Generalization. *CIO - the magazine for information executives - 2*(8), (CIO).

OECD (Organization for Economic Cooperation and Development) (1981). Information Activities, *Electronics and Telecommunications Technologies, Impact on Employment, Growth and Trade* (Paris: OECD).

Palmer, J., and Dukes, A. (1986). Transborder Data Flow: A Corporate Concern. *Proc. National Computer Conference,* 29-33.

Palvia P., and Palvia S. (1990). Key MIS Issues in a Global Society: A Comparison between the U.S. and India. *Proceedings of the Hawaiian International Conference on Systems Sciences, IV,* 165-171.

Radice, H. (ed.) (1975). *International Firms and Modern Imperialism*. Penguin Books.

Rammurthi, R. (1985). High Technology Exports by State Enterprises in LDCs: The Brazilian Aircraft Industry. *Developing Economies, 23*(3), 254-280.

Richie, W., Hecker, D., and Burgen, J. (November, 1983). High Technology Today and Tomorrow. *Monthly Labor Review*.

Roberts, K. (1970). On Looking at an Elephant: An Evaluation of Cross Cultural Research Related to Organizations. *Psychological Bulletin, 74*(5), 327-360.

Saraswat, S., and Gorgone, J. (1989). A Perspective on the Global Implications of Information Technology. *Proceedings, Association of Human Resources Management and Organizational Behavior Annual Conference*, Boston, 273-277.

Sethi V., and Olson, J.E. (1991). An Integrating Framework for Information Technology Issues in a Transnational Environment. In the book on *Global Issues of Information Technology Management* edited by Palvia S., Palvia P., and Zigli Ron, Idea Group Publishing.

Shain, M. (1989). Security in Electronic Funds Transfer: Message Integrity in Money Transfer and Bond Settlements through GE Information Services' Global Network. *Computers and Security, 8*, 209-221.

Sikkink, K. (1986). Codes of Conduct for Industrial Corporations: The Case of the WHO/UNICEF Code. *International Organization, 40*(4), 815-840.

Smith, W.F., and Jaysiri, (1983). *Effective Computer Use in Developing Countries in Information Processing*. Amsterdam: North Holland Publishing Company.

Stampel, G.H., and Westley, B.H. (Eds.) (1981). *Research Methods in Mass Communication*. New Jersey: Prentice Hall.

Stix, G. (August, 1987). The High Cost of Global Reach. *Computer and Communications Decisions*, 52-57.

UNESCO Informatics. (1980). A Vital Factor in Development. Paris: UNESCO.

Vogel, D.J., and Wetherbe, J.C. (Fall, 1984). MIS Research: A Profile of Leading Journals and Universities. *Data Base*, 3-14.

Von Weizsacker, E., Swaminathan, M., and Lemma, A. (eds.) (1984). *New Frontiers in Technology Applications: Integration of Emerging and Traditional Technologies*. Dublin: Tycooly Press.

Werner, M. (1986). Transborder Data Flow: A Cost Benefit Analysis. *Canadian Banker, 93*(5), 34-36.

Wilder, C. (CW staff) (May 22, 1989). Foreign and US executives see eye-to-eye on the top IS issues. *Computerworld,* based on the Proceedings of the CIMS conference in Babson College, Wellesley, MA.

Wilson, J. (et. al.) (August, 1988). Computer Science Education in Peoples Republic of China in the Late 1980s. *Communications of the ACM*, 956-964.

Wright, K. (March, 1990). The Road to the Global Village. *Scientific American*, 83-95.

25 Planning Globally: Practical Strategies for Information Technology in the Transnational Firm

Peter G.W. Keen
International Center for Information Technologies
and **Fordham University**

OVERVIEW: PLANNING IN A CONTEXT OF UNCERTAINTY AS THE NORM

It is commonsense that firms with global business strategies for competing in a global marketplace must make sure their IT strategies move in parallel with them. How to do so is not at all commonsense. This is an area dominated by uncertainties and constraints, that are both managerial, technical, organizational and cultural. The main areas of uncertainty are:

1) How the firm itself will organize its transnational business operations. It has to balance many simultaneous and interdependent needs for central coordination plus local autonomy. In this context, the IS executive will not be presented with a clear business and organizational model that can provide a blueprint for the technical architecture.

2) Parochialism and ignorance about international differences in technology, regulation, procedures, constraints and options;

3) The lack of an organizational locus of expertise and authority for developing a global IT architecture. In most firms, IT has been handled on a country by country or regional basis. There is little momentum for creating an effective central coordinative and transnational planning function;

4) The many uncertainties, claims and variations in international IT standards and regulations relevant to creating a global IT platform.

This chapter aims at providing a practical framework for action for senior Information Services managers within this context of uncertainty. Its main recommendations are that IS managers and planners:

1) Establish a compelling business case at the level of top management for creating the transnational information technology platform. That platform is a shared information services and communications, whose business functionality is defined by two dimensions, Reach and Range. This is essential in order to create a counter to the natural movement towards distributing IT planning along with distributing the technology. Information Services planners need to highlight the likely losses of "business degrees of freedom" that results from a fragmented set of applications, instead of a flexible platform for applications.

2) Present a convincing economic model for applying IT to address the new realities of rapidly eroded profit margins across virtually every industry. Senior executives are increasingly concerned that they lack such a model. The business value of IT remains unproven and the costs continue to escalate. Vague claims about competitive advantage cannot substitute for showing where and how IT will directly and significantly contribute to economic performance.

3) Provide real news to grab business managers' attention about the opportunities a transnational perspective on IT provides for enhancing and not just supporting a transnational business strategy. IS planners and managers must highlight major, self-justifying and self-explanatory new sources of competitive and organizational advantage through ownership of the IT platform.

4) Build a cosmopolitan cadre of IT planners and staff. Here, "cosmopolitan" goes beyond "international"; it refers to a style of operating across cultures.

The recommendations rest on five assumptions, which will not be explained or justified in detail here. They are in effect the axioms driving the analysis:

1) Globalization will inevitably push the traditional multinational

corporation towards more tightly linked forms of cross-country operation and coordination. This will move firms towards the principles of transnational design summarized by Bartlett and Ghoshal: "Assets and capabilities are dispersed, interdependent and specialized; there are differentiated contributions by national units; and knowledge is developed jointly and shared worldwide." To this may be added their conclusion that "transnationalism" is more of a new "management mentality" than a specific organizational form.[1]

2) It will be extremely hard for most firms to make this shift smoothly, without mistakes and without massive cultural strains. Crossfunctional collaboration is difficult to create. Crossfunctional, crosscultural and crossorganizational collaboration will be much more difficult. Such collaboration is the hallmark of the transnational management mentality, with the world becoming awash with crossorganizational and crossborder joint ventures, mergers and acquisitions.

3) Information technology will be at least as important in transnational as in domestic operations, in terms of competitive opportunities and necessities and of organizational coordination. Computer-integrated manufacturing, electronic customer-supplier links, electronic data interchange, automated teller machines, and airline reservation systems are part of firms' core business drivers in domestic markets. These and other elements of the IT platform will inevitably be the base for managing in transnational firms as well, especially since coordination of operations across wide time zones in a context of time-based-competition depends on fast communications and hence on telecommunications.

4) The political, social and business context of 2001 will be at least as different from 1991 as 1991 was from that of 1981, and as unpredictable by even the wisest and most acute observer. Gorbachev, German reunification, the EC 1992 Open Market initiative, break up of AT&T and London's Big Bang are just a few of the surprises that reshaped the 1980s. There must be plenty of surprises coming in the 1990s.

5) The regulatory, technical and cost environment of international IT, particularly in the area of telecommunications, will remain volatile and unpredictable. International telecommunications is a battleground that resembles the international automotive industry, in terms of size, capital demands, political implications, impacts on national economic policy and regulation, and restrictive practices.

Most firms will have problems handling any one of these issues, let alone all of them together. The reason for stating these assumptions up front is that much of the discussion of both transnational business and international IT has an overtidy air of certainty and assertion, and offers oversimple recommendations about what firms should do. This is especially apparent in analyses of the EC 1992 Single Market initiative and of open systems and standards for information technology. Examples are the blanket statements about all seven layers of the Open Systems Interconnection reference model (OSI) being fully implemented by 1990 and predictions of a Fortress Europe or a "United States of Europe." Such assertions have an assuredness about them that easily encourages tidy conceptual schema and recommendations that finesse the huge uncertainties at the core of strategic positioning for global business.

MANAGEMENT CONCERNS

This will not be a tidy world for either business or IS managers. Firms have to take action in a context of many unresolved and partially unresolvable blockages. Concerns expressed by business and information services executives concerning transnational IT issues are summarized below. They were gathered in informal interviews in mid-1990 conducted as a preliminary stage to a major Fordham University research program.[2] They fall into four categories of concern:

1) *Organizational design*: what are the principles for evolving the transnational organization that should guide IT planning?

2) *The global IT platform:* how can the firm most effectively move towards a globally or regionally coordinated approach to IT planning?

3) *Cultural integration and technology adoption:* what are the main issues in managing not just across borders but across cultures? What is the role of IT, and what are the impacts of cultural differences on IT planning?

4) *Technology constraints, costs and opportunities:* how can a transnational IT base be most effectively built, given the wide variations in costs and degrees of regulation across key international markets?

The list of concerns is obviously not exhaustive but indicates the broad agenda of managers gearing up to deal with a new challenge, where they largely do not feel comfortable, well-briefed or ready to make commitments.

Uncertainty dominates both the tone and the nature of their questions. Any recommendations for management action that do not address those questions will lack impact and credibility.

The concerns are listed in detail in Appendix 1, where they are shown as questions, since that is how the managers usually expressed them. There is too short and limited an experience base for firms to be able to draw reliable conclusions from each other. The answer to many of the questions amounts to "No one is quite sure. Time will tell."

Taking Action: Building the Dialogue at the Top

Waiting for time to tell is not likely to help much. It pushes IS managers into a reactive mode. If one accepts the assumption that information technology will be at least as important to transnational business operations as it has been to domestic ones, this can mean pushing the organization into a position of competitive defensiveness and possibly competitive disadvantage.

Moving from reaction to anticipation and action rests on building an effective dialog at the top of the firm. Currently, there is more generally two monologs about IT. They are monologs in the sense that neither party is seen by the other as listening. The first monolog is that of the Information Services executive; he or she is primarily concerned about lead times, integration and the architecture for the firm's IT platform. The senior business executive is, by contrast, most concerned about the economics of IT: its high immediate costs, apparently uncontrolled cost growth, unproven overall benefits and lack of a coherent framework for assessing investment alternatives.

Making the case for an aggressive transnational strategy for IT primarily rests on these two management concerns: architecture and economics. There is ample evidence that senior business executives are not hearing any compelling business message even for their domestic IT planning about the need for an overall architecture and shared corporate information delivery base. There is also plenty of evidence that IS is not providing a convincing economic case for major IT infrastructure investments.[3]

The above assertions are partly based on a research study carried out by the International Center for Information Technologies (ICIT) in 1989. The research team interviewed chairmen, CEOs and other members of the top management team in 27 European and North American companies, all of which are among the top ten firms in their industry. The aim of the unstructured interviews was to find out how top executives think about IT and about their own role in planning and decision making.[4]

We found that most managers are well aware now of the business importance of information technology. That awareness mainly leads to increased delegation and pressures towards systems disintegration; executives raise their expectations of Information Services without feeling that they themselves should take a lead. We summarized our interpretation of the senior management decision process as a learning curve, with three distinct steps, shown in Figure 1:

> 1) Awareness of the business importance of IT: without this, top management essentially abdicates responsibility to an IS staff manager with limited authority. IT is then viewed as overhead, and managed as such;

> 2) A business vision to drive the deployment of IT; without this, management delegates to IS, expecting it to generate recommendations for using IT competitively;

> 3) A compelling business message for building a comprehensive and integrated IT platform, rather than a set of separate applications and facilities.

Only a third of the top managers interviewed had a clear and personal business vision for IT. Only a sixth saw a need for a corporate platform. The senior IS managers in almost all the companies reported their frustration with the lack of understanding of the need for an architecture and with their own inability to move senior executives away from reactive delegation.

The research team created a framework for helping relate business integration and technology integration. The goal is to turn the IS monolog about lead time, integration and architecture into a real dialog. The framework defines the business functionality of the firm's IT facilities in terms of two dimensions of Reach and Range (see Figure 2).

> *Reach* determines the locations the firm can link to, from workstations and computers in the same department via local area networks, to remote units within the company, to customers and suppliers domestically, to international locations, to anyone, anywhere;

> *Range* determines the information that can be shared directly and automatically across systems and services. At one extreme, only systems built on the same hardware, software and telecommunications base can process messages and transactions created by each of them. At the other, any computer-generated transaction, document, message, image or even telephone message can be used in any other system, regardless of its hardware or software.

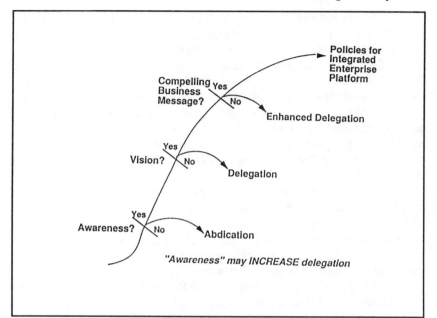

Figure 1: Senior Management Decision Process for IT

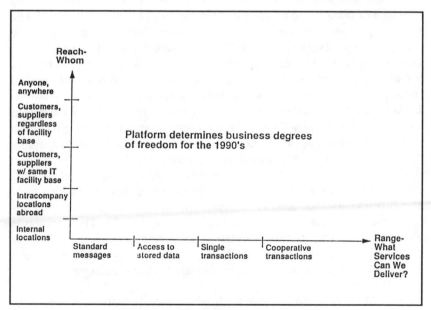

Figure 2: Explaining Integration

Reach and Range together determine the firm's "business degrees of freedom" for the 1990s: the extent of practical business options it can consider. Reach and Range enable or disable its choices of IT applications. In assessing the need for a transnational IT platform, IS planners have to start by asking "What degree of Reach and Range is implied by our own business plans?" The more critical an element information technology is or is likely to be in the areas of competitive positioning, geographic positioning, organizational redesign and human capital redeployment, the more dependent it will be on the characteristics of the IT platform. As the next section of this chapter shows, IS can provide plenty of real news about opportunities and necessities in each of these areas.

The Reach/Range framework focuses on the business functionality of the platform. The platform is defined in terms of its technology base through an architecture, which in turn is defined through a set of technical standards and a plan for evolving an integrated resource. It is outside the scope of this chapter to review specific choices of architecture and standards; the Reach/Range model establishes the business criteria for selecting them.

Figure 3 shows an extension of the Reach/Range model that specifically addresses the business and organizational policy decisions that can shift the terms of planning along the management learning curve shown in Figure 1, moving from delegation to top management's hearing the compelling message for the transnational platform. Figure 3 defines seven policy issues for all corporate IT planning. The question to answer for each policy is should it be a directive, where top management states "We insist that our IT plans be consistent with this policy", versus "It is desirable that they be consistent" or "This policy is not viewed as important". The policy issues provide a base for positioning the form's IT platform, without having to specify the detailed applications. This process respects the realities of business uncertainty. No one can know the likely mergers and alliances, opening up of such new markets as the U.S.S.R. and Eastern Europe, or new competitive forces that will depend on new IT applications. The policy issue is to determine how much flexibility the firm will ensure in its platform as a corporate decision.

The seven policies are summarized below. Can the IS manager provide "news" about transnational business, transnational information technology or transnational uses of IT that would make top management regard any of them as requiring the statement begin "We insist...."? The question is obviously rhetorical; there is plenty of interesting news.

Policy 1: *Business Practicality*: Our IT base must never be a blockage to a practical and important business initiative.

Many firms do not have the Reach in their IT platform to be able to extend their operations across the geography they expect to operate in;

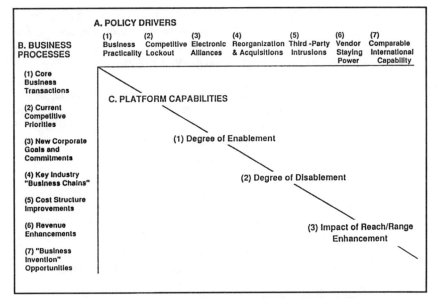

Figure 3: Business/Technology Platform Mapping

Policy 2: *Competitive Lockout:* If our competition uses IT as the base for an effective business initiative, we will not automatically be locked out of countering or imitating it.

The firms that have created global Reach to their business partners and international locations and added Range to be able to link processing systems for electronic data interchange, payments and logistics systems may have already locked a plurality of their competitors out; the reaction time for catching up and building the missing IT infrastructure is generally 5-7 years.[5]

Policy 3: *Electronic Alliances:* We will match all relevant firms in being able to make alliances, create "value-added" partnerships or enter consortia in intercompany or intra- and interindustry electronic business operations, such as EDI, payments systems and customer-supplier linkages.

Many top managers will be surprised by the extent to which EDI has already become an element in how cities like Hong Kong, Singapore and Amsterdam compete through IT and by the growth of value-added networks in Europe as the base for transnational logistics and trade.

Policy 4: ***Reorganization and Acquisitions:*** If we reorganize, make acquisitions or divestments, or relocate operations, our core operations, information systems, communications and processing will adapt quickly, simply and smoothly to the changes.

Is there any large firm anywhere in the world whose managers can reliably say that it will not be involved in a merger, acquisition, divestment or reorganization? Surely not. Meshing companies' operations means in practice meshing their communications and computing systems. Without a flexible and comprehensive platform, this is closer to chaos than to a mesh.

Part of the news about transnational IT is that firms with the platform are moving work to people and creating new labor markets and economies of expertise via the Reach and Range of their platform. Examples include offshoring back offices, engineering and software development to countries that provide a educated labor supply.

Policy 5: ***Third Party Intrusions:*** No one in our industry or third parties outside it will be able to intrude on our areas of strength or into the mainstream of our marketplace because their IT base provides them with advantages that they can turn into a competitive differentiator which we cannot match.

Policy 6: ***Vendor Staying Power:*** We will choose as our strategic vendors only those that have the R&D base, financial resources and technical capabilities to move with the mainstream of architectures and standards and towards integration as the same pace as the rest of the IT industry. "Integration" here refers to extending Reach and Range across all standard computing and communications services.

This is the topic that almost all discussions of standards and open systems ignore: the difference between defining standards and implementing them.

Policy 7: ***Comparable International Capability:*** All the above requirements will be as applicable in a transnational as in a domestic context.

In other words, a transnational business strategy will require a transnational planning process for IT and a transnational IT platform.

Figure 3 provides a base for mapping these seven policies (the columns of the diagram) into the firm's existing IT resources, under seven categories of business processes (the columns). Filling in the cells answers the question "Do we have the platform that will ensure we have the business degrees of freedom we need for the coming decade?":

> *Degree of enablement:* For each category of process and each policy driver, how well are we positioned in terms of having in place a platform that enables business initiatives?

> *Degree of disablement:* Where do we run the risk of not being able to move ahead in our business, in terms of competitive and/or organizational opportunities or necessities?

> *Impact of extending Reach and/or Range:* What impact would extending the business functionality of the platform have on our business degrees of freedom?

AN ECONOMIC MODEL FOR INFORMATION TECHNOLOGY: PROFIT AS THE "TOP LINE"[6]

The Reach/Range framework is useful in providing the base for helping senior managers and business planners understand the issues of integration and architecture. However, it does not in itself address their main concern: money. IT now amounts to around 50% of incremental capital investment in the Fortune 1000. It is generally the firm's third or fourth largest cost element, after salaries, real estate and interest payments. The payoff is largely unproven. Study after study finds no direct relationship between an industry or a group of firms' investment in information technology and its economic performance.

That does not mean that the payoff is not there; it may just be extremely hard to prove. As with the railroads in the 19th century, electricity in the early 20th, and the British Industrial Revolution, it is close to impossible to identify the economic impact of enabling infrastructures. It is the applications that they enable that provides the measurable benefits. The lead times before the payoff is apparent are often very long; in the case of the British Industrial Revolution, it was more than a century.

In many cases, the payoff depends on an apparently minor factor opening up new opportunities. For example, until the invention of the meter, electric power plants worked on fixed cost contracts to supply single large users. The meter made it practical to add consumer locations and small businesses. It is not at all easy to separate out the economic impact of the initial creation of power plants and the meter, anymore than it is to assess the contribution of an international telecommunications delivery base that adds Range to a firm's platform versus the international payments system that it enables and that provides quantifiable benefits.

Regardless of whether or not the massive investments in IT over the 1980s will later be shown to have provided real payoff, more and more senior business executives are wary and skeptical about IT. The problem is compounded by the apparently uncontrolled nature of IT costs. Most firms' accounting and IT budgeting systems do not track either the life cycle costs of systems development or the many hidden costs of IT. Every dollar spent on systems development typically generates around 60 cents of operations and maintenance a year. This means that a million dollar development expense is really a commitment of four million dollars of capital over a five-year period. Growing the systems development budget by just 10% a year increases the total IS budget by 40%, because of this compounding effect.

A $5,000 personal computer is a $20,000 capital cost, when support, telecommunications links and central disk storage are included. The purchase cost of a software package is around 20% of the full cost; support and education often add up to more than the original price.

In this context, senior business managers are not likely to listen to proposals about building new transnational platforms without a convincing economic model. Rallying cries about competitive advantage are no longer likely to carry much weight. After all, General Motors, Ford, Nissan and Toyota could gain immediate competitive advantage tomorrow by cutting the price of a car to $100 and throwing in a free house. Senior executives understand the potential competitive edge IT offers but worry about the price tag.

Globalization will make them worry even more. The painful reality for the transnational firm positioning for a new millennium is that there is no industry in the world, with the possible exception of sports, where profit margins are not decreasing. Deregulation is a major factor here. It reduces margins by around 30%. (This approximate estimate is derived from reviews of the US airline industry, European banking, UK telecommunications equipment prices, and the deregulated US long distance and data communications markets.)

Globalization similarly cuts operating margins. It opens up new sources of supply and reduces barriers to entry, pushing prices down to those of the leading providers. It also forces the requirements for levels of quality and service up to that of the leaders; companies then have to pay two new costs in order to compete on equal terms: a quality premium and a service premium.

This again puts pressures on margins. US firms have often been able to charge for quality. This may be termed the "European" view of quality; it is expensive but if you are willing to pay for it, we have it. Saville Row suits and Dom Perignon champagne are examples here: high quality, high price and high markup. The Asian view of quality is that it is like air; it must be there and you cannot charge a premium for it. Globalization also means that firms and governments can no longer easily keep out high quality providers to protect low quality domestic suppliers. The leading international firms set the standard for all.

The computer industry is an obvious example of margin erosion through globalization. The mainframe computer and software industry of the 1970's enjoyed high margins. The telecommunications, software, personal computer and mainframe markets of the 1990's have seen not just technical innovations driving down costs but aggressive and almost invariably international competition. Around 15 countries supply circuit boards for personal computers. Hitachi, Toyota, NEC, Amstrad, IBM, Hyundai, Olivetti and Toshiba are just a few of the worldwide players in the IBM and IBM-compatible personal computer market. The same international breadth is apparent in competition in mainframe computers, telecommunications equipment and, increasingly, software.

Figure 4 summarizes the implications of the increased margin pressures that mark the globalized and increasingly deregulated marketplace. It shows profit as the "top line" and not the "bottom line". It is worth examining why we routinely refer to profit as the "bottom line". At one level, the answer is obvious; the top line on the Profit and Loss statement shows revenues, followed by costs and taxes, with profit shown at the bottom. Profits are the byproduct of revenues. Growth creates profits. Providing that costs are kept under reasonable control, more revenues generate more profits.

For the 1990's, this commonsense picture is being turned upside down. When operating margins are being remorselessly driven down by global competition, deregulation and sophisticated consumers being in the driving seat, firms have to drastically change their cost structures and rethink the relationship between revenues and profits. Growth is now a way to go broke.

Figure 4 shows costs under three categories: traditional costs, quality cost premium, and service cost premium. Traditional costs are the obvious ones that all firms have managed throughout this century: labor, direct product costs, standard operating costs, etc. "Quality cost premium" refers to the often massive efforts firms have had to make to shift from quality being seen in "European" terms to how it is seen in "Japanese" terms. Firms cannot now treat quality as an add-on. They must pay a premium to improve it or see their position erode in the marketplace. Like it or not, firms must provide quality and pay whatever it takes to ensure it. That demands a cost premium over traditional costs, unless quality can be improved without adding cost.

The same is true for service as for quality. The old days when customer

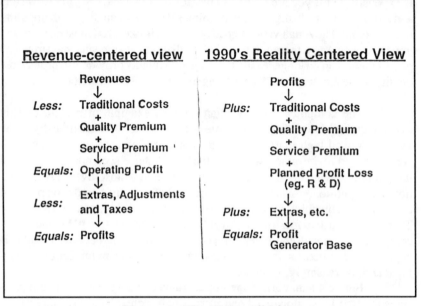

Figure 4: The "Bottom" Line

service departments were really the complaint departments, and when banks and phone companies could offer service with a scowl, have gone. The word "service" has even entered the vocabulary of government agencies. Customer power demands service and, as with quality, firms have to pay the premium to provide it.

The business context of the transnational firm is one where margins can be expected to erode and pressures to improve quality and service will be continuous and challenging. This will shift many aspects of business planning and operations. The airline industry may be a bellwether. It has made "yield management" a priority. When a plane takes off, it should contain the highest profit, not highest revenues. The airlines use their computerized reservation systems (CRS) for real-time inventory management and real-time pricing and for exploiting discounts and promotions as part of their revenue/profit trade-offs, with "yield" rather than revenue driving all elements of marketing. Yield management allowed the leading airlines to increase profits in 1986 by around 40% when Continental's price-cutting strategies cut fares by 60%. Companies like Frito Lay are similarly using real-time point of sale data to anticipate sales trends in days, rather than report on them weeks or months later, when it is too late to react.[7]

Transnational business trends almost guarantee that firms face a margin crunch for the rest of this century, together with a cost crunch. Unless IS managers and planners can show that investments in information technology directly and substantively improve the profit structures of the company, they should forget about trying to make the case for a transnational IT platform. No senior manager can afford to make additional capital investment in IT a priority otherwise. The interviews with CEOs and other top managers carried out for the ICIT research study strongly suggest that many of them see IT as a burden; they are aware that they must approve investments for competitive necessity, but the price tag is already high and growing. What are the reasons for adding to it by building new transnational infrastructures?

WHAT IS THE REAL NEWS ABOUT INFORMATION TECHNOLOGY IN THE GLOBAL MARKETPLACE?

Business and Information Services managers need "news" about the transnational impact of IT. Providing such news will be a growth area for research and education in the next few years: briefing managers and interpreting the general implications of particular industry, country and company developments.

Providing examples of transnational uses of IT that are directly relevant to helping turn the two management concerns about integration and economics into a dialog is directly reminiscent of the early 1980's discussion of information-technology-and-competitive-advantage, which became almost a breathless single word. The aim of many academics, consultants and management educators then was to raise senior management awareness about the new competitive implications of what had hitherto been largely treated as an overhead item.

They mainly relied on striking examples of successful firms stealing a competitive edge. These were often anecdotal, selective and didactic. A small number of companies formed the base for an entire literature. The most obvious of these were American Hospital Supply, Citibank, American Airlines, McKesson, Federal Express, Merrill Lynch and, more recently, Frito Lay and USAA. Many of the stories have since been challenged, either because the competitive edge turned out to be transitory or the initiative appeared to be as much serendipity as conscious strategy.[8]

There are obvious problems in trying to derive general principles from observation of selective examples, especially when much of the supporting data comes mainly from the business press, ad hoc interviews and subjective interpretations. That said, the examples often provided a richness of texture that stimulated discussion and insight. Whatever its limitations, the competitive advantage literature was "news" to managers; later, that news could be more rigorously analyzed by researchers.

The examples provided below of "news" about transnational IT aim at contributing to the senior management dialog. They appear to be more than just eccentric or specialized instances; they are presented here in the belief that they represent early indicators of a general trend. They fall into four categories:

1) *How cities compete* through information technology;
2) *Electronic data interchange* as the norm for transnational business;
3) *Location-independent work* opportunities;
4) Telecommunications costs and availability as the basis for *regionalization and rationalization* of operations.

In each instance, the main questions to address relate to the two management concerns of the economics of information capital and of the IT platform:

1) *Economics:* where does this trend or opportunity affect the cost and profit yield structures of the firm?

2) *Platform:* What implications does it have for the IT platform, and vice versa?

Ancillary questions, central to all IT planning, are:

a) Is this a competitive opportunity now?
b) When is it likely to become a competitive necessity?
c) By when must we have started moving to avoid competitive disadvantage?

One of the main conclusions that falls out of the examples below is that electronic data interchange is a critical element in any transnational strategy. Each of the four transnational IT opportunities is discussed below, in an individual section.

How Cities Compete through Information Technology[9]

One of the most striking emerging impacts of IT on transnational business is the explicit recognition by a number of cities that it can be used as a source of a competitive edge for themselves, in terms of making it attractive for businesses to locate facilities there or convenient for them to carry out operations. Some examples of this include:

Rotterdam, Netherlands: Using telecommunications and EDI to clear goods in 15 minutes, versus the more typical two days, of which 90% of the time is spent with the goods sitting on the ground waiting for documents to be processed.

Amsterdam, Netherlands: Complementing the Rotterdam INTIS system with HERMES, CARGONAUT and SAGITTAS for clearing rail freight, air cargo and customs via IT. Amsterdam is determined to maintain its position as the logistics center of Europe and sees IT as a central element for doing so.

Kawasaki and Yokohama, Japan: The development of an "intelligent city". The 20-story Recruit Cosmos building in Kawasaki has 13 floors dedicated to computer facilities, with provisions for cabling, communications backup, security and all other aspects of IT operations. Other intelligent buildings include ones for such specialized technologies as nuclear magnetic resonance equipment for groups of doctors. Yokohama is developing an intercompany telecommunications network link and shared information services and data bases. The Kanagawa Science park project envisages a mini-city built around first-rate IT facilities.

Hong Kong and Singapore: The use of EDI as a specific edge in manufacturing, international trade, shipping and freight. Both cities have established government value-added networks; the goal is to reduce the time needed to handle such matters as permits, processing of customs, shipping documents and any other aspect of trade down to 15 minutes.

Singapore's TradeNet has 500 company subscribers. Permits that took half a day or longer to obtain are produced electronically in 15 minutes or less and routed to port and aviation authorities to speed up clearance of goods. Excise duties, customs fees and funds transfers are processed by TradeNet. The Singapore agency for approving shipping bills receives over 10,000 requests daily.

Bombay, India: India has set itself a target of producing 2% of the world's software exports. It provides a skilled pool of IT labor at a fraction of the US and European cost. Companies such as Motorola and Citibank offshore software development to India, through satellite telecommunications links. The programmers "work" in the US, in the sense that that is where the physical computers are.

Dublin, Ireland: Ireland is a poor economy with one of the best-educated labor forces in the world. As with India, Dublin has become a center for firms offshoring people and processing. Aetna handles much of its data entry there. Bechtel recruits Irish engineers, who "work" in San Francisco through telecommunications.

Budapest, Hungary: Budapest is widely viewed as a major future software development city. It can provide highly-skilled programmers, experienced in engineering and scientific software development. Its Videoton company has 18,000 employees; the revenues of the computer division are over $150 million. Muszertechnika builds and sells its own personal computers. Novotrade is a fast-growing software house, with 1989 revenues of $44 million.

Heathrow, Florida and Breda, Iowa: Two striking instances of a city government, local Bell operating company and other parties getting together to provide fast service and high-quality IT facilities in order to persuade firms to relocate back office and headquarters operations there. The American Automobile Association moved its offices from Fairfax, Virginia, to Heathrow, largely because of the city's telecommunications strategy. Both cities have made fiber optics part of their physical infrastructure, geared the education system to providing the IT operations staff firms need, and developed a partnership with Pacific Bell and Ameritech to speed up installation of circuits. Heathrow will be the first city in the US to have residential ISDN.

Many other examples could be added. Omaha, Nebraska, has become the "800-number" capital of the US This was the result of a 1984 report by the governor's task force ("Nebraska as a World Class Center for the Communications Industry"). A group of public and private firms in the Paris region are developing a "teleport consortium", partly to meet the competition from London and Amsterdam in using IT as a competitive differentiator.

Perhaps the most striking example of the impacts on IT on competing as a trading city is London, especially in contrast to Frankfurt. London processes 40% of the world's daily foreign exchange, while Frankfurt handles under 10%. London's weekly foreign exchange transactions of over $500 billion exceed the *annual* physical exports of world's largest trading nation, West Germany. The U.K. has around 40% of Europe's value-added networks, for insurance, automotive and other industry shared electronic data interchange transactions. It has the largest number of local area network installations in Europe.

Britain was Europe's leader in liberalizing tele-communications, in the early 1980's. The West German Bundespost was the most aggressive protector of telecommunications as a government monopoly, moving to liberalize only in 1989. The Bundespost restricted business access to "private networks" (fixed cost networks, where large users could exploit economies of scale and technology). Britain became the lowest cost provider of telecommunications to business. In mid-1989, a basic analog leased circuit (9600 bits per second) cost $2,800 in Britain versus $9,400 in Germany (domestic) and $12,000 versus $20,000 (international). The costs per circuit were the same in both countries.[10]

West Germany has a larger share of world trade than Japan. In mid-1990, it took over from the U.S. as the world's largest exporter. Its currency is one of the three key ones internationally. These strengths are not reflected in its uses of telecommunications. The Bundepost's restrictive policies on telecommunications led a number of banks to locate their European offices in London and move out of not into Germany for back office processing and telecommunications-intensive operations. It fell well behind the practical state-of-the-art in telecommunications. In 1990, Germany expects to have just 12% of its telephone subscribers connected to the digital exchanges that are a cornerstone for modern telephony and data communications. France has 73% connected. Germany's trunk exchanges are just over 25% digital; France's are over 75% digital.

France has been by far the technical leader in telecommunications in Europe, and indeed in the world in many areas. Like Germany's Bundespost, France Telecom, the government monopoly, restricted business options and access to cost-efficient facilities in order to protect its existing revenue base. Despite the technical strengths of France Telecom, most business surveys rate Britain as the best provider of telecommunications.

Britain in general and London in particular have gained immensely from the other two nations' restrictiveness. Britain is a weak economy. Its GDP per capita in 1989 was $11,800 versus $18,600 for West Germany, $15,800 for France, and $13,300 for the EC, including Spain and Greece. The weaknesses are offset by its central role in foreign exchange, securities trading, back office processing and value-added networks.

This is news in itself: telecommunications as a major new element in a city's competitive positioning as a trading center. It is also directly relevant to the transnational firm. Where should a company locate transnational units? Amsterdam, London, Singapore and Stockholm stand out as cities that provide significantly lower costs of doing business in operations that depend on information technology than do Tokyo, Zurich, Frankfurt and Paris.

In terms of the two management concerns of economics and platform, this can have immense implications for basic aspects of business location and organizational design. Where should a manufacturing firm locate its Far East telecommunications node for coordinating computer-integrated manufacturing? Should an insurance company choose to centralize European back office functions in a city that provides the best combination of telecommunications and labor skills? Can a bank afford to locate time-critical and processing-intensive operations in specific cities?

Without adequate Reach and Range in its IT platform, many firms will be forced to locate business functions in specific locations and be unable to exploit the opportunities opened up by such examples as Heathrow (Florida), London and Amsterdam. The platform may determine the costs of doing business in many transnational activities.

Electronic Data Interchange as the Norm for Transnational Business

Electronic data interchange refers to the electronic transfer of business information from one independent computer application to another independent computer application, using agreed on standards to structure the data needed to carry out the transaction. The most simple example is eliminating paper documents and the people and steps involved in placing an order. The purchase order is sent as an EDI document directly into the supplier's computer system; invoices, delivery notices, bills of lading and the like are sent in electronic form between computers, instead of as paper through the mail.

EDI is rapidly growing in use in the United States, but not at the same pace as in Europe and Asia.[11] The main reason for the difference seems to reflect the many barriers to efficient transaction of business operations across borders. With just three time zones to bridge and no customs barriers between states, US firms do not have the same incentives to use EDI as the base for handling trade between them as do foreign ones. One commentator claims that EDI has doubled the speed of trucks across Europe; there is less time waiting for customs documents, bills of lading and the like.

Much of the rapid growth in shared industry value-added networks in Europe and Asia reflects the benefit all parties gain from eliminating paper, delays and people in transactions between them. The ODETTE network (automotive), TRADERNET (UK trading partners across industries) and SWIFT (international funds transfers) are well-established examples. In the area of standards for EDI, Europe took the lead; the EDIFACT standard was originally based on the X.12 standard developed by ANSI, the American National Standards Institute. ANSI voted by a huge margin in 1989 to adopt EDIFACT and make X.12 a subset of it.

As mentioned earlier, Hong Kong and Singapore have established

EDI value-added networks as a weapon in positioning their city in the wider worldwide trading network. Many US and European companies have begun to require that their suppliers link electronically to them as a requirement for doing business with the firm.[12]

The volume of documents involved in international shipping is absurd. In explaining why Hong Kong businesses asked the city government to set up its Tradelink EDI network, the general manager of one of its largest shippers provided figures on the volumes involved. Hong Kong has over 100,000 trading firms, each of which sends between 2,000 and 10,000 documents a year. His own company, Swire, has 300 employees, of whom 120 work full-time on documentation. The company handles nearly half a million bills of lading a year, supported by the same number of shipping sets, each of which usually comprises 7-8 documents.

Figure 5 shows reported benefits from EDI. They indicate the size of the target of opportunity it presents. Obviously, it will be firms involved in transnational transactions that have most to gain from EDI.

The questions here for the senior management dialog about IT planning are simple:

Is EDI a competitive necessity for transnational business?

Can we risk foregoing the benefits firms have been able to obtain from EDI in terms of direct costs and of providing improved service and quality?

Do we have the Reach and Range we need for this? What are the international standards we should adopt in our architecture so that we are able to meet the highest practical levels of EDI service?

Location-independent Work Opportunities

It is no secret to any manager that one of the biggest problems facing US business in the coming decade is the shortage of educated workers, especially young ones. The people coming into the labor force in the next few years will be the first generation of Americans less literate than its parents. Many firms spend substantial amounts of time and money now on teaching basic skills to new employees. One major hotel chain estimates it will have only two qualified applicants for every three jobs, and that its main competition is now Mcdonald and the US Army; each of them is trying to recruit the same scarce eighteen year olds.

A major opportunity for the firm with a comprehensive IT platform is to use it to bring work to people, instead of people to work. As more and more

Organization	Application	
Petroleum Industry Data Exchange (40 member companies)	Eliminate "joint interest billing" between partners in a producing well; often amounts to "thousands of pages"	• One firm reduced staff by 37%
Westinghouse/ Portland General Benefits	Procurement process for PGE Electric to obtain equipment	• EDI can reduce costs by 10% • Change the procurement process reducing the elapsed time from 15 days to 1/2 day from $90 to $10
Levi-Strauss	Levilink: EDI for electronic ordering, stock model management, bar coding carton tags, invoicing, packing slips, etc. Prior to Levilink, firm calculated that 70% of all its business data was manually entered into a computer and later manually entered into at least one other computer.	• Design Inc., chain of 60 stores, reduced replenishment cycle from 14 to 3 days. Order delivery turnaround dropped from 9 days to 3-5
Service Merchandising Corporation	Purchase orders	• Reduction in cost per order from $50 to $12. (Savings $7.5 million per annum.)
RJ Reynolds	Manufacturing-distribution-payments 100 Customers trading invoices and purchase orders with RJR	• $5 to $10 million savings on labor, inventory, lead times. Offering 5% discount to customers for payment through electronic funds transfer. 10 days faster collection on $100 million of funds a year.
United Parcel Service	Reading air freight documents: scan 700,000 labels a day, extract signature, weight, time of delivery, remarks. Shortage of data entry staff on "graveyard shift."	• One-year payoff in direct savings
Port of Rotterdam	INTIS cargo clearing system: trade documentation, insurance, letters of credit, customs documents, bill of lading, etc. Every export order has, on average, 25 to 30 documents. 50% of these have to be sent back because the information is innaccurate.	• 15 minute clearance of goods, versus typical 2 days. Dramatic reductions in error rate, time to repair errors.
Marks and Spencer, United Kingdom	90% of merchandise ordered via EDI.	
Super-Valu, Minneapolis	Largest U.S. grocery wholesaler. EDI for purchase orders, invoicing, etc., with 700 suppliers.	• Direct savings of $100,000 a year on purchase orders. Savings of $2 million in carrying costs through better inventory management. Indirect benefits from reduction in disputes about reconciliation, discounts, allowances, etc.

Figure 5: High Payoff Applications of EDI

work is computer-mediated - the workstation is the main tool for carrying it out - it can be made location-independent. A simple instance is 800 numbers used for customer service or telemarketing. When a customer phones in, he or she has no idea where the service is physically sited. The firm can place it anywhere. Omaha, Nebraska, has become the 800 number capital of the US, with 25 companies there handling over 100 million calls a year. Fireman's Fund, Union Pacific and Northwestern Bell chose Omaha for its customer service operations. The city offers low telecommunications costs, because of its unique position at the conjunction of a number of fiber optics networks, and provides a well-trained labor force.

A New York bank, concerned about the lack of a pool of available skilled labor can locate its New York customer service office in Omaha, or anywhere else. There are many indications that transnational firms will try to exploit this opportunity and that it will be a significant aspect of their organizational design. A primary issue for the transnational firm is to identify the best location for handling each specific activity. It may choose to locate manufacturing in one country, R&D in another, and marketing in a regional headquarters.

Software development is one area where firms are looking abroad to solve the problem of a scarcity of skilled labor at a reasonable price. India, Israel, Budapest, Singapore, Ireland and Shanghai are among the likely software cities of the 1990's. They will be connected to US and European companies via satellite telecommunications; the firm's IT platform will extend its organizational boundary to them, in the same way that electronic data interchange extends it to suppliers and customers.

American Airlines is similarly off-shoring clerical activities to the Caribbean, Aetna to Ireland and a number of banks to the Philippines. Mead is using South Korea as an offshore base for clerical operations. Bechtel is employing Irish engineers to work physically in Ireland but as if they are in the United States. One major pharmaceutical firm has 100 Japanese scientists "working" in its European headquarters.

In this context, the logic of decentralization is to choose where to place work, on the basis of either labor supply and costs, telecommunications availability and costs, tax advantages, logistics or other operating costs. The logic of interdependence and coordination is to tie all these decentralized activities together; that can be done efficiently and effectively only via IT. It is impossible otherwise to operate in a context of increasingly time-based competition across multiple time zones.

The issue for the senior management dialog is "What opportunities are there for us to make sure we get a first-rate labor force? What platform must we have to exploit the opportunities of location-independent work?" Simply locating an 800-number service in Omaha or Barbados does not require a platform; the company can just lease phone lines. For the customer service agents to have access to customer information, inventory and ordering systems, and financial payments records, however, the Reach of the platform must extend the transaction processing systems out from headquarters to the customer service location and its Range must make it easy for the agents to access all of this information as if it were in a single data base. That is not at all a simple matter technically; for many firms whose information systems are based on a variety of vendor equipment, operating systems, data structures, standards and telecommunications facilities, it will be close to impossible to implement in under a decade.

Is the effort worthwhile? Is it essential? The answer to this question rests on the emphasis the firm places on labor skills and costs in its transnational planning.

Telecommunications Costs and Availability as the Base for Regionalization and Rationalization

Regardless of the extent to which a firm uses information technology to exploit opportunities for location-independent work, it will be spending a lot of money on IT as part of its basic operations. There is no plausible scenario for the 1990s that reduces the use of IT in manufacturing, distribution, payments, service and coordination. Telecommunications will thus be a substantial and growing element in the firm's cost base.

There are wide variations in telecommunications availability, quality and prices across the world, many of them unjustifiable. These can be handled as part of the cost of doing business, with the firm paying whatever it must in each country. The alternative, however, is to exploit the firm's platform to locate IT-intensive functions on the basis of telecommunications costs and service. For example, instead of having, say, 12 data centers distributed across Europe, it may - only may - make sense to build a superdata center in a location that has the lowest overall international telecommunications costs and use this to minimize international telecommunications traffic into and out of particular countries.

For instance, one transnational firm located in Switzerland decided to consolidate its research computing centers in the UK. The cost of Switzerland to US communications in 1989 was almost exactly ten times per unit that of the same link from the US to Switzerland. Voice calls by satellite to the US were priced at $7,000 a month; the cost to the Swiss PTT was around $250 a month. The PTT did not permit firms to choose their own telecommunications switching equipment, a key issue in its development of an integrated international platform. The firm was required to use the national public data network. This was slow; the firm measured its speed in terms of how many computer screens of information it provides per second. The PDN operates at just 1 computer workstation screen per second for international communications and 7 domestically. A private network, widely available in the US and UK but not in many countries, would provide 26 screens a second. Several other countries in which the company has research centers have even more expensive and very unreliable telecommunications. Not surprisingly, the firm plans to centralize its research computing in London. This flies in the face of the "death of a mainframe" fad over the past few years that has argued that there is no need for large central systems, because of the increasing power of personal computers and departmental systems and local area networks. This company is willing to increase its computing costs if it can cut into its communications costs and provide the level of service its research teams worldwide need. It recognizes that the Reach and Range of its platform will either enable or block its ability to locate facilities in this way.

International telecommunications is a morass of regulatory, nationalistic and economic complexities. These complexities are one of the most difficult uncertainties the IS function faces in its planning. The impact of information technology on global communication and coordination is illustrated by the growth in international telephone traffic. This increased by close to 600% in the 1980's. Reliable estimates forecast an additional 500% growth in the 1990's. The total traffic in 1990 is running at the rate of 30 billion minutes a year. 60% of trans-Pacific traffic is by fax.

The Financial Times comments that telecommunications traffic is becoming a better way of gauging world economic activity than more traditional measures of imports and exports and gross national product: "The UK borders on the US; the Soviet Union is a tiny outpost on the margins of western civilization; sub-Saharan Africa is so unconnected with the rest of the world that it might almost be on another planet." Most economic statistics focus on tangible goods; telecommunications figures provide a clearer indicator of services growth.

There is one fundamental blockage to reducing telecommunications costs internationally. PTTs (Poste Telegraphe et Telephonique) are the government or quasi-government monopoly for telecommunications. While more and more of them recognize that they must liberalize telecommunications or lose the business of large transnational firms, non-U.S. telephone monopolies will not want to give up the huge free ride they get from the US on international telephone calls. 5.2 billion international call minutes a year are generated from the US (1990 estimates). Only 3.0 billion call minutes come into the country. The arrangements for handling international calls are based on cost-sharing at each end of the link. The formulae penalize the low-cost U.S. carriers, who have also cut their prices, and allocate most of the money charged to the U.S. caller to high-cost foreign PTTs. US carriers pay out on average

75% of the call charge to the destination country. In the case of a call to Brazil, a carrier pays the Brazilian PTT over 99 cents per dollar charged to the caller.

The distortions add up to overpayment by US business and consumers of $10-20 billion a year in international phone calls. The cost of a call from New York to Los Angeles averages 24 cents a minute, over a distance of 2,500 miles. The 3,500 miles from New York to London costs $1.00 a minute. British Telecom in 1988 made a profit of over $1 billion on international revenues of just over $3 billion; this was after changing its accounting system - the original profit figure was close to $1.5 billion.

PTTs are naturally very unwilling to see their cartel that has controlled international telephone pricing and revenue-sharing broken up. Deregulation of telecommunications slashes profit margins, largely because it brings price down to cost and costs are plummeting because of fiber optics. In the past seven years, the cost of fiber has dropped from around $3 a meter to 15 cents, with a hundredfold increase in capacity per meter. Deregulation immediately passes on some of the cost advantages of new technology. When British Telecom liberalized the telecommunications equipment market, prices dropped 30%.

Telecommunications has become intimately linked to national, economic and social policy. "Liberalization" is not "competition". The world's PTTs are on the whole only reluctantly loosening their monopoly. A few, in historically mercantile nations like Sweden, the Netherlands and Singapore, see liberalization as a major opportunity. By contrast, the West German Bundespost's labor unions, which have over 500,000 members, strongly opposed its split into three services, with gradual competition allowed. France Telecom and Belgium's PTT have sued the European Commission to prevent intrusion on PTTs' sovereign rights. Most PTTs have entirely ignored the Commission's voluntary guidelines concerning open tenders on telecommunications equipment bids.

Japan maintains a closed door to US equipment manufacturers, despite promises and pressures. In one notorious instance, AT&T lost a bid which went to the lowest tender. That was from a Japanese company, which bid $1. Korea's new National Telecommunications Association is under pressure to keep its technical standards "private" and thus protect domestic manufacturers.

The problem of "one-stop shopping" for transnational firms is a major stumbling block. Currently, firms have to negotiate each end of a crossborder linkage separately with the two PTTs involved. In 1988, 22 PTTs signed a formal agreement to set up a joint company, MDNS (Managed Data Network Services) to market data communications services throughout Europe. A single contact point, one of the 22 members, would coordinate every activity and provide consolidated international billing in a single currency, chosen by the customer.

MDNS collapsed before it got moving. The European Commission was concerned that the combined power of the PTTs would create a new supermonopoly that would stunt the growth of value-added networks. The proponents of MDNS argued that their overall competitiveness would be hampered if they could not offer services comparable with those of GEIS, INFONET and Federal Express, which is positioning to become a mini-PTT worldwide, including providing an electronic data interchange service to Hong Kong. Individual PTTs wanted to restrict MDNS's range of services to protect their own more profitable segments. MDNS is now dead.

Compounding the problems of one-stop shopping and uncertainties about liberalization and competition are the wide differences in technical standards worldwide. It is not at all easy to define a standard; the relatively simple X.25 standard which is the proven base for international data communications and public data networks took fifteen years to implement. The comprehensive OSI model has taken several decades to evolve and is only gradually being implemented in products and services.

The timetable for the far simpler international standard for electronic messaging, X.400, has taken almost a decade before products using it have become available. X.400 is a likely cornerstone for many aspects of the platform for transnational coordination; it links previously incompatible electronic mail systems and provides a base for simple EDI applications. The first international committees for X.400 met in 1980-83. The first recommendations were defined in 1984. Only in 1988 were agreements made concerning implementation of the X.400 protocols and products began to be tested in late 1989.

A major European initiative in telecommunications has been ISDN (Integrated Services Digital Network), developed in the 1970's. It was intended to provide a common infrastructure for all communications, integrating voice, data, image and video. In theory, European-wide compatible ISDN will be available in 1992, based on a set of common standards which were to be completed by mid-1990. Not a single standard had been issued when the deadline passed. Europe still has ten incompatible telecommunications switching systems.

None of these problems would be important, though they would remain a major inconvenience, if and only if there is no need for a transnational platform across business functions and international locations, and if and only if telecommunications costs, availability and quality are not key elements in business efficiency and effectiveness, and do not affect cost structures and margins. The obvious question at the level of top management policy is "Is the IT platform sufficiently critical to the firm's business degrees of freedom and margin and cost structures to make coordinated transnational planning essential?" If it is, then the IS function has to position itself and build a cadre of planners that can try to sort through the uncertainties and constraints of international IT.

PLANNING GLOBALLY: THE AGENDA FOR ACTION

There are scattered examples of firms that have successfully matched transnational business and transnational IT strategies. There has been little indepth case studies and surveys about the management process that created them, their approach to building the platform and the economics of their operations. Digital Equipment corporation operates a private network linking 41,000 locations across the world. 60% of DEC's employees have access to it. DEC reports many benefits in terms of organizational coordination and crossnational teamwork. The Mitsubishi Group's network links its 28 "family" companies and around 100 others. Mitsubishi is spending $20 billion to create what is in effect the firm's transnational organizational structure in action. Its 1989 annual statement contains a senior manager's comments about the importance of global computing and communications to Mitsubishi on roughly every other page.

General Motors spent over $3 billion between 1987 and 1990 to link its dealers and suppliers. To that may be added its more recent expenditures on payments systems and on satellite links to dealers and plants for training, communication and coordination. Federal Express's COSMOS system links the firm's own locations and over 60 subsidiaries world wide, in real-time. Digital radio and voice radio extend that link to 85% of Federal Express's courier fleet. Much of Citibank's success in the international banking market-place of the early 1980s came from its development of a fragmented network with global Reach and wide Range across its products; the degree of Range came from its COSMOS processing system, which provided a common infrastructure across products.

Many other firms are building transnational facilities on an application by application basis, rather than aiming for a comprehensive corporate platform. Some rely on value-added networks for selected applications, especially EDI. Many have developed a corporate backbone telecommunications network, linking major business locations. The most typical example of this provides a transatlantic bridge, with gateways in the US and Europe; London has a disproportionate share of these gateways.

Fewer companies appear to have determined where their Far East gateway will be. In the 1980's, firms like Citibank adopted Manila as the main node. The political instability of the Philippines, uncertainties about Hong Kong's future, the high costs of operating in Japan, plus doubts about the Lee regime in Singapore have all resulted in new uncertainties, in a context where electronic data interchange and telecommunications linkages between firms have become essential for gaining business in almost all trade-related industries.

With few proven guidelines and models to follow, firms have difficult choices to make, one of which is wait and see. However, the very uncertainties are in themselves a potential source of competitive edge. If innovation were easy, anyone and everyone could innovate. The firms that can work their way through the issues, opportunities and constraints discussed throughout this chapter have a chance of drawing ahead of the pack.

The agenda for action to take charge of change was outlined at the start of the chapter. It is partly a political agenda for mobilizing senior business managers to elevate the need for a comprehensive platform to the policy level. It is partly a research agenda. The brief examples of electronic data interchange, how cities compete, location-independence and telecommunications relative cost and location advantages need more detailed and systematic review; firms should look at their own geographic spread and identify where the issues discussed are an opportunity and where and when they will be a necessity.

The agenda is:

1) Establish a compelling business case at the level of top management for creating the transnational information technology platform.

2) Present a convincing economic model for applying IT to address the new realities of rapidly eroded margins.

3) Provide real news to grab business managers' attention about the opportunities a transnational perspective on IT can provide.

4) Build a cosmopolitan cadre of IT planners and staff.

The last of the recommendations is implicit in the others. A headquarters-centered view of IT, whether that view is from New York, London or Tokyo, will almost surely misread the world of international IT, especially the geopolitics of telecommunications. Firms must break open the parochial mindsets that many commentators see as a limitation of US business thinking and that is very marked among IT specialists, few of whom are familiar with standards, practices and regulation across the three main global markets of North America, Western Europe and the Pacific Rim.

The strategy for action here rests on the dialog at the top resulting in IT being seen as a transnational necessity, not international overhead. It requires that the firm then:

1) Review the need for international cooperation, collaboration and coordination. The firm's own business plans through the mid-1990's are the obvious guide here;

2) Establish a clear responsibility for defining the international platform and shared facilities, such as regional data centers;

3) Make it unambiguous which aspects of IT planning and operations require central coordination and what is left to local initiative;

4) Require the corporate IT group to travel to the field regularly and focus on the business rather than just technical context of their activities;

5) Fund the corporate backbone network as a shared business asset;

6) Build knowledge of international IT issues among all technical and business units; hammer business managers into becoming aware of the opportunities and necessities of IT within a transnational business plan.

There are no domestic markets anymore. There are really no large domestic firms. Each of the following companies earns over 50% of its revenues from outside its home country: Coca Cola, Corning, Dow Chemical, Gillette, Hoffman La Roche, IBM, ICI, Johnson and Johnson, Nestle, Northern Telecom, Sony, Volvo and Xerox. Of the world's 500 largest companies, slightly over a third are headquartered in North America and just under a third each in Europe and Japan. The world is splitting into three major markets, of roughly equal size: North America, the Pacific Rim and Business Europe, which includes the EC and EFTA. Firms will need a presence in each to be major players in their industry.

Information technology is an enabler of new business and organizational initiatives. In the world of transnational business, transnational thinking about IT represents the next major evolution in the Information Services field.

References and Notes

1. Christopher A. Bartlett and Sumantra Ghoshal, *Managing Across Borders* (Boston: Harvard Business School Press,, 1989)

2. Fordham Graduate School of Business: Information Technology in the Transnational Firm, 1989.

3. See, for example, Paul A. Strassman, "Management Productivity as an IT Measure," in *Measuring Business Value of Information Technologies* (Washington, DC: ICIT Press, 1988) and

Peter Weill, *Do Computers Pay Off?* (Washington, DC: ICIT Press, 1991).

4. The interviews are discussed in Peter G.W. Keen, *Shaping the Future: Business Design through Information Technology* (Boston: Harvard Business School Press, 1991). They are the basis for the Reach/Range platform framework discussed in this section.

5. For examples and evidence, see Peter G.W. Keen, *Competing in Time* (Cambridge, MA: Ballinger, 1988).

6. The material in this section is covered in more detail in Peter G.W. Keen, *Shaping the Future,* chapter 6, which examines managing the economics of information capital. The "Top line" framework for profit engineering through IT is addressed in chapter 1 and 8.

7. Frito-Lay's use of IT has been widely-covered in the business press and is likely to become a model for many other firms. A compact and accurate summary is provided in Barnaby J. Feder, "Frito-Lay's Speedy Data Network", New York Times, November 8, 1990.

8. For reviews of competitive applications of information technology and assessments of the resulting advantages, see F. Warren McFarlan, "Information Technology Changes the Way You Compete," Harvard Business Review (May-June 1984), pp 98-103, C. Wiseman, *Strategy and Computers* (Homewood, IL: Dow Jones-Irwin, 1985), and Keen, *Competing in Time* (op. cit.)

9. Much of this section is based on data gathered in a research study carried out by The International Center for Information Technologies in 1989. See M.L. Manheim, J. Elam, and P.G.W. Keen, "Using Telecommunications to Gain Competitive Advantage: A Strategy for Cities," and D.W. Edwards, J. Elam, and R.O. Mason, "Securing an Urban Advantage," (Washington, DC: ICIT Press, 1989).

10. Obviously, such cost figures are often altered by volatile shifts in currency exchange rates and by price changes made by individual PTTs as part of liberalization, exploitation of new technologies, or response to growing pressures to rationalize unreasonable price distortions. That said, the range of prices for the same telecommunications capability remain as broad as shown here.

11. Figures on EDI growth and usage vary widely, partly because of the lack of a common definition and partly because the growth is built on a relatively small base. The evidence for its likely continued and dramatic growth comes from looking at leading individual firms, industries, cities and countries. Firms such as General Motors, Marks and Spenser, Philips, and Sears show that major companies are increasingly demanding EDI linkages as a condition for doing business with suppliers. The shipping, automotive, retailing, and grocery industries have made EDI a basic aspect of operations. Rotterdam, Singapore, Amsterdam, and Hong Kong are early examples of cities embedding EDI in their economic strategies.

12. A recent example is the letter sent to all Sears' 6,000 suppliers by Sear's Chairman in July 1990, informing them that they must adopt Sears' software (provided free, together with free training) by early 1991; otherwise, they will no longer be suppliers to the firm.

APPENDIX 1

The following questions summarize the concerns of managers interviewed as part of a study of information in the transnational firm, carried out by Fordham University's Graduate School of Business.

Organizational Design

1.1. What are the opportunities for and implications of particular product/market strategies, such as "Euro products", regionalized manufacturing with national distribution, or global products? What technology platform issues does each of these raise?

1.2. How should transnational joint ventures be defined and managed? What has been the experience of firms with transborder alliances and joint ventures?

1.3. Where should firms locate back office and regional headquarters functions in rationalizing fragmented operations? Where is IT an opportunity or a blockage?

1.4. What business and technical functions need to be centralized and which ones decentralized? Why? Where? How?

2. Building the Transnational Technology Platform
2.1. What is an effective way of ensuring adequate coordination of transnational IT resources without intruding on local autonomy in an organization structured around separate operating units? Does there need to be a Chief Information Officer in each country? With what authority and responsibility?

2.2. How can transnational firms solve the continuing problem of lack of a base for "one-stop" shopping for telecommunications?

2.3. What are effective approaches to developing international private and virtual private facilities instead of depending on public data networks?

2.4. How can firms reliably anticipate and interpret trends in international standards, in terms of their practical implementation rather than their definition, and do the same for the pricing and technical strategies of PTTs, value-added networks and private network providers?

2.5. What are the likely trends in policy and availability of IT capabilities in individual countries and regions, particularly Eastern Europe and Asia, and what are their implications for business and technical planning?

3. Cultural integration and technology adoption
3.1. What are the impacts of cultural differences on development and management of business and IT?

3.2. How can firms merge, expand and acquire in a world of cultural diversity? Where can IT contribute to or hinder effective crosscultural collaboration?

3.3. What are effective strategies for diffusion of innovations and rollout of products?

3.4. What are the new human resource issues created by rapid globalization, such as different standards of education and work force supply, parochialism of managers, union and work regulations, and access to information and technology?

3.5. How should development of transnational information systems be managed? Where should teams be located? What are the relative responsibilities of the field and regional and head offices?

4. Costs, infrastructure needs and technology opportunities and constraints

4.1. Given the wide variations in costs across the world for the same IT facilities and services, how can firms get the best deal? How should internal pricing, cost recovery, auditing and business justification be handled?

4.2. How can end-to-end network management be handled across a multi-vendor, multi-technology, multi-geography environment?

4.3. How can firms assess the risks, costs and benefits relevant to backup, disaster recovery, hot standby, etc?

4.4. How can firms bypass local PTT facilities? What are the likely opportunities for VSAT and cellular communications? (This question raises the more general issues of how to track PTT strategies and work with the Ptts.)

4.5. What new problems of security, reliability and network management does a shift from national to transnational operations create and what are effective solutions?

26

Global Information Technology as a Strategic Weapon for MNCs: A Conceptualization

A.G. Kefalas
University of Georgia

Multinational Corporations (MNCs) are the greatest data creators and consumers. Their hundreds of subsidiaries thrive on information on market, product and people trends around the globe. They, in turn, transmit trillions of records to the headquarters in order to inform the MNC about the degree of accomplishment of their goals. The 1990s ushered in the era of the information economy — i.e., an economy in which both nation-states and MNCs will manage to compete in the global market not by directly using their natural endowments more efficiently, but rather by creating useful information and knowledge out of massive amounts of data. MNC and nation-state competitive advantages will be derived from better use of information in the process of innovation and continuous improvement and upgrading. This chapter provides a framework for the design and management of a Global Information System (GLOBIS) which can be used to integrate data processing, office automation and telecommunications into an integrated system.

INTRODUCTION

This last decade of the Twentieth Century will prove to be the official introduction of the "information economy." While most people are aware of the explosively escalating importance of information-related industries in a country's composition of its gross domestic product (GDP), most of us have ignored the equally, if not more, significant escalation of information as the newest competitive weapon. A quick perusal of the popular business and scientific press will convince one of the preeminence achieved by the concepts of speed, time, and information as competitive weapons. In an age where product-and-technology life cycles are now counted in months and not in years, where national and geographical borders have been practically eliminated, where the conventional clock has been stretched to read daytime (i.e., worktime) 24 hours around, where one's inventions are turned into innovations by somebody else thousands of miles away virtually overnight, and where the entire globe has been turned into a giant Global Village, minimization of the information float becomes management's main task.

MNCs have been known as the world's best scanners. Their ability to scan the world has been characterized as one of the most important competitive weapons very early. As Vernon and Wells (1981, 1987) put it, "The competitive power of an effective information-gathering network in international business is evident not only in the occasional big decisions to establish a new foreign source or invade a new foreign market but also in the day-to-day operations of some foreign business activities."

Evidence of the strategic role of information is provided by the great success of the Japanese trading companies (sogoshoshas) both in aiding Japanese manufacturing companies to establish themselves at home (by importing standardized bulk commodities and raw material) and conquering the world (by exporting their products overseas), but also in literally cornering global trade. In both cases, sogoshoshas gain competitive advantages by collecting information about sources and markets, scheduling shipments, and financing transactions in such a way as to minimize the time lag (information float) between sensing an opportunity in one part of the world and finding a firm to take advantage of this opportunity in another location thousands of miles away.

The panoply of technologies — hardware (machines) and software (program instructions), — is the INFOstructure which is superimposed on the MNC's INFRAstructure of land, people, material, equipment and money. In other words, the individual information systems, when integrated into the global information system (GLOBIS), form a powerful managerial tool which enables MNC managers to identify and exploit business opportunities across the globe.

A GLOBIS consists of the integration of the three main islands of the information archipelago (McFarlan & McKenney, 1983): (1) the conventional Electronic Data Processing (EDP), (2) the recently popularized Office Auto-mation (OA,) i.e., the widespread use of wordprocessing, spreadsheets, data base and expert systems/artificial intelligence microcomputer supported end-user off the shelf inexpensive packages, and (3) telecommunications systems linked and operating in concert with both EDP and OA systems known as

Computer and (Tele) communications systems or C² systems.

The MNC's ability to compete in the global markets will depend on the speed with which its management espouses the C² philosophy and begins building the necessary organizational strategy and structure which will facilitate the free movement of information along "noise free channels" across the globe. Most of the hardware and software technology is already available. However, its life cycle is extremely short. Beer's aphorism ABSOLUTUM OBSOLETUM, i.e., if it works it is out of date, is more true today than it was when he first coined it several decades ago.

The last decade experienced great changes in the strategies and structures used by the global firms. A quick review of the international business literature will reveal a dramatic shift away from the traditional MNC strategy and structure, which is usually called the Multinational Enterprise, towards Global and even transnational firms. An integral part of this shift is a combination of "global strategy and operations integration and local responsiveness," as it is called in the U.S. academic literature (Prahalad & Doz, 1987) or "Glocalization" in the Japanese practitioner language (Townley, 1990). The emphasis on global integration of strategy and operations (Globalization) makes the collection of data in a central databases an absolute necessity. By the same token, the quest for local responsiveness necessitates the ability to access and "drill-down" the MNC databases with great ease and speed.

The main thesis of this chapter is that the missing link between the two developments (globalization of business strategy and information technology) is the lack of a conceptual framework which will enable the two parties (business managers and IT managers) to relate each other's needs and approaches to need satisfaction. This is the aim of this chapter: to provide a conceptual framework which will enable business managers to express their needs to IT managers, and to allow the IT managers to "show off" their wares in an effort to maximize IT utilization to enhance users' productivity. The framework does indeed provide a win-win opportunity for both parties and the MNC as a whole.

The chapter begins with an explanation of the main concepts of the phenomenon of information technology. These concepts are (1) Information, i.e., the object, the fundamental building block of decision making and (2) Information Systems, the means of creating and "moving" information. The second section deals with the task of preparing an MNC for the development of an information system which will tie all its affiliates into an integrated system. Finally, the third section describes a framework for a Global Information System (GLOBIS) for an MNC.

THE BASIC CONCEPTS: INFORMATION AND INFORMATION SYSTEMS

The Concept of Information

Information is a peculiar word. Even though it is one of the most commonly used words, most people do not know its true origins and significance. What most people know is that having information is good and the more information one has the better off he/she is. Thus, managers learn very early in their careers that information is the key to good decisions and making good decisions is the key to success. In this way the causal relationship between success and the amount of information is established. What actually constitutes information, how it is measured, and when the point of diminishing return to information acquisition is reached are esoteric subjects which will eventually be dealt with by some expert individual.

Information systems professionals are the last to realize the importance of the distinction between data and information. In the words of Lee Foote, manager of DuPont's Electronic Data Interchange Section at Wilmington, Delaware, "There are many misconceptions about what the right stuff-information-actually is...Data spewed out by legions of mainframes should not be confused with information. Properly structured data will result in information, but only in the minds of the individuals and under certain contexts and time frames." IS groups that don't understand this distinction and haven't found out what data client organizations really need will simply print everything out. And the results? Data overload (Carlyle, 1988).

Academic literature connects the concept of information to the decision making process. In relating information to uncertainty reduction one distinguished between the concept of data as the raw material in the information-creation process and information as the end result of that process. This information is, in turn, distinguished from knowledge by defining knowledge as the outcome of usage of information in the specific situation of uncertainty reduction (Schoderbek, Schoderbek & Kefalas, 1990). Finally, the concept of wisdom is distinguished from knowledge by assigning the adjective "appropriate" to the use of knowledge (Cleveland, 1985; Ackoff, 1988; Gore, 1991).

Information Systems: An Evolution

The use of information technology, i.e., mechanical devices (hardware) with the appropriate instructions (software), underwent three main stages. As can be seen from Exhibit 1 during Epoch A, the Data Processing Era, the majority of the use of the technology dealt with the acquisition and

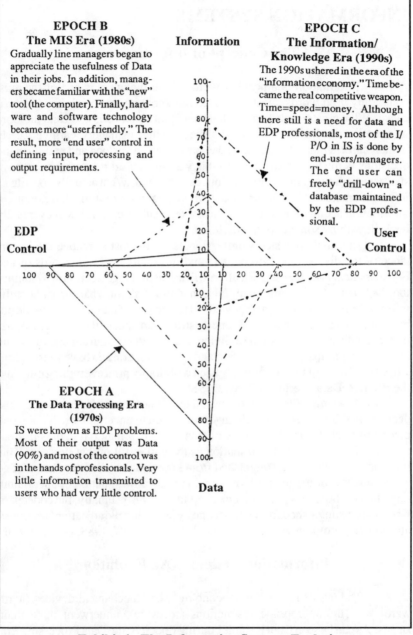

EPOCH B
The MIS Era (1980s)
Gradually line managers began to appreciate the usefulness of Data in their jobs. In addition, managers became familiar with the "new" tool (the computer). Finally, hardware and software technology became more "user friendly." The result, more "end user" control in defining input, processing and output requirements.

Information

EPOCH C
**The Information/
Knowledge Era (1990s)**
The 1990s ushered in the era of the "information economy." Time became the real competitive weapon. Time=speed=money. Although there still is a need for data and EDP professionals, most of the I/P/O in IS is done by end-users/managers. The end user can freely "drill-down" a database maintained by the EDP professional.

**EDP
Control**

**User
Control**

**EPOCH A
The Data Processing Era
(1970s)**
IS were known as EDP problems. Most of their output was Data (90%) and most of the control was in the hands of professionals. Very little information transmitted to users who had very little control.

Data

Exhibit 1. The Information Systems Evolution

processing of data. The entire process was controlled by the EDP professional with very little freedom on the part of the user (manager).

The second phase, Epoch B, began with the increase in the manager's ability to directly use the technology with minimum interaction with the EDP professional. This is the Era of Management Information Systems (MIS). The ability of the manager, who is confronted with the problem, to relate it to a set of data and create information, without having to go through the EDP professional, greatly enhanced both the use of the technology and its effectiveness.

The future belongs to the Era of Information and Knowledge. Here (Epoch C) the user has almost absolute control over the use of the technology. Direct linkages to large data bases, thousands of miles away, give their user tremendous opportunity to create information in a fraction of the time required before. This is the age of the C^2: Computers and Communications. MNCs are the primary users of C^2.

In sum, the brief treatise on the conceptual issues pertaining to IT provided a partial explanation of the lack of satisfactory inroads made by the IT managers in integrating the various IT architectures in parallel with the MNC's strategic global reach. At the same time, it points to the direction of future "homework" that must be done by both the line executives in familiarizing themselves with IT's main concepts and systems and the IT manager's need to expand his or her knowledge of the line executive's tool kit. This chapter is a small step towards that goal and is intended as a crude map for the journey.

PREPARING FOR THE DESIGN OF A GLOBAL INFORMATION SYSTEM

Creating a global information system is a major challenge for MNC managers. The novelty, volatility and complexity of the technology, combined with the relative lack of understanding of the tasks which it is designed to perform, makes the management of an information system extremely difficult. This situation becomes visibly unmanageable when compounded by the differences in social, technical, ecological, political and economic characteristics across national borders. For this reason most MNCs are very reluctant to integrate data flows globally, choosing instead to, in the words of Martin D.J. Buss (1982), "let sleeping dogs lie where information processing is concerned."

An effective information system requires the collection, storage, organization and transmission of enormous types and amounts of data. This demand for data requires that some of these data processing activities will be performed in one country and then merged with some other activity in another country for still further processing by the Data Processing or Information Systems department at the headquarters. While there are cost and (decision-making) efficiency reasons which dictate the amount and type of data processing which should be done at certain countries, the MNC is not completely free in implementing a cost effective strategy. There are many constraints which must be taken into consideration. For brevity, the next few pages highlight the legal constraints imposed by different agencies in the context of TBDF. Industry, firm and technology specific constraints are treated in detail in the fast increasing literature (McFarlan & McKenney, 1983).

Political and Legal Considerations of TBDF

The forces which led to political and legislative interest in data processing and transmission across national borders relate to the recognition that information is a vital ingredient in corporate and government decision-making. Since in the past the majority of information-generation activity was performed by MNCs headquarter in the U.S.A., U.S. - based corporations were caught in the so-called Transborder Data Flows (TBDF) controversy early on.

The legislative and political initiatives have created a multitude of problems for some MNCs, in particular in industries where data processing and information creation and use are very essential in their ability to function— such as, for example, banking, financial services, transportation and shipping, and construction industries. Even though new technological developments (e.g., Fax) have or may soon render some of these legislative constraints obsolete, it still behooves the MNC manager to keep them in mind while the design of a global information system is contemplated.

The first reason for legislation of TBDF is the recognition that, in the words of Louis Joinet, French Magistrate of Justice:

> Information is power, and economic information is economic power. Information has an economic value, and the ability to store and process certain types of data may well give one country political and technological advantage over other countries. This, in turn, leads to a loss of national sovereignty through supranational data flows (cf. Grub & Settle, 1986).

Legislative efforts were first directed toward "Personal Privacy," which, in the context of automated data record keeping systems, refers to the right of individuals in relation to the collection, processing, storage, dissemination, and use in decision making of personal data. Exhibit 2 provides a list of the "essential principles of privacy."

At the Nation-State level, the privacy issue is translated into the so-

1.**The Social Justification Principle**—the collection of personal data should be for a general purpose and specific uses which are socially acceptable.

2.**The Collection Limitation Principle**—the collection of personal data should be restricted to the minimum necessary and such data should not be obtained by unlawful or unfair means but only with the knowledge or consent of the data subject or with the authority of law.

3.**The Information Quality Principle**—personal data should, for the purposes for which they are to be used, be accurate, complete and kept up to date.

4.**The Purpose Specification Principle**—the purpose for which personal data are collected should be specified to the data subject not later than at the time of data collection and the subsequent use limited to those purposes or such others as are not incompatible with those purposes and as are specified on each occasion of change of purpose.

5.**The Disclosure Limitation Principle**—personal data should not be disclosed or made available except with the consent of the data subject, the authority of law, or pursuant to a publicly known usage of common and routine practice.

6.**The Security Safeguards Principle**—personal data should be protected by security safeguards which are reasonable and appropriate to prevent the loss of, destruction of, unauthorized access to use, modify, or disclose the data.

7.**The Openness Principle**—there should be a general policy of openness about developments, practices, and policies with respect to personal data. In particular, means should be readily available to establish the existence, purposes, policies, and practices associated with personal data as well as the identity and residence of the data controller.

8.**The Time Limitation Principle**—personal data in a form that permits identification of the data subject should, once their purposes have expired, be destroyed, archived or de-identified.

9.**The Accountability Principle**—there should be, in respect of any personal data record, an identifiable data controller who should be accountable in law for giving effect to these principles.

10.**The Individual Participation Principle**—an individual should have the right (a) to obtain from a data controller, or otherwise, confirmation of whether or not the data controller has data relating to him; (b) to have communicated to him, data relating to him (i) within a reasonable time, (ii) at a charge, if any, that is not excessive, (iii) in a reasonable manner, and (iv) in a form that is readily intelligible to him; (c) to challenge data relating to him and (i) during such challenge to have the record annotated concerning the challenge, and (ii) if the challenge is successful, to have the data corrected, completed, amended, annotated, or if appropriate, erased; and (d) to be notified of the reasons if a request made under paragraphs (a) and (b) is denied to be able to challenge such denial.

Source: P.D. Grub and S.R. Settle, "Transboder Data Flows: An Endangered Species?" in, P.D. Grub, F. Ghadan and D. Khambata, Editors, *The Multinational Enterprise in Transition*, 3d Edition, (Princeton: The Darwin Press, Inc., 1986), pp. 280-81.

Exhibit 2: Principles of Privacy

called national sovereignty issue. Most countries, due to their lack of control over the inflow and outflow of information, attribute considerable loss of the ability to set their own policies and laws and secure their execution.

Closely linked to the national sovereignty issue is the concept of vulnerability to foreign influence. This issue is more acute in the developing countries which tend to feel overwhelmed with or by the MNC's ability to collect and transmit vast amounts of data about the country's economic and political performance. When computers are tied to telecommunication systems which instantly transmit audio and video images from and to a given country there is the fear that an unsolicited change agent is undermining the country's pursuit of a self-reliant development.

Developed countries are not immune to the vulnerability complex. France is a classic example of a country which recognized very early the importance of information technology. In a clear indication of economic nationalism, a report to the French government made the following points:

1.The "informatization" of society will have serious consequences for France, socially, economically, and culturally.

2.Foreign firms (particularly IBM) must not be allowed to be instruments of foreign (primarily U.S.) dominance.

3.Post, Telephone and Telegraph Administration (PTTs) should be restructured so that the telecommunications portion can be redirected to work more closely with other high technology agencies.

4.Mastery of component technology is as important as nuclear mastery for national independence (cf. Grub & Settle, 1986).

Some other reasons for legislation of TBDF are (a) Balance of Payments (currency outflows for expensive computer and communications equipment) (2) Employment losses of national workers (data processing outside the country "exports" jobs) (3) Technology Dependence (lack of data processing opportunities deter hardware and software industry development thereby making the country dependent on foreign technology) (4) National and Cultural Values (developing countries and East Block countries seem to feel invaded by cultural and political messages which conflict with their own aspirations) and (5) National Defense (easy and quick access to information gives the enemy an added advantage) (Samiee, 1984; Baker, 1981; Burton, 1980).

The above concerns have tremendous implications for MNC management since they impact the majority of management decisions from the choice of the appropriate entry strategy to employee or human resource management (Bushkin, 1981; Kirchner, 1981; Nanus, 1978; United Nations, 1982; *The Economist*, 1981).

Organizational Considerations

In addition to the political and legal factors, the design of a global information system for an MNC is made more complicated by a number of concerns that relate to managerial choices regarding organizational strategy, structure, and systems on the one hand and staff, skills and styles, on the other.

Strategy is a very important determinant of both structure and systems. Currently most MNCs are confronted with the phenomenon of "Globalization" which conceives the world as a giant market in which superficial regional and national differences are unimportant. The implications of the choice of a globalization strategy for the IS designer and manager are numerous. A decentralized organizational structure staffed with people with multiple skills and styles can play havoc with an IS designer who may wish to follow the advice of William Rush, VP of Prudential-Bache Securities, "Centralized decision-making is key to implementing an aggressive communications strategy successfully...If you Balkanize those decisions, you get a lot of neat things that don't work" (Carlyle, 1988).

Operational changes relate to the growing interdependence of overseas affiliates, the introduction of the microcomputer and the acceleration of end user computing and telecommunication, and unionization of data processing personnel. These developments, directly or indirectly, affect policies regarding personnel selection, development and evaluation, budgets and so on. For example personnel, hardware, software and data communication costs are in most parts of the world considerably higher than in the U.S. Wages and fringe benefits for information processing personnel in West Germany, for example, are twice as much as those in the U.S. Hardware cost are about 60% more than those in the U.S., while a line of data transmission in Spain would cost six times more than a comparable line in the U.S.

The Basic Steps

Before embarking on the design of a global IS for an MNC, the firm must study the existing IS architectures at the headquarters and the affiliate levels. Since very little research has been done in this area, this brief discussion is intended to offer a few guidelines to a rather complex task.

Step 1: Diagnosis. The first step in creating a GLOBIS is to assess the capability of the existing information handling systems at the headquarters

NATURE OF THE INFORMATION PROVIDED

1. Can I compare operating results across affiliates in a way that helps me form conclusions on relative product costs, margins, and sales volumes? YES NO
2. Do I know whether my subordinates are satisfied with their information resources? YES NO
3. Do I know whether my competitors have better information systems than I do? YES NO

BUSINESS AND DATA PROCESSING PLANNING

4. Have I approved a long-range information systems plan? YES NO
5. Do I know whether the data processing plan supports my business plans for the key regions? YES NO
6. Has data processing been on the agenda of high-level operations reviews in the past 6 months? YES NO
7. In the past 12 months have I been involved in any major decisions on an information processing issue? YES NO
8. Have I been briefed in the past 12 months on the implications of new information processing technology for my business? YES NO

ORGANIZATION OF DATA PROCESSING

9. Do I know how international data processing responsibilities are organized? YES NO
10. Do I have the authority and responsibility to get the information processing I want? YES NO
11. Do I have a source that keeps me informed as to how well data processing is working? YES NO

COST OF INFORMATION PROCESSING

12. Do I know how much I am spending on data processing in my key regions? YES NO
13. Do I know whether these regions are spending enough, too much, or too little? YES NO
14. Do I know on which functions data processing emphasis is being placed for the current levels of expenditure? YES NO
15. Do I think this emphasis is in the right place? YES NO

TOTAL:
Scoring: A score of 12 or more yeses indicates that information processing operations are sound and well coordinated. A score of 6 to 11 yeses suggests that management intervention in some areas is needed. Fewer than 6 yeses indicates serious problems; senior international managers should almost certainly take action in the following three ways: (1) Orchestrate the process by which the organization plans its approach to international data processing, (2) create the right organizational framework for the international information system activity, and (3) define the roles of the key players.

Source: Martin D.J. Buss, "Managing International Information Systems," p. 158.

Exhibit 3: Rating the International Data Processing Operation

and its ability to relate to the several systems used by the foreign affiliates. Exhibit 3 depicts a diagnostic tool which is designed to give a senior executive a quick perspective on the situation.

The most likely outcome of this diagnostic exercise will be the discovery that the MNC is an archipelago of EDP and MIS departments which experience frequent storms and occasional hurricanes relative to their ability to handshake and communicate with each other and with the MNC. The purpose of this brief discussion on GLOBIS is to provide a framework which will enable the MNC to bring these isolated islands into a coherent and integrated communication and control system.

Step 2: Policy Setting. The second step involves the installation of policies which will secure the uniform use of information technology by all subsidiaries around the globe. A brief description of the possible IT policy content is offered in Exhibit 4. However, IT utilization policies must be integrated with other policies designed to guide the utilization of the conventional resources, such as people, money, material and equipment. The items listed under the "issues" column of the table are very representative of the "areas that must be covered."

Step 3: Integration. This step is designed to enable the MNC to begin conceptualizing "information as a strategic weapon." In other words, the purpose of integration is to create the appropriate *INFO*structure which will accommodate the MNC's need to communicate (inform and be informed) and control the complex *INFRA*structure of its physical, human and monetary resources around the globe. In the words of James L. McKenney and F. Warren McFarlan, the goal of this step is to "bring the islands that make up an archipelago of information — office automation, telecommunications, and data processing — under integrated control" (McFarlan & McKenney, 1982).

To be able to merge these three islands of information technology for its subsidiaries into one coherent whole, the MNC must first merge (1) data processing (DP) and (2) office automation (OA) both at the headquarters and subsidiary levels into an integrated Information System (IS). Once this task is accomplished, then the MNC must link the numerous local ISs at the subsidiaries with the headquarters IS into Global Information System (GLOBIS) via a telecommunications system.

The remainder of the chapter provides a conceptual framework to designing a global IS. The "client" for this GLOBIS is the field manager at the MNC headquarter who is charged with providing answers to the MNC's diverse stakeholders.

ISSUES	BRIEF DESCRIPTION OF POLICY CONTENT
A. HARDWARE: CPU and PERIPHERALS	**Central Hardware Concurrence or Approval:** Avoid mistakes in vendor viability and lack of compatibility; pursue economies of scale in purchasing decisions; local vendor patronizing.
B. SOFTWARE: SYSTEMS, APPLICATIONS, HEADQUARTERS TRANSFER, IN-HOUSE DEVELOPMENT, OUTSIDE PURCHASE	**Central Software Development and Standards:** Uniform standards must be set which will secure software documentation, maintenance, compatibility and economy; software transferability must be maximized. Development and updating must take into consideration the local needs, availability of well-trained personnel, costs and willingness of the headquarters staff to support and update programs made by the affiliates. Feasibility studies for the development of new software or upgrading of old ones must follow uniform procedures. Purchases of software from outside vendors must adhere to the same rules as the purchase of hardware (compatibility and economy).
C. DATA: GATHERING, PROCESSING, TRANSMISSION	**Data Gathering, Processing and Communication:** Instruments for gathering data such as forms, question-naires, terminals must be uniform to avoid duplication, confusion and incompatibility. Naming, labeling and classifying data must be done so as to lead to the development of an international corporate data dictionary. Storage of data both in terms of form and medium must also follow a corporate model to allow the use of tapes, discs, and other storage devises by data processing equipment across the globe.
D. ORGANIZATION AND PERSONNEL	**Organization and Staffing:** Selection, hiring, training, appraising and career development procedures must be uniform to avoid "job hopping" and "brain drain" from subsidiary to headquarters and from developing to developed countries. Job rotation, visitations, confer-ences, schools and joint educational programs must be encouraged across the globe. Particular attention must be given to nationals in promotions.
E. CONSULTING SERVICES	**Corporate and Outside Consultation:** Corporate and Regional headquarters personnel are usually more aware of leading-edge hardware and software developments. Policies and procedures must be set up for both requesting and accepting unsolicited head-quarters assistance. In some cases, outside consulting might be preferable.
F. TBDF AND OTHER LEGAL MATTERS	**Legal and Transborder Data Transfer:** Care must be taken to assure compliance with local , regional and international restriction on data transfer across national boundaries in particular when name-carrying data transmission is concerned.

Source: F. Warren McFarlan and James L. McKenney, Corporate Information Systems: The Issues Facing Senior Executives. (Homewood, IL: Richard D. Irwin, Inc., 1983), Chapter 9, p. 165-182.

Exhibit 4: Policy Guidelines for MNC Information Processing

DESIGNING A GLOBAL INFORMATION SYSTEM (GLOBIS) FOR AN MNC

Multinational Corporations are huge networks of information which are created by complex and sophisticated computer and telecommunication systems. The diverse activities of a typical MNC create vast amounts of data which are symbolic representations of events gathered, stored and transmitted in many different forms and languages. For the MNC to be able to control its own and its subsidiaries' activities and to be able to comply with the multitude of laws, rules and regulations around the globe, it must create an equally complex global information system.

Exhibit 5 provides a sketch of a global information system (Kefalas, 1990). The lefthand side of the graph is called the "External Global Information Subsystem" (EXGLOBIS). The purpose of this subsystem is to allow the MNC to identify the constraints, threats and opportunities which are hidden in the external business environment. The right hand side of the graph depicts the "Internal Global Information Subsystem" (INGLOBIS). Both subsystems are, of course, linked via feedforward and feedback mechanisms to guarantee adequate control.

The External Information Acquisition Global System (EXGLOBIS)

Information about the external environment is exceedingly difficult to acquire. Unlike the internal information creation processes of the MNC where both problems and available data sources are agreed upon by conviction, convenience and convention, external environment data sources are riddled with hidden problems. The lack of uniformity in definitions, measurements and meaning of issues over which data are gathered makes their accuracy, timeliness, ease of access, and in general, reliability/integrity exceedingly questionable. Most private and public—national and international—sources of environmental data make considerable disclaimers about the confidence they assign to the reliability of the data.

For this reason, this paper offers a "framework" for gathering, analyzing, evaluating and using data. The framework consists of a series of resolutions starting with a very broad approach which is designed to provide an adequate understanding of the external business environment, the so-called "big picture," and ends with a rather specific and precise calculus of the problem at hand, the "detail picture."

Phase I, is Environmental Scanning. In a nutshell, the purpose of

---

THE EXTERNAL GLOBAL INFORMATION SUBSYSTEM (EXGLOBIS)

I. ENVIRONMENTAL SCANNING: ISSUE MANAGEMENT APPROACH

Issue Identification	Brainstorming on events, trends, issues. List top 10 Issues/Megatrends
Issue Evaluation	Assesses Issue Magnitude, Importance and Meaning of Top Ten Issues
Issue Incorporation	Develop Scenarios using the Top Five Issues Identified in Issue Evaluation
Issue Translation	Relate chosen Strategies to the three scenarios: Optimistic, Pessimistic, and Most Likely

II. POLITICAL ECONOMY APPROACH
  A. MACROECONOMIC ASSESSMENT: $Y + M = A + X$
representing real flows of goods and services in an economy where Y is output, M is imports, A is domestic absorption (consumption, investment and public-sector spending) and X is exports, all in real terms. Or the money equivalent:
$VX - VM = DS + FDI + U - K_o = DR - NBR$. Here VX and VM represent the money value of exports and imports, respectively. DS represents debt-service payments to foreigners (usually part of VM in conventional balance-of-payments accounting); FDI is net flows of nonresident foreign direct investments; U represents net flows of private and public-sector grants such as foreign aid. K_o is net capital flows undertaken by residents, DR is the change in international reserves of the country in question, and NBR is its net borrowing requirement.

  B. EXTERNAL/COMMERCIAL SERVICES
     BERI, EUROMONEY, NBI, PSSI, WPRF, FROST & SULLIVAN.

THE INTERNAL GLOBAL INFORMATION SUBSYSTEM (INGLOBIS)

III. STATUTORY REQUIREMENTS
  A. INCOME/PROFIT AND LOSS STATEMENT
  B. BALANCE SHEET STATEMENT
  C. CHANGES IN FINANCIAL POSITION STATEMENT
  D. NOTES ON CONSOLIDATED FINANCIAL STATEMENTS

IV. OPERATIONAL/TACTICAL MANAGEMENT REQUIREMENTS
  A. FINANCIAL MANAGEMENT REQUIREMENTS
         - Exposure Management   - Capital Budgeting
         - Cash Management   - Investment Evaluation and Funding

  B. NON-FINANCIAL MANAGEMENT REQUIREMENTS
         - Organizational Structure
         - Sourcing/Production Strategy
         - Marketing Strategy
         - Human Resource Development Strategy

V. STRATEGIC MANAGEMENT REQUIREMENTS
  A. RATIONALIZATION/RESTRUCTURING
     - Downsizing, Pruning, Retrenching, Deinvesting
  B. INTERNAL GROWTH
     - New Markets
     - New Products
  C. EXTERNAL GROWTH
     - Joint Ventures   - New Plants: Greenfield
     - Acquisitions   - New Plants: Brownfield
  D. STRATEGIC ALLIANCES
     - Existing Business Domain
     - New Business Domain

Source: A.G. Kefalas, (1990).

Exhibit 5. The Global Information System (GLOBIS)

environmental scanning is to give the manager an adequate understanding of the main issues which seem to preoccupy the organizational's external environment. The process of environmental scanning is depicted in the upper left side of Exhibit 5. The ultimate result of this process is a relation of a set of scenarios to known MNC strategies.

Phase II is a more traditional approach used by academicians and practitioners. This approach uses the so-called "Political Economy" viewpoint. In Phase II (A) a macroeconomic model is exhibited which is designed to give a "quick and dirty" idea of the country's ability to "pay its way" in the international business game (Walter, 1984).

In Phase II (B) a more detailed assessment of the country is provided using professional commercial sources which a manager may wish to hire. Most of these have on-line capabilities. Some of the most well-known sources are (Kennedy, 1987):

(1) The Business Environmental Risk Index (BERI)
(2) The Business International (BI) system
(3) Nikkei's Business Index (NBI)
(4) Political System Stability Index (PSSI)
(5) World Political Risk Forecasts (WPRF) or the Prince Model, and,
(6) The Gladwin-Walter Model
(7) Political Risk Services/Political Risk Letter

Internal Global Information Subsystem (INGLOBIS)

The complexity of the financial transactions between the MNC's headquarters and its numerous subsidiaries, and among the subsidiaries themselves, is a true nightmare for the information systems specialist whose task is to provide the information required by the company's diverse stakeholders. These diverse and complex informational needs require an equally complex system which will gather, organize, process, store, and retrieve data from all subsidiaries, convert these data into useful information and supply this information into the decision-making centers all over the globe.

The input needs of such a MIS are determined by many factors such as organizational structure, product and geographical diversification, management philosophy and above all, management attitude toward computerized data bases and use of computers in managerial decision-making. In most firms, however, due to the current fashionable emphasis on rationalization, the need for timely, accurate, speedy, and cost-efficient information gathering and dissemination systems available to, and accessible by, all pertinent decision-making centers is an idea whose time has definitely come.

An added demand for efficient internal information systems is caused by the complex financial instruments. The inability or unwillingness on the part of the world's governments to create some kind of managed exchange rates system imposes another severe demand on the MNC's information handling capacity. In short, one can argue that a firm which will possess an efficient international financial information management system would most definitely have the only true competitive advantage left in this extremely competitive world (Pennon & Wallace, 1988).

There are essentially three sources from which demand for accurate and timely internal data emanates. Exhibit 5 presents a tabular picture of these sources.

Statutory Requirements. Every country treats every private, for-profit organization as its own citizen subject to taxation and other regulations. Therefore, an MNC must comply with both its own government's requirements and the governments of every one of its subsidiaries. In addition, the company's other stakeholders such as investors (shareholders), bankers, and employees desire to know management's handling of their resources invested in the firm. While government and other formal stakeholder requirements vary considerably from country to country there are enough similarities upon which a system can be built to handle all reporting requirements globally.

Every stakeholder wishes to know (1) what resources a firm has (2) who owns these resources (3) how were these resources being utilized for wealth creation and finally, (4) what share of this wealth is due to them. A firm satisfies these information needs of its stakeholders by creating and making available the following four documents:

A. Income Statement (P&L Statement)
B. Balance Sheet
C. Changes in Financial Position
D. Notes on Consolidated Financial Statements

All four of these documents are contained in the Annual Report which the company makes available to its stakeholders including concerned citizens (e.g., pressure groups and students).

Operational/Tactical Management Requirements. Statutory information and reporting requirements are designed to satisfy the demands imposed by the company's "external stakeholders." Operational/Tactical Management Requirements are information gathering and reporting demands imposed by the "internal stakeholders." Internal stakeholders are individuals and units which have "a right to know" an individual's or company's handling of organizational resources and their own share of the outcome. Tactical management requirements refers to the demand for control of a subsidiary's items which appear in all four main documents, i.e., income statement, balance sheet, cash flow and notes.

Unlike the statutory requirements, for which predetermined dates and frequency of reporting is set by the requestor, tactical management control requirements vary from company to company and from case to case within the company. As a matter of fact, the magnitude and frequency of reporting by the subsidiaries to the parent company is one of the most "hidden" battlegrounds in every MNC. Frequent reporting keeps headquarters informed but, at the same time, deters subsidiary management from performing their true tasks of making the most efficient use of organizational resources.

Frequently smaller subsidiaries are asked to report on matters which are completely "strange" to them. As one managing director of a subsidiary in a small country confided to the author:

> I think I am going crazy. I just finished the monthly report on leasing private aircraft by my executives for the third time this year. . .I put all zeroes or NA everywhere. . .that's what they told me to do when I called up and told them that over here there is no such thing as private aircraft. . Nobody leases airplanes to go and do business or attend a meeting which is a very common practice in Chicago. You have no idea how much time I spend doing things like that. . .Our turnover (sales) is barely over $10 million a year and yet we have to report on things that pertain to hundreds of millions of dollars. Every time I do this kind of thing my whole day is shot. I just go home and play with the kids.

In general, the purpose of insisting on subsidiary inputs to the corporate INGLOBIS is to facilitate (1) planning (2) following-up of plans (3) detection of deviations from plans (4) evaluation of these deviations (5) taking timely corrective actions and (6) adjustment of plans.

Exhibit 5, Section IV, divides the need for tactical management information into two main sets of requirements. Set A, Financial Management Requirements, includes data required to carry out the task of the Financial Manager and the Comptroller. In summary, this task includes exposure management, cash management, and project evaluation and funding. Set B, Non-Financial Management Requirements include data gathering and processing pertinent to the designing and updating of the organizational structure, sourcing and production strategy, marketing strategy and human resource development strategy.

Appraising operations is perhaps the most legitimate reason for an INGLOBIS from the tactical non-financial management viewpoint (See IV, B). Managers' performance appraisal and its importance for their immediate and future compensation is a pure function of headquarters' ability to stitch together an accurate picture of managerial performance which would reflect the manager's true ability to lead and accomplish corporate objectives. In the international business sphere, however, events beyond the control of a manager (e.g., currency exchange fluctuations) could easily convert a successful managerial performance into a disastrous document of managerial incompetence.

Strategic Management Requirements. The purpose of the Strategic Management Requirements is to provide the management of the MNC with the information it needs to chart the company's long range journey through a turbulent globe.

The Strategic Management Requirements outlined in Section V in Exhibit 5 pertain to the formidable task of relating the firm's strength and weaknesses to the environment's constraints, threats and opportunities and setting the organization's objectives and goals. This task is translated into four options:

      A. Rationalization/Restructuring of Existing Activities
      B. Internal Growth Options
      C. External Growth Options, and
      D. Strategic Alliances

In sum, the process of identifying the informational needs of the MNC and designing the appropriate information systems to create, organize and disseminate this information to the appropriate decision makers begins with Step I at the extreme upper left corner of Exhibit 5 and ends at the extreme upper right corner with Step III. In other words, the Global Information System of an MNC brings together informational requirements for both strategic and tactical management. The system is energized by assessing the firm's External Business Environment via the EXGLOBIS whose purpose is the identification and evaluation of threats and opportunities. The output of the EXGLOBIS becomes the input to the INGLOBIS via the Strategic Management System. This system relates the firm's Strengths and Weaknesses to environmental threats and opportunities and sets the future objectives and goals for the MNC. Financial and operational subsystems continuously monitor and evaluate the MNC's progress toward the accomplishment of its goals.

CONCLUSION

Information is to the contemporary manager/decision maker what energy was to the engineer of the past: energy augmented human muscle power; information augments human cognitive capacity. The use of information for commercial and industrial purposes created a brand new technology known as information technology (IT). Today this technology encompasses the use of information handling systems whose primary inputs are data (EDP), office automation systems (OA) which deal with the processing of words and reprocessed data (i.e., information in the conventional and colloquial meaning of the word) and telecommunications and computer (C^2).

One of the most powerful competitive advantages of the multinational corporation is its ability to scan the entire globe and gather data about resource availability and accessibility and customer needs and wants. The MNC's need to evaluate these data and convert them into powerful information is the contemporary manager's prime challenge.

This chapter has provided a broad framework of some basic ideas which should be the main pillars upon which the edifice of a truly global information system will be built and managed.

Designing an information system for a MNC is a very difficult task. The complexity of the task does not come only from the complexity inherent in the MNC's operations (which span many countries with different languages and legal and accounting systems), but it is also aggravated by the existence of legal and political restrictions imposed on the transfer of data across national boundaries.

Competing in the Global Village of tomorrow will involve turning it into an Electronic Global Village of today. MNCs, with electronic linkages of their local MISs into an integrated GLOBIS will minimize the information float and thereby will manage effectively and efficiently the modern information/ knowledge-intensive, lean, fast, and flexible organization. MNCs whose infostructure resembles that of today's fragmented, non-compatible, data-intensive MISs will be deprived of the growth opportunities of tomorrow. The task for the future-oriented information managers is clear: align, connect, relate, simplify, and globalize your information systems today to minimize the information float and maximize flexibility and speed of decision making.

References

Ackoff, R. (1988). *From data to wisdom.* Paper presented at the meeting of the International Systems Science Society.

Ackoff, R.L. (1967, December). Management misinformation systems. *Management Science*, pp. 147-156.

Ashby, W.R. (1960). *Design for a brain.* New York: Barnes and Noble.

Baker, S.W. (1981, March). Importing information: Current U.S. customs control. *American Import-Export Bulletin*, pp. 50-54.

Beer, S. (1972). *The brain of the firm.* New York: McGraw-Hill.

Brightman, H.J., & Harris, S.E. (1987, September/October). A comparison of modeling practices in domestic and foreign firms. *Managerial Planning*, pp. 30-34.

Bruns, W.J., & McFarlan, E.W. (1987, September/October). Information technology puts power in control systems. *Harvard Business Review*, pp. 89-94.

Burton, R.P. (1980, June). Transnational data flows: International status, impact and accommodation. *Data Management*, pp. 27-34.

Bushkin, A.A. (1981, August 3). The threat to international data flows. *Business Week*, pp. 10-11.

Buss, M.D.J. (1984, May/June). Legislative threat to transborder data flow. *Harvard Business Review*, pp. 111-118.

Buss, M.D.J. (1982, September/October). Managing international information systems. *Harvard Business Review*, pp. 153-162.

Carlyle, R.E. (1988, March 1). Managing IS at multinationals. *Datamation*, pp. 54-66.

Cleveland, H. (1985). Educating for the information society. *Change*, pp. 13-21.

Cleveland, H. (1985). *The knowledge executive.* New York, NY: E.P. Dutton.

Drucker, P. (1988, January/February). The coming of the new organization. *Harvard Business Review*, pp. 45-53.

Gore, A. (1991). Information superhighway. *Futurist*, January-February, pp. 21-23.

Grub, P.D., Settle, S.R., Transborder data flows: An endangered species? In Grub, P.D., Ghadan, F., & Khambata, D. (Eds.), *The multinational enterprise in transition*, 3rd edition (pp. 280-81). Princeton: The Darwin Press, Inc.

The information edge. (1988, February 2). *Financial Times*, p. 7.

Jenster, P.V. (1987, February). Using critical success factors in planning. *Long Range Planning*.

Keen, P.G.W. (1986). *Competing in time: Using telecommunications for competitive advantage.* Cambridge, MA: Ballinger Publishing Company.

Kefalas, A.G. (1990). *Global business strategy: A systems approach.* Cincinnati: South-Western Publishing Company.

Kennedy, C.R., Jr. (1987). *Political risk management: International lending and investing under environmental uncertainty.* New York: Quarum Books, 41.

Kirchner, J. (1981, August 3). TDF barriers seen hitting U.S. firms in pocket: Executives tell Congress. *Computerworld*, p. 5.

McFarlan, W. E. (1984, May/June). Information technology changes the way you compete. *Harvard Business Review*, pp. 98-103.

McFarlan, W.E., & McKenney, J.L. (1983). *Corporate information systems management: The issues facing senior executives.* Homewood: R.D. Erwin, Inc., pp. 165-182.

McFarlan, W.E., & McKenney J.L. (1987). *Corporate information systems: Text and cases.* Homewood, IL: Richard D. Irwin, Inc.

McKenney, J.L., & McFarlan, E.W. (1982, September/October). The information archipelago — steps and bridges. *Harvard Business Review*, pp. 109-119.

Nanus, B. (1978). Business, government and the multinational computer. *Columbia Journal of*

World Business, pp. 19-26.

Narchal, R.M., Kittappa K., & Bhattcharya, P. (1987). An environmental scanning system for business planning. *Long Range Planning, 29*(6), 96-105.

New OECD guidelines on privacy. (1980, November). *OECD Observer,* pp. 26-41.

Nigh, D., & Cochran, P. L. (1987). Issues management and the multinational enterprise. *MIR,* Vol. 27, pp. 4-12.

Pennon, K., & Wallace, G.D. (1988, February 22). The economy: Uncertainty isn't about to go away. *Business Week,* pp. 52-53.

Peters, T. (1990). Prometheus barely unbound. *The Executive, IV*(4), 70-84.

Porter, M.E., & Miller, V.E. (1985, July/August). How information gives you competitive advantage. *Harvard Business Review,* pp. 149-160.

Prahalad, C.K., & Doz, Y.L. (1987). *The multinational mission: Balancing local demand and global vision.* New York: Free Press.

Radhakrishnan, K.S., & Soenen, L.A. (1987, July/August). Why computerized financial reporting and consolidation systems? *Managerial Planning,* pp. 32-36.

Richman, L.S. (1987, June 8). Software catches the team spirit. *Fortune,* pp. 125-136.

Roy, P.S., & Cheung, J.K. (March/April). Early warning systems: A management tool for your company. *Managerial Planning,* pp. 16-21.

Samiee, S. (1984, Spring/Summer). Transnational data flow constraints: A new challenge for multinational corporations. *JIBS,* pp. 141-150.

Shannon, G.E., & Weaver, W. (1964). *The mathematical theory of communication.* Urbana, IL: The University of Illinois Press.

Toffler, A. (1970). *Future shock.* New York, NY: Random House.

Toffler, A. (1980). *The thirdwave.* New York, NY: W. Morrow Company, Inc.

Toffler, A. (1990). *Power shift.* New York.

Transnational corporations and transborder data flows: A technical paper. New York: United Nations Centre on Transnational Corporation, 1982.

Vitro, R.A. (1984, January/February). The information engine. *Managing International Development,* pp. 24-39.

Wallace, W.A. (1987, February). International accounting and likely approaches to future inquiry: An overview of research. *MIR, 27,* 4-25.

Walter, I. (Ed.) (1984). *Handbook of international business.* New York: John Wiley & Sons.

27

Managing Systems Development in Multinational Corporations: Practical Lessons from Seven Case Studies

Edward M. Roche
University of Arizona

Today's multinational corporation (MNC) is an old structure which is being forced to adapt to new levels of international competition. To do this requires that the CIO must adopt new global strategies. He must first understand the implications of corporate strategy, then respond with the appropriate systems development efforts. There are many practical problems which must be faced including mustering sufficient political authority, managing across cultures and time zones, and coping with varied requirements in different countries. In addition, he must make the correct decisions regarding architecture. This chapter contains seven case studies of how different IS organizations have attempted systems development projects aimed at matching information technology strategy to business strategy.

INTRODUCTION

The most fundamental challenge facing the multinational corporation (MNC) today is how to match its systems development efforts with corporate business strategy. Meeting this challenge involves assessing factors such as how the MNC interacts between its headquarters and subsidiaries, the nature of the relationship with host country governments and markets, its foreign direct investment (FDI) patterns, the fundamental nature of its business, and

I would like to acknowledge the generous help of the Index Group, Inc. for its assistance in compiling these case studies. However, Index Group is not responsible for the Content herein and the statements do not necessarily reflect Index Groups philosophy or approach.

how it intends to respond to the competition.

Such factors as national regulations and barriers, rules on Foreign Direct Investment (FDI), currency and trading arrangements, the degree of control over the technology being used, and competitive pressures from host country firms provide more variables with which the MNC must cope in devising its strategy (Doz, 1980; Behrman, 1969). Even in highly informational sectors such as financial services, the regulatory environment is a critical force shaping how business strategy responds to new opportunities. Information technology is then used to support day-to-day operational tactics once the basic strategy has been decided upon. Although these external factors certainly condition the grand strategy of the MNC, they have little to do directly with information technology and the practical realities of systems development.[1,2]

It is true that the CIO must ensure that information strategy is in sync with business strategy, (Nanus, 1969,78) but unfortunately, as CIOs assess their current systems, rather than finding a well-functioning empire, many find a splintered haphazard configuration of different national data processing centers facing the challenge of how to work more effectively together. These information systems might be called United Nations-type[3] or polycentric information systems because the MNC uses a semi-autonomous data center in each country[4]. Most often these data centers were set up when assumptions about the nature of international competition were quite different. In the 1950s-1970s, MNCs concentrated on serving each national market separately, and this strategy usually implied separate data processing facilities in each country[5]. Although this type of strategy fits with the general business strategy of adapting to local conditions in each market, it does not meet the global imperative.

In formulating a global response, the CIO finds his competitors are implementing many new technology strategies which raise the stakes in the game. Global logistics systems; complex order processing systems; multiple country sourcing of components; global R&D, instantaneous world-wide financial reconciliation — these types of new applications can give competitive advantage to the MNC and they compel the CIO to undertake a new generation of international systems development projects.

As the CIO embarks on these projects, many times using as a guide the lessons learned from years of operating in a domestic environment, he begins to encounter specific types of barriers and difficulties which are unique at the international level. Strong country managers may hinder or stop altogether systems development efforts which are coming from "headquarters". The logistics and coordination difficulties of international projects are in themselves difficult enough to wear down a team no matter how energetic; and the requirement to operate across many different time zones makes things even more difficult. Finally, the CIO and his team face many technical questions, the answers to which are by no means obvious: which data or applications to centralize or decentralize?; whether to build national or regional data centers?; how to integrate incompatible systems and applications?; how to get reliable telecommunications services?, etc. Even worse, the CIO frequently lacks a clear "global" mandate and accompanying power base; and as a result may find that the different subsidiary-based IS organizations which he supposedly controls may resemble more a group of independent warring states, than a well coordinated army. In addition, all of this takes place in a cross-cultural environment which complicates even further the management process (Negandhi, 1983). Yet, these are some of the conditions under which the CIO must manage his systems development projects.

This chapter presents seven case studies which highlight different aspects of systems development in the international environment[6]. Some of the cases are "successes," while others are "failures". They point to the variety of challenges faced by the CIO as he first feels the pressure of changing business strategy, then responds with a new systems development effort in the highly uncertain international environment.

INFORMATION SYSTEMS SUPPORT OF GLOBAL MANUFACTURING — "CAR" (1983-1990)

"Car" faces tremendous competitive pressures to reduce costs, increase innovation, and shrink the new car development and introduction cycle. As a company which had to respond to these pressures, "Car" developed the "globe car" in the early 1980's. The globe car concept involves making a car which will sell in many different national markets of the world, using the cheapest components available.

After the information systems department was informed of the new strategy concept, it scrambled to develop the required systems which would link together its different key locations. For example, it developed a second data communications network dedicated to linking together computer aided design (CAD) workstations and tools on a world-wide basis. This network is set up as a separate system, not digitally integrated into the regular data communications network used for other applications hosted in the various data centers around the world.

Another major innovation was the Engineering Release System (ERS). Engineering releases occur when the product or component design department hands over the technical design details to the manufacturing engineers who are located in the different manufacturing plants around the world. Although an automobile company changes its models on a yearly basis, engineering releases, many times containing changes which are invisible to the consumer, occur very frequently and automobile manufacturing is correspondingly improved step-by-step. This approach does not apply to lean manufacturing (Roos, 1990).

"Car's" engineering release system was started in 1983 and has taken approximately 6 years to ramp up to full operation. In the U.S., Europe and Mexico, approximately 10,000 to 12,000 persons access the system on a regular basis. The database is managed centrally in the United States and this gives an advantage of having only one set of code in a single location. This is an advantage with updating information because the changes are made to a single location, and the system to coordinate file locking is less cumbersome than with multiple databases. Applications development and maintenance of the database is also much easier as well in terms of coordination between different parts of the systems development team.

The nature of the transformation of the data processing environment involves an apparent decentralization of databases, without losing the control which has been traditionally exercised by the central computing installations. In order to accomplish this, the large core system will be replaced eventually with an infrastructure of six local satellite systems located in various parts of the world. These systems will interact with the main core system which in any case will retain its function as a home database for the satellite systems. Products engineered in several different locations can distribute their design and engineering specifications from the core system as a type of "broadcast". Each of the satellite systems will support an on-line capability for users.

Knowing the strategy, however, is not enough to carry it out. The information systems department finds itself standing in the center of a complex development and engineering process being coordinated on a world-wide basis. Getting agreement from the different parts of the information systems function is time consuming and difficult.

The IS management team believes that one key factor causing this difficulty is the absence of a world-wide line manager for engineering. For example, if there were a world-wide line manager and if the IS team had this level of management support, then it would be far more easy to get the required agreement for faster planning and implementation of the system. This level of support is not there. It is therefore more difficult to manage the consensus between the far-flung parts of the information technology "empire".

The most important lesson concerns making local data processing professionals view their work in a global context. This is completely different from the style of the past when the existing systems were developed behind national boundaries. The new view implies a focus on common systems. Without this type of consensus view, it is immeasurably more difficult to develop corporate-wide systems because each national data processing group will continue to place priority only on its own data processing requirements.

The IS management also values a management-by-consensus approach to strategic planning for information technology. Although it is clearly important to make quick progress on the various "global" initiatives underway, the IS management team at headquarters strives to get a sense of common agreement before rushing ahead. It recognizes the need to develop global economies of scale in data processing.

Lessons Learned from "Car"

This case points to some interesting lessons which may have wider implications for other firms attempting the same type of project:

Decentralized "global" manufacturing may use centralized IS: The most advantageous alignment of information systems with corporate strategy in the MNC does not automatically mean adoption of a similar structure. In the case of "Car", a centralized IS was necessary in order to support a global manufacturing operation which was highly decentralized.

Strike a balance between national and global interests: In any systems development operation spanning borders, the project manager in charge will inevitably encounter resistance from national IS organizations. People's priorities are determined locally, and not at headquarters. The firm must find some way to strike a balance between the different priorities so that everyone is satisfied and the project goes through.

Seek economies of scale in international data processing: Particularly when facing the requirement for operation and maintenance of a large database responsible for coordinating activities in different countries, a firm may be able to gain significant economies of scale in data processing by centralization. There is a complicated trade-off between the efficiencies of centralization and the costs of operating international systems. Although "Car" was not able to rely completely on a single centralized location for processing, a regiocentric approach still provided significant economies of scale in contrast to having processing done in each country.

ACQUISITION FORCES THE INFORMATION SYSTEMS DEPARTMENT TO MERGE A GLOBAL PROFS NETWORK — "TOBACCO" (1989-1990)

"Tobacco" Corporation is now a large consumer oriented conglomerate which recently acquired "Food". Because of the world-wide nature of the cigarette business, "Tobacco" has built up very large data processing systems which operate throughout the world. When the merger with "Food" took place, "Tobacco" IS management was fortunate in finding that "Food" had roughly similar types of systems, i.e. the same vendor and operating systems.

After the merger took place, a survey of data processing requirements suggested the need to develop a common world-wide data center which would coordinate global operations. This meant that the information systems organization was planning on changing from a United Nations (polycentric) model to a global model. This centralized concept would have been the ultimate in world-wide coordination and consolidation of many different critical functions in the organization.

Unfortunately, as soon as work began on this project, it ran into problems. The central organization became the target point for all requests for resources. Each data processing group was focused on getting support and funding only for its own interests. No one seemed to have enough political power to coordinate a corporate-wide strategy. When volumes of uncoordinated facility requests started pouring in from data centers around the world, it became quickly impossible to satisfy all of the demands.

The reaction was so strong, "Tobacco" had to abandon the "global" approach. It had worked fine on paper but in practice was impossible to carry out. "Tobacco" adopted a regiocentric (Perlmutter) strategy with data centers in three locations: Europe, the United States, and Asia. It had been simply impossible to build a comprehensive data processing facility to service global operations.

Even though it had abandoned globalism in favor of regionalism in data processing, "Tobacco" found it still needed global telecommunications capabilities. The requirement for more data centers had shifted the burden to the telecommunications network. This was particularly important for the corporate-wide electronic mail facility which was available through the IBM product PROFS[7]. The IS team found that at the time of the merger, "Foods" had implemented a world-wide PROFS system which was fully operational by September of 1989. As it began the detailed work of patching together the different parts of the "Tobacco" businesses, IS management found that the tobacco section of the business also had a large PROFS installation. The task then focused on using the network to tie together all of the different PROFS installations into a coherent system. This would enable executives from all parts of the new organization — both "Tobacco" and "Food" — to communicate with one another electronically and transfer a variety of documents back and forth as needed. However, tying together the different systems was not easy, altogether it took approximately 1 1/2 years of development and programming effort. The IS team in charge found that there were many PROFS installations which had to be tied together. The major problems occurred in the consolidation of electronic mail directories based on addressing schemes accepted on a corporate-wide basis.

Tying together the PROFS installations was viewed by top IS management as being a "good, low cost way to test the infrastructure initiatives." This initiative was undertaken because it was felt that "infrastructure platform systems are the least risky." It was certainly less risky than the failed centralization strategy which had been attempted earlier. The effort served as a type of "fire drill" for more complicated initiatives in the future. The skills exercised in the development of these global systems can be sharpened for more complex efforts later on. One might call it a piecemeal approach to building global systems.

"Tobacco" Identifies Barriers to Globalism

In assessing the future development of international information systems strategies for "Tobacco", the IS management team identified several barriers for IS development and implementation:

Language Barriers: "Tobacco" finds that although management may speak English well; the "information workers" who will actually be using the system do not have the same command of the language.

Lack of "Global" Suppliers: Although "Tobacco" finds it necessary to build large international systems, it finds it impossible to locate "global" suppliers of computer systems and related services. Instead, the company has been forced to negotiate and sign separate agreements in each country for equipment and services. Software support may not be available everywhere.

Cultural Problems: Cultural problems can inhibit the effectiveness of management teams engaged in systems development because different management styles and values may clash making difficult decision-making and a delay in arriving at the required consensus.

Inadequate Facilities: IS management at "Tobacco" has found that on a global basis, vendors of many services, particularly telecommunications, are many times unable to provide truly consistent global services. Some products and network capabilities are available in only selected countries and are very unevenly distributed around the world. For example, there is no global Integrated Services Digital Network (ISDN) and leased line circuits are hard to get. Firms are forced to sign dozens or even hundreds of agreements with different telecommunications authorities in order to build international networks, and this requirement is complicated even further by the uneven nature of services available.

National Variances in Tax Laws: The variances in tax laws is a major headache because it adds tremendous complication to the accounting conventions used in purchasing equipment. Depreciation scales for tax purposes vary from country to country and so do the rules concerning expense items and deductions. As firms attempt moving towards a global (geocentric) model of data processing, it may discover an emerging need for complex staffing requirements to handle this aspect of the business.

Inadequate Justification Methods: "Tobacco" also points to the difficulty faced in collecting valid cost data uniformly from all countries on a world-wide basis for making capital investment decisions for computer systems. This makes it very difficult to make an accurate analysis of infrastructure costs and adds great complexity to any analysis. National variations in exchange rates, costs of infrastructure support such as electrical supply, programming, and telecommunications, change the underlying assumptions about the economics of computing. Many traditional estimations of pay-off have to be revised on a case-by-case basis.

"International" Lacks Political Clout: There is a conflict in work priorities between domestic operations and international operations. The interviewees stated that "most domestic IS groups are running lean, with a full plate of work, characterized by heavy maintenance requirements." As a result, domestic operations get priority in allocation of both human and financial resources over international operations.

Skill Shortage: Information systems management at "Tobacco" also mentioned an "eroding skill base threat." They observed that there is a shortage of people with the correct talent for designing and building complex systems at the international level. If shortages result in having to place heavy international travel demands against skilled staff, the rate of "burn out" will inevitably rise.

IS Subservient to Corporate Strategy: Information systems management at "Tobacco" does not see IS as taking on an important role in re-designing the way business works. Instead, they see the role of IS as being to "map to the business" by which they mean that information systems must adapt to the organizational structure of the business rather than attempt to introduce change into the way employees go about their work. This is the received way IS is expected to support business units in their operations. This supporting role at the domestic level by implication should extend to the international level. The idea of IS somehow shaping global corporate strategy is viewed as being absurd.

In order to better implement change on an international scale, the IS management is attempting to draw their executives from the international business units. This gives the IS department a direct connection with the business unit for which it might be developing an application or building a new system.

GLOBAL STRATEGY MEANS CENTRALIZED COMPUTING — "PLASTIC" (1987-1989)

"Plastic" is the world leader in manufacturing plastic kitchen storage systems. It conducts business in over 35 countries, and has 17 plants located around the world in North America, South America, Europe, and the Pacific region.

In spite of repeat attempts at careful market research, "Plastic" is not able to anticipate demand of products. For example, a simple flat stencil set for children suddenly "caught fire" and vastly exceeded all earlier demand projections. This raises significant problems. If it is unable to supply the booming demand for "hot" products, it risks alienation of independent distributors who see a chance to make a quick profit. According to management, maintaining the loyalty and excitement of independent distributors is critical to corporate survival because selling this type of product is a "highly emotionally-charged business".

"Plastic" has the ultimate United Nations (polycentric) data processing system. Computing and telecommunications resources are scattered world-wide with a large IBM mainframe located at headquarters. A mixture of mini- and micro-computers in different countries make up the remaining portions of the installation. Equipment from IBM, Digital, Wang, NCR, Compaq, Apple, and various DOS PC compatibles constitute "Plastic's" rich texture of international computing.

In the past, the world-wide businesses were run independently, supported by autonomous data centers in each major country. As the competitive picture changed during the mid-1980's, it became more difficult to both meet market demands and contain operating costs. Top management decided to reorient the company and its information systems towards global operations. For "Plastic" a global business strategy included world-wide sourcing of raw materials, and the central coordination of the sharing and shuttling of molds[8] from location to location in order to meet demand. In order to follow this strategy, the information systems department had to create an information systems infrastructure which tied together the cacophony of different systems in various locations around the world. It needed a responsive telecommunications network, combined with a portfolio of applications which operated the same way from all locations. Order processing, distribution and logistics control, mold data and tracking information, as well as their associated accounting systems all needed to be delivered through the international telecommunications system.

The information systems management at "Plastic" faced two major challenges: First it had to make an accurate estimation of the resources required to implement its world-wide system. Second, "Plastic" had to learn how to organize, staff, and operate a project on an international basis involving as it did so many countries, cultures, and time zones. If the project had been located within only a single country, it would have been considerably easier and routine in nature. Since it was international in scope, it became much more difficult because of the need to coordinate the activities of heretofore independently minded data processing professionals in several different countries.

As "Plastic" set about its task, it brought together the key IS professionals from around the world. A conscious strategy was devised to ensure a good balance of information systems technical skill combined with a strong knowledge of the business and its problems in each geographic location, thirteen in Europe alone.

After several brainstorming and problem-solving sessions, it was realized that the problem could be handled by an Electronic Document Interchange[9] (EDI) solution. The core IS management group then assigned the project to several teams, each one of which would then go to their respective geographical location and build the standard interfaces and transaction systems needed to handle the processing of orders and the other associated functions, particularly inventory control and management.

There were some very important advantages by adopting the strategy of interfacing each system to a common EDI standard rather than to other systems in the organization. The developmental work could be done with the local staff familiar with the system without having to coordinate with many overseas locations. In addition, since each machine was interfacing to a single standard, the interface problems were reduced in complexity to $n/(n^2 - n)$ where n is the number of different systems being connected together[10]. If several different systems are interfacing to a single standard, then new applications code will be required for n systems, where n is the number of different machine standards which must be adapted. However, if a machine-to-machine approach is used, then the number of specialized applications required to tie together the system increases very rapidly as given by $(n^2 - n)$. This represents the maximum amount of leverage obtained by having different machines interface to a common standard. If a few compatible machines are in the system, the problem becomes less difficult, although the number of locations keeps increasing.

The project was implemented over a period of one year, with project teams working at each of the key locations. The total project staff consisted of approximately thirty information systems and business function specialists.

Communication between the various work groups was difficult because of language barriers, as English was the second language in most cases. The groups were located around the world, spanning at least six major time zones. A rigorous project management approach was adopted so as to ensure frequent checkpoints in the systems development process. Local project plans were consolidated by the project coordinator and weekly reviews of progress were conducted via teleconference with all key personnel. Periodic teleconference sessions were also held to discuss requirements and design specifications. Furthermore, periodic face-to-face review sessions were held at key project milestones to review the status of the project and revise plans if necessary.

As this project was completed, several benefits to the organization became clear. The shipment and supply of the plastic products can now be processed centrally on a global basis. All relevant data is now available at any local data processing center. As a result, the largely independent sales force has found it much easier to conduct business, and the rapid accounting of sales gives "Plastic" much better warning when a "hot" product starts to emerge. In this case, a global business strategy required centralization of data processing.

Lessons Learned from "Plastic"

By all indications, the project was a success, and offers some lessons namely:

Interface to common standards: When tying together diverse information systems it is more efficient to have all machines interface to a common standard rather than attempting to build all of the different interfaces between each of the different information systems.

Maintain local ownership and pride: Allowing the information system employees at the remote locations in other countries to continue using their expertise on their systems was a morale booster compared to a strategy in which a centrally developed system is imposed uniformly upon the different locations scattered around the world.

Develop consensus: The project managers from the foreign locations were brought into the systems development process from the very beginning. After agreement was achieved regarding the design approach, these same people were sent back to their respective foreign installations to implement the system. Everyone felt they had an important impact on the design of the solution, and most did.

USING THE LEAST COMMON DENOMINATOR — "DRUG" (1988)

"Drug" Corporation is one of the largest and most successful pharmaceutical companies in the world. It has been elected as the "most admired" U.S. corporation several years in a row by leading U.S. business publications[11]. As a pharmaceutical company, "Drug" faces intense regulation in each market where it conducts business. Each country has a different and highly restrictive regime for managing the legal pharmaceutical trade in order to protect the public welfare, provide sufficient accountability for manufacture of pharmaceuticals, and to prohibit oligopolistic market practices. As a result, this regulatory environment strongly influences how business is conducted in each country, and also has a large effect on the nature of the information systems which are used. It means in practice that the data processing environment is virtually self-contained in each country. For most applications, this regulatory and business operations structure drives the information technology support system. According to "Drug", it has a "United Nations" type of organization in its information systems function — it has separate IS departments in each country and virtually no centralized applications.

In contrast to the extreme decentralization of computing facilities, "Drug" had a need to consolidate its financial position — sales volume, expenses, etc. — on a world-wide basis each month at headquarters. The United Nations model of data processing had optimal data processing in each country, but not for the corporation as a whole. As a result, the international financial consolidation process was essentially manual. The various subsidiaries around the world would create their local financial reports, then use facsimile to transmit these to headquarters. After the summary reports arrived, they would go through data-entry and consolidation. The format of the incoming reports was not entirely standard, thus producing a need for a great deal of manual accounting work at the headquarters. This process is called "closing the books".

In order to simplify this process, management decided to work towards building an information system which would link headquarters with all of the satellite locations. This would be done by uploading the reports from the field to headquarters through dedicated telecommunications linkages. A high level task force was appointed to solve this problem. After much study and more than one year, the team developed a way to solve the problem.

The proposed solution was highly complex because it called for creating a mainframe-based application at headquarters which would be capable of accommodating the many different incoming formats of each of the different subsidiaries reporting the financial data. It would require re-writing code at each location. Unfortunately this was beyond the capability of the number of team members they had allocated for this project. In addition, the particular solution which they had adopted would have required constant re-coding, and the number of programs would have proliferated. A project management team estimated that in order to create this system, it would have cost approximately $500,000 as a conservative estimate, and this was far beyond the budget allocation.

Another complication was that the subsidiary satellite locations did not all possess the same type of equipment. Some of the locations had IBM S/36's, others S/38's.

A new management team was brought in to assess the situation. The alternative solution developed was based on a spreadsheet type program which would work with a database application. Only 40 programs were required. They were written in RPG, and in any case were far less complex. This was a great simplification over the original plan which would have required more than 700 programs of much greater complexity.

This solution was based on the S/36 architecture, which was less advanced than the S/38[12], but was a common architecture to both. Programs and applications developed on the S/36 would run on the S/38, but not the other way around. The S/38 platform was more sophisticated, and ran better software. The S/36 was a common denominator amongst all of the platforms available. When this idea of using the common denominator came up, there were complaints that the solution would "not be using the full capabilities of the S/38." From the point of view of the locations which were operating S/38's, the solution being proposed was "running inferior software on a superior machine." On the surface, this appeared to be a waste of computing capacity, and it was; but only if measured at each separate location.

By using an application which was common to all of the machines, however "Drug" could radically reduce the amount of coding required to get the operation up and running. The simplicity of this solution quickly won out over other alternatives because it was less complex, required considerably less implementation time, and was easier to modify as would inevitably be required by changes taking place at the various satellite locations.

Lessons Learned From "Drug"?

This particular example provides some important lessons which might be learned:

The United Nations model may pose hidden dangers: The existence of different types of equipment in the various satellite IS installations complicated the optimum solution and ultimately resulted in some underutilization of some equipment (the S/38's) which had to interface to the "common denominator."

Use of a common denominator as a quick way to get compatibility: The solution of the S/36 for the base solution brought out an important strategy for coping with inherited incompatibility of equipment. Even though it was not the most advanced equipment available, the trade-off in performance was balanced against the need to write different types of code to accommodate the variety of equipment.

Global approaches may be technically feasible, but impossible in practice: The nature of the pharmaceutical trade, and the fact that it is so heavily regulated in each country is responsible for the persistence of the United Nations (polycentric) model in data processing. Testing and health data on individuals can generally not be removed from a country via transborder data flows without special permission from the host government. All pricing, sales and accounting data must be open to inspection at any time, and there are complex linkages which must be maintained with customers. None of these factors call for global data processing; in fact, they argue strongly against it.

FOREIGN ACQUISITION BRINGS NIGHTMARE TO INFORMATION SYSTEMS —"WHITE GOODS" (1989-1991)

The "White Goods" corporation is a leading manufacturer of major household appliances. Home laundry appliances account for 34% of net sales, home refrigeration and room air conditioning equipment 39%, and other household appliances make up the remaining 25% or so of the product mix. "White Goods" has minority interests in concerns making appliances in Mexico, Canada, and Brazil. In the past, the Canadian, Mexican, and Brazilian operations ran their own data centers autonomously. It also provides advice and assistance to foreign manufacturers for fees based on sales.

Most of "White Goods"'s domestic (U.S.-based) computing is centrally managed out of headquarters. Its systems handle manufacturing, sales, and engineering. All of the manufacturing plants located in different parts of the United States employ computer technology to receive and transmit information to and from the central site. The plant's computer equipment supports local manufacturing requirements including materials control, production scheduling, and inventory management. Manufacturing schedules are produced daily at the central site and downloaded to local computers nightly.

Engineering applications include computer aided design (CAD) technology which is located throughout the major domestic manufacturing plants and in the research and development centers.

In early 1989, "White Goods" greatly increased its international presence by acquiring 53% of a European appliances manufacturer. This acquisition was a complete surprise to the information systems department. In the past it had focused 100% of its attention on domestic issues. Now it was suddenly forced to become 100% international in its orientation. It is having to cope with an entirely new set of problems, and face issues which are changing its assumptions about how to plan, build, and operate information systems. Its assumptions about the past are of only minimal help in preparing for the new international challenges it must face.

The acquisition of the European manufacturer represented an increase of approximately fifty percent in revenues and geographical market area supplied by the company. The necessity to understand the European acquisition in terms of the evolving structure of information technology poses a challenge to management.

A Lesson in Fear

The acquisition literally sent shock waves through IS management as it was confronted with many unfamiliar international problems:

Uncertainty in working effectively with Europeans: The interviews revealed that the IS management team is worried about possible difficulties in working with Europeans. It has no skills or experience base in working closely with non-Americans. The deficit in knowledge makes matters worse, as it is unsure what types of managerial problems will be encountered and is thus unclear on how to prepare. The result will more than likely be a slow beginning in some areas.

How to wean the subsidiary away from its former parent company: The question of how the IS of the new company is going to be separated from its former parent and integrated into the "White Goods" system remains the most formidable challenge. It is difficult to dis-entangle the data processing requirements of its acquired European subsidiary from its former parent which operated fairly well integrated data processing systems.

Lead times in building telecommunications networks in Europe: "White Goods" is facing major difficulty adjusting to the telecommunications environment in Europe — an environment which is much more highly regulated than in the U.S. The types of services, the conditions under which those services might be purchased, and the general level of flexibility available to the IS function is highly variable from one country to another. Although "White Goods" realizes that learning to cope with this uncertainty is a critical skill, one would anticipate problems in getting efficient networks established.

Assessment of information technology requirements on an international basis: In planning its strategy, the "White Goods" IS management must conduct a world-wide inventory survey of its information technology base, but is unsure exactly how to make meaningful measurements. What are the most important aspects to measure, and how can one interpret the data which is obtained? Without this information, it will be impossible to begin the comprehensive planning process which will be required should IS attempt to integrate the European operations as closely into its data processing system as are its domestic U.S.-based manufacturing facilities.

Assumptions regarding the availability of technology must be re-examined at the international level: As part of its expansion overseas, "White

Goods" must be prepared to integrate a highly diverse technology base. It is clear that the management team which made the acquisition did not take into consideration the difficulties involved with integrating together the information systems based as they are on completely different mainframe technologies.

TECHNICAL BEAUTY, POLITICAL DISASTER —"LITTLE DRUG"

"Little Drug" is a worldwide health care company. Its product focus is in human pharmaceuticals, diagnostics and animal health. Backing all these businesses is a substantial research and development operation which is at work on the discovery, development and registration of tomorrow's medicines. Information technology is utilized and directed at a local level. The company has a decentralized philosophy. The headquarters is in the United States and the company maintains financial centers in Central America and the Caribbean. It has manufacturing and distribution facilities in Japan, and most countries of Western Europe. All is held together by a central holding company registered at an off-shore location. In addition, its family of companies also operate in many developing nations.

Many of the countries where "Little Drug" is operating its business do not have the level of investment in the country infrastructure found in developed countries. For example, electricity and phones do not work efficiently, the transportation networks are not as smooth, and the newest generations of information technology are slow to become available. As a result, technical support is hard to find.

Being relatively small, "Little Drug" did not have a sophisticated information system which linked together its different companies around the world. For international communication, it used telex and couriers to transmit the bulk of its information manufacturing, sales and profit data. As company sales continued to grow, the bureaucratic overhead of this arrangement was becoming unbearable and unworkable.

A corporate decision was taken to introduce a worldwide network to transmit messages among the companies in "Little Drug's" family. The selected platform was a Wang minicomputer using the Wang application product *Mailway* over dial-up public telephone lines. By the early 1980's, the systems were in place and attempts were made to introduce automatic transmission using all the features of the Mailway package. Although the system was operational at the functional level, the subsidiaries did not have access to an acceptable quality telecommunication system in all locations. Dial-up was unreliable, and relatively expensive. In addition, it was not transparent to the user and was difficult to use. The subsequent attempts to correct this situation and get a reliable system into production took a great deal of time on the part of the information systems planning group. Although this arrangement constituted a type of world-wide network it was unreliable. The user community began to bypass the network with courier services, telex and an accelerating use of facsimile machines.

Wang demonstrated a new turnkey applications package called *Office*, which could run on "Little Drug's" installed base of computer equipment and would have universal support. With more than 60 systems world-wide, this solution presented the type of low cost option that "Little Drug" had been seeking. The solution enabled the IS team to use X.25 public packet switched networks for its data communication system. This was to replace the dial-up networking which it had been using with decreasing returns. Public packet switched networks are available from the PTT organizations in each of the countries where "Little Drug" operates.

A Steering Committee was formed to oversee the launch, testing, financing and implementation of the project. In order to win top management approval of the new information system plan, a thorough presentation was developed for the corporate vice president and vice chairman of the main board of the central holding company. The multi-million dollar project won swift approval at corporate headquarters and the information systems team assumed that everything was in order to proceed.

As the system implementation phase was started, a pilot project was set up to verify the performance of all the technical elements of the system. A detailed implementation plan was prepared and the necessary equipment was received from the vendor to run the new network in readiness for the full system roll out.

Corporate money had set aside when top management joined in agreement with the plan to improve corporate information systems on a global scale. The critical barrier which ultimately proved to be the undoing of the entire plan turned out to be the country managers, who generally represented the most senior corporate officer in each country where the company does business. Getting the country managers to share the same vision proved to be a more challenging proposition. In spite of the funding commitment by the corporate levels, regional and local management led by the country managers were unwilling to spend their own resources on a "global" project. It took only a single rejection from one of the regional or country managers to quash the carefully laid plan and completely wreck the entire project, and this is exactly what happened. The entire plan was killed, and the company is still struggling to develop a global strategy.

Lessons Learned from "Little Drug"

This example represents the "worst case" possible in trying to put together a global information system. What was a technically beautiful solution turned into a political disaster which severely damaged the credibility of the corporate information systems department. This experience suggests the following lessons:

Assess the Political Power of the Different Players: The IS team failed to appreciate the political power of the country managers. The assumption that because there was corporate approval and support for the project it would automatically be approved was a serious error which led to a tremendous psychological blow when the plan was rejected. In addition, it does not appear that top management at corporate headquarters was willing to support IS on a "global basis. The information systems department did not read the signals well enough.

DECENTRALIZATION OF MANUFACTURING CALLS FOR RE-CENTRALIZATION OF COMPUTING —"COMPONENTS" (1985-1989)

"Components" is a manufacturer of parts for the automobile industry. One of its major customers is the "Car" Motor Company (See Case study 1). The interviews revealed that the information technology strategy of "Components" is driven first of all by its relationship with "Car" which is the dominating partner. "Components" is a large organization. It has approximately 130 manufacturing locations world-wide, each of which must be linked together into the information system.

In the 1980"s, "Car" developed a strategy to move towards using a single supplier in each market where it manufactured. As a result "Components" was forced into changing the way it did business. The information system which had coasted through the 1970's began to change rapidly.

Since "Car" was its main customer, it could almost dictate the terms of the business relationship. In the past, each of the foreign subsidiaries of "Car" had regularly placed orders with the nearest subsidiary of "Components". The new strategy of "Car" called for an arrangement which was much more centralized. "Car" now wanted a single world-wide point of contact for placing orders. In order to respond, "Components" began to develop an information system which would take orders for components at a single location, then auto-distribute the orders through its private telecommunications network to the appropriate manufacturing site at any one of the 130 locations around the world. The information technology infrastructure which supports this new strategy is based on the IBM AS/400 distributed processing system using IBM's software. There is a system of consolidation of orders at the top level of the corporation.

In the 1990's, the IS management team sees an even closer relationship between the customer and the supplier and a heightened degree of communications to support this strategy. This will imply a move towards global networking in order to make it easier to share engineering data — including CAD/CAM information — between different manufacturing locations of the firm and with its principal customer base. This will be particularly helpful because there is a tendency for parts and components being manufactured to be identical in many different locations of the world. Information systems management planning calls for financial, manufacturing and engineering data to be moved around the world in roughly equal proportions and expects that much will be done through networked engineering workstations.

The nature of the telecommunications network and data processing infrastructure will not be the same for all types of data. A work team within the information systems department estimated that it would require less effort and complexity to share financial data than to share manufacturing data which is more complex. Although it is therefore possible to centralize financial consolidation reporting, engineering data will be treated differently. It will be processed in three regional data processing locations; one in the U.S., one in Europe and one in the Far East — probably the Phillipeans.

"Components" has worked hard to develop a system which is reasonably consistent from country to country. But in so doing, it encountered several major problems the most serious of which appears to be the language barrier.

Unreadable system documentation: The volumes of systems documentation may not be understandable by less educated employees who do not have working knowledge of a foreign language. If the end-user interface for the information system is going to be made available throughout the 130 plant locations, spanning many different countries; then the multinational corporation must be able to deliver the translation of documentation into the different languages required. Either the vendor or the user must provide this information. However, for documentation of in-house applications, the vendor is not responsible and the translation and dissemination must be done in-house.

Urgent system error messages on the system may not be understood: This language problem becomes even more severe when we give consideration to a manufacturing environment. There, an urgent error message from the system must be immediately and clearly understood by the machine operator. To rely on the English comprehension of the overseas working population is not a viable course.

Even limited software programming and systems development using higher level languages may be beyond the capabilities of the local workers: Another related factor resulting from the language barrier is that the end-user programming advantages of object-oriented languages and 4GL's are negated by the inaccessibility of these programs in other languages. The effect of this is to shift more strain to the programming staff than would normally be the case in an English-speaking environment.

"Components" is moving towards an infrastructure which is both centralized and decentralized. Surprisingly, it has tended to decentralize financial control under an umbrella of centralized financial consolidation. Decisions about the utilization of software have also been decentralized. However, it has attempted to tie together its manufacturing control into a centralized system which is driven by orders coming from customers.

As it moves towards its current strategy, the IS management team says that the transition towards global coordination of their 130 plants world-wide did not cause resistance on the part of the local IT executives "because it was handled correctly". As the system was rolled out, the various European IT executives were brought fully into the process and shown the advantages of moving towards a common type of system.

Lessons Learned from "Components"

Telecommunications continues to be a major problem (as of late 1990): The IT management team reported that it "can't get decent communications". There are problems with high cost, delays, and quality of the telecommunications circuits which are used. Western Europe is particularly difficult in this regard. For example, "Components" has a design center in Germany, and a manufacturing plant in Spain. There is still after more than two years of attempts at getting service no telecommunications network available which enables these two locations to be efficiently connected.

Europe may face a critical skills shortage: In spite of the excitement in Europe arising from the prospects of a common market by "1992", not all of the countries of Europe have an adequate skill base for information technology, particularly Portugal. The "Components" IS management does not believe that the transition to a Pan-European market will be "as easy as it says in the press". In addition, there are fears the "open market" will actually turn out to be a "closed club" reserved for European corporations, with restrictions against non-Europeans remaining in place (particularly against the Japanese).

The entire global information technology strategy can be driven by your customers: Although within "Components", the IS function is leading the transformation of the corporation; this is being driven by the information technology interface requirements of "Car", the largest and most powerful customer. Whether they like it or not, there is no choice but to respond to the demands of the customer base, even if the demands are concerning information technology.

International telecommunications are still a major headache, even in developed countries: It is a surprise that even in developed countries, such as those of Western Europe, Components is encountering severe problems which in some cases are more severe than found in developing countries. The types of problems encountered involve availability of leased lines, unstable tariff problems, complex and lengthy approval processes, restrictive licensing and interconnection equipment certification processes, and other generally restrictive administrative practices. Once approvals are finally achieved, the major difficulty remains delays in getting the service installed in a reasonable period of time.

Building a central order processing center may have advantages for world-wide management of production: There may be a lesson in "Component's" effort to build a single order point for its entire world-wide operation. Labor and bureaucratic effort will be reduced, and the coordination for manufacturing, inventory control, and related functions will become more efficient.

Language can be a significant problem in international manufacturing Systems: If a multinational corporations is involved in manufacturing in a significant number of countries, it must inevitably cope with the need to generate factory-floor intelligibility of information technology and information systems at the lowest levels. Otherwise, the average worker will not be able to read the messages on the information system. Although many of the information systems professionals in the organization may have a working knowledge of a foreign language, such as English, in which most documentation is prepared, this is not true for the average worker. The workers on the manufacturing floor rarely excel at foreign languages. Any global system may have significant parts of its database or other critical functions centralized, however, its user interfaces must be decentralized and multi-lingualized.

CONCLUSIONS

The international environment provides some very different challenges from the domestic one. Systems development efforts which might be relatively simple within a country can turn into cultural, administrative, and logistical nightmares when attempted internationally. In addition, there is the omnipresent "political" factor — IS must be constantly on the look-out for the strong country manager or other corporate actor who can strangle off "global" developments with the flick of a pen. Finally, there is the technical and operational complexity of it all: getting international computer communications systems up and running can be a much stiffer challenge because of the "Tower-of-Babel" effect of different protocols, standards, and software interfaces.

The successful international systems development efforts appear to be those which bring in national managers from each location involved, aim for relatively simple solutions, and strive to make significant but not revolutionary changes.

    In the end, it is clearly the business strategy of the multinational corporation which determines the challenge to IS, driven as it is by external factors found in each host country. Although IS has come onto the scene relatively late, the effective CIO constantly seeks to shape his priorities for systems development by keeping a close watch on the international business strategy.

SUMMARY OF LESSONS LEARNED

	"Car"	"Tobacco"	"Plastic"	"Drug"	"White Goods"	"Little Drug"	"Components"
Global strategy means centralized IS	•						•
Balance national and global interests	•	•	•			•	
Economies of scale in data processing	•						
Language Barriers hinder operations		•					•
Availability of vendor support	•	•			•		•
Cultural problems in the host country		•			•		•
Inadequate host country infrastructure		•			•	•	
Host country tax regime		•					
International cost justification techniques		•			•		
Skill shortages overseas		•					•
IS strategy driven by business strategy	•	•	•				•
International standards			•	•			
Difficulties of the U.N. model			•	•		•	•
Host country legal regime				•			
Merger Acquisition		•			•		
International telecommunications					•		•

References

Aronson, J.D., & P.F. (1988). *Cowhey When Countries Talk: International Trade in Telecommunications Services.* Cambridge, Massachusetts: Ballinger Publishing Company.

Bartlett, C.A., & Sumantra, G. (Fall, 1988). Organizing for Worldwide Effectiveness: The Transnational Solution. *California Management Review,* 54-74.

Bartlett, C.A., & Sumantra, G. (Summer, 1987). Managing Across Borders: New Strategic Requirements. *Sloan Management Review.*

Bartlett, C.A., & Sumantra, G. (November-December, 1986). Tap Your Subsidiaries for Global Reach. *Harvard Business Review.*

Behrman, J.N. (March-April, 1969). Multinational Corporations, Transnational Interests and National Sovereignty. *Columbia Journal of World Business.*

Boddewyn, J.J., Marsha Baldwin Halbrich, & Perry, A.C. (Fall, 1986). Service Multinationals: Conceptualization, Measurement and Theory. *Journal of International Business Studies,* 41-57.

Chakravarthy, B.S., & Perlmutter, H.V. (Summer, 1985). Strategic Planning for a Global Business. *Columbia Journal of World Business.*

Doz, Y. (Fall, 1980). Multinational Strategy and Structure in Government Controlled Businesses. *Columbia Journal of World Business.*

Dunning, J.H. (Ed.) *Multinational Enterprises, Economic Structure and International Competitiveness.* John Wiley & Sons, New York: 1985); see also The Multinational Enterprise (George Allen & Unwin Ltd, London: 1971)

Dunning, J.H., & Norman, G. (1983). The Theory of the Multinational Enterprise: An Application to Multinational Office location. *Environment and Planning A,* 675-692.

Feketekuty, G. (1988). *International Trade in Services.* Cambridge, Massachusetts: Ballinger Publishing Company.

Ghoshal, S. (1987). Global Strategy: An Organizing Framework. *Strategic Management Journal,* 8, 425-440.

Hamelink, C.J. (1984). *Transnational Data Flows in the Information Age.* (Lund: Student litterateur,) Edited by Transnational Data Reporting Service, Amsterdam.

Jussawalla, M., & Chee-Wah Cheah. (1987). *The Calculus of International Communications: A Study in the Political Economy of Transborder Data Flows.* Littleton, Colorado: Libraries Unlimited, Inc.

Herman, B., & van Holst, B. (1984). *International Trade in Services: Some Theoretical and Practical Problems.* Rotterdam: Netherlands Economic Institute.

Katzan, H.S., Jr. (1980). *Multinational Computer Systems: An Introduction to Transnational Data Flow and Data Regulation.* New York: Van Nostrand Reinhold Company.

Al-Muhanna, I.A. (1987). *The World System in Transition: Information Technology and Transnational Banking.* Doctoral Thesis, The American University.

Nanus, B. (November-December, 1969). The Multinational Computer. *Columbia Journal of World Business.*

Nanus, B. (Spring, 1978). Business, Government and the Multinational Computer. *Columbia Journal of World Business*, 19-26.

Negandhi, A.R. (Fall, 1983). Cross-Cultural Management research: Trend and Future Directions. *Journal of International Business Studies.*

Novotny, E.J. (1985). *Transborder Data Flows and World Public Order: Law and Policy Problems in Controlling Global Computer Communication Technology.* Doctoral Thesis in Government. Georgetown University.

Perlmutter, H.V. (January-February, 1969). The Tortuous Evolution of the Multinational Corporation. *Columbia Journal of World Business.*

Roche, E.M. The Computer Communications Lobby, the U.S. Department of State Working Group on Transborder Data Flows and Adoption of the O.E.C.D. Guidelines on the Protection of Privacy and Transborder Data Flows of Personal Data. Doctoral Thesis, Columbia University, 1987; "Knowledge-Processing Technologies and the Global Strategies of Transnational Corporations: Issues for Developing Countries." In Teng, Weizao & N.T. Wang *Transnational Corporations and China's Open Door Policy* (Lexington, Massachusetts: Lexington Books, 1988); "Managing Information Technology in Multinational Corporations" Working paper. MIS Department, The University of Arizona, 1990.

Roos. (1990). *The Machine That Changes The World.* Cambridge, MIT Press.

Sambharya, Rakeshkumar Bi *The Impact of Transborder Data Flows on the Strategy and Operations of U.S. Based Multinational Corporations.* Doctoral Thesis, Temple University, 1987.

Samiee, S. (Spring-Summer, 1984). Transnational Data Flow Constraints: A New Challenge for Multinational Corporations. *Journal of International Business Studies.*

Samiee, S. (Winter, 1983). Developments in Transnational Data Flows: Regulations and Perspectives. *Journal of International Business Studies*, 159-162.

Sauvant, K.P. (Spring, 1983). Transborder Data Flows and the Developing Countries. *International Organization*, 359-371.

United States Trade Representative. (1982). *Trade Barriers to Telecommunications, Data and Information Services.* Washington: No Pub.

Endnotes

[1]The only major area where national regulations play such a direct role is in transborder data flow (Roche, 1987,88; Novotney,1985; Katzan, 1980; Jussawalla, 1987; Hamelink, 1984; Sambharya, 1987) controls over importation and registration of computer equipment (USTR, 1982) and in administrative regulations involving database maintenance. These regulations may be particularly important in trade in services (Sauvant, 1983; Al-Muhanna, 1987; Feketekuty, 1988; Aronson,

1988; Samiee, 1983, 84; Boddewyn, 1986; Herman, 1984), but they have not amounted to much more than a nuisance in most cases.

[2]The nation state which wishes to control a business can do so much more directly to exercise policy than through indirect control over data processing.

[3]I owe a debt to Mr. Brad Power of the Index Group for use of this term. Polycentric comes from Perlmutter

[4]Whether or not this is an optimal solution depends upon the nature of the business of the MNC.

[5]In addition, many countries used a variety of means to encourage all data processing be done within their national borders.

[6]It is based on interviews conducted with various information systems professionals in the companies studies who are involved in building international systems and on notes and survey responses prepared by the corporations in preparation for the interviews. The names of the companies have been withheld.

[7]PROFS is the Professional Office System provided by IBM corporation. It runs on IBM mainframes and minicomputers equipment and provides services for the office such as electronic mail, file editing, calendar service, word processing, etc.

[8]The plastic injection molds are complex pieces of industrial equipment weighing thousands of pounds.

[9]Using Electronic Document Interchange (EDI) companies build inter-organizations systems to electronically transmit documents which in the past were handled manually. Examples of such documents include: purchase orders, purchase order acknowledgements, invoices, functional acknowledgements, freight details and invoices, plan schedules with releases, status details reply, shipment information, acceptance/rejection advice, commercial invoices, etc. For more details see Roche, 1991.

[10]If several different systems are interfacing to a single standard, then new applications code will be required for n systems, where n is the number of different machine standards which must be adapted. However, if a machine-to-machine approach is used, then the number of specialized applications required to tie together the system increases very rapidly as given by (n^2-n). This represents the maximum amount of leverage obtained by having different machines interface to a common standard. If a few compatible machines are in the system, the problem becomes less difficult, although the number of locations keeps increasing.

[11]The name of this and other cases herein are omitted.

[12]The System 38, made by IBM, represents an advancement over the System 36 which, although not as advanced, is upwardly compatible in many respects. Most of these series have been replaced by the ES/9000 seris.

GLOSSARY

Absorptive Strategy: *A Strategy for acquisition of technology, which involves initial participation of a foreign partner either through joint ventures or direct investment, with the degree of foreign investment phased out over time.*

Analog: *Pertaining to data in the form of continuously variable physical quantities.*

Analysis: *The systematic investigation of a problem and the separation of the problem into smaller interrelated units for further detailed study.*

ARCNET: *A set of protocols developed by Datapoint Corporation to facilitate communication across different hardware devices.*

Broadcast: *The simultaneous transmission to a number of stations.*

CDoT: *In India, the Center for Development of Telematics.*

Coding: *The process of translating systems specifications into actual programs in the computer system. Also, the process of modifying computer programs to meet custom specifications.*

Common Denominator: *The highest standard for operating systems or architecture which is compatible with all of the systems throughout the organization.*

Competitive Advantage: *Superior market share, sales growth, or financial performance relative to competitors.*

Computer Aided Design (CAD): *The use of computers in the design, modeling and drafting process for creating specifications for manufacturing of goods.*

Computer Network: *A group of interconnected computers and/or peripheral devices that allows data to be transmitted from one of the devices to another. The network may be local within an office, building, or adjacent group of buildings or it may encompass a wide geogrphic area. Examples of local area networks (LANs) are ARCNET and EtherNet. Examples of wide area networks (WANs) are BITNET, INTERNET, TELENET, SWIFT, EURONET, and COMSHARE.*

Concentrator: *(1) In data transmission, a functional unit that permits a common transmission medium to serve more data sources than there are channels currently available within the transmission medium. (2) Any device that combines incoming messages into a single message (concentration) or extracts individual messages from the data sent in a single transmission sequence (deconcentration).*

Crossbar Switch: *A relay-operated device that makes a connection between one line in each of two sets of lines. The two sets are physically arranged along adjacent sides of a matrix of contacts or switch points.*

Data Architecture: *The design and relationship among an organization's databases.*

Distributed Processing: *A family of computer architectures in which access to files and databases is available through different computers located apart from one another.*

Doordarshan: *India's government-owned television broadcasting serivce.*

Earth Station: *The ground based unit used to transmit and/or receive communication signals from a satellite.*

Economic Evaluation of IT: *An assessment of the efficiency and costs with which information technology activities are conducted.*

Electronic Document Interchange (EDI): *The substitution of electronic messages for standardized commercial documentation so as to eliminate the need for actual physical copies of the documents.*

Ethnocentric Systems: *Computer systems which support a multinational cor-*

poration that is dominated by a particular ethnic or cultural style in its operations and organization.

***Europe 1992**—The year when the member nations of the European Community will implement the 279 actions needed to bring about a single internal European Market for its members.*

***Exchange:** A room or building equipped so that telecommunications lines terminated there may be interconnected as required. The equipment may include manual or automatic switching equipment.*

***Facsimile Machine:** A machine that scans a sheet of paper and converts the light and dark areas to electrical signals that can be transmitted over telephone lines.*

***File Locking:** An event in database updating when access to a file is prevented for more than a single function at a time.*

***Foreign Direct Investment (FDI):** The form of equity participation used by a multinational corporation to set up operations and business in a foreign country.*

***Fourth-Generations Languages (4GL's):** Applications packages which are easy enough to use so that average information workers can make reasonably complex queries into a corporate database.*

***GIO (Global Information Officer):** A CIO of a multinational corporation who is responsible for IT issues on a global level.*

***Global Enterprise:** Any organization that centrally controls its foreign subsidiaries' activities from its headquarters so that the entire business enterprise achieves economies of scale and cost efficiencies.*

***Global Systems:** International computing systems that support a business strategy by the multinational corporation that treats the entire world as a single marketplace, rather than as a series of individual markets.*

***GNP:** Gross National Product, the most popular measure of a country's economical performance.*

***Graphical User Interface:** A visual interface, typically using a mouse for input. Contrasted with the text-based interface of DOS. GUI examples include the Macintosh Operating System, Windows, and OS/2 Presentation Manager.*

Harmattan: *Cold, dry wind from the north that blows in West Africa from December to March.*

Hausa: *Chief language spoken in northern Nigeria, also popular in Niger, Benin and Cameroon.*

Host Country: *The foreign country that allows a multinational corporation to conduct business within its national borders.*

IIP: *Intergovernmental Informatics Program established by UNESCO with the aim of solving some problems of disparity in the development of Informatics around the world.*

Information Resource Management: *The economical and efficient management, servicing, and support of all information that is of value to the organization.*

Information Services Professional: *Cross-trained, highly-integrated staffs of information technology professionals that act as facilitators, catalysts for change, standards monitors, and resource managers for complex, user-driven and controlled, information storage/delivery systems.*

Information Systems Strategic Assessment: *That portion of the information technology planning process that evaluates the relative imporance and value-added contribution of factors including the size of information technology facilities, the ease of transferring knowledge from providers to users in multiple sites, local environmental conditions (e.g. legal, cultural, and human resources), and the approximate location of linked activities.*

Information Technology Architecture: *A blueprint for network, application, and data structures and interrelationships.*

Information Utility: *Within any organization, the information utility includes all those resources, services, and facilities that comprise, process, and deliver information to the end user.*

Information Workers: *(General)— Any employee of a firm who is not engaged directly for manual labor. (Specific)— Non-manual labor and non-top management workers in the firm who are responsible for the bureaucracy of the organization.*

Informatization: *A term used in Soviet Bloc governments which means the effort to introduce information technology.*

INRs: Indian Rupees, the currency of India.

INSAT: Indian national satellite.

Insular: Having a restricted or isolated natural range or a narrow provincial viewpoint.

Integrated Services Digital Network (ISDN): A telecommunications standard that divides a circuit into several different digital channels. For example, a regular telephone line can have two voice channels and a data channel over the same wires which in the past only carried a single voice channel.

International Business: Any organization that has one or more activities that cross international borders.

International Subscriber Dialing (ISD): In India, international direct dialing service available to subscribers.

Interconnection Equipment Certification: The process of getting official approval from telecommunications authorities in foreign countries to the effect that equipment can be interconnected directly into the telecommunications network without harming the network itself.

International Systems: Information systems which link together businesses across national borders.

Lagos: The capital of Nigeria, located at the Gulf of Guinea coast, having a population of approximately 3 million.

Lead System: The use of the project teams that have the greatest expertise relative to specific problems being considered, regardless of where in the geographic scope of the organization they come from.

League of Nations: The international organization responsible for international peace and security which existed prior to the United Nations, before the second World War.

Leased Lines: Telecommunications linkages which are purchased from the telecommunications authority and dedicated solely to the use of the leasing corporation.

Local Area Network: A network of computers that communicate with each other, typically in close proximity but in any case over distances less than one mile.

Locus of information technology management: *The relative power exercised by information technology management of corporate headquarters and subsidiary organizations.*

Mean Time Between Failure: *The average time that a device operates without failure.*

Micro-Processors: *An integrated circuit that accepts coded instructions for execution. The instructions may be entered, integrated, or stored internally.*

Microwave Radio: *Radio transmissions in the 4 to 28 gHz range. Microwave radio transmissions require that the transmitting and receiving antennas be within sight of each other.*

Modulation: *The process of varying some characteristic of one wave in accordance with another wave or signal.*

Multi-Access Rural Radio (MARR): *A radio system particularly useful in rural areas. The long distance public telephone (LDPT) can be installed as a terminal in the MARR rural radio circuits, thus providing communications service to more than one user.*

Multi-Lingualization: *The process of insuring that systems documentation and display of information and data on the computer screen is in the native language of the foreign information worker.*

Multinational Corporation: *A form of business organization in which its owned assets are located in more than one country.*

NEPA: *Nigerian Electrical Power Authority, a state-owned company and sole producer and distributor of electric power in Nigeria.*

NICNET: *In India, a nationwide satellite-based two way data communication network, developed by India's National Informatics Center. It links the various central and state government offices across the country.*

Niger State: *One of the 19 Nigerian states, located near the geographical center of Nigeria. Easily confused with Niger an independent country, sharing its southern border with Nigeria.*

Novell: *A software company; one of the leaders in the field of providing* *software for local area networks.*

Off Shore Locations*: Usually small countries, located away from the major developed nations, and having liberal tax and regulatory requirements for corporate financial reporting, thus providing a convenient location for incorporation.*

Organization of Petroleum Exporting Countries (OPEC)*: A cartel formed by the thirteen major petroleum-producing and exporrting countries for the purpose of controlling supply and world market prices, and advancing members' interests in trade and development dealings with industrialized oil-consuming nations. The member countries are Saudi Arabia, Kuwait, Libya, Iran, Iraq, Venezuela, Ecuador, Algeria, Gabon, Nigeria, Qatar, the United Arab Emirates, and Indonesia.*

Open Skies Policy: *No limitations on the fundamental right of sovereign nations to acquire data from space.*

Optical Fiber: *A communications medium made of very thin glass or plastic fiber that conducts light waves.*

Organizational Complexity: *A measure of the number of intra-organizational linkages. A simple structure has relatively few intra-organizational linkages, a more complex structure has many.*

Organizational Linkages: *The design of the subsidiary IS organizational structure, control systems, and reporting procedures as well as the subsidiary's participation in the functions of the corporation as a whole.*

Point-to-Point Circuit: *A circuit connecting two nodes as contrast and with a multipoint circuit.*

Polycentric Systems: *Information systems in multinational corporations in which many different semi-autonomous data processing installations support business operations in each country.*

Postal, Telephone and Telegraph (PTT): *The state-owned telecommunications monopoly present in most countries and responsible for provision of all telecommunications services. In some countries (U.S., U.K., Japan) the PTT's are becoming privatized.*

Presentation Graphics: *Pictorial aids that are usually viewed in groups. Typically includes transparencies and color slides, but the current emphasis is on computer-generated graphics files.*

Regiocentric Systems: *Information systems which support the activities of the multinational corporation in several countries of a region of the world. For example, a company may do business in many countries of Europe, but operate a single regional data processing center in either London or Brussels.*

Remote Sensing: *The detection, recording, and analysis of electromagnetic radiation.*

S-band: *Radio transmissions band in the 2 and 4 range.*

Satellite Locations: *Locations in the multinational corporation which are not in the country where the headquarters of the corporation is incorporated.*

Special Telecommunications Action for Regional Development (STAR): *A program designed to develop the infrastructure for telecommunications of Ireland, Greece, Portugal, and Spain.*

Strowger Switch: *A step-by-step switch named after its inventor, Almon B. Strowger.*

Switching Exchange: *An exchange that terminates multiple circuits. It is capable of interconnecting circuits or transferring traffic between circuits.*

System Documentation: *Books provided by either the hardware or software vendor which contain instructions on how to use the product.*

Tariff (telecommunications): *The published rate for a specific unit of equipment, facility, or type of service provided by a telecommunications carrier. Also, the vehicle by which regulating agencies approve or disapprove such facilities or services. Thus, the tariff becomes a contact between the customer and the telecommunications facility.*

Techno-nationalism: *The movement to develop and nationalize discrete information industries.*

Trade in Services: *International trade in non-manufactured items. Examples include banking, insurance, consulting, legal services, advertising, data and information services, etc.*

Transborder Data Flow (TDF or TBDF): *International telecommunication of computer generated data, including personal information, across international borders.*

Transfer Network: *The lines of communication and diffusion corresponding to the paths that the technology (data, equipment, training, etc.) take as it is disseminated.*

Transnational Enterprise: *Any enterprise that transfers product, capital, and knowledge between its central organization and foreign subsidiaries, and facilitates such transfers among subsidiaries, to create a competitive advantage in any of its markets from any combination of resources in the eneterprise system.*

Transnational Interactions: *The movement of tangible or intangible items across national boundaries when at least one actor is not an agent of a government or an international organization.*

Transnational Systems: *International computer systems which operate without reference to national borders.*

Transponder: *(1) (Rader)—A receiver-transmitter facility, the function of which is to transmit signals automatically when the proper interrogation is received. (2) (Communication satellite)—A receiver-tranmitter combination, often aboard a satellite, or spacecraft, which receives a signal and retransmits it at a different carrier frequency. Transponders are used in communications satellites for reradiating signals to earth stations or in spacecraft for returning ranging signals.*

Turnkey Applications Package: *Computer software that provides a complete solution to a business problem or need without any major modification to fit the needs of the business in which it is being used.*

UNESCO: *United Nations Educational, Scientific and Cultural Organization, one of the United Nations-sponsored organizations with headquarters in Paris.*

United Nations Model *(See Polycentric Systems): A form of business organization in which the entire operation structure, including all functions, are replicated in each country in which it conducts business. For data processing, a complete computer data center is created in each country in which the firm operates.*

X.25 Networking: *A telecommunications standard accepted by the International Telecommunications Union which enables transmission over packet switched networks.*

AUTHORS

Maryam Alavi is an Associate Professor of Information Systems at the College of Business and Management, University of Maryland at College Park. Her areas of expertise include decision support systems, end-user computing, system development teams, and information technology strategies.

George Ballester is a Senior Systems Analyst at the Boston Company and a part-time lecturer in MIS at Northeastern University.

William B. Carper is Associate Dean of the School of Business at Georgia Southern University in Statesboro where he teaches in the areas of Strategic Management, Social Issues, and Information Systems. His recent research has focused on a variety of strategy related issues including mergers and acquisitions and on the social impacts of information technology. Professor Carper has authored more than two dozen scholarly papers which have been presented at various professional meetings or published in such journals as the *Academy of Management Journal and Review, Business Horizons,* and the *Journal of Management.*

Elia V. Chepaitis is an Associate Professor of Information Systems at Fairfield University and a consultant in New Haven, Connecticut. She specializes in global information resource management and medical systems. Her research focuses on computer technology transfers and developmental issues in the Third World and in Eastern Europe. Her work appears in *International Science and Technology: Philosophy, Theory and Policy,* in the proceedings of numerous international conferences, *Fairfield, Business Review, Interface,* and *Managing Microcomputer Technology as an Organizational Resource.*

Roger Clarke is Reader in Information Systems in the Department of Commerce at the Australian National University. Prior to taking up that appointment, he spent 17 years in professional, managerial and consulting positions in the information technology industry, in Sydney, London and Zürich. His research and consulting interests are in application software technology and its management; economic and legal aspects of information technology; and information privacy and data surveillance.

Gordon B. Davis is Honeywell Professor of Management Information Systems, an endowed professorship in the Graduate School of Management, University of Minnesota. He is a pioneer in management information systems research and education. Professor Davis is the author of fifteen texts and numerous articles in management information systems, data processing, programming, and EDP auditing. His international activities have included seminars in all parts of the world. He serves as the USA representative to and Chairman of Technical Committee 8, Information Systems, of the International Federation for Information Processing. From July 1986 to September 1987, he was the first Shaw Professor of Information Systems and Computer Science at the National University of Singapore.

Persio DeLuca is one of the partners responsible for the Business Systems Consulting Practice of Arthur Andersen in Brazil. He has worked in the Management Information Consulting Division of Arthur Andersen since 1971, and has been responsible for the division in Sao Paulo and subsequently for Brazil, for the last 6 years. During his career, he has been directly responsible for the design and implementation of a variety of business information systems involving EDI.

Krishna S. Dhir is a Professor of Business Administration at The Citadel, and a Professor of Health Services Administration at The Medical University of South Carolina, both in Charleston, South Carolina. Previously he was Head of the Department of Business Administration at The Citadel, Director of the M.I.M. degree program at the University of Denver, advisor to the top management of the Pharmaceutical Division of CIBA-GEIGY AG in Balse, Switzerland, and the manager of a pilot plant at Borg-Warner Chemicals' International Division in Parkersburg, West Virginia. Dr.Dhir received his D.B.A. in Management Science and Administrative Policy from the University of Colorado, M.B.A. from the University of Hawaii, M.S. in Chemical Engineering and Physiology from Michigan State University and B. Tech. in Chemical Engineering from the Indian Institute of Technology, Bombay. He is a member of the Decision Sciences Institute, Academy of Management, Academy of International Business, Pan Pacific Business Association, and the Indian Institution of Industrial Engineering.

A. Lee Gilbert began his information systems practice for Marathon Oil in 1960, and has since consulted to governments and corporations in North America, Europe, the Middle East and Asia. From 1982 through 1986, he directed executive education programs for the Institute of Systems Science at the National University of Singapore. Selected as 1987-88 Harvard Business School Information Systems Fellow, he has also developed and taught management courses at Babson and Linfield Colleges and the

University of Oregon. He serves the United Nations Secretariat as its Regional Advisor for Technology Transfer and Development in the Asia-Pacific region, based in Bangkok.

Ernie P. Goss is Associate Professor of Management Information Systems at the University of Southern Mississippi. Prior to his current position, he taught at the University of Alabama in Huntsville, where he also served as Chairman of the Department of Management Information Systems. He received his Ph.D in economics from the University of Tennessee. In addition to numerous journal publications and consulting assignments, Dr. Goss is completing a book on Database Management and Spreadsheet Applications Development.

Joze Griçar is Professor of Management Information Systems at the University of Maribor's School of Organisational Sciences in Yugoslavia. His Masters degree in Business and Ph.D. in Information Systems are from the University of Ljubljana. He teaches in systems engineering, information systems development and management of information systems. The areas of his current research are systems re-engineering, inter-organisational systems and EDI, and executive information systems.

Takeshi Imai is Executive Director of the Intelligence Engineering Association, and is based in Tokyo.

Tom Iverson is an Associate Professor of Management at the University of Guam. He was previously an associate professor of public administration at Kentucky State University and has taught at Midwestern State University (Texas), the University of Texas, and Hawaii Loa College. He has worked in the public sector as a research analyst, a manpower planner, and an employment and training project coordinator. Since 1988 he has served as CEO of the consulting firm Tom Iverson and Associates, with projects on the islands of Truk, Majuro, Palau, and Guam. Dr. Iverson's current research interests include executive information systems, economic development strategies, technology transfer and labor force analysis.

Leon J. Janczewski has 25 years of experience in the computer/information systems field in the roles of hardware designer, computer system analyst, large computer installation manager, and managerial consultant. His senior positions include serving as director of the largest IBM installation in Poland and supervising the design of the first computer center in the Niger State of Nigeria. Janczewski has taught numerous computer science and information system courses at the University of Toronto, Technical University of Warsaw and Economical Academy in Warsaw.

Jerry Kanter is the Director of Babson College's Center for Information Management Studies, a cooperative effort of business and academia to improve the use of information systems. Prior to starting the center, Mr. Kanter served in a variety of information systems management and technical positions with the Honeywell Company in Boston and with the Kroger Company in Cincinnati. His most recent position was as a consultant where he specialized in systems planning, end-user computing, and organizational issues. Prentice-Hall has published five of his books, the latest being Computer Essays for Management in 1987. He has also written many articles for professional journals and has lectured at Harvard, Dartmouth, Baylor, Northwestern, Oxford (UK), and Cambridge (UK).

Asterios G. Kefalas, Professor of Management, The University of Georgia, earned an undergraduate degree in Greece and a graduate degree at the University of Hamburg, West Germany, and his Doctor of Philosophy in Business Administration at the University of Iowa. He has co-authored *Management Systems: Conceptual Considerations; Management: Making Organization Perform;* and *Management: Book of Readings.* He has also participated in the writing of several reports, including Goals for Global Societies: A Report to the Club of Rome (Chapter 10 - Goals for Multinational Corporations), and World Order Studies, Reshaping the International Order (RIO) Foundation, the Netherlands. His most recent books are: *Global Business Strategy: A Systems Approach and Management Systems: Conceptual Considerations, 4th Edition.*

Richard M. Kesner currently serves as Chief Information Officer for Babson College, Wellesley, Massachusetts, where he is responsible for all aspects of the College's use of information technologies. He is also President and Senior Consultant for RMK Associates, Inc., a management, strategic planning, and MIS consulting firm. Prior to forming RMK Associates, Richard Kesner served as the Vice President of Development and Systems for the Parkman Companies, a diversified real estate development and management company. He also spent nearly four years as the Vice President of General Services and MIS for Multibank Financial Corporation, a $2.3 Billion bank headquartered in Dedham, Massachusetts.

William R. King is University Professor in the Katz Graduate School of Business (KGSB) at the University of Pittsburgh. He is the author of more than a dozen books and 150 technical papers that have appeared in the leading journals in the fields of management science, information systems and strategic planning. Dr. King is past-president of the Institute of Management Sciences (TIMS) and was the Senior Editor of the *MIS Quarterly.*

Edmund Marcarelli is an Assistant Vice President in the Custody Systems Department at the Boston Company.

Donald J. McCubbrey is Chair of the Department of Management Information Systems in the Graduate School of Business at the University of Denver. From 1957 until 1983 he worked in the Management Information Systems Consulting Division of Arthur Andersen & Co. At various times, he was Director of Consulting Practice in several U.S. and Canadian offices, and regional Partner-in-Charge of Consulting in Colombia, Ecuador, Mexico, Peru and Venezuela. Since joining the University of Denver in 1984, his research interests have included international MIS issues, the use of IS for competitive advantage, creativity in systems analysis and design, and inter-organisational systems. He is co-author of a text-book, and an associate editor of the *Journal of Information Systems.*

F. Warren McFarlan is the Ross Graham Walker Professor of Business Administration at the Harvard Business School whose faculty he has been on since 1964. He has published a number of books and articles in the field of information technology, most recently focusing on the competitive uses of information technology and the management problems which must be addressed if success is to be achieved. He is a member of several corporate and non-profit boards of directors and is currently on the executive committee of the Society of Information Management (SIM).

Timothy S. Mescon is Dean of the School of Business Administration at Kennesaw State College. Dr. Mescon is the author of more then seventy-five articles and cases, and a graduate text in Strategic Management by Harper & Row. Dr. Mescon is a contributing editor to Delta Airlines' *Sky Magazine*, where his management column is read by more than twenty-five million readers yearly. His second book, a collection of the *Sky* articles, coupled with essays by CEOs from around the world, was recently published by Peachtree Publishers.

Josephine E. Olson is Associate Professor of Business Administration and of Economics at the Joseph M. Katz Graduate School of Business at the University of Pittsburgh, where she teaches course in international economics and international business as well as macroeconomics. Prior to moving to Pittsburgh, she taught in the Department of Economics and Finance at the Bernard M. Baruch College of the City University of New York. She also worked briefly for the Federal Reserve Bank of New York and the U.S. Interstate Commerce Commission. Dr. Olson has an A.B. from Wellesley College and a Ph.D. in economics from Brown University. Her research has focused on economic regulation, various aspects of international economics, and human capital economics.

Prashant C. Palvia is Associate Professor of Management Information Systems in the Department of Management Information Systems and Decision Sciences at Memphis State University. Previously, he spent 9 years in industry. His research interests include international information systems, strategic information systems, database design, software engineering, SDLC Methods, and MIS in small business. He has published in several journals including *Decision Sciences, ACM Transactions on Database Systems, Information and Management, Information Resources Management Journal, Information Systems, Interface,* and *Information Sciences.*

Shailendra Palvia is Assistant Professor of Information Systems at Babson College in Wellesley, MA. He also taught at Kent State University for two years. He has been in industry for twelve years with the Federal Reserve Bank, Hennepin County, Control Data Corporation, and IBM. His research interests include implementation of MIS/DSS, mode of presentation for problem framing and problem solving, managing the system development process, and global issues of information technology management. Professor Palvia has published in *MIS Quarterly, Information & Management, Information Resources Management Journal, Journal of Information Systems,* and *International Journal of Information Management.* He has also published twenty-four papers in several regional, national, and international conference proceedings. He is a member of the Decision Science Institute (DSI), the Institute of Management Sciences (TIMS), Society for Information Management (SIM), and American Statistical Association (ASA).

P.K. Prabhakar is a member of the technical staff at AT&T Bell Laboratories. He specializes in designing networks and planning operations support systems for multinational corporations. Previously, he was chief engineering manager for Hindustan Petroleum Corporation (formerly ESSO) in India. He has worked as a project manager for several nuclear engineering projects in the U.S. before that. He holds an MBA in international business.

Edward M. Roche is an Assistant Professor of Management Information Systems at the University of Arizona. He earned an M.A. in International Relations from the Johns Hopkins University School of Advanced International Studies in Washington, D.C. He earned an M.Phil. in Political Economy and a Ph.D. in Political Science from Columbia University in New York City. His doctoral work focused on transborder data flows and international computer communication systems. He has done research on international computing issues in China, Japan, Korea, Brazil, and the USSR. Prior to entering academia, Dr. Roche worked as a consultant for The Diebold Group Inc., and Booz, Allen and Hamilton, Inc., both in New York. His current research centers on the use of information and telecommunications technologies in multinational corporations.

Sundeep Sahay currently is a doctoral candidate in the Decision Sciences and Information Systems Department, College of Business Administration at Florida International University. He has a Masters Degree in Management Studies and a Masters Degree in Industrial Development from Birla Institute of Technology and Science, Pilani, India. His research interests is in the areas of Information Systems and Public Policy.

Chetan S. Sankar researches and teaches in MIS as a faculty member at the Auburn University College of Business. He received his Ph.D from the Wharton School, University of Pennsylvania. He taught for four years at Temple University and was a Systems Engineer at AT&T Bell Laboratories for another four years. He performs research in telecommunications management, information resources management, standardization of data elements, and global information systems. A recent paper of his co-authored with three others won the third prize in the prestigious Society for Information Management 1990 Papers Awards Competition. His papers have appeared in *Information Management Review, Management Science, MIS Quarterly, IEEE Transactions on Professional Communications, Naval Logicts Quarterly and Decision.*

Satya Prakash Saraswat is an Assistant Professor of Computer Information Systems at Bentley College. Before joining Bentley College, Dr. Saraswat was a faculty member at San Diego State University and he also taught Information Systems courses at Georgia State University. He has published several articles on global implications of information technology, transborder data flow, developmental issues in informatics and organizational aspects of information systems. Dr. Saraswat is a member of ACM,

Association of Management, and Association of Computer Educators.

Vicki L. Sauter is an Associate Professor of Management Science and Information Systems at the University of Missouri - St. Louis. She received her Ph.D. in Systems Engineering from Northwestern University. She has published widely in the areas of decision support and expert systems. Her articles have appeared in various journals including *Journal of MIS, Omega: The International Journal of Management Science, Information and Management* and the *International Journal on Policy and Information*. Dr. Sauter has pursued research in the area of information and model usage. Her current research interests include transnational DSS development and international issues in MIS.

James A. Senn is Director of the Information Technology Management Group at Georgia State University in Atlanta and Vice-President for International Affairs of the Society for Information Management, an organization of corporate information executives. He is known internationally as a dynamic speaker on management and information technology and on developing winning strategies for personal and corporate success. Senn consults widely with business and is the author of several leading books on information technology along with numerous articles and papers.

Vikram Sethi is a doctoral candidate in the MIS area at the Joseph M. Katz Graduate School of Business, University of Pittsburgh. He received his MBA degree in Marketing and Finance from Wright State University, Dayton, Ohio and his undergraduate degree in electrical engineering from Thapar Institute of Technology, India. His research has focused on transnational information systems, telecommunications policy

Christine N. Specter currently is Assistant Professor of International Business at Florida International University. She has been with the University since 1986, teaching courses in international business. Dr. Specter's research efforts are directed at managing the transfer of remote sensing technology to developing countries. An article appearing in *Photogrammetric Engineering and Remote Sensing* about her dissertation research, "The Transfer of Remote Sensing Technology to Developing Countries: The Landsat Experience, 1970," referred to it as "the most comprehensive study of the impediments to technology transfer that has ever been undertaken in the field of remote sensing." In July 1990 Dr. Specter was asked to participate as an interdisciplinary task force member for the Consortium for International Earth Science Information Network.

Ewan Sutherland is a lecturer in management information systems in the School of Management at the University of Stirling. He previously worked at the Polytechnics of Central London and Wolverhampton and at the European Business School. His research interests include the interactions between strategic management and information technology, particularly telecommunications and in the more general areas of business use of telecommunications. He is co-editor of *Business Strategy and Information Technology* and deputy editor of the *International Journal of Information Resource Management*.

Paula Swatman spent 10 years in Information Systems in the private sector, including EDI consultancy work with G.E. Information Services. She subsequently moved into academe in Perth, first at Curtin and currently at Murdoch University, where she specialises in the fields of I.S. management and implementation. Her current research interests are in the integration of EDI systems into wider organisational applications. She has published widely in the field of EDI, presented invited papers at many academic and industry conferences, and consulted to the Western Australian Government and private corporations.

Kranti V. Toraskar is Assistant Professor in the Management and Organizational Sciences department at Drexel University. His research interests include MIS/DSS, IS evaluation, cost-benefit analysis, end-user computing, forecasting, and Modeling in Operations Management. He has published in *MIS Quarterly, Information: Technology and Peoples, Manufacturing Review,* and*The IS Research Arena of the 1990s.*

George S. Vozikis is the Alvah H. Chapman, Jr. Endowed Chairholder at the Citadel in Charleston, South Carolina, where he teaches Strategic Management and Entrepreneurship. Prior to his current position, he has taught at Memphis State University, the University of Alabama in Huntsville, the University of Miami, the University of Oklahoma, and the University of North Texas. He received his Ph.D is Business Administration from the University of Georgia under the direction of the then President of the Academy of Management, the late William F. Glueck. In addition to numerous business conference papers, journal publications, and textbooks, Dr. Vozikis has conducted executive development seminars and served as a consultant for many organizations, such as Aramco, Goldstar, McDonnell Douglas Corporation, GTE, and the U. S. Army Missile Command.

Greggry Young is a doctoral student at the College of Business and Management, University of Maryland at College Park. His research area is focused on information processing perspectives of strategic management.

Ronald M. Zigli holds a joint appointment as a Professor of Business Administration at The Citadel and Professor of Health Services Administration at the Medical University of South Carolina. He also serves as the Director of the MBA Program at The Citadel. His research interests include strategic information systems, strategic management, and ideation techniques such as Nominal Grouping and Delphi. He is professionally active having served as regional president, national vice president, and member of the board of directors of the Decision Sciences Institute. Prof. Zigli is the author of several books and has published in a variety of journals including the *International Journal of Information Management, Journal of Management, Business, University of Michigan Business Review, Atlantic Economic Review, Production and Inventory Management,* and *Quality Progress.*

INDEX